**THIRD EDITION**

# Racial and Ethnic Relations

## Joe R. Feagin

*University of Texas (Austin)*

PRENTICE HALL, Englewood Cliffs, New Jersey 07632

*Library of Congress Cataloging-in-Publication Data*

Feagin, Joe R.
   Racial and ethnic relations.

   Includes bibliographical references and index.
   1. Minorities—United States . 2. United States—
Race relations. 3. United States—Ethnic relations.
I. Title.
E184.A1F38  1989       305.8'00973      99-23189
ISBN 0-13-750209-5

Editorial/production supervision and
interior design: Serena Hoffman
Cover design: Ben Santora
Manufacturing buyer: Peter Havens

**1989, 1984, 1978 by Prentice-Hall, Inc.
A Division of Simon & Schuster
Englewood Cliffs, New Jersey 07632**

Printed in the United States of America

10  9  8  7  6  5  4  3  2  1

ISBN 0-13-750209-5

Prentice-Hall International (UK) Limited, *London*
Prentice-Hall of Australia Pty. Limited, *Sydney*
Prentice-Hall Canada Inc., *Toronto*
Prentice-Hall Hispanoamericana, S.A., *Mexico*
Prentice-Hall of India Private Limited, *New Delhi*
Prentice-Hall of Japan, Inc., *Tokyo*
Simon & Schuster Asia Pte. Ltd., *Singapore*
Editora Prentice-Hall do Brasil, Ltda., *Rio de Janeiro*

# Contents

## PART II    A Nation of Immigrants: An Overview of the Economic and Political Conditions of Specific Racial and Ethnic Groups   45

# Preface

This third edition of *Racial and Ethnic Relations* is designed for social science courses variously titled Minority Groups, Minority Relations, Race Relations, or Racial and Ethnic Relations, as well as a variety of ethnic studies and multicultural education courses in college and noncollege settings.

My purpose is to provide the reader with access to the social science literature on race and ethnic groups in the United States. I have drawn on a broad array of sources, including articles, books, and other data analyses by sociologists, political scientists, social psychologists, historians, economists, journalists, and legal scholars. I have focused on a modest number of major racial and ethnic groups, preferring to accent depth rather than breadth. And I have chosen to concentrate on groups primarily important in the United States, rather than to compare race and ethnic relations around the globe. Social science analyses of the United States have begun to dig deeper into the "what," "why," and "how" of racial and ethnic relations here, particularly relations involving such little-studied groups as the Italian Americans, recent Asian Americans, and Puerto Ricans. Until we do that analytical and descriptive task well, it is difficult to compare the situation in the United States with that in other countries. I have set myself this task: an exploration of the diversity, depth, and significance of racial and ethnic relations in one country—the United States.

This edition of *Racial and Ethnic Relations* is thoroughly revised and updated with reference to the research literature of the mid to late 1980s. The book has been restructured so that the substantive chapters are prefaced by introductory (overview) sections that introduce the concepts in the chapters that follow. The introduction to Part I accents the racial and ethnic mosaic that is the United States and traces the study of racial and ethnic relations. It serves as an introduction to Chapters 1 and 2, which discuss the major concepts and theories in the study of racial and ethnic relations. The introduction to Part II provides a broad overview of the political and economic history of the United States—the backdrop and context of adaptation and discrimination for each of the major immigrant groups that, voluntarily or involuntarily, came to these shores. Only one group, Native Americans, cannot be viewed as immigrants; indeed, they were often the victims of this continuous stream of immigrants from elsewhere.

Chapter 2 has been thoroughly revised to include new theories of racial and ethnic relations, such as the economic niche and competitive race relations theories, as well as new perspectives on older theories. The substantive chapters on the various groups have been rewritten to include recent research studies and new demographic data on those racial and ethnic groups. An entirely new chapter, Chapter 12, describes several important Asian immigrant groups, including the Vietnamese, the Chinese, the Pilipinos ("Filipinos"), and the Koreans, groups made up to a substantial degree of relatively recent immigrants to the United States. In addition, this edition has been carefully corrected and copyedited for clarity and readability, in line with the helpful suggestions from numerous students, teachers, editors, and reviewers.

I am indebted to a long list of insightful readers and colleagues whose help, advice, and suggestions have made this a better book: Graham Kinloch, Edward Múrguía, Louis Schneider, Nestor Rodríguez, Gilberto Cardenas, David Roth, John S. Butler, Andrew M. Greeley, Joseph Lopreato, Clairece Booher Feagin, Anthony Orum, Eric Woodrum, Lester Hill, Edna Bonacich, Chad Oliver, Marcia A. Herndon, Rogelio Nuñez, Tom Walls, Samuel Heilman, Phylis Cancilla Martinelli, José Limon, Devon Peña, Diana Kendall, Leslie Inniss, Robena Jackson, Mark Chesler, David O'-Brien, and Bradley Stewart. I am indebted to Suzanne Harper for research assistance in preparing this edition and for coauthoring Chapter 12 on Asian American groups. I am also indebted to Clairece Booher Feagin for assistance in proofreading and for preparing the index.

Joe R. Feagin

# PART I

# *The Racial and Ethnic Mosaic*

Two hundred years ago the new United States severed its colonial ties with Europe. Born in revolution, that nation has been portrayed as forging an era of patriotic unity and dedication to freedom and equality. Over the next two centuries a vigorous nation would emerge, with great racial and ethnic diversity. Yet the new society had its seamy side. Racial and ethnic oppression and conflict—these too were imbedded in the founding period and in the history of the new republic. Thus by the end of the seventeenth century the enslavement of black Africans was fundamental to the economy of the North American colonies, and slave revolt was a recurrent problem. Other nonwhite peoples such as Japanese Americans, would later suffer yokes of oppression.

But non-Europeans were not the only ones to face oppressive conditions. Discrimination against later white immigrant groups was part of the sometimes forgotten history of both the pre- and postrevolutionary periods. In the earliest period the colonial population on the prospering Atlantic coast was predominantly English in its origins and basic social institutions.

Because of their huge appetite for raw materials and new markets, English authorities encouraged non-English immigration to the colonies. Yet there was popular opposition, verbal and violent, to the long line of new white immigrants. "Foreigners" soon became a negative category for the colonists. "Despite the need for new settlers English colonials had mixed feelings about foreign arrivals. Anglo-Saxon mobs attacked Huguenots in Frenchtown, Rhode Island, and destroyed a Scotch-Irish frontier settlement in Worcester, Massachusetts."[1] In the 1700s colonies such as Virginia, Pennsylvania, and Rhode Island attempted to block non-British immigrants.[2]

1

The basic documents of the new republic reflect its patterns of race relations and racial subordination, and some of the republic's first laws were aimed at hampering groups of non-English origin. The otherwise radical Declaration of Independence, prepared by Thomas Jefferson, had originally contained language accusing King George of pursuing slavery, of waging "cruel war against human nature itself, violating its most sacred rights of life and liberty in the persons of a distant people who never offended him, captivating them and carrying them into slavery in another hemisphere, or to incur miserable death in the transportation thither."[3] Jefferson noted that the English king had not attempted to prohibit the slave trade, had even encouraged the slaves to "rise in arms" against white colonists. But because of pressure from slaveholding interests in the South and slave-trading interests in New England, this critique of slavery was omitted from the final version of the Declaration. Even in this revolutionary period the doctrine of liberty could not be extended to the black population, for criticism of King George was in fact criticism of the North American economic system. Jefferson himself was a slaveholder whose wealth was tied to an oppressive slaveholding agricultural system.

The Constitution recognized race subordination in three places. First, as a result of a famous compromise between northern and southern representatives to the Constitutional Convention, Article I originally stipulated that three-fifths of a given state's slave population was to be counted among the total in apportioning the state's legislative representation and taxes—that is, each slave was officially three-fifths of a person. Interestingly, in this case southern slaveowners pressed for full inclusion of the slaves in the population count, while northern interests were opposed.

In addition, a section was added to Article I permitting the slave trade to continue until 1808. The Constitution also incorporated a fugitive-slave provision requiring the return of runaway slaves to their owners, a provision opposed by very few at the time.[4] Neither the statement in the Declaration of Independence that "all men are created equal" nor the Constitution's Bill of Rights was seen as applying to what was a very large proportion of the population at that time—people of African descent. Black slavery, strangely enough, would last much longer in the new republic than in imperial Britain.[5]

Blacks were not the only group to suffer from government action. Numerous other non-English groups continued to find themselves less than equal under the law. Anti-immigrant legislation in the late 1700s and early 1800s included the Alien, Sedition, and Naturalization Acts.[6] Irish, German, and French immigrants were growing in number by the late eighteenth century, and concern with the political sentiments of these and other immigrants was acute. The Naturalization Act stiffened residency requirements for citizenship from five to fourteen years, while an Alien Act gave the president the power to expel foreigners. President Adams was frequently pressed to issue exclusion warrants and did so in two cases. Shiploads of foreign immigrants left the country out of fear of exclusion.

Inequality in life chances along racial and ethnic lines was a fundamental fact of the new nation's institutions. At first liberty and justice seemed to be for British males only. Yet this situation did not go unchallenged. By the late eighteenth century many Irish and German immigrants had come into the colonies. Indeed, a significant proportion of the four million persons enumerated in the first United States Census were of non-English origins.

Over the next two centuries English domination was modified to include other northern Europeans. These groups in turn were challenged by southern and eastern European and nonwhite groups trying to move up in the social, economic, and political systems. Gradually the new nation became a complex and unprecedented mixing of peoples.

Most in the non-British immigrant groups eventually came to adopt the English language and institutions, the core of American society and culture. Most groups adapted to the dominant culture and ways, some gaining substantial power and status in the process. Yet other groups remained in a subordinate position politically and economically. Thus racial and ethnic diversity and inequality became early and continuing dimensions of the foundation of this society. Intergroup relations were not always peaceful, nor was equality a basic fact of group life. In some cases, racial and ethnic stratification intensified, with some groups taking precedence over others.

These issues of race and ethnicity in the United States are at the heart of the sociological study of racial and ethnic relations. In the two chapters of Part I we will define basic terms used by social scientists and examine these concepts from a critical perspective. Chapter 1 examines terms such as *race*, *racism*, *ethnic group*, and *prejudice*. Chapter 2 reviews the major conceptual frameworks, including assimilation theories and internal colonialism theories, for interpreting the complex structure and long-term development of racial and ethnic relations in the United States.

## NOTES

1. Leonard Dinnerstein and Frederic C. Jaher, "Introduction," in *The Aliens*, ed. Leonard Dinnerstein and Frederic C. Jaher (New York: Appleton-Century-Crofts, 1970), p. 4.
2. Leonard Dinnerstein and Frederic C. Jaher, "The Colonial Era," in ibid., p. 17.
3. Quoted in Peter M. Bergman, *The Chronological History of the Negro in America* (New York: Harper & Row, Pub., 1969), p. 52.
4. John Hope Franklin, *From Slavery to Freedom*, 2nd ed. (New York: Knopf, 1963), pp. 141–43.
5. Ibid., p. 143.
6. Samuel E. Morison, *The Oxford History of the American People* (New York: Oxford University Press, 1965), p. 353.

# CHAPTER 1

# Basic Concepts in the Study of Racial and Ethnic Relations

In the early 1980s Susie Guillory Phipps, the wife of a white businessman in Sulphur, Louisiana, went to court to try to get the racial designation on her birth certificate at the Louisiana Bureau of Vital Records changed from "colored" (black) to "white." A 1970 Louisiana "blood" law required that persons with one thirty-second or more "Negro blood" (ancestry) were to be designated as colored on birth records; prior to 1970 "any traceable amount" of black ancestry had been used to define a person as colored. The white-skinned Phipps was the descendant of an eighteenth-century white plantation owner and a black slave, and her small amount of black ancestry was enough to get her classified as colored on her official Louisiana birth certificate. Because other records supported the birth certificate designation, Phipps lost her case against the state of Louisiana. Even one black ancestor among many white ancestors resulted in the black classification. The controversy raised the question of how a person comes to be defined as white or black in U.S. society. This recent story illustrates the persisting ambiguity of the designations *Negro* and *colored* in the United States and the fact that racial group definition is in fact *social* and *political*, *not scientific*.[1]

## SOME BASIC TERMS

A logical place to start making sense out of this controversy is with basic terms and concepts. People have often used such terms as *racial groups* and *prejudice* without specifying their meaning. Since these terms are basic concepts in the study of intergroup relations, we will analyze them in detail.

### Race

Both *racial group* and the common term *race* have been used in a number of senses in social science and popular writings. *Human race, Jewish race, Negro race*—such terms in the literature suggest a range of meanings. The earliest use of *race* in six-teenth- and seventeenth-century Europe was in the sense of descendants of a common ancestor, emphasizing kinship linkages.[2]

It was only in the late eighteenth century that the term *race* came to mean a dis-tinct category of human beings with *physical* characteristics transmitted by descent. Prior to the late eighteenth century, however, humans were being categorized by Europeans on physical grounds. In the late 1600s François Bernier was one of the first Europeans to sort out human beings into a number of basic and distinctive categories, relying heavily on facial character and skin color. Soon a hierarchy of groups (not yet termed *races*) came to be accepted, with white Europeans at the top. The Negro or black African category was usually relegated to the bottom, in part because of black Africans' color and allegedly primitive culture, but primarily because they were then best known to Europeans as slaves. Economic subordination meant a "lower" posi-tion in the classification system.[3]

Immanuel Kant's use of the German phrase for "races of mankind" in the 1770s was probably the first explicit use of the term in the sense of biologically distinct categories of human beings. The use of *race* by physical anthropologists in the late eighteenth and nineteenth centuries was with this biological meaning. Basic to this in-creasingly prevalent view was the idea of a set number of genetic groups with distinc-tive physical characteristics, together with the idea that these characteristics made for a hierarchy of groups. By the late nineteenth century numerous European and American writers were systematically downgrading all peoples not of northern European origin as inferior "races," particularly southern and eastern Europeans.[4]

## Ideological Racism

It was in this context that ideological "racism" emerged. Although this term has often been used loosely, for our purposes we can define *ideological racism* specifically as *an ideology that considers a group's unchangeable physical characteristics to be linked in a direct, causal way to psychological or intellectual characteristics, and on this basis distinguishes between superior and inferior racial groups.*[5] The "scientific racism" of such European writers as Count de Gobineau in the mid-nineteenth cen-tury was used to morally justify the imperialism of northern European states in Asia, Africa, and the Americas. A long line of "scientific racists" followed in de Gobineau's footsteps, including German Nazi leaders such as Adolf Hitler. In their hands the ideol-ogy of racial inferiority was broadly applied to culturally distinct white European groups, such as the Jews; in this perspective, real or alleged physical characteristics were coupled with cultural traits considered undesirable.

This racism was common in the United States as well. In 1935 an influential University of Virginia professor wrote that

> the size of the brain in the Black Race is below the medium both of the Whites and the Yellow-Browns, frequently with relatively more simple convolutions. The frontal lobes are often low and narrow. The parietal lobes voluminous, the occipital protruding. The psychic activities of the Black Race are a careless, jolly vivacity, emotions and passions of short duration, and a strong and somewhat irrational egoism. Idealism, ambition, and

the co-operative faculties are weak. They love amusement and sport but have little initiative and adventurous spirit.[6]

We see in this ideological racism the linking of physical and personality characteristics. Although this portrait often passed for science prior to World War II—and in today's racist organizations much of it still does—it is really pseudoscience. For the most part the ideological racists assumed the stereotyped characteristics traditionally applied to black Americans to be true; they did not scientifically prove their assertions.

Modern biologists and anthropologists have demonstrated the wild-eyed irrationality of much of this racist mythology. The basic tenet of racist thinking is that physical differences such as skin color or nose shape are intrinsically tied to meaningful differentials in intelligence or culture. No convincing scientific support for this assumed linkage exists. Many social scientists have come to reject attempts at constructing complex typologies of inferior and superior racial categories. But the lack of scientific support has hardly lessened the tremendous impact of racist ideologies.

Montagu has noted that this ideological racism is dangerous, a view shaped in part by his observation of the German Nazi ideology, which argued for distinctive Aryan and Jewish races.[7] The ideology was linked to the killing of millions of European Jews in the 1930s and 1940s. As a result, a 1950 *UNESCO Statement on Race*, prepared by a distinguished group of social scientists, pointed out that race, even from a strict biological standpoint, could refer *at most* to a group with certain distinctive gene concentrations. Whatever categorization social scientists apply to human beings, the document further asserted, they should never include "mental characteristics as part of those classifications."[8] The UNESCO statement also noted that inherited genetic factors are not the major forces shaping cultural or intellectual differences among human groups; environment is far more important.

## Racial Group

In the last few decades a major concern among social scientists has been with the *social* definition of race and racial groups. In 1948 Oliver C. Cox was one of the first to underscore this perspective by defining a race as "any people who are distinguished, or consider themselves distinguished, in social relations with other peoples, by their physical characteristics."[9] From the social-definition perspective, characteristics such as skin color have *no self-evident meaning*; rather, they primarily have *social* meaning, so much so that one can speak of "social races." Similarly, *racial group* has been defined by van den Berghe as a "human group that defines itself and/or is defined by other groups as different from other groups by virtue of [presumed] innate and immutable physical characteristics."[10] This definition relates to the everyday use of racial distinctions in the social world.

A person's race is most typically determined by and important to certain outsiders, although a group's self-definition can also be important. Thus *a racial group is not something naturally generated as part of the self-evident order of the universe, but is a social group that persons inside or outside the group have decided is impor-*

*tant to single out as inferior or superior, typically on the basis of real or alleged physical characteristics subjectively selected.*

In the United States a number of groups would fit into this definition. As we will see in a later chapter, black Americans have been defined as racially different by white groups for centuries on the basis of certain physical characteristics. Asian Americans, Native Americans ("Indians"), and Mexican Americans have also seen their physical characteristics, such as skin color and eye shape, singled out as badges of racial inferiority. Note too that some social groups once defined as racial groups— and as physically and mentally inferior groups at that—are no longer defined that way. In later chapters we will see the way the Irish and the Italians were at one time defined as *inferior racial groups* by Anglo-Saxon Protestants. Later, definition as a racial group was replaced by definition as an *ethnic group*, a term to be examined shortly. It became clear that there were no significant *physical* differences between the Irish, or the Italians, and Anglo-Saxon Americans.

Why are some physical characteristics, such as skin color, selected as a basis for distinguishing human groups, whereas other characteristics, such as eye color, seldom are? These questions can be answered not simply in biological terms but primarily by historical and sociological analysis. Such characteristics as skin color are, as Banton has argued, "easily observed and ordered in the mind."[11] But they also become highlighted in a social interaction process. More important than ease of observation is the way in which economic or political exploitation often leads to the need to identify the exploited group in a certain way. The real or alleged physical characteristics singled out to typify the exploited group often become seen as inferior racial characteristics in the process of justifying exploitation. Technological differences in military firepower between European and African peoples facilitated the subordination of Africans as slaves in the English and other European colonies. In turn, darker skin color and selected other physical differences came to signal the different obligations and privileges of the two groups. Skin-color characteristics had no inherent meaning; in intergroup interaction they became important only because they could be used easily to classify most members of the dominant and subordinate groups.

Knowledge of one's kinship and relatives sometimes affects one's assignment to a racial group, particularly for those who lack the obvious physical characteristics. People have been distinguished not only on the basis of their own physical characteristics but also on the basis of a socially determined "rule of descent."[12] Descent is not determined scientifically, but on the basis of social perception of ancestry. With regard to black Americans, for example, as the clear-cut color characteristic accented in the early colonial period became more problematical over time, the ancestry aspect became more critical in the identification process. Pettigrew has noted that "black" Americans in the United States today "evidence an unusually wide range of physical traits. Their skin color extends from ebony to a shade paler than many 'whites'; their nose-shape from extremely flat to aquiline; their stature from basketball giant to dwarf."[13]

In some communities, particularly in the southern United States, the *social* aspect of the defining process becomes obvious when a light-skinned person without some of the physical traits usually associated with blacks is treated as black because one of his or her ancestors or relatives is remembered to have been of African ancestry. Even in the case of groups traditionally distinguished on the basis of physical characteristics, ambiguity arises in the actual defining process. Moreover, since the distinctive physical characteristics of subordinate racial groups are assumed to be linked to intellectual or cultural characteristics, dominant groups regularly mix their racial definitions with notions about intelligence and cultural distinctivenss. For example, in an employment situation a black applicant may suffer discrimination not only because of darker skin color but also because he or she dresses or speaks oddly in the view of a white personnel interviewer.

## Ethnic Group

The term *ethnic* has been used by social scientists in two different senses, one narrow and one broad. Some definitions of the term are broad enough to include socially defined racial groups. For example, in Gordon's broad definition an ethnic group is a social group distinguished "by race, religion, or national origin."[14] As in the case of racial group, here is a notion of set-apartness. But here the distinctive characteristics can be physical *or* cultural, and language and religion are seen as critical signs of ethnicity even where there is no physical distinctiveness. Glazer has expressed this inclusive view of the ethnic group:

> Thus one possible position on ethnicity and race, and the one I hold, is that they form part of a single family of social identities—a family which, in addition to races and ethnic groups, includes religions (as in Holland), language groups (as in Belgium), and all of which can be included in the most general term, ethnic groups, groups defined by descent, real or mythical, and sharing a common history and experience.[15]

These definitions illustrate the broad definition of an ethnic group.

Other analysts prefer a narrower definition of ethnic group, one that omits groups defined *primarily* in terms of racial characteristics and limits the term to groups distinguished *primarily* on the basis of cultural or nationality characteristics. Indeed, the word *ethnic* comes from the Greek *ethnos*, originally meaning "nation." In its earliest English usage the word referred to culturally different "heathen" nations (those not Christian or Jewish). Apparently the first usage of *ethnic group* in terms of national origin developed in the period of heavy immigration from southern and eastern European nations to the United States in the early twentieth century. Since the 1930s and 1940s a number of prominent social scientists have suggested that the narrower definition of ethnic group, in line with the literal Greek meaning, makes the term more useful.[16]

W. Lloyd Warner distinguished between ethnic groups, which he saw as characterized by cultural differences, and racial groups, characterized by physical differences. The greater the cultural and racial differences between a group and the core society, the slower its assimilation into the core society.[17] More recent scholars have also preferred the narrower usage. In van den Berghe's translation of this view, ethnic groups are "socially defined but on the basis of cultural criteria."[18] When the term *ethnic group* is used in this book, the usual meaning will be the narrower one—that of *a group socially distinguished or set apart, by others or by itself, primarily on the basis of cultural or nationality characteristics.*

Reviewing different definitions of *ethnic group*, one soon sees that the definitions sometimes vary because of different underlying assumptions. Those who prefer the broader definition often argue that the experiences of people defined as nonwhite are essentially similar to the experiences of white groups.* Some have argued that in the United States the situation and experiences of nonwhite Americans are essentially similar to those of white immigrant groups. Often a further assumption is that the experiences of both white and nonwhite groups are adequately explained using the same theoretical framework—usually an assimilationist framework.[19] Researchers who prefer the narrower definition, who see ethnic groups as a category separate from racial groups, usually have different underlying assumptions. These include the view that the experiences of non-European racial groups have been distinctively different from those of European groups.[20]

Whether *ethnic group* is defined in a narrow or a broad sense, ancestry is important. Perception of common ancestry, both real and mythical, has been important both to outsiders' definitions and to ethnic groups' self-definitions. German sociologist Max Weber saw ethnic groups broadly as "human groups that entertain a subjective belief in their common descent—because of similarities of physical type or of customs or both, or because of memories of colonization or migration—in such a way that this belief is important for the continuation of the nonkinship communal relationships."[21] Gordon has described an ethnic group as one having a shared sense of being one people.[22] Consciousness of one's own kind is accented.

The social definitions of *racial group* and *ethnic group* move us away from a biological determinism that sees groups as self-evident and genetically fixed with unchanging physical or mental characteristics. People themselves, both outside and inside differentiated groups, determine when certain physical or cultural characteristics are important enough to single out a group for social interest, whether for good or for ill.

A given social group may be viewed by different outsiders or at different times as a racial or an ethnic group. And some groups have been defined by the same outsiders as important on the basis of both physical and cultural criteria. German Jews, for example, were spoken of as a "race" in Nazi Germany, in part because of both real and alleged differences in physical characteristics. However, in Nazi Germany, routine identification of specific Jews for persecution was based more on ethnic characteristics—on cultural characteristics such as religion or language and on known genealogical ties to Jewish ancestors—than on physical characteristics. As later chapters should make clear, outsiders have frequently placed more emphasis on one or the other of these sets of socially distinguished criteria—physical or cultural characteristics—in defining a given group's societal position.

---

*In this book the term *nonwhite* will ordinarily refer to groups basically of non-European origin, such as black Americans. The term *white* will be used for groups basically of European origin and often will encompass different ethnic groups.

## Minority and Majority Groups

Other terms have been used for racial and ethnic groups. Prominent among these has been the term *minority group*.[23] Louis Wirth explicitly defined a minority group in terms of subordinate position, as "a group of people who, because of their physical or cultural characteristics, are singled out from others in the society in which they live for differential and unequal treatment and who therefore regard themselves as objects of collective discrimination."[24]

Wagley and Harris have defined minority groups as: suffering discrimination and subordination within a society; set apart by physical or cultural traits disapproved of by the dominant group; units with a sense of collective identity and common burdens; having membership that is determined by the socially invented rule of descent; and characterized by marriage within the group.[25]

The term *minority group* implies the existence of a "majority group," a dominant group with superior rights and advantages. These concepts point up racial and ethnic *stratification*, a ranking system in the form of a hierarchy of more and less powerful groups. It is more accurate to use the term *dominant group* for a majority group, as well as *subordinate group* for a minority group, since the "majority group" can be numerically a minority, as with the ruling white Europeans in a number of African countries. The "minority groups" in these situations are actually numerical majorities. In this book the terms *dominant group* and *subordinate group* will be the preferred designations for groups in a race-ethnic hierarchy.

## Prejudice and Stereotyping

Another common term is *prejudice*, which in popular discourse is tied to negative attitudes. Understanding how and why negative attitudes develop is best approached by first defining *ethnocentrism*, which was long ago described by Sumner as the "view of things in which one's own group is the center of everything, and all others are scaled and rated with reference to it."[26] Members of social groups develop, on the one hand, *positive ethnocentrism*, a loyalty to the values, beliefs, and members of one's own group. This kind of ethnocentrism, however, often becomes linked with negative views of outgroups, views manifested in prejudices and stereotypes. Such negative views, which seem to grow out of a constant evaluating of outgroups in terms of one's own values and ways, are inextricably linked to social, economic, and political interaction among groups.[27]

Prejudice has been defined by Gordon Allport as "thinking ill of others without sufficient warrant."[28] The term comes from the Latin word *praejudicium*, which referred to a judgment made on the basis of prior experience. In English the word evolved from meaning "hasty judgment" to the present connotation of unfavorableness that goes with the meaning of an unsupported or biased judgment. Although prejudice can theoretically apply to biases favoring a group, its current meaning in both popular usage and social science analysis is almost exclusively in terms of negative views. Prejudice can be defined more precisely as "*an antipathy based upon a faulty and inflexible generalization. It may be felt or expressed. It may be directed toward a group as a whole, or toward an individual because he [or she] is a member of that group.*"[29] Prejudice is here viewed as involving a negative feeling or attitude toward the outgroup and an inaccurate belief as well; it has both emotional and cognitive aspects. An example might be "I hate black and Mexican people, because black and Mexican people always smell worse than whites." The first part of the sentence expresses the negative feeling (the hatred), the last part an inaccurate generalization. This latter cognitive aspect has been termed a *stereotype—that is, an overgeneralization associated with a racial or ethnic category that goes beyond existing evidence.*

In "All in the Family," a television show popular for several years, the prominent character, Archie Bunker, is supposed to be an example of a white bigot. He verbally attacks outgroups, calls blacks "jungle bunnies," and worries deeply about white women marrying blacks. Supposedly only the blue-collar people of America, such as Bunker, are bigots. But that is simply not the case. Social science surveys have found that prejudices and stereotypes aimed at nonwhites are common among all classes of white America.

Why do some people stereotype others? Why have Irish Americans long been stereotyped as lazy drunkards; blacks as indolent, violent, and oversexed; Italians as "Mafia" types; the Japanese as treacherous Orientals? Such questions force us to examine the role that prejudices and stereotypes play in the lives of individuals and groups. Sociologically oriented analysts tend to emphasize the group pressures on the individual for conformity or rationalization, while psychological analysts tend to stress individual irrationality or personality defectiveness. Much psychological research and analysis has underscored the expressive function of prejudice for the individual. Frustration-aggression theories, psychoanalytic theories, and authoritarian-personality perspectives focus on the *externalization* function of prejudice—the transfer of an individual's internal psychological problem onto an external object as a solution to that internal problem. Many psychologically oriented interpretations stress "sick" or "abnormal" individuals whose race or ethnic prejudice is intimately linked to special emotional problems in their psychological life-economy, such as hatred of their fathers.[30]

In a classic study of prejudice and personality, *The Authoritarian Personality*, Adorno and colleagues argue that persons who hate Jews or blacks differ from tolerant persons in central personality traits—specifically, that they exhibit "authoritarian personalities."[31] Those with authoritarian personalities differ from others in their greater submission to authority, tendency to stereotyping, superstition, and concern for social status. They view the world as sinister and threatening, a view easily linked to intolerant views of outgroups in subordinate positions in the social world around them.

Some scholars have raised serious questions about this traditional stress on the expressive function of prejudice and of stereotypes. Williams and Pettigrew have suggested that *conformity* may be a much more important factor.[32] Most people seem to accept their own social and community situation as given and to hold the prejudices they have been taught at home and at school. Conformity to prevailing beliefs is seen as a major source of prejudice. From this perspective, prejudices are not so much individually determined preferences, but rather shared social definitions of racial and ethnic groups. This points to the social-adjustment function of prejudice. Indeed, most of us can think of numerous situations in which northerners or southerners have had to adjust to new racial beliefs as they moved from one region to another or from one setting to another. As Schermerhorn notes, "prejudice is a product of *situations*," not "a little demon that emerges in people simply because they are depraved."[33]

These explanations partly explain why people hold prejudices and stereotypes; an additional factor is that stereotypes help rationalize a subordinate group's position. Whereas prejudice is deeply rooted in human history, stereotyping in the form of a fully developed racist ideology may be relatively recent, perhaps developing with the rise of the European colonization of peoples of color around the world. Modern prejudice, Cox argues, "is a divisive attitude seeking to alienate dominant group sympathy from an 'inferior' race, a whole people, for the purpose of facilitating its exploitation."[34]

When peoples are subordinated, as in the case of the white enslavement of black Africans in the American colonies or in the case of the restrictive quotas for Jews in American schools in the 1920s and 1930s, stereotypes develop, at least in part, to justify that subordination. Indeed, the ideological racism noted previously can be viewed as a complex set of stereotypes aimed at rationalizing the imperialism of certain white European nations exploiting southern and eastern European immigrants and expanding at the expense of non-European peoples.

## Discrimination: Distinguishing Dimensions

Discussions of discrimination and of government programs that attempt to eradicate it are often confusing, in part because the dimensions of discrimination are not distinguished. As a first step in sorting out discrimination, I suggest the diagram in Figure 1–1. The dimensions of discrimination include (a) motivation, (b) discriminatory actions, (c) effects, (d) the relation between motivation and actions, (e) the relation be-

**FIGURE 1-1**   The Dimensions of Discrimination

Larger societal
context (g)

Immediate institutional
context (f)

(a) Motivation

(d)

(b) Discriminatory actions

(e)

(c) Effects

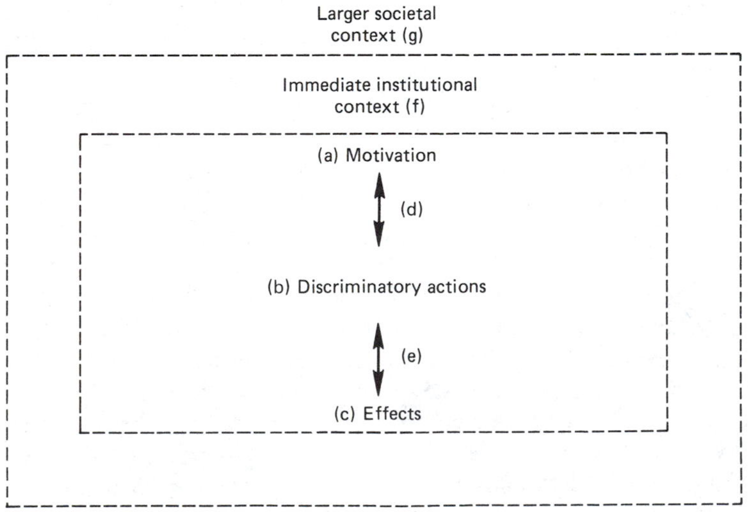

tween actions and effects, (f) the immediate institutional context, and (g) the larger societal context.[35] For example, a given set of discriminatory acts—such as the legalized exclusion of black children from all-white schools from the nineteenth century to the 1960s—can be looked at in terms of these dimensions. One can ask what the motivation was for this legalized discrimination. Was it prejudice, or what? One can also ask what form the exclusionary practices actually took. In some cases principals refused black children entrance into their school buildings. Also of importance are the effects of these practices. One effect was the poorer facilities and education many black children received. But these practices were often not the isolated actions of principals and other administrators. They were part of an institutionalized pattern of segregated education, the effects of which are still a part of U.S. society. Finally, such legalized patterns of school discrimination have been part of a larger social context of general racial subordination of black Americans across many institutional areas. Discrimination is a multidimensional problem encompassing schools, the economy, and politics.

## Traditional Research on Prejudice and Discrimination

Much research and discussion on discrimination has focused on one type of motivation (*a* in Figure 1–1)—prejudice—to the virtual exclusion of others. Much traditional analysis emphasizes the relation between prejudice and discrimination (*d* in Figure 1–1), viewing prejudice as the critical cause of discriminatory treatment of a singledout group. For example, Gordon Allport suggested that few prejudiced people keep their prejudices entirely to themselves; rather they act out their feelings in a variety of ways, ranging from speaking against to discriminating against to exterminating an outgroup.[36] In his classic study *An American Dilemma* (1944), Gunnar Myrdal saw race prejudice as "the whole complex of valuations and beliefs which are behind discriminatory behavior on the part of the majority group."[37] A few years later Robert K. Merton argued that discrimination might be practiced even by an unprejudiced person who was afraid of the prejudices of others.[38]

Over the last several decades laboratory research studies have focused on the relationship between personal prejudice and discrimination. Researchers have tried to determine if prejudiced people do in fact discriminate and to see how prejudice is linked to discrimination. In these research studies prejudice is typically determined by means of questions on questionnaires. Discriminatory action is often measured in a weak way, as, for example, by the readiness of a white subject to sign a release form indicating a willingness to be photographed with blacks. Such studies have found a low positive correlation between expressed prejudice and the measured discriminatory behavior; that is, knowing how prejudiced a subject is may not help predict his or her actions. The weakness of this correlation has been explained in various ways. One problem may be the wording or character of the questions on attitudes; another may be the mild form of discrimination measured in the laboratory. Most significantly, racial discrimination in the outside world is usually far more substantial than that measured in the lab.[39]

## Institutional and Individual Discrimination

The heavy emphasis on individual prejudice and on bigoted individuals in assessments of discrimination has been questioned by those researchers concerned with privilege theories of discrimination and with institutional discrimination. Some authors have pointed out that the intent to harm lying behind much discrimination may not reflect prejudice but simply a desire to protect one's own social and economic privileges. Some white people discriminate because they gain economically or politically from racial restrictions on the nonwhite competition. In the historical struggle over resources, systems of race stratification were established in which the dominant groups, such as whites, benefit economically, politically, and psychologically. They strive to maintain their privileges, whether or not they rationalize the striving in terms of prejudice. Wellman has argued that discrimination is a "rational" response to struggles over scarce resources." In this struggle a system of stratification has been established in which the dominant racial group benefits economically, politically, and psychologically.[40]

A related issue is the institutionalization of privilege and thus of discrimination. Hamilton and Carmichael apparently were the first to develop the concepts of *individual racism*, exemplified by the actions of white terrorists bombing a black church, and *institutional racism*, illustrated by societal practices that lead to large numbers of black children suffering constantly because of inadequate food and medical facilities.[41] Hamilton and Carmichael's book *Black Power* is an attempt to move beyond a focus on individual bigots. Institutional racism can involve actions in which people have "no intention of subordinating others because of color, or are totally unaware of doing so."[42] In his analysis of racism and mental health, Pettigrew distinguishes between *direct* and *indirect* racial discrimination, applying the latter to situations where restrictions in one area are shaped by racial discrimination in yet another.[43]

Drawing on this literature, one can define discrimination without mentioning prejudice or intent to harm. The working definition of discrimination in this book is as follows: *actions carried out by members of dominant groups, or their representatives, that have a differential and harmful impact on members of subordinate groups.* The dominant and subordinate groups here are racial and ethnic groups. Thus discrimination involves actions, as well as one or more discriminators and one or more victims. The distinction between *intentional* (motivated by prejudice or intent to harm) and *unintentional* (not motivated by prejudice or intent to harm) is useful for distinguishing basic types of discrimination.[44]

Drawing on these two dimensions of scale and intention, I would suggest four basic types of discriminatory practices:

*Type A*  Isolate discrimination
*Type B*  Small-group discrimination
*Type C*  Direct institutionalized discrimination
*Type D*  Indirect institutionalized discrimination

Type A, *isolate discrimination*, is harmful action taken intentionally by a member of a dominant group against members of a subordinate racial or ethnic group, without being socially embedded in the larger organizational or community context. An example might be a white police officer who implements antiblack hostility by beating up black prisoners at every opportunity, even though police department regulations specifically prohibit and punish such actions. (If the majority of officers in that department behaved in this fashion, these beatings would no longer fall into this category.) The term *isolate* should not be taken to mean that Type A discrimination is rare in the United States, for it is indeed commonplace. Rather, the term can be used to indicate an individual's action taken without the immediate support of norms (standards of conduct) in a large-group or organizational context.

Type B, *small-group discrimination*, is harmful action taken intentionally by a small number of dominant-group individuals acting in concert against members of subordinate racial and ethnic groups, without the support of the norms or rules of a larger organizational or community context. The bombing of Irish Catholic churches in the 1800s or of the homes of black families in northern cities by small Ku Klux Klan–type groups in the 1960s and 1970s might be viewed as examples of this type.

Type C, *direct institutionalized discrimination*, refers to organizationally prescribed or community-prescribed action that by intention has a differential and negative impact on members of subordinate race and ethnic groups. Typically, these actions are not episodic or sporadic, but are routinely carried out by a large number of individuals guided by the norms of a large-scale organization or community. With Type C we come to the *institutionalization* of discrimination. Historical examples of this type include the intentional segregation of black or Jewish persons in inferior facilities or jobs. Type C discrimination can be seen in real estate companies that "steer" blacks away from white housing areas, a practice documented by Diana Pearce in a study of Detroit. A study of minority medical students by Diana Kendall has also demonstrated the persistence of institutionalized patterns of informal discrimination that batter the lives of nonwhite Americans.[45]

Type D, *indirect institutionalized discrimination*, consists of practices having a negative and differential impact on members of subordinate race and ethnic groups even though the organizationally or community-prescribed norms or regulations guiding those actions have been established, and are carried out, with no intent to harm the members of those groups. For example, intentional discrimination institutionalized in the education and training of subordinate groups—resulting in poor education—has often handicapped their attempts to compete with dominant-group members in the employment sphere, where hiring and promotion standards often incorporate educational requirements. Many nonwhite workers have suffered indirect discrimination because of job seniority practices established with no intent to harm them. For example, in businesses that were intentionally segregated in the past, recently hired members of subordinate groups have little job seniority; thus in a recession they are the first workers to be laid off.

## Subtle and Covert Discrimination

Recent conceptual work has examined the more covert and subtle types of institutionalized (mostly Type C) discrimination, focusing particularly on differential treatment in the workplace. For example, with the gradual expansion of black employment in the 1970s and 1980s to include jobs once unavailable to nonwhite Americans have come new forms of discrimination. These forms of discrimination are usually supported by the informal norms and beliefs that guide the behavior of people working in organizations. *Subtle discrimination* can be defined as *unequal and injurious treatment of members of subordinate racial and ethnic groups that is visible but not as blatant as the traditional door-slamming varieties of discrimination*. This type of discrimination often goes unnoticed in the modern bureaucratic settings where most Americans work because white employers and employees have internalized the discriminatory behavior as normal and acceptable.[46]

In his research on black managers who have been able to secure decent-paying entry-level positions in white corporations, Ed Jones has found a predisposition among whites, both co-workers and bosses, to assume the best about persons of their own color and the worst about people different from themselves when it comes to evaluating job performance. This stereotyping (Jones calls it *colorism*), which can be conscious or subconscious, is more subtle than the old-fashioned blatant racism, but it nonetheless plays a major role in generating discrimination against black (and other nonwhite) employees in modern corporations and other employment settings. For example, black managers report that their achievements are often given less attention than their failures, while the failures of comparable white managers are more likely to be excused in terms of situational factors or even overlooked by their white superiors. Pettigrew and Martin have described this subtle stereotyping as the "ultimate attribution error." Whites in organizations tend to prefer racially stereotyped explanations of black managers' failures, rather than the situational explanations they would choose for the failures of comparable whites. In turn, this negative feedback on a black worker's performance makes it more difficult for him or her to perform successfully in the future. Indeed, one result of these more subtle barriers to recognition and promotion is that many talented black (and other nonwhite) managers have become very angry, frustrated, and inclined to drop out of corporations in favor of other employment.[47]

*Covert discrimination* is unequal and injurious treatment of members of subordinate racial and ethnic groups that is hidden, malicious, and very difficult to document. Common types of covert discrimination include manipulation, tokenism, and sabotage. Intentional sabotage is especially serious. An example of this comes from a black female mail carrier:

> I've been in this job nine years and I still have problems with the guys. About a year ago, whenever I returned from my route, I'd find a bunch of mail that I hadn't picked up. The district manager said I wasn't doing my job and gave me an undesirable [high-crime] route. I found out later that the district manager gave my route to a new guy who was a friend of the family.[48]

Nonwhite employees, such as Asians, blacks, or Hispanics, are sometimes intentionally hired as "tokens" or "window dressing": they may be stereotyped in terms of race (a "credit to their race") and placed to make the corporation or other organization look good rather than being evaluated in terms of their abilities, talents, and accomplishments for higher-level positions. And in many organizations the hiring of a few minority employees is used to reduce pressures to expand the number of nonwhite employees to more representative numbers, particularly in positions of power such as middle-level or top-level management positions. Tokenism thus becomes an intentional barrier to minority group advancement.

These concepts extend our conceptualization of institutionalized discrimination in that they force us to think about subtle and covert forms of race discrimination embedded deeply in the institutions of U.S. society. Moreover, subtle and covert discrimination are much more difficult to eliminate with civil rights legislation than the old-fashioned door-slamming discrimination.

Various combinations of the types of discrimination can coexist in a given organization or community. Members of subordinate groups can suffer both from institutionalized regulations intended to have a harmful effect and from those not so intended, as well as from the flamboyant actions of bigots who focus their hostility on racial or ethnic targets within their reach. From a broader point of view, the patterns of discrimination interlocking political, economic, and social organizations in this society might even be termed *systematic* discrimination. For a given victimized group, oppression can be interlocking and cumulative, involving many institutional sectors.

Contrary to some views of more conservative analysts of American racial patterns, racial discrimination is not rapidly disappearing from U.S. society. The Mathematica survey research firm interviewed 3,000 black households nationwide. Two-thirds of the heads of these households felt black Americans were still discriminated against "a great deal" in this country.[49]

## SUMMARY

This chapter has examined the key terms *race*, *racial group*, *racism*, *ethnic group*, *minority (subordinate) group*, *majority (dominant) group*, *prejudice*, *stereotyping*, and *discrimination*. These critical concepts loom large in discussions of race and ethnic issues. More than a century of discussion of these concepts lies behind the voyage we have set out on here and in the following chapters. We must carefully think through the meaning of such terms as *race* and *racial group*, because such concepts have themselves been used in the shaping of ethnic and race relations.

Indeed, ideas about race and racial groups have been dangerous for human beings, playing an active role in the triggering, or the convenient rationalizing, of societal processes costing millions of lives. Ideas can have an impact. The sharp cutting edge of race, as in "racial inferiority" theorizing, can be seen in the enslavement by white Europeans of black Africans between the seventeenth and nineteenth centuries and in actions taken by German non-Jews against Jews in the 1930s and 1940s.

Sometimes it is easy to consider words and concepts as harmless abstractions. However, a moment's reflection on both recent and distant Western history gives the lie to this naive view. The concept may not be "mightier than the sword," to adapt an old cliché, but it is indeed mighty.

## NOTES

1. Frances F. Marcus, "Louisiana Repeals Black Blood Law," *New York Times*, July 6, 1983, p. A10.
2. Wilton M. Krogman, "The Concept of Race," in *The Science of Man in the World Crisis*, ed. Ralph Linton (New York: Columbia University Press, 1945) p. 38.
3. Winthrop D. Jordan, *White over Black* (Baltimore: Penguin, 1969), p. 217.
4. Peter I. Rose, *The Subject Is Race* (New York: Oxford University Press, 1968), pp. 32–33; Thomas F. Gossett, *Race* (New York: Schocken Books, 1965), p. 3.
5. See Pierre L. van den Berghe, *Race and Racism* (New York: John Wiley, 1967), p. 11.
6. Robert Bennett Bean, *The Races of Man* (New York: University Society, 1935), pp. 94–96, as quoted in *In Their Place: White America Defines Her Minorities*, 1850–1950, ed. Lewis H. Carlson and George A. Colburn (New York: John Wiley, 1972), p. 106.
7. Ashley Montagu, *Race, Science and Humanity* (Princeton, N.J.: D. Van Nostrand, 1963).
8. *UNESCO Statement on Race*, reprinted in ibid., p. 174.
9. Oliver C. Cox, *Caste, Class, and Race* (Garden City, N.Y.: Doubleday, 1948), p. 402.
10. Van den Berghe, *Race and Racism*, p. 9.
11. Michael Banton, *Race Relations* (New York: Basic Books, 1967), p. 57; see also p. 58.
12. Charles Wagley and Marvin Harris, *Minorities in the New World* (New York: Columbia University Press, 1958), p. 7.
13. Thomas F. Pettigrew, *A Profile of the Negro American* (Princeton, N.J.: D. Van Nostrand, 1964), p. 69.
14. Milton M. Gordon, *Assimilation in American Life* (New York: Oxford University Press, 1964), p. 27.
15. Nathan Glazer, "Blacks and Ethnic Groups: The Difference, and the Political Difference It Makes," *Social Problems* 18 (Spring 1971): 447; see also Nathan Glazer and Daniel P. Moynihan, "Introduction," in *Ethnicity*, ed. Nathan Glazer and Daniel P. Moynihan (Cambridge: Harvard University Press, 1975), p. 4.
16. William M. Newman, *American Pluralism* (New York: Harper & Row, Pub., 1973), p. 19.
17. W. Lloyd Warner and Leo Srole, *The Social Systems of American Ethnic Groups* (New Haven: Yale University Press, 1945), pp. 284–86.
18. Van den Berghe, *Race and Racism*, p. 10.
19. See Glazer, "Blacks and Ethnic Groups."
20. D. John Grove, *The Race vs. Ethnic Debate: A Cross-National Analysis of Two Theoretical Approaches* (Denver: Center on International Race Relations, University of Denver, 1974); Robert Blauner, *Racial Oppression in America* (New York: Harper & Row, Pub., 1972).
21 Max Weber, "Ethnic Groups," in *Theories of Society*, ed. Talcott Parsons et al. (Glencoe, Ill.: Free Press, 1961), 1:306.
22. Gordon, *Assimilation in American Life*, pp. 23–25.
23. This term was suggested by Donald M. Young in *American Minority Peoples* (New York: Harper, 1932), p. xviii.
24. Louis Wirth, "The Problem of Minority Groups," in *The Science of Man in the World Crisis*, ed. Linton, p. 347.
25. Wagley and Harris, *Minorities in the New World*, pp. 4–9.
26. William G. Sumner, *Folkways* (New York: Mentor Books, 1960), pp. 27–28.
27. Robin M. Williams, Jr., *Strangers Next Door* (Englewood Cliffs, N.J.: Prentice-Hall, 1964), pp. 22–25.

28. Gordon Allport, *The Nature of Prejudice*, abridged ed. (New York: Doubleday, Anchor Books, 1958), p. 7 (italics omitted); see also pp. 6–7.

29. Ibid., p. 10 (italics added).

30. See Thomas F. Pettigrew, *Racially Separate or Together?*. (New York: McGraw-Hill, 1971), pp. 134–35.

31. T.W. Adorno et al., *The Authoritarian Personality*. (New York: Harper, 1950), pp. 248–79.

32. Williams, *Strangers Next Door*, pp. 110–13; Pettigrew, *Racially Separate or Together?* p. 131.

33. R.A. Schermerhorn, *Comparative Ethnic Relations* (New York: Random House, 1970), p. 6.

34. Cox, *Caste, Class, and Race*, p. 400.

35. Figure 1–1 and portions of this discussion are adapted from Joe R. Feagin, "Affirmative Action in an Era of Reaction," in *Consultations on the Affirmative Action Statement of the U.S. Commission on Civil Rights* (Washington, D.C.: U.S. Government Printing Office, 1982), pp. 46–48.

36. Allport, *The Nature of Prejudice*, p. 14.

37. Gunnar Myrdal, *An American Dilemma* (New York: McGraw-Hill Paperback, 1964; originally published 1944), 1:52.

38. Robert K. Merton, "Discrimination and the American Creed," in *Discrimination and National Welfare*, ed. Robert MacIver (New York: Harper, 1949), pp. 103ff. See also Graham C. Kinloch, *The Dynamics of Race Relations* (New York: McGraw-Hill, 1974), p. 54.

39. See Lester Hill, "Prejudice and Discrimination" (Ph.D. diss., University of Texas, 1978). This paragraph draws on Joe R. Feagin and Douglas L. Eckberg, "Discrimination: Motivation, Action, Effects, and Context," in *Annual Review of Sociology*, ed. Alex Inkeles, Neil J. Smelser, and Ralph H. Turner (Palo Alto, Calif.: Annual Reviews, 1980), pp. 3–4.

40. David M. Wellman, *Portraits of White Racism* (Cambridge: Cambridge University Press, 1977).

41. Charles Hamilton and Stokely Carmichael, *Black Power* (New York: Random House, 1967), p. 4. See also Louis L. Knowles and Kenneth Prewitt, eds., *Institutional Racism in America* (Englewood Cliffs, N.J.: Prentice-Hall, 1969), p. 5.

42. Anthony Downs, *Racism in America and How to Combat It* (Washington, D.C.: U.S. Commission on Civil Rights, 1970), pp. 5, 7.

43. Thomas F. Pettigrew, "Racism and the Mental Health of White Americans: A Social Psychological View," in *Racism and Mental Health*, ed. Charles V. Willie, Bernard M. Kramer, and Bertram S. Brown (Pittsburgh: University of Pittsburgh Press, 1973), p. 271.

44. Joe R. Feagin, "Indirect Institutionalized Discrimination," *American Politics Quarterly* 5 (April 1977): 177–200.

45. Diana M. Pearce, "Black, White, and Many Shades of Gray: Real Estate Brokers and Their Racial Practices" (Ph.D. diss., University of Michigan, 1976); Diana Kendall, "Square Pegs in Round Holes: Nontraditional Students in Medical Schools" (Ph.D. diss., University of Texas, 1980).

46. Nijole V. Benokraitis and Joe R. Feagin, *Modern Sexism* (Englewood Cliffs, N.J.: Prentice-Hall, 1986), pp. 30–33.

47. Ed Jones, "What It's Like to Be a Black Manager," *Harvard Business Review*, 64 (May/June 1986): 84–93; Thomas Pettigrew and Joanne Martin, "Shaping the Organizational Context for Black American Inclusion," *Journal of Social Issues* 43 (Spring 1987): 41–78.

48. Quoted in Benokraitis and Feagin, *Modern Sexism*, p. 109.

49. *Initial Black Pulse Findings*, Bulletin No. 1, Research Department, National Urban League (New York, 1980).

# CHAPTER 2

# Adaptation and Conflict: Racial and Ethnic Relations in Theoretical Perspective

## RACIAL AND ETHNIC HIERARCHIES

How do racial and ethnic groups develop? How do they come into contact with one another in the first place? How do they adjust to one another beyond the initial contact? There are a number of theories of how intergroup contact leads to initial patterns of racial and ethnic interaction and stratification. Various other theories explore the persistence of racial and ethnic patterns. Group control and stratification, as well as intergroup conflict, are critical issues in these racial and ethnic theories.

There is a diversity of racial and ethnic groups in this society. As in the 1790s, so in the 1980s the number of racial and ethnic groups in North America remains impressive, although the exact mix of groups is different. Racial and ethnic diversity is basic in the history of this society.

Yet diversity, as the common terms *majority group* and *minority group* suggest, has often been linked to a racial and ethnic *hierarchy*, to stratification. Human beings organize themselves in a number of different ways—for example, for earning a living, for religious rituals, and for governing. Among the important features of social organization are ranking systems. Such systems rank categories of people, not just individuals. Several ranking systems coexist, shaped by differences in such aspects as race or ethnic group, sex, handicapped status, and class position. There are a number of categories in each ranking system. Rewards tend to parallel these categories. Some categories, such as English Americans and males, have greater privileges and resources than others, such as black Americans and women, and ranked classifications persist from one generation to the next. Class stratification in Western capitalist countries has been a focus of concern since the middle of the nineteenth century; it is exemplified in the distinction among the working class, the small-business class, and the capitalist class. Racial and ethnic stratification occurs in ranking systems where *ascribed* (that is, attributed, not achieved) group characteristics such as race or ethnicity are major criteria for social positions and social rewards. Class stratification and race–ethnic stratification, as we will see in the chapters that follow, are often overlapping systems.[1]

The image of a ladder will make the concept of racial and ethnic stratification clearer. In Figure 2–1 the positions of five selected racial and ethnic groups at a specific time are diagramed on a ladder. Some groups are higher than others, suggesting that they have greater privileges than the lower groups. The privileges can be thought of as economic, political, and social or cultural. A group substantially higher than another on an important dimension is usually viewed as a dominant group; one substantially lower than another is seen as a subordinate group. The more groups in a society, the more complex the image, with middle groups standing in a relation of dominance to some groups and in a relation of subordination to others.

Take the United States in 1790, the time of its founding. For that year one might roughly diagram the five groups in Figure 2–1 in terms of such factors as overall economic power or cultural status, so that the top group would be English Americans,

**FIGURE 2-1**    A Ladder of Dominance: The United States as of 1790

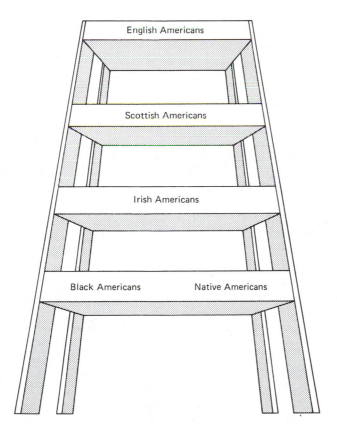

with Scottish Americans a bit down the ladder. A little farther down might be the Irish immigrants, a group composed substantially of poor farmers and indentured servants. At the bottom would be black Americans, most of whom were still locked in slavery in the South. Those Native American tribal groups and individuals within the boundaries of the new nation—many others were still outside it—were also at the bottom of the hierarchy. The North American experience reveals the presence of race–ethnic, class, and gender hierarchies from the very beginning.[2]

## Some Basic Questions

A number of social science theories have been developed to explain this diversity and stratification and the intergroup adaptation that creates them. For some, *theory* means vague speculation, but in the social sciences the term usually refers to a conceptual framework by which one attempts to interpret important social phenomena. Barth and Noel have summarized some of the major questions raised in the theoretical analysis of racial and ethnic relations:

1. How does one explain the origin and emergence of racial and ethnic diversity and stratification?
2. How does one explain the continuation of racial and ethnic diversity and stratification?
3. How does one interpret internal adaptive changes within systems of racial and ethnic diversity and stratification?
4. How does one explain major changes in systems of racial and ethnic diversity and stratification?[3]

## MIGRATION AND GROUP CONTACT

The origin of race and ethnic relations lies in intergroup contact. Different groups, often with no common ancestry, come into one another's spheres of influence. Contact can be between an established or native people and a migrating people (group A → land of group B) or between migrating groups moving into a previously uninhabited area (group A → new land ← group B). The movement of the English colonists into the lands of Native Americans in the 1600s is an example of the first case.

Migration has been viewed by sociologist Charles Tilly in terms of:

1. The actual migrating units (for example, families)
2. The situation at the point of origin (for example, the home country)
3. The situation at the destination (for example, a U.S. city)
4. The social and political framework within which the migration occurs (for example, corporate capitalism)[4]

Certain characteristics of the precontact situation are critical to shaping both the migration and the outcome of the contact generated by the migration. What groups bring to contact is important. The characteristics of the migrating group (such as education) and its home society, and of the receiving group (or other migrating group) and its home society, are extremely critical. Push and pull factors generating migration stem from each of these areas. The technological level of each group, particularly its transportation and firepower, is an important shaping factor. Technological development has played a major role in giving advantage. Native Americans lost out to European settlers because of their less developed military technology. The ability of each group to organize for expansion and competition also shapes the migration as well as the outcome of contact. Critical too is the social and economic (for example, the job) situation at the point of origin of the migrants. A depressed economy or painful religious conflict in the sending countries often underlies major migrations to other countries; the migrants are attracted by the portrayal, accurate or inaccurate, of better conditions—such as "lots of jobs"—at the destination.[5]

## Types of Migration

The types of migration generating race and ethnic relations can be seen as a continuum running from involuntary to completely voluntary migration:

1. Movements of forced labor (slavery)
2. Contract labor movement
3. Movement of displaced persons and refugees
4. Voluntary migration[6]

*Movements of forced labor* include the forcible removal of African slaves to North America; *contract labor* transfer includes the migration of indentured Irish servants to the English colonies and of Chinese laborers to western North America. The *displaced persons* category is exemplified in the streams of refugees coming in the wake of numerous U.S. wars. *Voluntary migration* covers the great Atlantic migration of southern and eastern European groups to the United States in the early twentieth century. Another important type of migration often precedes the types just examined. This is the voluntary migration of colonizers, sometimes termed *colonization migration*. External colonization can be seen in the English trading companies whose employees founded early American colonies, a development that led to the engulfing and dispersal of the Native American population.[7]

# PATTERNS OF RACIAL AND ETHNIC ADAPTATION

## The Initial Contact

What happens once different human groups come into contact as the result of migration? A close look at racial and ethnic contact reveals a variety of outcomes. In the initial stage the range of outcomes includes:

1. Exclusion or genocidal destruction
2. Egalitarian symbiosis
3. A hierarchy or stratification system

*Genocide* is the killing off of one group by another—a common outcome of contacts between British settlers and Native Americans on the Atlantic coast of North America. *Egalitarian symbiosis* consists of peaceful coexistence and a rough economic and political equality between the two groups. A few examples of this outcome can be found in the history of world migrations, but they are rare, especially in North America. Some authors argue that by the late eighteenth century the Scots were approaching approximate equality with English Americans in many areas. A more common result of migration and contact is hierarchy or stratification. Lieberson has listed two hierarchies that can result from intergroup contact. *Migrant superordination* occurs when the migrating group imposes its will on indigenous groups, usually through superior weapons and organization. The Native American populations of the United States and Canada were subordinated in this fashion. *Indigenous superordination* occurs when groups immigrating into a new society become subordinate to groups already there, as in black slave importation to North America.[8]

## Later Adaptation Patterns

Beyond the initial period, the range of outcomes of intergroup contact includes:

1. Continuing genocide
2. Continuing egalitarian symbiosis
3. Replacement of stratification by inclusion along "core-conformity" lines
4. Replacement of stratification by inclusion along cultural pluralism lines
5. Continuing stratification with some acculturation, ranging from moderate to extreme exploitation of the subordinate race/ethnic group

One type of outcome can be a continuing thrust by the dominant group to kill off the subordinate group. Some Native American groups experienced white attempts to exterminate them until the early twentieth century. Egalitarian symbiosis can also persist. The initial hierarchy can be modified in the direction of full assimilation of the incoming group within the core culture and society.

This can take two forms. In the first, inclusion in the dominant sphere is along cultural conformity lines, with the incoming group conforming to the dominant group. Here rough equality is attained by surrender of much of one's cultural heritage, though some ingroup ties may be retained. Some have argued that certain North European immigrant groups, such as Scottish and Scandinavian Americans, gained rough equality in this way. Others, in contrast, might argue that the initial stratification can also be replaced by rough egalitarian inclusion along cultural pluralism lines; thus the eventual outcome for certain white immigrant groups (such as Irish Catholic and Jewish Americans) was substantial socioeconomic and political assimilation along with substantial retention of major cultural (e.g., religious) and primary-group distinctiveness. According to this view, the absorption trend was primarily in the realm of economic or political matters.

A fifth outcome of continuing intergroup contact is persisting racial or ethnic stratification. The extent and inequality of the stratification can vary, but for many nonwhite groups in the United States political and economic inequality has remained so great that it has been described accurately as *internal colonialism*. Even here, however, partial assimilation usually occurs in terms of adaptation to the core culture (for instance, to the English language).

## Types of Theories

In the United States explanatory theories of racial and ethnic relations have been concerned with migration, adaptation, and stratification. Most such theories can be roughly classified as order theories or power–conflict theories. *Order theories* tend to accent assimilation, as in the third and fourth of the outcomes just described, concentrating on progressive adaptation to the dominant culture and stability in intergroup relations. *Power–conflict theories* give more attention to first and fifth outcomes—genocide and continuing stratification—and to the social control and conflict associated with exploitation and subordination. Assimilation analyses are examples of order theories; the internal colonialism theory and class-oriented neo-Marxist viewpoints are examples of power–conflict theories.

## ASSIMILATION AND OTHER ORDER PERSPECTIVES

In the United States much theorizing has emphasized assimilation, the orderly adaptation of a migrating group to the ways and institutions of an established host group. Hirschman has noted that "the assimilation perspective, broadly defined, continues to be the primary theoretical framework for sociological research on racial and ethnic inequality." The reason for this dominance, he suggests, is the "lack of convincing alternatives."[9] The English word *assimilate* comes from the Latin *assimulare*, "to make similar." This meaning has been taken literally by assimilation analysts, who have not been significantly concerned with hierarchy and stratification outcomes of intergroup contact.

## Robert Park

Robert E. Park, one of the first major American theorists of racial and ethnic relations, argued that European out-migration has been the major catalyst of world reorganization. Intergroup contacts and relations regularly go through stages of a race relations cycle. Fundamental social forces such as out-migration lead to recurring cycles in intergroup history: "The race relations cycle which takes the form, to state it abstractly, of *contacts, competition, accommodation* and eventual *assimilation,* is apparently progressive and irreversible."[10] In the contact stage migration and exploration bring peoples together, which in turn leads to economic competition and thus to new social organization. Competition and conflict flow from the contacts between native peoples and the migrating groups. Accommodation, an unstable condition in the Park cycle, often takes place rapidly. It involves a forced adjustment by a migrating group to a new social situation. Park seems to have viewed accommodation as involving a stabilization of relations, including the possibility of permanent caste systems. Sometimes he spoke of the race relations cycle as inevitably leading from contact to assimilation. At other times, however, he recognized that the assimilation of a migrant group might take centuries.

Nonetheless, Park and most scholars working in his tradition have argued that there is a long-term trend toward assimilation of racial and ethnic minorities in modern societies. "Assimilation is a process of interpenetration and fusion in which persons and groups acquire the memories, sentiments, and attitudes of other persons or groups, and, by sharing their experience and history, are incorporated with them in a common cultural life."[11] This final stage of intergroup interaction is basically a melting pot stage resulting in new amalgamated peoples. Even racially subordinate groups are expected to assimilate.[12]

## Stages of Assimilation: Milton Gordon

Since Park's pioneering analysis in the 1920s, many U.S. theorists of racial and ethnic relations and textbook writers have adopted an assimilationist perspective, although most have departed from Park's framework in a number of important ways. Milton Gordon, author of the influential *Assimilation in American Life*, distinguishes a variety of initial encounters between race and ethnic groups and an array of possible outcomes. He gives substantial attention to European immigrants to America, viewing them primarily in terms of assimilation to the dominant *Anglo-Saxon–Protestant* culture and society. The actual trend of immigrant adaptation is typically in the direction of *Anglo-conformity*, of immigrants giving up much of their heritage for the dominant, preexisting Anglo-Saxon (English) core culture. The touchstone of the process of adjustment is viewed thus: "If there is anything in American life which can be described as an overall American culture which serves as a reference point for immigrants and their children, it can best be described, it seems to us, as the middle-class cultural patterns of, largely, white Protestant, Anglo-Saxon origins, leaving aside for the moment the question of minor reciprocal influences on this culture exercised by the cultures of later entry into the United States."[13]

How has the general trend in the adaptation of immigrant groups in the United States been described? Gordon notes that Anglo-conformity has been substantially achieved, at least in regard to cultural assimilation. Most groups following the English have adapted to the core culture. Gordon is more concrete than Park, distinguishing seven processes within the adaptation of one group to the core society:[14]

1. *Cultural assimilation*: change of cultural patterns to those of the core society
2. *Structural assimilation*: penetration of cliques and associations of the core society at the primary-group level
3. *Marital assimilation*: significant intermarriage
4. *Identification assimilation*: development of a sense of identity linked to the core society
5. *Attitude-receptional assimilation*: absence of prejudice and stereotyping
6. *Behavior-receptional assimilation*: absence of intentional discrimination
7. *Civic assimilation*: absence of value and power conflict

Particularly important is Gordon's distinction between cultural and structural as-similation. Whereas Park believed structural assimilation, including primary-group ties such as intergroup friendships, flowed from cultural assimilation, Gordon stres-ses that this may not be inevitable. Although acculturation is an inescapable outcome of initial contact for Gordon, primary-group assimilation or marital assimilation is not.

Gordon conceptualizes structural assimilation as relating to primary-group rela-tions. He does not highlight as a separate type of structural assimilation the movement of a new immigrant group into what sociologists term the *secondary groups* of the host society—that is, preexisting employing organizations, such as corporations or public bureaucracies, as well as educational and political institutions. Moving into the core society's secondary organizations does *not necessarily* mean entering the preexisting primary groups, such as friendship cliques. In addition, the dimension Gor-don calls *civic assimilation* is confused in his discussion, since it includes "values," which are really part of the cultural assimilation dimension, and "power," which is an aspect of structural assimilation at the secondary-group level.

In *Human Nature, Class, and Ethnicity* (1978) Gordon admitted neglecting the power and conflict issues in his model of assimilation and proposed bringing these is-sues into the model. But in this book his analysis of power and conflict is very brief. Gordon mentions in passing the different resources available to competing racial and ethnic groups and refers briefly to black–white conflict, but he gives no serious atten-tion to economic power, inequalities in material resources, or capitalistic economic history in examining racial and ethnic relations.[15]

Focusing on the millions of European immigrants and their adjustment to the core culture, Gordon's assimilation model emphasizes *generational* changes in im-migrant groups. From this perspective, substantial acculturation to the dominant Anglo-Saxon core culture has often been completed by the second or third generation for many European immigrant groups. The partially acculturated first generation formed protective immigrant communities and associations, but the children of those immigrants were considerably more exposed to Anglo-conformity pressures, in the mass media and in the public school system.[16]

Gordon suggests that substantial assimilation along other dimensions, such as the civic, behavior-receptional, and attitude-receptional ones, has occurred for numerous white European groups. Most white groups have made considerable progress in gaining equality at the secondary–structural levels of employment and politics, although the dimensions of this secondary–structural assimilation are neither named nor discussed in any detail by Gordon.

For these white groups, structural assimilation at the primary-group level is another matter. Structural integration at the primary-group level is far from complete even in present-day America for many European immigrant groups, particularly non-Protestant ones. Gordon suggests that substantially complete cultural assimilation (for example, adoption of the English language) along with structural (primary-group) pluralism form a characteristic pattern of adaptation for certain white ethnic groups. Even these people, though, tend to go outside their immediate groups in making in-formal friendships and marriage ties with *similar* groups that are part of their religious community. Following Will Herberg, who argued that there are three great community "melting pots" in the United States—Jews, Protestants, and Catholics—Gordon suggests that primary-group ties beyond one's own group are usually developed within one's socioreligious community, whether that be Protestant, Catholic, or Jewish.[17]

In recent writings Gordon takes an optimistic view of the assimilation of nonwhite Americans, including black Americans, into the core culture and society. He argues in regard to blacks that the United States has "moved decisively down the road toward implementing the implications of the American creed [of equality and justice] for race relations"—as in the spheres of employment and housing. Because of this tremendous progress for black Americans, the new governmental policy dilemma is the choice between a traditional political liberalism that ignores race and a "corporate liberalism" that recognizes group rights along racial lines. Gordon includes under corporate liberalism the governmental programs of affirmative action, which he apparently rejects in favor of traditional liberalism and its emphasis on individual rights. Gordon's optimism about the implementation of the American creed of equality for black Americans is not well founded, as we will see.[18]

## Cultural Pluralism and Ethnogenesis

Some assimilation theorists do not accept the argument that most European-American groups have become substantially assimilated to the Anglo-Saxon way of life. A few social scientists have begun to explore models that depart from Anglo-conformity in the direction of cultural pluralism. Most analysts of pluralism accept a substantial amount of Anglo-conformity as inevitable, if not desirable. In *Beyond the Melting Pot*, Glazer and Moynihan agree that the original customs and ways of European immigrants were lost by the third generation. But this did not mean the decline of ethnicity. The European immigrant groups often remained culturally distinct in terms of name, identity, and other cultural attributes.[19]

The theme of ethnic group persistence in later generations as part of the adaptive process has been elaborated under the conceptual term *ethnogenesis*. Andrew Greeley has applied an ethnogenesis model to groups defined by nationality and religion. A revisionist in the assimilation tradition, he is critical of the traditional assimilation perspective because it assumes "that the strain toward homogenization in a modern industrial society is so great as to be virtually irresistible."[20] Traditionally, the direction of this assimilation in the United States is assumed to be toward the Anglo-Saxon–Protestant core culture. But from the ethnogenesis perspective, adaptation has meant more than this one-way conformity. The traditional assimilation model does not explain the persistence of ethnicity in the United States—the emphasis among immigrants on ethnicity as a way of becoming American and, in recent decades, the self-conscious attempts to create ethnic identity and manipulate ethnic symbols.[21]

The complex ethnogenesis model proposed by Greeley is illustrated in Figure 2–2. This model of intergroup adaptation suggests that in many cases host and immigrant groups had a similar *cultural* inheritance. Some European immigrant groups had a cultural background distantly related to that of English settlers. As a result of interaction in schools and the influence of the media, over several generations the

**FIGURE 2-2**    The Ethnogenesis Perspective

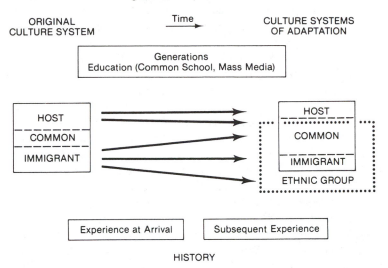

Source: Andrew M. Greeley, *Ethnicity in the United States* (New York: John Wiley, 1974), p. 309.

number of cultural traits common to the host and immigrant groups grew. Yet in the adaptive process some nationality traits persist and certain aspects of the heritage of the home country still receive emphasis. From this perspective, ethnic groups share traits with the host group *and* retain major nationality characteristics as well.[22] A number of field studies in the United States have documented the persistence of distinctive white ethnic groups such as Irish Americans, Italian Americans, and Polish Americans in U.S. cities, not just in New York and Chicago but in San Francisco, New Orleans, and Tucson as well. Yancey and associates have suggested that ethnicity is an "emergent phenomenon"—that its importance in cities depends a lot on the specific social and economic situations.[23]

## Problems with Assimilation Theories

Most assimilation theorists take as their examples of ethnic adaptation white European groups migrating more or less voluntarily to the United States. But what of the adaptation and assimilation of non-European groups beyond the stage of initial contact? Some analysts of assimilation include nonwhite Americans in their framework, despite the problems that arise from such a classification. Some analysts have argued that assimilation, cultural and structural, is the necessary answer to the race problem in the United States—and the likely result of the long-term trend as well. One prominent European writer on U.S. race relations, Gunnar Myrdal, argued that as a practical matter it is "to the advantage of American Negroes as individuals and as a group to become assimilated into American culture, to acquire the traits held in esteem by the dominant white Americans."[24] In Myrdal's view there is a fundamental ethical dilemma in the United States, which can be seen in the contradiction between the democratic principles of the Declaration of Independence and the institutionalized subordination of black Americans. For Myrdal this represents a "lag of public morals," a problem solved in principle but still being worked out in an assimilation process that may or may not be completed.

More optimistic analysts have emphasized progressive inclusion, which will eventually provide black Americans and other nonwhites with full citizenship. For that reason, they expect ethnic and racial conflict will disappear as various groups become assimilated into United States society. Nathan Glazer, Milton Gordon, and Talcott Parsons have stressed the egalitarianism in the institutions of the United States and what they view as the progressive emancipation of nonwhites. As we have noted, Gordon has underscored the cultural and structural assimilation of black Americans, particularly those above the poverty level, over the last several decades. Full membership for black Americans seems inevitable, notes Parsons, for "the only tolerable solution to the enormous tensions lies in constituting a single societal community with full membership for all."[25] The importance of racial, as well as ethnic, stratification is expected to decline as powerful, universalistic societal forces wipe out the vestiges of earlier value systems. White immigrants have desired substantial assimilation, and most have been absorbed. The same is expected to happen for non-European groups.

Assimilation theories have been criticized as having an "establishment" bias, as not distinguishing carefully enough between what *has* happened to a given group and what the establishment at some point felt *should have* happened. For example, a number of Asian American scholars and leaders have reacted vigorously to the application of the concept of assimilation to Asian Americans, arguing that the concept originated in a period (1870–1925) of intense attacks by white Americans on Asian Americans. The term was tainted from the beginning by its association with the dominant European American group's ideology that the only "good groups" were those that assimilated (or could assimilate) in Anglo-conformity fashion.

One of the serious weaknesses in recent assimilationist analysis is that some of that work abandons historical assessments of the immigrants being considered. Unlike Park, who paid substantial attention to the historical and world-economy context of migration, many assimilationists seldom analyze the centuries-long development of racial and ethnic relations, including the relationship of racial and ethnic conflict and exploitation to the capitalistic search for profits in an expanding world economy. As Geschwender has noted, "they seem to have forgotten that exploitation is the driving force that gives meaning to the study of racial and ethnic relations."[26]

## Biosocial Perspectives

Some assimilationists have recently turned to a biosocial perspective on racial and ethnic relations. The idea of race and ethnicity being deeply rooted in the biological makeup of human beings is an old European and American notion that began to receive attention from a few social scientists and biologists in the United States in the 1970s. This perspective has been adopted by order-oriented social scientists such as Milton Gordon and Pierre van den Berghe. In *Human Nature, Class, and Ethnicity* Gordon suggests that ethnic ties are rooted in the "biological organism of man." Ethnicity is a fundamental part of the physiological as well as the psychological self. Ethnicity "cannot be shed by social mobility, as for instance social class background can, since society insists on its inalienable ascription from cradle to grave." What Gordon seems to have in mind is not the old racist notion of the unchanging biological character and separateness of racial groups, but rather the rootedness of intergroup relations, such as racial and ethnic relations, in the everyday realities of human grouping, kinship, and socially constructed group boundaries. Gordon goes further, however, emphasizing that human beings tend to be "selfish, narcissistic and perpetually poised on the edge of aggression." And it is these selfish tendencies that lie behind racial and ethnic tensions.[27] Gordon is here adopting a Hobbesian (dog-eat-dog) view of human nature. Critics of Gordon's biosocial view have suggested that he is reading back into fundamental "human nature" what are in reality only the specific characteristics of an individualistic value system that has evolved under modern capitalism. That is, under capitalism selfishness and narcissism are *learned* rather than rooted deeply in the human biological makeup.

Pierre van den Berghe has emphasized that ethnic and racial sentiments are grounded in kinship relations, and that the kinship favoritism underlying ethnic and racial relations is in turn grounded in the evolutionary and selfish struggle of human "genes" to perpetuate themselves. Like Gordon, and unlike American and European racial theorists of the past decades such as Madison Grant and Adolf Hitler, van den Berghe does not defend racist thinking, which accents racial differences grounded in biology, but rather emphasizes the common biological characteristics of human beings. He does argue that the *social* significance of genetically determined characteristics, such as dark skin color, can be very important, and he further suggests that this social significance is often far greater than biological or evolutionary significance—which in the case of skin color is relatively trivial. Then how does racist thinking arise? Van den Berghe argues that racist categorizing almost always occurs where there is long-distance migration "across a genetic gradient"—that is, where there are wide differences in skin color between migrating and host groups. He sees this as the most important cause of racism. However, he fails to discuss the economic and political conditions that frequently spur the kind of migration that pushes a darker group (such as black Africans) into the clutches of a lighter-skinned group (such as European Americans).[28]

Though decidedly different from the earlier biological theories, this biosocial analysis of Gordon and van den Berghe remains problematical. The exact linkages between the deep genetic underpinnings of human beings and concrete racial or ethnic behavior are not spelled out beyond some vague analysis of kin selection and selfish behavior. A more convincing sociobiological analysis might attempt to show more exactly how the "desires" of the human genes are changed, through several specified levels or techniques, into social phenomena such as slavery or language assimilation. As yet, this important task has not been done.

Another difficulty with the biosocial approach is that in the real world, racial and ethnic relations are *immediately social* rather than biological. As Edna Bonacich has pointed out, many racial and ethnic groups have mixed biological ancestry. Jewish Americans, for example, have a very mixed ancestry: as a group, they share no distinct biological characteristics. Biologically diverse Italian immigrants from different regions of Italy gained a sense of being Italian American (even Italian) in the United States. The bonds holding Jewish Americans together and Italian Americans together were not genetically based or biologically primordial, but rather the result of real *historical* experiences in settling into the United States. Moreover, if ethnicity is primordial in a biological sense, it should always be a prominent force in human affairs. Sometimes ethnicity leads to intense conflict, as in the case of Jews and Gentiles; in other cases, as with Scottish and English Americans, it quietly disappears in the assimilation process. Sentiments based on common ancestry are important, but they are activated primarily in concrete experiences of specific migrating and host groups.[29]

## Emphasizing Migration: Competition Theory

A recent example of the exploration of migration and adaptation issues in the Robert Park tradition can be seen in the framework called *competition theory*. Park emphasized the migration of peoples in the creation of ethnic contacts, which led in turn to competition for scarce resources, then to accommodation and assimilation. Recent competition theorists have explored the contact and competition parts of this "race relations cycle." They focus on how competition leads to certain types of racial and ethnic conflict. There is a tradition in sociological thought, called *human ecology*, that draws on the ideas of Park and other ecologists and that emphasizes the "struggle of human groups for survival" in their natural environments. This tradition, which highlights demographic trends such as the migration of groups and population concentration in cities, has been adopted by recent competition analysts researching racial and ethnic groups.[30]

Competition theorists such as Susan Olzak and Joane Nagel view ethnicity as a social phenomenon distinguished by boundaries of language, skin color, and culture. The tradition of human ecology and demography is considered valuable because it emphasizes the stability of ethnic population boundaries over time, as well as the impact of shifts in these boundaries resulting from migration; ethnic group membership often coincides with the creation of a distinctive group niche in the labor force. Competition occurs when two or more ethnic groups attempt to secure the same resources, such as jobs or housing. Competition theorists have accented the ways in which ethnic group competition and the accompanying ethnic solidarity lead to collective action, mobilization, and protest.[31]

According to competition theorists, collective action is fostered by immigration across borders and by the expansion of once-segregated minorities into the same labor and housing markets to which other ethnic groups have access. A central argument of these theorists is that collective attacks on immigrant and nonwhite workers increase at the local level when subordinate ethnic groups move up and out of segregated jobs, and not, as one might expect, in cities where ethnic groups are locked into ethnic segregation and poverty. For example, empirical data presented by Susan Olzak in an article on ethnic and racial violence in the late nineteenth century support the view that ethnic collective action, such as Anglo-Saxon–Protestant crowds attacking

European immigrants coming into the United States, increases when immigration expands and economic recessions occur. Olzak uses such data to argue that the ethnic boundary of the native-born was mobilized against immigrant and black workers "when ethnic competition was activated by a rising supply of low wage labor and tight labor markets."[32]

Competition theorists explicitly contrast their analyses with the power–conflict views we will discuss in the next section, perspectives that emphasize the role of capitalism, the significance of economic subordination, institutionalized discrimination, and routine economic exploitation. As the competition theorists see the ethnic world, class-linked labor exploitation and economic hardship are not major forces in ethnic and racial conflict. Migration and population concentration, as well as other demographic factors, seem to be more important. Using the traditional ecologists' language, competition theorists speak of ethnic groups competing in job, housing, and other markets. But they study markets without a clear sense of the structural character of job and housing markets in Western capitalist countries. The markets in which the immigrant groups are competing are not in fact free competitive markets, but are often severely distorted by the economic reality of a few big companies controlling jobs or sales and the reality of major government intervention. Ethnic immigrant groups do not compete on an equal playing field. Since the economic markets are already structured along oligopoly capitalist lines when the ethnic and racial immigrants come in, it is essential to probe more deeply than migration and group mobility and to research the larger political and economic context of the immigrant adjustment. Missing from much of the new competition theory is a systematic concern with the inequality, power, exploitation, and discrimination issues accented by the power–conflict theories.

## POWER–CONFLICT THEORIES

The last few decades have witnessed the development of alternative conceptual frameworks explaining racial and ethnic relations, perspectives that place greater emphasis on economic stratification and power issues than one finds in assimilation and competition theories. Within this broad category of power–conflict theories are a number of subcategories: the caste perspective, the internal colonialism viewpoint, and a variety of class-based and neo-Marxist theories.

### The Caste School

One early exception to the assimilation perspective was the *caste school* of race relations, which developed in the 1940s under W. Lloyd Warner and Allison Davis.[33] Focusing on black–white relations in the South, these researchers viewed the position of black Americans as distinctively different from that of other racial and ethnic groups. After the Civil War a new social system, a caste system, replaced the old slavery system of the South. In addition to economic and social inequality, the white and black castes were separated by a total prohibition of intermarriage. Warner and his associates were critical of the heavy emphasis in traditional analysis on prejudiced attitudes and feelings.[34]

## An Early Class Theory of Race Relations

Another early power–conflict analyst was Oliver C. Cox, a brilliant black scholar whose work has been neglected because of its explicitly Marxist approach, one emphasizing the role of the capitalist class in racial exploitation and discrimination. Cox systematically analyzed the economic distinctiveness of black slave migration and the oppressiveness of later adjustment patterns of blacks. White-on-black stratification arose out of the expansion of European capitalism. The African slave trade was "a way of recruiting labor for the purpose of exploiting the great natural resources of America." The color of Africans was not important: they were chosen "simply because they were the best workers to be found for the heavy labor in the mines and plantations across the Atlantic." A search for cheap labor by a profit-oriented capitalist class led to a system of race subordination. Racial prejudice developed later as an ideology rationalizing the exploitation of Afro-Americans.[35]

## Internal Colonialism

The persistence of racial stratification in the U.S. capitalistic system over time has underscored its distinctiveness. For that reason, analysts of internal colonialism prefer to see racial stratification and the class stratification of American capitalism as *separate but related* systems of oppression. Neither should be reduced in social science theories to the other. An emphasis on power and resource inequalities, particularly white–nonwhite inequalities, is at the heart of the internal colonialism model.

The framework of internal colonialism owes a debt to the analysis of *external colonialism*—the imperialism of the capitalist nations, including the United States and European nations.[36] For example, Balandier has noted the impact of capitalist expansion on non-European peoples since the fifteenth century: "Until very recently the greater part of the world's population, not belonging to the white race (if we exclude China and Japan), knew only a status of dependency on one or another of the European colonial powers."[37] External colonialism involves the running of another country's economy and politics by an outside colonial power. Many colonies became independent of their colonizer, such as Britain or France, but continued to have their economy directed by its capitalists and corporations. This system of continuing dependency has been called *neocolonialism*. Neocolonialism is common where there were few white settlers in the colonized country. Colonies experiencing a large in-migration of white settlers often show a different pattern. In such cases external colonialism becomes *internal colonialism* when the control and exploitation of subordinate (for example, nonwhite) groups in the colonized country passes from whites in the home country to dominant (often white European) groups within the newly independent country.[38]

Nonwhite groups entering later, such as African slaves and Mexican farm workers in the U.S. case, can be viewed in terms of internal colonialism. Internal colonialism emerges out of classical European colonialism and imperialism, but it takes on a life of its own. The historical origin and initial stabilization of internal colonialism in North America predates the Revolutionary War. The process of systematic subordination of non-Europeans began with "genocidal attempts by colonizing settlers to uproot native populations and force them into other regions."[39] Native Americans were killed or driven off desirable lands. Later, Asians and Pacific peoples were imported as indentured workers or annexed in an expansionist period of United States development. Slaves from Africa were a cheap source of labor for capital accumulation both before and after the Revolution. Robert Blauner, a colonialism theorist, notes that agriculture in the South depended on black labor; in the Southwest, Mexican agricultural development was taken over by force by European settlers, and later agricultural development was based substantially on cheap Mexican labor coming into what was once northern Mexico.[40]

In this process of exploiting the labor of nonwhite people, who were made slaves or were paid low wages, enormous profits were reaped by agricultural and industrial capitalists. This accumulation of capital contributed substantially to the growth of this capitalist economy. From the internal colonialism perspective, contemporary racial and ethnic inequality and stratification have a base in the economic *interests* of the whites in cheap labor, an underpinning of economic exploitation. Nonwhite, non-European groups were subordinated to certain European-American requirements for *labor* or *land*. Moreover, internal colonialism theorists have recognized the central role of *government* in supporting the exploitation of nonwhite minorities. For example, the colonial and U.S. governments played an important role in legitimating slavery in the sixteenth through the nineteenth centuries and in providing the troops that subordinated Native Americans across the nation and Mexicans in the southwest.

Internal colonialism theorists are not concerned primarily with white immigrant groups, many of which entered the United States after the nonwhites were subordinated. Instead, they wish to analyze the establishment of racial stratification and the control processes that maintain white dominance. Stokely Carmichael and Charles Hamilton, who in their writings in the 1960s were among the first to use the term *internal colonialism*, accented institutional racism—discrimination by the white community against blacks as a group.[41] Blacks are a "colony" in white America in regard to education, economics, and politics. Racial discrimination is thoroughly institutionalized.

## A Renewed Emphasis on Class

Some recent analysts of racial and ethnic relations have combined an internal colonialism perspective with an emphasis on class stratification that draws on the Marxist research pioneered by Oliver Cox. Mario Barrera, for example, has suggested that the heart of the current systems of internal colonialism is an interactive structure of class *and* race stratification that divides our society. A clear discussion of class, in the economic-exploitation sense of that term, needs to be central to an internal colonialism perspective. Basic to the U.S. system of internal colonialism are four major classes that have developed in American capitalism:

1. *Capitalists*: that small group of people who control capital investments and the means of production and who buy the labor of many others
2. *Managers*: that modest-sized group of people who work as administrators for the capitalists and have been granted control over the work of others
3. *Petit bourgeoisie*: that small group of merchants who control their own businesses and do most of their work themselves, buying little labor power from others
4. *Working class*: that huge group of blue-collar and white-collar workers who sell their labor power to employers in return for wages and salaries

The dominant class in the U.S. political-economic system is the capitalist class, which in everyday practice subordinates working people, nonwhite and white, to its investment needs and other economic requirements. And it is the capitalists who decide whether and where to create jobs.

Barrera argues that each of these classes contains important segments that are set off in terms of race and ethnicity. Figure 2–3 suggests how this works. Each of the major classes is cross-cut by a line of racial segmentation that separates those suffering institutionalized discrimination, such as black Americans and Mexican Americans, from those who do not. Take the example of the working class. Although minority workers share a similar *class* position with white workers in that they are struggling against capitalist employers for better wages and working conditions, they are in a subordinate economic position because of structural discrimination along racial lines. Barrera notes that the dimensions of this structural discrimination include lower wages for minority workers, their concentration in certain lower-status occupations, and their use as a reserve labor force.[42]

**FIGURE 2–3**    The Class and Race Structure of Internal Colonialism

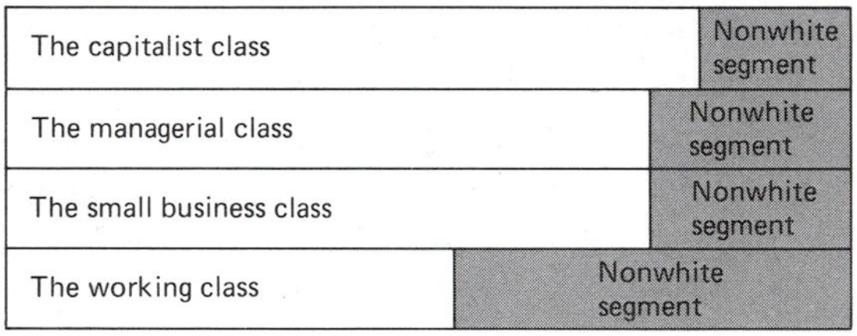

| The capitalist class | | Nonwhite segment |
|---|---|---|
| The managerial class | | Nonwhite segment |
| The small business class | | Nonwhite segment |
| The working class | Nonwhite segment | |

## Culture and Ideology

Internal colonialism theorists have also studied the role of cultural stereotyping and ideology in delimiting the opportunities of dominant and subordinate groups. A racist ideology often dominates an internal colonialist society, intellectually dehumanizing the colonized. Stereotyping and prejudice, seen as more or less temporary problems in many traditional assimilation theories, are viewed by internal colonialism analysts as a way of rationalizing exploitation over a long period. Discrimination is a question not of individual bigots but rather of a system of exploitation rationalized by prejudice. The dominant group's economic gains become linked to its psychological gains. Inequality in economic power becomes linked to a broad system of exploitation on economic, political, and cultural fronts.[43]

In his book on the English colonization of Ireland, Michael Hechter has developed a theory of internal colonialism that emphasizes how the subordinate group utilizes its culture to *resist* subordination. Hechter argues that in a system of internal colonialism, cultural as well as racial markers are used to set off subordinate groups such as black Americans in the United States and the Irish in the United Kingdom. Resistance to the dominant group by the subordinate group often takes the form of cultural solidarity in opposition to the dominant culture. This solidarity can become the basis for protest movements by the subordinated group.[44] Hechter's emphasis on cultural markers is somewhat different from that of other colonialism analysts, such as Robert Blauner, who see resistance movements, including the black ghetto riots of the 1960s and 1980s, as territorial rebellions against white agents of territorial domination. However, Blauner also notes the importance of cultural nationalism in providing the ideological support for rebellions.

## Some Problems with Colonialism Theories

A number of social scientists sympathetic to a power–conflict viewpoint have questioned whether the internal colonialism model fits subordinate groups in the United States. Joan Moore, for example, focuses on the use of the term *neocolonialism.* As we noted above, a neocolonial situation is one in which a Third World country (for example, an African country) has just separated itself politically from a European colonial power (for example, Great Britain) but continues to be dependent on that power. It still needs "foreign experts." It has a class of indigenous leaders to help the former colonial power to exploit the local population. It has a distinct territorial boundary. Moore suggests that this neocolonialism model does not apply very well to subordinate nonwhite groups in the United States, because they are not generally confined to a specific bounded territory and because the exploitative intermediary elite of Third World neocolonialism is not present in nonwhite communities in the United States. This space-centered critique has been repeated more recently by Michael Omi and Howard Winant, who argue that the extensive interpenetration of white and nonwhite societies in the United States casts doubt on the internal colonialism argument about territorially bounded colonization.[45]

However, most internal colonialism researchers have recognized the differences between internal-colonial and neocolonial oppression. These theorists note that the situations of nonwhite groups in the United States are different from those of Africans in a newly independent nation still dependent on a European country. In response to Moore's critique, internal colonialism analysts might argue that there are many aspects of colonialism evident in U.S. racial and ethnic relations; they might emphasize that in the United States nonwhites (1) are residentially segregated, (2) are "superexploited" in employment and deficient in other material conditions when compared with white immigrants, (3) are culturally stigmatized, and (4) have seen some of their leaders co-opted by whites to help exploit their poorer brothers and sisters. While these conditions in the United States are not defined as precisely as they are in Third World neocolonialism, they are similar enough to allow the use of the idea of colonialism to assess the U.S. situation. Note too that the internal colonialism viewpoint has the advantage of including the broad sweep of American history, for it emphasizes the ways in which racial inequalities have developed from the 1600s to the late twentieth century.

## The Split Labor Market View: Another Class-Based Theory

Colonialism analysts such as Blauner are sometimes unclear about whether all classes of whites benefit from the colonization of nonwhites, or just the dominant class of capitalist employers. A power–conflict perspective that helps in assessing this question is the split labor market view, which treats class in the sense of position in the means of production. This class-oriented viewpoint has been defended articulately by Edna Bonacich. From this point of view, in U.S. society the majority-group (white) workers do not share the interests of the dominant political and economic class, the capitalists. Yet both the dominant employer class and the white part of the working class discriminate against the nonwhite (e.g., black American) part of the working class.[46]

Using a traditional Marxist emphasis on class explanations of racial subordination, Oliver Cox and Robert Allen argued that it was the capitalist class, motivated by a desire for profit and cheap labor, that sought cheap African labor for the slave system in the United States. Ever since, this employer class has played its role in keeping nonwhite Americans in a subordinate economic position in U.S. society. Al Szymanski argues that since employers have not created enough jobs for all Americans wishing to work, black and white workers are pitted against each other for too few jobs, often to the broad advantage of employers as a class. Employers benefit from the lower wages of black workers and from the divisions created between black and white workers, divisions reducing the likelihood of large working-class unions. Economists Paul Baran and Paul Sweezy see this reserve army of black labor as functional for capitalism, since it gives employers flexibility in times of expansion and recession.[47]

In contrast, Bonacich emphasizes that discrimination against nonwhite workers by ordinary white workers seeking to protect their own privileges, however limited these may be, is important. Capitalists bring in nonwhite laborers to decrease labor costs, but white workers resist because they fear economic harm in the form of job displacement or lower wages. Over the last century organized white workers have successfully restricted the access of black workers to many of this society's better job ladders, thus splitting the general labor market, reducing black incomes, and increasing black unemployment problems.

Research on unions in Alabama by Stanley Greenberg provides historical evidence for this argument. Greenberg concludes that from the 1880s to the 1960s the industrial unions in Alabama "helped forge a labor framework" that created and perpetuated rigidly segregated white and black jobs.[48] In coal mining, aircraft, retail trade, shipbuilding, and textiles, union rules specifically set up separate white and black lines of promotion, black and white seniority lists, and superior jobs for whites only. White workers gain and lose from this structural racism. They gain in the short run, because there is less competition for the privileged job categories from the nonwhites they have excluded. But they lose in the long run because the cordoned-off labor sector of non-whites can be used by capitalist employers to undercut white workers.[49]

## "Middleman" Minorities and Ethnic Enclaves

Drawing on the insights of earlier scholars, Bonacich has also explored the in-between position, in terms of power and resources, that certain racial and ethnic groups have occupied in stratified societies. These groups find their economic niche as go-betweens serving elites and workers, as small business people positioned between producers and consumers. Some ethnic and racial groups become small-scale traders, merchants, and entrepreneurs doing certain jobs that the dominant groups in the society are not eager to do. For example, in the face of exclusion from mainstream employment by white Protestants, many Jewish and Japanese Americans became small-scale peddlers, tailors, restaurant operators, or gardeners. Thus these groups occupy "a distinctive class position that is of special use to the ruling [capitalist] class." They "act as a go-between to society's subordinate classes."[50]

Bonacich and Modell have found that Japanese Americans fit the middleman-minority model. Before World War II Japanese Americans resided in highly organized and socially integrated communities and concentrated their economies in self-employment, such as gardening and truck farming, and in nonindustrial family businesses. The ethnic solidarity of the first generation of Japanese Americans helped them establish successful small businesses. However, they faced hostility from the surrounding society, and in fact were driven into the businesses they developed because they were denied most other employment opportunities. By the second generation there was some breakdown in the middleman position of Japanese Americans, for many of that generation moved into professional occupations outside their ethnic economy.[51]

Some middleman minorities, such as Jewish American merchants in U.S. central cities, become the targets of hostility from less well off groups, such as poor blacks. In addition, strong ethnic bonds can make the middleman group an effective competitor. Even Anglo-Saxon–Protestant capitalists may become hostile toward a white immigrant middleman minority that competes too effectively. Thus Jewish Americans have been viewed negatively by better-off Anglo-Saxon–Protestant merchants, who had the power to discriminate against them, as well as by poor blacks with whom Jews dealt as "middleman" landlords and merchants. Recently, some scholars of racial and ethnic relations have criticized the middleman minority theory as applied to Asian Americans, arguing that historically Japanese Americans and Chinese Americans, although substantially involved in trade, have rarely been a *middle* group of entrepreneurs actually situated between a poor nonwhite group and a richer white group. More generally, the middleman minority perspective does not deal adequately with the movement of large numbers of the middleman minority into the majority group, as has happened for large numbers of Jewish Americans. One must also be careful in generalizing the theory to settings outside the United States, such as the Middle East, where dominant (majority) groups have often been the trading "minorities" (small merchants) in particular historical periods.

A related perspective, *enclave theory*, emerged in the 1980s. Both the middleman and ethnic enclave perspectives examine secondary–structural incorporation into the U.S. economy, a topic neglected by the assimilation theorists. Both recognize the importance of racial and ethnic stratification and economic incorporation in niches. They assess the ways in which certain immigrant groups have created distinctive niches for themselves in the ethnic complexes of U.S. cities. The similarities between the enclave view and the middleman view lie in the mode of incorporation into a capitalistic society; both stress the incorporation of certain immigrant groups, such as Asian or Cubans, into a society like the United States in the guise of small businesses and specialized economies. The major differences between the two viewpoints stem from the concrete examples examined. Groups accented by the enclave theorists, such as Cuban and Korean Americans, have created ethnic enclaves that are more than merchant or trading economies—they often include manufacturing enterprises, for example. In addition, these ethnic enclaves usually compete with established Anglo-Saxon–Protestant elites. Enclave theorists argue that in contrast, the middleman minorities develop trading economies and are likely to fill an economic niche that complements that of the established elites. However, the aforementioned research of Bonacich on Jewish Americans suggests that there is little difference between the real-world experiences of the middleman minorities and the enclave minorities, for example, Jewish Americans also engaged in manufacturing enterprises.

An example of the ethnic enclave perspective can be seen in the work of Portes and Manning, who examined the enclave communities and economies of the Cubans in Miami and the Koreans in Los Angeles, groups that have developed many small businesses catering to customers inside and outside the ethnic communities. The researchers suggest that strong enclave economies require a substantial number of immigrants with business capabilities, available capital, and a large pool of low-wage labor. These are the characteristics that enabled the Cuban Americans in Miami to build a better life for themselves. Ethnic enclaves, unlike the "colonies" of internal colonialism, do not relegate newcomers to a permanent position of inferiority and exploitation. For that reason Portes and Manning are critical of the internal colonialism and split labor market viewpoints for trying to encompass the situations of all non-European minorities. (Portes and Manning do note that the situations of blacks, Mexican Americans, and Indians can best be explained in terms of internal colonialism.) However, much enclave analysis pays insufficient attention to the exploitation of enclave low-wage labor by ethnic (e.g. Cuban American) capitalists, as well as to the surrounding political–economic system—in this case multinational capitalism—which shapes the enclave economies.[52]

## Class, the State, and Racial Formation

Michael Omi and Howard Winant have developed what they call a theory of "racial formation." Most innovative in this perspective on race relations is a central emphasis on the role of government in the social and political definition of racial and ethnic relations. Racial and ethnic relations are substantially defined by the actions of governments, ranging from the passing of legislation (for example, restrictive immigration laws) to the imprisonment of immigrants defined as a threat (for example, Japanese Americans in World War II). Although the internal colonialism viewpoint gives some emphasis to the state's role in the exploitation of nonwhite minorities, it has not developed this argument sufficiently.

Omi and Winant note that from the beginning the United States government has been concerned with and actually shaped the politics of race: a lengthy series of laws have defined racial groups and interracial relationships. For example, the Naturalization Law of 1790 explicitly declared that only *free white* immigrants could qualify for naturalization. Many non-Europeans, including Africans and Asians, were for decades prevented from becoming citizens. Japanese and other Asian immigrants, for example, were banned by law from becoming citizens until the 1950s. In 1854 the California Supreme Court even ruled that Chinese immigrants should be classified as "Indians"(!) and therefore denied the political rights available to white Americans.[53]

For centuries, the American state officially favored northern European immigrant groups over non-Europeans and less favored European groups such as Italians. For example, the Immigration Act of 1924 was used to exclude Asian immigrants and most immigrants from southern and eastern Europe, whom leaders in Congress and the White House saw as racially inferior. In this way the American government has created and reinforced the existence of racial and ethnic groups.

### Recurring Themes

We can conclude this discussion of the critical power–conflict theories by underscoring certain recurring themes in the writings of scholars such as Oliver Cox, Edna Bonacich, Robert Blauner, and Michael Omi:

1. A central concern for racial and ethnic inequalities in economic position, power, and resources
2. An emphasis on the roots of racial inequalities and hierarchies in the economic institutions of capitalism
3. A major concern with the class structure of capitalism and its impact on racial relations
4. An emphasis on the role of the state in legalizing racial exploitation and segregation and thus in defining racial and ethnic relations
5. An emphasis on intergroup relations and conflict in a broad historical perspective

Critical power–conflict theories emphasize racial and ethnic inequalities and their deep roots in the history of the U.S. economy and government.

## SUMMARY

This chapter has reviewed the ways in which major conceptual frameworks have dealt with migration and subsequent patterns of adaptation. Migration—varying from the movement of conquerors to slave importation to voluntary immigration—creates intergroup contact. Adaptation can have different outcomes in the initial period, ranging from extreme genocide to peaceful symbiosis to some type of stratification. Further adaptation leads not only to further genocide and symbiosis but also to Anglo-conformity, cultural pluralism, or continuing stratification.

Assimilation theories emphasize Anglo-conformity or cultural pluralism outcomes, whereas power–conflict theories accent substantial inequality and stratification. Both perspectives offer insights into race and ethnic realities. Assimilation analysts have pointed out the different dimensions of intergroup adaptations, such as acculturation and marital assimilation, and have accented the role of value consensus in holding a race and ethnic system together. Power–conflict analysts have pointed up the forced character of much cultural and economic adaptation, particularly for non-whites, and have underscored the role of coercion, segregation, colonization, and institutionalized discrimination in keeping groups on the bottom rungs of the societal ladder.

Power–conflict theorists have emphasized the importance of examining racial and ethnic relations in the long-term perspective of historical development. In the introduction to Part II we will explore the utility of such an approach in evaluating the broad contours of racial and ethnic relations in three and a half centuries of American history.

## NOTES

1. See Tamotsu Shibutani and Kian M. Kwan, *Ethnic Stratification* (New York: Macmillan, 1965), pp. 28–33; and Donald L. Noel, "A Theory of the Origin of Ethnic Stratification," in *Majority and Minority*, eds. Norman R. Yetman and C. Hoy Steele (Boston: Allyn & Bacon, 1971), p. 32.
2. William M. Newman, *American Pluralism* (New York: Harper & Row, Pub., 1973), pp. 30–38.
3. Ernest A. T. Barth and Donald L. Noel, "Conceptual Frameworks for the Analysis of Race Relations: An Evaluation," *Social Forces* 50 (March 1972): 336.
4. Charles Tilly, *Migration to an American City* (Wilmington: University of Delaware Agricultural Experiment Station, 1965).
5. Barth and Noel, "Conceptual Frameworks," pp. 337–39.
6. R. A. Schermerhorn, *Comparative Ethnic Relations* (New York: Random House, 1970), p. 98.
7. Ibid., p. 99.
8. Stanley Lieberson, "A Societal Theory of Racial and Ethnic Relations," *American Sociological Review* 29 (December 1961): 902–10.
9. Charles Hirschman, "America's Melting Pot Reconsidered," *Annual Review of Sociology* 9 (1983): 397–423.
10. Robert E. Park, *Race and Culture* (Glencoe, Ill.: Free Press, 1950), p. 150 (italics added).
11. Robert E. Park and Ernest W. Burgess, *Introduction to the Science of Society* (Chicago: University of Chicago Press, 1924), p. 735.
12. Janice R. Hullum, "Robert E. Park's Theory of Race Relations" (M.A. thesis, University of Texas, 1973), pp. 81–88; Park and Burgess, *Introduction to the Science of Society*, p. 760.
13. Milton M. Gordon, *Assimilation in American Life* (New York: Oxford University Press, 1964), pp. 72–73.
14. Ibid., p. 71.
15. Milton M. Gordon, *Human Nature, Class, and Ethnicity* (New York: Oxford University Press, 1978), pp. 67–89.
16. Gordon, *Assimilation in American Life*, pp. 78–108.

17. See Will Herberg, *Protestant—Catholic—Jew*, rev. ed. (Garden City, N.Y.: Doubleday, Anchor Books, 1960).

18. Milton M. Gordon, "Models of Pluralism: The New American Dilemma," *Annals of the American Academy of Political and Social Science* 454 (1981): 178–88.

19. Nathan Glazer and Daniel P. Moynihan, *Beyond the Melting Pot* (Cambridge: Harvard University Press and MIT Press, 1963).

20. Andrew M. Greeley, *Ethnicity in the United States* (New York: John Wiley, 1974), p. 293.

21. Ibid., pp. 295–301.

22. Ibid., p. 309.

23. William L. Yancey, D. P. Ericksen, and R. N. Juliani, "Emergent Ethnicity: A Review and Reformulation," *American Sociological Review* 41 (June 1976): 391–93. See also Greeley, *Ethnicity in the United States*, pp. 290–317.

24. Gunnar Myrdal, *An American Dilemma* (New York: McGraw-Hill, 1964), 2:929.

25. Talcott Parsons, "Full Citizenship for the Negro American? A Sociological Problem," in *The Negro American*, ed. Talcott Parsons and Kenneth B. Clark (Boston: Houghton Mifflin, 1965–66), p. 740.

26. James Geschwender, *Racial Stratification in America* (Dubuque, Iowa: Wm. C. Brown, 1978), p. 58.

27. Gordon, *Human Nature, Class, and Ethnicity*, pp. 73–78. See also Clifford Geertz, "The Integrative Revolution," in *Old Societies and New States*, ed. Clifford Geertz (New York: Free Press, 1963), p. 109.

28. Pierre L. van den Berghe, *The Ethnic Phenomenon* (New York: Elsevier, 1981).

29. Edna Bonacich, "Class Approaches to Ethnicity and Race," *Insurgent Sociologist* 10 (Fall 1980): 11.

30. Frederik Barth, "Introduction," *Ethnic Groups and Boundaries: The Social Organization of Culture Difference* (Oslo: Universitets Forlaget, 1969), pp. 10–17.

31. Susan Olzak, "A Competition Model of Collective Action in American Cities," in *Competitive Ethnic Relations*, ed. Susan Olzak and Joane Nagel (Orlando, Fla.: Academic Press, 1986), pp. 17–46.

32. Susan Olzak, "Have the Causes of Ethnic Collective Action Changed over a Hundred Years?" (technical report, Department of Sociology, Cornell University, 1987), p. 18.

33. W. Lloyd Warner, "Introduction," in Allison Davis et al., *Deep South* (Chicago: University of Chicago Press, 1941), pp. 4–6; W. Lloyd Warner and Leo Srole, *The Social Systems of American Ethnic Groups* (New Haven: Yale University Press, 1945), pp. 295–96.

34. Compare Robert Blauner, *Racial Oppression in America* (New York: Harper & Row, Pub., 1972), p. 7.

35. Oliver C. Cox, *Caste, Class, and Race* (Garden City, N.Y.: Doubleday, 1948), p. 332.

36. Ronald Bailey and Guillermo Flores, "Internal Colonialism and Racial Minorities in the U.S.: An Overview," in *Structures of Dependency*, ed. Frank Bonilla and Robert Girling (Stanford, Calif.: privately published by a Stanford faculty–student seminar, 1973), pp. 151–53.

37. G. Balandier, "The Colonial Situation: A Theoretical Approach," in *Social Change*, ed. Immanuel Wallerstein (New York: John Wiley, 1966), p. 35.

38. Pablo Gonzalez-Casanova, "Internal Colonialism and National Development," in *Latin American Radicalism*, ed. Irving L. Horowitz et al. (New York: Random House, 1969), p. 130; Bailey and Flores, "Internal Colonialism," p. 156.

39. Bailey and Flores, "Internal Colonialism," p. 156.

40. Blauner, *Racial Oppression in America*, p. 55. This analysis of internal colonialism draws throughout on Blauner's provocative discussion.

41. Stokely Carmichael and Charles Hamilton, *Black Power* (New York: Random House, Vintage Books, 1967), pp. 2–7.

42. Mario Barrera, *Race and Class in the Southwest* (Notre Dame, Ind.: University of Notre Dame Press, 1979), pp. 214–17.

43. Guillermo B. Flores, "Race and Culture in the Internal Colony: Keeping the Chicano in His Place," in Bonilla and Girling, *Structures of Dependency*, p. 192.

44. Michael Hechter, *Internal Colonialism* (Berkeley: University of California Press, 1975), pp. 9–12; Michael Hechter, "Group Formation and the Cultural Division of Labor," *American Journal of Sociology* 84 (1978): 293–318; Michael Hechter, Debra Friedman, and Malka Appelbaum, "A Theory of

Ethnic Collective Action," *International Migration Review* 16 (1982): 412–34. See also Geschwender, *Racial Stratification in America*, p. 87.

45. Joan W. Moore, "American Minorities and 'New Nation' Perspectives," *Pacific Sociological Review* 19 (October 1976): 448–55; Michael Omi and Howard Winant, *Racial Formation in the United States* (New York: Routledge & Kegan Paul, 1986), pp. 47–49.

46. Bonacich, "Class Approaches to Ethnicity and Race," p. 14.

47. Cox, *Caste, Class, and Race*; Robert L. Allen, *Black Awakening in Capitalist America* (New York: Doubleday, 1969); Al Szymanski, *Class Structure* (New York: Praeger, 1983), pp. 420–40; Al Szymanski, "Racial Discrimination and White Gain," *American Sociological Review* 41 (1976): 403–14; Paul Baran and Paul Sweezy, *Monopoly Capital* (New York: Monthly Review Press, 1966).

48. Stanley B. Greenberg, *Race and State in Capitalist Development* (New Haven: Yale University Press, 1980), p. 349.

49. Barrera, *Race and Class in the Southwest*, pp. 201–3; Bonacich, "Class Approaches to Ethnicity and Race," p. 14.

50. Bonacich, "Class Approaches to Ethnicity and Race," pp. 14–15.

51. Edna Bonacich and John Modell, *The Economic Basis of Ethnic Solidarity* (Berkeley: University of California Press, 1980), pp. 1–37. For a critique, see Eugene Wong, "Asian American Middleman Minority Theory: The Framework of an American Myth," *Journal of Ethnic Studies* 13 (Spring 1985): 51–87.

52. Alejandro Portes and Robert D. Manning, "The Immigrant Enclave: Theory and Empirical Examples," in *Competitive Ethnic Relations*, ed. Susan Olzak and Joane Nagel (Orlando, Fla.: Academic Press, 1986), pp. 47–68.

53. Omi and Winant, *Racial Formation in the United States*, pp. 75–76.

# A Nation of Immigrants: An Overview of the Economic and Political Conditions of Specific Racial and Ethnic Groups

In the detailed chapters that follow we will examine a number of important racial and ethnic groups in U.S. society. For each we will look at many aspects of its history and analyze its current situation in terms of the racial and ethnic theories reviewed in Chapter 2. Before examining these groups in detail, we can here provide the reader with an overview by setting the groups in the broad historical context of U.S. society over nearly four centuries of economic and political development. We will accent two important dimensions of that society in this brief overview: the changing capitalistic economy and the expanding political and governmental framework. Within these broad frameworks each group worked out its own family and other cultural patterns in the new mosaic nation called the United States.

## IMMIGRATION, THE ECONOMY, AND GOVERNMENT

American economic development has proceeded through several stages: mercantilism, a plantation economy, competitive industrial capitalism, and multinational (oligopoly) capitalism. Economic institutions, realities, and developments have shaped the character of all waves of immigration and the subsequent patterns of immigrant adjustment.

**TABLE II-1  An Overview Of Immigrant Groups In Selected Periods**

| Immigrant Groups | Time of Entry | Economic Conditions in North America | Government Conditions and Actions |
|---|---|---|---|
| *Phase One: Mercantilism, Commercial Capitalism, and Plantation Slavery: 1600–1865* | | | |
| 1. English | 1600s–1800s | Mercantilism; land taken from Native Americans; English entrepreneurs and yeomen farmers; commercial capitalism emerges. | English state creates land companies; and later colonial governments define individualized property and protect property. |
| 2. Africans | 1600s–1800s | Enslaved as property; became major source of low-wage labor for plantation capitalism. | Colonial governments establish slave codes; U.S. Constitution legitimates slave trade; U.S. government controlled by plantation oligarchy. |
| 3. Irish Catholics | 1830s–1860s | Driven out of Ireland by famine; labor recruited for low-wage jobs in transport, construction. | U.S. government opens up western lands; Irish take urban political machines from British Americans. |
| *Phase Two: Industrial Capitalism: 1865–1920* | | | |
| 4. Chinese | 1850s–1870s | Contract labor and low-wage work in mining, railroad, construction; menial service work for Anglo-Saxon settlers. | Local government helps recruit Chinese labor; later, anti-Chinese laws passed in California; 1882 Exclusion Act. |
| 5. Italians | 1880s–1910s | Moved as peasants into industrial capitalism; overseas recruitment for low-wage industrial and construction jobs in the cities. | Government backing for labor recruitment; U.S. treaties with Europe; invervention in European affairs (World War I); numbers reduced by 1924 Immigration Act. |
| 6. Jews of East Europe | 1880s–1910s | Industrial capitalism utilized their skilled and unskilled labor; small entrepreneurs reestablished themselves; much anti-Semitic discrimination. | Government backing for labor recruitment; U.S. treaties with Europe; numbers reduced by 1924 Immigration Act. |

| | | | |
|---|---|---|---|
| 7. | Japanese | 1880s–1900s | First recruited as agricultural laborers to Hawaii; later migrated to West Coast as agricultural labor; served in domestic work; create small businesses. | Government backing for contract and agricultural recruiting; U.S. imperialism in Asia; conquest of Philippines and Hawaii; 1924 Immigrant Act excludes Asians. |

*Phase Three: Advanced Industrial (Multinational) Capitalism: 1920s–1980s*

| | | | | |
|---|---|---|---|---|
| 8. | Mexicans | 1910s–1980s | With Asian/European labor cut off, Mexicans recruited for farms and urban industry; low-wage jobs in construction. | U.S. government provides bracero and other programs; fosters U.S. agribusiness in Mexico, stimulating outmigration; U.S. Border Patrol monitors immigration. |
| 9. | Puerto Ricans | 1940s–1980s | Early farm labor migration; U.S. corporations recruit labor in 1950s–1960s for sweatshops; low-wage blue-collar work in expanding service economy. | Conquest of Puerto Rico in 1898; U.S. government-supported agribusiness takes over economy, creates surplus labor, stimulates migration to U.S.; later, "Operation Bootstrap" gives corporate tax breaks. |
| 10. | Recent AsianGroups (Koreans, Vietnamese, Chinese, Pilipinos*) | 1960s–1980s | Many refugees; some entrepreneurs and professionals created economic niches, making use of expanding service economy. | From 1853 to1970s U.S. imperialism in Asia; government action in South Korea, Vietnam, Taiwan, Philippines stimulates outmigration. |

*Note: Pilipino is now the preferred term for the group often called Filipino (see Chapter 12).

Table II–1 briefly outlines most of the immigrant groups discussed in this book. Each of these groups immigrated to North America; among these groups black Americans experienced a second major migration, from the rural South to the cities, and could be listed a second time. Each group entered America under particular historical circumstances. Many started in slavery, low-wage jobs, or small businesses. Political and economic conditions at the time of entry were very important; for example, some groups entered when low-wage jobs were plentiful in the cities, whereas others entered when fewer jobs were available. And the extent of racial and ethnic discrimination varied considerably, as we will see in the chapters that follow. Also important were the economic and educational resources brought by certain of the immigrant groups. Those white European immigrants who came with a little capital, some education, or entrepreneurial experience could take better jobs or develop small businesses—opportunities not available to many nonwhite immigrants.

Note too that Native Americans (not listed here) were the original inhabitants of the land the English and subsequent immigrants migrated to; many lost lives and lands as a result of the European invasion and conquest.

## COMMERCIAL CAPITALISM AND THE SLAVE SOCIETY: 1600–1865

### Colonial Society and Slave Labor

The United States began as a colonial society which by the end of the 1600s was tied closely to England and the expansionist policies of the English governmental and economic elites. The early economic system in the North American colonies was a combination of state enterprises under the English king and private enterprises developed by independent entrepreneurs, including by the eighteenth century the large plantation owners in the South and the merchant entrepreneurs in the North. In the 1600s the objective of English colonization was securing raw materials and markets for goods. The first joint stock companies were formed by merchants under the auspices of James I of England. Employees of the Southern Company settled Jamestown; this was the English colony that bought enslaved Africans from a Dutch ship in 1619.

The English merchants and entrepreneurs sought to invest their capital in the production of raw materials for English industries. Basically agricultural, the colonies served the empire as a source of raw materials and as a dumping ground for the surplus workers and peasants displaced by the expansion of capitalism in Europe. Production for profit was not the only important economic dimension, for the colonies also became home to many English and other north European immigrants—people displaced from the land—seeking to become small farmers. In the colonies there were two modes of production, the household mode and the capitalist (slave-plantation and merchant) mode.[1] The American colonies had so much free land that it was difficult for English entrepreneurs to secure enough European labor, particularly for large-scale agriculture. They tried using white indentured servants, but these immigrants eventually worked off their terms of servitude and went into farming for themselves.

In the 1600s African slaves became the cheap labor source used by merchant and agricultural capitalists in the colonies. After 1790 the emergence of cotton and sugar as international commodities produced by large-scale plantation agriculture created a very strong demand for slaves. The number of slaves increased from 59,000 in 1714 to 3.9 million in 1860. The forced labor of African and Afro-American slaves built up profits (capital) not only for further slaveowner investments in expanding plantations and allied processing enterprises, but also for the merchants, shippers, and industrialists of the North and South.

There is some debate over whether the slave-plantation agriculture was capitalist, but Bonacich's evaluation seems convincing:

> Although colonial producers of raw materials came to depend upon coerced labor, their orientation was essentially capitalist. They were involved in the investment of capital in the enterprise whose purpose was the production of commodities for a market, while profits were created by the extraction of surplus from labor by having the slaves work longer hours than was necessary for their own subsistence.[2]

### Civil War: The Southern Plantation Oligarchy versus Northern Entrepreneurs

The slave mode of production was profitable; the South was the most prosperous and powerful region in the country from the late 1700s to the 1850s. Southerners owned most of the productive land, much of the agricultural produce for export, tools and mills, and the slave labor. They controlled U.S. politics, as most presidents between Washington and Lincoln were slaveholders or were sympathetic to slavery; few decisions made by the federal legislative and judicial branches went against the interests of the slaveholding oligarchy. The U.S. Civil War was, to a substantial degree, a struggle for power between northern industrialists and small farmers on the one hand and the southern plantation oligarchy on the other. The victory of the North marked the arrival of the northern industrialists as the dominant force in the United States economy and government.[3]

### Immigrant Laborers in the North

In the northern states, beginning in the 1820s, the growing industrial working class and the class of small farmers were peopled with immigrants from

Ireland, Germany, and Scandinavia. Immigrant labor often became the labor of new industrial enterprises—the textile mills, the railroad shops, and the foundries. The factors motivating millions of Irish Catholics and Germans to cross the Atlantic after 1820 were the same as those that have attracted European immigrants for centuries to a United States portrayed by industrial recruiters as the land of golden opportunity. In Ireland a potato disease created food shortages and starvation; this crisis plus political and economic oppression by England generated the movement of 1.6 million Irish to the United States in two decades. Many small farmers and artisans from Ireland sold their labor to U.S. industrialists; they became domestic servants, farm workers, railroad laborers, miners, and unskilled workers in cities.

The arrival of large numbers of white immigrants from northern Europe laid the foundation for new patterns of racial conflict. Blacks became a smaller percentage of urbanites in the North. Free blacks were used by the industrial entrepreneurs in the North as cheap labor, even as strikebreakers—a fact of economic life that increased the hostility of white immigrant workers toward black Americans. By the 1840s some of the free black workers in the North were being replaced by new white immigrants. Irish workers, for example, took over some skilled job categories.

### Western Expansion: Native Americans and Mexican Americans

Fostered by U.S. governmental decrees and military protection, the great westward expansion in the nineteenth century brought not only Native Americans but also a new group—the Mexicans—into the orbit of exploitation by white European-American entrepreneurs, soldiers, and settlers. The ideology of the "white man's civilizing responsibility" for nonwhites was used by white expansionists to justify the taking of Mexican and Indian lands in the West. For example, expansionists believed the "Mexican race" should assimilate to the "Anglo-Saxon race." The first Mexican citizens did not migrate; they and their land were brought into the United States by force after the Mexican-American War in the 1840s.

## THE PERIOD OF INDUSTRIAL CAPITALISM: 1865–1920

### Industrial Capitalism and Government Expansion Overseas

The Civil War was followed by a great industrial boom. An economy dominated by competitive capitalism and by small- and medium-sized businesses gradually became dominated by large enterprises. The growth of industrial enterprises was dramatic, and the United States soon surpassed Great

Britain in numerous production categories. The proportion of Americans engaged in agriculture declined sharply between the 1860s and the 1920s while the proportion in manufacturing doubled. By the last two decades of the nineteenth century U.S. corporations were growing larger through mergers and acquisitions.

Leading industrialists were expanding corporate activities in numerous countries overseas, backed by a U.S. government that was beginning to grow in size and military power. The movement of U.S. Navy ships, as well as private merchants and missionaries, into Asian countries such as China, Japan, and the Philippines disrupted the rural economies of these countries, thereby increasing their surplus of farm workers. This show of U.S. power gave Asian workers a clear image of U.S. military and economic superiority. U.S. labor recruiters enticed many Asian workers to Hawaii and the West Coast of the United States. More than 200,000 Chinese laborers came to the United States between 1848 and 1882 to undertake the "dirty work" along the West Coast, including mining, railroad, and service jobs. After the Chinese were excluded by law, Japanese immigrants were recruited for low-wage jobs. Japan sent 400,000 emigrants to the United States, a migration triggered by Western influence and by labor recruiting by U.S. employers in Japan.[4]

The U.S. victory in the Spanish-American War of the 1890s resulted in the annexation of Puerto Rico and the Philippines by the expansionist U.S. government and the effective domination of Cuba. When the United States took over Puerto Rico much of that land was owned by smaller farmers, but by 1930 large U.S. absentee-owned companies were monopolizing production. Puerto Rico and the Philippines would later send large numbers of emigrants to the U.S. mainland.[5]

## Black Americans: Exclusion from Western Lands

The second half of the nineteenth century was a period of major governmental growth and bureaucratization in the United States. Government action had a major influence on racial and ethnic relations. One of the first actions of Abraham Lincoln and the new Republican legislators in 1862 was to pass the Homestead Act, an "affirmative action" program for the many immigrant families seeking land, including poor Germans, Scandinavians, and Irish. A European-American family wishing to farm was given 160 to 320 acres of land if it would develop it. After the Civil War the U.S. Land Office ruled that most black Americans were ineligible for these land grants because they were not citizens when the act was passed. While some land was made available in portions of the former slave states, black families for the most part did not have the opportunity to build up the landed wealth that many white American families garnered.[6]

In the late 1800s and early 1900s black labor from the South was one possible source of labor for northern industries, but the white oligarchy in the South, after the brief Reconstruction period, took control of the South's economy, and governments and saw to it that the freed blacks and their children became cheap labor for southern agriculture. There was little distribution of slave-plantation land to the black slaves who had made that land fruitful. Most freed slaves found themselves in new forms of government-sanctioned subordination to white agricultural entrepreneurs, including tenant farming.

## Southern and Eastern European Immigrants

Unable to use southern black labor, or preferring not to use it, northern industrialists turned to Europe. The majority of the 20.7 million immigrants to the United States between 1881 and 1920 were from southern and eastern Europe. Labor shortages and increasing wages for native workers encouraged the U.S. industrialists to seek immigrant labor. A 1910 survey of twenty major manufacturing and mining industries found that six out of every ten workers were foreign-born. Without this immigrant labor the great industrial expansion of the United States would not have been possible. There was a tremendous need for workers in this dramatically growing industrial society.[7] In some cases these new workers displaced native-born workers; and they were also used as strikebreakers. Anti-immigrant hostility among the workers from older European American groups increased as a result.[8]

## European Immigrants and Black Americans

Irving Kristol has argued that "The Negro Today Is Like the Immigrant of Yesterday." His argument illustrates the common view that the experience of black Americans moving to the industrial cities is not significantly different from that of recent white immigrant groups—that black Americans will move up just as the white immigrants did.[9]

This argument overlooks important differences between the experiences of white and nonwhite immigrants. In the case of European immigrants, group mobility was possible because

1. Most arrived at a time when urban jobs were available, when capitalism was expanding and opportunities were relatively abundant.
2. Many had some technical or other skills or a little capital, resources available to only a few nonwhite Americans.
3. Most faced far less severe employment and housing discrimination than blacks did.
4. Most found housing, however shabby and inadequate, reasonably near the workplace.
5. The political system was changing from business dominance to shared power between business elites and the political machines oriented to immigrant voters.[10]

In the critical periods of European immigration, cities such as New York, Philadelphia, Boston, and Chicago were expanding centers of manufacturing. Blue-collar jobs were frequently available, if not plentiful. In the mid-nineteenth century Irish and German immigrants were attracted to rural areas and to cities, where most found industrial, service, or government jobs. From 1890 to 1930 southern and eastern Europeans came in large numbers to the cities, sometimes to the same cities as earlier immigrant groups and sometimes to newer cities. One study notes that "the Italian concentration in construction and the Polish in steel were related to the expansion of these industries as the groups arrived."[11] Many workers migrated as a result of labor recruiting by U.S. industrialists in Europe.

Also among the immigrants in the 1880–1920 period were large numbers of Jewish immigrants fleeing oppression in Europe. Although poverty-stricken, many Jewish immigrants came as an urban-industrial proletariat with some experience in skilled trades. One study in 1911 found that two-thirds of the Jewish immigrants were skilled workers, whereas other southern and eastern European immigrants were primarily peasant farmers or farm workers. When Jewish immigrants entered in large numbers around 1900, the clothing industry was moving to mass production and offered plenty of jobs for tailors and seamstresses, as well as unskilled jobs, and chances for small-scale entrepreneurs.

The situation for the Afro-Americans who began to move to the northern cities after 1910 was different. Black workers who migrated from the South had no access to government jobs and were regularly displaced by the new white immigrant groups, who forced them out of job after job, such as construction and transport jobs, and into marginal, low-paying jobs. Stanley Lieberson has explored why the white southern and eastern European immigrants have done so well in northern cities, compared with black Americans. Among his important conclusions are that: (1) blacks were the victims of more severe racial discrimination over a longer period than were the white immigrant groups; and (2) the economic competition between whites and the very large and growing group of black Americans in the urban North led to extensive racist antagonism on the part of whites.[12]

## ADVANCED INDUSTRIAL (MULTINATIONAL) CAPITALISM: 1920s–1980s

### Other Non-European Immigrants

With the industrialization accompanying World War I came a sharp decline in the number of laborers available for agricultural work. The need was filled in part by Mexican labor, recruited with substantial help from the federal government. Thus Mexican labor and allied migrations increased significantly in the 1920s. Los Angeles and San Antonio had labor agencies recruiting Mexican workers for agriculture as well as for jobs in the steel, auto, and other urban industries. Blauner has captured the contrast between the nonwhite and the white immigrant workers of this period and later: "America has used African, Asian, Mexican, and, to a lesser degree, Indian workers for the cheapest labor, concentrating people of color in the most unskilled jobs, the least advanced sectors of the economy, and the most industrially backward regions of the nation."[13]

## Large Corporations and the U.S. Business Cycle

Since the 1920s very large multinational corporations, many with an international orientation, have come to dominate the American economy and politics. By the late 1920s a very large number of Americans, including many of the recent immigrant workers, were working in some part of the auto industry or in related industries such as steel or rubber. Aggressive competition among the large auto firms in the 1920s resulted in the production of more cars than were needed in the American economy. This overproduction, a chronic problem in a market economy, resulted in major cutbacks in employment in many cities, helping to trigger the Great Depression of the 1930s. The Depression was a hard blow to recent black and Hispanic migrants to the cities. Unemployed whites, including recent European immigrants and their children, took over the menial "Negro jobs." Government grew as the business leaders in Washington tried to develop economic and social programs to save the foundering capitalist system. However, racial discrimination was institutionalized in the dramatic relief programs. In New Deal relief programs blacks often received lower wages than whites, were employed only as unskilled laborers, and were employed after whites.[14]

## The Postwar Era: The United States and the World

For three decades after World War II the U.S. government, the U.S. military, and American multinational corporations substantially dominated the world economy, in large part because industrial societies elsewhere, such as Germany and Japan, had been destroyed by the war. Since World War II it has become easier for corporations to move capital investments from the central city to the suburbs, from northern to southern cities, and from a U.S. city to cities overseas. Much of this capital "flight" has resulted in economically abandoned central cities, as in Detroit, Newark, and Pittsburgh. The U.S. government facilitated this outward expansion of the economic system. Government-funded highway systems changed to reflect the needs of companies developing plants and workers living outside the central cities. As a result, after World War II many white ethnic Americans—the children and grandchildren of European immigrants—followed the new industrial plants to the suburbs.

Into the central cities came many nonwhite Americans—blacks, Puerto Ricans, Mexican Americans, Mexicans, and Native Americans. After World War II these nonwhite immigrants to the larger cities in the North frequently inhabited areas abandoned by industry and by the more affluent children of the earlier European immigrants. Among these were the Puerto Ricans, many of whom were recruited for low-wage manufacturing jobs in the cities in the 1950s and 1960s. U.S. industrial and agribusiness development in Puerto Rico helped to stimulate a large outmigration. Although many older cities have seen an increase in black and Hispanic political and governmental influence in recent years, several of these cities are economically troubled. What the future holds for these nonwhite minorities in central cities remains unclear, politically as well as economically.

## Government Involvement Overseas and Asian Immigration

Until the mid-1960s U.S. immigration legislation was so restrictive that most people desiring to emigrate from Asia could not get in. By the mid-1960s discriminatory quotas for Asians had been lifted, and since then there has been a great increase in Asian immigrants, especially the Chinese, Koreans, Pilipinos, and Vietnamese. Not surprisingly, U.S. support for South Korea during and after its war with North Korea built strong ties between the two countries. The political dictatorship in South Korea drove out some of the Korean dissenters who migrated to the United States; others came for economic or education reasons. The immigration of the Chinese (especially from Taiwan), the Pilipinos, and the South Vietnamese has also been related to U.S. involvement overseas. U.S. arming and support of the Philippine government and the Chinese government on Taiwan, and U.S. participation in the war in South Vietnam, created a large group of Pilipinos, Chinese, and Vietnamese dependent on the United States; large numbers of them eventually emigrated.

## Latin American Immigration and the Sunbelt Boom

Caribbean immigrants to the United States since the 1960s have included Haitians and Cubans moving to Florida. The U.S. government long supported a dictatorship in Cuba, which was overthrown by a guerrilla movement led by Fidel Castro. Many Cuban business people and professionals fled in the first waves of emigration. Conservative politically, these Cubans established an economic niche in the city of Miami. After 1980 poorer Cubans migrated to the United States, many of them expelled as "undesirables" by the Castro government. Some immigrant groups, such as Cuban Americans and Korean Americans, have brought educational skills or modest capital to the United States. Their economic success is often called an "ethnic miracle." This success can be partially explained by the fact that their skills, education, or capital exceeded those of other groups—such as black Americans—with whom they are sometimes compared.[15]

One important feature of U.S. society is the shift of investment capital and federal grants to Sunbelt cities in recent decades. The booming economy of the Sunbelt states created a large demand for low-wage workers in sectors such as construction and agriculture. Many people have immigrated from Mexico and Central America, some for economic reasons, others for political reasons. Mexican immigrants make up more than half of all the undocumented immigrants to the United States. U.S. corporations operating in Mexico have played a role in generating Mexican migration. U.S. agribusiness firms stimulated the development of export-oriented agriculture in Mexico, thereby driving many Mexican peasants off land desired for export crops.

### Immigration Restrictions

During the 1950s European immigrants made up half of the 252,000 persons coming to the United States in an average year. By the 1970s Europeans constituted only 17 percent of the 462,000 entering in an average year. The change was the result of the abolition of discriminatory national origins quotas by the 1965 Immigration Act. However, the many Asian and Hispanic immigrants to the United States since the 1960s have come to be seen as a "problem" by native-born Americans. The 1986 Immigration Reform and Control Act was passed with a number of provisions limiting immigration to the United States.

Native workers and leading politicians were concerned that the United States could not absorb so many new immigrants, even though the ratio of immigrants to the native-born population was much higher earlier in the twentieth century. In the 1980s the United States population has a smaller percentage of foreign-born than that of many other nations, including Argentina, France, England, Germany, and Switzerland. Implicit in many discussions of the migrants seemed to be a concern that most of the new immigrants were from Asia and Latin America—that is, they were not white and European.[16]

### SUMMARY

In this introduction we have briefly reviewed the economic and governmental contexts within which particular groups have immigrated and adjusted. We have seen that the time of entry for particular groups and the resources they bring affect their economic and political success. A complete understanding of the streams of migration to the United States requires an analysis of immigration in light of the political and economic contexts of entry and upward mobility. Capitalist development and expansion, as well as related U.S. political involvement overseas and governmental expansion and action, have not only shaped the context and character of U.S. immigration and the patterns of race and ethnic relations in North America for several centuries, but also provided crucibles within which family patterns, distinctive cultures, and political responses of specific groups have developed.

## NOTES

1. Edna Bonacich, "United States Capitalist Development: A Background to Asian Immigration," in *Labor Immigration under Capitalism*, ed. Lucie Cheng and Edna Bonacich (Berkeley: University of California Press, 1984), p. 82.
2. Ibid., p. 81.
3. Herbert Aptheker, lectures on American history, University of Minnesota, 1984.
4. Lucie Cheng and Edna Bonacich, "Imperialism, Distorted Development, and Asian Emigration to the United States," in Cheng and Bonacich, *Labor Migration under Capitalism*, pp. 214–17.
5. Bonacich, "United States Capitalist Development," pp. 99–110.
6. Coretta Scott King, "It's a Bit Late to Protest Preferential Treatment," *Detroit Free Press*, December 13, 1985, p. 9A.
7. Stephen Steinberg, *The Ethnic Myth* (New York: Atheneum, 1981), p. 36.
8. Bonacich, "United States Capitalist Development," pp. 112–15.
9. Irving Kristol, "The Negro Today Is Like the Immigrant of Yesterday," *New York Times Magazine*, September 11, 1966, pp. 50–51, 124–42.
10. Theodore Hershberg et al., "A Tale of Three Cities: Blacks, Immigrants, and Opportunity in Philadelphia: 1850–1880, 1930, 1970," in *Philadelphia,* ed. T. Hershberg (New York: Oxford University Press, 1981), pp. 462–64.
11. William Yancey, E.P. Ericksen, and R.N. Juliani, "Emergent Ethnicity," *American Sociological Review* 41 (June, 1976): 393.
12. Stanley Lieberson, *A Piece of the Pie* (Berkeley: University of California Press, 1980), pp. 377–83.
13. Robert Blauner, *Racial Oppression in America* (New York: Harper & Row, Pub., 1972), p. 62.
14. H. Sitkoff, *A New Deal for Blacks* (New York: Oxford University Press, 1978), pp. 37–38; C. G. Wye, "The New Deal and the Negro Community," *Journal of American History* 59 (December 1972), 634.
15. Steinberg, *The Ethnic Myth*, pp. 104–5.
16. Charles B. Keeley, "Population and Immigration Policy: State and Federal Roles," in *Mexican American and Central American Population Issues and U.S. Policy*, ed. Frank D. Bean, Jurgen Schmandt, and Sidney Weintraub (Austin, Tex.: Center for Mexican American Studies, 1988).

# CHAPTER 3

# English Americans and the Anglo-Saxon Core Culture

Cleveland Amory tells a story about prominent English American families in Massachusetts. A Chicago banking firm wrote a Boston investment company for a letter of recommendation on a young Bostonian. Eloquently praising the young man's virtues, the company's letter pointed out that his mother was a member of the Lowell family, his father a member of the Cabot family, and his other relatives members of other prominent New England families. The bank wrote back, thanking the company but noting that this was not the type of letter of recommendation they had in mind: "We were not contemplating using Mr._____ for breeding purposes."[1] Apocryphal or not, this story illustrates the elite status of the "proper Bostonians" and suggests their wealth and prominence in the history of New England.

The story underscores the importance of inbreeding, descent, and interlocking family ties over generations. Ethnicity involves cultural or nationality characteristics that are distinguished by the group itself or by important outgroups, but lines of descent are the channels for passing along ethnic characteristics to later generations.

Who are these English Americans? What is their significance? The phrase *English Americans* itself may sound a bit strange. We hear discussions of Mexican Americans, black Americans, even Irish Catholics, but few speak of English Americans. One reason for this is that other labels are used to designate the group. Perhaps the most common are *Anglo-Saxon* and *White Anglo-Saxon Protestant*. Although in-depth analyses of this group are rare, numerous authors have commented on the central importance of the Anglo-Saxons. For example, a prominent historian of immigration takes the impact of the Anglo-Saxon group for granted: "Our American culture, our speech, our laws are basically Anglo-Saxon in origin."[2]

Milton Gordon's view of the shaping impact of this first large group of European immigrants on the *core culture* of the United States has already been noted: "If there is anything in American life which can be described as an overall American culture which serves as a reference point for immigrants and their children, it can best be described . . . as the middle-class cultural patterns of, largely, white Protestant, Anglo-Saxon origins."[3] This comment suggests the importance of the core culture in the adaptation process faced by later immigrant groups. To take another example, Herberg has noted the influence of this Anglo-Saxon group on the self-image of Americans: "It is the *Mayflower*, John Smith, Davy Crockett, George Washington, and Abraham Lincoln that define the American's self-image, and this is true whether the American in question is a descendant of the Pilgrims or the grandson of an immigrant from southeastern Europe."[4] This is the result of an essentially one-way cultural assimilation, whereby everyone adapts to the Anglo-Saxon core culture.

Two troubling problems come to mind here. One is that no social science analyst has undertaken a comprehensive analysis of these English Americans, the immigrant group of paramount importance in U.S. history. Why has this group been among the most neglected? The answer is unclear. A second question regards the term *Anglo-Saxon*. Numerous sources use the term loosely for persons or institutions of English extraction. In one sense, *Anglo-Saxon* is an inadequate designation for the immigrants from England and their descendants. The term derives from the names for the Germanic tribes, the Angles and the Saxons, that came to the area now called England in the fifth and sixth centuries A.D. But there were other people there already—the Celts—and the Germanic tribes were followed by the Normans from France. The English settlers of the American colonies embodied several centuries of fusion of nationality types.[5] So, at best, the term *Anglo-Saxon* is shorthand for a complex heritage.

Some authors use Anglo-Saxon and such related terms as "old-stock Americans" in two broader senses. The terms are sometimes used in a loose way to include British groups other than the English—the Scots and the Welsh. In addition, certain other closely related white north European groups which substantially assimilated to the English core culture—particularly Scandinavian and German Protestants—are sometimes included in the Anglo-Saxon terminology. In any event, when the terms Anglo-Saxon and British are used, English Americans and the core culture they generated are at the heart of the discussion.

# THE ENGLISH MIGRATIONS

## Some Basic Data

What was the origin of those English Americans whose company now numbers in the tens of millions? As every schoolchild probably knows, it was migration. Although the English were not the first to come to North America, they were the first to colonize it in large numbers. Only rough estimates exist for the number of English migrants prior to the early 1800s, because no careful records were kept. By the early eighteenth century there were approximately 350,000 English and Welsh colonists in North America. At the time of the Revolution this number had increased to between one and two million.[6]

Much of this growth seems to have derived from colonial birth rates rather than from migration. Migration to the American colonies was very heavily English until 1700, after which time English migration receded. Migration remained at modest levels in the few decades after the Revolution. "Most people who have studied the history of the period and whatever local records were available," note the Taeubers, "believe that something less than a quarter of a million white immigrants entered the country in the 30 years from 1790 to 1819."[7] Most of these came from Britain and Germany.

Nearly three million English migrated to the United States between 1820 and 1950, with the two decades between 1880 and 1900 seeing the heaviest flow. The English migration to the colonies, and later to the United States, was one of the largest population flows in this period. The English were not only the first sizable European group in what was to become the United States; they continued to be an important part of the migration flow until World War I.[8]

## The First Colonial Settlements

The migration of the English settlers in the seventeenth century, together with the establishment of settlements, was different from later European migration streams. This migration can be viewed as *colonization*. Colonization, unlike other types of migration, involves the subordination of native people. Unlike the French and Spanish, who also explored North America, the English had come to establish permanent colonies. A range of economic interests was involved.[9] The colonies developed under the auspices of the English king and his merchants and were often viewed as an extension of the mother country.

Why did the English Crown become interested in North American colonies? Why were colonies developed at all? Various explanations for colonial development were put forth by English advocates in the colonial period. Commercial objectives were often mentioned; much attention was given to the need for trading posts and for new sources of raw materials. Emphasis was placed on the creation of new markets for English goods.[10] Other colonial advocates emphasized Protestant missionary objectives, the search for a passage to Asia, the need to stop Spanish and French expansion, and the need for some place for surplus English population and for criminals and other undesirables. Nonetheless, the central objective of colonization was economic gain: "What England primarily looked for in colonies was neither expansion of territory *per se* nor overseas aggregations of Englishmen, but goods and markets."[11]

Colonization had dire consequences for Native American ("Indian") tribes. Geographical expansion proceeded rapidly. Native Americans were perceived as a threat. The French were interested in the fur trade, but the English wanted land for economic colonization and farming.[12] At first, attempts were made to convert the "heathen" natives and certain tribes were treated in a friendly fashion. The settlers, few at first, soon gained superiority over the Native Americans, forcing them into frontier areas or killing them.[13] Few settlers seemed concerned over the genocidal consequences of colonialism. In Massachusetts a plague had wiped out many Native Americans prior to the *Mayflower's* landing. The famous minister Cotton Mather commented: "The woods were almost cleared of those pernicious creatures, to make room for a better growth."[14]

The English established large settlements in North America. The first joint-stock companies were formed by merchants under the auspices of James I of England in the early 1600s. Employees of the Southern Company settled Jamestown, a colony where the primary goal was economic. This was the English colony that bought Africans from a Dutch ship in 1619, laying the foundation for racial oppression. The northern colony of Plymouth was settled in 1620 under the auspices of another royal company. These Plymouth settlers, the famous Pilgrims, had seceded from the Anglican church.[15]

Both settlements nearly expired in their early years because of disease and starvation. The development of tobacco agriculture and the granting of private property to settlers saved Jamestown. Thousands of English immigrants came to Jamestown, and a healthy and vigorous agricultural settlement gradually developed. The Plymouth colony managed to survive with the aid of friendly Native Americans. By 1640 there were thousands of English colonists in the New England area; it was these colonists who first regarded themselves as English *Americans*.[16]

What was the racial and ethnic mix of this colonial population? As late as the 1740s the English still made up the majority of immigrants to North America.[17] But shortly thereafter immigration from England became less central. The fears of overpopulation and the political dissent that had originally fueled the large outmigration from England had lessened by the late seventeenth century because of better economic conditions, and outmigration was now discouraged. The Irish and the Germans came to dominate the migration flow by the 1760s.[18]

The American Historical Association has developed estimates of the national stocks of the white population in 1790 based on a surname analysis:[19]

| | |
|---|---|
| English | 60.1% |
| Scotch, Scotch-Irish | 14.0 |
| German | 8.6 |
| Irish (Free State) | 3.6 |
| Dutch | 3.1 |
| French, Swedish | 3.0 |
| Other | 7.6 |
| Total | 100.0% |

These estimates give the English the primary position, with a significant proportion of the rest of the population composed of other British groups. In most states the English constituted more than half the white population. Of course, the largest single group in the South was black Africans. Slaves made up one-fifth of the population in revolutionary America.[20]

## The Nineteenth-Century Migration: Capital and Workers

There was a modest flow of immigrants from the British Isles and the rest of Europe between the Revolution and 1820, but the century following 1820 saw the greatest Atlantic migration in history. The English and other British contributions to this nineteenth-century migration have been neglected.[21] This neglect underscores the ease with which the later English immigrants blended in. As we have seen, nearly 3 million came between 1820 and 1950. Yet by the 1910s the great English migration stream had declined significantly.[22]

Economic motives were of paramount importance for the nineteenth-century immigrants. There were numerous depressions, and thus widespread unemployment in the textile industry, the largest employer in Britain. Emigration came to be seen as one solution to unemployment.[23] The skills of textile workers facilitated their mobility. As with their predecessors, this immigrant group attained a relatively successful position in a country just beginning to industrialize. Their skills spurred the dramatic industrialization in the nineteenth-century. The English Americans in the United States received high wages in the iron and copper mining and silk industries; together with other British groups, they were top wage earners in many other industries. They moved in large numbers from the British manufacturing and mining industries to comparable positions in American industry.[24]

When English American workers were eventually displaced by machines or later immigrant groups, they often moved up into managerial and technical positions. With their help, American industry surpassed the industry of the mother industrial society. The English immigrants were not just skilled blue-collar workers. Some were unskilled laborers; some were professionals; some were farmers. But all were welcomed and generally did well.[25]

Was adaptation to the core culture difficult for these English immigrants? The ease with which many moved into industry indicates the swiftness of their assimilation at the level of secondary organizations. Their skills kept most from the poverty that usually faced other immigrants. Larger numbers moved into clerical and professional jobs than was the case with most other white immigrant groups. Acculturation was easy for the English immigrants. They would be more readily hired where the ability to speak English was important. These English immigrants avoided most of the anti-immigrant agitation others faced. Indeed, new English immigrants often shared the ethnocentric or racist views held by previous English settlers, including the stereotyping of Jews, hostility towards blacks, and hatred of southern Europeans. The English immigrants encountered relatively little prejudice or discrimination. Structural assimilation in the primary-relations sphere, to use the concept developed by Milton Gordon, was rapid for them. Marriage with citizens was common. Kinship and friendship ties were easily developed. Enforced residential segregation did not develop for these immigrants.[26]

Ties to the homeland were not immediately severed. The monarch was widely revered. British taverns flourished in American cities. Although English newspapers were published for immigrants, they seldom lasted more than a year to two. Societies such as the St. George's Society were created to aid destitute English settlers, and there were also social clubs. However, the organizations for preserving English culture were fewer and less exclusive than similar organizations among other immigrant groups. Many of the children of English immigrants left these organizations. Berthoff quotes a young son of a Chicago Englishman who was reviewing the Revolutionary War for his father: "You had the King's army, and we were only a lot of farmers, but *we*

English Americans and the Anglo-Saxon Core Culture

thrashed you!"[27] Here the pinnacle of identificational assimilation has been reached, even in the second generation; the son's identity is English *American*.

## Twentieth-Century Migration

Smaller numbers of English immigrants have come to the United States since 1910—only 11,000 a year in the late 1920s. In the 1930s, indeed, more people returned to England than came in as immigrants. Between the 1950s and the 1980s one distinctive aspect of English migration has been the "brain drain." A large proportion of immigrants in this period was composed of managerial, professional, and technical workers, including physicians and academics. Though relatively few compared with the immigrants of earlier decades, these immigrants generated a controversy in Great Britain over the costly loss of highly skilled workers.[28]

## Other Protestant Immigrants

Because the term *Anglo-Saxon* has sometimes included not only the English but also the Scots, the Welsh, and even Scandinavians and Germans, we need to touch briefly on these groups. The Welsh entered the colonies in relatively small numbers, beginning in the early 1600s. The total number who came has been estimated at just over 100,000, with many going into industrial jobs or farming. The first generations retained their customs, language, and distinctive communities, but they were soon assimilated to the white Protestant mainstream.[29]

In terms of power the Scots were perhaps the closest to the dominant English group from the first century onward, although they would feel Anglo-conformity pressures. Scottish Highlanders and Lowlanders, as well as Scottish emigrants to Ireland, came to the new nation in its formative centuries. By the late eighteenth century there were perhaps 250,000 Scots, a number to be supplemented over the next century by three-quarters of a million migrants. In the colonial period many were merchants, clerks, soldiers, and middle-income farmers, although the majority probably were servants, laborers, and poor farmers. Assimilation to the English core culture accompanied inclusion in the economic system, so that by the early 1800s the Scots had probably moved up to near parity with the English. They too became an important segment of the white Protestant mainstream.

German immigrants made up the largest non-British group. Germans were perhaps 9 percent of the colonists in the eighteenth century; in the century after 1820 several million would come to the United States. Some were Catholics and Jews, but the largest proportion was Protestant. Many became farmers, laborers, merchants, and, later, industrial workers. Over several generations much, but by no means all, of the German culture was reshaped by the well-established Anglo-American patterns. Cultural assimilation, together with substantial mobility in the economic and political spheres, came in a few generations for these Protestants. Yet some distinctiveness did persist, in the form of German communities.

Scandinavian immigrants, such as Swedes and Norwegians, did not enter in really large numbers until the 1870s and 1880s. In all perhaps two million came. Many immigrants entered as farmers and laborers, but the next generation moved up into skilled blue-collar and white-collar positions. Here too substantial assimilation to the core culture and society came in a few generations, and much of the Scandinavians' ethnic distinctiveness was lost as they became part of the Anglo-Saxon Protestant mainstream. Yet some community distinctiveness persists today.

These Protestant groups, together with other groups, assimilated relatively rapidly to the core culture, particularly in the cultural, economic, and political spheres. Although maintaining some communal distinctiveness, as in informal group life, most became part of the Protestant mainstream by the early twentieth century.

Yet this assimilation was not always peaceful. In earlier periods some of these Protestant groups suffered physical attacks and cultural pressure from the established English group. By the nineteenth century English Americans were marrying with other British Americans, some even with Scandinavians and Germans. So it is not surprising that by the early twentieth century the designation white Anglo-Saxon Protestant increasingly came to blur the distinction between the original Anglo-Saxons—the English—and those later groups that had substantially assimilated to the English core culture and society.

## ANGLO–SAXON PROTESTANT REACTIONS TO IMMIGRANTS

Not all immigrant groups had the easy reception that nineteenth-century English immigrants had. Established groups, though descendants of earlier immigrants, were often hostile to new immigrant groups. The most important group was the English Americans, although they were by no means the only northern European group involved in anti-immigration agitation, or *nativism,* as it is often termed. Nativism goes far back into American history, but the term was apparently first used in the 1840s and 1850s. Nativists were nationalists who saw themselves as the only true Americans. Higham notes three themes in reactions to immigrants: anti-Catholic, antiforeign, and racist (Anglo-Saxonism).[30]

At an early stage some immigrants were discouraged from entering the colonies—certain religious groups (such as Catholics), paupers, and convicts.[31] In the earliest period, concern was centered in religious and moral desirability. Historically, antiforeign sentiment was first directed primarily at non-English immigrant groups. French Huguenot refugees are one example. Virginia tried to prohibit their immigration, and other colonies placed restrictions on them. At least one Huguenot community was violently attacked.[32]

The Huguenots were followed as targets by the Irish and Germans. As Jordan notes, "in the early years Englishmen treated the increasingly numerous settlers from other European countries, especially Scottish and Irish servants, with condescension and frequently with exploitative brutality."[33] Many resented the intrusion of new peoples onto English soil. In Virginia and Maryland discriminatory duties were placed on non-English servants coming into the colonies. The Scottish faced the least discrimination, the Irish more, and the blacks the most. The Catholics among the Irish were "doubly damned as foreign and Papist."[34]

There was some ambivalence about the new immigrants. On the one hand, immigrants provided needed labor, ship captains profited from immigration, and new immigrants were encouraged to settle in frontier areas to increase frontier security. On the other hand, immigrants were often seen as a threat, and English American mobs occasionally tried to prevent their landing. In 1734 a "Scotch-Irish" Presbyterian church was destroyed by a mob in Worcester, Massachusetts.[35]

## Fear of Foreigners

Antiforeign sentiment took legal form in the late 1700s with Federalist concern about immigrant radicalism and fear of the growth of the Jeffersonian Democrats, who were supported by non-British immigrants. The 1798 Alien Act empowered the president to deport immigrants considered a threat to the new nation. The period of residence required for citizenship was raised from two to five years in 1795 and to fourteen years in 1798. Attempts were also made to set an exorbitant fee for naturalization. These strategies were designed to limit the political power of the new immigrants.[36]

Numerous attempts were made to reduce the influence of foreigners by pressuring them to assimilate to the English core institutions. When Benjamin Franklin set up a Pennsylvania school in the 1740s, he was concerned about the many foreigners who did not know the language and customs.[37] A Swedish Moravian minister visiting the colonies in 1745 complained of the interaction of Swedes with the English: "The English are evidently swallowing up the people and the Swedish language is so corrupted, that if I did not know the English, it would be impossible to understand the language of my dear Sweden."[38]

The pressure of the English language was great, accelerating acculturation for many northern European immigrant groups. Homogeneity was clearly the goal of the English founding fathers and prominent educators of the eighteenth century. George Washington believed in a homogeneous citizenry. Thomas Jefferson and Benjamin Rush expected those who were educated to fit into a culturally homogeneous mass of citizens. But such unity could be had only by the subordination of other ethnic identities to that of the core society.[39]

Anti-Catholic sentiment was at the core of nativist agitation. The Irish and German influx of the 1840s and 1850s generated a burst of agitation and a variety of secret societies, sometimes termed the Know-Nothing movement, that sought to combat immigration and Catholicism. (When questioned, members of these societies would supposedly say, "I don't know nothing.") Some have viewed this movement as a Puritan revival because of its concern for the moral training of immigrants. In the 1850s avowed and suspected Know-Nothings were elected to state legislatures, Congress, and state executive offices. Know-Nothings stimulated numerous violent attacks against immigrants and Catholics, attacks that apparently slowed the immigration flow itself.[40]

Race-oriented nativism developed in the second half of the nineteenth century, with other north European Protestants now joining the English Americans. From their perspective American development was the perfect example of what could be accomplished by the Anglo-Saxon "race." Higham notes the source of these notions:

"By another irony, the Americans who attributed the uniqueness and distinction of their nation to the Anglo-Saxon race were simply echoing the prior claims of the English. Proud appeals to Anglo-Saxon origins and ancestors came into vogue in England in the seventeenth and eighteenth centuries among the champions of Parliament."[41]

This Anglo-Saxonism, arising in the United States by the 1840s, was picked up by the expansionists who lusted after Mexican land in California and Texas. The vigorous thrust into those areas was seen as directed and legitimated by a racial mandate to colonize the inferior races. One expansionist commented that "the Mexican race now see in the fate of the aborigines of the north, their own inevitable destiny. They must amalgamate or be lost in the superior vigor of the Anglo-Saxon race, or they must utterly perish."[42] Anglo-Saxonism was to play an important role in racist thought after the Civil War, for it provided the rationalization for U.S. imperialism in places such as the Philippines.

The upper classes in the United States became a stronghold of Anglo-Saxonism after the Civil War. One influence, "scientific" historians in England, argued for the superiority of the Anglo-Saxon background of England's greatness. Anglo-Saxons were viewed as God's Chosen People. There was an Anglo-Saxon school among American social scientists; its guiding idea was that democratic institutions in this country had come from England, whose institutions had in turn derived in part from early Germanic tribes.[43] These social scientists were convinced that English ways, institutions, and language were the most civilized in the world. American intellectual thought came under the influence of social Darwinism, replete with notions of racism based on "survival of the fittest." There was a strong movement to expand the teaching of the Anglo-Saxon language in colleges and universities, and some suggested it be taught at lower levels of public education. One prominent intellectual advocate of biological evolution, John Fiske, celebrated the superiority of English civilization and claimed it was the destiny of the English people to populate the world's empty spaces.[44] Even more influential were popular writers such as Josiah Strong, a Congregationalist minister whose book *Our Country* (1885) sold thousands of copies. Strong was a vigorous advocate of Anglo-Saxon myths in combination with attacks on Catholics and other white immigrants. The English peoples were rapidly multiplying, he argued, and the United States was destined to be the seat of a great Anglo-Saxon "race" approaching, by the 1980s, a billion strong. Survival of the fittest, he argued, dictated the ultimate superiority of the Anglo-Saxon race throughout the world.[45]

## Racism and Nativism since 1890

The increase in immigration from southern and eastern Europe and from Asia around the turn of the twentieth century focused anti-immigration sentiment on these groups. The economic and political troubles facing late-nineteenth-century America moved some intellectuals and other leaders away from their confidence that new immigrants could readily be assimilated. Henry Cabot Lodge, an English American from New

England, was fiercely determined to defend the English "race" against immigrant threats in the 1890s. A prominent political figure, Lodge did a study of entries in a biographical listing to prove the dominance of the English over all others. English American aristocrats from Boston formed the Immigration League to fight the flood of southern and eastern European migrants. The league worked diligently for a literacy test, which easily passed Congress, and associated itself with the eugenics movement started by Sir Francis Galton, a prominent English Darwinist. The eugenicists argued that heredity shaped moral as well as biological characteristics, and that perpetuation of the unfit could thus lead to the destruction of the superior race. A basic idea was that the unfit should be eliminated.[46]

Perhaps the most prominent American to contribute to the development of racial nativism was Madison Grant, an American of English extraction. An amateur scientist, Grant fused various racist ideas in his influential book *The Passing of the Great Race* (1916). Particularly worried about the influence of certain newer European groups, Grant claimed that interbreeding various "races" would lead to mongrelization. The northern Europeans, the "Nordic race," were the superior "race."[47]

Such "scientific" racism resulted in the restrictive immigration legislation of the 1920s, legislation that discriminated against non-British groups. Various "national origin" quotas were spelled out to restrict immigration, with Britons allowed to constitute nearly half the total.

The 1920s saw an outpouring of racial nativism on many fronts. Journalists such as Kenneth L. Roberts continued to write about racial mongrelization.[48] Nativist organizations such as the revived Ku Klux Klan provided a social outlet for such views for those who wished to subordinate black people and preserve the Anglo-Saxon race against "niggers, Catholics, and Jews."[49] Anti-Catholic, anti-Semitic, antiforeign, antiblack—all these attitudes were expressed in the Klan. Nor did opposition die after the Depression and World War II. Opposition to foreign immigration resurfaced after World War II, when various members of Congress and "old stock" organizations spoke up in opposition to legislation permitting displaced persons, such as Jews and Catholics, to migrate to the United States. In the 1970s and 1980s nonwhite immigrants from Asia, Latin America, and the Philippines became the targets of modern-day nativists, including those in the again revived Ku Klux Klan.

## THE IMPACT OF THE ENGLISH CORE CULTURE ON BASIC INSTITUTIONS

Virtually all analysts of the U.S. scene have assumed a core culture and society basically English or Anglo-Saxon. During the first century of colonial development an English heritage integrated the colonies, and the English core culture adapted to the new physical environment. Colonial political, legal, and economic institutions were based on familiar English models. This is not to say that American institutions were identical to the English; they were not. The dominant Anglican church in the colonies soon gave way to a moderate amount of religious liberty. There was also no hereditary ruling class, as was found in England. The availability of land—the basis of wealth—

guaranteed greater democracy in the colonies. The wilderness gave settlers greater freedom and mobility; traditional English ways and laws were modified to take into account these new conditions.[50]

## Language

The lasting dominance of the English language in America makes conspicuous the impact of the English. Our central language is not a blend of early immigrant languages. Language sets off ethnic groups in fundamental ways. The pressures on non-English speaking immigrants first took the form of language pressures. Anglo-conformity pressures on non-English speakers could be great. Warner and Srole conclude that "our customary way of life is most like the English, and our language is but one of the several English dialects."[51]

As we just noted, many native-born Americans of British background attacked later immigrants to the United States for their alleged mongrelization of the Anglo-Saxon "race" and culture. From then to the present the dominance of the English language has been a major concern of nativists. They have worried that the entrance of millions of immigrants would cause the English language to be watered down or to become only one of several important languages. Interestingly, in the 1980s the dominance of the English language has been reasserted by organized nativists. More recently, modern nativists have worried that many in the latest group of immigrants, especially the Hispanic and Asian immigrants, have not accepted English as the dominant language. They have been concerned that Spanish, now spoken by 5 percent of all Americans at home, is challenging the dominance of English. One result of lobbying by new nativist organizations has been the introduction in many states of legislation to make English the official language. By 1987 such bills had been introduced or passed in twelve state legislatures, including those in Alabama, Missouri, and New Hampshire. Late in 1986 California passed a ballot proposition (by 73 percent of the vote) that declared English to be the official language of the largest state in the Union.[52]

Recent nativist organizations such as the California English Campaign and the national group called U.S. English have argued that they are not trying to discriminate against Hispanic immigrants to the United States. Rather, they wish the immigrants to quickly become part of the mainstream by adopting English as their primary language. These pro-English advocates have also asserted that they are not racist. However, leaders of Hispanic civil rights groups have pointed out that the pro-English advocates openly advocate stopping the spread of Spanish as a major language and cutting off governmental expenditures for bilingual programs in schools. Hispanic leaders have argued that pro-English campaigns promote racist stereotyping of and discrimination against Spanish-speaking Americans. Recent nativist campaigns to promote the English language underscore the traditional dominance of the English language—and the uneasiness that descendants of earlier immigrants to the United States still feel in the presence of the language and culture brought by newcomers to this "nation of immigrants" and in the presence of the English language that so often adopts "foreign" words.

## Religion and Basic Values

The English religious influence on the United States has been of great importance. For the first two hundred years English churches, or derivatives thereof, dominated the American scene. The Anglican church received some government support, but this privileged position was lost in the Revolution. The disproportionate number of Anglican and Congregational churches was obvious at the time of the Revolution, although Baptist and Presbyterian churches were by then more numerous than Anglican churches. Gradually, in the century after 1776, English dominance of American religious institutions gave way in the face of the numerous Catholic, Presbyterian, and Jewish groups that grew as a result of immigration.[53]

Herberg argues that the Catholic and Jewish faiths, as well as non-British Protestantism, have been distinctively shaped by the "American way of life," his phrase for the Anglo-Saxon core culture.[54] For example, one important study of Judaism has shown the substantial impact of Protestant institutions on eastern European Judaism. Sklare found that the immigrant synagogue made major changes over time in response to the core culture. Religious school adaptations were made in scheduling and in format, with Torah schools replaced by congregational schools. Among Reform Jews, English came to be the language of worship, and worship itself was modified with the introduction of Friday night services.[55]

The impact of the core culture on the non-Protestant religions of later immigrants was mixed. The immigrant has been expected to adapt in language and in many other areas, but some of the religious heritage has been preserved. One area where "cultural pluralism" has descriptive accuracy for the American scene is religion.

Perhaps more important than religious organization has been the impact of English Protestant values. The importance of the ascetic Protestantism that many of the early English settlers brought to the colonies cannot be underestimated. *Puritanism was important in* establishing the Protestant work ethic at the center of the American value system. Basic was the idea of work as a duty of every person. Originally, the idea was that hard work glorified God. Richard Baxter, an important English Puritan divine, exemplified this important perspective in his advocacy of hard work and abstinence from personal pleasures.[56] "Continuous work was seen as a major defense against the sinful temptations of the flesh; the primary objective of work was to glorify God. Idleness was regarded as sin."[57]

This view fostered the dominance of the work ethic so distinctive of the United States. The emerging capitalistic system in the late 1700s and the 1800s was pervaded by "pursuit of profit, and forever *renewed* profit, by means of continuous, rational, capitalistic enterprise."[58] Benjamin Franklin personified this spirit of capitalism with his famous maxims about time being money, about punctuality, and about the virtues of hard work.[59]

There is much one could add here about the influence of the English on general American culture, on such areas as music and art, but we have the space for only a few comments. Musical and artistic developments were initially linked to the English religious tradition. The first book published in the New England colonies was the *Bay*

*Psalm Book* (1640), which drew on English tradition.[60] "Yankee Doodle" was probably an English tune, the original lyrics satirizing ragtag colonial soldiers. Only when the Revolution began did American soldiers take it over from the British. Thus before, during, and after the Revolution, English melodies were the basis of most popular and political songs.[61] Even our national anthem, "The Star-Spangled Banner," draws on an English drinking song for its melody.

## Education

English and other British Americans took advantage of what few educational opportunities were available in the colonial period; better-off parents sent their children to the few private schools and colleges established before 1800. With the public school movement, which began in earnest in the first decades of the nineteenth century and spread throughout the nation, English and other British dominance of the public schools became a fact of life. Working-class and middle-class British Americans took advantage of these schools. Public schools in urban areas were seen as a particularly important means of socializing non-Protestant immigrants into Anglo-Saxon Protestant values and the emerging industrial system. British American industrialists and educators usually established the public schools, shaped their curricula and teaching practices, and supervised their operation. Although some educators, such as John Dewey, believed education gave greater opportunity to poor immigrants, many educators emphasized the social-control aspects of the schools. In many of the schools the Americanization pressures on immigrant children were intense; whether the children were Irish, Jewish, or Italian did not seem to matter. Anglicization of the children was designed to ferret out the harmful non-Anglo-Saxon ways, to assimilate the children in terms of manners, work habits, and the Protestant ethic.[62]

## Political and Legal Institutions

American political and legal institutions have been shaped in critical ways by the English and British heritage. We can think of this impact in two basic ways: in terms of laws inherited from the English and in terms of the influence English immigrants and their descendants have had in important political organizations and government institutions.

Given the near monopoly of English settlers among the early colonists of the eastern seaboard, it is not surprising that English legal institutions were dominant. A concern for the rule of law and for the "rights of Englishmen" was manifest in the first settlements. The famous Mayflower Company, which set up a political framework theoretically providing for equality and justice under the law, has often been praised. New England, with its Puritan institutions, provided the model for later American political and legal developments.[63]

Huntington has argued that the North American colonies took on a very distinctive set of political institutions—those characteristic of sixteenth-century England. Although many of these constitutional features were being *abandoned* in England, they became part of the political structure on this side of the Atlantic. The basic ideas in this system include unity of government and society, subordination of government to law, a balance of power between the legislature (Parliament in England) and the executive (the king), and substantial reliance on local governmental authorities.[64] American political and legal institutions, including the U.S. Constitution itself, have reflected these ideas ever since. Authority and power were centralized in England, but in the United States there was a separation of basic authority into three governmental branches—the executive, judicial, and legislative. There is the unusual position of the president. The United States, unlike almost every other modern political system, does not distinguish between the head of government and the (often nominal) chief of state. In the 1970s the Watergate scandal of the Richard Nixon administration and in the 1980s the "Contragate" scandal of the Ronald Reagan administration made this executive power clear. America was a new society, but an "old" political state.

One of the most important English political influences can be seen in the representative assemblies in the colonies and the United States. By the 1600s the British Crown had begun to establish representative assemblies in the English colonies based on the parliamentary model.[65] Gradually these assemblies grew in power vis-a-vis the London government. Eventual Crown infringements on the operations of these assemblies were among the critical issues leading to the Revolution.

The American legal framework also reflected English influence. Prior to the Revolution, English common law was asserted to be "the measure of rights of Americans."[66] The colonies had similar legal frameworks, but negative feeling arose over English common law because of the tension between the new United States and England. Some wanted a new American code, "but," as Pound notes, "most lawyers sought to reshape or add to the existing stock of authoritative legal materials."[67] Although there was variation in the way English statutes were incorporated into the legal systems of the colonies and later the states, their implementation was thoroughgoing: "the use of English statutes was provided for at an early stage in twenty-six of the twenty-eight jurisdictions organized between 1776 and 1836."[68]

These statutes were incorporated sometimes by direct action of the new state governments, sometimes by indirect action that had the effect of continuing previous statutes. Although the American legal system has been patched many times, the basic cloth has remained English common law. The legal system in England, in which some colonial leaders were trained, had a direct impact on the development of American law.[69]

## Officeholding

In addition to their impact on laws and political institutions, the English have had an impact on the operation of those institutions. English Americans have filled offices in various political contexts throughout United States history. There have been only a few studies of the English, or British, influence on sectors of the political structure. Davie notes that "the colonial assemblies were almost exclusively English in makeup, and the English were inclined to look upon other ethnic groups as inferior."[70] The founding fathers were also quite distinctly English. The Declaration of Independence was signed by fifty-six European males, thirty-eight of whom were English by background or birth; nine were Scottish or "Scotch-Irish," three Irish, five Welsh, and only one Swedish.[71]

This predominance of the English among the new nation's political leaders is found in numerous other political gatherings of that period. Indeed, the Constitution clearly reflects the interests of English with wealth. The Constitutional Convention was predominantly English, judging from the last names. Most men of wealth in the new nation—merchants, financiers, shippers, wealthy farmers, and their allies—supported the Constitution out of economic self-interest. Slaves, indentured servants, poor farmers, laborers, and women had no say in the framing of the Constitution. The framers of the Constitution perpetuated the class lines that were the substance of English social structure.[72]

Studies of national political leaders—presidents, Supreme Court justices, and members of Congress—have revealed a distinctive pattern persisting to the present. Presidents and presidential candidates have been "required" to possess ancestry qualifications, preferably British American or northern European origins. Of the thirty-six presidents from Washington to Nixon, about 60 percent had English origins; all but six had English, British, or Scotch-Irish backgrounds, and all the remainder had northern European backgrounds.[73] A study of the ethnic origins of Supreme Court justices from 1789 to 1957 found that over half were English or Welsh. In all periods English Americans have been heavily represented on the nation's highest court.[74]

Analysis of the 1901–1910 period provides additional data on officeholders. One study of 162 prominent political leaders (including presidents, representatives, senators, and Supreme Court justices) in this period found that over half were of English or Welsh origin. Most were at least fourth-generation, with family lines predating the Revolution.[75]

Baltzell has traced the rise of English American leaders such as Robert Todd Lincoln, the son of Abraham Lincoln, at the turn of the twentieth century. Educated at Phillips Academy and Harvard, Lincoln became a millionaire corporation lawyer at the heart of the ruling elite in Chicago and Washington. In 1901, the year of Queen Victoria's death, the Lincoln heir was part of a British and British American establishment that dominated much of the world. A northwestern European Protestant, Theodore Roosevelt, was in the White House, and J.P. Morgan, a leader in the (Protestant) Episcopal church, had just put together the first billion-dollar corporation. The Senate of the United States was a Protestant millionaires' club. British American influence extended throughout all institutional sectors.[76]

Baltzell further argues that in the next few decades of the twentieth century this establishment developed into a rigid caste. Even when the new immigrants managed to break into politics, as in the case of Irish and Italian Americans, they were usually subservient to Protestant leaders. The Irish Catholic Kennedy administration (1961–1963) marked a brief shift from a homogeneous political establishment. Yet Kennedy was soon followed by more men of "old stock" lines.[77] However, apart from Baltzell's study only a little research has been undertaken on explicit English political dominance in the mid-twentieth century.

What of the English impact on local government? One study of New Haven, Connecticut, has pointed up English dominance. The old patrician elite there "completely dominated the political system. They were of one common stock and one religion, cohesive in their uniformly conservative outlook on all matters, substantially unchallenged in their authority, successful in pushing through their own policies, and in full control of such critical institutions as the established religion, the educational system (including not only all the schools but Yale as well), and even business enterprise."[78]

Even the nineteenth-century entrepreneurs and industrialists who succeeded the old patrician elite in New Haven could trace their lineage back to the *Mayflower*. Moreover, a study of the mayors of Cleveland in the 1836–1901 period found that most were part of an Anglo-Protestant elite, with strong family and friendship ties to New England. Their governing framework was guided by the "New England creed," proposition one of which was "The good society is white and Protestant."[79] Presumably much Anglo-Saxon Protestant political dominance has persisted into the late twentieth century.

## Economic Institutions

The English heritage is reflected in U.S. economic institutions—in the values that shape those institutions and in the actual dominance of English American individuals. Just as the legal system incorporated portions of the English legal system, the colonies developed initially under a combined mercantilist-capitalistic economic system that dominated much of Europe at the time; the attempt was made to increase the raw materials and the markets available for the king's control. As we have seen, the first English colonies were set up by state-chartered trading companies. Others were proprietary colonies set up by men of wealth and power. While the colonies generally did not have the payoff that these speculators had hoped, they did bring significant economic benefits.

Mercantile capitalism, the economic system that still existed in the colonies at the time of the Revolution, was a state-directed capitalism closely linked to a vigorous nationalism that worked constantly for a favorable balance of trade for one's own country—in this case, England. The American Revolution was basically a clash between English and English (or British) American commercial interests, a clash that unified the colonies and brought a political break between two generally similar economic systems.[80]

Although full-fledged industrial capitalism in the United States developed several decades later, its guiding philosophy had intimate connections with the English system. The basic ideas for U.S. industrial development arrived through English channels, and English capitalists and skilled workers provided much of the knowhow for American capitalistic development. After the Revolution, as before, Britain and the United States formed a single Atlantic economy, so close and important were their economic connections. From 1820 to the Civil War about half of United States exports went to British ports; 40 percent of their imports came from those same ports. Cotton exports from the slave plantations of the south to Britain were particularly significant, as were British textiles in the return flow.[81]

## Direct Participation in the Economy

The English have had a significant impact on the operation of the U.S. economy through their participation in critical positions. In the beginning they established the colonies and controlled the land, and thus the wealth. Colonial society was not democratic. In the early period economic and political control of the colonies lay primarily in the hands of English (and other British) landowners and merchants.[82] Morison has argued, however, that the men who eventually came to dominate many of the colonies in the late prerevolutionary period were yeoman farmers.[83] The founders had included English aristocrats, but they had died or returned to England by the mid-1650s.

Whatever their background, men with land and wealth needed labor, and the demand for labor was tremendous. The eighteenth-century Atlantic migration was spurred primarily by the labor demand.[84] Because there was no surplus population in the colonies for economic enterprises, labor from Europe and Africa was imported.[85] By the 1730s a substantial Irish migration had begun. A large proportion of these immigrants were indentured servants. The African slave trade eventually supplanted the trade in white servants.[86]

As we move toward the Civil War period and then into the twentieth century, we again find few specific studies on the dominance of the economy by English (or British) Americans. A recent study of the wealth of males living in the United States in 1860 concludes only that the wealth of "native-born males" was about twice that of "foreign-born males."[87] The industrialization in the nineteenth century was partially fueled by imported English and Dutch capital. American railroad development was bankrolled by English capital and produced fortunes for several English investors. English capital also played a role in the development of agriculture (for instance, wheat farming) in the Mississippi Valley.

U.S. capitalist elites were substantially dominated by Americans of British descent. In the nineteenth century the most famous of these leaders were the chief industrialists and financiers of the new industrial nation, many of whom have been regarded as "robber barons." Most were relatively young at the time of the Civil War: John D. Rockefeller, Leland Stanford, J.P. Morgan, Jay Gould, and Jim Fisk. All were men of great wealth and power. Their ethnic heritages were typically English, with a few other northern Europeans scattered among them. Most were well versed in the private accumulation of profit. Political influence was theirs as well. Many of these men, or their associates or family members, became senators, representatives, and governors. The impact of these men and their descendants on the economy and the political sphere is incalculable. Their economic system increasingly exploited immigrant labor.[88]

A study of top executives and entrepreneurs in the late-nineteenth-century iron and steel industry found that few came from immigrant families recently arrived in the United States. Most were native-born and had fathers with capitalist or professional backgrounds. Most did *not* fit the image of a poor immigrant "making good," as did the steel magnate Andrew Carnegie, who came to America as a poor boy. Over half were of English or Welsh ancestry; most of the rest were either Scottish or (early) Protestant Irish. A study of the social origins of a broader group of business leaders in the late nineteenth century found that 90 percent were of English, Scottish, or Welsh ancestry. In both studies English Americans were dominant.[89]

One study of persons of wealth and influence (millionaire and multimillionaire manufacturers, bankers, and merchants) in the first decades of the twentieth century found that the backgrounds of about half were English; a significant percentage of the rest were Scottish or Irish. In another study twentieth-century executives in major businesses were found to be predominantly of northern and western European ancestry. A substantial majority of the major European-origin business executives belonged to Episcopalian, Presbyterian, or Congregational churches. Newcomer concludes that "for the most part, the religious preference is inherited from the family, and the dominance of British family backgrounds is sufficient in itself to account for the large proportion of executives belonging to these churches."[90] A survey of two hundred major executives in the largest companies and corporations from 1901 to 1910 found that 53 percent were of English or Welsh origin, 7 percent were Scottish, 14 percent were Irish, and 8 percent were Canadian or British (unspecified).[91]

## Local Economies

A few studies bearing on American towns and cities have made clear the extent of English (or British) dominance in local economies. Thernstrom's study of nineteenth-century Newburyport, Massachusetts, for example, revealed the dominance of New Englanders, presumably of English or British origin. In the mid-nineteenth century English and Scottish workers had significant advantages over Irish and other immigrants. "The immigrant workman in Newburyport," writes Thernstrom, "was markedly less successful than his native counterpart in climbing out of the ranks of the unskilled in the 1850–1880 period."[92] One reason was that immigrant workers such as the Irish were discriminated against by the factory owners. An examination of Newburyport in the 1930s found half the population still to be Yankee. This predominantly Yankee group still dominated upper income groups.[93]

Burlington, Vermont, was dominated in the 1930s by "Old Americans"—those who had been in the United States for four generations, probably heavily English and English Canadian. They controlled banking, manufacturing, and the university there. They constituted a disproportion of professional and political officials. "Old Americans" were the model for the community, a model with a racist dimension. Anderson underscores this point: "Traditions of family and name, of power and influence, in the financial and civil life of the community, of race-consciousness, plus a very deep conviction that the Protestant traditions of their forefathers are basically important to the development of free institutions in America, set the Old Americans apart as a group distinct from other people."[94]

A few studies of economic influentials have been done since the 1930s. The "proper Philadelphians" about whom Baltzell has written typically have English or British backgrounds. The English and their descendants long had a heavy influence on the development of the middle colony of Pennsylvania. This is suggested, for example, by the decided dominance of Episcopalians and Presbyterians in the Philadelphia *Social Register* for the year 1940. Of the 147 *Register* members with religious affiliations listed, most were Episcopalian or Presbyterian. And of the 513 Philadelphians in *Who's Who*, well over half belonged to one of these two denominations.[95]

These Philadelphians were persons of great power and influence in the 1940s, particularly in banking, law, engineering, and business. To sum up, a typical member of the Philadelphia elite in 1940 would be "of English or Welsh descent" and "his great-great-great-grandfather would have been a prominent Philadelphian in the great age of the new republic."[96]

In an analysis of the 1950s and 1960s, Baltzell has underscored the continuing dominance of English and other British Americans at the national level as well. Although non-British groups have significantly penetrated the economic and political system, as in the case of the Irish Catholics, they had not been as successful in the executive suites of large corporations, where the leadership is "still mainly composed of managers of Anglo-Saxon Protestant background."[97] In the 1950s Dalton's impressive study of one large industrial corporation found ethnic stratification; 60 percent of the management was of British American origin.[98]

## A Study of Contemporary Elites

A 1970s study by Dye of the top decision makers in the United States identified 4,000 people in the top positions in major employment areas, including the corporate sector (industry, communication, banking), government, and the public interest sector (education, mass media, law). Dye concluded that "great power in American is concentrated in a tiny handful of men. A few thousand individuals out of 200 million Americans decide about war and peace, wages and prices, consumption and investment, employment and production, law and justice, taxes and benefits, education and learning, health and welfare, advertising and communication, life and leisure."[99]

Decisions of importance are reached at the middle and lower levels of the society, but it is the few thousand people in these top positions who make the most critical decisions—those affecting the lives of members of all racial and ethnic groups. Dye's research revealed that the social origins of the 4,000 elites were not typical. They were generally affluent, white, Anglo-Saxon males. There were only a few blacks and virtually *no* Mexican Americans, Native Americans, or Japanese Americans. Dye has estimated that these elites were "at least 90 percent Anglo-Saxon" and noted that "there were very few recognizable Irish, Italian, or Jewish names" in the group.[100]

In looking at social and economic mobility in the United States, one must be careful to distinguish the reality from the Horatio Alger rags-to-riches myths. For all their movement from the lower to the higher levels of the working class over several generations, Catholic and Jewish Americans still are not well represented at the very top of the economic and political pyramids of power. However, it is important to note that by the 1980s the upper reaches of American institutions had broadened to include not only the British Americans but also those with other northern European ancestry, particularly German, "Scotch-Irish," and Scandinavian Americans. And by the 1980s a scattered handful of Catholic and Jewish Americans were at least beginning to penetrate the upper levels of elite bastions of power in the United States. Nonetheless, research studies by Dye and others in the 1980s found a continuing pattern of overwhelming White Anglo-Saxon Protestant dominance at the top levels in industrial, public interest, and governmental organizations.

A number of critics, usually representing emerging non-British ethnic groups, have been outspoken about the influence of Anglo-Saxon Americans. The following is Michael Novak's intriguing assessment:

> In the country clubs, as city executives, established families, industrialists, owners, lawyers, masters of etiquette, college presidents, dominators of the military, fundraisers, members of blue ribbon committees, realtors, brokers, deans, sheriffs—it is the cumulative power and distinctive styles of WASPs that the rest of us have had to learn in order to survive. WASPs never had to celebrate Columbus Day or march down Fifth Avenue wearing green. Every day has been their day in America.[101]

It is important to note the caustic character of this generally accurate assessment of the economic power of the Anglo-Saxon Protestants given here. By the 1960s and 1970s the term *WASP*, originally shorthand for *White Anglo-Saxon Protestant*, was increasingly being used in a derogatory way, particularly by writers of southern and eastern European heritage. Another example is the title of Peter Schrag's book *The Decline of the WASP*.[102] One significance of this greater derogatory use of *WASP*, and of the stereotyping associated with the term, was that English and other Anglo-Saxon Americans were increasingly being *challenged* for political and economic dominance by Americans from southern and eastern Europe.

## English Americans as a Group: U.S. Census Data

It is clear from the foregoing discussion that English Americans have done well in the higher echelons of U.S. society. Still, it is important to ask as well about the fortunes of ordinary English Americans, a group who according to the 1980 census totaled 50 million. U.S. Census Bureau data for 1950 and 1970 on English Americans are not very useful for estimating the general social and economic position of the group in U.S. society because they are limited to recent immigrants and their children. But in 1980 a more general question on national ancestry was asked, a question that provides a picture of a larger group of English Americans. By supplementing these more recent data with the earlier figures we can evaluate the position of English Americans as a whole in the areas of education, income, and occupation. For example, looking at the median years of education completed for English American and all U.S. adults, we find this pattern:[103]

|      | Native-born with Foreign Parent(s) | | All U.S. Adults | |
|------|------|-------|------|-------|
|      | Men  | Women | Men  | Women |
| 1950 | 10.7 | 11.4  | 9.0  | 9.6   |
| 1970 | 12.4 | 12.3  | 12.1 | 12.1  |

In the years 1950 and 1970 the native-born children of more recent English immigrants to the United States had median levels of educational attainment higher than those for all persons twenty-five and over. The 1980 data are available for a larger group, those who identified themselves in terms of nationality group or country of origin in reply to a census question on ancestry. In 1980 the median number of years of school completed for all those reporting English ancestry was 12.5, a figure virtually identical to the medians for all men (12.6) and women (12.4) in the United States.[104]

Family income data are available for 1969 and 1979. In 1969 the median income of second-generation English American families and unrelated individuals (those living alone in households) was $11,374; the figure for all families and unrelated individuals in the United States was lower—$9,590. In the late 1960s these children of recent English immigrants were doing better in terms of income than the typical U.S. household. The 1980 census figures for Americans of English ancestry, a much larger group than that just mentioned for 1969, show a different pattern. Those Americans with English ancestry reported a median family income of $19,807 for the year 1979; the median income for all U.S. families was $19,917. Thus, in 1980 English American families, taken as a group, had a median income close to that of the typical American family.[105]

Occupational data show a somewhat similar pattern. An examination of the occupational distribution of second-generation English Americans for 1950 and 1970 reveals that these children of immigrants were more likely to be found in professional, technical, managerial, and crafts jobs than the employed population as a whole. They were less likely to be found in the less skilled blue-collar positions. The 1980 occupational distribution for all Americans of English ancestry is generally similar to that of the general population. There was a slightly smaller proportion of English Americans in professional and technical occupations (12.8 percent) than in the population as a whole (15.4), but the proportion of managers and officials was larger (14.7 percent) than for the population as a whole (10.4 percent). Taken together, these two better-paying, white-collar job categories accounted for a bit more than one quarter of English American workers and about one quarter of the American population as a whole. The proportions of English Americans in the clerical/sales, skilled blue-collar, unskilled blue-collar, and service categories were similar to the corresponding proportions for the American population in general. The disproportionate influence of English Americans in corporate America and the impact of the English culture on the American core culture do not mean that this nationality, taken as a whole, is today better off in terms of income and occupational position than white Americans in general.[106]

## Anglo-Saxon Protestants and Catholic Americans: Poll Data

The relative mobility and achievements of Anglo-Saxon Protestant Americans and Catholic Americans have been debated by social scientists. The groups being compared in this debate are broader than the English Americans we examined in the last section; the data used are drawn from opinion polls. For example, Greeley found that Catholic American groups had occupational and income achievements comparable to or exceeding those of Protestants as a group, even those of British Protestants. Greeley concludes that U.S. society has in recent decades "bestowed economic, occupational, and education success" on its British Protestant and Irish Catholic populations.[107]

However, other survey research suggests that Catholic Americans have not yet surpassed the educational, income, and occupational achievements of the elite white Protestant groups. Using survey data, Clark Roof has demonstrated that Americans in the latter groups (the Episcopalians, Presbyterians, and Congregationalists) rank substantially above white Catholic Americans, including Irish Catholics, in family income level, educational achievement, and occupational prestige. Roof concludes that even with the upward movement of Catholic Americans, "upper-class Protestants maintain a hold on their [top] position too, and are not likely to be displaced any time soon in the status hierarchy."[108]

## BLENDING IN WHITE AMERICA: A NOTE ON THE SOUTHERN CASE

Numerous studies of whites loosely mix large non-English groups such as the "Scotch-Irish" and the Dutch with English Americans. In such discussions one cannot be sure about the experiences or impact of English Americans. In order to illustrate this problem, and also to emphasize the regional variation in white Protestant America, we can turn briefly to the case of whites who live in the South.

In his *White Southerners*, a study of this distinctive regional group, Lewis Killian refers to its members by that term, and occasionally as *white Anglo-Saxon Protestants*. It is clear that he is grouping many white ethnic groups besides English Americans under these labels. A particularly large segment of the southern white population is descended from early Irish immigrants, those often called *Scotch-Irish*. There are also large proportions of French, Spanish, and German descent. Killian notes that English and other British Americans have become submerged in a larger and ethnically diverse white population that, nearly unanimously until the 1960s, emphasized "whiteness" above all else. "For a southerner, the salient fact was and is whether he was white or black; all else was secondary."[109] Although it is possible that white southerners of English descent remain influential in southern politics and the southern economy, they are not examined by Killian as a specific group. What Killian provides is an important portrait of white southerners as a distinctive regional group.

In a number of ways the subcultural distinctiveness of American regions is similar to their ethnic distinctiveness. This is particularly true for the Old South. Southern culture has perhaps been the most distinctive regional culture, because of the racial oppression of black Americans and the subsequent rationalizations for that thoroughgoing racial discrimination. Slavery and later discrimination against black Americans have been moral problems for white Americans, North and South, for centuries. Agonizing over the immorality of racial oppression has not been limited to northern whites, for, as Cash notes, "the South itself definitely shared in these moral notions—in its secret heart [it] always carried a powerful and uneasy sense of the essential rightness of the nineteenth century's position on slavery."[110] This is clear in that prior to 1827 most of the nation's 130 abolition (antislavery) societies were in the South.

After the Civil War and Reconstruction southern whites rapidly rebuilt a dismantled slave-plantation society, and the New South was intentionally structured to keep black southerners "in their place." The New South has long been riddled with a massive array of discriminatory practices, legal and informal, aimed at handicapping blacks; the rationale for these practices has been a racist ideology. Killian notes that whites and their leaders have "offered apologies for indefensible practices," such as lynchings and segregation. The weight of this racist system has shaped the cultural system of whites in fundamental ways, even retarding literary and intellectual developments. Ever resentful of the regional dominance of the North in the southern economy, loyal sons and daughters of the white South have clung to "the belief that there is some mystical superiority in 'the southern way of life.'"[111] Even the economic resurgence in the Sunbelt in the 1970s and 1980s has not eliminated southern racial problems or the southern resentment of the North.

Books such as Killian's lead us to think about regional diversity in the United States and the ethnic diversity of the South. They also lead up to questions about the role of English Americans among white southerners. Unfortunately, Killian provides no answers to those questions; a specific history of English Americans in the South has not yet been published.[112]

## SUMMARY

The purpose of this chapter has been to examine that most neglected of all white ethnic groups, English Americans. Their blending into the background makes it difficult to assess the power, location, and achievements of these first immigrants and their descendants. It was the English who first colonized on a large scale the area now known as the eastern United States. In this chapter we have spelled out in some detail just what the original English colonization and migration have meant for American institutions, past and present. *Dominance* would seem to be the appropriate term, for the basic influence on American religious, economic, and political institutions has been English.

The colonization migration of the English led to a dominant core culture and society to which subsequent groups were required to adapt. The study of assimilation begins here. For several centuries English migrants and their descendants have been disproportionately represented in key social, economic, and political positions. Between the mid-1800s and the 1980s they were slowly joined in their dominant position by certain other Protestant groups. The result was a more diverse Anglo-Saxon Protestant group.

If we had the space, we would have explored the class and regional diversity of this Anglo-Saxon grouping more deeply. The tremendous impact of Anglo-Saxon Protestant Americans does not mean that substantial segments have not stayed working-class or even poor. There have long been regional and denominational differences within the Anglo-Saxon Protestant group. Episcopalians are a bit different from Congregationalists, and southerners are different from New Englanders.

In recent decades Anglo-Saxon dominance has been seriously and vigorously challenged by Catholic Americans, Jewish Americans, and numerous nonwhite groups. Some have argued that Anglo-Saxon influence, particularly in the arts, is on the wane. Schrag has argued that Anglo-Saxon Protestants are on the road to cultural demise. According to this view, white Anglo-Saxon Protestant domination came to an end after World War II; reflecting the "decline of the WASP" is the increasing non-Anglo-Saxon dominance of American music, writing, and art. But even Schrag modifies his overall estimation for the economic sphere: the Anglo-Saxon Protestant "elite still controls its own corporate offices, its board rooms, its banks and foundations."[112]

# NOTES

1. Cleveland Amory, *The Proper Bostonians* (New York: Dutton, 1947), p. 11.
2. Carl Wittke, "Preface to the Revised Edition," in *We Who Built America*, rev. ed. (Cleveland: Case Western Reserve University Press, 1967).
3. Milton M. Gordon, *Assimilation in American Life* (New York: Oxford University Press, 1964), p. 72.
4. Will Herberg, *Protestant—Catholic—Jew*, rev. ed. (Garden City, N.Y.: Doubleday, Anchor Books, 1960), p. 21.
5. Rowland T. Berthoff, *British Immigrants in Industrial America* (Chicago: University of Chicago Press, 1953), p. 1.
6. Wilbur S. Shepperson, *British Emigration to North America* (Oxford: Basil Blackwell, 1957), p. 3.
7. Conrad Taeuber and Irene B. Taeuber, "Immigration to the United States," in *Population and Society*, ed. Charles B. Nam (Boston: Houghton Mifflin, 1968), p. 316.
8. Immigration and Naturalization Service, *1975 Annual Report* (Washington, D.C.: U.S. Government Printing Office, 1975), pp. 62–64.
9. Alice Marriott and Carol K. Rachlin, *American Epic* (New York: Mentor Books, 1969), p. 105.
10. Samuel Eliot Morison, *The Oxford History of the American People* (New York: Oxford University Press, 1965), pp. 48–49.
11. Klaus E. Knorr, *British Colonial Theories, 1570–1850* (Toronto: University of Toronto Press, 1944), p. 126.
12. Marriott and Rachlin, *American Epic*, p. 106.
13. Ibid., pp. 104–6; Winthrop D. Jordan, *White over Black* (Baltimore: Penguin, 1969), p. 89.
14. Quoted in John Collier, *Indians of the Americas*, abridged ed. (New York: Mentor Books, 1947), p. 115.
15. The next three paragraphs draw on Morison, *Oxford History of the American People*, pp. 50–154; and Maldwyn A. Jones, *American Immigration* (Chicago: University of Chicago Press, 1960), pp. 10–38.
16. Morison, *Oxford History of the American People*, p. 74.
17. Ibid., p. 131.
18. Henry P. Fairchild, *Immigration* (New York: Macmillan, 1920), p. 32. Leonard Dinnerstein and Frederic C. Jaher, "Introduction," in *The Aliens*, ed. Leonard Dinnerstein and Frederic C. Jaher (New York: Appleton-Century-Crofts, 1970), p. 4.
19. *Proceedings of the American Historical Association*, vol. 1 of *Annual Report of the American Historical Association* (Washington, D.C.: U.S. Government Printing Office, 1932), p. 124.
20. Jones, *American Immigration*, pp. 34–35.
21. Berthoff, *British Immigrants in Industrial America*, p. vii.
22. Ibid., p. 5.

23. Shepperson, *British Emigration to North America*, p. 20.

24. Berthoff, *British Immigrants in Industrial America*, pp. 28–29; Charlotte Erickson, "English," in *Harvard Encyclopedia of American Ethnic Groups*, ed. Stephan Thernstrom (Cambridge: Harvard University Press, 1980), pp. 324–32.

25. Shepperson, *British Emigration to North America*, pp. 27–32, 84; Berthoff, *British Immigrants in Industrial America*, pp. 46–87, 122; Charlotte Erickson, "Agrarian Myths of English Immigrants," in *In the Trek of the Immigrants*, ed. O. Fritiof Ander (Rock Island, Ill.: Augustana Library Publications, 1964), pp. 59–64.

26. Berthoff, *British Immigrants in Industrial America*, p. 125.

27. Ibid., p. 210. See also pp. 143–83.

28. Erickson, "English," pp. 335–36.

29. This section draws heavily on Charles H. Anderson, *White Protestant Americans* (Englewood Cliffs, N.J.: Prentice-Hall, 1970), pp. 28–71, 79–87. See also Ian C. Graham, *Colonists from Scotland* (Ithaca, N.Y.: Cornell University Press, 1956); and Albert B. Faust, *The German Element in the United States* (New York: Steuben Society, 1927).

30. John Higham, *Strangers in the Land* (New York: Atheneum, 1963), p. 4.

31. Fairchild, *Immigration*, p. 47.

32. Jones, *American Immigration*, p. 44.

33. Jordan, *White over Black*, p. 86.

34. Ibid., p. 87.

35. Jones, *American Immigration*, pp. 41–46.

36. Fairchild, *Immigration*, pp. 57–58.

37. Michael Kammen, *People of Paradox* (New York: Knopf, 1972), p. 66.

38. Quoted in Jordan, *White over Black*, p. 338.

39. Kammen, *People of Paradox*, p. 74; Jordan, *White over Black*, p. 339.

40. Higham, *Strangers in the Land*, p. 6; Marcus L. Hansen, *The Immigrant in American History* (New York: Harper Torchbooks, 1964), pp. 111–36; Wittke, *We Who Built America*, p. 505.

41. Higham, *Strangers in the Land*, p. 9.

42. Quoted in Richard Hofstadter, *Social Darwinism in American Thought*, rev. ed. (Boston: Beacon Press, 1955), pp. 171–72.

43. Higham, *Strangers in the Land*, p. 32; Hofstadter, *Social Darwinism in American Thought*, pp. 173–74.

44. Higham, *Strangers in the Land*, p. 33.

45. Hofstadter, *Social Darwinism in American Thought*, pp. 178–79; Lewis H. Carlson and George A. Colburn, *In Their Place* (New York: John Wiley, 1972), pp. 305–8. Carlson and Colburn provide excerpts from the writings of Strong.

46. Higham, *Strangers in the Land*, pp. 96–152.

47. E. Digby Baltzell, *The Protestant Establishment* (New York: Random House, Vintage Books, 1966), pp. 96–98; Higham, *Strangers in the Land*, pp. 148–57.

48. See, for example, the excerpt from Roberts's *Why Europe Leaves Home* in *In Their Place*, ed. Carlson and Colburn, p. 312.

49. David M. Chalmers, *Hooded Americanism* (Chicago: Quadrangle, 1965), pp. 28–38.

50. Jones, *American Immigration*, pp. 36–38.

51. W. Lloyd Warner and Leo Srole, *The Social Systems of American Ethnic Groups* (New Haven: Yale University Press, 1945), p. 287.

52. Susanna McBee, "A War over Words," *U.S. News & World Report*, October 6, 1986, p. 64.

53. Edwin S. Gaustad, *Historical Atlas of Religion in America* (New York: Harper & Row, Pub., 1962), pp. 1–20.

54. Herberg, *Protestant—Catholic—Jew*, p. 82.

55. Marshall Sklare, *Conservative Judaism* (Glencoe, Ill.: Free Press, 1955), pp. 31–117.

56. Max Weber, *The Protestant Ethic and the Spirit of Capitalism* (New York: Scribner's, 1958), pp. 158–60.

57. Joe R. Feagin, *Subordinating the Poor* (Englewood Cliffs, N.J.: Prentice-Hall, 1975), p. 22.

58. Weber, *The Protestant Ethic*, p. 17.

59. Ibid., p. 50.

60. David Ewen, *History of Popular Music* (New York: Barnes & Noble, 1961), pp. 1–4.

61. Ibid., pp. 5–10.

62. See Samuel Bowles and Herbert Gintis, *Schooling in Capitalist America* (New York: Basic Books, 1976).

63. Morison, *Oxford History of the American People*, p. 55.

64. Samuel P. Huntington, "Political Modernization: America versus Europe," *World Politics* 18 (April 1966): 147–48.

65. Jack P. Greene, *The Quest for Power* (Chapel Hill: University of North Carolina Press, 1963), pp. 1ff.

66. Roscoe Pound, *The Formative Era of American Law* (Boston: Little,Brown, 1938), pp. 7–8.

67. Ibid., p. 12.

68. Elizabeth G. Brown and William W. Blume, *British Statutes in American Law, 1776–1836* (Ann Arbor: University of Michigan Law School, 1964), p. 44. See also Lawrence M. Friedman, *A History of American Law* (New York: Simon & Schuster, 1973), pp. 96ff.

69. Pound, *The Formative Era of American Law*, p. 81.

70. Maurice R. Davie, *World Immigration* (New York: Macmillan, 1939), p. 36.

71. Henry J. Ford, *The Scotch-Irish in America* (Princeton, N.J.: Princeton University Press, 1915), p. 491.

72. Charles A. Beard, *An Economic Interpretation of the Constitution of the United States* (New York: Macmillan, 1947), p. 17.

73. This tabulation was drawn from the profiles in Joseph N. Kane, *Facts about the Presidents*, 3rd ed. (New York: Wilson, 1974).

74. John R. Schmidhauser, "The Justices of the Supreme Court: A Collective Portrait," *Midwest Journal of Political Science* 3 (February 1959): 1–57.

75. William Miller, "American Historians and the Business Elite," *Journal of Economic History* 9 (November 1949): 202–3.

76. Baltzell, *The Protestant Establishment*, pp. 10–12.

77. Ibid., p. 21.

78. Robert A. Dahl, *Who Governs?* (New Haven: Yale University Press, 1961), pp. 15–16.

79. Matthew Holden, Jr., "Ethnic Accommodation in a Historical Case," *Comparative Studies in Society and History* 8 (January 1966): 172.

80. Rowland Berthoff, *An Unsettled People* (New York: Harper & Row, Pub., 1971), p. 13; Oliver C. Cox, *Caste, Class, and Race* (Garden City, N.Y.: Doubleday, 1948), pp. 338–39; Barrington Moore, Jr., *Social Origins of Dictatorship and Democracy* (Boston: Beacon Press, 1966), pp. 112–13.

81. Frank Thistlewaite, *The Anglo-American Connection in the Early Nineteenth Century* (Philadelphia: University of Pennsylvania Press, 1959), pp. 5–11.

82. Jesse Lemisch, "The American Revolution Seen from the Bottom Up," in *Toward a New Past*, ed. Barton J. Bernstein (New York: Random House, 1968), p. 8; J. O. Lindsay, ed., *The Old Regime*, vol. 7 of *The New Cambridge Modern History* (Cambridge: Cambridge University Press, 1957), pp. 509–11.

83. Morison, *Oxford History of the American People*, p. 89.

84. Abbot E. Smith, *Colonists in Bondage* (Chapel Hill: University of North Carolina Press, 1947), p. 25.

85. Jordan, *White over Black*, p. 47.

86. Howard Zinn, *The Politics of History* (Boston: Beacon Press, 1970), p. 68; Smith, *Colonists in Bondage*, p. 336.

87. Lee Soltow, *Men and Wealth in the United States, 1850–1870* (New Haven: Yale University Press, 1975), p. 149.

88. Matthew Josephson, *The Robber Barons* (New York: Harcourt, Brace & World, 1934), pp. 32–35, 315–452.

89. John N. Ingham, *The Iron Barons* (Westport, Conn.: Greenwood Press, 1978), pp. 14–16; Francis Gregory and Irene Nau, "The American Industrial Elite," in *Men in Business*, ed. William Miller (New York: Harper & Row, Pub., 1962), p. 200.

90. Pitirim Sorokin, "American Millionaires and Multi-millionaires," *Social Forces* 3 (May 1925): 634–35; Mabel Newcomer, *The Big Business Executive* (New York: Columbia University Press, 1955), p. 46.

91. Miller, "American Historians and the Business Elite," p. 202.

92. Stephan Thernstrom, *Poverty and Progress* (Cambridge: Harvard University Press, 1964), pp. 99–101.

93. W. Lloyd Warner and Paul S. Lunt, *The Social Life of a Modern Community* (New Haven: Yale University Press, 1941), pp. 213–25; Samuel Koenig, "Ethnic Groups in Connecticut Industry," *Social Forces* 20 (October 1941–May 1942): 105.

94. Elin L. Anderson, *We Americans* (Cambridge: Harvard University Press, 1937), p. 137; see also pp. 21–247.

95. E. Digby Baltzell, *An American Business Aristocracy* (New York: Collier Books, 1962), p. 267.

96. Ibid., p. 431.

97. Baltzell, *The Protestant Establishment*, p. 321.

98. Melville Dalton, *Men Who Manage* (New York: John Wiley, 1959), pp. 183–84.

99. Thomas R. Dye, *Who's Running America?* (Englewood Cliffs, N.J.: Prentice-Hall, 1976), pp. 3–8, 150–53. See also Thomas R. Dye, *Who's Running America? The Carter Years* (Englewood Cliffs, N.J.: Prentice-Hall, 1979), pp. 171–77.

100. Thomas R. Dye, letter to the author, April 11, 1977.

101. Michael Novak, "The Nordic Jungle: Inferiority in America," in *Divided Society*, ed. Colin Greer (New York: Basic Books, 1974), p. 134; compare Thomas R. Dye, *Who's Running America? The Conservative Years* (Fourth ed., Englewood Cliffs, N.J.: Prentice-Hall, Inc., 1986), pp. 185–199.

102. Peter Schrag, *The Decline of the WASP* (New York: Simon & Schuster, 1971).

103. U.S. Bureau of the Census, *U.S. Census of Population, 1950: Special Reports—Nativity and Parentage*, P-E No. 3A, 1954, p. 137; U.S. Bureau of the Census, *U.S. Census of Population, 1970: Subject Reports—National Origin and Language*, PC(2)-1A, 1973, p. 368.

104. U.S. Bureau of the Census, *U.S. Census of Population, 1980: General Social and Economic Characteristics*, PC 80-1-C1, 1983, pp. 21, 172.

105. U.S. Bureau of the Census, *U.S. Census of Population, 1970: Subject Reports—National Origin and Language*, PC(2)-1A, 1973, p. 368; U.S. Bureau of the Census, *Census of Population, 1980: General Social and Economic Characteristics*, PC 80-1-C1, 1983, pp. 51, 177.

106. U.S. Bureau of the Census, *U.S. Census of Population, 1950: Special Reports—Nativity and Parentage*, P-E No. 3A, 1954, p. 137; U.S. Bureau of the Census, *U.S. Census of Population, 1970: Subject Reports—National Origin and Language*, PC(2)-1A, 1973, p. 125; U.S. Bureau of the Census, *U.S. Census of Population, 1980: General Social and Economic Characteristics*, PC 80-1-C1, 1983, p. 174.

107. Andrew M. Greeley, *Ethnicity in the United States* (New York: John Wiley, 1974), pp. 63–89; Andrew M. Greeley, "Catholics and the Upper Middle Class: Comment on Roof," *Social Forces* 59 (March 1981): 824–30.

108. Wade Clark Roof, "Socioeconomic Differentials among White Socioreligious Groups in the United States," *Social Forces* 58 (September 1979): 285–89.

109. Lewis M. Killian, *White Southerners* (New York: Random House, 1970), p. 16.

110. W. J. Cash, *The Mind of the South* (New York: Random House, Vintage Books, 1941), p. 63.

111. Killian, *White Southerners*, p. 42.

112. Schrag, *The Decline of the WASP*, p. 164.

# CHAPTER 4

# *Irish Americans*

Numerous discussions of ethnicity have focused on the *white ethnics*, a term often used for Catholic and Jewish Americans. Anglo-Saxon Protestant Americans have, on occasion, blamed these groups for corruption and racial discrimination in American cities. They have spoken of white ethnic "hardhats" as though they were uneducated buffoons with a corrupt, racist, or authoritarian bent. Not surprisingly, white ethnics have counterattacked, arguing that hypocritical Anglo-Saxon Protestants have little consciousness of the experiences of white Catholic and Jewish Americans. It is the purpose of this chapter on the Irish, and the following chapters on Italian and Jewish Americans, to analyze the neglected experiences of the non-English white Americans who helped build the United States.

The Irish are one of the major groups that come to mind when white ethnic groups are mentioned, especially in the cities. The traditional view of the Irish contains images of parading leprechauns in funny suits, shamrocks, Saint Patrick's Day, and big-city political machines. The Irish, furthermore, are supposed to be among the most conservative and racist of white Americans, with greater alcoholism problems than other Americans. This superficial imagery is an inaccurate portrayal of the past and present realities of the Irish American experience. The Irish contribution to the development of the United States has been major.

How did the Irish come to these shores in the first place? What was their immigration experience? What proportions were Protestant and what Catholic? What conflicts have occurred? How does the assimilation model fit the Irish experience? How successful have the Irish been? Let us turn now to these basic questions.

## IRISH IMMIGRATION: AN OVERVIEW

On the migration continuum from slave importation to voluntary immigration, the Irish migration to North America would be toward the voluntary end. Even so, this movement was less voluntary than the migrations of some other European groups, for there was great economic and political pressure to leave Ireland. Yet there was a choice in the points of destination. Perhaps 200,000 to 400,000 Irish left for the colonies prior to 1787; between 1787 and the 1820's approximately 100,000 migrated.[1] The period 1841–1860 saw the heaviest migration, with about 1.6 million immigrants. Migration peaked again in the 1880s and the 1890s, but then dropped off sharply in subsequent decades to a trickle after World War II. From 1941 to 1980 the total number of immigrants was less than 170,000.[2]

## The Eighteenth-Century Migration

The first Irish came prior to 1700, in small numbers. In the 1650s Captain John Vernon supplied 550 persons from southern Ireland as servants and workers for the English colonists and entrepreneurs in New England, and by 1700 a few Irish Catholic families had settled in Maryland.[3] Not until the 1700s did large numbers of Irish arrive on North American shores. A significant proportion of these were from northern Ireland (Ulster) and had Scottish ancestry, but many were from southern Ireland and could trace their ancestry back into ancient Irish history.

There were push and pull factors. The image of North America as a land of opportunity was for most immigrants a major pull factor, but domestic pressures were also important. In the 1100s Ireland was conquered by the English. By the 1600s, Scots, in increasing numbers, were encouraged to migrate across the channel to Ireland and to develop lands given to English and Scottish landowners by the king of England. Subsequently the English drove many of the native Irish off the land.[4]

As a result of this English colonizing of Ireland, the Ulster (northern) Irish who migrated to North America contained a significant number of persons of Scottish ancestry. Yet those who migrated were the fourth or fifth generation in Ireland. They had become Irish; Ireland was their home.[5] There is some debate among scholars as to how much the Scottish settlers blended with the Irish, but it is clear that some intermixture, cultural and marital, did occur. Their nationality, as they themselves would say, was not Scottish but Irish.

To what extent were the migrants from northern Ireland in the 1700s joined by those from southern areas? To what extent were these migrants Celtic* or Catholic? These questions are debated by scholars. The traditional view has been that virtually all the immigrants before 1800 were "Scotch-Irish," Protestants from northern Ireland. Ford and Leyburn claim that the immigrants were generally persons from the North with Presbyterian backgrounds.[6] Other authors have provided evidence of a large southern (and thus Catholic) component to this migration. O'Brien cites "unquestionable proof that every part of Ireland contributed to the enormous emigration of its people, and while there are no official statistics now available—for none were kept—to indicate the numerical strength of those Irish immigrants, abundant proof of this assertion is found in authentic records."[7]

---

*Celtic refers to those inhabitants of Ireland whose ancestry dates back far before the Roman and English invasions of the island.

For example, tens of thousands of people with old Celtic names appear in various records. Evidence of the significant quantity of non-Ulster immigrants is suggested by data on passenger ships. Of 318 such ships sailing between 1767 and 1769, 60 percent neither came from nor ended up in northern Irish ports; in the 1771–1774 period, the figure was 57 percent of 576 ships. Such evidence is only suggestive, however, since an unknown number of ships from northern Ireland stopping in southern ports for provisions gave the latter as their points of departure. Prior to 1787 perhaps one third of the immigrants were Catholic.[8]

O'Brien argues that southern Irish immigrants gave up the traditional faith, in part because there were few Catholic churches in the colonies, in part because in many areas (in Ireland and in the colonies) practicing the Catholic faith was dangerous because of the hostile Protestant environment.[9] Local laws often required children to be baptised protestant, and great antagonism was directed at "papists." Conversion of the Catholic Irish to Protestantism was common in the early migration. One Episcopalian clergyman wrote to a missionary society that "there were many Irish Papists in Pennsylvania who turn Quakers and get into places as well as Germans."[10]

The northern Irish in the first waves of immigration regarded themselves as Irish rather than Scotch-Irish. In the first two centuries of Irish presence the term **Scotch-Irish** was seldom used. The new migrants gave Irish names to their settlements and joined organizations such as the Friendly Sons of Saint Patrick rather than Scottish American societies.[11]

The term *Scotch-Irish* came into heavy use after 1850, when some Irish Protestant immigrants and their British friends sought to distinguish themselves from the Irish Catholic immigrants who were then the focus of discrimination.[12] The issue of the "Scotch-Irish race" and its impact became a heated one by the late nineteenth century. Prominent politicians praised the members of the "Scotch-Irish race" as great pioneers and democrats while damning the "Catholic Irish race." Consider Henry Cabot Lodge writing in an 1891 issue of *Century Magazine*: "I classified the Irish and the Scotch-Irish as two distinct race-stocks, and I believe the distinction to be a sound one historically and scientifically."[13]

In his book *Winning the West*, Theodore Roosevelt dramatized the contributions of the Scotch-Irish frontier people. We had not understood, Roosevelt argued, the important part "played by that stern and virile people," the brave "Puritans" of the West.[14] In the early 1900s scholars argued that the Scotch-Irish were not really Irish, that they saw themselves as Scots resident in Ireland, a distinct and superior racial type with a different "type of frame and physiognomy."[15]

The view that the Scotch-Irish were part of the Anglo-Saxon or Teutonic "race" was so vigorously argued that it reached the absurd point of denying any Celtic (i.e., Catholic) part in the mixture: "Whatever blood may be in the veins of the genuine Scotch-Irishman, one thing is certain, and that is that there is not mingled with it one drop of the blood of the old Irish or Kelt."[16] The data showing large numbers of Celtic Irish in the early migration pose serious questions for this racist glorification of the Protestant Irish.

### Early Life

What was life like for the Irish settlers in an English-dominated society? Perhaps half became indentured servants; others became farmers or farm workers, often in frontier areas. The English treated Irish servants as lowly subordinates, even to the point of brutality. Discriminatory import duties and longer indenture terms were placed on Irish servants.[17] Irish Catholic servants suffered because of their nationality and their religion. As early as 1704 heavy taxes were placed on Irish Catholic immigrants. Laws were passed excluding them or discouraging their importation.[18] With times as hard as this, significant numbers of the Irish gave up their Catholicism. Not all converted, however. Irish immigrants in some Pennsylvania counties were predominantly Catholic. Pressing for religious tolerance, several prominent Irish Catholics wrote President Washington in the late 1700s asking that the full religious rights of Catholics be protected.[19]

Pennsylvania and New England received the first waves of Ulster Irish, in the decades before 1740. After 1740 many migrated to the valleys of Virginia and the Carolinas. Many of these also were indentured servants; others became farmers. Immigrants' letters to Ireland reveal that America was considered a land of hope.[20] Many eighteenth-century Irish immigrants, encouraged to settle in frontier areas as a barrier against the Native Americans, came into conflict with the latter, as well as with British landowners, on whose land they sometimes squatted.[21]

By 1790 almost 10 percent of the white United States population of 3.2 million was Irish. The Ulster Irish, somewhat more numerous, constituted large populations of the Georgia, Pennsylvania, and South Carolina populations, while those from the southern areas of Ireland were most substantially represented in Maryland, Virginia, Delaware, and North Carolina. The Irish were a large nationality group at the time of the new nation's birth.[22]

The pull factors motivating millions of Irish Catholics to cross the Atlantic after 1830 were the same as those that attracted European immigrants for centuries to North America, which was portrayed, often in exaggerated terms, as the land of golden opportunity. Push factors loomed even larger. The famine that came to Ireland in the 1840s spurred emigration to the United States. Irish peasants relied heavily on potatoes for food. The potato blight caused a massive failure of that crop, and many people starved to death or died from diseases such as hunger typhus. During these famine years Ireland actually produced more than twice the food, including corn and cattle, that was needed to feed the hungry. The dominant English landlords saw to it that these foodstuffs were exported to England and elsewhere or consumed by those in Ireland with money. The Irish were right when they said that "God sent the blight, but the English landlord sent the famine."

In addition, English leaders advocated emigration to the United States and elsewhere as the proper solution for the poor Irish. Many Irish who emigrated to the United States mourned their departure with a sad, all-night farewell ceremony called the "American wake"; they saw their new land as a place of involuntary exile, a condition Kerby Miller sees as the foundation of Irish-American homesickness and nationalism. The long history of English conquest and oppression of the Irish lies behind the persisting conflict between the two peoples, in places such as Northern Ireland, in the late twentieth century.[23]

The Atlantic crossing was dangerous. Few ships arrived that had not lost a number of their poorly accommodated passengers to starvation or disease. The survivors usually chose urban destinations. New York became a major center, eventually housing more Irish than Dublin. Like most urban migrants, the new immigrants went where relatives or fellow villagers had settled.

Residential segregation for Irish Americans in the nineteenth century had a distinctive form. Huge ghettos, such as black Americans now live in, were not the rule. The Irish newcomers found housing wherever they could, usually in the little houses and shanties on the side streets or in the alleys beside or behind the fashionable homes of affluent Anglo-Saxon urbanites. As blue-collar workers, they often lived within walking distance of manufacturing jobs. They clustered in smaller, more dispersed settlements than would be the case for later immigrant groups.[24]

These scattered settlements were reinforced by a second, equally large wave of immigrants from Ireland between 1870 and 1900, and by significant but declining numbers of immigrants from 1900 to 1925. These later immigrants were forced out not by famine, but primarily by poverty and the hope for a better life. In New York, Boston, and Philadelphia, slum housing with its attendant disease, was frequently their lot. An analysis of New York revealed that the 1877 death rate for the Irish-born was high, as was the mortality rate for their American-born children. Whole families were consigned to a single room in crowded apartment houses called *rookeries*. The Irish were overrepresented in the almshouses of some cities. Irish crime rates, high for some categories of minor offenses, were exaggerated by nativists; the rate for *serious* offenses was low. The poverty of Irish immigrants had several causes. Many of the immigrants had few skills, but more important reasons were hard jobs, low wages, and direct institutionalized discrimination against those of Irish descent.[25]

One distinctive aspect of the Irish immigration was the presence of large numbers of young women. These women decided that Ireland held no hope for them and that America was the land of opportunity. More women than men migrated to the United States, and there were more foreign-born women than men in the Irish American communities. Once in America these women did not subscribe to the cult of womanhood, which emphasized that the woman's place was only in the home. Most did not live lives of sheltered domesticity, but rather became self-sufficient persons with distinctive work histories. And they made important contributions to the later mobility of Irish Americans into middle-income America.

The famine in Ireland destroyed many Irish families, and for six decades young, unmarried women came to the United States to avoid the terrible life awaiting them in Ireland. In contrast with male Irish immigrants and female immigrants from other countries, these women were willing to postpone or forego marriage and to work in the homes of native-born Americans as domestic servants. Later, many became schoolteachers. And many supported families in the old country. Their values, expressed in the decisions they made about work, were fundamental life-choice values that persisted into the late twentieth century. Among them was a strong commitment to their Irish heritage and to personal independence. Interestingly, the daughters of these women often became schoolteachers or clerical workers.[26]

## STEREOTYPING THE IRISH

The resistance of English Americans to the Irish immigration dates back to the seventeenth and eighteenth centuries. "Papists" were the targets of open hatred. Protestant and Catholic Irish Americans suffered from nativistic concern over their political persuasions, as in the conflicts in the 1790s between the Federalists and the Jeffersonians. Yet it was the nineteenth-century Irish, poor Catholics from the famine-ridden Emerald Isle, who were attacked the most.

Dale Knobel studied the Civil War public literature on the Irish and found what he terms the Paddy stereotype, a view of the Irish that gradually changed. From the 1820s to the mid-1840s the dominant view of the Catholic Irish in North America emphasized their morality, style, and lack of intelligence. Alleged character faults such as ingratitude, foolishness, wickedness, and ignorance were accented in this early stereotype. With the surge in Irish migration in the late 1840s and early 1850s the image in the literature came to emphasize conflict, hostility, and emotionality. Words such as *temperamental*, *dangerous*, *quarrelsome*, *idle*, and *reckless*—characteristics emphasizing conduct as much as character—came into use after 1845. The Anglo-American image of the Irish had hardened and become less tolerant as the numbers of Irish immigrants grew.[27]

Attacks on Irish Catholics took the form of cartoons that stereotyped the Irish by means of outrageous symbols—an apelike face, a fighting stance, a jug of whisky, a shillelagh. The influential caricaturist Thomas Nast published cartoons of this type in *Harper's Weekly* and other magazines. One of his caricatures shows a stereotyped southern black man and a nasty, apelike Irishman, both portrayed as ignorant voters and a threat to orderly politics. "New York's leading cartoonists of the 1870s and 1880s," notes Curtis, "certainly did not refrain from simianizing Irish-American Paddies who epitomized the tens of thousands of working-class immigrants and their children caught up in urban poverty and slum conditions after their flight from rural poverty and famine in Ireland."[28]

### The Ape Image

Not surprisingly, the apelike image of the Irish was imported from England. With the rise of debates over evolution in England, the poor Irish came to be regarded by many in England and America as the "missing link" between the gorilla and the stereotyped Negro. With the constant threat of Irish rebellion on the one hand and the press of Darwinism on the other, "it was comforting for some Englishmen to believe—on the basis of the best scientific authority in the Anthropological Society of London—that their own facial angles and orthognathous features were far removed from those of apes, Irishmen, and Negroes as was humanly possible."[29] In rationalizing the exploitation of the Irish and black Africans, racists on both sides of the Atlantic developed dehumanizing stereotypes.

Notice the comparable position of black and Irish Americans in this mythology. Greeley has underscored the parallels in prejudice and stereotyping:

> Practically every accusation that has been made against the American blacks was also made against the Irish: Their family life was inferior, they had no ambition, they did not keep up their homes, they drank too much, they were not responsible, they had no morals, it was not safe to walk through their neighborhoods at night, they voted the way crooked politicians told them to vote, they were not willing to pull themselves up by their bootstraps, they were not capable of education, they could not think for themselves, and they would always remain social problems for the rest of the country.[30]

Early stage shows made fun of the Irish by using these stereotypes, just as they did with black Americans. In the nineteenth century the Catholic Irish were often socially defined by those in dominant groups as physically different, and thus as a "race." In the twentieth century, the emphasis on this alleged physical distinctiveness would disappear.

## Recent Decades

In 1932 white male students at Princeton University were given a list of eighty four positive and negative traits and asked to identify those traits they associated with ten racial and ethnic groups, including Irish Americans. Fifty years later, a similar questionnaire was given to a predominantly white sample of male and female students at Arizona State University. In 1932 the Princeton students rated among the top ten traits of Irish Americans: pugnacious, quick-tempered, quarrelsome, aggressive, and stubborn. This rather negative stereotype accented images of aggression and fighting on the part of the Irish. This aggression imagery decreased significantly in the 1982 sample, for the Arizona State students listed only "quick-tempered" and "stubborn" in their top ten traits for the Irish. More positive traits now appeared in the top ten, including "intelligent" and "loyal to family ties." Moreover, at neither point did the Irish receive the most negative stereotypes available to the students—the traits of "treacherous" and "sly," which groups such as the Jews, Japanese, and blacks received. These results suggest a reduction since the 1930s in the traditional stereotyping of Irish Americans and signal substantial attitude-receptional assimilation, to use Milton Gordon's conceptual term.[31]

Irish Catholic Americans have been seen by some analysts as a particularly antiblack group of white Americans. Compared with most other white Americans, though, Irish Catholics are relatively liberal. A review of opinion polls came to this conclusion:

> Surveys in the 1970s revealed that in the North Irish Catholics were more sympathetic to integrated neighborhoods, integrated schools, and interracial marriages than other white Catholics and white Protestants. Among whites only Jews are more liberal on racial issues than Irish Catholics.[32]

Irish Catholics in the North are more likely than other whites to live in racially integrated neighborhoods. Of course, relatively liberal racial attitudes sometimes do not carry over into actual behavior, for Irish Catholics, like other whites, have played a role in discrimination against nonwhite Americans.

## PROTEST AND CONFLICT

From their first decades in North America, Irish Americans have suffered not only verbal abuse and stereotyping but also intentional discrimination and violent attacks. Irish Americans have on occasion retaliated, even to the point of violence. In other situations they have inaugurated conflict. As noted in Chapter 2, ethnic conflict means a struggle over resources and can be generated by inequality. Conflict can take both nonviolent and violent forms, and it often involves groups with differing power and resources.

Assimilation theorists have usually neglected the conflict that has characterized interethnic and interracial relations. Indeed, some views of American history embody a myth of peaceful progress. In this view the members of each white ethnic group have advanced higher on the social ladder by pulling themselves up by their bootstraps— by hard work and diligent effort, not by active protest and collective violence. This image is incorrect. As with other white groups, the Irish have struggled for their "place in the sun" with many groups, from established Anglo-Saxon Protestants to Native Americans. They have been involved in conflict with groups above and below them in the racial and ethnic hierarchy.

### Early Conflict

The first major conflict was with the established groups that controlled the major institutions in the North American colonies at the time of the initial Irish Immigration. A few eighteenth-century Irish settlements were damaged or destroyed by attacks. British Americans attacked and destroyed an Irish community in Worcester, Massachusetts, in the eighteenth century. There was a great deal of vigorous opposition from the colonists to both Catholic and Protestant Irish migrants.[33]

Conflict arose between the Irish Protestant farmers in the frontier areas and the plantation gentry of British connections in the coastal areas. In the early period, the backcountry Irish were sometimes seen as crude frontier people. Settling in frontier areas, the Ulster Irish defied laws made by eastern interests and engaged in aggressive protest and collective violence in the Whisky Rebellion and the Regulation movement, movements to extend their control when it suited their own ends.[34]

Conflict with Native Americans was part of the Irish experience. The Irish were encouraged to settle the frontier areas of the colonies so that the dominant eastern interests would be protected from Native Americans. Scalping was institutionalized by English and Irish settlers. Placing bounties on the scalps of Native American men and women became common in New England and the middle colonies. Conflict between Irish who were taking Native American lands and Native Americans who were protecting their way of life became widespread in Virginia and the Carolinas.[35]

In the 1790s there were violent attacks on Irish Catholics in Maryland and elsewhere. In 1798 a disturbance known as the Federal Riot took place at Saint Mary's Church in Philadelphia: opponents of the new Alien Law who had come to the church with a petition for the congregation to sign were beaten up by a group of Federalist rioters.[36] Although the Irish had a valid reputation for aggressiveness, much of the rioting after 1800 was directed against them because they were immigrants and Roman Catholics. Most "Irish riots" were triggered by anti-Irish incidents, often by anti-Catholic acts. An 1806 riot in New York was generated by Protestant attempts to break up a Catholic religious service.[37]

Churches were destroyed in several cities.[38] By 1850 most large cities had seen anti-Catholic demonstrations and riots. Philadelphia became a center for anti–Irish Catholic violence. There, in 1844, two major riots "resulted in the burning of two Catholic churches...; the destruction of dozens of Catholic homes; and sixteen deaths."[39] In the 1850s new nativist groups such as the Know-Nothings played a major role in conflict with the Irish.[40]

## Group Conflict

Conflict in the mine fields was a major feature of the Irish experience in the latter half of the nineteenth century. Irish workers and better-paid English workers often did not get along.[41] Old feuds were renewed. In the early days of copper mining in Michigan, English and Irish miners struggled for jobs.[42] Similar struggles characterized the coal-mining areas of Pennsylvania, where the Irish had played a major role in developing the anthracite coal mines. Here they found English and Welsh capitalists and English control of skilled work.[43] Conditions were oppressive. Pay rates were low, perhaps $20 to $30 a month. Often pay was in the form of a "bobtail check": money owed the company for groceries and rent equaled one's wages, a situation of wage slavery.[44] Such oppression and poverty led to violent conflict between predominantly British Protestant owners and superintendents and Irish Catholic miners.

As early as the Civil War, trouble between the Irish and the older groups flared up in Pennsylvania. There was opposition to the Union cause and to the draft among Irish workers who saw the Civil War as "a rich man's war." Many feared blacks would come north and take their jobs. The use of troops against Irish groups protesting the war was narrowly avoided.[45]

The coal strike of 1875, called the Long Strike, forced many miners into near-starvation conditions. The capitalists broke the strike and crushed attempts at unionization.[46] In response, secret Irish organizations linked to the Ancient Order of the Hibernians (AOH) resorted to assassination and sabotage. The owners reacted with violence against the AOH groups. Numerous shootings were engineered by the Anglo-Saxon establishment, and the miners replied with armed defense and guerrilla warfare.[47] Although called Molly Maguires (an older organization in Ireland), the protesting miners were not part of that secret organization. Instead, they were members of miners' organizations who went underground when moderate protests failed to improve their living and working conditions.

Rather than yield to the reasonable requests of the miners for better wages, British American and other capitalists hired an army of private detectives to put down the workers' rebellion. One detective, sent into the fields to spy, gathered information used in court cases; twenty Irish miners were publicly hanged for engaging in protest. The owners' counterattack in the courts was reinforced by nativist portrayals of the members of the secret societies as undisciplined, violent Irishmen.[48] This nativism was evident in the trials of the miners, whose convictions were influenced by Irish stereotypes.[49]

## Violence and Rioting

Irish Americans have found themselves competing economically with groups lower on the socioeconomic ladder, as we have seen in the case of Irish Protestants and Native Americans on the frontier. As early as the 1840s, Irish competition with black Americans in northern cities engendered substantial distrust and hostility between the two groups. Between the 1840s and the 1860s Irish workers attacked black workers in several cities in the North. During the Civil War Irish hostility toward black Americans increased, for the two groups were major competitors in the struggle for the low-paying jobs at the bottom of the employment pyramid. Irish opposition to blacks was basically economic: "they feared the competition of the hordes of freed slaves who might invade the North, and valued the security that came from the existence in the country of at least one social class below them."[50]

Excluded from unions, blacks sometimes were used as strikebreakers. The use of black strikebreakers spurred the 1863 Irish riot, usually termed the Draft Riot, the most serious riot in American history. Perhaps four hundred rioters were killed in the streets, together with some free blacks and some white police and soldiers. Rioters attacked Yankees, the police, and blacks.[51] At the front of the rioters were Irish workers upset at the recent use of black strikebreakers. This tension has persisted in the cities. Irish and other white ethnic frustration at black gains from the 1960s to the 1980s was a familiar topic in the mass media. Many felt that blacks were receiving a disproportional share of government benefits, more than the urban white ethnics were receiving. Today there are serious tensions between black and Irish residents in a few major cities, such as Boston and Chicago.

On the West Coast Irish workers fought to maintain their economic position in the mid-nineteenth century. Competition from Chinese laborers led to anti-Chinese attacks in Irish papers, as well as meetings and parades demanding prohibition of further Chinese immigration. Anti-Chinese protest was led by Irish immigrants and their descendants.[52]

## Struggles with Immigrants

By 1900 the new immigrants from southern and eastern Europe were confronting Irish Americans with a new type of economic competition. In Chicago and Boston, Irish control of the church and of political parties was also major source of friction with these new immigrant groups. The southern and western immigrants resented Irish control of city governments and jobs.

In the 1930s Father Charles Coughlin and his organization the Christian Front spread anti-Jewish views among the Irish and other Americans. In 1938 Coughlin serialized an anti-Semitic document, the Protocols of the Elders of Zion, a well-known forgery, in his magazine. The Christian Front went so far as to make a list of non-Jewish merchants who promised not to hire Jews or to deal with Jewish businesses.[53]

## POLITICS AND POLITICAL INSTITUTIONS

When the Irish began arriving in the seventeenth century, much of the general political framework was already fashioned by the English. Those Irish who came in the eighteenth century played a minority role in shaping the nation's basic institutions.[54] Some were to be found among the founding fathers. There were a number among the signers of the Declaration of Independence—altogether eight of the fifty-six, five from the north and three from the south of Ireland.[55]

Only four men born in Ireland were members of the Constitutional Convention, together with three other men of Irish descent. Several of these seven were Catholics. At least two Irish Americans were members of the first U.S. Senate, and two were members of the first U.S. House. Before 1800 a few could be found participating in state and local government as governors of territories and states and as mayors.[56]

Most of the Irish migrating after the Revolutionary War settled in eastern cities, where they became involved in politics. The Irish, not unexpectedly, were anti-Federalist and supported the democratic factions. Here again was interethnic competition. The Federalist-sponsored Alien and Sedition Acts of 1798 were directed in part against them. Irish immigrants taking offense at such actions led to the downfall of the Federalists, turning out en masse to help elect Jefferson. In this period the Irish from the south and north of Ireland were united. A few decades later the same Irish vote would play an important role in electing the first Irish (Protestant) president, Andrew Jackson.[57]

### Political Organization in the Cities

Traditionally discussion of the Irish in politics has focused on the Irish Catholics. The common terms are *boss* and *machine*. The theme of corrupt urban machines has been tied to hostile views of immigrants. Protestant views have tended to be pious: "In general, the Irish Catholic political machines in the United States have been notoriously and flamboyantly corrupt—a disgrace to Catholicism, to American democracy, and to the Irish people."[58] Commenting on the Irish machine in New York, William Adams argued that "the 'horrible example' of New York politics combined with a rapid increase of pauper immigrants to check the advance of liberal ideas."[59] The tone of such analyses is that the Irish were more unscrupulous and corrupt in their political activities than other ethnic groups. In fact the Irish entered a political system that already had many weaknesses, including no secret ballot and much corruption. Machines existed *before* the Irish ever controlled them. Political organizations by which those in power secured their poor constituents jobs, housing, and food were already the rule in cities.

Why, then, the strong Irish involvement in local politics? Politics was one means to social mobility, a means of achieving power in the face of great Anglo-Saxon Protestant opposition. The dominant perspective on government in the nineteenth and early twentieth centuries tended toward a hands-off view, with government staying out of economic affairs as much as possible. It was against this do-nothing background that desperate urban residents, plagued with unemployment, low income, and poor housing, joined large urban political organizations. Taking control of local party organizations, immigrant leaders shaped government programs benefiting the poor. Providing jobs—for example, in real estate and transportation construction—was one of the machines' most critical functions. The political bosses could make a great deal of money as brokers of construction, acting illegally, but poor immigrants were less concerned about corruption than they were with jobs.[60]

One of the first great political machines was New York City's Tammany Society. In 1817 a group of Irish Americans, incensed at discrimination at the hands of this machine, broke into one of its meetings and demanded the nomination of an Irish person for Congress. Although they were driven away this time, a few decades later the Irish penetrated the New York political organization. Irish political power brought new leadership to Tammany Hall in the 1860s and 1870s.

One major figure in Tammany Hall, William M. "Boss" Tweed, has long been cursed for his alleged greed and corruption. Numerous articles and textbooks have heralded this image of Boss Tweed. Yet this image is largely myth. In reality, William M. Tweed was a political leader who represented the underdog, including the Irish and the Jews, in nineteenth-century New York. He was tolerant of religious beliefs, he was a family man, and he was ambitious. He identified with New York's poor immigrants and worked to build schools and hospitals. He was hated by Anglo-Saxon Protestant Republicans because of his identification with immigrants. Yet Tweed's own ethnic background remains unclear; he was apparently of Scottish or Irish descent. Because of growing Irish political power, Tweed became a powerful New York political leader and rewarded Irish and other immigrant constituents with jobs, schools, and social services. Research on Tweed indicates that he may well have been less corrupt than many of the Anglo-Saxon Protestant politicians who dominated urban politics before and after.[61]

New York City finally elected an Irish mayor in the 1880s and the Irish have played a major role in New York politics to the present. Not surprisingly, heavy Irish representation in appointed public jobs has characterized New York politics up to the present.[62]

Numerous cities with large Catholic populations have seen the Irish gain important positions. In vigorous fights with English and other British Americans, the Irish gradually won a place in the political sun in Boston, Brooklyn, Philadelphia, New Haven, and Chicago. In New Haven, for example, after initial Irish Catholic occupancy of the mayor's office in 1899, the Irish became an increasingly significant political force.[63]

The Irish political organizations, except in Chicago, were gone by the 1960s. The paramount Irish boss, maintaining power into the 1970s, was Chicago Mayor Richard J. Daley. In 1962 the Irish constituted 10 to 15 percent of Chicago's population, but had a quarter of its fifty aldermanic positions, the mayor's chair, and 42 percent of the fifty ward committee seats.[64] But by the 1980s Daley was dead and the machine was weakening. There have been complexities to the Chicago machine: tremendous urban development and renewal, allowing friends to get city construction contracts, keeping old people on the payrolls even when their work ability has diminished.[65] Moreover, in the 1980s a black mayor was elected against the wishes of the declining political machine.

## Pragmatism in Politics

For the Irish, politics is an honorable profession. Family and friends provide the necessary networks for entry into political positions.[66] The Irish developed a political style based on concern for individuals and personal loyalty to leaders.[67] Individual charity is a major feature. One Irish official is quoted by Levine: "When a man is ill in government and without enough time for retirement or health benefits, an efficient man fires him. Yet the Irish administrator says, 'What the hell, he has two kids,' and keeps him on. He knows this is a risky thing, letting him come in at ten and leave at two. So what happens? He gets a little more work out of the others to make it up."[68]

In recent decades Irish politicians have been influenced by reform movements to clean up blatant corruption. Some Irish politicians have been reformers themselves, playing a major role in bringing down the corrupt leaders of political machines in New York and other cities. Yet the personal, pragmatic, nonideological style of Irish politics remains.[69]

Pragmatic politics, with its coalition and compromise themes, is a major Irish contribution to American politics. One principle is that a city is a mosaic of racial and ethnic groups and the political machine is a broker, balancing these groups so that a coalition can hang together. The leaders believe in balanced tickets, for they know that people vote along ethnic lines: they are aware of the hopes and fears of the voters. Such politicians are also aware of the tendency in these same groups toward trust, rationality, and sympathy for humanistic reforms.[70] Irish politicians have been critical to urban coalition building.

Irish organizations have also made a major contribution to the bricks-and-mortar development of cities. Without the Irish contractors tied to the machines, who would have met the need for public buildings, streets, and subways in many cities?[71]

With suburbanization and marriage with other Catholics Americans, this Irish political style has begun to fade, but it has by no means disappeared. A study of fifty-one cities by Clark found that those with large Irish populations were more likely than other cities to have a local government (often Irish-dominated) that provided a high level of public services for city residents. There was more responsiveness to poorer groups, including blacks, in these Irish-populated cities than in other cities. Irish political machines may be fading, but their humane, services-oriented, patronage approach to government persists. Even in the suburbs Irish Catholicism undergirds Irish ethnicity. Some analysts have attempted to link the upward mobility of the Irish to a growing "conservatism." Since the 1960s the Irish electorates in New York and Connecticut have tended to prefer the more conservative political candidates in mayoral, gubernatorial, and senatorial races. Elsewhere, however, they continue to vote for liberal and moderate Democrats.[72]

Taken as a whole, Irish Americans are generally more liberal than numerous other white Gentile groups. Irish Catholic Americans have a progressive political tradition. Today they are substantially Democratic, with a large proportion of liberal Democrats among them. And they have been central figures in labor unions fighting for workers' rights.

## National and International Politics

After 1840 the Irish electorate was increasingly sought by presidential and congressional candidates. Grant, the Republican presidential candidate in 1868, wooed Irish voters; after he was elected he made a few Irish appointments to his administration. In most succeeding elections the Irish vote has been sought by presidential candidates of both parties.[73]

One study of the 1901–1910 period found that 13 percent of 162 prominent political leaders, including presidents, senators, representatives, and Supreme Court justices, were Irish, compared with 56 percent who were English or Welsh.[74] Irish *Catholic* influence at the national level was weak. In a letter to Theodore Roosevelt, Finley Peter Dunne, a prominent Irish writer, commented on the lack of Irish influence: "As for the point about Irishmen holding office, I simply wanted to emphasize the fact that Irishmen are the most unsuccessful politicians in the country. Although they are about all there is to politics in the North between elections, there is not, with one exception, a single representative Irish man in any important cabinet, diplomatic, judicial or administrative office that I know about."[75] Penetration at the city level did not necessarily lead to important positions in the federal executive or judicial branches for Irish Catholics.

Most research literature on the Irish in politics at the national level, as well as at the local level, focuses on Irish Catholics. Millions of Irish Protestants, many in the rural South, have received little attention in analysis of the last century's politics. One Irish Protestant who has received attention was the Scotch-Irish president Woodrow Wilson, who held office at a crucial time in the history of Ireland. Wilson was not sympathetic to Irish national consciousness or Irish Catholic causes. Because of his background and lack of support for the Irish fight against England, he was opposed by the Irish Catholic press. Irish Americans, primarily Catholics, have reacted to the oppression of their brothers and sisters in Ireland. Numerous Irish nationalist groups came to public attention in the late 1800s and early 1900s and attempted to shift American foreign policy away from its pro-English stance.[76]

After World War I, a critical issue for Irish Catholic Americans was Wilson's, and many other Protestants', stand on the question of Ireland's independence. In the 1918 British elections several dozen Irish representatives were elected to Parliament, but they met separately, set up an Irish Republic, and were arrested by the British. Guerrilla warfare developed, the rebellion was brutally suppressed, and its leaders were executed. The brutality and the other issues surrounding independence racked Irish communities in the United States, leading to organization and protest meetings.[77] In subsequent decades the issue of an independent, united Ireland became less important, but it continued to periodically generate financial and political support among Irish Americans into the 1980s. In 1971 Senator Edward Kennedy of Massachusetts introduced a U.S. Senate resolution asking for the removal of British soldiers from Irish soil.

The controversy over Ireland not only illustrates the interethnic struggle up to the present, in this case over foreign policy within the traditional political arena, but also shows how events in the country of origin of a segment of the population can long affect ethnic relations within the United States. This theme will reappear in the chapters that follow, as, for example, in the effect of events in Italy on Italian Americans and in Japan on Japanese Americans. The world is the ultimate context of interethnic and interracial relations in the United States.

## An Irish Catholic President

By the late 1920s Irish Catholics had become visible in national politics. Alfred E. Smith was the first Irish Catholic to carve out an important role in presidential politics. In 1928 he became the Democratic candidate for president. But his Catholic religion, his calls for modification of Prohibition, his lack of knowledge of much of the United States—all these factors counted against him in this first Irish Catholic presidential campaign. Though he lost the election, he managed to equal or exceed the Republican vote in eleven of the nation's twelve largest cities, pulling the new urban immigrants into a national voting bloc in the Democratic party for the first time. No candidate could again ignore the growing importance of the non-Protestant vote in the booming cities.[78]

In 1930, with the exception of one Supreme Court justice, there were still no Irish Catholics holding major positions in the judicial and executive branches of the federal government. Franklin Roosevelt was the first president to appoint Irish Catholics to important positions, including ambassador to Great Britain, postmaster general, and attorney general. In the New Deal electoral landslides many were sent for the first time to Congress. Both Roosevelt and Truman appointed far more Irish Catholic judges and executive officers than any previous president.[79]

Not until 1960, three hundred years after the first few Irish Catholics had come to the United States and more than a century after there were sizable Irish Catholic communities, was the first (and only) Irish Catholic president elected. Six of the thirty-six presidents from Washington to Nixon had Irish backgrounds, but except for Kennedy all of these men were Protestant Irish, as was a more recent president, Ronald Reagan.

President Kennedy was a descendant of Irish Catholic politicians in Boston; he was elected on the "backs of three generations of district leaders and county chairmen."[80] His grandfather had been mayor of Boston; his father was the first Irish Catholic to serve as ambassador to Great Britain. John Kennedy came from the small, wealthy elite. Yet he was a pragmatic politician. Day-to-day problems of food and shelter were critical issues to him. In the 1960 presidential election Irish Catholic votes in New England, New York, and Pennsylvania helped to shape Kennedy's victory. Nationwide he received an estimated 75 percent of the Irish vote, but only 50.1 percent of the total vote. As president, Kennedy acted to some extent on behalf of America's newer and emergent urban groups, appointing the *first* Italian American and the *first* Polish American to a presidential cabinet and the first black American to head an independent government agency.[81]

In later elections the Irish vote would remain important. Thus in 1976 Gerald Ford got the majority of the white American vote, but Jimmy Carter drew 5 percent of the Irish and East European Catholic vote in his successful presidential bid that year.

## THE IRISH IN THE ECONOMY

As we noted in Chapter 2, one type of structural assimilation involves large-scale movement by members of an immigrant group into the secondary-organization levels of a society, such as governmental agencies. Another critical movement is into the ecomomic organizations—the farms, and factories—of the core society. Such movement is termed *social mobility*.

The majority of Irish immigrants started out at the bottom of the economic pyramid, filling the hard, dirty, laboring jobs on farms and in cities. The eighteenth-century Irish migrants, among whom were a large number of northern Irish, contributed significantly to the economic development of the colonies and the new nation by providing low-paid agricultural labor. They contributed to fledgling industries, providing weavers for the textile industry and laborers for the road and canal systems. In New England they were important in commerce; in the South they became farm laborers, farmers, and owners of small businesses. Few data are available on the mobility patterns of these Irish immigrants or their descendants over the next century or two. Many moved from indentured service to their own farms. Most seem to have moved up the economic ladder over the next few generations, sometimes at the expense of later Catholic immigrants.[82]

### Male and Female Work: The Irish after 1830

Irish immigrants after 1830 typically became urban workers, miners, or transportation workers. Irish Catholic labor was critical to industrial and commercial development. Hard, low-paying work was the lot of most immigrants. They had migrated looking for work. Irish men found it in unskilled jobs, on the docks and in the factories of large cities, and Irish women found it as servants in Anglo-Saxon Protestant homes. In the 1855 census of New York city three-quarters of the domestics (the maids and other servants) were Irish. Yet the Irish were only one-quarter of the population. Many Irish immigrants were single females unattached to family groups. Impoverished and alone in an alien land, these women moved into domestic work where they could live with a family. Later immigrant women, such as Italians and Jews, were not as likely to go into domestic work. This had little to do with differences in cultural backgrounds, but resulted simply from the different character of later migration: Jewish and Italian women generally came with their families. Irish women often came alone, not by choice but because of the terrible economic conditions in Ireland under English rule.[83]

Male Irish immigrants became farm laborers, canal and railroad laborers, miners, and textile workers. Many died helping build transportation systems, as the old saying "There's an Irishman buried under every railroad tie" indicates. As late as

1876, half of Irish-born Americans were still in the worst-paid, dirtiest jobs, compared with 10 to 20 percent of certain other white ethnic groups.[84]

Irish Catholics encountered direct institutionalized discrimination in employment. Few capitalists would hire them except for unskilled positions. By the 1840s Boston newspapers were carrying advertisements with the phrase "None need apply but Americans."[85] The Irish in Boston were relegated to the least-skilled occupations. Stereotyped as unskilled or rowdy, Irish men and women were denied jobs by Protestant employers.

Numerous observers have blamed these Irish immigrants for the emergence of urban poverty. Against the contributions of such immigrants, argues Adams, "must be set certain intangible social burdens on the whole community and some definite expenditures, of which poor relief through almshouses, hospitals, and dispensaries was most costly."[86] Many among the Irish became dependent on charity or public aid. But local and state governments in that period actually provided rather little in the way of support for the poor—the majority of whom were *not* Irish.

Few among the millions of immigrants and their children moved from rags to riches. Many did save some money, sending a great deal back to Ireland. This charitable impulse reduced their own chances for mobility in the United States. One study of Newburyport, Massachusetts, revealed that Irish working-class families were more likely to have accumulated some property (housing) than was commonly thought. But one price of accumulated property of this type was a spartan life and the early employment of children, so that the education of this latter generation was reduced. Economic advance in one generation did not necessarily mean upward mobility for subsequent generations. In addition, building a separate church and parochial school system meant some drain on individual and family resources.[87]

Even with these burdens, some Irish Catholics had begun to move up the socioeconomic ladder after the Civil War. For example, in Newburyport, Massachusetts, structural movement upward in the economy came early for a small group.[88] The Irish in Philadelphia, by the decade after the Civil War, had already begun to move into middle-income residential areas. Although many still found themselves in segregated, inferior housing, a significant number had begun to move to better housing. Philadelphia had become a major eastern center for manufacturing and transportation and the Irish concentrated in unskilled labor there later gained semiskilled and skilled positions. New economic gains were reflected in the erection of churches, parochial schools, and charitable institutions.[89]

Significant numbers of Catholic Irish became upwardly mobile near the turn of the twentieth century. A major reason was the point at which they entered an ever-expanding, labor-hungry capitalism. New cities emerged as capitalists centered new types of manufacturing in the industrial heartland, from Pittsburgh to Chicago and Detroit. In the late nineteenth century occupational success for the Irish seems to have come a bit more rapidly in midwestern cities than in older East Coast cities.

Powerful urban political machines facilitated mobility by providing some economic resources—menial jobs at the least—for the start of the upward trek. Machines channeled money into building projects, facilitating the emergence of a business elite. By the end of the nineteenth century the Irish in Philadelphia could boast of twice the proportion of contractors and builders that other immigrant groups had. The growing number of worker organizations aided Irish mobility. As early as the 1850s the Irish controlled a few labor organizations in Massachusetts and New York. By the early 1900s unions had emerged among dockworkers, construction workers, and miners, with some providing, as we have seen, the base for organized protest. To the present day, the Irish have been prominent in labor organizations, including the AFL–CIO.[90]

The Irish, especially Irish Protestants, had begun to penetrate business and professional areas by the middle of the nineteenth century. A few wealthy entrepreneurs could be found among the Irish Protestants. A study of the handful of native-born U.S. millionaires in the 1761–1924 period found that 8 percent were Irish, apparently Protestant Irish. Of course, this proportion was considerably smaller than the English and Scottish contingent.[91]

Although some progress was obvious for rank-and-file Catholics by the turn of the century, discrimination and poverty were still having an impact. One study of Irish-born immigrants in 1890 Boston revealed them to have an occupational distribution that included 0 percent in the professions, 10 percent in other white-collar jobs, and 65 percent in low-skilled jobs. This employment situation contrasted greatly with that of the native-born Boston residents, mostly non-Irish, 47 percent of whom had white-collar jobs. The second-generation Irish fared better, not nearly as well as the native Yankees. The 1890 Census showed, moreover, only a small proportion of the foreign-born Irish population in professional positions—1.7 percent for males.[92]

## Mobility in the Twentieth Century

A study of Philadelphia's Irish population in 1900 found that 70 percent were in manufacturing, laboring, and domestic service jobs. Less than 10 percent of employed men and women held professional or managerial jobs. By that year the Irish had begun to move slowly up the social and economic ladder: some held political office in the urban political organizations, there was a small but growing middle-income group, and a few brethren had become prosperous in business, mining, and construction. But a majority were still rather poor. Interestingly, the middle-income group grew to the point of being stereotyped as "lace curtain" Irish. (The term comes from the prosperity that enabled this group to put up lace window curtains.)[93]

The little information available on mobility among the Irish, Catholic and Protestant, after 1900 suggests increasing economic security for a growing segment of that population. Apparently the Irish Protestant descendants of pre-1840 immigrants were still disproportionately concentrated in farming areas, in towns, and in southern and border states. In the late nineteenth and early twentieth centuries, and probably in later decades as well, a significant proportion had become relatively prosperous farmers, owners of small businesses, and skilled blue-collar workers, as well as part of the growing clerical-job category. Many were blending into the Anglo-Saxon Protestant mainstream. Whether the overwhelming majority were moving up the socioeconomic ladder is unclear, for many remained poor and isolated in rural areas.

Some concrete data are available on the Irish Catholics. By the 1930s they had not blended into the Anglo-Saxon Protestant mainstream. In their study of Newburyport, Massachusetts, in the 1930s Warner and Srole found that the Irish were moving ever closer to native Yankee residents in socioeconomic status. None, however, could be found at the top. The Depression hit the Irish hard, probably postponing for a decade the major economic breakthrough that was just within their reach. Baltzell's study of Philadelphians in 1940 revealed that few people of wealth and influence were Catholic; at the top white Protestants still dominated.[94]

Baltzell has suggested that business leadership in the 1950s and 1960s was still British American Protestant. In those decades Irish Catholics were less conspicuous in the ranks of leading scientists and industrialists than expected. This may be in part because their ancestors brought little scientific or management experience from the homeland. Some have suggested that modest representation in scientific fields may be due to Catholic education, with its classical emphasis. But it is also because of anti-Catholic discrimination at higher levels in business and industry.[95]

## Recent Successes

Irish Catholics have often been employed in politics, in police and fire departments, in the courts, and in colleges and schools. Government employment has been central. A 1964 study of a large urban police department revealed that about 25 percent of the sergeants were second-generation Irish, although, as one might expect, by this time very few were first-generation Irish.[96]

In the 1960s and 1970s Irish Catholics moved up economically in comparison with other ethnic groups. The Irish are now one of the most prosperous of the white ethnic groups. One analysis of opinion poll data revealed that Irish Catholic males had increased significantly in proportion in low- and high-level white-collar positions compared with their fathers. The proportion for the respondents was 66 percent white-collar, versus 38 percent for their fathers. In both generations the Irish Catholics were more likely to be found in better-paying white-collar positions than most other Catholic groups.[97]

In many discussions of the Irish, the human symbols of success have typically been athletes, entertainers, politicians, or, more recently, entrepreneurs such as Joseph Kennedy. But another group of Irish heroes has received little notice—the growing group of Irish Ph.D.'s and academics since the 1960s. Catholics now make up one-fourth of faculty members in top state colleges and universities, and about half of these are *Irish*. Irish Catholics are heavily represented in numerous humanities departments. Moreover, many graduate-trained Irish Catholics have moved into local, state, and federal government as lawyers, administrators, researchers, and elected officials.

Data on family income for 1969 and 1979 are available from the Census Bureau. In 1969 the median income of second-generation Irish American families and unrelated individuals was $11,776; the figure for all families and unrelated individuals in the United States was $9,590. In the late 1960s these children of immigrants were doing better in terms of income than the typical U.S. household. The 1980 census figures for all Americans of Irish Catholic and Irish Protestant ancestry—a much larger group than that just mentioned for 1969—show a similar pattern. In the 1980 census those with Irish ancestry reported a median family income of $20,719 for the year 1979; the median income for all U.S. families was $19,917. In 1980 Irish American families, taken as a group, had a median income somewhat higher than that of the typical American family. In addition, the Irish family income was higher than the median income for English American families ($19,807).[98]

Occupational data show a similar pattern. An examination of the occupational distribution of second-generation Irish Americans for 1950 and 1970 reveals that these children of immigrants were more likely to be found in professional-technical, managerial, and crafts jobs than the employed population as a whole. They were less likely to be found in less-skilled "operative" positions. The 1980 occupational distribution for all Americans of Irish ancestry is similar. There was a slightly smaller proportion of Irish Americans in professional and technical occupations (15 percent) than in the population as a whole (15.4 percent), and the proportion of managers and officials was significantly larger (15.3 percent) than that for the population as a whole (10.4 percent). The proportions of Irish Americans in the clerical/sales and service categories were a bit higher than those for the U.S. population as a whole, but the proportion in operative and laborer jobs was lower. Overall, most Irish Americans were employed in white-collar jobs in 1980. This Irish mobility is particularly noteworthy, given the long history of low-wage, blue-collar employment for the first Irish generations in North America.[99]

## EDUCATION

Organized education on a significant scale for Irish Protestants probably began after the Civil War. In the South, public schools spread in the Reconstruction period, and by the early twentieth century many of the Protestant Irish had taken advantage of them.

The Catholic Irish, in contrast, relied on parochial and public schools in urban areas of the North for organized education. Because of the heated anti-Catholicism of the period, no Catholic schools of any kind existed in 1790. It was not until the 1820–1840 period that numerous parochial schools were established. In cities some Irish Catholic children were beginning to receive public education, although the intense Americanization pressures in the public schools gave strong impetus to the development of separate, church-related schools as a means of retaining ethnic identity. By the late 1800s and early 1900s the center of the Irish Catholic community in numerous cities was a church and a parochial school system, attached to which were hospitals and charitable organizations[100]

By 1960 there were nearly 13,000 elementary and secondary Catholic schools, with an enrollment of five million children. At the center of this immense network are Irish Catholic Americans. In recent decades Catholic parochial schools have become a center of controversy in the United States. Financed by Catholic Americans, these private schools have gradually come to receive some public aid as well. This aid has brought extensive opposition from Protestant and Jewish groups and not a few court cases.[101]

Even in the 1920s Irish Catholics were going to college in large numbers, above the national average for all whites. By that decade, the educational achievements of Irish Catholic Americans were impressive, with Catholic colleges being built and college attendance for Irish Catholics on the increase. The Presbyterian Irish had already made important contributions in the area of education, including the establishment of institutions such as Princeton to provide an educated ministry for local Presbyterian churches.[102]

Drawing on the 1950 and 1970 census surveys of immigrants and their children, we can evaluate the position of the children of Irish immigrants in education. These figures primarily represent Irish Catholics. Looking at the median years of education completed for adults, we find this pattern:

|      | Native-born with Foreign Parents | | All U.S. Adults | |
|      | Men | Women | Men | Women |
| --- | --- | --- | --- | --- |
| 1950 | 10.3 | 10.9 | 9.0 | 9.6 |
| 1970 | 12.3 | 12.2 | 12.1 | 12.1 |

In both years the native-born children of Irish immigrants had median levels of educational attainment higher than those for all persons twenty five and over. The 1980 data cover a much larger group—those who identified themselves in terms of Irish nationality or Ireland as their country of origin in reply to a census question on ancestry. This group includes those with Irish Catholic heritages and those with Irish Protestant heritages. In 1980 the median number of years of school completed for all those reporting Irish ancestry was 12.5 years, a figure *identical* to the median for all men and women in the United States.[103]

# RELIGION

In the political and economic spheres the Irish have been pressured to assimilate, more or less nonreciprocally, to the established Anglo-Saxon Protestant core society and culture. But in the religious sphere the Irish have played the major role in firmly establishing what may well be the most important non-Protestant institution in the United States—the Roman Catholic Church.

While the Presbyterians from northern Ireland seem to have gradually blended into the Protestant religious institutions from the eighteenth century onward, Irish Catholics have fought intense anti-Catholic prejudice and discrimination to root the Catholic church in Anglo-Protestant soil. New churches sprang up wherever Catholic laborers went. Priests had long suffered with the poor in Ireland and in the United States, so the church was respected. In addition to church organizations there were related community organizations of great consequence, including benevolent and charitable organizations, of which the Ancient Order of Hibernians is perhaps the most famous.[104]

The Catholic church's hierarchy has long been disproportionately Irish. After the immigration of millions of Catholics, Irish influence became great. One analysis of Catholic bishops from 1789 to 1935 revealed that 58 percent were Irish. While 17 percent of the total Catholic population was Irish in the 1970s, a third of the priests and half of the upper hierarchy were Irish. Nonetheless, Irish influence seems to be declining. In recent years some Irish church leaders have been replaced by Polish, Portuguese, and Italian prelates.[105]

Although the Catholic church has had to adapt to some extent to the preexisting Protestant system, it has had its impact, sharpening the separation of church and state in the United States and reinforcing the right of all Americans to choose any faith. The strong tie between the Irish and the Catholic church has a historical basis. The longtime English oppression in Ireland had burned Catholic loyalty into Irish immigrants.

### Parishes and Irish Neighborhoods

In northern cities many Irish neighborhoods have been built around the parish church. Local politics blends with church and school, as do the local grocery stores and taverns:

> Among Irish Americans, that particular part of the urban turf with which you are identified and in which live most of the people on whom you have a special claim...is virtually indistinguishable from the parish; when asked where they are from, Irish Catholics in many cities give not the community's name but the name of the parish—Christ the King, St. Barnabas, All Saints...and so forth.[106]

Today in suburbs of cities such as Chicago the Irish Catholic parish survives. Loyalty to the church remains relatively strong: one survey found that over half of Irish Catholics go to mass every week.

Irish Catholic priests have dominated U.S. Catholicism, shaping the U.S. church in a number of distinctive ways, some conservative and some progressive. Irish archbishops and cardinals have mostly been a conservative lot, but priests and bishops have led many progressive fights. For example, the longtime president of Notre Dame University, Father Theodore M. Hesburgh, symbolizes the liberalism in Irish Catholicism. For many years, including his service as head of the U.S. Commission on Civil Rights, Father Hesburgh has been outspoken in his support for civil rights laws, antisegregation action, and affirmative action benefiting black Americans.[107]

## ASSIMILATION THEORIES AND THE IRISH

Now we can examine how the theories and concepts discussed in Chapter 2 help illuminate the experiences of Irish Americans. As we have seen, some power-conflict analysts (such as students of internal colonialism) specifically omit immigrant groups such as the "white ethnics" from their analyses, preferring to focus on nonwhite groups because most of these have endured much greater violence and repression while being subordinated in the North American colonies and the United States.

The assimilation theories of Gordon and Greeley are the most relevant for analysis of groups such as the Irish, Italians, and Jews. Yet in looking at these groups from the assimilation perspective we must keep in mind something many assimilationists tend to forget—the substantial conflict and ethnic stratification that has characterized the experiences of white ethnic Americans.

Compared with many other ethnic and racial groups, the Irish are several steps higher on the ladder of economic success and dominance. Among Irish Americans each new generation has become more incorporated in the core culture and society than prior generations.

The eighteenth-century Irish moved up the social and economic ladders quietly but surely; they were typically Protestants. Substantial assimilation on a number of dimensions apparently came by the late nineteenth century for many of the descendants of these Irish. One observer argues that this group blended in rather quickly, for "their social and political activities have mixed freely and spread freely through the general mass of American citizenship."[108] While the Scotch-Irish propagandists have exaggerated the rapidity of this cultural and structural assimilation, there is doubtless truth to the view that the early Irish immigrants and their descendants assimilated relatively rapidly at the level of culture, slowly but surely at the level of structural integration into the economy and the polity, and gradually into more intimate social ties and even identification with English and other British American families. Sometime in the last century many Scotch-Irish became a difficult-to-distinguish part of the Anglo-Saxon Protestant mainstream.

Assimilation came more slowly for Irish Catholics, who entered in increasing numbers after 1840. Rapid adaptation to the core culture, particularly in learning the language and basic values, is necessary to movement within United States institutions. In this regard, assimilation had come early for most Irish immigrants. Clark argues that the Irish Catholic adjustments were not as difficult as some have argued. American cities offered hope for escape from the oppressive conditions of Ireland. There was the greater chance for mobility, the expanding industrial environment. The customs had some similarities. While assimilation at all levels took several generations, cultural assimilation did proceed.[109]

Religion was an exception. Most Irish Catholics did not become Protestants. In new Irish communities external hostility and a common background reinforced a protective separatist reaction. Conflict with the nativists intensified Irish commitment to the Catholic church. The core culture eventually came to accommodate Protestant, Catholic, and Jewish religious communities. Yet the Catholic community did make adjustments to the English-dominated milieu in language and church organizations. Such adaptation made the Catholic church and school system an important medium within which new immigrants began their acculturation and even structural assimilation (for example, priests helped in securing employment).[110]

Did commitment to the Catholic religion decline in later generations of Irish Catholics? Some analysts have claimed this, arguing that cultural assimilation will thus soon be complete. Recent studies have not found this to be the case, however. As a group, the Irish are among the most likely to attend mass of all the Catholic groups studied. Andrew Greeley has presented information on Irish Catholics that indicates an increase in religious devotion—particularly among those in their thirties—over the last few decades.[111]

In regard to the dimensions Milton Gordon calls behavior-receptional assimilation and attitude-receptional assimilation—in effect, discrimination and prejudice—there have been substantial changes since the mid-nineteenth century for the Catholic Irish. Stereotyping has declined substantially since the days of the apelike image, although there is still some negative feeling directed against Irish Catholicism and urban machine politics. Discrimination has declined significantly, although it is still felt at the very highest levels of the U.S. economy and government. The U.S. has, as yet, had only one Irish Catholic president.

## Patterns of Structural Assimilation for the Irish

At the structural-assimilation (secondary-group) levels the Irish have made slow but significant movement into the Anglo-Saxon Protestant core society. We have seen the steady movement of the Irish from unskilled work into white-collar occupations and the relatively high income and occupational levels of the Irish Catholics in recent decades. Housing upgrading has paralleled these developments, although some self-segregation persists in the East and Midwest. After a century of struggle in the political sphere, Irish Catholics are now substantially integrated at local and state levels; in the last two or three decades they have moved significantly into the judicial, legislative, and executive branches of the federal government, if not yet in large numbers to the top. At the local level, the Irish have shaped urban politics in a number of cities.

Some have argued that with their economic assimilation, their movement into higher economic status, the Irish have of late been moving away from the Democratic party. Looking at the period since the 1940s, Glazer and Moynihan have argued that the "mass of the Irish have left the working class, and in considerable measure the Democratic party as well."[112] Yet voting data for roughly the same period suggest that the Irish are still tied to the Democratic party. Urban politicians, particularly Democrats, still pay great attention to this ethnic community, and many liberal Democratic leaders are still Irish. This suggests that one assimilation theory of ethnic politics—that economic mobility weakens traditional ethnic voting patterns—is not necessarily correct. Absorption into the Republicanism of many Anglo-Saxon Protestants has not happened for Irish Catholics as a group.[113]

As for structural incorporation at the level of primary-group ties, data on informal groups and voluntary associations point up some interesting trends. Ethnic clubs and organizations, since World War II if not before, have apparently declined in importance for the Irish Catholics. Benevolent societies have declined in numbers; so have the great fund drives to support Irish causes. This indicates increasing integration into the voluntary associations of the larger society. There has also been a decline in Irish attendance at Catholic parochial schools over recent decades, which may mean that Irish children are making more friendships across ethnic lines than ever before.[114]

Intermarriage may be the ultimate indicator of adaptation at the primary-group level. Abramson's study points up an increasing intermarriage rate for Irish Catholics. There is still substantial endogamy for Irish Catholics, with 65 percent of respondents with Irish fathers in one national survey also having Irish mothers; 43 percent of men who had married had a wife with an Irish father. Given the several generations that the majority of Irish Catholic families had been in the United States by the 1960s, the extent of inmarriage may be surprising. Marital assimilation with older Protestant groups has been slower than one might have expected. Still, just over half the respondents to the national survey had a non-Irish spouse. The trend does seem to be in the direction of increased outmarriage.[115]

## Is There an Irish Ethnic Identity Today?

Among the final stages of assimilation is what Gordon and Greeley have seen as identificational adaptation. Ultimately, this type of adaptation would mean a loss of a sense of Irishness and the development of a sense of peoplehood that is solely American or Anglo-Saxon Protestant American. One's sense of identity would no longer be Irish. This may have happened for many Irish Protestants but most Catholics still have a feeling of Irishness, although for many it may be a vague sense.

Some Irish Catholic writers, such as Daniel P. Moynihan, have argued that the Irish are losing their ethnic identity because of the decline in immigration. In her book *Irish Americans: Identity and Assimilation,* Marjorie Fallows argues that the American Irish are fully acculturated to the core culture. Irish Catholicism has become "Americanized" and fully in line with the Protestant ethic. In her view distinctive ethnic traits that are culturally significant are rare among the American Irish today, except in isolated ethnic enclaves. Scholars such as Fallows have argued that even though there are still a few ethnically distinct Irish Catholic communities in northern cities, this does not mean that most Irish Catholics live in such communities. Indeed, they assert that cultural and structural assimilation are all but complete for those Irish Catholics living outside ethnic neighborhoods.[116]

Other scholars emphasize the persistence of some ethnic distinctiveness. The Irish Catholic group has changed over generations of contact with the school system and media, but it has retained enough distinctiveness to persist as an ethnic group into the last decades of the twentieth century. The theory of ethnogenesis discussed in Chapter 2 seems appropriate to Irish Catholic Americans. This ethnic group has been more than a European nationality group. The Irish who came in large numbers after 1840 forged, over several generations, a distinctive American ethnic group. Ethnicity was an important way for the Irish Catholics to attach themselves to the new scene, a way of asserting their own identity in a buzzing confusion of diverse nationality groups. For Irish Catholics, because of nativisitic attacks and discrimination, ethnic identity was less voluntary in the first few decades than it was to become later. In the beginning the Irish group had a cultural heritage that was distinctly different from that of the British-dominated host culture. Over several generations of sometimes conflictual interaction the Irish adapted substantially to the host society. In this process was created a distinctive Irish ethnic group that reflected elements *both* of its nationality background and of the host culture.

The research of scholars such as Andrew Greeley confirms the persistence of ethnic distinctiveness, particularly in certain northern cities:

On the basis of the evidence available to us, the Irish-American subculture is likely to persist indefinitely. The Irish Catholic Americans will continue to be different in their religion, their family life, their political style, their world view, their drinking behavior, and their personalities.[117]

Drawing on his extensive analysis of survey research data, Greeley further concludes:

The Irish will continue to be affluent and probably will become even more affluent as they settle down securely amidst the upper crusts of the middle class with a firm foothold in the nation's economic and political, if not intellectual and artistic, elites.[118]

Furthermore, Greeley and associates even see evidence of a return to higher levels of self-conscious identification among young Irish. Whether this trend will continue remains to be seen. Whatever happens, however, it is clear that the impact of the Irish background on Irish behavior remains strong.[119]

An example of the persistence of Irish ethnicity and its positive and negative functions can be seen in the desegregation struggle that has taken place in Boston since the 1970s. There a predominantly Irish working-class community, South Boston, was involved in a judge's school desegregation plan; the plan was vigorously, even violently, opposed by the Irish. This has been more than a legal desegregation struggle. Different views of schooling and of urban communities are reflected in the controversy; the South Boston Irish see the central-city schools as a socializing force, reinforcing traditional family and community values, whereas many nonwhites and suburban whites view them as avenues of upward mobility for nonwhite minorities. Irish resistance to racial desegregation of central-city neighborhoods is based in part on racial prejudice. But perhaps most of all, it is based on protecting their ethnic community against all intruders, whoever they may be.

## SUMMARY

The Irish began moving to North America quite early, with indentured servants and farmers entering in the 1700s. The earlier immigration apparently included more southern, or Celtic, Irish than exaggerated accounts about the Scotch-Irish have suggested. The majority of the descendants of these early migrants were, or became, Protestants, settling disproportionately in the rural South and in frontier areas. The descendants of these early settlers often became part of the Anglo-Saxon mainstream over the next several generations. However, a significant proportion remained poor. The Protestant Irish in particular have received little attention in recent decades from scholars.

After the 1830s large numbers of Catholic immigrants settled in the cities of the North, where many suffered violence at the hands of Catholic-hating nativists and discrimination at the hands of employers. Poverty-stricken, Irish Catholics slowly began moving toward economic equality with older groups. Conflict, sometimes violent, marked their climb. Political innovators, the Irish Catholics shaped the political organizations of the cities to facilitate their integration into the core institutions.

Economic mobility between 1860 and 1980 became so dramatic as to place Irish Catholics in a position of near parity with established white Protestant groups on a number of important dimensions. Irish Protestant mobility since 1900 has received little scholarly attention, although at least one study suggests that those still identifying themselves as Irish Protestants lagged behind Catholics in economic attainments as recently as the 1970s. Nonetheless, today both Irish American Catholics and Protestants constitute major segments of Middle America.

## NOTES

1. U.S. Department of Justice, Immigration and Naturalization Service, *Annual Report* (Washington, D.C.: U.S. Government Printing Office, 1973), pp. 53–5. The figures for 1820–1867 represent "alien passengers arrived"; for later periods they represent immigrants arrived or admitted.

2. Cited in William Peterson, *Population*, 2nd ed. (New York: Macmillan, 1969), p. 260.

3. Philip H. Bagenal, *The American Irish* (London: Kegan Paul, Trench & Co., 1882), pp. 4–5).

4. Henry Jones Ford, *The Scotch-Irish in America* (Princeton, N.J.: Princeton University Press, 1915), pp. 125–28.

5. James G. Leyburn, *The Scotch-Irish* (Chapel Hill: University of North Carolina Press, 1962), pp. 142–43.

6. Ford, *The Scotch-Irish in America*, pp. 183–86; Leyburn, *The Scotch-Irish*, pp. 160ff.

7. Michael J. O'Brien, *A Hidden Phase of American History* (New York: Devin-Adair Co., 1919), pp. 249; see also pp. 287–88.

8. See Robert J. Dickson, *Ulster Immigration to Colonial America, 1718–1773* (London: Routledge & Kegan Paul, 1966), pp. 66–68.

9. O'Brien, *A Hidden Phase of American History*, p. 267.

10. Quoted in ibid., p. 254.

11. Thomas D'Arcy McGee, *A History of Irish Settlers in North America* (Boston: Office of American Celt, 1851), pp. 25–34.

12. Leyburn, *The Scotch-Irish*, pp. 331–32.

13. Quoted in Ford, *The Scotch-Irish in America*, pp. 520–21.

14. Theodore Roosevelt, *The Winning of the West* (New York: Review of Reviews Co., 1904), 1:123–25.

15. Ford, *The Scotch-Irish in America*, pp. 522, 539.

16. John W. Dinsmore, *The Scotch-Irish in America* (Chicago: Winona Publishing Co., 1906), p. 7.

17. Winthrop D. Jordan, *White over Black* (Baltimore: Penguin, 1969), pp. 86–88.

18. Edwin S. Gaustad, *Historical Atlas of Religion in America* (New York: Harper & Row, Pub., 1962), pp. 34–35; Dennis Clark, *The Irish in Philadelphia* (Philadelphia: Temple University Press, 1973), p. 8.

19. Quoted in McGee, *A History of Irish Settlers in North America, p. 79*.

20. Ford, *The Scotch-Irish in America*, pp. 180–240; E. R. R. Green, "Ulster Immigrants' Letters," in *Essays in Scotch-Irish History*, ed. E. R. R. Green (London: Routledge & Kegan Paul, 1969), pp. 100–102.

21. Leyburn, *The Scotch-Irish*, pp. 262–69.

22. American Historical Association, *Annual Report* (Washington, D.C.: U.S. Government Printing Office, 1932) 1:255–70.

23. Arnold Shrier, *Ireland and the American Emigration, 1850–1900* (Minneapolis: University of Minnesota Press, 1958), pp. 13–16; T. A. Jackson, *Ireland Her Own* (New York: International Publishers, 1970), pp. 243–45; Kerby A. Miller, *Emigrants and Exiles* (New York: Oxford University Press, 1985), p. 556.

24. Carl Wittke, *The Irish in America* (Baton Rouge: Louisiana State University Press, 1956), pp. 24–27; Theodore Hershberg et al., "A Tale of Three Cities," in *Majority and Minority*, 3rd ed., ed. Norman Y. Yetman and C. Hoy Steele (Boston: Allyn & Bacon, 1982), pp. 184–85.

25. Bagenal, *The American Irish*, p. 72 (the statistics crime and poverty are found on pp. 70–71); Wittke, *The Irish in America*, p. 46.

26. Hasia R. Diner, *Erin's Daughters in America* (Baltimore: Johns Hopkins, 1983), pp. xiii–xv.

27. Dale T. Knobel, *Paddy and the Republic* (Middletown, Conn.: Wesleyan University Press, 1986), pp. 24–27.

28. Lewis P. Curtis, Jr., *Apes and Angels: The Irish in Victorian Caricature* (Washington, D.C.: Smithsonian Institution Press, 1971), p. 59.

29. Ibid., p. 103.

30. Andrew M. Greeley, *That Most Distressful Nation* (Chicago: Quadrangle, 1972), pp. 119–20.

31. Leonard Gordon, "Racial and Ethnic Stereotypes of American College Students over a Half Century" (paper presented at meetings of the Society for the Study of Social Problems, Washington, D.C.:, August 1985), pp. 14–15.

32. Andrew M. Greeley, *The Irish Americans* (New York: Harper & Row, Pub., 1981), p. 167.

33. Leonard Dinnerstein and Frederic C. Jaher, "Introduction," in *The Aliens*, ed. Leonard Dinnerstein and Frederic C. Jaher (New York: Appleton-Century-Crofts, 1970), p. 4.

34. Leyburn, *The Scotch-Irish*, pp. 234, 301–16.

35. Ford, *The Scotch-Irish in America,* pp. 291–324; Leyburn, *The Scotch-Irish*, pp. 225–30.

36. Nathan Glazer and Daniel P. Moynihan, *Beyond the Melting Pot* (Cambridge: MIT Press and Harvard University Press, 1963), p. 220; McGee, *A History of Irish Settlers in North America*, p. 88.

37. Wittke, *The Irish in America,* pp. 47ff.

38. Ibid., p. 119; Wayne G. Broehl, Jr., *The Molly Maguires* (Cambridge: Harvard University Press, 1964), p. 75.

39. Clark, *The Irish in Philadelphia,* p. 21.

40. Wittke, *The Irish in America,* p. 120.

41. Rowland T. Berthoff, *British Immigrants in Industrial America* (Cambridge: Harvard University Press, 1953), pp. 190–93.

42. Ibid., p. 187.

43. Broehl, *The Molly Maguires*, p. 85.

44. Leonard P. O. Wibberly, *The Coming of the Green* (New York: Henry Holt & Co. 1958), pp. 101–3.

45. Broehl, *The Molly Maguires*, pp. 87–90.

46. Ibid., pp. 198–99.

47. Anthony Bimba, *The Molly Maguires* (New York: International Publishers, 1932), pp. 70–73.

48. Broehl, *The Molly Maguires*, pp. vi, 361.

49. Ibid., p. 359.

50. Oscar Handlin, *Boston's Immigrants, 1790–1865* (Cambridge: Harvard University Press, 1941), p. 137.

51. See James McCague, *The Second Rebellion* (New York: Dial Press, 1968).

52. Wittke, *The Irish in America,* pp. 191–92.

53. Richard Polenberg, *One Nation Divisible* (New York: Penguin, 1980), pp. 40–41.

54. Ford, *The Scotch-Irish in America*, p. 462.

55. Ibid., p. 491.

56. Ibid., p. 246; McGee, *A History of Irish Settlers in North America,* p. 71; Shane Leslie, *The Irish Issue in Its American Aspect* (New York: Scribner's, 1919), p. 8.

57. Maldwyn A. Jones, "Ulster Emigration, 1783–1815," in *Essays in Scotch-Irish History*, ed. Green, p. 67.

58. Paul Blanshard, *The Irish and Catholic Power* (Boston: Beacon Press, 1953), p. 282.

59. William F. Adams, *Ireland and Irish Emigration to the New World* (New Haven: Yale University Press, 1932), p. 377.

60. Wittke, *The Irish in America*, p. 104; Edward M. Levine, *The Irish and Irish Politicians* (Notre Dame, Ind.: University of Notre Dame Press, 1966), pp. 6–9.

61. Leo Hershkowitz, *Tweed's New York* (New York: Doubleday, Anchor Books, 1987), pp. xiii–xx.

62. Glazer and Moynihan, *Beyond the Melting Pot*, pp. 218–62.

63. Robert A. Dahl, *Who Governs?* (New Haven: Yale University Press, 1963), p. 41.

64. Levine, *The Irish and Irish Politicians*, p. 146.

65. Mike Royko, *Boss: Richard J. Daley of Chicago* (New York: Dutton, 1971).

66. Levine, *The Irish and Irish Politicians*, pp. 145–55.

67. Ibid., p. 155.

68. Ibid., p. 174.

69. Wittke, *The Irish in America*, pp. 110–12.

70. Greeley, *That Most Distressful Nation*, pp. 206–9.

71. Dennis J. Clark, "The Philadelphia Irish," in *The Peoples of Philadelphia*, ed. Allen F. Davis and Mark H. Haller (Philadelphia: Temple University Press, 1973), p. 145.

72. Terry N. Clark, "The Irish Ethnic and the Spirit of Patronage," *Ethnicity* 2 (1975): 305–59; Mark R. Levy and Michael S. Kramer, *The Ethnic Factor* (New York: Simon & Schuster, 1972), pp. 130–35; Greeley, *The Irish Americans*, pp. 168–69.

73. Maldwyn Jones, *American Immigration* (Chicago: University of Chicago Press, 1960), p. 236.

74. William Miller, "American Historians and the Business Elite," *Journal of Economic History* 9 (November 1949): 202–3.

75. Quoted in Elmer Ellis, *Mr. Dooley's America* (New York: Knopf, 1941), p. 208.

76. Donald H. Akenson, *The United States and Ireland* (Cambridge: Harvard University Press, 1973), pp. 40–42.

77. Wittke, *The Irish in America*, pp. 281–91.

78. William V. Shannon, *The American Irish* (New York: Macmillan, 1963), pp. 151–81.

79. Ibid., pp. 332–52; Samuel Lubell, *The Future of American Politics*, 2nd rev. ed. (New York: Doubleday, Anchor Books, 1955), pp. 83–84.

80. Glazer and Moynihan, *Beyond the Melting Pot*, p. 287.

81. Ibid; Shannon, *The American Irish*, pp. 395–411; Levy and Kramer, *The Ethnic Factor*, pp. 126–127. Compare John R. Schmidhauser, "The Justices of the Supreme Court: A Collective Portrait," *Midwest Journal of Social Science* 3 (February 1950): 1–57.

82. Leyburn, *The Scotch-Irish*, p. 322 and elsewhere.

83. Stephen Steinberg, *The Ethnic Myth* (New York: Atheneum, 1981), pp. 160–64.

84. Bagenal, *The American Irish*, p. 69.

85. Handlin, *Boston's Immigrants*, p. 67.

86. Adams, *Ireland and Irish Emigration to the New World*, p. 358.

87. Stephan Thernstrom, *Poverty and Progress* (Cambridge: Harvard University Press 1964), pp. 154–58.

88. Ibid., p. 184.

89. Clark, *The Irish in Philadelphia*, pp. 59, 167–75

90. Greeley, *That Most Distressful Nation*, p. 120; Clark, "The Philadelphia Irish," p. 143; Wittke, *The Irish in America*, pp. 217–27.

91. Pitirim Sorokin, "American Millionaires and Multi-Millionaires," *Social Forces* 3 (May 1925): 634–35. Data are based on father's ancestry.

92. Stephan Thernstrom, *The Other Bostonians* (Cambridge: Harvard University Press, 1973), p. 131; Berthoff, *British Immigrants in Industrial America*.

93. Hershberg et al., "A Tale of Three Cities," p. 190.

94. Lloyd Warner and Leo Srole, *The Social Systems of American Ethnic Groups* (New Haven: Yale University Press, 1945), pp. 93–95; E. Digby Baltzell, *An American Business Aristocracy* (New York: Collier Books, 1962), pp. 267–431; E. Digby Baltzell, *The Protestant Establishment* (New York: Random House, Vintage Books, 1966), pp. 320–21.

95. Shannon, *The American Irish*, pp. 436–37.

96. Cited in James Q. Wilson, "Generational and Ethnic Differences among Career Police Officers," *American Journal of Sociology* 69 (March 1964): 527.

97. Harold J. Abramson, *Ethnic Diversity in Catholic America* (New York: John Wiley, 1973), pp. 41–44; Levy and Kramer, *The Ethnic Factor*, p. 125; see also Greeley, *The Irish Americans*, p. 111.

98. U.S. Bureau of the Census, *U.S. Census of Population, 1970: Subject Report—National Origin and Language*, PC(2)-1a, 1973, p. 152; U.S. Bureau of the Census, *Census of Population, 1980: General Social and Economic Characteristics*, PC80-1-C1, 1983, pp. 51, 177; U.S. Bureau of the Census, *U.S. Census of Population, 1970: General Social and Economic Characteristics*, Final Report PC(1)-C1, United States Summary, 1972, p. 368; U.S. Bureau of the Census, *U.S. Census of Population, 1980: General Social and Economic Characteristics*, PC80-1-C1, 1983. p. 21.

99. U.S. Bureau of the Census, *U.S. Census of Population, 1950: Special Reports—Nativity and Parentage*, P-E No. 3A, 1954, p. 139; U.S. Bureau of the Census, *U.S. Census of Population, 1970: Subject Reports—National Origin and Language*, PC(2)-1A, 1973, p. 126; U.S. Bureau of the Census, *U.S. Census of Population, 1980: General Social and Economic Characteristics*, PC 80-1-C1, 1983, p. 174; U.S. Bureau of the Census, *U.S. Census of Population, 1950: Vol. II, Characteristics of the Population,* Part 1, United States Summary, 1953, p. 102; U.S. Bureau of the Census, *U.S. Census of Population, 1970: General Social and Economic Characteristics*. Final Report PC(1)-C1, United States Summary, 1972, p. 392; U.S. Bureau of the Census, *Statistical Abstract of the United States: 1984* (104th ed.), 1983, p. 416.

100. John T. Ellis, *American Catholicism* (Garden City, N.Y.: Doubleday, Image Books, 1965), p. 62; Clark, *The Irish in Philadelphia*, p. 123.

101. David O. Moberg, *The Church as a Social Institution* (Englewood Cliffs, N.J.: Prentice-Hall, 1962), p. 193.

102. Andrew M. Greeley, *Ethnicity, Denomination and Inequality* (Beverly Hills, Calif.: Sage Publications, Inc., 1976) pp. 45–53.

103. U.S. Bureau of the Census, *U.S. Census of Population, 1950: Special Reports—Nativity and Parentage*, P-E No. 3A, 1954, p. 139; U.S. Bureau of the Census, *U.S. Census of Population, 1970: Subject Reports—National Origin and Language*, PC(2)-1A, 1973, p. 100; U.S. Bureau of the Census, *U.S. Census of Population, 1980: General Social and Economic Characteristics*, PC 80-1-C1, 1983, p. 172; U.S. Bureau of the Census, *U.S. Census of Population, 1950: Vol. II, Characteristics of the Population*, Part 1, United States Summary, 1953, p. 96; U.S. Bureau of the Census, *U.S. Census of Population, 1970: General Social and Economic Characteristics*, Final Report PC(1)-C1, United States Summary, 1972, p. 368; U.S. Bureau of the Census, *U.S. Census of Population, 1980: General Social and Economic Characteristics*, United States Summary, PC80-1-C1, 1983, p. 21. The 1950 ancestry figures are for persons fourteen and older.

104. Wittke, *The Irish in America*, pp. 52–61, 205.

105. Owen B. Corrigan, "Chronology of the Catholic Hierarchy of the United States," *Catholic Historical Review* 1 (January 1916): 267–389; Gaustad, *Historical Atlas of Religion in America*, p. 103; Ellis, *American Catholicism,* p. 56; Wittke, *The Irish in America*, p. 91; Greeley, *That Most Distressful Nation*, p. 93.

106. Greeley, *The Irish Americans*, p. 145.

107. Ibid., pp. 130–32.

108. Ford, *The Scotch-Irish in America*, p. 538.

109. Clark, *The Philadelphia Irish*, p. 178.

110. Thernstrom, *Poverty and Progress*, p. 179.

111. Abramson, *Ethnic Diversity in Catholic America*, p. 111; Greeley, *The Irish Americans*, pp. 149–51.

112. Glazer and Moynihan, *Beyond the Melting Pot*, p. 219.

113. Raymond E. Wolfinger, "The Development and Persistence of Ethnic Voting," *American Political Science Review* 60 (1965): 907.

114. Joseph P. O'Grady, *How the Irish Became American* (New York: Twayne, 1973), p. 141; Majorie R. Fallows, *Irish Americans: Identity and Assimilation* (Englewood Cliffs, N.J.: Prentice-Hall, 1979), p. 147.

115. Abramson, *Ethnic Diversity in Catholic America*, p. 53.

116. Fallows, *Irish Americans*, pp. 148–49. See also Richard D. Alba, "Social Assimilation among American Catholic National-Origin Groups," *American Sociological Review* 41 (December 1976): 1032.

117. Greeley, *The Irish Americans*, p. 206.

118. Ibid.

119. Ibid. Compare Andrew M. Greeley, *Ethnicity in the United States* (New York: John Wiley, 1974). p. 311.

# CHAPTER 5

# *Italian Americans*

For many decades Italian Americans found themselves targets of Anglo-Saxon Protestants. As late as the 1970s, this Catholic group was attacked for being prejudiced against blacks, for being unsophisticated, superpatriotic "hardhats" with connections to the "Mafia." By the late 1960s a counterattack was already developing. Many white ethnic leaders, including Italian Americans, came to view Protestant intellectuals and officials critically: "The ethnic American is sick of being stereotyped as a racist and a dullard by phony white liberals, pseudo black militants and patronizing bureaucrats.... He pays the bill for every major governmental program and gets nothing or little in the way of return."[1] Richard Gambino, an Italian American scholar, noted that "the white elite has shown little understanding of Italian-American history, culture, or problems and less empathy with them."[2]

The militant defense of things Italian and the achievements of Italian Americans had by the 1980s begun to change the situation. Italian Americans were gaining greater acceptance among other Americans, including many Anglo-Saxon Protestant voters. Clear signals of the rising prominence of Italian Americans in the United States could be seen in the selection of Geraldine Ferraro as the vice-presidential candidate of the Democratic party in 1984 and the mention of Mario Cuomo, governor of New York, and Lee Iacocca, chief executive at Chrysler Corporation, as possible Democratic presidential nominees in 1988.

## ITALIAN IMMIGRATION

Italian explorers, including Cristoforo Colombo (Christopher Columbus), played a major role in opening the Americas to European exploitation. An Italian navigator, Amerigo Vespucci, made a number of voyages to the Americas shortly after Colombo's voyages. Because of his early maps the continents came to be named after him.[3]

## Numbers of Immigrants

A few Italians migrated to the colonies prior to the 1800s. Schiavo notes that "in Virginia, a small group of Italians settled with Filippo Mazzei in 1774 in order to introduce wine making and Italian agricultural methods."[4] Thomas Jefferson was so impressed that he relied on Mazzei's intellectual talents and also invited other Italian agricultural experts and crafts workers to Virginia.

Between 1820 and 1980 more than five million Italians migrated to the United States.[5] Until 1860 the migration was quite small.[6] Between 1861 and 1880 migration picked up a little, totaling 67,500.[7] In the next four decades, Italian immigration became heavy, with more than four million recorded immigrants. Prior to 1880 most immigrants were from northern Italy; now they came in very large numbers from the south.[8] The heavy migration of poor farmers and laborers had begun three decades after the formerly independent regions of Italy were unified into one state.[9]

Certain factors are relevant to the study of this migration: the point of origin, the destination, the migrating units, and the larger context. As with the Irish, land and agricultural problems triggered much of the Italian out-migration. National unification, with the new Italian government controlled by northern Italians, had brought heavy taxes to southern Italy. Low incomes, poor soil and weather, poor health conditions, a feudal land system, unreasonable taxes, corruption in government—these were the important push factors at the point of origin. Areas with a large and militant working-class population sent fewer migrants in spite of their poverty. Agricultural organization and labor militancy in Italy significantly lowered out-migration rates.[10]

The main pull factor at the destination was the image of the United States as an economic paradise. Emigration was a means of expanding opportunity. Many came to stay. Others came with the idea of building capital for enterprises back home; of these, some returned and others remained. Most who came were poor. Many migrated as a result of labor recruiting in Italy; a considerable portion of the immigration was stimulated by aggressively expanding industrial capitalism in the United States.[11]

Migration along family and kinship networks, typical for poor and working-class migrants from most countries in Europe, lessened the pain of migration. Italians migrated in large numbers from the same village areas. Italian men often would migrate first.[12] There were chains of kin migration across the Atlantic linking areas in Italy and America. Most immigrants headed for urban points; like the Irish, they had had enough of farm life. Cities of the industrialized East Coast, such as Boston, New York, and Philadelphia, were popular destinations. Migration was to the "Little Italies" in larger cities, where fellow villagers from Italy resided. Today most Italian Americans live in the larger cities of the northeastern and north-central regions.[13]

Remigration was an important feature of the migration. Between 1908 and 1920 the number returning to the homeland in some years reached 60 to 70 percent of the number of new immigrants, placing the Italians well above other groups in terms of remigration.[14] A small portion of these were temporary sojourners, "birds-of-passage" whose aim was to make money in the United States and then return to invest it in enterprises at home.[15]

Between 1924 and 1965 Italian immigration was sharply curtailed by laws passed under pressure of nativist agitation. Previous Italian immigration was one of the factors in this anti-immigration legislation. Beginning in 1897, numerous legislative attempts were made to restrict immigration.[16] The Immigration Act of 1924 established a small, discriminatory quota for Italians. By 1929 an annual quota of 5,802 Italians had been established, compared with quotas of 65,721 for Great Britain and 25,957 for Germany. (These discriminatory quotas were altered little by the 1952 Walter-McCarran Act.) The quota system was based on the prejudiced notion of Anglo-Saxon nativists that those countries that had furnished the most "good American citizens"—that is, citizens prior to the immigration waves after 1880—should be the ones with the largest quotas. The British, Germans, Irish, and Scandinavians were given 76 percent of the total, although the demand from those countries had slackened considerably by that time.

Pressure on Italy's small quota was great. A backlog of 250,000 applicants developed. Not until 1965 was a new Immigration Act passed, replacing the discriminatory national-origin quota system in two stages. In the first stage the unfilled quotas of some countries could be used to augment the filled quotas of certain other countries. As a result, the number of Italian entrants increased significantly. In 1966 some 26,447 Italian immigrants were admitted; in 1967, 28,487. However, the 1965 act dictated that after 1968 no country should exceed 20,000 in any one year, again increasing the backlog of Italians trying to migrate to the United States. Italian migration continued at a high level in the early 1970s, to the point that the years 1972 and 1973 saw twice as many entrants from Italy as from any other European country. However, by the late 1970s and the early 1980s the number of Italian immigrants had fallen off significantly; the backlog had been exhausted.

## Life for the Immigrants

What was life like for the large waves of Italians who immigrated in the peak 1880–1920 period? Work took the form of unskilled labor on transportation systems such as canals and railroads and on city water and sewer systems. Pay was typically low, and individuals as well as families were poor. The immigrants and their children were discriminated against in many ways, economically, politically, and socially. Italian immigrants found themselves segregated in "Little Italies," ghettos within cities.

There is irony here, since *ghetto* is thought to be an Italian (Venetian) word first applied to the practice of segregating Jews in Italy in the sixteenth century. In the United States it was the Italian Catholics who found themselves in ghettos. In many cities Italians replaced earlier groups as part of an invasion-succession process. Other groups would follow on the heels of the Italians.[17]

Some analysts have viewed working-class communities in cities as disorganized "slum" areas with little positive social life. This was certainly not true for such Italian communities. As with the Irish before them, Italians developed their own extensive friendship and kinship circles, political clubs, avenues for mobility, and community celebrations. Central to Italian communities were indigenous organizations and festivals, including clubs and mutual-benefit societies—societies whose members made small monthly payments to ensure a proper funeral and a decent burial upon their demise. In 1927 there were two hundred mutual-aid societies in Chicago and many other clubs and lodges. Legal agencies developed; Italian newspapers flourished.[18]

Italian communities were laid on the bedrock of extensive kinship networks. Kinship was important in areas such as the North End of Boston, where extended-family members lived near one another. As a result, and contrary to nativist propaganda, few among first-generation Italians ended up in almshouses. As they had been in Italy, Italian families in the United States tended to be patriarchal; kinship solidarity was emphasized. A high value was also placed on home ownership. The community was a critical factor in cementing Italians to certain northern and midwestern cities.[19]

## STEREOTYPES

Nativist images of the Irish had been harsh, but by the end of the nineteenth century the stereotype of the apelike Irish was being replaced by stereotypes of southern and eastern Europeans. Italian Catholics were one target of stereotyping. The stereotype was strong and frequently absurd:

> It is urged that the Italian race stock is inferior and degraded; that it will not assimilate naturally or readily with the prevailing "Anglo-Saxon" race stock of this country; that intermixture, if practicable, will be detrimental; that servility, filthy habits of life, and hopelessly degraded standard of needs and ambitions have been ingrained in Italians by centuries of oppression and abject poverty.[20]

Such indictments appeared in national magazines. In the 1888 *North American Review,* labor activist T. V. Powderly alleged that southern and eastern Europeans were an inferior stock that lived immoral lives centered in liquor.[21]

### Myths of Biological Inferiority

Popular writers, scholars, members of Congress—all warned of the peril of allowing inferior stocks from Europe into the United States. Kenneth L. Roberts, a prominent journalist, wrote of the dangers of the newer immigrants making Americans a mongrel race: "Races can not be cross-bred without mongrelization, any more than breeds of dogs can be cross-bred without mongrelization. The American nation was founded and developed by the Nordic race, but if a few more million members of the Alpine, Mediterranean and Semitic races are poured among us, the result must inevitably be a hybrid race of people as worthless and futile as the good-for-nothing mongrels of Central America and southeastern Europe."[22] The "Alpine, Mediterranean, and Semitic races" generally covered countries of heavy emigration other than those of northern Europe; the Italians and Jews were thought by such writers to be examples.

Half-truths about disease and illiteracy were circulated about the southern and eastern European immigrants. It was true in some years between 1880 and 1920 that half the adult Italian immigrants could not read and write, but in other years the overwhelming majority were literate.[23] In no year were the charges of total illiteracy leveled at Italian Americans by the press and politicians accurate.[24] Particularly hostile was the leap from the proportions illiterate to assumptions of low intelligence.

In the first three decades of the twentieth century intellectual inferiority stereotypes were based in part on misreading the results of new psychological tests inaccurately labeled intelligence (IQ) tests. The term *intelligence test* is inaccurate because the tests measured selected, learned verbal and quantitative *skills,* not a broad or basic intelligence. In 1912 Henry Goddard gave Binet's diagnostic test and related tests to a large number of immigrants from southern and eastern Europe. His data showed that 83 percent of Jewish and 79 percent of Italian immigrants were "feeble-minded," a category naively defined in terms of low scores on the new tests.[25]

With the coming of World War I some prominent psychologists became involved in large-scale testing of draftees. Verbal and performance tests were developed. Although the results were not used for military purposes, detailed analyses were published in the 1920s and gained public and congressional attention because of the racial-inferiority interpretation placed on test results of southern and eastern Europeans by some psychologists.[26]

In 1923 Carl Brigham, a Princeton psychologist who would later play a role in developing college entrance tests, wrote a detailed analysis of the intellectual inferiority of immigrant groups, including Italians, drawing on data from Army tests. The average scores for foreign-born draftees ranged from highs of 14.87 for English and 14.34 for Scotch draftees, to an average of 13.77 for all white draftees, to lows of 10.74 for Polish draftees and 11.01 for Italian draftees. The low test scores for such groups as the Italian Americans were boldly explained in racial terms. Those groups with lower results were considered inferior racial stock. These "scientific" results were interpreted by psychologists such as Brigham as support for the prevalent ideology of "Nordic" intellectual superiority being espoused by racial theorists such as Madison Grant. Brigham went on to argue that the sharp increases in southern and eastern European immigration had lowered the level of American intelligence.[27]

The political implications of Brigham's analysis were proclaimed: immigration limits were necessary. Political means should be developed within the United States to prevent "the continued propagation of defective strains in the present population." Here was pseudoscientific support for such government action as passage of the 1924 Immigration Act, which would soon restrict Italian and other southern European immigration.

An important aspect of this stereotyping of Italian and other European immigrants is the role of the *state*, of government. The definition of these immigrants as undesirable ethnic groups was stimulated by social psychologists working with and for state agencies, in this case the U.S. armed forces. And this research was used by another branch of government, the Congress, to restrict immigration.[28]

The "intelligence" differences measured by psychological tests were considered to reflect the inferior or superior genetic background of European "racial" stocks. In those decades few seriously considered the possibility that the linguistic (English), cultural (northern European–American), and educational bias in the tests and in interpretative procedures could account for the differentials. These debates over the inferiority of European "racial" groups are now a historical curiosity. No social scientists today would advance these arguments of inferiority on the basis of such test data.[29]

Some immigrant leaders developed strategies for dealing with concern over "blood" lineage. One prominent Italian leader, Fiorello La Guardia, suffered personal attacks that incorporated stereotypes. For his criticism of officials such as President Herbert Hoover he received letters like the following: "You should go back where you belong and advise Mussolini how to make good honest citizens in Italy. The Italians are preponderantly our murderers and boot-leggers."[30] La Guardia's countertactic was often biting humor. When asked to provide material on his family background for the *New York World,* he saw the ghost of "blood" inferiority behind the request and commented: "I have no family tree. The only member of my family who has one is my dog Yank. He is the son of Doughboy, who was the son of Siegfried, who was the son of Tannhäuser, who was the son of Wotan. A distinguished family tree, to be sure— but after all he's only a son of a bitch."[31] Such humor has been one response to hostile stereotyping.

## The Mafia Myth

The most persistent aspect of the stereotyping of Italian Americans has been the criminality image. As early as the 1870s Italians were depicted as lawless, knife-wielding thugs looking for a fight.[32] A report of the influential United States Immigration Commission argued that certain types of criminality were "inherent in the Italian race."[33] Data from the early decades of this century raise questions about the validity of the criminality stereotype at that time. The arrest rate for drunkenness and disorderly conduct for the Italian foreign-born in 1910 was quite low—158.1 per 100,000 people, versus 202.6 for the American-born. The arrest rate for prostitution was very low, and the imprisonment rate in 1910 was much lower than public stereotypes would suggest: 527.3 prisoners per 100,000 for the Italian-born, 727.4 for English and Welsh foreign-born, and 371.3 for the white American-born population.[34]

Small-scale crime was a problem in urban ghettos, but it did not involve a sinister conspiracy, an organization later known by the term *Mafia.* Italian crime in the cities began on a small scale, fostered in part by poverty and discrimination. Prohibition catapulted Italian Americans into organized crime, which at that time was controlled by Irish and Jewish Americans. For immigrant groups crime was an avenue of mobility. Increasingly, the Sicilian term *Mafia* was used to describe these gangsters, whether Sicilian or not; indeed, many were not even Italian. Yet Italian Americans had low crime rates in the 1920s and 1930s. What data there are suggest that foreign-born Italian Americans had relatively low crime rates, close to those for all native-born Americans.[35]

The image of Italian criminality has taken on a widespread mythological character; the stereotype of the Italian American as a Mafia hoodlum committed to crime and violence persists. A Louis Harris opinion poll found that 78 percent of the national sample reported a belief in a secret crime organization called the Mafia.[36] Into the late 1980s the mass media continued to provide TV series and movies whose criminals had Italian American names, clearly a signal of ties to the "Mafia." Reruns of "The Untouchables" still appeared, and there was a short-lived series called "Our Family Honor." The *Godfather* and *Rocky* films were available on videotape, and there were new films such as *Prizzi's Honor*, about a Mafia hit man and hit woman, and *Wise Guys*, a comedy about Mafia criminals. The *Godfather* films created a Mafia mystique even in the 1980s, with businesses using that name and toys being associated with the Mafia.

That organized crime continues as a major enterprise cannot be disputed. That a small proportion of Italians play a role in it is not disputed. That these Italians control a nationwide crime syndicate with no help from other racial and ethnic groups can be disputed; that the Italian (Sicilian) term *Mafia* should be used to describe such a syndicate can be rejected. Organized crime is a *multi-ethnic* enterprise, with criminals drawn from most racial and ethnic groups. FBI statistics show that Italian Americans make up only 4 percent of the 500,000 Americans estimated to be involved in organized crime.

Many law-enforcement officials and mass media people have assumed that organized crime was, and is, primarily an Italian conspiracy. Smith has argued that a major reason for perpetuation of this myth is the desire of law-enforcement officials to divert public attention from their own incompetence by picturing organized crime as a sinister, foreign conspiracy too powerful for their agencies to handle with conventional methods.[37] All Italian Americans are made to bear the burden not only for the sins of a small minority but also for the shortcomings of law-enforcement agencies seeking to displace the blame for their failure. To put the matter simply, there is no evidence that current Italian American crime rates are higher than those of other major ethnic groups.[38]

## Stereotypes and Discrimination

A study of the portrayal of Italian Americans on primetime television examined a sample of 263 programs in the 1980–1981 season. The study found that negative images of Italian Americans outnumbered positive images by two to one. Most of the 96 Italian characters in the shows studied were males and had low-status jobs. A significant percentage were portrayed as criminals, and many were pictured as "lovable or laughable dimwits who worked in jobs that offered little pay and less prestige." The majority of Italian Americans portrayed on television made grammatical errors, misunderstood English words, or spoke broken English.[39]

In a more recent study in northern California cities, a number of respondents reported various kinds of stereotyping and discrimination. One Italian American described his experience with ethnic slurs: "When I joined the office in the new location I became a member of the Rotary Club, and of course there were very few Italian members. So the minute I came on board, they started referring to me as the Godfather of the country." He went on to say that he found this humor very degrading, since he seemed always to have to explain that he had no ties to the Sicilian "Mafia." Numerous other Italian Americans reported similar experiences, including discrimination in corporations and much barbed "Mafia" joking.[40]

## CONFLICT

The myth of peaceful progress is again dispelled by the history of struggles of Italians with Anglo-Saxon Protestant nativists, Irish Catholics, and black Americans. Irish and Italians were fighting on the streets of Boston by the 1860s, and Italian parents often accompanied their children to school for protection. In the 1870s Irish workers on strike in New York attacked Italian strikebreakers; four Italians were killed in Pennsylvania in a clash with striking Irish miners.

By the 1880s immigrants from southern Italy had become targets of nativist attempts to control them, sometimes under the guise of "legal action" to prevent alleged crime, sometimes in the form of vigilante action. In the 1880s in Buffalo, New York, more than three hundred Italians—most of the local Italian population—were detained by police after an incident in which one Italian had killed another; only two of the three hundred were found holding weapons. The Italian community protested to the Italian government. Replying to the governor of New York, the police chief of Buffalo explained that he thought Italians as a rule carried concealed weapons and were a threat to social order.[41] Much violence was directed against southern Italians; several dozen were killed by mobs in numerous places in the South and a few northern areas.[42]

Attacks in the South were motivated by a variety of reasons, from labor competition to a desire to maintain racial lines. Italian Americans were more likely than other whites to support black political rights. Thus Italian immigrants were a threat to white solidarity in the South. They worked alongside blacks as laborers or sold to them as small shopkeepers. In one town five Sicilian shopkeepers were lynched for this reason.[43]

A publicized attack occurred in New Orleans after the 1891 murder of a police superintendent investigating crime among Italians. A number of Italians were jailed for the deed, and when the jail was stormed by a large group led by prominent citizens, there was no police interference; eleven of the Italians were killed. Newspapers praised the deed, as did major political figures, with most developing the stereotypical theme of criminality. Theodore Roosevelt made negative comments about Italian Americans, calling the 1891 lynchings in New Orleans "a rather good thing."[44]

## More Legalized Killings

Italians were fired on and forced to leave Marksville, Louisiana, for violating southern racial taboos. Two hundred were driven out of Altoona, Pennsylvania, in 1894. In some areas, Italians counterattacked. In 1899 an Italian agricultural community in Arkansas suffered vandalism and the burning of its schoolhouse at the hands of other whites. Groups of Italians armed themselves and patrolled their area, effectively ending the attacks.[45]

Sometimes killings were legalized. One of the most famous murder trials of all time was that of Nicola Sacco and Bartolomeo Vanzetti, Italian-born workers who were tried for robbery and murder in Massachusetts. Numerous witnesses testified that the defendants were elsewhere at the time of the crime, but the testimony of Italian-born witnesses was ignored by the court. Anti-Italian prejudice was evident in the trial and in the presiding judge. The two men did not receive a fair trial. As suspected political radicals, they were executed in 1927 in the midst of an era of hysteria over left-wing, un-American activities. In the 1980s several books reassessed the prosecution's case; the most important points made by the prosecution were brought into question by new evidence presented in these books.[46]

## Conflict with Blacks

Since the 1930s conflict between Italian Americans and groups lower on the socioeconomic ladder has been part of the urban scene. "Law and order" has been a major issue, as have school desegregation and busing, in the large metropolitan areas of the North. Italian leaders and writers have sometimes complained that blacks are the "darlings" of the white Protestant liberals and get disproportionate press coverage and federal aid.[47]

Italian Americans in such cities as Newark and Philadelphia have found themselves surrounded by large numbers of immigrating blacks. With these poor immigrants came increased crime and drug problems. Realistic fears about crime became coupled with exaggerated views of blacks.[48]

A number of surveys have shown significant antiblack prejudice and strong opposition to neighborhood desegregation among Italian Americans. One survey found that 70 percent of Italians would object if a black family moved into their area, a figure higher than for whites in general.[49] In addition, some civil rights demonstrations by blacks in the cities, particularly demonstrations tied to housing and school desegregation, have provoked hostile verbal attacks and even violence by white ethnics, including Italian Americans. Yet such data must be interpreted in a broader context. Italian Americans have been among the few white groups willing to remain in some central-city areas. They are also among those most likely to own their own homes there. Thus Italian Americans, along with other southern and eastern Europeans, were found in research studies in the 1970s to be more likely to live in naturally integrated neighborhoods, or at least integrated areas of cities, than were members of British American groups.[50]

# POLITICS

The first meaningful Italian influence on American politics was that of Filippo Mazzei, a friend of Thomas Jefferson who, as we have seen, came to the colonies to help with agricultural development. As it turned out, he helped Jefferson bring legal reforms to Virginia. Mazzei's writings speak vigorously of freedom and equality and include phrases similar to those Jefferson later used in the Declaration of Independence—for example, the phrase "All men are by nature created free and independent."[51]

## Italians in City Politics

During and after the great migration of 1880 to 1920, southern Italians were recruited into the Democratic party by Irish Americans. In Chicago, Italians benefited from the political patronage system; many were employed by the city in the 1890s, mostly in menial positions such as street sweeping. Italians had elected an alderman there by 1892, and they had a few representatives in the Illinois legislature by the mid-1890s. Italians began to be elected to office in New York by 1900; by 1920 Italians were central to city politics, for example, in passing out life-sustaining job favors.[52]

By the late 1930s a few cities, such as New York, San Francisco, and New Orleans, had Italian mayors. Nonetheless, the typical picture was of an Italian community governed by non-Italian politicians. Substantial political gains were made in the next few decades. A number of smaller cities, particularly in New Jersey, elected Italian mayors. In 1947 New York City's political machine came under the control of Italian Americans. In New Haven Irish control of local government had kept Italians from moving up for a number of decades, and as late as 1940 the latter were still underrepresented. Yet by the late 1950s Italian Americans were well represented in city government positions. Over the next two decades, the number of Italian Americans serving as mayor or city-council member became conspicuous in many northern cities.[53] Prominent Italian American mayors in recent decades have included Anthony Celebrezze (Cleveland), Joseph Alioto (San Francisco), George Moscone (San Francisco), and Frank Rizzo (Philadelphia). Of the dozen or so who have served as chief executives in major cities, most have been liberal Democrats.

As with the Irish, Anglo-Saxon Protestant reform movements reduced the benefits going to the Italian working class. These movements were aimed at ridding urban politics of machine bosses and corruption. But defeating the machine meant decreasing the political power of working-class ethnics.[54]

Reform in the guise of urban renewal and urban redevelopment has also hurt Italian communities. For example, the West End of Boston once contained a large, viable, Italian working-class community with relatively little political clout. In the late 1950s the area was officially designated a "slum" by the politically powerful city fathers and razed for urban renewal. New apartment buildings were built, development that was expected to improve the tax base of the central city. But several thousand Italians had been forced to relocate, a move that brought them great pain.[55]

Moreover, Italians particularly suffered during the 1919–1922 Red Scare. The infamous Palmer raids conducted by the attorney general in this period were aimed largely at immigrant families, often Italian, thought to be radical or subversive. Many aliens were illegally detained or arrested, and some were deported as a result.[56] This had a dampening effect on political participation.

## State and National Elections

Few Italians served in state and national legislatures in the North prior to 1900. One was Francis Spinola, a brigadier general in the Union Army, a member of the New York legislature, and a member of the U.S. House of Representatives. After 1900 the few successes at state and national levels were often based on the concentration of voters in urban communities. Prior to 1950 a major state such as New York had had only six Italian representatives in Congress. Perhaps the most famous of these was Fiorello La Guardia, a man proud of his heritage. La Guardia won elections in part on the strength of the Italian vote. In Congress he became the most vigorous supporter of Italian immigration, attacking Anglo-Saxon nativism and the anti-Italian quota system it had fostered. He was the first Italian American to rise through the ranks of Irish politics in New York City, where he later served as mayor. First elected mayor in 1934, La Guardia showed that Italians and other white ethnics could support reform movements aimed at urban machines, in this case Tammany Hall, and promote efficient, honest government.[57]

International politics affected Italian American political activities, just as the Ireland–Britain struggle has affected Irish Americans. During the Depression Mussolini became a hero for many Italian Americans, as well as for many non-Italian Americans. Yet antifascist activity was also a significant force in many Italian communities. During World War II Italian Americans suffered some discrimination. There was much talk about alleged Italian subversion, although the action taken against Italian Americans was far less substantial than that against Japanese Americans. The use of the Italian language was prohibited on the radio in New York and Boston. Several thousand Italians were arrested, and nearly two hundred aliens were placed in internment camps after the U.S. declaration of war.[58]

On the other hand, Richard Alba has argued, the war contributed to eventual Italian American mobility and assimilation, particularly after the war. The solidarity generated by the struggle against fascism in Germany and Japan brought these white ethnic immigrants and their children more rapidly into the American melting pot. Italian Americans enlisted in the armed forces and served in integrated units. (In contrast, black Americans and Japanese Americans served in segregated units.) Many became citizens. In this period novels and films about the armed forces celebrated the ethnic diversity of U.S. soldiers. The war contributed to what Alba terms "a different vision of America, which included ethnic Americans, or more precisely those who were white, in the magic circle of full citizenship."[59]

Since the Great Depression Italian Americans have slowly penetrated the middle levels of state and federal government, including the judicial system. Italian Americans finally made it into the judiciary in New York State by the 1930s. It was not until Franklin Roosevelt's administration that the first Italian American judge was appointed in the federal courts; President Harry Truman appointed the second and third.[60] Only one Italian American (Antonin Scalia) has served on the Supreme Court. Progress in congressional representation has been more substantial. By the late 1940s there were eight Italians in Congress; by the 1950s Italians were serving in ever larger numbers in state legislatures. John Pastore of Rhode Island became the first Italian governor (1946) and the first senator shortly thereafter. In 1962 Anthony Celebrezze became the first Italian American to serve in a presidential cabinet. In 1968 Governor John Volpe of Massachusetts was considered a likely vice-presidential choice for the Republicans.[61]

By the 1970s and 1980s there were more Italian American cabinet members and more governors and state legislators. Mario Cuomo, governor of New York in the 1980s, was a keynote speaker at the 1984 Democratic party convention that nominated Geraldine Ferraro as its vice-presidential candidate. In 1987 three Italian Americans, including Alfonse D'Amato of New York, were serving in the U.S. Senate. And in 1988 as we have seen, Cuomo was considered for the presidential nomination, as was Lido (Lee) Iacocca, chief executive at Chrysler Corporation.

Since the 1968 and 1972 presidential elections Republican strategists have worked hard for the white ethnic vote, including the Italian vote. Fears about civil rights actions fueled discontent. Nor surprisingly, this strategy has had a few successes, most notably in the 1972 presidential election. Yet in most contests the votes of Italian Americans have continued to go for the Democratic party. Survey data for the late 1970s showed Italian Americans to be leaning strongly toward the Democratic party. Only 22 percent called themselves Republicans. In addition, the percentage of younger voters leaning toward the Democratic party was about the same as that of older voters.[62]

There is an image of Italians as incapable of community or political organization in their own behalf. An example is the 1950s urban renewal in the West End of Boston, discussed earlier; Italians were unable to organize politically to defend their neighborhood against the urban renewal carried out destructively by the city fathers. But this view has been exaggerated, for there are also examples of political organization. Thus in 1968 East Bostonians organized against further encroachment upon their neighborhoods by Boston's Logan International Airport, preventing construction of a new runway. East Bostonians have worked to prevent inroads by other outsiders. In 1972 a Save East Boston organization was established to protect the community from a number of external threats.

There has also been nationwide organization. In 1976 the National Italian American Foundation was created; from its headquarters in Washington D.C., this organization operates as a clearinghouse of information on Italian politicians and political issues of importance to Italian Americans. In the mid-1960s the 130 chapters of the American Committee on Italian Immigration were an effective force in changing the racist U.S. immigration law. These Italian American organizations held rallies and lobbied successfully to get the 1965 Immigration Act passed.[63]

## THE ECONOMY

Structural adaptation includes the movement of immigrant groups into secondary-organization levels of the core society—into the economic, as well as the political and educational, organizations of the society. Economic mobility entails the penetration of higher levels of employment and attendant economic benefits. Italian Americans started out at the bottom of the ladder. The immigrants prior to 1880 were smaller in number, mostly artisans, street sellers, and political exiles, and primarily from northern Italy. The southern Italian immigrants, who came after 1880, were economically oppressed; they responded to the tremendous demand for unskilled labor that existed in the late nineteenth century.[64]

Large numbers came to the United States with the aid of *padroni*, labor bosses or work sponsors who linked the new immigrants to employment, food, and housing. Some claim this system was imported from Italy, but others have argued that it was a normal part of the United States' industrialization, which virtually devoured immigrant workers. The padroni acted primarily as agents who secured cheap labor for transportation, construction, and manufacturing enterprises within the United States. Exploitation often resulted from the padrone system. Exorbitant prices were charged by the labor bosses for housing and food; labor abuses were heaped on workers iso-lated in camps.[65] By 1909, because of legislation passed in several states, contractors and other business operators had begun to change from the extralegal padroni to legitimate agents.[66]

## Early Poverty and Discrimination

Urban poverty was the lot of most immigrants. Coupled with this were working con-ditions so dangerous that workers were killed or disabled. Stella sums this up: "The Italian immigrant may be maimed and killed in his industrial occupation without a cry and without indemnity. He may die from the 'bends' working in the caissons under the river, without protest; he can be slowly asphyxiated in crowded tenements, smothered in dangerous trades and occupations (which only the ignorant immigrant pursues, not the native American); he can contract tuberculosis in unsanitary factories and sweatshops."[67] A number of studies documented poor community conditions—overcrowding and exorbitant rents in run-down housing, as well as inadequate water and sewage facilities. In the cities such as New York, death rates from infectious dis-eases were often high.[68]

Lack of skills affected the first generation. Some were semi-skilled workers, but overall this group had the highest percentage of unskilled laborers among major im-migrant groups in this period. One study found that of the immigrants around 1900, 0.2 percent were professional workers, 12.7 percent trade or industrial workers, and 64.9 percent farmers or farm workers, with the rest being women and children.[69] Poor farmers and their families made up the majority. A study of Italian-born males in the United States found few employed in agriculture, but a high proportion employed as unskilled workers—miners, laborers, and fishermen. Many replaced the Irish in build-ing roads and railroads. Few were in clerical fields or the professions. In the domes-tic and personal service areas they were mostly barbers and restaurant workers. Italian women were employed primarily in trade.[70]

Background handicaps such as a poor command of English and lack of voca-tional skills were not the only restrictions on occupational opportunity. Discrimina-tion played an important role. Isolate, small-group, and direct and indirect institutionalized discrimination—all four types outlined in Chapter 1—held Italians back. From the first years of heavy migration the new Italian residents were, Higham asserts, "abused in public and isolated in private, cuffed in the works and pelted on the streets, fined and imprisoned on the smallest pretext, cheated of their wages, and crowded by the score into converted barns and tumble-down shanties that served as boarding houses."[71] Direct discrimination was well institutionalized; the discrimina-tion in wages was often blatant. Thus when a major New York City reservoir was built in 1895, ads for laborers listed the daily wages as $1.30 to $1.50 for "whites" and $1.15 to $1.25 for "Italians."[72] Just as important was indirect discrimination in the form of recruitment practices with a built-in bias. Informal social networks were a major means of circulating job information. Anglo-Protestant and Irish sponsors were important in job networks, protecting their own kind and discriminating against Italians.[73]

## Unions

One additional factor operating against Italians, at least in the beginning, was discrimination by worker organizations. Such discrimination kept Italians from moving into many blue-collar jobs. Some poor Italians became strikebreakers because of that discrimination and because their poverty-stricken condition led them to be hired as scabs by employers seeking to destroy unions. In their first decades in the cities southern Italians were not as active in unions as native whites.

However, some later immigrants became very active in labor unions, bringing radical working-class ideas with them from Italy. Some were union leaders and took part in major strikes, such as that in Lawrence, Massachusetts, in 1912. Joseph Ettor, Italian American organizer of the Industrial Workers of the World (IWW), was asked to assist textile factory workers, including Italian women, in their strike over reduced wages. The woolen company there refused arbitration; the ensuing strike was sometimes violent. The state militia, made up of native-born white-collar workers, was called in, and one woman striker was killed in clashes between the militia and 25,000 strikers. The 7,000 Italian Americans were the largest nationality group among the strikers, and Italian Americans were prominent leaders. By the early 1900s there was extensive Italian involvement in the union rank and file and leadership. Italians have been among the strongest union members for decades.[74]

## Upward Mobility

Progress for the great mass of Italian Americans came slowly but steadily. An early study of Italian workers found that half were still laborers in 1916, but only 31 percent fifteen years later. Data on occupation show a decline from 33 percent in unskilled positions in 1916 to 11 percent in 1931. Small-business and skilled blue-collar positions were more common by 1931.[75]

Mobility was evident, but so was the persisting differential between Italians and others. A study in Newburyport, Massachusetts, in the early 1930s revealed that Italians there were lower than other whites on the "prestige" ladder and somewhat lower on the occupational ladder. The Depression slowed advancement, but did not stop it. By 1939 Italians had begun to supplant Jews as the major group in a number of important unions of skilled workers. They had become numerous in the garment industry and in building trades. The Italians paralleled the economic pattern of the Irish, moving up from unskilled to skilled blue-collar positions in a few generations.[76]

Since the 1920s organized crime has provided better-paying jobs for some Italians in northern cities. The non-Italians, the "good citizens" of the cities, kept bootlegging, prostitution, and gambling operations going with their patronage.[77] Later, money from organized crime would flow to legitimate enterprises, just as it had earlier for other ethnic groups. Members of families successful in organized crime would move out of illegitimate enterprises altogether. This trend, according to Ianni, supports "the thesis that for Italian Americans, as for other ethnic groups, organized crime has been a way station on the road to ultimately respectable roles in American society."[78] But only a few Italian Americans ever made it up this way. The line between legitimate and illegitimate business, moreover, has often been fuzzy in this society, and not just in the case of white ethnics in organized crime. The Anglo-Saxon Protestant heroes of industry were involved in a variety of economic and political activities, including illegal ones.[79]

A few Italians became nationally prominent entrepreneurs and scientists. One was Amadeo Giannini, founder of the Bank of America. He made his fortune in California, bankrolling generations of small businesses and ranches; he even permitted his poor depositors a voice in bank management. Italians such as Di Giorgio and Gallo began to play major roles in restaurant, agricultural, and contracting businesses. Nobel Prizes were won by the scientists Fermi and Kuria. As with groups before and after them, Italians also found upward mobility in sports, as is indicated by the careers of such men as Rocky Marciano and Joe DiMaggio.[80]

## Recent Decades

By the 1950s further advances had become evident, though not to the level of major Protestant groups. One urban study in the 1950s suggested that second-generation Italian Catholics had yet to equal white Protestants in the proportion possessing higher-level white-collar jobs.[81] An examination of the occupational distribution of all second-generation Italian Americans in the 1950 and 1970 censuses reveals that these children of immigrants were less likely to be found in professional and technical jobs and clerical/sales positions than the employed population as a whole. They were more likely than the general population of workers to be employed as managers or officials. They were also more likely than the general population to be found in skilled blue-collar jobs.

In the 1980 census the occupational distribution for all Americans of Italian ancestry showed mobility. There was a slightly smaller proportion of Italian Americans in professional and technical occupations (13.7 percent) than in the population as a whole (15.4 percent), but the proportion of managers and officials was significantly larger (15.4 percent, versus 10.4 percent). The proportions of Italian Americans in the clerical/sales (30.9 percent) and crafts (13.9 percent) categories were higher than those of the U.S. population as a whole, while the proportion in operative and laborer jobs (15.8 percent) was lower. Overall, a greater percentage of Italian Americans was employed in white-collar jobs in 1980 than in the general population as a whole.[82]

Richard Alba analyzed national survey data on Italian Americans and white Anglo-Saxon Protestant Americans for the late 1970s. He found that as a group Italian Americans were less likely than Anglo-Saxon Protestants to hold professional, technical, and managerial jobs. But he also found that this occupational gap had been significantly narrowed by the third- and fourth-generation Italian American men in his sample. (Italian American women in these later generations had not yet closed the gap.) Alba predicts that as the third and fourth generations come to be the majority of Italian Americans, the differences between Italian Americans and Americans of British ancestry will disappear.[83]

Family income data are available from the Census Bureau for 1969 and 1979. In 1969 the median income of second-generation Italian American families and unrelated individuals was $11,857; the figure for all families and unrelated individuals in the United States was $9,590. In the late 1960s these children of Italian immigrants were doing better in terms of income than the typical U.S. household. The 1980 census figures for all Americans of Italian ancestry—a much larger group than that just mentioned for 1969—show a similar pattern. In the 1980 census those with Italian ancestry reported a median family income of $21,842 for the year 1979; the median income for all U.S. families was $19,917. In 1980 Italian American families, taken as a group, thus had a median income somewhat higher than that of the typical American family. In addition, the Italian American income was higher than the median income for English American families ($19,807). Italian American achievement is impressive, but ethnic stratification, with elite Protestant groups at the top of corporations, persists in the United States in the late 1980s.[84]

## Persisting Problems of Discrimination and Poverty

Discrimination against Italian Americans is still a problem at the highest levels of society: direct and indirect discrimination are barriers to higher-level managerial, administrative, and professional positions. In northeastern cities Italian Americans are heavily represented among rank-and-file workers in police, fire, and sanitation departments and in public utilities. Yet higher-level administrative positions in city departments sometimes have a low representation of Italian Americans.[85] A New York City study found that 25 percent of New Yorkers and 22 percent of the city's professional and managerial white-collar category are Italian. But these proportions have not been reflected in higher-level employment at the City University of New York. The study concludes: "In decision-making positions of Dean, Director and Chairman of the system's 18 colleges, there are only 20 Italian Americans out of a total of 504 positions."[86] A small percentage of the faculty was Italian. These faculty members tended to be at the lowest ranks. This underrepresentation of Italian Americans, particularly in top positions, persisted into the late 1980s. Hostility and discrimination are part of the explanation. The general lack of hiring at CUNY since the mid-1970s and the small number of Italian Americans who went to graduate school before the 1950s are also factors in a full explanation.

Some exclusive residential areas and top business clubs still discriminate against Italian Americans, if subtly. Into the 1970s and 1980s some important private clubs barred Italian Americans. One finds relatively few Italian Americans, such as Lee Iacocca, in the top management of major corporations. One study of the 106 largest Chicago-area corporations compared the Italian percentage in the Chicago population (4.8 percent) with the numbers of Italians among directors (1.9 percent) and officers (2.9 percent).[87] In addition to being generally underrepresented, *no* Italians were found in these positions in *most* of the major corporations studied: 79 percent of the corporations had no Italian directors at all, and 71 percent had no Italian officers. The majority of these industrial firms, retailers, utilities, transportation companies, and banks are national businesses; many are among the top national companies.

Poverty remains a problem for a portion of Italian American communities. In the 1970s Italian communities in some cities faced a growing number of poverty-stricken residents. Investigating census tracts with 50 percent or more foreign-born

Italians, one report found significant percentages of Italians living in poverty in New York City. From 15 to 18 percent of families in these tracts had incomes below the federal poverty level. Some of these poor Italian Americans were probably aged immigrants who came in the first two decades of the twentieth century. Others were more recent immigrants who came to New York in the thousands in the late 1960s and 1970s. Moreover, in the late 1980s Boston's North End, once a vigorous Italian American community of 10,000, had become a much more diverse area of older Italian residents and young non-Italian professionals who found the North End a chic place to live. The economic pressures on the older Italian Americans, especially those with modest incomes, were serious. Many were forced out by the gentrification and condo expansion brought on by the young urban professionals. The quality of life deteriorated and many longtime community residents were now living in poverty.[88]

Yet we should view such poverty in perspective. The overall picture of recent occupational and income mobility for a white ethnic group oppressed on a large scale just a few years ago is impressive. Compared with their past, the majority of Italian Americans have made strides up the socioeconomic ladder, so much so that on some indexes they are at least at parity with Anglo-Saxon Protestants taken as a group.

## EDUCATION

Organized education for Italian Americans began toward the end of the nineteenth century. Many immigrants came from areas in Italy where the poor were provided with little schooling. Half could not read or write. In the United States many adopted a pragmatic approach to education, valuing it but asking, "What is the practical value of this for jobs, for later life?" Many poor families made sacrifices to get their first child through elementary school. And the first children were expected to help, with a job, to get later children through school.

One hurdle was thrown up by the Protestant establishment. As with the Irish, Protestant educators were very concerned about the alleged corruption and cultural inferiority of Italian Americans; many sought to Americanize them as quickly as possible, teaching them Anglo-Saxon ways. Schools became pressure cookers of Americanization. Anglo-Saxon Protestant norms about health, dress, work, and language were pressed on immigrants and their children. Discrimination was a fact of life. These pressures were especially strong for second-generation children, most of whom went to public schools. (Conflict with the Irish, as well as economic problems, kept many Italian parents from sending their children to parochial schools.) These adaptation pressures did *not* mean that public schools took all poor Italian immigrants and gave them the necessary skills to make it in American society. Public schools were Procrustean beds shaped in Anglo-centric form, with the effect that some children left school rather than give in to hostile pressures.[89]

Over the next few decades Italian Americans overcame these barriers in a dramatic way. Progress could be seen in rising educational levels between the 1920s and the 1950s, and in recent decades educational attainments have been impressive. Drawing on the census for 1950 and 1970, we can evaluate the educational achievement of the children of Italian immigrants. Looking at the median years of education completed for these adults, we see this:

| | Native-born with Foreign Parent(s) | | | All U.S. Adults | |
|---|---|---|---|---|---|
| | Men | Women | | Men | Women |
| 1950 | 10.4 | 10.2 | | 9.0 | 9.6 |
| 1970 | 11.9 | 11.7 | | 10.3 | 10.9 |

In both years the native-born children of Italian immigrants to the United States had median levels of educational attainment higher than those for all persons twenty-five and over. The 1980 data are available for a much larger group—those who identified themselves in terms of Italian nationality or Italy as their country of origin in reply to a census question on ancestry. In 1980 the median number of years of school completed for all those reporting Italian ancestry was 12.3 years, versus 12.5 years for all men and women in the United States.[90]

One analysis of national opinion survey data found that by the late 1970s only 19 percent of first- and second-generation Italian Americans had college training. But 42 percent of third- and fourth-generation Italian Americans had at least a year of college. Among the men in these later generations, the percentage of college *graduates* was 29 percent, versus 13 percent for women. (The gender imbalance in college attendance was also significant.) Driven by the work ethic of hard labor and saving, many Italian American families have sacrificed to put their children through school.[91]

## RELIGION

The Catholic church has been important in the lives of Italian Americans. The male peasant in southern Italy infrequently attended mass, primarily on feast days, holy days, or other ceremonial occasions. Older women were the most active church members. There the Church was associated with an oppressive landlord system. In the United States, Protestant opposition to Catholicism was an obstacle to the free practice of religion. For Protestants, urban political machines and Catholicism conjured up images of immigrants from southern and eastern Europe. Protestant social workers in settlement houses attempted to Americanize the new Catholic population. One Protestant minister argued that "public schools, mission schools and churches will do the work to evangelize the immigrants. And it must be done, business pleads for it, patriotism demands it, social considerations require it."[92]

Many Irish Catholic churches were overwhelmed by the number of Italian immigrants. For the Italians, the Irish were too orthodox. For the Italian immigrant, religion was not an intimate part of political identity, but for the Irish, religious expression was tied to a nationalist heritage of anti-English agitation. Italian immigrants were Catholic, but not fanatically so. Saints were dear to Italians, as were religious festivals, which played an important role in cementing the Italian community.[93]

Irish pastors often saw the new parishioners in a negative light. They were not considered to be as serious as the Irish. Sometimes this tension escalated. Once ethnic parishes for Italians had developed, Italians were warned away, on occasion forcefully, from Irish parishes. Italians reciprocated. Many first-generation Italian Americans preferred to send their children to public schools rather than to the Irish-dominated parochial schools, a reaction that would not be as vigorous in later generations.[94]

Gradually, Italian Catholicism, with its distinctive festivals and ceremonies, took its place alongside Irish Catholicism. By 1900 there were fourteen Italian parishes in New York, by 1924 fifty-three, and by 1961 seventy-four.[95]

Italian Catholicism persisted. However, one study found that among seven major Catholic ethnic groups, the parents of Irish respondents were among the highest in mass attendance, while the parents of Italians, particularly fathers, were among the lowest. Italian parents were much less likely to have had any parochial schooling than any of the other groups.[96]

A study of Italian and Irish Catholics in New York City suggests the controversial conclusion that third-generation Italians may be becoming more "Irishized" in their religious practices; the data show less emphasis on the Virgin Mary, fewer masses said for deceased relatives, and more emphasis on generous contributions to the church than in earlier generations.[97] Adaptations to a multi-ethnic church may be coming most rapidly in suburban areas, where even Italian men are playing a more active role in church life. Upward mobility has brought a concern with the social milieu of the suburbs, one part of which is church life. Yet even in the suburbs Italians differ from other groups. Lopreato notes that "the Italians' tradition of secularism and skepticism toward church authority. . .has not disappeared and remains ingrained in the younger generations of the suburbs."[98] This is evident, for example, in the widespread use of banned contraceptives among Italians. The Italian immigrants and their descendants have forced the American church to take into account different ethnic brands of Catholicism.

## ASSIMILATION OR ETHNOGENESIS?

Acculturation pressures came early for southern and eastern European immigrants. Unlike the British before them, they spoke no English, nor were they familiar with the customs of Anglo-Saxon Protestant society. Concentrated in "Little Italies," Italian immigrants had to learn Italian dialects other than their own, but most could get by with minimal English. Cultural adaptation was slowed by factors other than language and community: poverty, the intention of some to return home, and hostility in the new environment.[99]

The first-generation family was in transition, cross-pressured between old Italian and new American ways. Families became less patriarchal and kin solidarity weakened somewhat, as did ties to religion. Children were more on their own. Speaking Italian at home was a point of intergenerational conflict, since the younger members felt school pressures to speak only English.[100]

A second point of intergenerational conflict was marriage. First-generation parents saw it as a family matter, while the children tended to see it as an individual matter. Given this tension, it is not surprising that second-generation families adapted in different ways. One type abandoned the old ways, changing the Italian name and moving out of an Italian residential area. This was rare. A second type rejected the old ways in part, perhaps by moving out of the Little Italy but remaining near enough to maintain close ties to the first generation. This was the largest group. A third type stayed in the old community and retained many of the old ways. In the late 1970s most Italian Americans were still first and second generation; they were thus close to the immigration experience. But the third and fourth generations were coming into their own by the 1980s. However, most still lived in large central cities or their suburbs in the North.[101]

## Structural Assimilation

Structural assimilation can be seen as movement into the secondary organizations—the businesses and bureaucracies—of the larger society, as well as into its primary social networks: social clubs, neighborhoods, and friendship circles. Structural movement of Italian Americans over the first several decades came with considerable violence and resistance from earlier groups. Positioning at the lower socioeconomic levels was a fact of life for a time.

In recent decades Italian Americans have made impressive gains in employment, income, and education and advances in politics. Alba has noted that this upward educational and occupational mobility contributed to assimilation in other areas, since in the workplace, the suburbs, and the colleges there was equal-status contact between Italian Americans and members of other white groups, contacts that created cross-ethnic friendship and kinship networks.[102]

The success of Italian Americans and other white ethnic groups is often compared with the relative lack of success of other groups, such as black Americans. Why were the Italian Americans so successful in assimilating to core-society institutions and organizations? The answer to this question lies not just in the hard work and sacrifice of several generations of Italian Americans, for those factors are also characteristic of nonwhite Americans. It lies also in the timing of Italian immigrants' entry into the United States: jobs and housing near jobs were available to the masses of Italians who arrived in the last decades of the nineteenth century and the first decades of the twentieth century. The second and third generations emerged with enough economic support from their parents to get the education they needed for the better-paying jobs opening up during and after World War II. The expansion of jobs on the middle rungs of the occupational ladder made possible the upward mobility of many white ethnic Americans. The poverty and discrimination faced by these immigrants, though very serious, was never as thoroughgoing as the extreme poverty and institutionalized racism faced by such groups as black Americans.

World War II helped in another respect as well. Wartime solidarity brought white ethnics, including Italian Americans, into core institutions, such as the ethnically integrated units of the armed forces, more rapidly. As we have noted, nonwhite minorities, such as black Americans and Japanese Americans, were kept in segregated units. After the war many Italian Americans also took advantage of the

G.I. grant programs to get college educations. At that time, nonwhites were still excluded from many white colleges.

Many Italian American families, both in the suburbs and in central cities, have remained enmeshed in kinship and friendship networks composed at least partially of other Italian Americans. Contemporary studies have revealed the persisting importance of these networks, particularly in working-class communities. In his classic 1962 study Gans wrote about an "urban village" in Boston, a blue-collar Italian American community with intimate ties between relatives and friends. Today ethnic enclaves can be found in cities, but most Italian Americans now live outside them. Primary-group ties remain strong. A study of Italian Americans in New York City found that most preferred Italian American neighborhoods and that primary-group relationships in all generations tended to be with other Italians. Structural assimilation at the primary level had not occurred for this sample of Italian Americans.[103]

A 1975 study of Italian Americans in the Bridgeport, Connecticut, metropolitan area found a continuation of close kinship ties, particularly among the first and second generations. Among the later generations there was a decline in reported closeness to distant relatives (such as aunts); closeness to parents and siblings, however, remained high. Italian Americans beyond the second generation were more likely than earlier generations to have close friends who were not relatives and not Italian. Even for the younger generations, about 80 percent of friends were Catholic. While kinship ties have remained strong, the large, extended families of the old Italian American enclaves seem to be disappearing with suburbanization. Less than a fifth in the Bridgeport sample still lived in predominantly Italian American neighborhoods.[104]

Johnson's 1985 study of Italian Americans in another northeastern city found strong family systems persisting among the several hundred people interviewed. She found that inmarried Italian Americans were more family-centered than those who had intermarried and those in a control sample of white Protestants. She also found that older Italian Americans were more likely than non-Italians to have younger relatives nearby. There were strong bonds between parents and their children. Although most of these Italian Americans had friends and co-workers who were not Italian, they spent much of their time with close relatives. Ninety-two percent of the inmarried respondents reported seeing parents daily or weekly, compared with 81 percent of the outmarried Italians and 71 percent of the non-Italian Protestants. Sixty-three percent reported seeing siblings daily, compared with 32 percent of the outmarried respondents and 12 percent of the non-Italians. Those who had intermarried had weaker ties to Italian relatives, including parents, than the inmarrieds, but most still lived near these relatives. Johnson predicts that with increasing intermarriage there will be a diminishing of this family orientation among Italian Americans.[105]

Complete marital assimilation is probably the last stage of structural assimilation. Studies of marriages in New Haven in 1870 and Chicago in 1920 found high rates of inmarriage for Italians: 94 to 98 percent of all marriages were endogamous. In subsequent decades inmarriage decreased: the New Haven figure was 77 percent by 1950. A more recent study suggests a similar pattern. In the Bridgeport study, 84 percent of the respondents reported both of their parents were of Italian ancestry. However, only 44 percent were themselves married to Italian Americans. The rate of exogamous marriage was higher for those with higher-status educational and occupational achievements. Yet there was a high level of religious endogamy: most marriages outside the Italian group were with persons raised as Catholics. Moreover, assessing 1979 census data on Italian Americans, Alba found that 43 percent of the men and 48 percent of the women had Italian American spouses, a decline of about 10 percent since the 1960s. In addition, the youngest age group, those under thirty in 1979 with unmixed Italian ancestry, had an outmarriage rate of nearly 80 percent. In addition, using opinion survey data for the late 1970s, Alba estimated that 80 percent of second-generation Italian American Catholics had married other Catholics. The rate of ethnic outmarriage seems to be increasing over time.[106]

Alba has argued that Italian Americans are becoming more structurally integrated into the mainstream of American society, that ethnicity is receding for the third and fourth generations. While ethnicity is still important for the first and second generations, a transition is under way for later generations. Intermarriage rates are relatively high in recent years, and this means that most of the younger Italian Americans are of mixed ancestry. As the younger generations succeed the earlier ones, this will mean a more assimilated Italian American group.[107]

## An Italian Identity?

Identificational assimilation involves giving up one's ethnic identity for that of the core culture. This has not happened for most Italian Americans. Interviews with Italians in one New York City study found that most saw themselves as Italians or Italian Americans. A project in Providence, Rhode Island, found that a majority of those interviewed also saw themselves as Italian, with greater pride in ethnicity being expressed among third-generation respondents than among earlier generations.[108]

A prominent historian of immigration, Marcus Lee Hansen, once argued that there is inevitably an increase in ethnic awareness in the third generation of an immigrant group; this substantially assimilated generation vigorously searches out its roots. Whether or not this theory is correct, it is true that many white ethnic Americans have by the third generation developed an ethnic consciousness that their parents and grandparents perhaps could not afford to articulate. Ironically, then, the assimilation of older Italian Americans has made it possible for younger generations to express their ethnicity more openly. Younger Italian Americans face less discrimination and stereotyping than the older generations did, and can therefore write and speak of their ethnicity more forthrightly. Indeed, this greater freedom may partially account for the ethnic resurgence found among some Italian Americans in the third and fourth generations. The current of assimilation is strong in these younger generations, but there is a vocal minority resisting assimilation and working to highlight and preserve their heritage and Italian community institutions.[109]

In addition, the distinctive Italian American neighborhoods in northern cities, the large numbers of older Italian Americans still residing in those communities, and the new Italian immigrants in the 1960s and 1980s have helped to keep alive the visible cultural characteristics of Italian Americans. Ethnic ties and accents are greater in older generations and among all generations in the persisting ethnic enclaves. Ethnicity, then, is a variable, stronger in some areas than in others. This point was accented in the study of Micaela di Leonardo on Italian Americans in California. Di Leonardo makes the important point that *where one works* shapes ethnic networks and identity. She found that working-class Italians in California no longer worked with large numbers of other Italians. They therefore expressed their ethnic identity differently from shopkeepers and independent professionals, who can stress their ethnicity in their work, often in serving an ethnic clientele. The latter groups are more likely to participate in Italian American voluntary organizations and to accent the continuing cohesiveness of the Italian American community. Participation in the economy may or may not destroy ethnic identity; it depends on the character of one's participation and on where one works.[110]

The sense of ethnic identity among Italian Americans is weakening, but it is not likely to disappear as long as there is significant stereotyping and discrimination against Italian Americans in the larger society. Italian Americans remain underrepresented at the higher economic and political levels of U.S. society, in spite of a recent appointment to the Supreme Court and a vice-presidential nominee in 1984. Even an author who has written about the "twilight of ethnicity" among Italian Americans has noted, "Because networks of sponsorship tend to perpetuate the ethnic patterns of the past, elite levels register only slowly the ethnic changes at lower levels, and the Italian-American gap in representation is unlikely to close anytime soon."[111]

The ethnogenesis model of Andrew Greeley (see pp. 28–29) seems to fit the Italian experience. Italians came to the United States with significant differences from the dominant British group, but they shared some historical background and a Christian tradition with that group. Through interaction in public schools and the influence of mass media, the gap narrowed substantially, but by no means completely. Italian Americans became similar in some ways to the host culture, but in other ways they retained their distinctiveness. Because of their heritage, together with segregation and strong community and kinship networks, a distinctive American ethnic group was spawned over time. No longer an Italy-centered group dominated by its heritage, neither has it simply become British Protestant American or simply American. Substantial adaptation without complete assimilation currently characterizes Italian Americans.

## SUMMARY

Today most descendants of the Italian immigrants who entered around the turn of the century live in cities on the East Coast and in the Midwest. Most remain Catholic. These Americans play an important role in the United States. We have focused primarily on the descendants of the 1880–1920 and earlier waves of migration, examining the beginnings of this migration and tracing its impact. Poverty and hard working conditions greeted these immigrants. They were ill prepared for the intense nativist attacks, which falsely stereotyped them as an inferior, immoral, and corrupt people. IQ testing in this early period seemed to be aimed at proving their inferiority.

The Mafia myth further stigmatized their communities. Even violent attacks were suffered.

Political avenues were closed for a time; the economy consigned them to low-paying jobs; schools tried to make carbon-copy Anglo-Saxon Protestants out of them. Yet in spite of these problems the immigrants and their descendants persevered and prospered. After World War II they began to make their mark in politics, the economy, and education. Their mobility has made them another American success story, although a considerable price was exacted for that success. Nonetheless, Italian Americans have retained a significant degree of ethnic distinctiveness.

## NOTES

1. From *The New York Times*, June 17, 1970, p. 31. © 1970 by the New York Times Company. Reprinted by permission.
2. Richard Gambino, *Blood of My Blood* (Garden City, N.Y.: Doubleday, Anchor Books, 1975), p. 344.
3. Giovanni Schiavo, *The Italians in America before the Civil War* (New York: Vigo Press, 1934), pp. 55–180.
4. Ibid., p. 135.
5. U.S. Department of Justice, Immigration and Naturalization Service, *Annual Report* (Washington, D.C.: U.S. Government Printing Office, 1973), pp. 52–54. Figures for 1820 to 1867 represent alien passengers arrived; for 1868–1891 and 1895–1897, immigrant aliens arrived; for 1892–1894 and 1898–1973, immigrant aliens admitted.
6. Schiavo, *The Italians in America*, p. 204.
7. Carl Wittke, *We Who Built America*, rev. ed. (Cleveland: Case Western Reserve University Press, 1964), p. 441.
8. Humbert S. Nelli, *The Italians in Chicago, 1880–1930* (New York: Oxford University Press, 1970), p. 5.
9. Grazia Dore, "Some Social and Historical Aspects of Italian Emigration to America," in *The Italians*, ed. Francesco Cordasco and Eugene Bucchioni (Clifton, N.J.: Augustus M. Kelley, 1974), p. 7.
10. Joseph Lopreato, *Italian Americans* (New York: Random House, 1970), pp. 23–27; John S. MacDonald, "Agricultural Organization, Migration, and Labor Militancy in Rural Italy," *Economic History Review*, 2d ser., 16 (1963–1964): 61–75. I am indebted to Phylis Cancilla Martinelli for her useful suggestions concerning the sections that follow. I draw on her suggestions in this paragraph and in the rest of this chapter.
11. Luciano J. Iorizzo and Salvatore Mondello, *The Italian-Americans* (New York: Twayne, 1971), pp. 57–59; Lopreato, *Italian Americans*, p. 36.
12. Antonia Stella, *Some Aspects of Italian Immigration to the United States*, reprint ed. (San Francisco: R & E Associates, 1970), p. 33.
13. Rudolph J. Vecoli, "*Contadini* in Chicago," in *Divided Society*, ed. Colin Greer (New York: Basic Books, 1974), p. 220.
14. Data cited in William Petersen, *Population*, 2d ed. (New York: Macmillan, 1969), p. 260.
15. Stella, *Some Aspects of Italian Immigration*, p. 15; Lopreato, *Italian Americans*, pp. 14–16.
16. John Higham, *Strangers in the Land*, rev. ed. (New York: Atheneum, 1975), pp. 312–24.
17. See Stanley Lieberson, *Ethnic Patterns in American Cities* (Glencoe, Ill.: Free Press, 1963), pp. 209–18.
18. William F. Whyte, *Street Corner Society*, 2d ed. (Chicago: University of Chicago Press, 1955), pp. 272–73; Walter Firey, *Land Use in Central Boston* (Cambridge: Harvard University Press, 1947), pp. 187–88; Wittke, *We Who Built America*, p. 446.
19. Firey, *Land Use in Central Boston*, p. 193; Paul J. Campisi, "Ethnic Family Patterns: The Italian Family in the United States," in *The Italians*, ed. Cordasco and Bucchioni, pp. 311–14; Lopreato, *Italian Americans*, pp. 51–53; Whyte, *Street Corner Society*, p. 274.

20. Eliot Lord, John J. D. Trenor, and Samuel J. Barrows, *The Italian in America,* reprint ed. (San Francisco: R. & E Associates, 1970), pp. 17–18.

21. Quoted in Iorizzo and Mondello, *The Italian-Americans,* p. 64.

22. Kenneth L. Roberts, *Why Europe Leaves Home,* excerpted in "Kenneth L. Roberts and the Threat of Mongrelization in America, 1922," in *In Their Place,* ed. Lewis H. Carlson and George A. Colburn (New York: John Wiley, 1972), p. 312.

23. Mary F. Matthews, "The Role of the Public School in the Assimilation of the Italian Immigrant Child in New York City, 1900–1914," in *The Italian Experience in the United States,* ed. Silvano Tomasi and M. H. Engel (New York: Center for Migration Studies, 1970), p. 127; Stella, *Some Aspects of Italian Immigration,* p. 54.

24. Stella, *Some Aspects of Italian Immigration,* p. 38.

25. Cited in Leon J. Kamin, *The Science and Politics of I.Q.* (New York: John Wiley, 1974), pp. 15–16.

26. Ibid., pp. 16–19.

27. Carl C. Brigham, *A Study of American Intelligence* (Princeton, N.J.: Princeton University Press, 1923), especially pp. 124–25, 177–210. Later Brigham recanted.

28. See Woodrow Wilson, *History of the American People* (New York: Harpers, 1901), 5:212–14.

29. See Kamin, *The Science and Politics of I.Q.,* p. 30.

30. Quoted in E. Digby Baltzell, *The Protestant Establishment* (New York: Random House, Vintage Books, 1966), p. 30.

31. Quoted in ibid.

32. Iorizzo and Mondello, *The Italian-Americans,* pp. 35–36.

33. Quoted in Nelli, *The Italians in Chicago, 1880–1930,* p. 126.

34. Stella, *Some Aspects of Italian Immigration,* pp. 60–61, 73.

35. Gambino, *Blood of My Blood,* pp. 293–98; Lopreato, *Italian Americans,* p. 126; Nelli, *The Italians in Chicago, 1880–1930,* pp. 154–55.

36. Reported in Francis A. Ianni, *A Family Business* (New York: Russell Sage Foundation, 1972), p. 194.

37. Dwight C. Smith, Jr., *The Mafia Mystique* (New York: Basic Books, 1975), pp. 289ff.

38. Ibid., 324, Gambino, *Blood of My Blood,* pp. 300–301.

39. Robert Lichter and Linda Lichter, "Italian-American Characters in Television Entertainment" (report prepared for the Commission for Social Justice, Order of Sons of Italy, May 1982).

40. Micaela di Leonardo, *The Varieties of Ethnic Experience* (Ithaca, N.Y.: Cornell University Press, 1984), pp. 160–161.

41. William F. Whyte, "Race Conflicts in the North End of Boston," *New England Quarterly* 12 (December 1939): 626; Iorizzo and Mondello, *The Italian-Americans,* pp. 35, 66.

42. Luciano J. Iorizzo, "The Padrone and Immigrant Distribution," in *The Italian Experience in the United States,* ed. Tomasi and Engel, pp. 49–51.

43. Gambino, *Blood of My Blood,* p. 119; Higham, *Strangers in the Land,* p. 169.

44. Gambino, *Blood of My Blood,* p. 118, 280–81.

45. Ibid., pp. 104, 119; Higham, *Strangers in the Land,* p. 90; see also Andrew F. Rolle, *The American Italian* (Belmont, Calif.: Wadsworth, 1972).

46. See, for example, William Young and David Kaiser, *Postmortem* (Amherst: University of Massachusetts Press, 1985). See also Gambino, *Blood of My Blood,* pp. 120–21.

47. Iorizzo and Mondello, *The Italian-Americans,* p. 207; Gerald D. Suttles, *The Social Order of the Slum* (Chicago: University of Chicago Press, 1968), pp. 102–3.

48. Richard Krickus, *Pursuing the American Dream* (Garden City, N.Y.: Doubleday, Anchor Books, 1976), p. 280.

49. Cited in Mark R. Levy and Michael S. Kramer, *The Ethnic Factor* (New York: Simon & Schuster, 1972), p. 174. Other data on racist attitudes can be found in Andrew M. Greeley, *Why Can't They Be Like Us?* (New York: Dutton, 1971), pp. 67ff.

50. Norman M. Bradburn, Seymour Sudman, and Galen L. Gockel, *Racial Integration in American Neighborhoods* (Chicago: National Opinion Research Center, 1970), pp. 147–49.

51. Schiavo, *The Italians in America before the Civil War,* pp. 163–66.

52. Nelli, *The Italians in Chicago, 1880–1930*, pp. 75–76; Wittke, *We Who Built America*, p. 447; Lopreato, *Italian Americans*, pp. 113–17; Giovanni Schiavo, *Italian American History* (New York: Vigo Press, 1947), 1:499–504.

53. Rolle, *The American Italian*, p. 85; William F. Whyte, *Street Corner Society*, p. 276; Samuel Lubell, *The Future of American Politics*, 2d ed. (Garden City, N.Y.: Doubleday, Anchor Books, 1955), p. 70; Lopreato, *Italian Americans*, p. 114.

54. Joel H. Spring, *Education and the Rise of the Corporate State* (Boston: Beacon Press, 1972), pp. 86–87.

55. Herbert J. Gans, *The Urban Villagers* (Glencoe, Ill.: Free Press, 1962), pp. 285–87.

56. See Gambino, *Blood of My Blood*, p. 117.

57. Salvatore J. LaGumina, "Case Studies of Ethnicity and Italo-American Politicians," in *The Italian Experience in the United States,* ed. Tomasi and Engel, p. 147; Krickus, *Pursuing the American Dream*, pp. 174–81.

58. Wittke, *We Who Built America*, p. 450; Iorizzo and Mondello, *The Italian-Americans*, pp. 200–205, 208; Gambino, *Blood of My Blood*, p. 316.

59. Richard Alba, *Italian Americans* (Englewood Cliffs, N.J.: Prentice-Hall, 1985), pp. 78–81.

60. See Lubell, *The Future of American Politics*, pp. 83–84; and John R. Schmidhauser, "The Justices of the Supreme Court: A Collective Portrait," *Midwest Journal of Political Science* 3 (February 1959): 19–20.

61. Lubell, *The Future of American Politics*, p. 70; LaGumina, "Case Studies of Ethnicity and Italo-American Politics," p. 145.

62. Alba, *Italian Americans,* p. 143. See also Andrew M. Greeley, *Ethnicity in the United States* (New York: John Wiley, 1974), pp. 94–101.

63. Krickus, *Pursuing the American Dream*, p. 92; Sylvia Pellini Macphee, *Changing Perspectives of Italian Americans* (Cambridge, Mass.: Center for Community Economic Development, 1974), pp. 10–15.

64. Iorizzo, "The Padrone and Immigrant Distribution," p. 43.

65. Nelli, *The Italians in Chicago, 1880–1930*, pp. 56–60; anonymous, "The Philanthropists' View of the Italian in America," in *The Italian in America: The Progressive View*, ed. Lydio F. Tomasi (New York: Center for Migration Studies, 1972), p. 79. This article is reprinted by Tomasi from *Charities*, an early journal of social and settlement workers.

66. Iorizzo and Mondello, *The Italian-Americans*, pp. 138–58; Nelli, *The Italians in Chicago, 1880–1930*, pp. 64–66.

67. Stella, *Some Aspects of Italian Immigration*, p. 94.

68. Nelli, *The Italians in Chicago, 1880–1930,* pp. 13–14; Antonio Stella. "Tuberculosis and the Italians in the United States," in *The Italians*, ed. Cordasco and Bucchioni, pp. 449ff.

69. Gambino, *Blood of My Blood*, p. 85; Leonard Covello, "The Influence of Southern Italian Family Mores upon the School Situation in America," in *The Italians*, ed. Cordasco and Bucchioni, p. 513.

70. Lord, Trenor, and Barrows, *The Italian in America*, pp. 16–19; E P. Hutchinson, *Immigrants and Their Children, 1850–1950* (New York: John Wiley, 1956), pp. 137–38.

71. Higham, *Strangers in the Land*, p. 48.

72. Gambino, *Blood of My Blood*, p. 77.

73. Stephan Thernstrom, *The Other Bostonians* (Cambridge: Harvard University Press, 1973), p. 161.

74. Elizabeth Gurley Flynn. "The Lawrence Textile Strike," in *America's Working Women*, ed. R. Baxandall, L. Gordon, and S. Reverby (New York: Random House, Vintage Books, 1976), pp. 194–99; Nelli, *The Italians in Chicago, 1880–1930*, pp. 78–85; Gambino, *Blood of My Blood*, p. 115–17.

75. John J. d'Alesandre, "Occupational Trends of Italians in New York City," *Italy-America Monthly* 2 (February 1935): 11–21.

76. W. Lloyd Warner and Leo Srole, *The Social Systems of American Ethnic Groups* (New Haven: Yale University Press, 1945), pp. 96–97; Gambino, *Blood of My Blood*, p. 101; Wittke, *We Who Built America*, p. 443.

77. Nelli, *The Italians in Chicago, 1880–1930*, pp. 211–14; Smith, *The Mafia Mystique*, p. 322.

78. Ianni, *A Family Business*, p. 193.

79. Smith, *The Mafia Mystique*, p. 323.

80. Rolle, *The American Italians, pp. 89–93.*

81. Thernstrom, *The Other Bostonians*, p. 171.

82. U.S. Bureau of the Census, *U.S. Census of Population, 1950: Special Reports—Nativity and Parentage*, P-E No. 3A, 1954, p. 155; U.S. Bureau of the Census, *U.S. Census of Population, 1970: Subject Reports—National Origin and Language*, PC(2)-1A, 1973, p. 166; U.S. Bureau of the Census, *U.S. Census of Population, 1980: General Social and Economic Characteristics*, PC 80-1-C1, 1983, p. 174; U.S. Bureau of the Census, *U.S. Census of Population, 1950: Vol. II, Characteristics of the Population,* Part 1, United States Summary, 1953, p. 102; U.S. Bureau of the Census, *U.S. Census of Population, 1970: General Social and Economic Characteristics*, Final Report PC(1)-C1, United States Summary, 1972, p. 392; U.S. Bureau of the Census, *Statistical Abstract of the United States: 1984* (104th ed.), 1983, p. 416.

83. Alba, *Italian Americans*, pp. 126–128.

84. U.S. Bureau of the Census, *U.S. Census of Population, 1970: Subject Reports—National Origin and Language*, PC(2)-1A, 1973, p. 167; U.S. Bureau of the Census, *U.S. Census of Population, 1980: General Social and Economic Characteristics*, PC80-1-C1, 1983, p. 177; U.S. Bureau of the Census, *U.S. Census of Population, 1970: General Social and Economic Characteristics,* Final Report PC(1)-C1, United States Summary, 1972, p. 368; U.S. Bureau of the Census, *U.S. Census of Population, 1980: General Social and Economic Characteristics*, PC80-10C1, 1983, p. 21.

85. Gambino, *Blood of My Blood*, p. 89.

86. *National Center for Urban Ethnic Affairs Newsletter* 1, no. 5:8.

87. National Center for Urban Ethnic Affairs, "The Representation of Poles, Italians, Latins, and Blacks in the Executive Suites of Chicago's Largest Corporations," *Minority Report*, no date, pp. 2–5.

88. Congress of Italian-American Organizations, *A Portrait of the Italian-American Community in New York City* (New York, 1975), pp. 7–10, 49–51; "Ferraro's Mixed Blessing," *Newsweek*, October 1, 1984, p. 12.

89. Lawrence A. Cremin, *The Transformation of the School* (New York: Knopf, 1961), pp. 67–68; Colin Greer, *The Great School Legend* (New York: Basic Books, 1972), pp. 3–6.

90. U.S. Bureau of the Census, *U.S. Census of Population, 1950: Special Reports—Nativity and Parentage*, P-E No. 3A, 1954, p. 155; U.S. Bureau of the Census, *U.S. Census of Population, 1970: Subject Reports—National Origin and Language*, PC(2)-1A, 1973, p. 165; U.S. Bureau of the Census, *U.S. Census of Population, 1980: General Social and Economic Characteristics*, PC 80-1-C1, 1983, p. 172; U.S. Bureau of the Census, *U.S. Census of Population, 1950: Vol. II, Characteristics of the Population,* Part 1, United States Summary, 1953, p. 96; U.S. Bureau of the Census, *U.S. Census of Population, 1970: General Social and Economic Characteristics*, Final Report PC(1)-C1, United States Summary, 1972, p. 368; U.S. Bureau of the Census, *U.S. Census of Population, 1980: General Social and Economic Characteristics*, United States Summary, PC80-1-C1, 1983, p. 21. The 1950 ancestry figures are for persons fourteen and older.

91. Alba, *Italian Americans*, pp. 120–21.

92. Quoted in Silvano M. Tomasi, "The Ethnic Church and the Integration of Italian Immigrants in the United States," in *The Italian Experience in the United States,* ed. Tomasi and Engel, p. 168.

93. Rudolph J. Vecoli, *"Contadini* in Chicago: A Critique of *The Uprooted,"* in the *The Aliens,* ed. Leonard Dinnerstein and Frederic C. Jaher (New York: Appleton-Century-Crofts, 1970), p. 226; Harold J. Abramson, *Ethnic Diversity in Catholic America* (New York: John Wiley, 1973), pp. 136–39.

94. Tomasi, "The Ethnic Church," p. 167.

95. Ibid., pp. 187–88; Nelli, *The Italians in Chicago, 1880–1930*, p. 195.

96. Abramson, *Ethnic Diversity in Catholic America*, pp. 111–15.

97. Nicholas J. Russo, "Three Generations of Italians in New York City: Their Religious Acculturation," in *The Italian Experience in the United States,* ed. Tomasi and Engel, pp. 200–206.

98. Lopreato, *Italian Americans*, p. 93. Compare Gambino, *Blood of My Blood*, p. 239.

99. Covello, "The Influence of Southern Italian Family Mores," p. 515.

100. Paul J. Campisi, "Ethnic Family Patterns: The Italian Family in the United States," *American Journal of Sociology* 53 (May 1948): 443–49; Covello, "The Influence of Southern Italian Family Mores," pp. 525–30.

101. Irvin L. Child, *Italian or American?* (New Haven: Yale University Press, 1943) (an important excerpt from this book can be found in *The Italians*, ed. Cordasco and Bucchioni, pp. 321–36); Alba, *Italian Americans*, p. 114.

102. Alba, *Italian Americans*, p. 166.

103. Herbert Gans, *The Urban Villagers*, rev. ed. (New York: Free Press, 1982), pp. 412–13; Greeley, *Why Can't They Be Like Us?*, p. 77. See also Phylis Cancilla Martinelli, "Beneath the Surface: Ethnic Communities in Phoenix, Arizona," (paper, Arizona State University, 1980).

104. James A. Crispino, *The Assimilation of Ethnic Groups: The Italian Case* (New York: Center for Migration Studies, 1980), pp. 80–86.

105. Colleen L. Johnson, *Growing Up and Growing Old in Italian American Families* (New Brunswick, N.J.: Rutgers University Press, 1985), pp. 221–28.

106. Francis X. Femminella and Jill S. Quadagno, "The Italian American Family," in *Ethnic Families in America*, ed. Charles H. Mindel and Robert W. Habenstein (New York: Elsevier, 1976), pp. 74–75; Ruby Jo Reeves Kennedy, "Single or Triple Melting Pot? Intermarriage in New Haven, 1870–1950," *American Journal of Sociology* 58 (July 1952): 56–59; Nelli, *The Italians in Chicago, 1880–1930*, p. 196; Crispino, *The Assimilation of Ethnic Groups*, p. 105; Alba, *Italian Americans*, pp. 146–47.

107. Alba, *Italian Americans*, pp. 159–62.

108. P. J. Gallo, *Ethnic Alienation* (Rutherford, N.J.: Fairleigh Dickinson University Press, 1974), p. 194; John M. Goering, "The Emergence of Ethnic Interests: A Case of Serendipity," *Social Forces* 49 (March 1971): 381–82.

109. Marcus Lee Hansen, "The Third Generation," in *Children of the Uprooted*, ed. Oscar Handlin (New York: Harper & Row, Pub. 1966), pp. 255–71; Krickus, *Pursuing the American Dream*, p. 362.

110. di Leonardo, *The Varieties of Ethnic Experience*, p. 156.

111. Alba, *Italian Americans*, p. 162.

# CHAPTER 6

# *Jewish Americans*

Jews have been the scapegoats for the hatreds of dominant peoples around the globe for thousands of years. From the Egyptian and Roman persecutions in ancient times, to the massacres and expulsions in Spain in the late 1400s, to the brutal pogroms of the Russian czar in the 1880s, to the German Nazi massacres, Jews might be regarded as the most consistently and widely persecuted ethnic group in world history. Residing in many lands, the constantly harassed ancestors of Jewish Americans forged distinctive traditions. Indeed, the intellectual pillars of modern civilization—Karl Marx, Sigmund Freud, and Albert Einstein—were Jewish.

Under the ancient law of the rabbis, a Jew is a person whose mother is Jewish—a definition of ethnicity with an accent on ancestry. Many Jewish writers define Jews as those who identify themselves as Jews. In the last century Jews have been regarded by some non-Jews as a religious group, a racial group, and an ethnic group. They have been socially defined on the basis of real or alleged physical or cultural characteristics. In the early 1900s, in the 1930s and 1940s, and even to the present, they have been considered by some non-Jews to be a biologically inferior "race." Today Jews are generally considered by social scientists to be an ethnic group, a group distinguished by others and by themselves primarily on the basis of cultural characteristics, including Jewish religion or identity.[1]

## MIGRATION

### From 1500 to World War II

Jewish immigration to the United States can be divided into three periods: (1) the Sephardic (Spanish and Portuguese) migration, (2) the central European migration, and (3) the eastern European migration. The Sephardic migration was triggered by late-fifteenth- and sixteenth-century oppression in Europe. A Spanish decree forced thousands of Jews to emigrate or convert on penalty of death. A chief sponsor of Columbus at the Spanish court was Luis de Santangel, a Jew who had been converted to Christianity. Santangel and his associates, sometimes called Marranos, were doubtless hoping that these voyages would open up lines of escape for Jews. In the 1500s and 1600s a few thousand Sephardic immigrants came to the European colonies in North America. By 1820 there were five thousand in the United States.[2]

Between 1800 and the 1840s European persecution of Jews increased. Letters espousing the economic prosperity of the United States attracted migrants; many settled in the Midwest. They were peddlers, merchants, and craftworkers such as tailors and shoemakers. Synagogues and other institutions were adapted to the English core culture. By 1880 eight of every ten Jewish Americans were of German descent. The size of the Jewish population grew from 15,000 in the early 1840s to more than 250,000 by 1880.[3]

The third major group of immigrants were eastern European. By the 1880s and 1890s waves of Russians, Poles, Rumanians, and other eastern Europeans had migrated west. The overwhelming majority came from Russia or Russian-controlled areas. Direct discrimination in education and the economy, as well as government-sponsored killings of Jews, generated emigration from Poland and western Russia. In the 1880s a chief adviser to the Russian czar, Alexander III, recommended that the official "Jewish solution" should be to force one-third to leave the country, one-third to convert to Christianity, and one-third to starve or be killed.[4]

This Jewish immigration from 1881 to 1920 has been estimated at more than two million. Most migration occurred between 1890 and 1914 and in the five years following World War I. Unlike the German Jews, these eastern European Jews constituted a large proportion of the larger immigrant group of which they were a part. Also unlike the Germans, they were concentrated in a few destinations—the large East Coast cities. As peddlers, street vendors, and unskilled workers they became part of the growing urban working class. These new immigrants brought with them a distinctive language and culture (both Yiddish), an Orthodox Jewish religious orientation, and an emphasis on scholarship and literature.[5]

After the restrictive 1924 Immigration Act, an act aimed at limiting eastern and southern European immigration, the numbers began to decline rapidly. Between 1921 and 1936 fewer than 400,000 Jews entered the country. During the Great Depression there was a sharp reduction in the number of immigrants coming from all parts of the globe. President Franklin Roosevelt's administration did permit some increase in Jewish refugees from Germany, yet Roosevelt, and particularly his state department, did less than they could have to allow persecuted Jews to flee to the United States. The obstacles to Jewish immigration were a scandal: the U.S. State Department adopted the callous policy of requiring affidavits of financial solvency and good character and used visa regulations to slow the flow of refugees from the threat of Hitler's death camps. And in June 1940 the State Department put an end to most immigration from Germany and central Europe. This action left unused the remainder of the legal quotas of 20,000 to 25,000; in effect these unfilled quotas represent lives lost to extermination by Hitler because of American immigration policy.

Among the 150,000 refugees who did enter between 1935 and the early 1940s were many talented people. One-fifth were professionals, and many of the rest had trade skills. They set up businesses from New York to San Francisco; contrary to the prevailing stereotype, they were no burden on their new homeland. Among these refugees were some of the world's most talented scientists and artists, including Albert Einstein, Leo Szilard, and Edward Teller—who played a critical role in the U.S. nuclear research program—and scholars such as Eric Fromm, Herbert Marcuse, and Bruno Bettelheim.

## World War II to the Present

After the arrival of thousands of postwar refugees, Jewish migration again tapered off significantly. By the 1950s and 1960s an estimated 8,000 were entering each year. However, by the 1970s a significant number of Israelis—estimated at 100,000 or more—had come to the United States. Large numbers were "illegals." Between 1966 and 1982 nearly 250,000 Soviet Jews left their country. Prior to 1975 most went to Israel, but by the late 1970s most were coming to the United States. By 1980 nearly 100,000 had entered. The cost of helping the immigrants was borne largely by the American Jewish community. In a recent survey most of these immigrants said they were proud of their Jewish heritage and had left the Soviet Union because of fear that they or their children would be victims of anti-Semitism. In the late 1980s the American Jewish population was estimated at six million—half the world's total Jewish population. After World War II many Jewish Americans participated in the migration from cities to suburbs in the United States. Even with some shift to the Sunbelt in the 1980s, a majority of Jewish Americans today reside in the East in the larger cities and their suburbs, with a large number in the New York City area.[6]

By the early twentieth century the various American Jewish streams were blending into one ethnic group. The 1840s' German immigrants coalesced with earlier groups, substantially acculturating to the core culture within a generation or two. Then came the eastern Europeans. This new group of Russians and others eventually coalesced and were called "Russians," a group predominantly Yiddish in culture. Rosenberg has argued that in each case the earlier immigrant groups had already become American Jews by the time of the next group; that is, they had given up much of their European nationality character by the time the new Jewish group came in. This made for easier absorption of later immigrants. The synagogue sometimes brought German and eastern Europeans together; fraternal and communal organizations played an important role in mutual adaptation. Increasing contacts, as well as the intensifying attacks on Jews at home and abroad, eventually brought increasing ethnic homogeneity.[7]

As Herberg notes, by the 1920s "American Jewry, despite all internal divisions, already constituted a well-defined ethnic group."[8] However, this blending of Jewish American groups did not eradicate the distinctiveness of German and East European

Jews. Some distinctiveness in region of residence and religious affiliation persisted into the 1970s and 1980s.

## STEREOTYPING AND PREJUDICE

No white group in history has suffered under a broader range of stereotypes for a longer period than have the Jews. For centuries, Jews have been targets for intensely held prejudices. This complex of hostile attitudes has its own name—*anti-Semitism*. Anti-Semitism has rocketed tragic political movements into prominent positions in history. The term has been used to refer both to attitudes and to discriminatory behavior.

For almost two thousand years Jews have been cursed and killed because they were seen as "Christ killers." From the earliest Christian period to the present, the writings and liturgies of Christendom have been rife with anti-Semitism. Jews as a group have been held by many Christians as culpable for the death of their Christ and as deserving of death for their uniqueness. (Ironically, Jesus himself was a Jew.)

Christian groups in the North American colonies, beginning in the earliest period, brought the "Christ killers" view with them. Ministers and priests passed along these views to each new generation.[9] As late as the 1970s and 1980s, teaching materials used in a variety of Protestant and Catholic groups showed a significant amount of stereotyping, including stories of "the wicked Jews" who killed Christ.

Anti-Semitism has accented a number of other themes. One cliché is that the Jews are major examples of economic deviousness. Jewish Americans are stereotyped in different terms than blacks and Native Americans, who are frequently stereotyped as unintelligent. Jews have been seen as *too* hardworking, *too* intelligent, *too* crafty. McWilliams has suggested that this stereotype developed to rationalize the Jews' relative success as "middlemen" merchants and brokers. Because of rampant discrimination, Jewish Americans sought the crevices—marginal businesses—where they were allowed to operate. Success was downgraded as having been gained by cheating. By the 1850s, "to Jew" had become a phrase meaning "to cheat." The painful burden of this stereotyping lingers.[10]

After the Civil War the stereotype developed of Jewish Americans as social climbers. Parodies in the media of the day, including vaudeville, put clumsy Jewish figures speaking inflected English in high-society positions. By the 1880s newspaper and magazine cartoons were caricaturing Jewish Americans as long-nosed, garishly dressed merchants speaking in broken English.

Though some early leaders, such as John Adams, wrote tributes to the achievements of Jewish Americans, positive comments did not predominate in the next few generations. Even Adams's distinguished grandson, the intellectual Henry Adams, upset with the rapidly industrializing United States, was anti-Semitic. For him the Jew was a symbol of the money grubbing world he disliked. He saw certain financial operations as a Jewish conspiracy. These themes have persisted to the present day. Even as late as the 1970s, a Joint Chiefs of Staff head was quoted as saying, "They own, you know, the banks in the country, the newspapers; you just look where the Jewish money is in the country."[11]

## The Politics of Stereotyping

By the late nineteenth century Jewish Americans were seen as radicals with a genius for organizing. In the decades to follow, Jewish people would be stereotyped as radicals or "communist" sympathizers. In the 1900–1920 period political cartoons with these themes appeared in the mass media. A common theme was that Jews were taking over the government. By 1941 hatred of the Jews had risen to a fever pitch, with Jews being falsely accused of bringing the United States into war with Germany; the accusations came from members of Congress, the press, and prominent citizens. After that war a *Fortune* magazine poll found that three-quarters of those who felt some groups had more power than was good for the country's economy cited the Jews; the corresponding figure for a question on the country's political sphere was about half.[12] Subtle stereotypes of Jewish Americans cropped up in attacks by prominent politicians on the "eastern liberal" press as late as the 1980s.

In the early 1920s Brigham's book on IQ testing and immigrant soldiers accented not only the low scores of Italians but also the lower-than-average scores of the Russians, most of whom were probably Jewish Americans. Brigham argued that the test data disproved arguments for the high intelligence of Jewish Americans and supported the superiority of British Americans.[13]

## Modern Anti-Semitism

More recent surveys have confirmed the persistence of anti-Semitism among U.S. citizens. During World War II the famous book *The Authoritarian Personality* reported substantial support among samples of Californians for stereotypes: the Jew as clannish, the Jew as parasitic, the Jew as revolutionary. In 1980 the president of a major Baptist organization publicly stated that God does not hear the prayers of Jews, and a leader of the conservative Moral Majority repeated the age-old stereotype that Jews had a "supernatural" ability to make money. A 1981 poll of non-Jewish Americans found that many still harbored stereotypes of Jews. Fifty-three percent thought Jews always liked to be at the head of things. Thirty-three percent thought Jews engaged in shady business practices, and 22 percent believed Jews were dishonest. Although anti-Semitism was clearly apparent in these responses, it had declined since polls in the 1960s. Attitudinal anti-Semitism seems to have declined over the last several decades. Another 1981 poll, this one by the Gallup organization, found that 23 percent of non-Jewish Americans were prejudiced against Jews, but that older respondents were twice as likely to be prejudiced as younger respondents. Given this cohort pattern, one would expect a further decline in general American anti-Semitism as the younger generations mature.[14]

# VIOLENT OPPRESSION AND CONFLICT

Many eastern European immigrants had fled pogroms directed at Jewish communities. A *pogrom*, from Yiddish-Russian words for "destruction," is an organized massacre conducted with the aid of government officials. This and similar experiences led to an "oppression mentality" for many Jewish Americans, the acute awareness that anti-Jewish oppression "can happen again."

In the 1880s Jewish American merchants in the South suffered violent attacks from poor non-Jewish farmers who blamed them for economic crises. In the 1890s the farms and homes of Jewish American landlords and merchants were burned in Mississippi. In the early 1900s there were riots against Jewish American workers brought into factories in New Jersey. Just before World War I in Georgia, Leo Frank, the Jewish part-owner of a pencil factory, was convicted of killing a girl employee, though evidence pointed elsewhere. After being beaten up in prison, he was taken from the prison hospital and lynched by an angry crowd.[15]

Southern demagogues such as Tom Watson used the Frank case to fuel the flames of anti-Semitism for political purposes. About this time the Ku Klux Klan was revived; it waged violence against blacks, Jews, and Catholics. In the 1920s and 1930s crosses were burned on Jewish property; synagogues were desecrated and vandalized. On occasion, immigrants fought back. In the 1920s immigrant crowds, including Jews and Catholics, stoned or otherwise attacked parades and gatherings of the Ku Klux Klan members in Ohio and New Jersey.[16]

## Organized Anti-Semitism and Vandalism

Between 1932 and 1941 the number of openly anti-Semitic regional and nationwide organizations grew from only one to well over a hundred. Two dozen were large-scale operations holding numerous anti-Semitic rallies, some drawing thousands. Millions of anti-Semitic leaflets, pamphlets, and newspapers were distributed. Among the more prominent groups were the German-American Bund and the Silver Shirts. Father Charles Coughlin's organizations, the National Union for Social Justice and the Christian Front, became active in anti-Jewish agitation in the 1930s.[17]

Early in 1940 the FBI arrested more than a dozen members of a Christian Front group reportedly intending to kill "Jews and Communists, 'to knock off about a dozen Congressmen,' and to seize post offices, the Customs House, and armories in New York. In the homes of the group were found 18 cans of cordite, 18 rifles, and 5,000 rounds of ammunition."[18] Coughlin himself did not openly advocate violence, but he defended those who did. From the 1930s to the present, fascist organizations have attacked Jewish Americans and their property.

One important factor in anti-Jewish attacks was the increase in anti-Semitism in Nazi Germany. Germans had long portrayed their Jewish neighbors in negative stereotypes. This horror story began with restrictions on Jews in the Nazi sphere, soon to be followed by deportation to forced-labor camps and extermination by starvation, epidemics, and mass killings. These days of infamy would be etched in the minds of

Jews and non-Jews alike. An estimated six million Jews died in many countries. Extermination and forced migration reduced the Jewish population in countries such as Poland and Germany to 10 percent of the former numbers. The term adopted by American Jews to describe these horrors is *Holocaust*. The oppression mentality was invigorated not only by newspaper reports of European refugees but also by the growing knowledge that the United States government was actually aiding these actions in Germany, at first by continuing normal economic and diplomatic relations and later by turning its back on thousands of desperate refugees.[19]

Violent attacks on Jewish Americans, their property, and their synagogues were common after World War II. More than forty major incidents were reported in 1945–1946 in the United States. Between the mid-1950s and the 1980s there were numerous attacks, including the painting of Nazi swastikas on synagogues and violent attacks on the homes and stores of Jewish Americans. The Anti-Defamation League annually reports on anti-Semitic incidents. In its first survey (1979) there were 129 reported cases of vandalism, such as attempted arson and the painting of swastikas on tombstones or synagogues. The number jumped to 974 in 1981; the figure for 1984 was 715. Between 1979 and 1984 there were 3,694 reported incidents. In 1984 there were also 369 reported threats by mail or phone or assaults against Jewish individuals. Political pressures from Jewish and non-Jewish Americans have resulted in several states passing laws making religious desecrations special crimes; dozens of people were arrested in the 1980s for these incidents.[20]

Attacks on blacks and Jews by the Ku Klux Klan and similar organizations reappeared in recent decades, but by the late 1980s they seemed to be declining. One Klan group, the Invisible Empire, filed for bankruptcy. Other groups seemed to be limited to a few dozen members. Neo-Nazi groups also seemed to be on the decline. Even so, members of these groups have been very dangerous. In the 1980s several blacks were murdered in Oklahoma City, Indianapolis, and other cities by members or former members of neo-Nazi and Klan organizations. One neo-Nazi group, The Order, was formed in Idaho in 1983 to conduct a war against the "Zionist Occupation Government." Members of the group reportedly machine-gunned a Jewish American talk-show host in Denver, committed armed robberies, counterfeited money, set fire to a synagogue, and killed police officers trying to capture them.[21]

## Jewish Americans Fight Back

Since the 1960s there has been some conflict between Jewish Americans and blacks. Certain aspects of Jewish liberalism in central cities declined somewhat in the 1960s. Black rioters in the ghettos attacked Jewish businesses that they saw as exploitative, and black street criminals came to be seen as responsible for destroying the peace of Jewish neighborhoods. Fear of street crime led to the formation of militant self-protective associations in the late 1960s and the 1970s.

In 1968 Rabbi Kahane in New York City organized the Jewish Defense League (JDL) to deal with threats against Jewish communities in the cities. The JDL's goals included not only the reinvigoration of Jewish pride but also the physical defense of citizens wherever threatened. The JDL organized armed citizen patrols of city streets in New York specifically to protect Jewish communities from street crime. Chapters were established in a half-dozen cities. Since the 1970s disruptions of Soviet diplomatic activities have been undertaken by JDL members protesting the treatment of Jews in the Soviet Union. Strober argues that the movement touched a "middle-class nerve" and that for many the traditional organizations appeared unwilling to vigorously defend Jewish interests. Though most Jews disapproved of the JDL's violent tactics, many supported some of its aims.[22]

## POLITICS

The colonies generally limited voting and officeholding to Christians. Five states had removed these restrictions by 1790; six others carried Christians-only provisions for political participation as late as 1876.[23] The substantial Jewish American contributions to the revolutionary cause did not bring them political freedom. Although no anti-Semitism is reflected in the founding documents, some Federalist officials engaged in anti-Jewish practices. Federalist support for the Alien and Sedition Laws guaranteed that Jews would support the liberal Jeffersonian party, later to become the Democratic party. Though Jews supported Democrats for decades, their votes eventually gravitated to the antislavery Republican party.[24]

It was not until after the Civil War that Jewish Americans became significant in officeholding. In New York City Jewish Americans became active in Republican organizations; one became New York's Republican candidate for lieutenant governor in 1870.[25] As Jews became more concentrated in northern cities, their voting power increased. While some Socialist candidates received strong support, most Jewish Americans remained Republicans or began to gravitate to the Irish-dominated Democratic machines, which provided jobs and shelter. Jewish workers in Tammany Hall in New York were given patronage positions; many became active as district captains and poll watchers, and a few in New York and elsewhere eventually became leaders.[26]

Eastern European Jews became famous for exercising the franchise and undertaking volunteer political activity. Whereas the Irish used politics to advance their interests—to create jobs and patronage—Jewish Americans, though concerned with bread-and-butter matters, were more issue-oriented, particularly in commitment to civil rights.[27]

### Jews and the Democratic Party

In spite of their conscientious activity, by the 1910s few Jewish Americans had been able to win electoral office; few had been appointed to high-level positions. An occasional city-council member, one or two state legislators, a judge—this was the extent of their clout. At the national level the impact was modest as well, since many Jews voted for Republicans. When an internationalist Democratic candidate, Woodrow Wilson, came along, a majority of Jewish votes flowed to the Democrats for the first time in decades. Wilson appointed a few Jews to important positions, including Bernard Baruch to the War Industries Board and Louis Brandeis to the Supreme Court.[28]

After Wilson, Jewish American voters generally supported Republican presidential candidates until the late 1920s, although they were shifting to Democratic candidates at the local, state, and congressional levels. In 1920 there were eleven Jewish members of Congress, ten of them Republicans, but by 1922 a majority were Democratic. New York's Governor Al Smith, of poor Irish background, attracted a lot of Jews to the Democratic party and received substantial Jewish American support in his 1928 bid for the presidency.[29]

Although Jewish Americans have become increasingly more suburban and middle-income since the 1920s, their vote has not shifted heavily back to the Republican party. Franklin Roosevelt brought Jewish Americans firmly into the Democratic fold in 1932. Roosevelt's anti-Nazi rhetoric and his support of social security and union organization won over many Jewish liberals and Socialists. Until Roosevelt, few Jewish Americans had served in the executive or judicial branches of the federal government. Jewish Americans Benjamin Cohen, Felix Frankfurter, and Louis Brandeis served as close advisers to Roosevelt.

Yet Roosevelt's strong regard among Jewish Americans did not lead him to take dynamic action on behalf of refugees from Nazi-dominated Europe. One reason for this was his fear of the intense anti-Semitism prevailing in the United States during the 1930s and 1940s. Anti-Jewish discrimination was common in politics, social affairs, education, employment, jury selection in certain states, and residential restrictions.[30]

In recent decades at least one nationwide survey has revealed that 5 percent of Americans would like to vote for an anti-Semitic candidate for Congress and 33 percent said *it would not matter* to them if a candidate were anti-Semitic. Though such attitudes do not currently surface in political discrimination, they could in a crisis. An awareness of these attitudes, coupled with the fear that oppression such as that in Nazi Germany can happen again, has kept many Jewish Americans committed to liberal, civil-rights-oriented causes and politicians, a commitment documented in numerous opinion surveys since the 1940s. Recent concern among Jewish Americans for "law and order" has not kept them from remaining the most liberal of the white ethnic groups.[31]

The proportion of the Jewish American vote going to Democratic presidential candidates has remained substantial. Though in 1948 this vote fell off from Roosevelt's 90-percent landslides, three-quarters of Jewish voters still supported Harry Truman. Three-quarters voted for Adlai Stevenson during the Eisenhower landslides, and more than three-quarters supported John Kennedy in 1960. Considerably more than three-quarters voted for Lyndon Johnson in 1964 and for Hubert Humphrey in 1968. George McGovern got 65 percent of the Jewish vote in 1972—an achievement, considering that Richard Nixon attempted to capitalize on Jewish American alienation from the old coalitions.

In 1976 Democrat Jimmy Carter received 70 percent of the Jewish vote, up from the percentage for McGovern in 1972. In 1980 one poll found that Carter received only 45 percent of the Jewish vote in his second bid for the presidency, with the rest split between Ronald Reagan and the independent candidate. This, the lowest percentage given to a Democratic since Franklin Roosevelt, apparently reflected Jewish concern over Carter's attempts to build bridges to the Arab world. Jewish Americans feared that Israel's security might be jeopardized by Carter's peace initiatives in the Middle East. Nonetheless, most Jewish Americans voted against Ronald Reagan in 1980. In 1984, according to a *Times*/CBS report, Jewish Americans were the *only* major white ethnic group to give a majority (66 percent) of their votes to Walter Mondale; only a minority voted for Reagan in his landslide election. One reason for the large anti-Reagan vote among Jewish Americans was Reagan's close ties to the religious right, including some fundamentalist Christian ministers. Some of these preachers have been associated with intolerant attitudes toward non-Christian Americans and have tried to assert the dominance of Protestant Christian values over those of other religious traditions in the United States. Not surprisingly, a 1984 opinion poll found that 57 percent of Jewish respondents identified themselves as Democrats, 31 percent as independents, and only 12 percent as Republicans.[32]

Recent opinion polls have shown strong support among Jewish Americans for civil rights progress and for causes such as women's rights. Jewish Americans generally remain progressive in their political views.

Historically, Jewish Americans have been underrepresented among elected and appointed officials. Just over a hundred Jewish Americans have been senators, members of Congress, and governors. The current scene shows an improvement. By 1981 there were 33 Jewish Americans in Congress; most were Democrats. So far, only a half-dozen Jewish Americans have served on the United States Supreme Court, although perhaps a fifth of the nation's lawyers in recent decades have been Jewish. By 1976 only nine Jews had served in presidential cabinets, including Oscar Straus under Theodore Roosevelt, Henry Morgenthau under Franklin Roosevelt, Lewis Strauss under Eisenhower, Abraham Ribicoff under Kennedy, Arthur Goldberg and Wilbur Cohen under Johnson, and Henry Kissinger under Nixon and Ford. A half-dozen more served under the Ford, Carter, and Reagan administrations. Jewish Americans have served in significant (although less than representative) numbers in local and state executive and legislative offices. It was not until 1974 that Abraham Beame became the *first* Jewish mayor of New York City. He was succeeded by another Jew, Edward Koch. Also in the 1970s, Diane Feinstein became the first Jewish woman chosen mayor of a major city, in this case San Francisco.[33] Koch and Feinstein were still serving as mayors in the late 1980s.

While statistics on members of Congress and governors are impressive compared with the limited political clout of nonwhite groups, they still reflect discrimination. Currently, the proportion of Jewish Americans in elected office is less than one might expect, given their high proportion (perhaps 20 percent) among political activists. Isaacs has stressed that although there are more Jews than Presbyterians or Episcopalians in the United States, Jewish Americans have not held a fifth of the congressional offices held by those powerful white groups in recent years. Discrimination plays a role in limiting the number of Jewish Americans who occupy the political front lines. Because of discrimination and the oppression mentality, many Jewish Americans have preferred to work as political advisers, fund raisers, and speech writers.[34]

## Union and Community Organization

Jewish Americans have participated in protest activities other than those associated with electoral politics. Large-scale protest against oppressive conditions was first mounted by eastern European Jews. By the 1890s they were organizing to fight long hours, low pay, and unsafe working conditions in the sweatshops. Tens of thousands of workers struck the garment industry; the 1910 strike, the Great Revolt, lasted two months, with heavy costs to the "bosses" and destitution for workers. The New York strikers inspired union militants elsewhere.[35]

Figures on unions in the 1930s for New York City show large numbers of Jewish workers in food, entertainment, clothing, and jewelry unions. Jewish union leaders went beyond the problems of wages and working conditions to grapple with broader issues. Jewish unions pioneered health, pension, and educational programs that would be imitated by all major unions. Working-class Jews played an important role in the growth of the Socialist party between 1905 and 1912 and other labor–liberal parties later on.[36]

The organized Jewish American community is impressive. One important aspect of this "civic Judaism," to use Woocher's term, is the North American Jewish federation movement, made up of approximately 225 local community federations and many social service and educational agencies representing and serving Jewish Americans. The federation movement originally emphasized philanthropy and Jewish immigrant adjustment to life in the United States, but now stresses Jewish activism and survival in the modern world.[37]

## Civil Rights and Affirmative Action

By the 1930s there were several civic and civil rights organizations whose importance would persist: the Anti-Defamation League of B'nai B'rith, the American Jewish Congress, the American Jewish Committee (AJC), and the United Jewish Appeal. Since 1906 the AJC has vigorously fought anti-Semitic prejudice and discrimination in the United States. By the 1970s it had a large budget and forty thousand members. The American Jewish Congress, established in the 1910s by eastern European Jews, has fought for the civil rights of Jewish Americans, but it has been more pro-Israel than the American Jewish Committee. By 1980 it had a large budget and thousands of members. The Anti-Defamation League, a branch of the fraternal organization B'nai B'rith, was set up in 1913. It has carried out perhaps the most vigorous civil rights campaign, attempting to root out anti-Semitism. The United Jewish Appeal, established in 1939, has been an extraordinarily successful fund-raising organization aiding Jewish causes, including war refugees and the state of Israel.[38]

Israel was established, and has survived, with substantial support from Jewish Americans. During the Eisenhower administration Jewish American pressure to support Israel often went unheeded, but by the 1960s American political support for Israel had sharply increased and required less Israeli lobbying and indigenous pressure. In the 1970s and 1980s Jewish political pressure has been mobilized for other causes, such as laws supporting Soviet Jews and punishment of liberal political candidates taking a tolerant position toward Arab nations hostile to Israel. American policy in these decades seemed to be becoming more flexible and sympathetic to the Arab position. As a result, many Jewish leaders began to worry about the apparently declining support of Jewish causes in the United States.[39]

The important Jewish groups have not focused exclusively on anti-Semitism. Several have sought to eliminate all racial and ethnic prejudice and discrimination and to keep church and state separate. Jewish commitment to the black civil rights movement has been strong since its beginning. Numerous Jewish congregations and their rabbis were active in the black civil rights protests of the 1950s and 1960s. They provided substantial money for the movement and swelled the ranks of demonstrators across the South. Young Jewish Americans were active in the antiwar movements.[40]

By the 1970s black criticism of Zionism had alienated a significant number of Jewish Americans from active participation in the black cause. As part of their rhetoric a few black leaders were broadcasting anti-Semitic statements aimed at the white merchants and landlords they believed were exploiting their ghettoized brothers and sisters. Jewish commitment to black civil rights also came in conflict with black inner-city programs for police reform, school reforms, and desegregated schools. For example, in a 1966 New York City referendum Jews voted in the majority against establishing a police-review board desired by non-whites. In 1968 a new community-controlled school board in a black area of Brooklyn fired a number of teachers; a teachers' strike ensued, pitting protesting Jews against blacks.

Affirmative action programs, seeking to improve job chances for minorities, have come under attack by Jewish leaders since the late 1960s. One objection seems to be that these programs' "goals" become quotas benefiting certain groups and violating the principle of merit. Memories of quota restrictions in higher education against Jews in the 1930s and 1940s are a major reason for this commitment to the abolition of affirmative action programs. A second reason for opposition is that Jewish Americans have made a heavy commitment to higher education; so where there are a limited number of job openings requiring college degrees, preferences for non-Jewish minorities will disproportionately affect Jewish Americans. Since this commitment to securing college degrees partially reflects the earlier reactions of Jews to anti-Semitic discrimination in the business world, affirmative action programs preferring non-Jewish minorities and cutting the chances for Jews to be hired perpetuate the effects of past anti-Jewish discrimination.[41]

A recent survey of the members of the boards of the American Jewish Committee, the American Jewish Congress, the United Jewish Appeal, and the Anti-Defamation League found them to be relatively affluent with a median income of $135,000. Some Jewish Americans have accused these well-off *leaders* of being more sympathetic to the needs of employers and capitalists and to critiques of affirmative action than to the traditional Jewish concerns for the workers, the poor, and racial discrimination against blacks and other nonwhites. While this criticism of the leaders may be to some extent unfair, it does point up the dilemma faced by Jewish Americans today. As the most affluent of "white ethnic" groups, Jews might be expected to develop the generally conservative orientation of other high-income white groups.[42]

Yet, given their Jewish past and the periodic recurrence of anti-Semitism in the United States, most affluent Jewish Americans remain far more liberal, politically and economically, than their non-Jewish white counterparts. In the late 1980s opinion surveys continue to show that among *all* whites, Jewish Americans as a group are *the most sympathetic* to black Americans' civil rights struggle and economic problems.

## THE ECONOMY

Two dozen Sephardic Jewish immigrants contributed to an increase in Dutch prosperity in America when they came to New Amsterdam in the 1650s. A Jewish immigrant from Poland, Haym Salomon, played a critical role in financing the American Revolution with a loan to the struggling revolutionary government; Salomon worked hard to secure European aid for the revolutionary cause.[43]

The opening of commerce in the Americas presented a golden opportunity for European Jews, because exclusion from land ownership and skilled-worker guilds had forced them into commercial pursuits in Europe, where they excelled. For centuries in Europe one critical "trading" minority was the Jewish group. Because they have been so successful in this role, Jews have been an accessible scapegoat for the non-Jewish poor, who see them as exploiters, and for the non-Jewish rich, who view them as a political threat. The marginal nature of their enterprises, as well as outside hostility, fostered the growth of an *ethnic economy*, where Jews would turn to other Jews for economic aid in order to maintain their enterprises and communities.[44]

### Establishing an Economic Niche: A "Middleman Minority"?

The rate of penetration of a new immigrant group into the core society depends on its own economic background as well as the economic conditions at the point of destination. German Jews entered the American economy just as frontier development and industrial growth were exploding. The urban and commercial backgrounds of this new wave of immigrants were useful in establishing a niche. Itinerant peddlers roamed city streets and the countryside in the South and West, engaging in trade and commerce.[45]

By 1889 census figures showed 58 percent of employed Jewish Americans in trading or financial occupations, 20 percent as office workers, and 6 percent as professionals. The rest were blue-collar workers or farmers. Jewish entrepreneurs were concentrated in clothing, jewelry, meat, and leather businesses. By the 1890s a majority of Jewish Americans seemed to be moving up. Though they had prospered by the second generation, they had come in when British American entrepreneurs firmly controlled the central enterprises in the industrial economy. Most German Jews came "without capital, with the natural consequence that they have remained to this day outside the top positions of the economic life of the country."[46]

The influx of Jewish migrants from eastern Europe hit the expanding industrial system at a particularly appropriate time. They entered with considerable experience in coping with oppression and with a cultural heritage replete with strategies for finding economic niches in which they could survive. It was in the industrial cities that these poor Jewish immigrants settled. Many who had been small merchants in eastern Europe continued as such in the United States. A few eventually worked their way to the head of clothing firms; by 1905 a proportion of the clothing industry in New York City was under eastern European Jewish management. A number went into the professions; by 1905 eastern European Jews had a toehold in law, medicine, and dentistry in New York.[47]

Most went into working-class occupations, such as carpentry and manual labor. Tabulations for 1900 indicate that the occupational distributions of Russians (mostly Jewish Americans) in larger cities showed 60 percent in manufacturing, which usually meant blue-collar labor in factories. Another 8 percent were servants, while the rest were in clerical or public service jobs. Scholars have estimated that one-third of eastern European Jews were workers in clothing industries and one-quarter were manual workers in industries such as jewelry and liquor.

Though many eventually moved out of manual occupations, new immigrants kept filling their places—until discriminatory quotas finally ended Jewish migration in the 1920s. These new residents were generally at the bottom rungs of the mobility ladder. Men, women, and children—whole families—were engaged in manufacturing work that brought wages of $10 to $12 a week for men in 1900. Hours were long; poor conditions resulted in employment settings becoming known as *sweatshops*, as indeed they were. Reform and union movements were generated in part by the agitation of these workers against such conditions.[48]

Jewish women contributed significantly to the family income. A Philadelphia study found, in this early period, that one in three Jewish American households had a woman working outside the home. Most unmarried Jewish American women worked. Because of the low wages of male and female workers, most families needed the women to work outside or to take in sewing or laundry in the home. In addition, wives often joined their husbands in the system of small retail shops that supplied many Jewish neighborhoods.[49]

Many eastern European wage earners set their sights on a business career. Some would move up the economic ladder from junk peddler to scrap-metal-yard owner, or from needleworker to clothing entrepreneur. But those in the second generation were encouraged by their parents to go into clerical and sales work. By the 1930s Jewish mobility had become conspicuous.

## From the Depression to the 1950s

About one-quarter of Jewish Americans in Detroit and Pittsburgh in the mid-1930s were owners or managers, compared with 9 percent of the total population in 1930. A study in Newburyport, Massachusetts, found Jews moving into the middle-income levels there; the proportion was estimated at just under half. Moreover, as in the case of Japanese Americans (see Chapter 11), the solidarity of the Jewish American community and its heavy involvement in small and medium-sized businesses brought aid to the unemployed in the Great Depression. Whenever possible, Jewish American businesses dealt with one another. Unemployed relatives were hired to do a variety of jobs, even if they were low-paying. Here the ethnic economy provided a basis for survival. A few Jewish Americans even became employed in organized crime in the 1920s and 1930s.[50]

The ethnic economy provided a fallback position for those who faced anti-Jewish discrimination in the 1930s. One of the goals of anti-Semitic organizations was to reduce the number of Jews in private and public employment. Discrimination became rampant as Jewish Americans moved into white-collar jobs. Non-Jewish whites in the teaching, banking, medical, legal, and engineering professions sought to prohibit Jews from employment in their sectors. In many areas, securing skilled blue-collar jobs and clerical jobs became difficult. The Depression accentuated the problem; anti-Jewish prohibitions or token quotas became commonplace. "No Jews need apply" signs were omnipresent, particularly in larger businesses and professional institutions.

Placement agencies throughout the Midwest, to take just one example, reported that from two-thirds to 95 percent of job listings specifically *excluded* Jewish Americans from consideration. A study of the teaching profession found discrimination directed against Jews, particularly in smaller cities and at colleges. Discrimination from 1900 to the 1950s was also rife in housing. Numerous real estate developments excluded Jewish Americans. Real estate agents discriminated against Jews from Philadelphia to Boston to Chicago, while neighbors made life miserable for those who managed to pioneer in desegregating an area. Later, even those who managed to move into the suburbs in significant numbers found Protestant-oriented organizations and recreational facilities off limits to them.[51]

One of the fears of anti-Semites has been alleged Jewish dominance of banking. Yet a *Fortune* magazine survey reported in 1936 found that very few Jews were in banking and finance. (A later survey found that only 600 of the 93,000 banking officials in the United States were Jewish.) Nor were they very numerous in heavy industries such as steel or automobiles or in the public utilities. Their representation was small in the press and in radio. The *Fortune* survey found that the only sectors Jewish Americans dominated were clothing, textiles, and the movies. Even in law and medicine Jews had little representation in powerful positions. The author of the 1936 *Fortune* article seemed puzzled at the clustering in certain industrial and business areas and explained the situation in the stereotypical terms of Jewish clannishness.

Such patterns were by no means mysterious; they reflected the extent to which Jewish Americans had to work outside mainstream industries and businesses because of institutionalized discrimination. As McWilliams had noted in *A Mask for Privilege*, discrimination forced Jews to become "the ragpickers of American industry." Jewish Americans were channeled into economic spheres marginal to the mainstream economy, areas filled with greater risk.[52]

After World War II, extensive employment discrimination continued to be directed at Jewish Americans. Job advertising included restrictions, and many employment agencies required applicants to list their religion or ethnicity; these listings were used to discriminate among applicants. In spite of this, many Jews were able to share in postwar prosperity, particularly in new and more risky industries such as television and plastics, and finally they overcame discrimination in areas such as engineering. The postwar economic pyramid for Jewish Americans had a small working-class base and no significant wealthy elite at the top. Jews remained concentrated primarily in trade, clothing, and jewelry manufacturing; commerce; merchandising; certain light industries; mass communications; and certain professions.[53] The 1957 Current Population Survey found that 78 percent of Jewish American men were employed in white-collar jobs, compared with 38 percent of white Protestants. Over half were in professional and managerial jobs, twice the percentage for white Protestants. Less than a quarter were found in blue-collar positions.[54]

Research on major corporation and business executives, presidents, and board chairmen indicates that in 1900 just under 2 percent were Jews; in 1925 and 1950 the figure was still between 2 and 3 percent. Given the preponderance of Jewish Americans in commercial and business employment, these proportions are much lower than they would be if there had been no anti-Jewish discrimination. Jews were still concentrated in certain types of manufacturing and mass communications businesses. Very few were in transportation or heavy industry. A very large proportion of the Jewish American executives—just under half—made it to the top in the ethnic economy, in Jewish businesses.[55]

## Jewish Americans in Today's Economy

Data from the 1950s shows a very sizable proportion (30 percent) of Jewish household heads with incomes above $7,500, compared with 13 percent of the total population. This advantaged economic position continued through the 1980s. Family income levels in the mid-1960s are suggested in a reanalysis by Glenn and Hyland of data in four opinion surveys: the median family income for the total sample was $5,856; the figure for Jews was $7,990. Jewish families averaged higher incomes than the total population in subsequent decades. Moreover, a 1984 estimate put the annual income of Jewish households at $23,300 versus $21,700 for Episcopalians. And in the 1983 General Social Survey, an opinion poll carried out by the National Opinion Research Center, data were collected on forty-three Jewish American respondents whose characteristics suggested they were representative of Jewish Americans. Thirty-nine percent reported family incomes above $35,000 annually, compared with 22 percent of white Protestants and 19 percent of Catholics in the same survey. Sixty-six percent reported incomes above $25,000, compared with 38 percent for white Protestants and 38 percent for Catholics. In the mid-1980s a majority of Jewish American families had incomes above the average for white Americans.[56]

One writer has estimated that among the 400 richest individuals examined by *Forbes* magazine in 1985, Jewish Americans constituted 23 percent, well above the 2 to 3 percent one would expect on the basis of population alone. However, these wealthy Jewish Americans were concentrated in the mass media, sports, clothing, trading, and real estate. Even among the rich there are very few Jewish American capitalists in the traditional American industries, where anti-Jewish discrimination has historically been so strong.[57]

## Occupational Mobility

Continuing occupational mobility has characterized Jewish Americans since the 1960s. In that decade an estimated one-quarter of male Jewish workers in New York City were still in blue-collar occupations. The blue-collar proportions in studies of other cities were lower. In five major cities (New York, Providence, Milwaukee, Detroit, and Boston) occupational data showed that 20 to 32 percent of Jewish American males were in professional positions and 28 to 54 percent were in managerial–official positions. Over half of all Jewish American workers in each city were in these two categories, while most of the rest were in other clerical or sales positions. In comparison, a majority of the total employed populations in those cities were in blue-collar positions. The 1981 *American Jewish Yearbook* reported data on the occupational distribution of Jewish men and women nationwide. Seventy percent of the men and 40 percent of the women held professional, technical, managerial, or administrative positions. Most of the rest were in other white-collar (clerical and sales) jobs.[58]

Studies of financial and banking institutions have found no Jews in the top jobs in forty-five of the fifty largest banks; Jewish Americans made up only one percent of senior executives in major banks. The pattern was similar for the thousands of executives below the top level—in New York as well as in other cities. Jewish Americans owned none of the twenty largest banks. Jews, contrary to the widely believed stereotype, have never controlled banking in the United States. This is true of agriculture, mining, and heavy industry as well. Jews were never concentrated in mining or agriculture, and were found only in certain manufacturing industries. They still are scarce in the executive suites of basic industries such as oil, steel, and autos. In recent decades Jewish American entrepreneurs and executives have been common only in certain industries they entered early; they have been successful in radio, TV, and publishing. Still, studies from the 1970s and the 1980s have found only 3 percent of U.S. newspapers owned by Jewish Americans—a figure that contrasts sharply with the stereotype of Jewish control of the news media.[59]

A major study of Jewish Americans in the U.S. corporate elite found that most were in Jewish-founded corporations or in peripheral positions in other corporations. Those who have cracked the corporate Protestant establishment, such as Irving Shapiro of du Pont, have usually done so by being brought in from the outside (Shapiro was brought in from government); they have rarely been given the chance to start at the bottom of the corporate hierarchy and work themselves up in the usual way. "They are not even remotely close to being the dominant force they are tragically and mistakenly thought to be by anti-Semites."[60]

Many of the nation's writers, scholars, and professors are Jewish. Jewish Americans are well represented among distinguished scholars at major universities and among top literary figures. They include Nobel laureate Saul Bellow and intellectuals such as Irving Howe. They have been the backbone of literary and critical magazines such as the *Partisan Review, Dissent,* and the *New York Review of Books.*

The effects of anti-Semitism keep many Jewish Americans in what has been termed "the gilded ghetto," economically successful but somewhat isolated from the social recognition and political power that success should have brought. Ghettoization in recent decades has been subtle. Much discrimination has been hidden by secrecy at higher economic levels. Exclusion from private social clubs and private schools creates economic and political disabilities in other spheres—a classic example of the indirect discrimination discussed in Chapter 1.[61] Thus in 1983 a bill was introduced before the New York City Council that would have banned discrimination, including anti-Jewish discrimination, in private clubs with more than 100 members. The bill was finally passed in 1985, but only after the limit it specified was changed to 400 members.

Discrimination and conformity to the dominant culture have exacted a price in cultural creativity, identity, and continuity. This price was heaviest for those whose mobility has carried them into professional, managerial, or white-collar clerical occupations. White-collar Jewish Americans have been forced by informal job requirements to spend much of their time in the non-Jewish world. Since non-Jews already held the dominant positions in the corporate and business world, it was the mobile Jewish Americans who had to conform. Non-Jews are the critical gatekeepers. The possibility of anti-Semitic rejection often pressures a Jewish white-collar worker to dispense with cultural distinctiveness and, to a certain extent, traditional connections. Sklare suggests that Jewish American success has brought serious problems of identity.[62] The core society again sought a cloning process with an Anglo-Saxon Protestant model. What would Jews have achieved, what creativity would have blossomed, and what would American society be like if the Jewish Americans had not been restricted by anti-Semitism?

While many Jewish Americans have prospered, others have not. There are still sizable poor populations in some areas of New York City, as well as in other cities. Many Jewish Americans still work in blue-collar occupations. One study in the 1970s found that one-sixth of the Jews in New York—272,000 people—were poor or near-poor by official standards, including many elderly people. Large numbers of poor and moderate-income Jewish Americans were also found in Chicago, Philadelphia, and Miami.[63]

## EDUCATION

In education Jewish Americans faced not only acculturation pressures but also anti-Semitic attitudes and discrimination. Significant participation in schools came with the surge of Russian and Polish Jewish immigrants, who brought an ancient tradition of respect for education. Numerous religious schools were established; thousands of adults attended evening schools, established by philanthropic organizations, to learn English after work. They sought acculturation at the level of language.[64]

By the early 1900s there were three dozen de facto segregated public schools in New York City with an estimated 61,000 Jewish pupils. Educational mobility for second- and third-generation Jewish Americans came swiftly. It was not long before large numbers of students were graduating from high schools in northern cities, with a significant number pursuing college educations. By 1920 the proportion of Jewish students in New York City colleges and universities was estimated to be greater than the proportion of Jews in the general population. Overall educational levels had increased remarkably by the late 1930s. In New York City just under 50 percent of Jewish students managed to complete high school, compared with only one-quarter of other students. Of the 1.1 million students in more than 1,300 colleges, 9 percent were Jewish Americans, a considerable overrepresentation.[65]

### Discriminatory Quotas for Jewish Students

Restrictive quotas limiting the number of Jewish American students were imposed at numerous colleges and universities from the 1920s to the 1950s. In a notorious 1922 proposal President A.L. Lowell of Harvard University openly called for discriminatory quotas on Jewish students; many schools followed his advice. In the 1920s, three-quarters of non-Jews applying to a major medical school in New York were admitted, compared with a percentage of Jews that peaked at half but eventually dropped to one-fifth. In the same decade restrictions were placed on Jewish admissions to law schools and to the bar in various states. Fraternities and sororities excluded Jewish Americans from membership; for many decades these were important grooming institutions whereby students from the "right" racial and ethnic backgrounds were given a boost onto the elevator to success.[66]

In the Great Depression it was difficult for Jewish students to gain admission to certain colleges and universities. Some of these schools continued to restrict Jewish American students to a zero or token quota. Few would admit they had quotas for Jewish Americans, but data on admissions to major East Coast colleges showed clearly that blatant discrimination was practiced. Professional schools continued such policies as well. Jewish American percentages of enrollments at prominent institutions such as Columbia, Syracuse, and Cornell medical schools dropped sharply between the 1920s and 1940s. Prominent schools were at the top of the list in enforcing an exclusion policy. These patterns of anti-Jewish discrimination continued into the 1940s, and have persisted to a lesser extent in the decades since.[67]

Coupled with anti-Semitic discrimination against students was discrimination against faculty members. Between the 1920s and the 1940s it was very difficult for Jewish Ph.D.'s, however distinguished, to get appointments at Anglo-Saxon-dominated universities. When the brilliant scholar Lionel Trilling was appointed to the English faculty at Columbia University, he was the first Jewish American ever in that department.

### Achievements in Education

Severe discrimination was on the decline by the 1950s and 1960s, and educational attainment was reaching ever higher levels. An analysis of 1963–1965 national data revealed that 36 percent of those adults identifying themselves as Jewish Americans had some college education, compared with 17 percent in the total adult sample. In those years median educational attainment was 12.6 years for Jewish Americans and 11.4 years for the total group. In recent decades the average educational attainment of Jewish Americans has remained significantly higher than that of the population as a whole. In the 1983 General Social Survey the median educational attainment for

Jewish American respondents was 15.9 years, versus 12.1 years for the white Protestants in this sample. Although the Protestant figure for this sample is lower than the 12.5 figure found in the 1980 census for all persons in the United States, the contrast with the median for Jewish Americans is dramatic. Fully two-thirds of the Jewish respondents reported that they had graduated from college, compared with 19 percent of the white Protestants in the sample. Twenty-two percent reported some graduate work, compared with 7 percent of the white Protestants. The commitment of Jewish Americans to education is graphically illustrated in these data.[68]

In recent decades surveys have found strong support among Jewish American parents for some type of Jewish education for their children. Between 1900 and World War I many second-generation eastern European Jews received some instruction in weekday religious schools. By 1918 about one-quarter of Jewish American children in New York City were getting at least a little Jewish schooling, usually in inadequate facilities. Jewish schools could not compete with public schools. Yet by 1980 an estimated eight in ten Jewish children had had some religious schooling, a proportion up sharply from figures for earlier decades. The renewed emphasis on formal learning of one's heritage and religion in the lower grades has carried over to colleges and universities. By the 1960s there were more than five dozen positions in Jewish studies; by 1980 there were more than three hundred.[69]

## RELIGION AND ZIONISM

Religious freedom in the colonies was variable, and most colonies restricted Jewish American participation in colonial life. After 1790 there was considerable support in the new nation, particularly among Jefferson and his followers, for maximizing religious freedom. Yet it was evident that the new nation and its component states were fundamentally Christian. Gradually, religious freedom became law in each of the new states, in most by 1850.

With the German influx Judaism began to thrive. Jewish Reform movement leaders began to question ancient religious traditions and to call for adaptations. The Reform movement accelerated with the waves of German immigration and became organized in the union of American Hebrew Congregations in the 1870s. Conservative Judaism also grew up in the nineteenth century, a movement making some concessions to the core culture, as in language and weekend time schedules for religious services, but retaining more of the traditional belief and ritual systems than the Reform movement considered necessary. By 1900, Orthodox Judaism, the oldest and most orthodox group, had received a major infusion from the eastern European immigrants. The synagogues of the eastern Europeans were ethnic centers where different nationalities came together in a religious context.[70]

In recent years substantial research has been focused on Orthodox Judaism. Many refugees fleeing the Nazis and turmoil in Europe in the 1930–1950 period were active members of Orthodox Judaism; they remained highly committed to it in the United States. Research on Jewish Americans in the 1970s and 1980s has demonstrated that commitment to Orthodoxy persists among many of the children of these immigrants. Highly visible, these traditional Jewish Americans have proudly asserted their religious traditions—and have rejected calls for cultural assimilation.

By the 1920s there were three divergent streams of religious commitment, with more than three thousand Jewish American congregations divided into Reform, Orthodox, and Conservative groups. The authority of the rabbi, as well as the traditional ritual and theology, became less important as one moved from Orthodox to Conservative to Reform congregations. The coordination of activities among the three groups has varied considerably over the years. Often it has been limited to specific issues rather than indicating a general trend toward a merger of the groups. During the 1920s and 1930s a secular movement began. A prominent scholar, Will Herberg, has argued that many of the second-generation eastern Europeans tended to turn away from all branches of Judaism; many became ardently secularist, Zionist, or radical unionist. Secularism and labor radicalism became the new "religions" of many younger Jewish Americans during the crises of the Depression and World War II.[71]

## Trends in Jewish Religion

With expanding suburbanization after World War II came an increase in the number of congregations relocating, or newly developing, in the rings around central cities. Suburbanized third-generation eastern European Jews came to accept their Jewishness more than their parents did, showing a greater interest in the ways of their ancestors. Herberg emphasizes that this interest is actually in a secularized Judaism, one without much traditional ritual or other religious trappings.

Yet the current picture of Jewish American religion is complex, with substantial evidence of interest in the traditional heritage and in maintaining the synagogue as a community center, and at the same time evidence of a decline in home religious practices and indications of a changing religious organizational structure. In recent years the suburban synagogues have moved more in the direction of the Protestant religious core, with Sunday schools and general synagogue organization similar to that of Protestant churches. Much traditional ritual has been retained, but regular participation in ritual has played a decreasingly important role in the lives of many.[72]

A study of a suburb in the Midwest discovered that most Jewish American respondents retained at most six of the many traditional home rituals of Judaism (lighting candles on Hanukkah, for instance) a decrease from the number of traditional observances reported for their parents' homes. A similar pattern was found in Providence, Rhode Island. The 1983 General Social Survey found that only 26 percent of the Jewish American respondents attended religious services once a month or more, compared with half of the Protestants. Forty-seven percent said they never attended services or went to one or two services a year at most. They attended less often than their parents had. This decline has been interpreted as part of a growing secularization, a movement away from the religious center of the Jewish heritage. While attendance may be relatively low, synagogues have remained in suburbia, providing an anchor for Jewish identity and the fountain of the Jewish heritage.[73]

J. L. Blau has suggested that much of Jewish religion has had a flexible character. In the United States it has developed a tolerance for different "denominations" of

Judaism. In this regard it is like American Protestantism. Modern American Judaism is also a "voluntary" faith: Jewish Americans can reject it or accept it to varying degrees. Moreover, much American Judaism is a "cardiac" religion, one that emphasizes the heart or one's morals rather than rigid ritual and doctrine. Judaism has become one of three American religious traditions. Of course, Blau's analysis does not apply to the Jewish Americans who are Orthodox.[74]

Over the last three or four decades the importance of Christian anti-Semitism in shaping the socio-religious context of Jewish Americans has persisted. Few Christian churches and organizations during the 1930s and 1940s took any position condemning the Nazi treatment of the Jews. Incredibly, after that war a few Christian groups even characterized the Holocaust as the *just retribution* for Jews' having persistently refused to accept Jesus Christ as their "savior." This interpretation of Jewish "sin" and of retribution was propounded even into the 1980s, particularly among fundamentalist Christian groups. In recent decades a number of Christian evangelical missionary organizations have sought to convert Jews to the Christian faith.[75]

Religious discrimination against Jewish Americans has been involved in a number of federal court cases. In the 1950s and 1960s Orthodox Jewish business owners fought local Sunday "blue laws" requiring businesses to close on Sundays; they argued that such laws violated their First Amendment right not to be penalized for religious practices. The Supreme Court rejected their case and upheld the blue laws. In addition, Christian religious observances, such as reciting the Lord's Prayer, were once standard in public schools. The imposition of these practices on Jewish American children was opposed in courts from New York to California. When a New York case reached the Supreme Court, the court ruled against officially sanctioned religious practices in the public schools.[76]

In 1986 the Supreme Court in a five-to-four decision decided that the U.S. Air Force could require an Orthodox rabbi employed as a chaplain to remove his religious cap, the yarmulke, when working indoors. Since his childhood Rabbi S. Simcha Goldman, an Orthodox Jew, had observed the Orthodox tradition of keeping his head covered, a tradition designed to remind individuals of God's omnipresence. The Pentagon decided, for unclear reasons, to spend a large amount of money in court defending its position of preventing Orthodox Jews from wearing the yarmulke while in uniform. Several dissenting justices asked why military authorities had the right to limit religious freedom when civil authorities could not.[77]

## Zionism

At the heart of modern Jewish political and religious commitments is the commitment to the prosperity of the state of Israel. Whether active in religious Judaism or not, many Jewish Americans share this Zionist commitment. Some social commentators have suggested that Zionism is like a religion in its fervor. This commitment has affected not only Jewish voting patterns and black–Jewish relations (because of pro-Arab sentiments among some blacks) but also Jewish American philanthropy. Jewish American financial support has been critical to Israel's survival in the face of hostility from surrounding Arab countries.

In the last decade there has been growing debate in Jewish American communities across the nation over the government of Israel and its actions, such as the 1982 invasion of Lebanon and the 1988 suppression of Palestinian protests in the occupied West Bank areas. While most in the debate remain strongly committed to Israel, many Jewish Americans have raised questions about the direction of Israel's development and the wisdom of Israeli leaders. A growing number have expressed the view that the "overriding challenge facing Western Jewry today is essentially that of discovering how it can contribute to Israeli–Arab reconciliation."[78]

## ASSIMILATION OR PLURALISM?

Two different theoretical perspectives have been used to interpret the experiences of Jewish Americans—assimilation perspectives and cultural pluralism views. Most scholarly analyses of Jewish Americans have reflected some type of assimilation perspective. A dominant perspective among Jewish Americans themselves has been at least partially assimilationist: the view that some defensive adaptation to the surrounding culture was critical to avoiding anti-Semitic prejudice and discrimination.[79]

Partial cultural assimilation came relatively quickly for each of the three major waves of Jewish immigrants and their children. Many German Jews rapidly adapted to their environment, picking up English and basic values, but they maintained a commitment to Judaism. Then came the waves of eastern Europeans. Completely separate Jewish American communities survived for a while; where they were close geographically the German and eastern European cultures and communities began blending. German Jews pressed the new immigrants to Americanize rapidly. In such cities as New York, German social workers and others came "downtown" to help assimilate the new eastern Europeans.[80]

Soon Sephardic and German distinctiveness seemed to have been all but lost in the overwhelming numbers of the eastern Europeans. Many of the latter group were committed to fighting acculturation pressures, with their strongest commitment to the retention of Judaism. Some heavily emphasized the crucial role Yiddish culture could play in perpetuating the Jewish heritage. The majority of the first generation adopted a partial commitment to cultural assimilation that was at bottom a survival strategy, a means of coping with anti-Semitic discrimination. In one sense, the eastern European immigrants were already partially acculturated when they stepped ashore: they came with a strong commitment to education, an urban–commercial background, and a desire to "make it" in North America.[81]

The second generation was more affected by assimilation pressures and rapidly picked up the language and values pressed on them in the media and the public school system. Like young Italian Americans, they were caught between the culture of their parents and the core culture, a situation guaranteed to create family tensions. The proportion of Jewish Americans speaking Yiddish declined substantially.[82]

Judaism, particularly the Reform and Conservative branches, was partially Americanized after 1900—with its Sunday schools, English-language services, and Protestant-like associational activities. The third East European generation, according to Herberg, was secure in the United States and eager to accent its "Jewishness," but without some of the religious trappings. What Herberg has in mind is a return to a secularized "Jewishness."[83]

The decline of certain traditional religious values and practices has not meant the demise of Judaism or of the synagogue as a community center. And the resurgence of Orthodox Judaism suggests that a minority of Jewish Americans are rejecting Jewish secularism. Recent research makes it clear that Orthodox Judaism is alive. A significant number of Jewish Americans, previously unaffiliated and raised in secular families, have become active in Orthodox religion, with its anti-assimilationist ideology and traditions. Liebman has suggested that Jewish Americans are going in two directions at the same time, most more or less assimilating culturally and a minority rejecting cultural assimilation as much as possible.[84]

## Patterns of Assimilation

In the sphere of structural assimilation at the secondary level of economics and politics, we have seen the rise of German and eastern European Jewish Americans up the ladder. Eastern European Jews moved from a blue-collar concentration to a white-collar concentration in three generations. The original occupational concentration in certain blue-collar and entrepreneurial categories largely reflected discrimination as well as the skills that Jewish workers brought with them. For many an ethnic economy was critical; Jewish Americans concentrated in "middleman" positions, where they prospered. Hard work and mastery of the core culture's educational system facilitated upward movement. Yet the present occupational distribution of Jewish Americans underscores the point that even the prosperous among them are not yet fully integrated. Indicative of discrimination, as we have seen, is the absence of Jewish Americans at the very top in most spheres of the economy. Substantial representation in the political sphere is recent.

Jewish Americans have, over a few generations, moved well up the economic ladder in the United States. Most came in poor; most today are part of middle-income America. Why were the Jewish Americans able to move up the ladder so successfully? Some have explained this in terms of basic values and religious traditions. Nathan Glazer has argued that "Judaism emphasizes the traits that businessmen and intellectuals require, and has done so at least 1,500 years before Calvinism.... The strong emphasis on learning and study can be traced that far back, too. The Jewish habits of foresight, care, moderation probably arose early."[85]

This image of success growing out of traditional values has been called by Steinberg the "myth of Jewish progress." Steinberg has demonstrated that Jewish American success had less to do with religious factors than with historical and structural factors. Jewish immigrants were not illiterate peasants lacking urban experience. Those in the 1880–1920 period came mostly from the urban areas of eastern Europe, where they had already worked in a variety of urban occupations, such as manufacturing, craftwork, and small-scale commerce. Many had experience as small merchants. Others were textile workers. Compared with most other immigrants at this time, their literacy level was high. Jews migrated to the United States at a time of expanding manufacturing and trade. Their urban backgrounds, skills, and education fit in well with the needs of capitalism, especially in the expanding textile industry. Steinberg concludes that, contrary to what Glazer and others have argued, Jewish immigrants did not need to rely only on their religious values; they came in with "occupational skills that gave them a decisive advantage over other immigrants." The fit between Jewish skills and economic circumstances at a critical time was also better than it would be for later nonwhite immigrants (such as blacks and Puerto Ricans) to the big cities.[86]

Because of ongoing discrimination, as well as Jewish choice, structural assimilation has proceeded slowly at the informal level. Concentration of informal social life still goes on within the Jewish American community. Lenski found this to be true of most Jewish Americans in Detroit; the study by Sklare and associates of a midwestern suburb found that most affluent Jews chose other Jews as close friends. One study of a Minnesota city suggested that the Jewish American community there is organized around friendships and family. More recent studies have shown an increase in Jewish American social ties outside the Jewish American community, coupled with strong traditional ties, particularly among younger generations.[87]

Discrimination has taken not only economic but also social form. From the late nineteenth century Jewish Americans were excluded from hotels, restaurants, social clubs, voluntary associations, and housing. Some discrimination has persisted into the present. The social ties of Jewish Americans have been firmly cemented in part for defensive reasons. The Jewish American community and family have provided the critical defensive context for survival in the face of anti-Semitism.

Even in cities such as Los Angeles, where the large Jewish American community has a reduced birthrate and a more dispersed housing pattern in the 1980s than in previous decades, group life is strong. As a study of Los Angeles Jews put it, "the picture that emerges from the survey is of a vibrant people whose closest personal associations are with other Jews in the family, friendship, and occupational groupings."[88]

A survey in the late 1950s found that only 7 percent of Jewish American marriages (that is, marriages in which at least one partner is Jewish) involved a non-Jew. Other studies in the 1950s and 1960s found variable rates; 17 to 18 percent of Jewish marriages in New York and San Francisco involved a non-Jewish partner. Rates have been found to be highest among third-generation Jews and in smaller Jewish American communities. In the 1970s and 1980s the rate of intermarriage seemed to be growing again, with 30 to 40 percent of Jewish marriages including a non-Jewish partner.[89]

Opinion surveys in the 1980s have demonstrated that Jewish Americans remain family-oriented. They are generally liberal on issues such as premarital sex and providing youths with birth control information, but have been opposed to extramarital sex. "By and large American Jews, for all their liberalism toward sex, continue to view the Jewish family as an institution that must be protected."[90]

Intentional discrimination played a major role in frustrating the rise of first-generation Sephardic, German, and eastern European Jews. Even the acculturated children of these immigrants faced anti-Semitic barriers, barriers that would stall structural assimilation. Discrimination channeled the eastern Europeans into familiar ghetto communities. In spite of the affluence of later generations, subtle economic and social discrimination seems to have survived. Gordon argued that while Jewish Americans have partially assimilated at the behavior-receptional level (that is, discrimination has declined), there has been less assimilation at the attitude-receptional level because of the persistence of anti-Semitism.[91] We have seen the persistence of anti-Semitic stereotypes among non-Jews surveyed in opinion polls even in the last decade.

## Recent Soviet Immigrants: Strong Jewish Identity

The social and economic adjustment of recent Jewish immigrants to the United States raises some interesting questions about assimilation and about American culture. In a survey of 900 recent Soviet immigrants, most reported that they had left the Soviet Union because of the anti-Semitism there. The opinion survey asked the immigrants to compare their lives in the United States with life in the Soviet Union. Most reported having trouble with English and initially finding a job but rated their life as Jews, as well as their housing, income, and overall standard of living, as *better* than that in the Soviet Union. But other answers were more surprising. Sixty-eight percent rated their cultural environment as *worse* in the United States. And large percentages felt their friendship, social status, and work atmospheres were worse in the United States. They liked the freedom and creativity of the United States, but disliked the vulgarity and "low" cultural tastes. This mostly well educated group of immigrants appears to be assimilating well to American life in material terms, but is having more trouble with sociocultural adjustments. Moreover, their strong Jewish identity means assimilation first in the Jewish American community, where their presence has boosted Jewish identity and commitment.[92]

## Modern Jewish Identity: Is It Changing?

In the World War II period many Jewish Americans changed their names. For example, in Los Angeles right after World War II, just under half of all those petitioning for name changes were Jewish, although Jewish residents made up about 6 percent of the population. For some this may have been the final rejection of their Jewish identity. For most, however, it may instead have been an action instrumental in securing a job, in facilitating structural mobility.

Numerous researchers have noted the continuing strength of Jewish identification, though coupled with a declining commitment to a specifically German or Yiddish heritage. The aforementioned 1983 General Social Survey found that a majority of the Jewish American respondents saw themselves as "strong" or "somewhat strong" Jews, even though most did not regularly participate in synagogue services. Substantially middle-income, the third and fourth generations have become more Americanized than their parents; at the same time, many have resisted what Gordon terms identificational assimilation.

Many Jewish parents have provided some education for their children in Hebrew schools. One 1970s study found that more than eight in every ten young Jewish males had attended Jewish parochial schools, as had seven in ten young Jewish women. Most parents want to preserve the Jewish ethnic identity. A Minnesota study found that only a small minority of a sample there denied their Jewish backgrounds when asked. And in their study of affluent suburbanites Sklare, Greenblum, and Ringer discovered that most of their respondents were committed to the maintenance of their heritage—and to the state of Israel. Israel has been a focus of Jewish American identity and consciousness, a focus reducing the possibility of identificational assimilation.[93]

An alternative to the traditional approach of Anglo-conformity assimilation, cultural pluralism can be seen in the views of many ethnic group leaders since the early 1800s. Interestingly, it was a Jewish American of Polish and Latvian origin who best formulated this perspective. Horace Kallen (1882–1974) argued that membership in ethnic–cultural groups was not a membership one could readily give up. Writing in *The Nation* in 1915, he argued that ethnic groupings had a right to exist in their own right—that is, democracy applied to ethnic groups. He argued against the ruthless Americanization advocated by some nativists. By the 1920s he had given the name *cultural pluralism* to the view that each ethnic group has the democratic right to retain its own heritage. However, other scholars have argued that cultural pluralism is not a useful perspective for understanding the United states, since massive acculturation and assimilation have been facts of life for immigrants.[94]

Greeley's *ethnogenesis* perspective is in part a call for recognition of the reality of cultural differences among contemporary ethnic groups. The ethnogenesis model seems to fit the Jewish experience. Jewish Americans are more than a European nationality group. They are a composite group of Sephardic, German, and eastern European origin. In the United States those groups forged a distinctive ethnic group, shaped partially by the European cultural heritage and partially by the core culture. Despite substantial changes, ethnic distinctiveness, including some cultural distinctiveness, remains.

Heritage, tradition, and socialization of children by parents still shape the behavior and beliefs of American Jews. Beyond this ethnic impact there is a question of ethnic identity. How strong is that identity? Is it, as Herbert Gans argues, only a "symbolic ethnicity," without much deep significance? History suggests that Gans is wrong. The sense of "Jewishness" is likely to remain strong for the majority of Jewish Americans for the foreseeable future.[95]

## SUMMARY

Jewish Americans, most of whom are descendants of eastern Europeans, have become partially assimilated in the cultural arena. An economically prosperous group, an ethnic group that made dramatic progress up the mobility ladder, Jewish Americans fought great discrimination and some violence. Theirs is a success story. But a price was paid for success, and today significant anti-Semitism persists, limiting movement to the very top. Coupled with vertical progress has been horizontal mobility in the form of suburbanization. The first-generation eastern European Jews were concentrated in central-city ghettos; the second and third generations began moving into suburban areas. In the last decade some have suggested that this trend toward suburbanization has ended, that there may even be a drift back to the cities. If so, the shape of Jewish American communities may again change.

Central to an adequate understanding of Jewish Americans today is an understanding of the ties to Israel. Periodic Arab–Israeli flare-ups have generated among Jewish Americans a strong commitment to Israel, philosophically and financially. Israel continues to be seen as the hope for a people that has survived the Roman persecution, the Spanish Inquisition, the Russian pogroms, and the Nazi Holocaust. Related to this hope has been the flow of thousands of Jewish Americans to the work camps, towns, and cities of Israel. Yet in recent years we have also seen a dramatic flow of Israeli and Soviet immigrants escaping the threat of war or seeking economic opportunities. Many new Jewish immigrants have settled in the United States. They provide a contemporary reminder of the continuing sojourner character of the Jewish experience.

Perhaps most important, we have demonstrated in this chapter just how diverse the American melting pot is—a diversity that makes for great vitality and creativity. The Jewish American presence and participation in U.S. institutions means that this nation is *not* by definition a *Christian* country; it is a nation of many religious groups, including Christians, Jews, and Muslims. One of the contributions of Jewish Americans has been to stand up for their religious and cultural heritage in spite of discrimination and opposition.

The presence of Jewish Americans has also contributed substantially to the American emphasis on education, to high achievement in the arts and sciences, and to the values of justice, tolerance, and fairness. Jewish Americans have not been only victims of past and present anti-Semitic prejudice and discrimination; they and their organizations have been in the forefront of the fight against the prejudice and racism that characterizes U.S. society even to the present day.

## NOTES

1. See David Sidorsky, "Introduction," in *The Future of the Jewish Community in America*, ed. David Sidorsky (New York: Basic Books, 1973), pp. xix–xxv; and Stephen D. Isaacs, *Jews and American Politics* (Garden City, N.Y.: Doubleday, 1974), pp. ix–x.

2. George Cohen, *The Jews in the Making of America* (Boston: Stratford Co., 1924), pp. 35–39.

3. Carl Wittke, *We Who Built America*, rev. ed. (Cleveland: Case Western Reserve University Press, 1967), pp. 324–30; Will Herberg, *Protestant—Catholic—Jew*, rev. ed. (New York: Doubleday, Anchor Books, 1960), pp. 175–77.

4. Lucy S. Dawidowicz, *The War against the Jews: 1933–1945* (New York: Holt, Rinehart & Winston, 1975), p. xiv; Wittke, *We Who Built America*, pp. 329–31.

5. Jacob Lestschinsky, "Economic and Social Development of American Jewry," in *The Jewish People*, vol. 4 (New York: Jewish Encyclopedic Handbooks, 1955), p. 56; Herberg, *Protestant—Catholic—Jew*, p. 178; Maurice J. Karpf, *Jewish Community Organization in the United States* (New York: Arno, 1971), p. 34; Samuel Joseph, "Jewish Immigration to the United States from 1881 to 1910," *Studies in History, Economics, and Public Law* 56 (1914): 509–12.

6. Karpf, *Jewish Community Organization in the United States*, p. 33; Sidney Goldstein, "American Jewry: A Demographic Analysis," in *The Future of the Jewish Community in America*, ed. Sidorsky, p. 71; Alvin Chenkin, "Jewish Population in the United States," *American Jewish Yearbook, 1973* (New York: American Jewish Committee, 1973), pp. 307–9; Arthur A. Goren, "Jews," in *Harvard Encyclopedia of American Ethnic Groups* (Cambridge: Harvard University Press, 1980), pp. 591–92; Rita J. Simon and Julian L. Simon, "Social and Economic Adjustment," in *New Lives*, ed. Rita J. Simon (Lexington, Mass.: Heath, Lexington Books, 1985), pp. 26–41.

7. Herberg, *Protestant—Catholic—Jew*, pp. 170–80; Stuart E. Rosenberg, *The Search for Jewish Identity in America* (New York: Doubleday, Anchor Books, 1965), pp. 47–68.

8. Herberg, *Protestant—Catholic—Jew*, p. 182.

9. Charles Y. Glock and Rodney Stark, *Christian Beliefs and Anti-Semitism* (New York: Harper & Row, Pub. 1966), p. 64 and elsewhere.

10. Carey McWilliams, *A Mask for Privilege* (Boston: Little, Brown, 1948), pp. 164–65, 170–73; John Higham, "Social Discrimination against Jews in America, 1830–1930," *Publication of the American Jewish Historical Society*, 47 (September 1957): 5.

11. Higham, "Social Discrimination against Jews in America, 1830–1930," pp. 9–10; Carey McWilliams, *Brothers under the Skin*, rev. ed. (Boston: Little, Brown, 1964), pp. 302–3. The quote appears in the *Los Angeles Times*, November 24, 1974, p. 1.

12. Gustavus Meyers, *History of Bigotry in the United States*, rev. ed. (New York: Capricorn Books, 1960), pp. 277–313; McWilliams, *A Mask for Privilege*, pp. 110–11; Isaacs, *Jews and American Politics*, pp. 51, 98.

13. Carl C. Brigham, *A Study of American Intelligence* (Princeton, N.J.: Princeton University Press, 1923), pp. 177–210.

14. T. W. Adorno et al., *The Authoritarian Personality* (New York: Harper, 1950), pp. 69–79; Gertrude J. Selznick and Stephen Steinberg, *The Tenacity of Prejudice* (New York: Harper & Row, Pub. 1969), pp. 6–8, 184. The 1981 polls are cited in Lenni Brenner, *Jews in America Today* (Secaucus, N.J.: Lyle Stuart, 1986), p. 64.

15. Henry L. Feingold, *Zion in America* (New York: Twayne, 1974), pp. 143–44; C. Vann Woodward, *Tom Watson* (New York: Oxford University Press, 1963), pp. 435–45.

16. Rufus Learski, *The Jews in America* (New York: KTAV Publishing House, 1972), pp. 290–91; John Higham, *Strangers in the Land* (New York: Atheneum, 1975), pp. 298–99.

17. Milton R. Konvitz, "Inter-group Relations," in *The American Jew*, ed. O. I. Janowsky (Philadelphia: Jewish Publication Society of America, 1964), pp. 78–79; Donald S. Strong, *Organized Anti-Semitism in America* (Washington, D.C.: American Council on Public Affairs, 1941), pp. 14–20.

18. Strong, *Organized Anti-Semitism in America*, p. 67.

19. Dawidowicz, *The War against the Jews*, p. 148; see also pp. 164, 403.

20. Lewis H. Carlson and George A. Colburn, "The Jewish Refugee Problem," in *In Their Place*, ed. Lewis H. Carlson and George A. Colburn (New York: John Wiley, 1972), pp. 290–91; Brenner, *Jews in America Today*, pp. 205–6.

21. Brenner, *Jews in America Today*, p. 209.

22. Gerald S. Strober, *American Jews* (Garden City, N.Y.: Doubleday, 1974), pp. 149–76.

23. Lawrence H. Fuchs, *The Political Behavior of American Jews* (Glencoe, Ill.: Free Press, 1956), pp. 23–25.

24. Mark R. Levy and Michael S. Kramer, *The Ethnic Factor* (New York: Simon & Schuster, 1972), p. 101; Feingold, *Zion in America*, pp. 83–89; William R. Heitzmann, *American Jewish Voting Behavior* (San Francisco: R & E Research Associates, 1975), pp. 27–28.

25. Heitzmann, *American Jewish Voting Behavior*, p. 29.

26. Irving Howe, *World of Our Fathers* (New York: Simon & Schuster, 1976), pp. 362–64; Emanuel Hertz, "Politics: New York," in *The Russian Jew in the United States, ed. Charles S. Bernheimer (Philadelphia: John Winston and Co., 1905), pp. 256–65*.

27. Edward M. Levine, *The Irish and Irish Politicians* (Notre Dame, Ind.: University of Notre Dame Press, 1966): Isaacs, *Jews and American Politics*, pp. 23–24; Feingold, *Zion in America*, p. 321.

28. Hertz, "Politics: New York," pp. 265–67; Heitzmann, *American Jewish Voting Behavior*, p. 37; Fuchs, *The Political Behavior of American Jews*, pp. 57–58.

29. Levy and Kramer, *The Ethnic Factor*, pp. 102–3; Howe, *World of Our Fathers*, pp. 381–88.

30. Heitzmann, *American Jewish Voting Behavior*, p. 49; Fuchs, *The Political Behavior of American Jews*, pp. 99–100.

31. Selznick and Steinberg, *The Tenacity of Prejudice*, p. 54; Fuchs, *The Political Behavior of American Jews*, pp. 171–91.

32. Isaacs, *Jews and American Politics*, pp. 6, 152; Heitzmann, *American Jewish Voting Behavior*, pp. 56–58; Strober, *American Jews*, pp. 186–88; Levy and Kramer, *The Ethnic Factor*, p. 103; Milton Plesur,

*Jewish Life in Twentieth Century America* (Chicago: Nelson Hall, 1982), pp. 134–52; William Schneider, "The Jewish Vote in 1984," *Public Opinion* 7 (December/January 1985): 58; Brenner, *Jews in America Today*, pp. 37, 128–31.

33. Isaacs, *Jews and American Politics*, pp. 23, 201; Levy and Kramer, *The Ethnic Factor*, p. 118; *Time*, March 10, 1975, p. 25; Plesur, *Jewish Life in Twentieth Century America*, pp. 143–45.

34. Isaacs, *Jews and American Politics*, pp. 12, 118–19.

35. Bernard Cohen, *Sociocultural Changes in American Jewish Life as Reflected in Selected Jewish Literature* (Rutherford, N.J.: Fairleigh Dickinson University Press, 1972), pp. 183–85; Learski, *The Jews in America*, pp. 158–59; Rudolf Glanz, *The Jewish Woman in America*, vol. 1, *The Eastern European Jewish Woman* (New York: KTAV Publishing House, 1976), pp. 48–57.

36. Nathan Reich, "Economic Status," in *The American Jew*, ed. Janowsky, pp. 70–71; Karpf, Jewish Community Organization in the United States, pp. 11–12; Howe, *World of Our Fathers*, pp. 391–93; Feingold, *Zion in America*, pp. 235–36.

37. Jonathan S. Woocher, *Sacred Survival* (Bloomington: Indiana University Press, 1986), pp. vii–viii.

38. Karpf, *Jewish Community Organization in the United States*, pp. 62–65; *Time*, March 10, 1975, p. 23; Naomi Cohen, *Not Free to Desist* (Philadelphia: Jewish Publication Society of America, 1972) pp. 3–18, 37–80, 433–52.

39. *Time*, March 10, 1975, pp. 18–28; Arnold Foster and Benjamin R. Epstein, *The New Anti-Semitism* (New York: McGraw-Hill, 1974), pp. 155–284; Strober, *American Jews*, pp. 7–42.

40. Wolfe Kelman, "The Synagogue in America," in *The Future of the Jewish Community in America*, ed. Sidorsky, pp. 171–73.

41. Strober, *American Jews*, pp. 120–30; Maurice R. Berube and Marilyn Gittell, "The Struggle for Community Control," in *Confrontation at Ocean Hill–Brownsville*, ed. Maurice R. Berube and Marilyn Gittell (New York: Praeger, 1969), pp. 3–12 and elsewhere; Joe R. Feagin and Harlan Hahn, *Ghetto Revolts* (New York: Macmillan, 1973), pp. 327–28; Nathan Glazer, *Affirmative Discrimination* (New York: Basic Books, 1975), pp. 33–76, 196–221.

42. Brenner, *Jews in America Today*, p. 10.

43. Wittke, *We Who Built America*, pp. 39–40; Cohen, *The Jews in the Making of America*, pp. 73–80.

44. Feingold, *Zion in America*, p. 12; McWilliams, *Brothers under the Skin*, pp. 305–6.

45. Wittke, *We Who Built America*, p. 325; Cohen, *The Jews in the Making of America*, pp. 120–22.

46. Lestschinsky, "Economic and Social Development of American Jewry," p. 78.

47. Ibid., pp. 74–77; Isaac M. Rubinow, "Economic and Industrial Condition: New York," in *The Russian Jew in the United States*, ed. Bernheimer, pp. 103–7.

48. Nathan Goldberg, *Occupational Patterns of American Jewry* (New York: Jewish Teachers Seminary Press, 1947), pp. 15–17; Marshall Sklare, *America's Jews* (New York: Random House, 1971), p. 61; Rubinow, "Economic and Industrial Condition: New York," pp. 110–11.

49. Charlotte Baum, Paula Hyman, and Sonya Michel, *The Jewish Woman in America* (New York: Dial Press, 1976), p. 98.

50. Karpf, *Jewish Community Organization in the United States*, pp. 9–14; Lestschinsky, "Economic and Social Development of American Jewry," pp. 91–92; W. Lloyd Warner and Leo Srole, *The Social Systems of American Ethnic Groups* (New Haven: Yale University Press, 1945), p. 112.

51. McWilliams, *A Mask for Privilege*, pp. 38, 40–41; Karpf, *Jewish Community Organization in the United States*, pp. 20–21; Higham, "Social Discrimination against Jews in America," pp. 18–19.

52. For the February 1936 *Fortune* survey, see Karpf, *Jewish Community Organization in the United States*, pp. 9–11; and McWilliams, *A Mask for Privilege*, pp. 143–50. See also Lestschinsky, "Economic and Social Development of American Jewry," p. 81.

53. Lestschinsky, "Economic and Social Development of American Jewry," pp. 71, 87; McWilliams, *A Mask for Privilege*, p. 159; Reich, "Economic Status," pp. 63–65.

54. Barry R. Chiswick, "The Labor Market Status of American Jews," in *American Jewish Handbook*, ed. M. Himmelfarb and D. Singer (New York: American Jewish Committee, 1984), p. 137.

55. Mabel Newcomer, *The Big Business Executive* (New York: Columbia University Press, 1955), pp. 46–48.

56. Donald J. Bogue, *The Population of the United States* (Glencoe, Ill.: Free Press, 1959), p. 706; Norval D. Glenn and Ruth Hyland, "Religious Preference and Worldly Success," *American Sociological*

*Review* 32 (February 1967): 78; Thomas R. Dye, *Who's Running America* (Englewood Cliffs, N.J.: Prentice-Hall, 1976), pp. 41–42; Brenner, *Jews in America Today*, p. 64.

57. Brenner, *Jews in America Today*, pp. 65–78.

58. Goren, "Jews," p. 593; Sklare, *America's Jews*, pp. 61–62; Sidney Goldstein, "Jews in the United States: Perspectives from Demography," in *American Jewish Yearbook, 1981* (New York: American Jewish Committee, 1980–1981), p. 54.

59. Reich, "Economic Status," p. 74; Sklare, *America's Jews*, p. 65; Richard L. Zweigenhaft and G. William Domhoff, *Jews in the Protestant Establishment* (New York: Praeger, 1982), pp. 24–27. The banking data are from American Jewish Committee reports summarized in Melvin L. DeFleur, William V. D'Antonio, and Louis B. DeFleur, *Sociology: Human Society*, 2d ed. (Dallas: Scott, Foresman, 1976), p. 268.

60. Zweigenhaft and Domhoff, *Jews in the Protestant Establishment*, p. 46.

61. Sklare, *America's Jews*, p. 65; McWilliams, *Brothers under the Skin*, pp. 310–11.

62. Sklare, *America's Jews*, pp. 67–69.

63. Naomi Levine and Martin Hochbaum, *Poor Jews* (New Brunswick, N.J.: Transaction Books, 1974), pp. 2–3, 36.

64. Cohen, *Sociocultural Changes*, pp. 158–59; Abraham Cahan, "The Russian Jew in the United States," in *The Russian Jew in the United States*, ed. Bernheimer, pp. 32–33.

65. J. K. Paulding, "Educational Influences: New York," in *The Russian Jew in the United States*, ed. Bernheimer, pp. 186–97; Cohen, *The Jews in the Making of America*, pp. 140–41; Karpf, *Jewish Community Organization in the United States*, p. 57.

66. Higham, "Social Discrimination against Jews in America, 1830–1930," p. 22; Karpf, *Jewish Community Organization in the United States*, p. 19; McWilliams, *A Mask for Privilege*, pp. 128–29.

67. McWilliams, *A Mask for Privilege*, pp. 136–38; Karpf, *Jewish Community Organization in the United States*, pp. 18–19; Goren, "Jews," p. 590.

68. Glenn and Hyland, "Religious Preference and Worldly Success," p. 79; *Time*, March 10, 1975, p. 24; Sklare, *America's Jews*, pp. 54–55; Goren, "Jews," p. 593; the 1983 General Survey data have been tabulated by the author for this book.

69. Cohen, *Sociocultural Changes*, pp. 163–67; Oscar I. Janowsky, "Achievements," in *The American Jew*, ed. Janowsky, pp. 129–30; Walter I. Ackerman, "The Jewish School System in the United States," in *The Future of the Jewish Community in America*, ed. Sidorsky, pp. 177–79; Robert Alter, "What Jewish Studies Can Do," *Commentary* 58 (October 1974): 71–74.

70. Anita L. Lebeson, *Pilgrim People*, rev. ed. (New York: Minerva Press, 1975), pp. 162; Feingold, *Zion in America*, pp. 29–31; Learski, *The Jews in America*, pp. 110–23; Marshall Sklare, *Conservative Judaism* (Glencoe, Ill.: Free Press, 1955): Rosenberg, *The Search for Jewish Identity in America*, pp. 174–75.

71. Samuel C. Heilman, "The Sociology of American Jewry," in *Annual Review of Sociology*, ed. Ralph Turner, vol. 8 (Palo Alto, Calif.: Annual Reviews, 1982), p. 145; Kelman, "The Synagogue in America," pp. 157–58; Herberg, *Protestant—Catholic—Jew*, pp. 185–96; Louis Lipsky, "Religious Activity: New York," in *The Russian Jew in the United States*, ed. Bernheimer, pp. 152–54.

72. Kelman, "The Synagogue in America," pp. 158–59; Herberg, *Protestant—Catholic—Jew*, pp. 190–93.

73. Marshall Sklare, Joseph Greenblum, and Benjamin B. Ringer, *Not Quite at Home* (New York: Institute of Human Relations Press, 1969), pp. 13–23; Sidney Goldstein and Calvin Goldscheider, *Jewish Americans* (Englewood Cliffs, N.J.: Prentice-Hall, 1968), pp. 195–97 et passim; Herberg, *Protestant—Catholic—Jew*, p. 197; Bernard Lazerwitz and Louis Rowitz, "The Three-Generations Hypothesis," *American Journal of Sociology* 69 (March 1964): 532.

74. J. L. Blau, *Judaism in America* (Chicago: University of Chicago Press, 1976), as summarized in Heilman, "The Sociology of American Jewry," p. 147.

75. Strober, *American Jews*, pp. 73–75, 83–98.

76. Konvitz, "Inter-Group Relations," in *The American Jew*, ed. Janowsky, pp. 85–95.

77. Robert F. Drinan, "The Supreme Court, Religious Freedom and the Yarmulke," *America* 155 (June 12, 1986): 9–11.

78. Noah Lucas, "Is Zionism Dead," in *The Sociology of American Jews*, 2d ed., ed. Jack N. Porter (Washington, D.C.: University Press of America, 1980), p. 261.

79. Howe, *World of Our Fathers*, p. 645; Karpf, *Jewish Community Organization in the United States*, pp. 37–39, 49–50.

80. Cohen, *Sociocultural Changes*, pp. 47–49; Baum, Hyman, and Michel, *The Jewish Woman in America*, pp. 29–33; Learski, *The Jews in America*, pp. 37–38.

81. Herberg, *Protestant—Catholic—Jew*, p. 183; Charles S. Liebman, "American Jewry: Identity and Affiliation," in *The Future of the Jewish Community in America*, ed. Sidorsky, p. 133.

82. Goldstein and Goldscheider, *Jewish Americans*, p. 226.

83. Herberg, *Protestant—Catholic—Jew*, pp. 183–87.

84. Goldstein and Goldscheider, *Jewish Americans*, pp. 8–10; Howe, *World of Our Fathers*, pp. 644–45; Milton M. Gordon, *Assimilation in American Life* (New York: Oxford University Press, 1964), pp. 190–94; C. Liebman, "Orthodox Judaism Today," *Mainstream* 25 (1979): 12–36; Heilman, "The Sociology of American Jewry," p. 139.

85. Nathan Glazer, "The American Jew and the Attainment of Middle-class Rank: Some Trends and Explanations," in *The Jews*, ed. M. Sklare (Glencoe, Ill.: Free Press, 1958), p. 143, as quoted in Stephen Steinberg, *The Ethnic Myth* (New York: Atheneum, 1981), p. 93.

86. Steinberg, *The Ethnic Myth*, pp. 94–102.

87. Gerhard Lenski, *The Religious Factor* (Garden City, N.Y.: Doubleday, Anchor Books, 1963), p. 37; Sklare, Greenblum, & Ringer, *Not Quite at Home*; Arnold Dashefsky and Howard M. Shapiro, *Ethnic Identification among American Jews* (Lexington, Mass.: Heath, 1974), pp. 117–18.

88. Quoted in Goldstein, "Jews in the United States," p. 28. Compare Isidore Chein, "The Problem of Jewish Identification," *Jewish Social Studies* 17 (July 1955): 221; Sklare, ed., *The Jews*; Dashefsky and Shapiro, *Ethnic Identification among American Jews*, pp. 115, 123–26.

89. U.S. Bureau of the Census, "Religion Reported by the Civilian Population of the United States," *Current Population Reports*, Series P-20 (February 1958), p. 8. The New York, San Francisco, and Providence studies are cited in Goldstein and Goldscheider, *Jewish Americans*, pp. 152–55. See also *Time*, March 24, 1975, p. 25.

90. Heilman, "The Sociology of American Jewry," p. 152.

91. Gordon, *Assimilation in American Life*, pp. 76–77.

92. Simon and Simon, "Social and Economic Adjustment," pp. 27–38.

93. Leonard Broom, Helen Beem, and Virginia Harris, "Characteristics of 1,107 Petitioners for Change of Name," *American Sociological Review* 20 (February 1955): 33–35; Dashefsky and Shapiro, *Ethnic Identification among American Jews*, pp. 120–21; Sklare, Greenblum, and Ringer, *Not Quite at Home*, pp. 82–83.

94. Milton R. Konvitz, "Horace Meyer Kallen (1882–1974)," in *American Jewish Yearbook, 1974–1975* (New York: American Jewish Committee, 1974), pp. 65–67; Gordon, *Assimilation in American Life*, pp. 142–59.

95. Herbert J. Gans, "Symbolic Ethnicity," *Ethnic and Racial Studies* 2 (1979): 1–20.

# CHAPTER 7

# *Native Americans*

It was the summer of 1977. Navaho medicine men came to Sante Fe, New Mexico, to take back religious and other ceremonial "artifacts" that a museum had collected. For the museum and its white visitors, these prayer sticks, medicine bundles, and other items were curiosities provided to entertain and perhaps inform white residents and tourists. But for the Navahos they were sacred objects that had been taken or stolen from their rightful Native American owners. After holding a ceremony with chants of joy, the medicine men reclaimed the sacred objects. One said, "We will take them home and teach the younger generation what these things mean." Many sacred objects belonging to Native American tribes remain in white hands.[1]

With this chapter we begin to consider several groups whose ancestry is substantially non-European and nonwhite. Some among them, such as the Native Americans, predate European entry into this continent. European colonization and expansion were the social processes that brought subordination to non-European groups. In subsequent chapters we will see critical differences in the past and present experiences of white and nonwhite Americans. We will discover the great relevance of power-conflict theories in interpreting the past and present of these subordinated groups.

The first victims of the European colonization process were those the Europeans called "Indians." Long erroneously called by this name, Native Americans have suffered from a variety of stereotypes, from the wooden cigar-stove figure to the bloodthirsty savage of the movies to the noble primitive of novels. Tomahawks, scalping, feathered headdresses, and red men on wild ponies—such images have been impressed on the Euro-American mind by mass-media sensationalism, including distorted images in magazines, newspapers, movies, and television.

Coupled with this has been a tendency to ignore the past and present reality of Native American life. Reflect for a moment on Europeans "discovering" an ancient continent *already* peopled by several million inhabitants. The Europeans were latecomers. The ancestors of the tribes encountered by the fifteenth-century explorers had discovered the continent at least twenty thousand years earlier, when they probably migrated across the Alaskan land bridge from Asia. Reflect too on the strange name these people have had to bear ever since, the "Indians" (*los Indios*), a name given to them by Europeans. Yet this name reflected a colossal error, the assumption that the early expeditions had found the Asian Indies they were seeking.

## CONQUEST BY EUROPEANS AND EURO-AMERICANS

Migration has been viewed as varying from voluntary migration to slave importation. Such a framework typically includes a dominant racial or ethnic group that is already established within certain boundaries and is assimilating a new human group. But the situation of Native Americans points up the need to look at the migration of the dominant group itself, in this case Europeans moving into the territories of the Native American groups. *Colonization migration* is an apt term for this process. This type of migration, unlike the others just mentioned, involves the conquest and domination of a preexisting group by outsiders. This process illustrates what some call *classical colonialism.*

How many Native Americans were there at the time Europeans came into North American history? Anthropologists and other analysts have estimated the native population of North America in 1600 at between 500,000 and 1,150,000 persons. In recent decades the estimate has been revised upward sharply. A considered estimate by Dobyns puts the number in North America at nearly ten million at the time of conquest, with tens of millions in Central and South America as well. While this figure may be high, it may also be more accurate than earlier figures. Older estimates have often been used for the purpose of legitimating the European conquest of an allegedly unoccupied land.[2]

European diseases and firepower sharply reduced the number of Native Americans in North America from one to ten million at the time of first contact to approximately 200,000 by 1850. The number of Native Americans remained between 200,000 and 300,000 from the low point in the mid-nineteenth century until the 1930s, when it began to grow again. The 1980 census counted 1.4 million people who said their background was American Indian. On another question 6.8 million Americans claimed some Native American ancestry. In the 1980s the 1.4 million Native Americans lived on 250 reservations, in other rural areas, and in cities; and most lived west of the Mississippi.[3]

The term *Indian* and most major tribal names are terms of convenience applied by European American settlers. The naming of Native American societies by outsiders reflects their subordination, for in most history books not one of the major tribes is recorded under its own name. This suggests one difference between colonized nonwhites and European immigrants: colonized peoples have had less control over the naming process. For example, the "Navahos" called themselves, in their own language, *Dine*, which meant "The People."[4]

## Native American Societies: Are They Tribes?

Native Americans have for centuries been a diverse collection of societies, with dramatic differences in numbers, languages, economies, polities, and customs. Some define the common term *tribe* as a group of relatives with a distinctive language and customs who are tied to a definite territory. Yet such a definition tends to obscure the great variety in size and complexity of Native American groups, which have ranged from very small hunting and gathering societies to the large, well-organized groups suggested by this definition. Although it is difficult to get away from the common usage of the term *tribe* for all groups, we will also use the term *society* for Native American groups in order to suggest that not all were well organized with definite territories.

There were perhaps two hundred distinct groups at the time of the European invasion. Traditionally, Native American societies have been grouped into geographical areas, including: (1) the societies of the East, who hunted, farmed, and fished, and whose first encounters with whites were with English settlers; (2) the Great Plains hunters and agriculturalists, whose first encounters were with the Spaniards; (3) the fishing societies in the Northwest; (4) the seed gatherers of California and neighboring areas; (5) the Navaho shepherds and Pueblo farmers in the Arizona–New Mexico area; (6) the desert societies of southern Arizona and New Mexico; and (7) the Alaskan groups, including the Eskimo. In this chapter we will sometimes be speaking of the two hundred past and present societies as though they were one group; at other times we will be speaking of one distinct group within this larger category.[5]

*Forced migration* at gunpoint was the lot of some native groups after they had been defeated. Among the famous forced marches was that of thousands of Cherokees, Creeks, Chicasaws, Choctaws, and Seminoles from their eastern lands to the Oklahoma Territory. Tribes in the West, such as the Navaho were rounded up after military engagements and forced to migrate to barren reservations. In the twentieth century, moreover, internal migration from rural areas to the cities has been very important. In the 1950s, under President Eisenhower's secretary of the interior, an earlier urban relocation program was expanded to cover more tribal groups and cities; a specific Bureau of Indian Affairs (BIA) branch was set up to oversee relocation services. The scale of this internal migration can be seen in the fact that 200,000 Native Americans moved to the cities between the late 1950s and the 1970s, settling for the most part in poverty-stricken areas.[6]

Why did they move to the cities? Analysts have pointed to voluntary choice, triggered by push factors of poverty and unemployment on reservations and the pull factor of expanding economic opportunities, which were concentrated in the cities.[7]

## The Colonial Period

Various strategies were developed by the Europeans for dealing with those Native Americans whose land they coveted. These ranged from honest treaty making with equals, to deceptive treaty making, to attempts to exterminate the "Indian menace," to enslavement in a form similar to that of Africans, to confinement in barren prison camps called reservations.[8]

On the East Coast in the 1600s, the Dutch established several communities. Several native groups were displaced or wiped out by Dutch settlers. A Dutch governor was one of the first to offer a government bounty for Native American scalps, used as proof of death; Europeans played a major role in spreading this bloody practice conventionally attributed only to Native Americans.[9] English settlers gained superiority over the Native Americans, forcing them into the frontier areas or killing them off.[10] Few seemed concerned for the genocidal consequences of their expansion. In spite of the often noted reliance of English settlers on friendly Native Americans in surviving the first devastating years, the new settlers soon turned on their neighbors. A war with the Pequots in 1637 ended when several hundred Native Americans in a village were massacred by whites, with the survivors sent into slavery. The 1675–1676 King Phillip's War with the Wampanoag tribe and its allies, precipitated by the oppressive tactics of the New England settlers, resulted in substantial losses on both sides. English retaliation was brutal. Hagan notes that the Native American leader, King Phillip, was "captured, drawn, and quartered: his skull remained on view on a pole in Plymouth as late as 1700."[11] Survivors were sold as slaves.

The enslavement of Native Americans was a major source of friction. A 1708 report mentioned 1,400 Native American slaves in the Carolina area. By the mid-eighteenth century the Native American proportion among slaves was between 5 and 10 percent. As late as the 1790 census, 200 of the 6,000 slaves in Massachusetts were Native Americans. Native Americans were replaced by Africans in part because escape was a constant problem with the former.[12]

The English defeat of the French after a ten-year war resulted in the French withdrawal from the continent in the mid-1700s. This move brought many tribes into contact with the less sophisticated policy of the English.[13]

## Treaties and Reservations: Of Utmost Good Faith?

With the founding of the new republic, Native Americans found themselves in a strange new political position. The U.S. Constitution briefly mentions Native Americans in giving Congress the power to regulate commerce with the tribes. And the 1787 Northwest Ordinance made the following solemn promises:

> The utmost good faith shall always be observed towards the Indians; their land and property shall never be taken from them without their consent; and in their property, rights, and liberty, they shall never be invaded or disturbed, unless in justified and lawful wars authorized by Congress; but laws founded in justice and humanity shall from time to time be made, for preventing wrongs being done to them, and for preserving peace and friendship with them.[14]

Washington's secretary of war, whose department had responsibility for "Indians," adopted a policy of peaceful adjustment. Supreme Court decisions in the early 1800s laid out principles that Native American societies had a right to their lands and that they were nations with a right to self-government. Chief Justice John Marshall argued that the United States government must take seriously its treaties with Native Americans. By the late 1700s the executive and legislative branches had become actively involved. In 1790 an act licensing "Indian traders" was passed. A treaty was signed with the Senecas in 1794, and in 1796 government stores were established to provide Native Americans with supplies on credit.[15]

Federal officials, by action or inaction, supported the recurrent theft of lands. In practice, these officials approved of ignoring Native American boundary rights wherever necessary.[16] A distinguished French observer of the 1830s noted the hypocrisy: "But this virtuous and high-minded policy has not been followed. The rapacity of the settlers is usually backed by the tyranny of the government."[17] The procedure was usually not one of immediate expropriation of land, but rather of constant encroachment by settlers, a process sanctioned after the fact by the government and legitimated by treaties.

The subordination of Native Americans was encouraged by Andrew Jackson, a president critical of treaty making, who even encouraged the states to defy Supreme Court rulings on Native Americans. Gradual displacement gave way to marches over hundreds of miles at gunpoint, a policy designed to rid entire regions of the so-called "red savages." Congress passed the Indian Removal Act in 1830, and within a decade many of the tribes of the East voluntarily or forcibly migrated to lands west of the Mississippi under the auspices of "negotiated" treaties. Atlantic and Gulf Coast tribes, such as the Cherokees, as well as midwestern tribes, such as the Ottawas and Shawnees, were forcibly removed to the Oklahoma Territory. Resisters were exterminated. This migration became known as the Trail of Tears. In addition to the large numbers of deaths in the forced march, there were problems in the new lands, with new agricultural techniques required and new animals to hunt.[18]

Westward-moving settlers sometimes precipitated a struggle with the Plains societies, many of whom had by that time given up agriculture for a nomadic hunting and raiding life-style. Most Native American groups in the region had participated in intertribal raiding, but the genocidal actions of federal troops and white settlers were a new experience. It was the nomadic, horse-oriented Plains peoples who forever came to symbolize "the Indian" in the public imagination. Yet the wars on the Plains were not as they have been pictured in the mass media. They usually did not involve glorious chiefs in warbonnets on stallions facing a brave collection of Army officers backed by their heroic men on a sunswept plain.[19]

## Myths about Conflict

The movies and television have portrayed the 1840–1860 era of white overlanders as one of constant conflict with western tribes. Wagon trains moving across the West, wagons in a circle, whooping Indians on ponies, thousands of dead settlers and Indians, treacherous "red men"—the movies and television have created many unforgettable images of the West. However, these images are largely mythological. Histories by John D. Unruh and others have made this clear. Between 1840 and 1860 approximately 250,000 white settlers made the long journey across the plains to the West Coast. Yet far less than 1 percent of those migrants died at the hands of the native inhabitants. Indeed, between 1840 and 1860 a total of *only 362 white settlers and 426 Native Americans* died in *all* the recorded battles between the two groups along wagon train routes. There is only *one* documented attack by Native Americans on a wagon train in which there were as many as two dozen casualties for the white settlers. Most of the accounts of massacres of whites by "wild Indians" are either fictions or great exaggerations of minor encounters.[20]

Unruh's research also highlights the cooperation between Native Americans and settlers. Native Americans provided food and horses for travelers. Some served as guides. Moreover, Unruh and other historians make clear the crucial role of the federal government and of federal troops in "pacifying" the native tribes. By the 1850s an army of federal agents, from the famous "Indian agents" to surveyors, road builders, and treaty agents, was assisting migrants westward.

There was a recurring pattern to the growing conflict between whites and natives. Settlers would settle on native lands to farm. Land for the resettlement of the Native American group affected would be provided by the federal government under the auspices of a treaty involving threat or coercion. More settlers, prospectors, and hunters moving along migratory paths from the East would gradually intrude on these new tribal lands. This land theft would then be legitimated by yet another treaty, and the process might begin again. Or perhaps a treaty promise of supplies or money to those living in their restricted area would not be kept, and some Native American men would leave seeking food or revenge. Such actions resulted in the Army taking repressive action, sometimes intentionally punishing an innocent group and thus precipitating further uprisings.

The treaties, part of United States law, were often masterpieces of fraud: consent was gained by deception or threat. Three hundred treaties with Native American tribes were made between 1790 and the Civil War. As time passed, treaties established regulations governing tribal behavior and provided restricted areas called reservations. Tribes became dependent on the federal Bureau of Indian Affairs and on Congress, which by the Civil War could change treaties without the consent of Native Americans. This treaty process had been abandoned by 1871.[21]

## Massacres of Native Americans

Treaty violations led to conflict. For example, in an 1862 uprising in Minnesota the eastern Sioux massacred settlers after losing much of their land and suffering at the hands of white Indian agents. Delays in payment of promised supplies resulted in warriors burning and killing throughout the Minnesota Valley; massive white retaliation followed. About the same time, conflict occurred in Colorado between local tribes and the militia left in charge when the army was withdrawn to fight the Civil War. The guerilla warfare of the tribes was met by savage retaliation. In 1864 Colonel John Chivington, a minister, and his Colorado volunteers massacred nearly two hundred Native Americans in a peace-seeking band at Sand Creek.[22] The massacre was one of the most savage in western history: "Children carrying white flags were slaughtered and pregnant women were cut open. The slaughter and mutilation continued into the late afternoon over many miles of the bleak prairie."[23]

After the Civil War, the large railroad corporations gobbled up millions of acres. The buffalo were slaughtered by the millions, and the economy of the Plains tribes was destroyed. In the late 1860s a federal peace commission met with numerous tribes at Medicine Lodge Creek in Kansas. Reservations were worked out for all the Plains tribes. But there would still be two decades of battles before all bands would agree to settle in these areas designated by the government.[24]

Settlers, miners, and the army violated treaties with the Sioux and moved into the Dakota Territory. Controversy over the invasion escalated; troops were sent in to force Sioux bands onto a smaller reservation, even though the bands were already on what the government regarded as "unceded Indian territory." In this force was Colonel George A. Custer. The most widely known battle of the Plains struggle occurred at Little Big Horn when an arrogant Custer and his soldiers were wiped out by a group of Sioux and allied tribes that had refused to settle on the reservation.

One of the last engagements was the massacre at Wounded Knee Creek fourteen years later. Attempting to round up the last few Sioux bands, the U.S. army intercepted one group near the Dakota Badlands and forced them to camp. The colonel in command ordered a disarming of the camp, which was carried out in ruthless fashion. One young Sioux shot into a line of soldiers; the troops replied by shooting at close range with rifles and machine guns. Perhaps three hundred Native Americans were killed on the spot or while running from the camp.[25]

In the Southwest, Native American resistance was, on occasion, substantial. Even after the United States took over the region by military conquest in the 1840s, slave raids on the Navaho by New Mexican settlers continued for a decade or two. Military expeditions were conducted in the Southwest against the scattered Navaho and Apache communities in an attempt to hem them in. Colonel Kit Carson succeeded in getting the Mescalero Apaches to agree to reside on a reservation. Establishing headquarters in Navaho territory, Carson began a scorched-earth program, destroying fields and herds. He then herded his captives three hundred miles to a small reservation—the famous Long Walk central to Navaho history. By 1890 virtually all the remnants of Native American tribes had been forced onto reservations.[26]

Toward the end of the nineteenth century native groups outside the (eventually) contiguous forty-eight states came under white American control. Native Hawaiians, previously subordinated by European plantation owners seeking cheap labor, came under United States jurisdiction when the country acquired Hawaii in 1898. The purchase of Alaska in 1867 led to thousands of Eskimo, Athabascan and Aleut peoples being brought under the control of the United States.

## STEREOTYPING

Stereotypes of Native Americans developed between the 1500s and the 1800s; they played a role in rationalizing land theft. One early myth, a mixture of appreciation and prejudice, was that of the "child of nature" or "noble savage." French philosophers such as Montaigne and Rousseau had read of European contacts with the Native Americans and utilized scanty data to argue for a golden age of human existence when there was only the unsophisticated "primitive" unspoiled by European civilization. The "child of nature" image, with its emphasis on *child* as well as *nature*, played an important role in the expectations of missionaries who saw their task as bringing Christianity to the "primitives."[27]

European settlers were shocked by the unwillingness of the indigenous residents to submit to the "civilizing" pressures of missionaries and farmers seeking land. Any violent resistance reinforced new stereotypes of the "cruel, bloodthirsty savage." This image became common after the first battles with Native Americans resisting encroachment on their lands. By the mid-1600s Europeans in New England and Virginia were writing that the Native Americans were wild beasts who should be hunted down like other savage animals. Puritan leaders such as Cotton Mather saw them as agents of the Devil.[28]

It was the era of westward expansion that imprinted on the public mind the image of a "savage race" attacking helpless settlers, in dime novels and later in movies and TV programs. Yet the savagery *of the settlers* has seldom been accented in the mass media. Carlson and Coburn have wondered aloud about the staggering number of Native Americans killed in the mass media: "The Indian, who had been all but eliminated with real bullets, now had to be resurrected to be killed off again with printer's ink."[29] The distorted image of Native Americans as savages can be found in many textbooks in U.S. schools.

Biased Euro-American accounts partly explain the exaggerated generalization that all Native Americans were savages. Brutality was manifest in the customs of some tribes, particularly in the treatment of prisoners captured by warlike tribes. A proper evaluation of this "savagery" requires an evaluation also of the practices of European settlers. The fate of Native Americans who were massacred or forced onto reservations suggests that brutality was part and parcel of European "civilization." The example of scalping, whose expansion was a result of European actions, suggests how stereotypes can be turned upside down.[30]

Another erroneous but persisting image is that of the "primitive hunter" who made little use of the land. Most tribes who were forced off lands or killed off were composed *not* of nomadic hunters but of part-time or full-time farmers. Tribes such as the Cherokee had by the removal period of the 1830s developed their own mills and other enterprises. Alexis de Tocqueville, that astute French observer of American life in the 1830s, accepted the myth, writing that it would be difficult to "civilize" the "Indians" without settling them down as agriculturalists.[31]

As early as the 1830s Dr. Samuel G. Morton argued that Native Americans were anatomically savage. In his 1931 book *Race Psychology*, Thomas R. Garth argued for the intellectual inferiority of Native Americans, basing his conclusions on the fact that they achieved the lowest average scores of any minority group on the omnipresent IQ test of the time. Racial inferiority theories have been aimed at Native Americans, who were increasingly defined after 1850 as a "racial group."[32]

A number of studies of elementary, high school, and college social science textbooks have found stereotypes about Native Americans. Most school texts have dealt briefly with the Native American, with a few references to Pilgrim or pioneer days and occasional use of derogatory terms such as *squaw* and *buck*. Recent studies of the mass media have pointed up grossly exaggerated images. One study of cartoons in the once widely read *Saturday Evening Post* found that virtually every Native

American had feathers in his or her hair; one-third of the cartoons of Native Americans showed them with bows and arrows. No modern-day Native Americans were to be found in the thousands of cartoons surveyed. The "Indian warrior" remains a common mass media image.[33]

Opinion poll studies of white attitudes have been rare. One study in the 1970s found that white views of Native Americans mixed romantic stereotypes with traditional negative stereotypes. The study updated research by Bogardus on the social-distance attitudes directed at Native Americans. White college students were asked how close, on a scale from 1 ("would marry") to 7 ("would not allow them in nation"), they would allow a given racial or ethnic group to themselves. In the earlier studies these white students rejected all close contact (such as friendships) with Indians. A 1970s study using the same attitude scale found Native Americans still being rejected by white respondents in regard to primary-group relations, such as marriage and club membership.[34]

## POLITICS

European communities at first dealt with Native Americans as independent nations; with growing strength came a shift in policy, so that tribes were treated as groups to be exterminated or as dependent wards. By the 1830s the eastern tribes were weak enough for the government to force them westward. About the same time, the Bureau of Indian Affairs (BIA) was established to coordinate federal relations with tribes, from supervision of reservations and land dealings to provision of much-needed supplies. Until the end of battles in the 1880s the position of the BIA was strange, since its attempt to protect Native Americans conflicted with the military policy of extermination.

Chiefs were set aside and replaced by Courts of Indian Offenses. Tribal religions were suppressed, and Christian missionaries were imported by the carload. BIA rations were usually provided to those who remained on reservations, while troops chased those who did not. Limited attempts were made to educate Native Americans to European ways in health and agriculture. With the termination of treaty making in 1871 and the reduction of all major groups to life on reservations by the 1890s, Native Americans entered into a unique relationship with white America. Here was the only subordinate racial or ethnic group whose life was to be routinely administered directly by a bureaucratic arm of the federal government.[35]

### From the Dawes Act to the New Deal

A major policy in shift on land took place in the late nineteenth century. Native Americans, liberal reformers argued, should be taught new rules of land use. The Dawes Act of 1887 provided that reservation lands be divided among individual families. The European tradition of private ownership and individual development of land was for many Native American groups an alien value system. Even so, advocates of the new policy hoped that small individual allotments (40 to 160 acres) would convert Native Americans into farm entrepreneurs. Unallotted lands left over could then be sold to white outsiders. The upshot of this new government policy was a large-scale land sale to white Americans; through means fair and foul the remaining 140 million acres of Native American lands were further reduced to 50 million acres by the mid-1930s.[36]

In 1884 a Native American named John Elk went to the city (Omaha, Nebraska), adapted to the white ways, and attempted to vote. Denied this right, Elk took his case to a federal court, where he argued that the Fourteenth Amendment made him a citizen and that the Fifteenth Amendment guaranteed his right to vote.[37] The court ruled that he was not an American citizen—that he was in effect a citizen of a *foreign* nation and thus not entitled to vote. Under the land allotment approach of the 1887 Dawes Act, the "wards" of the government could become citizens if they showed themselves competent in managing their individual land allotments. Some Native Americans were issued "certificates of competency" by special "competency commissions," which decided if they could function well in the white world. In 1924 Congress finally passed the Indian Citizenship Act, granting citizenship, including voting rights, to all Native Americans. Native Americans have been citizens for many decades.

The U.S. Supreme Court continued to hold that Native Americans were wards of the federal government, a status not changed by the Citizenship Act. As a result, many state governments refused to provide services or allow Native Americans to vote. On the other hand, the federal government on occasion tried to break off its services on the ground that Native Americans were officially citizens. Native Americans were caught in a political quandry.[38]

It was not until the New Deal that new federal policy was developed—in the 1934 Indian Reorganization Act. Native American groups were to vote on whether they wanted to come under the act, which ended land allotment and the sale of lands without careful supervision. Provisions were made for federal credit, for economic development, and for preferential hiring in the BIA. The changes seemed progressive. Very important was the new provision for tribal governments somewhat independent of the federal government. Many Native American groups incorporated themselves; many developed a central council, with constitutions reflecting the values of white culture. Others operated under traditional customs. Gradually, numerous tribes began some self-government, managing their own property, raising their own tax revenues, and governing their own affairs under federal supervision.[39]

Yet the New Deal policy had negative features. Oklahoma tribes were excluded; the Papago tribe lost control of its mineral resources; and great power was put in the hands of the secretary of the interior, who became what some called the "dictator of the Indians." The secretary made rules for elections, could veto constitutions, supervised expenditures, and made the regulations for land management on the reservations. As progressive as the law appeared, it ignored many problems, and the ward relationship to the government was maintained.[40]

## Fluctuations in Federal Policies

In the 1950s another shift in policy toward Native Americans could be seen, this time in House Concurrent Resolution 108, which called for the *termination* of federal supervision of Native American groups. The intent of the resolution was to reject the 1934 Indian Reorganization Act and return to the policy of forced conformity to individualistic values of land use. Supporters of termination included land-hungry whites outside reservations and members of Congress seeking to cut government costs, as well as some tribal members no longer on reservations. Between 1954 and 1960 several dozen groups were "terminated"; they were no longer under federal guardianship. Because of the resulting negative effects, including the problems of dealing with often unfriendly local officials and white land entrepreneurs, termination came to be viewed as a failure. In the famous case of the Menominee tribe, which became a new political unit under state law, per capita payments exhausted their joint funds and thus their development capital, their hospital had to be closed because it did not meet state standards, and their power plants were sold to an outside company. Termination has been costly for many such tribes unprepared to deal with the complexity and treachery of the outside white world.[41]

From the 1960s to the 1980s federal policy began to move away from termination. President Nixon called on Congress to maintain Native Americans' tie to the federal government and to prohibit termination without consent. Some of Nixon's specific proposals were soon legislated by Congress and put into effect, including the restoration of Blue Lake to the Taos Pueblo and the passage of an Indian Financing Act making credit available for business purposes. Congress passed an act settling certain land claims of Alaskan natives and passed self-determination legislation in 1974 that established a procedure for tribes to take over some of the administration of certain federal programs on reservations. In the late 1970s some Native American groups began to run their own schools and social-service programs.[42]

The most important government bureaucracy has been the Bureau of Indian Affairs. The BIA defines who is a Native American. It has kept records of "blood" lines in order to determine who is an "Indian" eligible for benefits. The BIA still supervises tribal government, banking, utilities, and highways, as well as millions of dollars in tribal trust funds. In the 1980s the federal government recognized 283 tribes and held in trust for them 52 million acres of land. The bureau supervises leasing and selling of lands. And until recently, all control of social services, including education, was in the hands of the BIA or allied federal agencies. By the 1980s there were in effect nearly 400 treaties and other governmental agreements, 5,000 federal statutes, 2,000 federal court decisions, 500 attorney general's decisions, and 30 volumes of BIA regulations covering federal relations with Native Americans. A large bureaucracy sits on top of a complex system of regulations.[43]

Today the BIA is regarded by many Native Americans as the lesser of two evils. To some extent, it has protected them against predatory exploitation from the outside. To terminate the BIA would be to terminate what protection now exists. Outside interests would have one less barrier. Even the Interior Department's other major branches have opposed the interests of Native Americans because of pressure from private ranching, lumbering, farming, and mineral interests. For example, the Bureau of Commercial Fisheries opposed Native American fishing rights in the Northwest. By the 1970s and 1980s the BIA, with growing numbers of representative Native

American administrators, had begun to provide protection from whites, coupled with the greatly expanded self-determination and community control.[44]

## Growing Pressures for Political Participation

Most Native American political participation has been limited to reservation elections and service in tribal governments. With some exceptions reservations have been exempt from state control and taxation, and tribes have made their own laws and regulations, subject to BIA approval. Tribal governments have often combined legislative and executive functions in one elected tribal council. Voter turnout for tribal elections has been substantial: one study of voting in forty-nine tribes found half the eligible voters turning out.

There has been political conflict on reservations. A power struggle on the Navaho reservation in the 1980s offers an example. The chair of the tribe, Peter Mac-Donald, was challenged by a faction that considered him too assimilated and accused him of mismanaging the budget and resources of the tribe. In 1983 Peterson Zah, a leader with a more traditional approach, was elected the new chair. In the late 1980s MacDonald regained his position, in part by promising better educational support for Navaho students.[45] In the 1970s and 1980s there have been numerous splits within reservations, sometimes between more and less radical leaders. Some Native Americans prefer to work with the BIA, while others, including American Indian Movement leaders Dennis Banks and Russell Means, wish to terminate the BIA and resurrect tribal sovereignty. These Sioux leaders want the federal government to honor its long-standing treaties with the Native American tribes and thereby recognize the tribes as the independent nations they once were. Less radical leaders wish to retain the relationship with the federal government and the BIA in order to resist termination and subordinated assimilation and to maintain the partial control of reservation laws and processes that they currently enjoy.[46]

To what extent have native Americans participated in electoral politics outside the reservation? It was not until the 1924 Indian Citizenship Act that Native Americans got the right to vote in elections outside the reservation. Even this right required protest for its implementation in states such as Utah, Arizona, and New Mexico, where reservation Indians were barred from voting until the 1940s; as late as the 1960s and 1970s some states made voting and jury participation difficult. Subtle mechanisms of direct and indirect discrimination, such as state literacy tests and the gerrymandering of district lines, have reduced the voting power of Native Americans in western states. Voter participation has been low in many areas. One study found only 40 percent of Native Americans of voting age registered, and only 17 percent voting in that year. By the 1960s and 1970s these figures were rising to substantial proportions in some areas. In the 1980s tribal leaders were talking about the Native American vote as a swing vote (a bloc that can throw close elections one way or another) and calling for increased voting. Several leaders also participated actively in the "Rainbow Coalition," a political coalition that backed Jesse Jackson , a black American, for the U.S. presidency both in 1984 and 1988.[47]

In 1964, because of increased voter turnout, Native Americans from predominantly Navaho counties in New Mexico were elected to the legislature there for the first time; attempts to bar them failed. In the mid-1960s the first Native American was elected to the state legislature in Arizona. By 1967 there were an estimated fifteen Native Americans serving in legislatures in six western states. At least a dozen others were elected to local positions.[48]

Although current trends in western states offer signs of modest change in representation, a broad reading of the situation in the first decades of the twentieth century suggests that the oldest Americans have had little access to American politics. Only a handful have served in state and federal legislatures, most of these since the 1950s. Two dozen have served in state legislatures since 1900. Very few have served in Congress—perhaps a half dozen representatives and two senators with some, often modest, Native American ancestry. The most famous, Charles Curtis, was born on the Kaw reservation in 1860. One-eighth Native American, Curtis was a representative for fourteen years, a senator for twenty, and vice-president under Herbert Hoover. Since then there has seldom been more than one Indian representative at any one time.[49]

The lack of representation in state legislatures and Congress is paralleled in town and city governments. In the 1950s and 1960s tens of thousands of Native Americans were encouraged to leave reservations for the greener employment pastures of the cities, so that by the 1980s about half of all Native Americans were living in metropolitan areas. Native Americans have suffered at the hands of urban whites; towns near reservations and areas of larger cities to which migrants have traditionally gone have frequently been strongholds of prejudice and discrimination. Nonetheless, by the 1970s and 1980s, Native Americans were being elected to city councils, school boards, and county governments in some of these local areas. For example, in the early 1970s there were 631 Native Americans serving on school boards in 232 districts; many of these districts were predominantly Native American. Progress in electing other city and county officials has been less dramatic.[50]

The extent of representation seems to vary by state and area. For example, the South Dakota Advisory Committee to the U.S. Commission on Civil Rights reported that few Native Americans have ever served as elected officials in that state, even though 5 percent of the population is Native American. In the early 1980s only one Native American was serving in that legislature. Very few had ever served there. Moreover, only one was mayor of a city, and only a very small number were serving on school boards, even where there was a large Native American population.

A few studies on the role of government in the lives of Native Americans in urban areas have focused on the police system. One study in Minneapolis and St. Paul found that Native Americans were underrepresented as employees in city government, including the criminal justice system, but heavily overrepresented among those arrested. A disproportionately small percentage of the Minneapolis police force was Native American. In the 1980s police harassment of Native American men in towns near reservations was a general problem, in part revealing discrimination by local white authorities. (Employment discrimination was also reported to be common in these areas.) Complaints by Native American leaders in numerous cities centered on the

lack of efforts to recruit Native Americans as police and parole officers and government attorneys, as well as the unnecessarily high arrest rates.[51]

## PROTEST AND CONFLICT

Native American protest against subordination has doubtless been the most sustained
of any group in the history of North America. Violent resistance between 1500 and
1900 produced some of the greatest protest leaders the continent has seen.

Yet the end of this period did not end protest. Rather the character of the protest
changed. By the late nineteenth century a number of protest organizations had sprung
up. One of the most important was the Indian Rights Association, founded by Quakers
concerned with protecting and "civilizing" Native Americans. By exposing the corruption and oppression on reservations, such early groups laid the basis for reforms in
policy. One of the first organizations formed by Native Americans was the Society of
American Indians, created in the early 1900s. A major pan-Indian organization (drawing together representatives of different tribes), it was self-help-oriented; goals included developing pride and a national leadership and improving educational and job
opportunities. In the decades that followed, the organization developed a pan-Indian
alliance and groomed a new leadership that pressed for citizenship legislation and
tribal self-determination.[52]

In the 1920s a prominent white defender of Native Americans, John Collier, organized the militant American Indian Defense Association to fight the attempts by
Republican officials to establish "executive order reservations," not covered by treaty
and accessible to greedy whites who wished to extract minerals. The National Congress of American Indians (NCAI) was formed in the 1940s and pressed for education, legal aid, and legislation. An influential organization, the NCAI worked
vigorously against the termination policy of the 1950s and 1960s and for the War on
Poverty of the 1960s and self-determination policy of the 1970s and 1980s. In 1961
the National Indian Youth Council was created. It has fought vigorously for the civil
rights of Native Americans, has organized civil disobedience, and has developed a
Red Power ideology. The Youth Council has been active in eduction and has taken up
causes critical to the protection of Native American lands. For example, one newsletter of the organization urged all to fight the development of coal-gasification plants
on the Navaho reservation.[53]

Since the 1960s a number of protest actions and civil disobedience movements
have been organized. One analysis of protest activities between 1961 and 1970 found
194 instances reported. Of these, 141 fell into the category of "facilitative tactics,"
such things as legal suits and formal complaints. This type of activity continues a long
tradition of trying to coax institutions into concessions—the great strength of organizations such as the National Congress of American Indians. The other 53 protest activities involved civil disobedience, such things as delaying dam construction,
occupying offices or other government facilities, picketing, and staging sit-ins. Over
the last two decades there have been numerous Native American protest actions, many
of which have brought changes.[54]

In one widely publicized action, students began a long occupation of California's Alcatraz Island late in 1969; they were replaced by one hundred Native Americans claiming *unused* federal lands under provisions of an old treaty. The intent of the Native Americans was both symbolic and concrete—to dramatize the plight of their people and to establish a facility where Native Americans could preserve tribal ways. Government agents forcibly removed the occupying group in the summer of 1971. In the same period several attempts were made to seize other unused federal property, including Ellis Island in New York Harbor, and BIA offices were occupied in protest against BIA policies.[55]

In the Midwest the Alexian Brothers' novitiate building was occupied by armed Menominees in 1975. A year earlier larger-scale occupation took place under the auspices of the American Indian Movement (AIM), a group organized to deal with problems ranging from police brutality to housing and employment. An Indian Patrol was established to supervise contacts between Native Americans and the police and was reportedly successful in improving police behavior. The movement spread until there were more than a dozen groups in cities and on reservations. Some leaders and several hundred members played an important role in the seventy-one-day armed occupation of Wounded Knee on the Pine Ridge reservation in the spring of 1973. Reform-minded leaders protesting the white-dominated tribal government began the occupation. Federal agents were sent in.

In its attempts to convict AIM leaders, the federal government, with President Nixon's encouragement, used illegal wiretaps, altered evidence, and paid witnesses—which led to dismissal of the case by a federal judge. Afterward, some government agents apparently participated in a campaign to destroy the movement, a campaign that probably included a dozen suspicious murders and accidents involving AIM members. Two hundred AIM members were harassed and arrested, but only a dozen or so were ever convicted. Here was a not-so-nonviolent confrontation between militant Native Americans and the Indian establishment propped up by white officials.[56]

Although plagued with internal divisions, the AIM persisted in its struggle into the late 1980s. There were AIM organizations in several Native American communities. "Survival" schools were organized for Native American children. A radio station operated in South Dakota. The AIM participated in an encampment at Big Mountain on the Navaho reservation to prevent the forced removal of Native Americans from their land. And in recent years the movement has developed relationships with liberation movements in Third World countries.[57]

The Native American civil rights movement and pan-Indian activism brought some modest gains in the 1970s and 1980s in raising the consciousness of the general public and the nation's mass media leadership. Some universities, including Stanford, dropped the name "Indians" for their sports teams. Films portraying Native Americans as savages and the "white people" as heroes were less evident, and new films such as *A Man Called Horse* and *Little Big Man* portrayed Native Americans in a more sympathetic light. A number of popular books, such as Dee Brown's *Bury My Heart at Wounded Knee*, and television shows also began to portray Native Americans more favorably.[58]

## Fishing Rights and Land Claims

At the heart of conflict between Native Americans and whites have been issues of law enforcement, fishing rights, and land claims. Law enforcement has been an issue across the country, but it is particularly important in the Midwest, as the AIM has demonstrated. Fishing rights have been a source of conflict on the West Coast. In the state of Washington, Native American nations have struggled with whites for a century over these rights. There have been shootings and court battles over tribal rights to catch fish, particularly salmon and trout—rights guaranteed by treaties between the nations and the federal government more than a century ago. White anglers and commercial fishing companies object to Native Americans exercising their ancient treaty rights because this reduces white fishing opportunities significantly. In a major court decision, *U.S. v. State of Washington* (1974), the judge ruled that the treaties did indeed reserve fishing rights for Native Americans that are different from those allowed whites. The court ordered the state of Washington to protect Native American fish catchers and recognized the tribal right to manage fishing resources.[59]

The court's decision was openly defied by white fish catchers, who protested that the decision discriminated against them. The federal government became heavily involved, spending millions of dollars to increase the fish available in the area and to compensate whites who suffered economic hardship. In 1979 the U.S. Supreme Court upheld the lower court ruling. Government enforcement has gradually reduced illegal fishing by whites. Slowly the government moved to uphold ancient treaties.

A report by the U.S. Commission on Civil Rights underlined the cause of the land claims conflict:

> The basic Eastern Indian land claim is that Indian land in the East was invalidly transferred from Indians to non-Indians in the 18th and 19th centuries because the Federal Government, although required to do so, did not supervise or approve the transactions.[60]

The historical record is one of the taking of Native American land without adequate compensation. Native American groups, such as the Oneida in New York and the Passamaquoddy in Maine, have gone to court to press land claims. A number of these cases have been won by tribal members, and some of the lands illegally taken have been restored.

The land claims have alarmed whites. A Maine legislator said of one court suit that it "threatens to bring the State of Maine to its knees.... Already there is a revolt beginning among the non-Indian citizens." The federal government, including President Jimmy Carter, became heavily involved in working out a settlement in the Maine case. An agreement providing for the acquisition of 300,000 acres of land (to be held in trust by the federal government) plus a $27 million trust fund was signed by Carter in 1980.[61]

A number of other land claims have been settled in recent years. In 1980, after a lengthy court battle, the U.S. Supreme Court awarded the Sioux tribe $191 million for more than 7 million acres taken from it illegally in the 1870s. An 1868 treaty had guaranteed the Sioux the land, but it was stolen in the gold rush a few years later.

However, several Sioux leaders and organizations have opposed the cash award, arguing that the land itself should be returned to the tribe. In 1985 a U.S. senator proposed that substantial land be returned to the Sioux in addition to the money. And in December 1987 Philip J. Stevens, a Sioux and former owner of an engineering firm, organized a campaign to pressure the federal government to return 1.3 million acres of land and to provide $3 billion in compensation for the other land illegally taken.[62]

One result of such pressures on the federal government has been an increase in the compensation paid by the Indian Claims Commission. Prior to 1960 the commission denied most claims for compensation for land taken, but in the 1970s it paid out $500 million in 180 cases involving tribal claims.[63]

Because of Native American land claims, fishing claims, and other militant protest, a white backlash developed, including the creation of a national organization called the Interstate Congress for Equal Rights and Responsibilities. Senator Mark Hatfield of Oregon publicly noted that this "very significant backlash... by any other name comes out as racism in all its ugly manifestations." Members of Congress, supporting the backlash, introduced bills to break treaties, overturn court decisions, and extinguish Indian land claims. These whites argued that the excessive demands by Native Americans had soured longtime "friendly relations." Native Americans responded that they were seeking what was legally theirs and not asking for special privileges. Whites were hostile because living up to U.S law was becoming costly. Whites were also hostile, as one tribal leader noted, "because of the lack of educational systems to teach anything about Indians, about treaties." White stereotypes about Indians and ignorance of treaties have played a critical role in recent struggles for social justice.[64]

Since the late 1950s Native Americans have won a number of legal battles over tribal law and jurisdiction. In a 1959 case, *Williams v. Lee*, the U.S. Supreme Court ruled that a non-Indian doing business on a reservation was subject to tribal law and courts. In a 1973 case the Supreme Court invalidated an Arizona state tax applied to reservation Indians. In addition the other branches of the federal government recognized some Native American rights in the 1970s and 1980s. The Menominee tribe in Wisconsin was restored to tribal status in 1975 (it was legally terminated earlier). And in 1975 a distinguished federal body, the American Indian Policy Review Commission, ruled that tribes are sovereign bodies with power to enforce their own laws and that a special trust relationship still exists between the tribes and the government.[65]

## THE ECONOMY

Structural assimilation can involve upward movement into ever higher levels of the economy. This movement has been modest for Native Americans. The colonialism model points up the way in which a group such as Native Americans can be incorporated into the U.S. economy without getting on the escalator to ultimate equality. Prior to being forced onto reservations, most groups were self-sufficient; there was diversity, ranging from the Pueblo agriculturalists of the Southwest to a few hunting societies on the Plains to the many mixed agricultural-hunting societies across the continent.

Land was the basis of the Native American economies; by the 1880s the tribes had lost millions of acres. With the breaking up of the remaining lands under the 1887 Dawes Act came the loss of millions more. Native American lands were frequently reduced to those having the least appeal to white entrepreneurs. Many reservations have faced problems such as poor utilities, roads, and transportation facilities. Those that retained important natural resources have typically not had the trained workers or capital to develop them.[66]

With the growth of industrial capitalism and urbanization in the late nineteenth century came waves of economic exploitation. The encroachment on Indian lands by lumbering, ranching, and railroad interests redirected resources from rural Native American lands to growing urban centers. The killing off of bison and other game for skins for people in Eastern cities and the taking of lands by white ranchers for cattle raising and by farmers for agriculture hastened the impoverishment of Native Americans in the West. Rural poverty increased as corporations reached out from metropolitan centers to exploit more and more land; this in turn pressured many to migrate to cities. Jorgensen argues that the poverty of rural Native Americans is "not due to rural isolation [or] a tenacious hold on aboriginal ways, but results from the way in which United States' urban centers of finance, political influence, and power have grown at the expense of rural areas."[67]

## Poverty and Land Theft

The poverty of reservation life has come from the destruction of tribal economies, encroachments on remaining lands, and mismanagement by BIA officials. Testifying before a congressional committee on the food situation in the winter of 1883, a member of the Assiniboine tribe pointed out that tribal members were healthy until the buffalo were killed off, and that the substitute BIA rations were not adequate:

> They gave us rations once a week, just enough to last one day, and the Indians they started to eat their pet dogs. After they ate all their dogs up they started to eat their ponies. All this time the Indian Bureau had a warehouse full of grub.... Early [the next] spring, in 1884, I saw the dead bodies of the Indians wrapped in blankets and piled up like cordwood in the village of Wolf point, and the other Indians were so weak they could not bury their dead; what were left were nothing but skeletons.[68]

Government agents were officially responsible for supplies, instruction in farming, and supervision of lands. By the 1880s many were notorious for their corruption and incompetence. Many desired to make their fortunes at the expense of those for whom they were responsible. The "agency towns" growing up on the reservations developed a stratified system in which there was little equitable contact between Native Americans and paternalistic white officials. After the 1890s attempts were made by the BIA to expand farming on some reservations. Here also white officials usually built paternalistic systems in which Native Americans had little part other than that of unskilled laborers or small farmers.[69]

The reorganization policy of the 1930s, which provided for tribal governments, put a partial brake on corruption and blatant land theft, but economic problems persisted. Federal policy fluctuated between tribal self-determination and forced individualism. Termination experiments have thrown some tribes to the "outside wolves." Lands have been sold to pay taxes, and tribes have fallen deeper into poverty as resources are further depleted.

Native American lands have been taken for dams, national parks, and rights-of-way for roads. The sale of lands to private lumbering and mineral interests continues. Attempts by tribes to control the use of their lands have led ranchers and other white interests to argue that self-government by Native Americans is an unreasonable threat to "rational" development. What substantial money is made in agriculture or ranching on reservations has frequently flowed to whites, who lease large proportions of the usable land. By the late 1960s the gross income from agriculture on reservations was $300 million a year. Native Americans received only a third of that; whites earned the majority. Facing discrimination and having limited technical schooling, little available technical assistance, and little capital to buy seeds, livestock, or machinery, the Native American farmer is faced with suffering a low yield or else leasing to outsiders.[70]

## Land, Minerals, and Industrial Development

In recent decades the federal government has taken some action to deal with the economic problems of reservations. War on Poverty programs came to the reservations in the 1960s, bringing some job and training benefits, mostly temporary. A major BIA strategy has been urban relocation and employment assistance. Thousands of Native Americans have moved to cities. Studies have found that urbanites earn more than those on reservations but are dissatisfied with urban life. One-half to three-quarters of urban relocates return to the reservation areas after a few years. Lack of economic success seems to be the major reason. Studies have shown a relationship between the negative economic experiences of urban migrants, such as low wages and unemployment, and their relatively high arrest rates. A basic problem is that Native Americans in cities continue to face poverty and discrimination; they find themselves in residential ghettos and in low-wage, dead-end jobs.[71]

Government attempts to attract industrial plants to reservations were ineffective in the early 1960s but improved with the tighter labor market of the late 1960s and the 1970s. Where there were only three such factories in 1959, by 1968 there were 110, and by 1972 there were 200. Yet many jobs in plants built on or near reservations went to workers other than Native Americans. Government funds have expanded corporate profits, with modest gains for tribal members. The BIA has also encouraged cottage industries, the revival of Native American arts and crafts; this revival has helped improve the financial situation on some reservations, although it does not integrate workers into the economic mainstream.[72]

In 1987 *Forbes* magazine ran an article on the difficulties of federal development projects such as vacation resorts and industrial parks on reservations. The 62 resorts and 55 industrial parks created between the 1960s and the late 1980s have generally been failures. The occupancy rate at the industrial parks has been 5 percent, largely because they are located in rural areas lacking the amenities many U.S. corporations desire. The *Forbes* article also noted that Native American "reservations do not seem fertile ground for the seeds of capitalism. Reservation resources are generally the province of the tribe rather than individuals and shared equally among the membership…" This comment in *the* magazine of American capitalism is noteworthy, since it recognizes that the values of Native Americans accent the *group* rather than the individual. Individualistic capitalism is alien to many tribal value systems. Moreover, under Ronald Reagan's administration an attempt was made to foster the "entrepreneurial spirit" on the reservations and to increase the number of Native Americans operating small businesses.[73]

Native American reservations in the United States encompass about one-third of all low-sulphur coal, one-fifth of oil and gas reserves, and half of all known uranium reserves. Underneath the fifteen-million-acre Navaho reservation lie an estimated 100 million barrels of oil, 25 trillion cubic feet of natural gas, 80 million pounds of uranium, and 50 billion tons of coal. For example, beneath the Northern Cheyenne reservation in Montana lies a huge deposit of coal, and below the Jicarilla Apache reservation there are some 154 million barrels of oil and 2 trillion cubic feet of natural gas. Some corporate executives have eagerly eyed these mineral resources; a few corporations have even called for the abolition of the reservations and the Bureau of Indian Affairs, so that these mineral resources could be more easily exploited.[74]

Historically, when mineral resources have been found on Native American land, the land has been taken over and exploited by white entrepreneurs and corporations. For example, when large copper deposits were found on the Papago reservation in Arizona in the 1920s, the ore-bearing land was taken from the tribe by a congressional law. Another example is the mineral extraction agreement that the Navaho Tribal Council made with the Kerr-McGee corporation in 1952. Mining uranium on the Navaho land for nearly two decades, Kerr-McGee employed 150 Navaho men as miners, initially at $1.60 an hour—about two-thirds of the prevailing off-reservation wage. Once the easy-to-reach deposits were mined, the company closed its Shiprock facility, leaving seventy-one acres of radioactive debris that threatened the water supplies of downstream communities. Enforcement of safety regulations in the Shiprock mine was reportedly lax. By 1980 twenty of the miners had died of cancers related to their mining of uranium.[75]

Three dozen tribes made national headlines in the 1970s when they announced the creation of the Council of Energy Resources Tribes (CERT) and hired a former Iranian oil minister to help them get better contracts with white-owned companies. Many whites worried that tribes were going to behave like OPEC and seek to be completely independent in making contracts with energy corporations. CERT was created because tribal leaders felt they were being cheated by energy companies and by the federal government. The federal Department of Energy tried to co-opt CERT by providing several million dollars in grants. CERT used the money to secure technical assistance and to develop proposals to industrialize reservations using royalties from resource development. CERT provided technical assistance to tribes and worked to increase engineering and other technical skills among Native American youths. Yet the close ties between CERT and the federal government led to internal conflict. Several tribes pulled out of CERT because of its stand for extensive uranium mining on Indian lands. Indian activists criticized expanded mining on traditional lands as a "destruction of Mother Earth." Many fear that such economic coalitions as CERT have adopted white ways of resource exploitation.[76]

## Persisting Economic Problems

The urban economy has been viewed as divided into two major sectors, a primary labor market and a secondary labor market. The primary labor market has been composed predominantly of white workers and has been characterized by skilled jobs, high wages, highly profitable companies, and significant mobility. The secondary labor market, on the other hand, has been composed predominantly of nonwhite workers and of white workers who have recently immigrated and has been characterized by instability, low wages, less profitable companies, and little job mobility.

Native Americans have been disproportionately concentrated in the secondary labor market. In 1940 one-third of all Native American males were unemployed, a figure far higher than that for white males. By 1960 the rate was even higher—38 percent, compared with 5 percent for all males. This increase reflected in part the move from agriculture to the less certain work opportunities in urban areas. By 1970 the rate had gone down to 12 percent for males, still three times the national figure. In 1980 the unemployment rate was more than double that of whites. These recent rates, one should note, do not include the large proportion of Native American workers who have given up looking for work. Rates for Native American women have also been high. Native Americans continue to face perhaps the longest "Great Depression" of any racial or ethnic group in the United States.[77]

Compare census data on occupational distribution since 1940:[78]

| | Native American Men | | | Native American Women | |
|---|---|---|---|---|---|
| | 1940 | 1960 | 1970 | 1960 | 1970 |
| Professional, technical | 2.2% | 4.9% | 9.2% | 9.1% | 11.1% |
| Managerial, Administrative | 1.4 | 2.8 | 5.0 | 2.0 | 2.3 |
| Clerical, sales | 2.0 | 4.9 | 8.0 | 17.8 | 29.1 |
| Craftworkers | 5.7 | 15.5 | 22.1 | 1.2 | 2.1 |
| Operatives | 6.2 | 21.9 | 23.9 | 15.2 | 18.7 |
| Nonfarm laborers | 11.4 | 20.2 | 13.2 | 1.7 | 1.3 |
| Farmers, farm workers | 68.4 | 23.5 | 8.0 | 10.5 | 2.3 |
| Service workers | 2.6 | 6.3 | 10.5 | 42.6 | 33.0 |
| | 99.9% | 100.0% | 99.9% | 100.1% | 99.9% |

In 1940 most men were poor farmers or unskilled workers. By 1960 the impact of the urban migration had become clear; there was a drop in farm occupations. (Some of this drop may reflect problems in data collection.) In 1960 men and women were heavily concentrated in the unskilled and semiskilled categories. There is evidence of upward mobility between 1960 and 1970, with substantially higher proportions of men and women at the white-collar levels and of men at the skilled-blue-collar level.

Yet the conclusion of significant economic mobility should be a cautious one. First, there is the problem of the censuses omission of large numbers of labor force dropouts who have given up looking for work—largely those on farms and the urban unskilled. Second, between 1960 and 1970 the census definition of "Native American" changed, with more emphasis on self-designation in 1970. The total number employed increased sharply in that decade; this probably means that more people with partial Native American ancestry opted for that designation, and that many of these were already at higher occupational levels.

We can assess 1980 data for male and female workers taken together. In that year 18.8 percent of Native Americans were in managerial, professional, and technical jobs, compared with about one-quarter of the general work force. Among Native Americans 21.4 percent were in clerical and sales jobs, versus 27.3 percent of the general workforce. The proportion in blue-collar jobs was generally higher than in the general workforce, with 14.9 percent in craft jobs, compared with 12.9 percent of the general population. The proportion in operative and laborer positions was 22.8 percent, compared with 18.3 percent of the general population. The proportion in service jobs was higher than in the general population—18 percent versus 12.3 percent. The proportion who were farmers was higher than in the general population—3.6 percent versus 1.5 percent. In the early 1980s more than four in ten working Native Americans were in unskilled laboring jobs, factory work, service positions, or farm jobs. And low wages remain characteristic of the blue-collar and white-collar jobs most Native Americans hold.[79]

For decades Native Americans on reservations have had perhaps the lowest incomes of any race or ethnic group. In 1939 males on reservations had a median income of only $500, compared with $2,300 for all U.S. males. That great imbalance was found for 1949, 1959, and 1970 as well. In 1970 the median income for Native American males was $2,749, compared with $6,614 for all U.S. males. The income level of Native American male earners was around one-quarter that of all males until 1970, when it surged to 42 percent, still under half of the national figure. The 1970 figure for Native American individuals in urban areas was better—$4,568, or about 69 percent of the national figure.

In 1970 the median income for Native American families was $5,800, well below the median for all U.S. families. While one in ten among all U.S. families fell below the government poverty line in 1970, fully one-third of all Native American families were officially classified as poor, including nearly half of those in rural areas. In the 1980 census the 1979 median income reported for all Native American families was still well below average, at $13,724, compared with $19,917 for all American families. Native American families still earned about 31 percent less than white American families. Families in urban areas had a median income of $15,160, rural families only $12,091.[80]

Poverty and unemployment mean inferior living conditions. Native Americans in rural areas face the worst economic and housing situation of any race and ethnic group, although the situation of rural blacks is not greatly different. Native Americans have the worst housing conditions in the United States. In the early 1970s, 6 percent of those in urban areas and 29 percent of those in rural areas lived in severely crowded conditions; 9 percent and 48 percent, respectively, had no toilet facilities. Two-thirds of those in rural areas had no plumbing. Today Native Americans are much more likely than European Americans to have inadequate nutrition, to live in small apartments or houses, and to have inadequate water and sanitation facilities. Illness rates, and death rates from accidents and illness, remain very high. The suicide rate is much higher than that of European Americans, and alcoholism rates are the highest in the nation. Disease rates for flu, strep throat, hepatitis, and pneumonia are several times the national figures. The infant death rate is twice the national average. As a result, life expectancy for Native Americans is about sixty-four years, far below the figure for European Americans. Inadequate medical facilities, coupled with poor nutrition resulting from low incomes, constitute a major part of the problem. Cutbacks in federal health programs in the 1980s, under the guidance of the Reagan administration, have reduced access to medical care for Native Americans. Native American conditions remain among the worst in the United States.[81]

Interestingly, since the 1970s a number of Native American tribes have developed gambling enterprises. Revenues have been used to pay for educational and health-care facilities, job training, and other social programs. This move into gambling has caused some Native American commentators, as well as BIA officials, to worry that organized crime might move onto the reservations. The extreme poverty of the reservations has led Native American leaders to try this extreme approach to creating jobs and boosting income for Native American families.

## EDUCATION

The formal educational experience of subordinated Native Americans began in the reservation period. Some influential whites were committed to the idea of education as the channel of forced acculturation. In the white-controlled school the "wild Indians" could be civilized. By 1887 the congressional appropriation for the education of Native Americans was $1.2 million; 14,300 children were enrolled in 227 schools, most operated by the BIA or by religious groups with government financial aid.[82]

By 1900 a small percentage of Native American children were receiving formal schooling; for most, schooling took place within tribal circles. In the Southwest perhaps one-quarter of the school-age children in the four decades after 1890 had some experience with boarding schools; a small percentage of the rest were in public schools. From the beginning the BIA and mission schools were run according to a strict Anglo-conformity approach; students were punished for speaking native languages.[83]

By the mid-1930s some boarding schools were being replaced by day schools closer to home, and a bilingual educational policy was at least being discussed. Increasingly, public schools became the context for Native American education. In the 1930s the Johnson-O'Malley Act provided some federal aid for those states developing public schools for Native Americans. Yet after World War II large proportions of Native Americans were not in formal schools—including, for example, three-quarters of those in the largest tribe, the Navaho. From the 1960s to the 1980s aid to primary, adult, and vocational education expanded substantially. Pressure mounted from Native Americans for improvement.[84]

Government attention was refocused on schools. In many federal schools advisory boards composed of Native Americans were developed. With the aid of War on Poverty funds, the first reservation community college opened on the Navaho reservation. By 1970 141,000 Native American children were recorded in public schools, 52,000 in BIA schools, and 11,000 in private schools. In the mid-1980s there were nearly 41,000 Native American students in BIA schools and another 166,000 in schools receiving special federal support. Several thousand Native American were in college. Moreover, some BIA schools were being operated by new tribal corporations. The shift away from heavy dependence on Anglo-centric boarding schools was the result of (1) parental pressures for schools closer to home, and (2) the movement of many Native Americans to the cities, where they used local public schools.[85]

Educational attainment levels have increased since the 1960s. The percentage of urban male Native Americans with fewer than nine years of schooling decreased from 46 percent in 1960 to 30 percent in 1970; for women this figure also went down. But in both cases the percentages were well above national figures. The gap at the high school level has persisted, even in the youngest groups. In 1970 two-thirds of the total U.S. male population aged sixteen to twenty-four finished high school, compared with only half of young Native Americans in urban areas and 26 percent in rural areas. In 1980, 57 percent of Native American males and 54 percent of Native American females were high school graduates, compared with 67 percent of all persons over twenty-five. The median years of school completed for Native Americans twenty-five and over was 12.2 years, somewhat below the national figure of 12.5 years.[86]

In the 1980s school enrollments varied greatly among reservations, with 95 percent of the children on the Pima and Papago reservations in Arizona enrolled, but only 35 percent of the Alaskan Eskimos. High school dropout rates remain high, at 40 percent of the students enrolled.[87]

For a century critical reports on the boarding schools have underscored the colonized position of Native Americans. Even the remaining boarding schools have sometimes been described as oppressive environments. In most the facilities and staff have been inadequate. Children have been pressured not to speak their native language and not to practice native traditions. The issue of enforced acculturation goes beyond the boarding schools. Native American cultures have long been viewed as a major problem by public school administrators as well. Conventional explanations of educational problems have zeroed in on cultural differences, emphasizing that the distinctive values of Native Americans contrast with those of white Americans. Heavy pressure has been placed by teachers attempting to make their pupils "less Indian." Little has been provided in school textbooks to make the children feel a link to their own culture.[88]

## RELIGION

Pressures for acculturation have been clear in the case of religion. The Spanish conquerors brought Roman Catholic priests to reduce southwestern tribes to a mission-centered life. Later white settlers sometimes attempted to convert the "heathen Indian" to Christianity. Some Native Americans have said of the Christian missionaries that "when they arrived they had only the Book and we had the land; now we have the Book and they have the land."[89]

With the reservation period came a jockeying among Christian denominations for control; reservations were divided up so that Episcopalians got one, Methodists another, and Catholics yet another. "Home mission" efforts by a dozen denominations were developed. Religious boarding schools and missions were placed alongside BIA operations. For a number of reasons, including fear, many Native Americans became affiliated with a Christian denomination.[90]

## Millenarian Movements as Protest

From the Pacific Islands to Africa to the U.S., colonized peoples have lashed out at European oppressors by joining millenarian movements. Such movements are often oriented to a "golden age" in which supernatural events will change oppressive conditions. Often the movements have been led by visionaries.

Among the most famous Native American millenarian movements were the Ghost Dance groups that emerged on the Great Plains. In the 1870s the prophet Wodziwob told of a vision in which the ancestors of Native America came on a train to Earth with explosive force, after which the Earth swallowed up the whites. Members of a number of tribes joined in the movement in the hope of salvation from white oppression. But when no cataclysm came, the movement died down. In the late 1880s there was a resurgence; the prophet Wovoka experienced a vision ordering him to found a new Ghost Dance religion. The religious fervor spread through the Plains tribes. Trancelike dances were a central part of the ritual; whites, it was said, could be driven out by means of the circle dance. Cooperation among all Native Americans was preached in this movement, and indeed, intertribal cooperation increased. Government officials were disturbed at the resurgence of millenarianism and tried to suppress it. The Sioux massacred at Wounded Knee in 1890 had gathered for Ghost Dance ceremonies.[91]

Peyotism surfaced as the Ghost Dance movement was being destroyed; it reflected another way of protesting white cultural pressures. Long used by individual practitioners to deal with sickness, peyotism did not become a group religion until 1880. Between 1880 and 1900 it spread throughout the Plains. The new religion reflected an ambivalence toward Christianity. Peyote rituals involved singing and praying, but were distinctive in the eating of peyote and in the visionary experiences this induced. Devoted to meditation, practitioners of peyotism aspired not to armed rebellion but rather to the establishment of an intertribal religion.[92]

Attacks by Christian missionaries and officials welded believers together. In 1918 intensive white opposition to peyote led to the introduction by a member of Congress of a bill to prohibit its use; although the bill passed the House, it went no further. Growing white opposition prompted the believers to organize formally, and in 1918 the Native American church was formally incorporated as an association of Christian groups protecting the Sacrament of Peyote. The new name and the development of its own offices made the movement more difficult to attack because of the

First Amendment guarantee of freedom of religion. Nonetheless, by the 1920s seven states had passed antipeyote laws, and proclamations were issued by the BIA banning its use. Opposition seemed to stimulate church growth, for in 1934 the Oklahoma Native American church amended its charter to include those churches in other states, a major step in the direction of national unity. In the 1930s the new commissioner of Indian affairs, the progressive John Collier, came to the defense of indigenous religions and allowed the resurgence of the old ways, although this brought charges that the government was fostering "paganism."[93]

Since World War II there has been yet another resurgence of tribal religions. The attempts to restrict peyotism did not have much effect. Membership continued to increase. On some Sioux reservations, 40 percent were Native American church members by the 1960s. Today there is a great variety of religious practice among Native American tribes, particularly on the reservations.[94]

By the 1960s a number of leaders were criticizing Christianity as a crude religion stressing blood, crucifixion, and bureaucratized charity rather than true sharing and compassion for people. The American Indian Historical Society requested that federal museums return thousands of Native American religious and art objects, particularly those illegally acquired. Closely tied to this criticism is the resurgence of criticism of the European core culture, stressing such themes as the following: The white Europeans are newcomers to the continent. They sharply accelerated war on the continent. They killed off many animal species. They betrayed the Native Americans who had aided them in establishing a place on the continent. They destroyed the ecosystem and polluted the environment. Respect for land and nature is a common theme in many Native American cultures. In 1970 a Hopi wrote to President Richard Nixon protesting strip mining and other forms of destruction of the western Indian lands: "The white man, through his insensitivity to the way of Nature, has desecrated the face of Mother Earth. The white man's advanced technological capacity has occurred as a result of his lack of regard for the spiritual path and for the way of all living things."[95] Many Native Americans now argue that the solution to problems of environmental damage lies in recognizing the superiority of Native American values, including a respect for the environment and a strong sense of community.

## ASSIMILATION AND COLONIALISM

Theoretical analyses in the field of race and ethnic relations have neglected Native Americans. Native Americans are distinctive among race and ethnic groups in that the classical (external) colonialism model is *relevant* to certain of their contacts with Europeans. In the earliest period Native American tribes on the Atlantic Coast saw their lands seized and their members driven off or killed by outsiders. For some tribes the European strategy was genocide, the killing off of those indigenous peoples who stood in the way of settlement by people with greater firepower. This process would recur as European Americans moved westward from the Atlantic in the next several centuries. Sometimes, as in the case of Plains tribes, genocide was the informal policy. Yet the policy of genocide coexisted with a reservation policy. Even in the earliest periods some whites felt that subordinating Native Americans and restricting them to certain areas, later called reservations, made for a better policy than killing them off. With the reservation period of the nineteenth century came new oppression for Native Americans. No longer were there wars and treaties with outsiders. The Native American "race," as they were termed, was now a subordinate segment of a U.S. stratification system, a segment placed at the very bottom. Movement up that ladder, or the lack thereof, can be viewed from both assimilation and power–conflict perspectives.

## Assimilation Theories

Some white observers have argued that the opportunity to assimilate is more open for Native Americans than for other minorities.[96] In the 1920s and 1930s even a few Native American professionals argued that Native Americans should voluntarily follow the lead of white immigrant groups and blend into the dominant white culture.

It is thus meaningful to ask how assimilation theorists today might view the past and present adaptations of Native Americans. Applying an assimilation model to Native Americans, one might accent the extent to which their traditional cultures have already undergone Europeanization. Schools and missions in the nineteenth century brought changes in religion, language, and dress styles. Other changes have been substantial, ranging from language changes to changes in land-ownership values. Assimilationists have argued that the major barriers to Indian acculturation are the Native American traditions. These analysts can seize on the cultural adaptations that many Native Americans have made and cite them as evidence of movement toward inclusion in the larger society. Yet some critics would note that much acculturation was forced. In addition, some data on acculturation suggest that it has been only partial, particularly for certain larger tribes.

There is great variation among the Native American tribes in living patterns—some are urban, some are rural—and in tribal identity—the Sioux and Navaho have strong tribal identity, other groups have lost their old ways and identities. Some groups, such as the western Pueblos, the Navaho, and the Sioux, confine their social contacts substantially to people of their tribe; other groups, such as a significant segment of the Blackfeet in Montana, have intermarried with whites and substantially acculturated to European American ways. Olson and Wilson note that some of the small California tribes, such as the Nomlaki and the Yuki, have "forgotten ancient customs, abandoned the native language, and look upon themselves more as extended families than as members of any particular tribe."[97]

In the early 1980s there were still three dozen Native American languages being spoken in the United States, and 30 percent of Native Americans spoke such languages as their primary tongues. The persistence of Native American languages has been significant. Intensive acculturation has not resulted in the demise of Native American cultures.

Structural assimilation at job levels above the lowest paid in the economy has come slowly for Native Americans. Mostly isolated on reservations until the 1950s and 1960s, many are still poor farmers or laborers. Not until the urban migration of the last few decades could many Native Americans be viewed as moving into the dominant urban economy. Yet urban integration has often been limited to less well paid positions in the blue-collar job market and to ghetto housing. Political integration has been very limited.

Structural assimilation at the primary-group level seems to have been limited as well. One study in Spokane, Washington, found little social integration of Native Americans into voluntary associations in that area. A few studies of urban migrants have accented their modest integration with outside whites, which is somewhat greater than that of rural dwellers. A shift can be seen in certain family values, with less emphasis in the urban area on extended families. Increases in marital assimilation have occurred in cities. One Los Angeles study found that one-third of the married respondents had white spouses. Census data showed the same pattern among urban Native Americans nationwide; the rural rate of intermarriage is about half that in urban areas. Inmarriage still seems the dominant pattern. Structural assimilation at the primary level has come very slowly. Though it is greater in urban areas than on the reservation, many urban migrants sooner or later return to the reservation.[98]

Other dimensions of assimilation suggested by Gordon—attitude-receptional, behavior-receptional, and identificational assimilation—reflect adaptation. Some movement can be glimpsed in the area of public attitudes; recent data point to some decline in negative stereotyping of Native Americans by the white population. Discrimination too is less, though, as we have seen in the economy, education, and politics, many types of direct and indirect discrimination still hamstring Native Americans.

Attachment to tribal identity seems strong, particularly for those who have predominant Native American ancestry. Some West Coast tribes have exemplified perhaps the weakest sense of identification. One study of the Spokane tribe in the late 1960s found over half identifying themselves in interviews as definitely Native American, while a third identified themselves as "definitely more white." Many Native American tribes persist as cultural islands. A number of pan-Indian organizations, including the National Congress of American Indians and the National Indian Education Association, have tried to build an "Indian" identity and promote unity among the more than 280 tribes. But this effort has been only partially successful. There have been conflicts within these organizations among members of various tribal groups—as well as in the BIA schools among students. Tribal membership remains very important for many Native Americans, and most Native Americans see themselves as Navaho or Sioux, rather than as "Indian."[99]

## Power-Conflict Perspectives

Because of the relatively low level of structural assimilation of Native Americans, some have persuasively argued that power-conflict models have greater relevance to the Native American experience. Analysts such as Blauner cite Native Americans as the clearest case of an externally colonized minority in United States history.[100]

Power-conflict analysis accents the deception and force involved in the subordination process. Much assimilation rhetoric—"civilizing the Indians"—was a cover for exploitation by land-hungry settlers. There was great pressure, even force, involved in treaties and laws providing for individual Native Americans to become "citizens" by taking individual land allotments and making other adaptations. In 1879 the commissioner of Indian affairs stated the government position clearly:

> Indians are essentially conservative, and cling tenaciously to old customs and hate all changes: therefore the government should *force* them to scatter out on farms, break up their tribal organizations, dances, ceremonies, and tomfoolery; take from them their hundreds of useless ponies, which afford the means of indulging in their wandering, nomadic habits, and give them cattle in exchange, and compel them to labor or to *accept the alternative of starvation.*[101]

On the reservations forced acculturation has been practiced in missions and boarding schools, where children are isolated from families. In recent decades the acculturation pressures from educational and religious sources have remained intense. Unlike assimilation analysts, power-conflict analysts would look at the broad sweep of the acculturation process and see the *force* behind it.

In the 1970s and 1980s serious problems of force assimilation to white values and behavior remained. One major problem is the taking of Native American children from their homes and placing them in white foster homes or institutions. In some areas 25 to 40 percent of all children are taken from their homes. Social workers argue the homes of poor Native Americans are not "fit" places for children and place the children in white homes. According to anthropologist Shirley Hill Witt, one Mormon child-placement program has reportedly been aggressive in seeking the placement of Indian children. The president of the Mormon church reportedly commented in this way:

> When you go down on the reservations and see these hundreds of thousands of Indians living in the dirt and without culture or refinement of any kind, you can hardly believe it. Then you see these boys and girls [placed in Mormon homes] playing the flute, the piano. All these things bring about a normal culture.[102]

Here we see the white culture held up as the "normal" culture against which Native Americans are judged. This is ironic, for the poverty and "dirt" in the lives of Native Americans are fundamentally the result of the destruction of Native American resources, the taking away of land, and the rank discrimination in urban areas over hundreds of years of oppression.

A recent study of Native American college students at the University of Oklahoma found that success in college was linked with two different sets of factors. On the one hand, those who had done well in high school and on college entrance tests tended to do well at the university. On the other hand, those with a strong Native American identity were more likely than assimilated Native Americans to fail and drop out, regardless of their academic ability. These researchers argued that the problem is the university context. The expected changes are unidirectional: the student is expected to conform to the white college environment. Educational institutions are not expected to adopt to the cultures and needs of nontraditional students.[103]

At all levels Native American children face tremendous assimilation pressures; many capitulate, adopting white stereotypes of themselves and dressing and behaving in Anglo-preferred ways. But this stylized behavior, notes Witt, damages "the inner self" and creates great stress for many. Caught between their native culture and Anglo pressures, some commit suicide. An Oklahoma study found that suicide rates among young males have been increasing; those with the highest rate were those who were the most assimilated to white culture. Traditionally, suicide has been rare among young Native Americans. Other young Native Americans, however, are fighting back aggressively against the vestiges of colonialism. The renaissance of Native American culture can be seen in the many protest movements in recent decades.[104]

A power–conflict analyst might also stress that many Native Americans remain isolated geographically—on the reservations, in rural areas, or in urban ghettos. They remain colonized on their own lands while European Americans prattle on about the "vanishing red man." For example, in Oklahoma there has been a prevalent white misconception that the reservation Cherokee tribe is dying out. Yet the tribe is one of the largest in the nation, clinging tenaciously to its language and values. Wahrhaftig and Thomas have suggested that this white "fiction serves to keep the Cherokees in place as a docile and exploitable minority population."[105] In effect, by denying the existence of viable and enduring Native American communities, whites can ignore the problems of their neighbors.

Perhaps the strongest argument for the relevance of a power–conflict (colonialism) model can be found in data on Native American income, employment, housing, education, and political participation. Although there have been some gains, Native Americans as a group remain on the lower rungs of the socioeconomic ladder. Poverty characterizes life for most in rural areas and many in cities. Since the late 1970s many reservations have had effective unemployment rates of 65 percent. In urban areas, Native Americans have had to face to a disproportionate degree low-wage jobs, absentee landlords, and widespread discrimination. Native Americans are latecomers to the industrial structure of the cities and have found their "place" defined by whites as the secondary labor market and urban ghettos. In the 1980s supply-side economic policy under president Ronald Reagan brought significant cutbacks in social programs for Native Americans on the reservations. The cutbacks forced many tribes to negotiate with corporations wishing to develop tribal mineral resources. The image of an *internal* colony remains highly appropriate for Native Americans on reservations.

## SUMMARY

Native Americans remain a subordinate group. They are the descendants of the only group that did *not* immigrate to North America in the last five hundred years. They were brought into the European American sphere over a long period, during which they fought bloody battles with the invaders. After the battles came a long reservation era, a long line of bureaucrats and officials seeking to dominate or exploit. Even social scientists got into the act. This is illustrated by the quip "What is a Navaho Family?" Answer: "Three matrilineal generations and one white anthropologist living together in an extended family."

Stereotyped as inferior, Native American tribes have suffered exploitation and discrimination in the economic, political, religious, and educational spheres. In the economic sphere they have seen their lands taken, their young forced by job circumstances to relocate in inhospitable cities, and their upward mobility limited by continuing discrimination. Recent decades have seen some gains. Yet the economic progress, however slow, has yet to be matched by substantial political progress, particularly off the reservations. The BIA, although more progressive and "Indianized," remains an outside governmental bureaucracy.

Protest organizations, secular and religious, have underscored the discontent of these subordinated peoples. In recent years Red Pride advocates have pointed up the cultural uniqueness of the Native American respect for community and for ecology. Groups have organized to regain fishing rights and lands that were stolen. Calls for maintaining cultural distinctiveness and recognizing the superiority of Native American values have also been heard. Some Native Americans have accented the uniqueness of their colonization. Native Americans have a unique position in regard to citizenship, since they existed in America prior to any European government. Indeed, some in groups such as the Iroquois have continued to argue that they are *not* citizens of the United States, and that they do not want to be citizens. They predate the European invasions, so they are citizens of their own nations.

## NOTES

1. Stan Steiner, "Sacred Objects, Secular Laws," *Perspectives* 13 (Summer–Fall, 1981): 13.

2. Henry F. Dobyns, "Estimating Aboriginal American Population," *Current Anthropology* 7 (October 1960): 395–116; Virgil J. Vogel, "How Many Indians Were There When the White Man Came and How Many Remain?" in *This Country Was Ours*, ed. Virgil J. Vogel (New York: Harper & Row, Pub., 1972), p. 250.

3. D'Arcy McNickle, *The Indian Tribes of the United States* (London: Oxford University Press, 1962), p. 1; Murray L. Wax, *Indian Americans* (Englewood Cliffs, N.J.: Prentice-Hall, 1971), p. 221; U.S. Bureau of the Census, *U.S. Census of Population, 1960* (Washington, D.C.: U.S. Government Printing Office, 1960); Alan L. Sorkin, *American Indians and Federal Aid* (Washington, D.C.: Brookings Institution, 1971), pp. 4–5.

4. Edward H. Spicer, *Cycles of Conquest* (Tucson: University of Arizona Press, 1962), pp. 20–23; Clyde Kluckhohn and Dorothy Leighton, *The Navaho*, rev. ed. (Garden City, N.Y.: Doubleday, Anchor Books, 1962), pp. 23–27 et passim.

5. U.S. Bureau of Indian Affairs, *The American Indians: Answers to 101 Questions* (Washington, D.C.: U.S. Government Printing Office, 1974), pp. 2–3.

6. Howard M. Bahr, "An End to Invisibility," in *Native Americans Today*, ed. Howard M. Bahr, Bruce A. Chadwick, and Robert C. Day (New York: Harper & Row, Pub., 1972), pp. 407–9; James E. Officer, "The American Indian and Federal Policy," in *The American Indian in Urban Society*, ed. Jack O. Waddell and O. Michael Watson (Boston: Little, Brown, 1971), pp. 45–60.

7. Bahr, "An End to Invisibility," p. 408.

8. Spicer, *Cycles of Conquest*, pp. 5, 306–7; Wax, *Indian Americans*, pp. 6–7; Lynn R. Bailey, *Indian Slave Trade in the Southwest* (Los Angeles: Westernlore Press, 1966), pp. 73–140.

9. Leo Grebler, Joan W. Moore, and Ralph C. Guzman, *The Mexican-American People* (New York: Free Press, 1970), pp. 320–21; Spicer, *Cycles of Conquest*, pp. 4–5; Carey McWilliams, *North from Mexico* (New York: Greenwood Press, 1968), pp. 20–33; Herbert Blatchford, "Historical Survey of American Indians," Appendix H in Stan Steiner, *The New Indians* (New York: Harper & Row, Pub., 1968), pp. 314–15.

10. McNickle, *The Indian Tribes of the United States*, pp. 13–17; Alice Marriott and Carol K. Rachlin, *American Epic* (New York: Mentor Books, 1969), pp. 104–8; John Collier, *Indians of the Americas* (New York: Mentor Books, 1947), p. 115.

11. William T. Hagan, *American Indians* (Chicago: University of Chicago Press, 1961), p. 14. The discussion of these wars is taken from ibid., pp. 12–15.

12. Almon W. Lauber, *Indian Slavery in Colonial Times within the Present Limits of the United States* (New York: Columbia University Press, 1913), pp. 107–69.

13. McNickle, *The Indian Tribes of the United States*, pp. 23–28; Ruth M. Underhill, *Red Man's America* (Chicago: University of Chicago Press, 1953), pp. 321–22; Wax, *Indian Americans*, p. 13.

14. Quoted on the title page of Vine Deloria, Jr., *Of Utmost Good Faith* (New York: Bantam, 1972).

15. McNickle, *The Indian Tribes of the United States*, pp. 32–35; National Indian Youth Council, "Chronology of Indian History, 1492–1955," in Steiner, *The New Indians*, pp. 318–19.

16. Blatchford, "Historical Survey of American Indians," pp. 316–18; Hagan, *American Indians*, pp. 41–44.

17. Alexis de Tocqueville, *Democracy in America* (New York: Random House, Vintage Books, 1945), 1:364.

18. Virgil J. Vogel, "The Indian in American History, 1968," in *This Country Was Ours*, ed. Vogel, pp. 284–87; McNickle, *The Indian Tribes of the United States*, pp. 40–41.

19. Ralph K. Andrist, *The Long Death* (London: Collier-Macmillan, 1964), p. 3.

20. John D. Unruh, *The Plains Across* (Urbana: University of Illinois Press, 1979), p. 185 et passim.

21. Vogel, "The Indian in American History," p. 285; Wendell H. Oswalt, *This Land Was Theirs* (New York: John Wiley, 1966), pp. 501–2.

22. Andrist, *The Long Death*, pp. 31–68, 78–91.

23. William Meyer, *Native Americans* (New York: International Publishers, 1971), p. 32.

24. Andrist, *The Long Death*, pp. 140–48.

25. Ibid., pp. 240–50, 350–53; Alvin M. Josephy, *The Indian Heritage of America* (New York: Bantam, 1968), pp. 284–342; Theodora Kroeber and Robert F. Heizer, *Almost Ancestors* (San Francisco: Sierra Club, 1968), pp. 14–20.

26. Spicer, *Cycles of Conquest*, pp. 216–21, 247–70.

27. Robert F. Spencer, Jesse D. Jennings, et al., *The Native Americans* (New York: Harper & Row, Pub., 1965), pp. 495–96; David Miller, "The Fur Men and Explorers View the Indians," in *Red Men and Hat Wearers*, ed. Daniel Tyler (Fort Collins, Colo: Pruett Publishing Co., 1976), pp. 26–28.

28. Peter Farb, *Man's Rise to Civilization as Shown by the Indians of North America from Primeval Times to the Coming of the Industrial State* (New York: Dutton, 1968), pp. 246–49; Tyler, *Red Men and Hat Wearers*, passim.

29. Lewis H. Carlson and George A. Colburn, in "Introduction," *In their Place*, ed. Lewis H. Carlson and George A. Colburn (New York: John Wiley, 1972), p. 44.

30. Farb, *Man's Rise to Civilization*, pp. 122–24.

31. Vogel, "The Indian in American History, 1968," pp. 288–89; Tocqueville, *Democracy in America*, 1:355–57.

32. Carlson and Colburn, "Introduction," pp. 32–33; Thomas R. Garth, *Race Psychology* (New York: McGraw-Hill, 1931), pp. 73–82.

33. U.S. Senate Subcommittee on Indian Education, *Hearings on Indian Education* (Washington, D.C.: U.S. Government Printing Office, 1969), passim; Jeanette Henry, "Text Book Distortion of the Indian," *Civil Rights Digest* 1 (Summer 1968): 4–8; Kathleen C. Houts and Rosemary S. Bahr, "Stereotyping of Indians and Blacks in Magazine Cartoons," in *Native Americans Today*, ed. Bahr, Chadwick, and Day, pp. 112–13 (see also p. 49).

34. Howard M. Bahr, Bruce A. Chadwick, and Robert C. Day, "Introduction: Patterns of Prejudice and Discrimination," in *Native Americans Today*, ed. Bahr, Chadwick, and Day, pp. 44–45; Emory S. Bogardus, *Immigration and Race Attitudes* (Boston: Heath, 1928); Beverly Brandon Sweeney, "Native American: Stereotypes and Ideologies of an Adult Anglo Population in Texas" (M.A. thesis, University of Texas at Austin, 1976), pp. 125–33.

35. U.S. Bureau of Indian Affairs, *Federal Indian Policies* (Washington, D.C.: U.S. Government Printing Office, 1975), p. 6.

36. Ibid., p. 7; Spicer, *Cycles of Conquest*, p. 348.

37. *Elk v. Wilkins,* 112 U.S. 94 (1884), See also Deloria, *Of Utmost Good Faith*, pp. 130–32.

38. U.S. Bureau of Indian Affairs, *Federal Indian Policies*, p. 7; S. Lyman Tyler, *A History of Indian Policy* (Washington, D.C.: U.S. Government Printing Office, 1973), pp. 95–107 et passim; Jack Forbes, *Native Americans of California and Nevada* (Berkeley, Calif.: Far West Laboratory for Educational Research and Development, 1968), pp. 79–80.

39. Spicer, *Cycles of Conquest*, pp. 351–53; McNickle, *The Indian Tribes of the United States*, p. 59; U.S. Bureau of Indian Affairs, *Federal Indian Policy*, p. 9.

40. Virgil J. Vogel, "Introduction," in *This Country Was Ours,* ed. Vogel, pp. 196–97.

41. W. A. Brophy and S. D. Aberle, *The Indian* (Norman: University of Oklahoma Press, 1966), pp. 179–93.

42. U.S. Bureau of Indian Affairs, *Federal Indian Policy,* p. 12.

43. Forbes, *Native Americans of California and Nevada*, pp. 80–82; Sorkin , *American Indians and Federal Aid*, pp. 48–65; Vogel, "Introduction," p. 205; James S. Olson and Raymond Wilson, *Native Americans in the Twentieth Century* (Provo, Utah: Brigham Young University Press, 1984), p. 209.

44. E. S.Cahn, *Our Brother's Keeper* (New York: World Publishing, 1969), pp. 157–58.

45. Brophy and Aberle, *The Indian*, pp. 33–44; Olson and Wilson, *Native Americans in the Twentieth Century*, p. 189.

46. Olson and Wilson, *Native Americans in the Twentieth Century*, p. 191.

47. Steiner, *The New Indians*, pp. 235–36.

48. Ibid., pp. 232–34.

49. Virgil J. Vogel, "Famous Americans of Indian Decent," in *This Country Was Ours,* ed. Vogel, pp. 310–51.

50. Theodore W. Taylor, *The States and Their Indian Citizens* (Washington, D.C.: U.S. Government Printing Office, 1972), pp. 82–84.

51. U.S. Commission on Civil Rights, Minnesota Advisory Committee, *Bridging the Gap: The Twin Cities Native American Community* (Washington, D.C.: U.S. Government Printing Office, 1975), pp. 65–67; Olson and Wilson, *Native Americans in the Twentieth Century*, p. 186.

52. Hazel W. Hertzberg, *The Search for an American Indian Identity* (Syracuse: Syracuse University Press, 1971), pp. 20–21, 42–76, 180–200.

53. Ibid., pp. 200–208, 291–93.

54. Robert C. Day, "The Emergence of Activism as a Social Movement," in *Native Americans Today*, ed. Bahr, Chadwick, and Day, pp. 516–17.

55. Vogel, "Famous Americans of Indian Decent," pp. 310–51.

56. Meyer, *Native Americans*, p. 88; "Pine Ridge after Wounded Knee: The Terror Goes on," *Akwasasne Notes* 7 (Summer 1975): 8–10.

57. Glenn T. Morris, "Resistance to Radioactive Colonialism: A Reply to the Churchill/La Duke Indictment," *Insurgent Sociologist* 13 (Spring 1986): 82.

58. Olson and Wilson, *Native Americans in the Twentieth Century*, p. 191.

59. U.S. Commission on Civil Rights, *Indian Tribes: A Continuing Quest for Survival* (Washington, D.C.: U.S. Government Printing Office, 1981), pp. 61–99.

60. Ibid., p. 103.

61. Ibid., pp. 118–19, 133.

62. "Give It Back to the Indians," *Newsweek,* December 7, 1987. p. 47.

63. Olson and Wilson, *Native Americans in the Twentieth Century*, p. 195.

64. U.S. Commission on Civil Rights, *Indian Tribes*, pp. 1–2.

65. Ibid., pp. 4–7.

66. Sar A. Levitan, Garth L. Mangum, and Ray Marshall, *Human Resources and Labor Markets*, 2d ed. (New York: Harper & Row, Pub., 1976), p. 441.

67. Joseph G. Jorgensen, "Indians and the Metropolis," in *The American Indian in Urban Society*, ed. Waddell and Watson, p. 85. This paragraph draws on Jorgensen's theory.

68. Quoted in Deloria, *Of Utmost Good Faith*, pp. 380–81.

69. Hagan, *American Indians*, pp. 126–27; Spicer, *Cycles of Conquest*, pp. 349–56.

70. Cahn, *Our Brother's Keeper*, pp. 69–110; Rupert Costo, "Speaking Freely," *Wassaja* 4 (November–December 1976): 2; Sorkin, *American Indians and Federal Aid*, pp. 70–71; Jorgensen, "Indians and the Metropolis," pp. 96–99.

71. Sorkin, *American Indians and Federal Aid*, pp. 105, 136–39, 201; Levitan, Mangum, and Marshall, *Human Resources and Labor Markets*, p. 443; Theodore D. Graves, "Drinking and Drunkenness among Urban Indians," in *The American Indian in Urban Society*, ed. Waddell and Watson, pp. 292–95.

72. Levitan, Mangum, and Marshall, *Human Resources and Labor Markets*, p. 443; Jorgensen, "Indians and the Metropolis," p. 83; Brophy and Aberle, *The Indian*, p. 99.

73. James Cook, "Help Wanted—Work, Not Handouts," *Forbes* 139 (May 4, 1987): 68–71.

74. Olson and Wilson, *Native Americans in the Twentieth Century*, p. 181.

75. Ward Churchill and Winona La Duke, "Native America: The Political Economy of 'Radioactive Colonialism,'" *Insurgent Sociologist* 13 (Spring 1986): 51–57.

76. Michael Parfit, "Keeping the Big Sky Pure," *Perspectives* 13 (Spring 1981): 44; Jeff Gillenkirk and Mark Dowie, "The Great Indian Land Power Grab," *Mother Jones* 7 (January 1982): 47–48.

77. U.S. Department of Health, Education and Welfare, *A Study of Selected Socio-economic Characteristics of Ethnic Minorities Based on the 1970 Census*, vol. 3, *American Indians* (Washington, D.C.: U.S. Government Printing Office, 1974), p. 49; Sorkin, *American Indians and Federal Aid*, p. 12. The 1970 figures are for males sixteen and over; earlier figures are for those fourteen and older.

78. U.S. Bureau of the Census, *1970 Census: American Indians* (Washington, D.C.: U.S. Government Printing Office, 1973); U.S. Bureau of the Census, *Population, 1960: Nonwhite Population by Race* (Washington, D.C.: U.S. Government Printing Office, 1963), p. 104; U.S. Bureau of the Census, *Population, 1940: Characteristics of the Nonwhite Population by Race* (Washington, D.C.: U.S. Government Printing Office, 1943), pp. 83–84. The data do not include those not reporting and, in 1960, states with less than 25,000 Native Americans.

79. U.S. Bureau of the Census, *U.S. Census of Population, 1980: General Social and Economic Characteristics*, PC80-1, 1981, p. 102.

80. U.S. Department of Health, Education and Welfare, *A Study of Selected Socio-economic Characteristics*, pp. 59–78; U.S. Bureau of the Census, *U.S. Census of Population, 1980: General Social and Economic Characteristics*, PC80-1, 1981, p. 112.

81. U.S. Department of Health, Education and Welfare, *A Study of Selected Socio-economic Characteristics*, pp. 59–78; Olson and Wilson, *Native Americans in the Twentieth Century*, p. 187.

82. U.S. Bureau of Indian Affairs, *Federal Indian Policies*, p. 5.

83. Ibid., pp. 5–6; Spicer, *Cycles of Conquest*, p. 349; Forbes, *Native Americans of California and Nevada*, passim.

84. U.S. Bureau of Indian Affairs, *Federal Indian Policies*, p. 9.

85. Tyler, *A History of Indian Policy*, pp. 228–29; Taylor, *The States and Their Indian Citizens*, pp. 83–85; Olson and Wilson, *Native Americans in the Twentieth Century*, p. 185.

86. U.S. Department of Health, Education and Welfare, *A Study of Selected Socio-economic Characteristics*, pp. 38–39, 43; Olson and Wilson, *Native Americans in the Twentieth Century*, p. 186; U.S. Bureau of the Census, *U.S. Census of Population, 1980: General Social and Economic Characteristics*, PC80-1-C1, 1983, p. 98.

87. Olson and Wilson, *Native Americans in the Twentieth Century*, p. 186.

88. Brophy and Aberle, *The Indian*, p. 142; Bruce A. Chadwick, "The Inedible Feast," in *Native Americans Today*, ed. Bahr, Chadwick, and Day, p. 141; Murray L. Wax, Rosalie H. Wax, and Robert V. Dumont, "Formal Education in an American Indian Community," in *The Emergent Native Americans*, ed. Deward E. Walker, Jr. (Boston: Little, Brown, 1972), pp. 638–40; American Indian Historical Society, "Textbooks and the American Indian," reprinted in U.S. Senate, *Hearings before the Special Subcommittee on Indian Education, 1967–1968*, part 1 (Washington, D.C.: U.S. Government Printing Office, 1969), pp. 397–405; Cahn, *Our Brother's Keeper*, pp. 35–36.

89. Quoted in Vine Deloria, Jr., *Custer Died for Your Sins* (London: Collier-Macmillan, 1969), p. 101.

90. Ibid., pp. 108–16.

91. Vittorio Lanternari, *The Religion of the Oppressed* (New York: Mentor Books, 1963), pp. 110–32; Spencer, Jennings, et al., *The Native Americans*, pp. 498–99; Wax, *Indian Americans*, p. 141.

92. Lanternari, *The Religions of the Oppressed*, pp. 99–100; Hertzberg, *The Search for an American Indian Identity*, pp. 239–40, 251, 280.

93. Hertzberg, *The Search for an American Indian Identity*, pp. 246, 257, 271–74, 280–84; Elaine G. Eastman, "Does Uncle Sam Foster Paganism?" in *In Their Place*, ed. Carlson and Colburn, pp. 29ff.

94. Deloria, *Of Utmost Good Faith*, pp. 177ff; idem, *Custer Died for Your Sins*, pp. 110–15.

95. Quoted in Olson and Wilson, *Native Americans in the Twentieth Century*, p. 219. See also Deloria, *Custer Died for Your Sins*, pp. 122–24; and Cahn, *Our Brother's Keeper*, pp. 175–90.

96. Lurie, as quoted in John A. Price, "Migration and Adaptation of American Indians to Los Angeles," *Human Organization* 27 (Summer 1968): 168–75.

97. Olson and Wilson, *Native Americans in the Twentieth Century*, p. 212; see also pp. 210–11.

98. Prodipto Roy, "The Measurement of Assimilation: The Spokane Indians," *American Journal of Sociology* 67 (March 1962): 541–51; Price, "Migration and Adaptation of American Indians to Los Angeles," pp. 169–74; U.S. Department of Health, Education and Welfare, *A Study of Selected Socioeconomic Characteristics*, pp. 35; Oswalt, *This Land Was Theirs*, pp. 513–14.

99. Lynn C. White and Bruce A. Chadwick, "Urban Residence, Assimilation, and Identity of the Spokane Indian," in *Native Americans Today*, ed. Bahr, Chadwick, and Day, p. 243; Brophy and Aberle, *The Indian*, p. 10; Spicer, *Cycles of Conquest*, p. 577.

100. Robert Blauner, *Racial Oppression in America* (New York: Harper & Row, Pub., 1972), p. 54; Spicer, *Cycles of Conquest*, pp. 573–74.

101. Quoted in Francis McKinley, Stephen Bayne, and Glen Nimnicht, *Who Should Control Indian Education?* (Berkeley, Calif.: Far West Laboratory for Educational Research and Development, 1969), p. 13 (italics added).

102. Quoted in Shirley Hill Witt, "Pressure Points in Growing Up Indian," *Perspectives* 12 (Spring 1980): 31.

103. Wilbur J. Scott, "Attachment to Indian Culture," *Youth and Society* 17 (June 1986): 392–94.

104. Witt, "Pressure Points in Growing Up Indian," pp. 28–31.

105. Albert l. Wahrhaftig and Robert K. Thomas, "Renaissance and Repression: The Oklahoma Cherokee," in *Native Americans Today*, ed. Bahr, Chadwick, and Day, p. 81.

# CHAPTER 8

# *Black Americans*

Black Americans have family trees in the United States extending back before 1800, well before the American Revolution, which should put them in good stead for membership even in such lineage-oriented organizations as the traditionally white Daughters of the American Revolution. There is a tragic irony here. That a people who have been here as long as the first white settlers should still find themselves in a subordinate position today is a fact of American life problematical both for the assimilation theory discussed in chapter 2 and for public policy in our democratic nation.

## MIGRATION AND SLAVERY

White immigrants came to North America voluntarily, for the most part. Most Africans had no choice; they came in chains. Afro-Americans exemplify the slave-importation end of the migration continuum we have discussed. Their destinations were determined by slave traders. The enslavement of black Africans was a solution to the need for cheap labor in the agricultural South and elsewhere.[1]

### The Slave Trade

Dutch and French companies early dominated the forcible importation of Africans; England came into the trade in the late 1600s. Fed by European piracy, the slave trade soon saw the institutionalization of trading alliances between certain African chiefs, who wanted horses and manufactured goods, and white slavers, who wanted human beings to sell. Some African coastal chiefs, out of greed or fear, succumbed to slave-trade pressure and established themselves as go-betweens in eastern Africa.[2]

Once captured, slaves were often chained in corrals called barracoons, where they were branded and held for transportation. The voyage was a living hell. Slaves were chained together in close quarters, with little room for movement and no sanitary facilities. The horror was summed up by a young slave:

> I was soon put down under the decks, and there I received such a salutation in my nostrils as I had never experienced in my life: so that with the loathsomeness of the stench, and crying together, I became so sick and low that I was not able to eat, nor had I the least desire to taste any thing.... On my refusing to eat, one of them held me fast by the hands, and laid me across, I think the windlass, and tied my feet, while the other flogged me severely.... One day, when we had a smooth sea and moderate wind, two of my wearied countrymen who were chained together (I was near them at the time), preferring death to such a life of misery, somehow made through the nettings and jumped into the sea.[3]

Slave suicides were common, and uprisings brought death to slaves and sailors alike. The myth of Africans' passive acquiescence is contradicted by the 155 recorded shipboard uprisings by slaves between 1699 and 1845; many other attacks went unrecorded.[4]

In 1619 twenty blacks were brought to Jamestown by a Dutch ship. In the early period some blacks were apparently treated like white indentured servants, but by the mid-1600s the slave status of Africans had been fully institutionalized in the laws of several colonies. For the next two and half centuries virtually all African immigrants were brought in for involuntary servitude. Estimates by Curtin of the number of slaves in the Western Hemisphere are 9.6 million for this period; most were brought to the West Indies and South America, only 5 percent to North America. Prior to 1790 an estimated 275,000 African slaves were brought into all the colonies; between 1790 and the end of the legal slave trade in 1808 another 70,000 were imported. The total for the entire slave period was approximately half a million.[5]

A number of founding fathers, including the slaveholders George Washington, James Madison, and Thomas Jefferson, spoke of the problems of slavery and saw its eventual demise. In an early draft of the Declaration of Independence, Thomas Jefferson went so far as to attack slavery by blaming it on King George. As a result of southern slave owners' opposition, however, his antislavery language was *not* included in the final draft of that founding document.[6]

Slave interests also forced recognition of slavery in several provisions of the United States Constitution. Slavery was recognized in a section that provided for the counting of each slave as three-fifths of a person, in a fugitive-slave section, and in a section postponing prohibition of slave importation to 1808. Although the slave trade was officially abolished as of 1808, the ban was not enforced. Thousands continued to be imported illegally.[7]

In 1860 an estimated one-quarter of the 1.6 million white families in the South owned 3.8 million black slaves. Most slave owners had fewer than ten slaves; only 46,000 white families owned twenty or more slaves. Most white farmers had *no* slaves. A majority of the slaves were chained to the larger farms or plantations, which produced surplus agricultural products to be marketed. Most plantation owners, tied to trade with the North and England, can be viewed as agrarian capitalists attuned to commercial trade and a money profit. The wealth, as well as power, of the slaveholding gentry rose as a result of slave agriculture. And this plantation gentry dominated the U.S. economy and the federal government from 1800 to the Civil War.[8]

## Slave Life

There has long been a magnolias-and-mint-julep mystique about the slave system, which lingers on, particularly in the South. According to this mythology, a paternalistic master cared kindly for contented, happy slaves. A big, white plantation house with multiple columns and magnolia trees all around was at the center of this idyllic existence. Black house servants were treated like members of the family. Popular writers and some scholars have painted sugar-coated views of slavery, downplaying the brutality and oppression as well as the violent rebellions.

Comparisons have been made with the living conditions of slaves in South America or poor workers in Europe, the point being that in terms of food and housing slaves in the South were apparently somewhat better off. Yet the apologists for U.S. slavery have ignored such issues as personal freedom, with regard to which southern slaves were worse off. The South's Anglo-Saxon Protestant religious and legal tradition had no prior experience with slavery. In the South there was little recognition of the slave as a person[9]

Slave autobiographies describe the oppressiveness of living conditions. Most slaves rose before dawn, then worked in the house or the fields until dark. Food was often insufficient. Clothing and housing were crude and inadequate. Social control depended to some extent on value consensus between slaves and masters, but even more on force. That many slaves came to accept the system was an important factor in its perpetuation. A white-supremacy ideology legitimated the position of slaves. Whites controlled the state militias and the courts.[10]

The whip and the chains were mechanisms in the control system. Some masters were extremely cruel, such as the owner of this slave, who told about moving from Georgia to Texas: "Then he chains all the slaves round the necks and fastens the chains to the hosses and makes them walk all the way to Texas. My mother and my sister had to walk. Emma was my sister. Somewhere on the road it went to snowing, and Massa wouldn't let us wrap anything round our feet. We had to sleep on the ground, too, in all that snow."[11] Other slave owners earned a reputation for kindness; they provided better material conditions and were less likely to use the whip. But most owners fell between the two extremes, caring somewhat for their "property" but resorting to cruel punishment when necessary for control.

At a tender age young slaves encountered a system of enforced deference to all whites and learned that docility was a virtue. White southerners developed an extensive racist ideology to back up the etiquette of deference. They liked to believe that slaves were happy with their lot. Stereotypes consistent with the alleged inferiority of blacks were developed by intellectuals and popular writers.[12]

The prominent historian of slavery Eugene Genovese sees Afro-American slavery as a paternalistic system, although he also stresses the role of violent oppression. For the masters, paternalism rationalized the subordination of other human beings; for the slaves, it meant some recognition of material needs. Yet a paternalistic system can be dangerous for the oppressed, for it tends to foster individualism and divisions in terms of privilege among the oppressed and thus to make organization for resistance difficult. Genovese has been criticized for exaggerating the paternalistic aspects of slavery, but his view remains important, for both accommodation and violent resistance were part of the slave reaction to an alternately brutal and paternalistic system.[13]

This paternalistic context may help us make sense out of family life. Slave families have been a concern of social scientists; even the contemporary problems of poverty and broken families have been traced back to the assumed constant breakup of black family units in slave days. Supportive family life has been viewed as nonexistent for the majority of slaves. Yet there is considerable evidence of paternalistic slave owners actually fostering families. Moreover, slaves themselves worked hard to preserve and protect their families, to the extent possible. Slave families were protective, supportive environments that helped slave communities to survive. Slaves often deserted brutal masters as family units, and a frequent cause of desertion was the desire to find lost loved ones. In an extensive analysis of families on large plantations, Gutman found that enslaved Afro-American women were expected to have their children by one man; that the names of fathers were given to sons; that adoption was a mechanism used to ease the disruption of death within and breakup of families; and that there was a continuity in many families over several generations. The threat to the slave family was also great. Slave marriages were likely to be broken up at some point, most often by death but frequently by masters. Clearly, an accurate picture of the slave family must include both the stability and the disruption.[14]

## Slave Resistance

Apologists for slavery have emphasized the submissive response, picturing a docile "Sambo." In scholarly debates over slavery a similar theme has received attention. Numerous scholars have underscored the severe impact of slavery on personality. Elkins argues that the major personality type created by the oppressive "total institution" was the childlike, docile one.[15]

Yet submissiveness was only one response. Most slaves did not adopt the "Sambo" personality in order to survive. An assertive aspect existed as well. Both aspects are likely to have been important components of a given slave's personality. Depending on the economic or other circumstances of life, one aspect or the other might come to the forefront. Many slaves used their wits to escape as much forced work and punishment as possible and observed the servile etiquette when necessary, but many also rebelled or attacked where that was possible.[16]

Rebellious behavior took different forms, including flight, suicide, and psychological withdrawal. Fugitive slaves were a serious problem for slave owners, serious enough to prompt inclusion of the fugitive-slave provision in the Constitution. Perhaps the most famous route of escape was the Underground Railroad, the network of antislavery citizens who secreted and passed along tens of thousands of slaves to the North between the 1830s and the Civil War. Thousands fled shorter distances.

Southerners committed to the "happy Sambo" view of their slaves sometimes went to absurd lengths to explain runaways. Physician Samuel Cartwright, incredibly, attributed the problem to a strange black disease, "drapetomania," by which he meant the unhealthy tendency to flee one's owner![17]

Nonviolent slave resistance took the form of a slow working pace, feigned illness, and strikes. Violent resistance was directed at the property and persons of slave owners or overseers. Black resistance could be seen in the destruction of tools, livestock, fields, and farmhouses. Masters and overseers were killed. Collective resistance could be seen in revolts and conspiracies to revolt. Aptheker found evidence of 250 slave revolts or conspiracies to revolt, a count that did not include numerous mutinies aboard slave ships. There is considerable evidence, in the newspapers of the day, of extensive white fear of uprisings.[18]

In 1800 a group of slaves led by Gabriel Prosser in Henrico County, Virginia, gathered weapons and planned to march on Richmond. Governor Monroe took action to protect the state capital. A thousand armed slaves rendezvoused, but a heavy rain cut them off from the city and they disbanded. Betrayed, the leaders were quickly arrested; at least thirty-five, including Prosser, were hanged. Perhaps the most serious slave revolt took place in 1811 near New Orleans. After several hundred armed slaves attacked whites on local plantations, white troops suppressed the rebellion. Several dozen slaves were killed during the encounter; others were executed later by a firing squad and their heads displayed along the route to New Orleans.[19]

The most famous rebellion took place in Southampton County, Virginia, in 1831. Nat Turner, the leader, was a self-taught slave with mystical-religious leanings. Turner recruited seventy slaves in a single day; his revolutionaries attacked, and dozens of white members of slaveholding families in the area were killed. Having delayed a planned attack on the county seat, the rebels were attacked and defeated by hundreds of militiamen and army soldiers. Turner, who had escaped, was executed several months later.[20]

Such slave revolts intensified the fears of whites, many of whom were near panic following a revolt. Revolts contradicted the apologists' notion of happy slaves. Given the opportunity, slaves would resist violently. Slavery, and the fears surrounding it, had a severe impact on whites in the South. Southern whites lost much of their humanity, as well as much of their own freedom of speech, press, and assembly, because of the slave system.

## Outside the Rural South

In the North slavery had long been seen by the *majority of whites* as legitimate. Significant numbers of slaves could be found in some northern states. The North was built in part on forced labor and in part on the surplus population of Europe. As Ringer puts it, "despite the early emancipation of slaves in the North [slavery] remained there, not merely as fossilized remains but as a *deeply ingrained coding for the future*."[21] Take Massachusetts, for example. In 1641, three years after slaves were brought in, slavery was made lawful. Massachusetts merchants and shippers played a central role in the North American slave trade. It was not until the 1780s that public opinion and court cases came together to effectively abolish slavery in New England. Even then, it was *not* recognition of the rights of blacks that ended slavery, but rather pressure from the growing number of white working people who objected to having to compete with cheap slave labor. To take another example, by 1786 slaves made up 7 percent of the New York population. Not until 1799 was a statute of emancipation passed there— and partial emancipation at that. Understanding that slavery was entrenched in the North's legal system is important for understanding the internal colonialism that blacks still face today in the North.[22]

Even before the Civil War Jim Crow laws (legally enforced segregation) had been given a boost in the states and cities of the North. There free blacks were segregated in public transportation, hospitals, jails, schools, churches, and cemeteries. Jim Crow railroad cars were early established in Massachusetts. All northern cities had black ghettos for free blacks at a time when there were no comparable ghettos in southern cities because black slaves there were allowed to live in the same areas as their masters.

## STEREOTYPING

Dominant groups develop beliefs to rationalize their domination. Racial theories of biological, mental, and moral inferiority were early devised by white theologians, intellectuals, and other southern leaders to rationalize the exploitation of blacks as slaves.

Negative views of African peoples existed in Europe before the founding of the American colonies, but these did not develop into full-blown racist ideologies until the late 1700s. Thomas Jefferson personified the moral dilemma of whites in the eighteenth century: He wrote a stinging indictment of slavery in the original draft of the Declaration of Independence, yet he was a major slave owner. He wrote vigorously of his opposition to interracial sex and miscegenation, yet he is reported to have had a black mistress who bore him children. He wrote of the inferiority of blacks, but he also argued that they should be free. In his 1786 *Notes on Virginia*, Jefferson argued that what he saw as the ugly color, offensive odor, and ugly hair of blacks were signs of their physical inferiority and that what he alleged to be their inability to create was a sign of mental inferiority. Jefferson's views on the inferiority of Afro-Americans were similar to the stereotypes of blacks that were popular in the eighteenth and nineteenth centuries.[23]

### Black Color as a Badge of Inferiority

At an early date, black people's dark color was singled out as unusual or ugly. By 1800 blackness was seen as a critical means of sorting out people; the terms *black* and *Negro* underscored the importance of color. By the mid-1800s advocates of slavery were arguing for acceptance of the supposed apelike characteristics of the Afro-American, a stereotype applied by Anglo-Saxons to Irish Americans a decade or two earlier.

Samuel Cartwright, in a famous article published in the 1850s, wrote that Africans were a different species than Europeans "because the head and face are anatomically constructed more after the fashion of the simiadiae [apes]."[24]

By the turn of the century this way of insulting black Americans had taken on ludicrous forms. The low point was probably reached in 1906 when the New York Zoological Society put a small African, Ota Benga, in a cage in the monkey house of the Bronx Park Zoo as part of an exhibit. Thousands came to view the African's new home. Some black ministers protested the degrading exhibition, but white officials as well as the white populace thought it great sport.[25]

Since the 1840s blacks have often been depicted by southerners as having an offensive odor. Black women were seen as immoral, black men as oversexed and potential rapists. This absurd fear of black sexuality reflected guilt over the widespread miscegenation between white men and black women slaves. Intermixing in the South had become a permanent feature of the sexual landscape, a point testified to by the lighter color of some black Americans.[26]

Afro-Americans were also charged with being mentally and morally inferior. Slavery advocates tried hard to depict slaves as childlike, happy-go-lucky "Sambos"; this stereotype did not die with slavery. Between 1900 and World War II, prominent white scientists, such as geneticist Edward East of Harvard University, took the position that "mentally the African negro is childlike, normally affable and cheerful, but subject to fits of fierce passion."[27]

Early discussions of blacks' inferiority assumed that blacks had a small brain and a lower mental capacity than that of Europeans. Southern apologists for slavery embraced views of racial inferiority, views routinely legitimated in the "scientific racism" of nineteenth-century writers in Europe. A burst of interest in this argument for mental inferiority occurred around 1900, when a number of American scientists argued for the inferiority of certain racial groups, including Americans of southern European and African descent. As we noted in Chapter 5, many observers, relying heavily on IQ tests, attempted to prove that southern and eastern Europeans were mentally inferior; others used the same tests to the same end with black Americans. Scholarly journals and popular magazines parroted this theme. Antiblack thought was coupled with theories of northern European racial superiority to other groups, southern European as well as African. Even American presidents have participated in the crude racial theorizing since the last decades of the nineteenth century.[28]

## "IQ" Testing and Race: Pseudoscience?

The theme of intellectual inferiority has received renewed attention since World War II—as, for example, in response to the 1954 Supreme Court decision desegregating public school systems. Social scientists Audrey Shuey and Henry Garrett wrote and spoke in support of inferiority theories, drawing on the extensive IQ-testing literature and alleging that blacks are so significantly different in mentality that they should not be educated with whites. Popular writers such as columnist James J. Kilpatrick and magazines such as *U.S. News & World Report* spread these arguments throughout white America.[29]

Since the 1960s a new group of social scientists have resurrected the old inferiority arguments on the basis of psychological test results available for blacks and whites. Arthur Jensen and Richard Herrnstein, among others, have argued that there are inherited IQ differences among racial groups. Groups at the lower social and economic levels are intellectually and genetically inferior to those at higher ones. In the past this perspective was applied to *white* immigrant groups considered inferior to Anglo-Saxons; in the last few decades the focus has been on *nonwhite* Americans. Jensen has argued that differences in IQ test scores reflect genetic differences between blacks and whites and that the two groups have different types of intelligence, perhaps requiring different educational techniques. Racial differences in mental ability, he has argued, are not just environmentally determined. Citing earlier studies by "scientific" racists, Jensen expressed concern about the higher birth rates of blacks and the alleged lowering of the national IQ.[30]

In the 1930s a number of social psychologists began questioning whether IQ test results could be used as evidence of genetically determined racial differentials. Citing data on the oppressive conditions suffered by blacks, they argued that black–white differences in IQ test scores reflected mainly *education* and *income* differences. A number of studies showed that IQ test scores of black children improved with better economic and learning environments, as when black children from segregated southern schools attended integrated northern schools. Results from large-scale IQ testing have shown blacks in some northern states scoring *higher* than whites in some southern states. Otto Klinberg retabulated the following data for selected states from World War I tests:[31]

| White Scores (Median) | | Black Scores (Median) | |
| --- | --- | --- | --- |
| Mississippi | 41.25 | New York | 45.02 |
| Kentucky | 41.50 | Pennsylvania | 42.00 |
| Georgia | 42.12 | Ohio | 49.50 |
| Arkansas | 41.55 | Illinois | 47.35 |

SOURCE:   Reprinted by permission of Louisiana State University Press from *Challenge to the Court* by I. A. Newby. Copyright © 1967 and 1969.

Using the logic of analysts from Carl Brigham to Jensen, one would be forced to conclude that southern whites in certain states are mentally and "racially" inferior to northern blacks. These writers avoid this interpretation; obviously they, as racist whites, do not wish to argue for black intellectual *superiority*. A few interpreters have used test data consistently showing lower scores for southern white children than for northern white children to make the tongue-in-cheek argument that southern whites are "racially inferior" to northern whites. Not even "scientific" racists would argue any longer for the racial inferiority of certain groups of white Americans. Rather, they would accept the environmental explanation for uncomplimentary regional differentials. So, too, overall IQ-score differentials between blacks and whites can reasonably be interpreted as reflecting environment.

Yet another problem has arisen for racial-inferiority interpretations of IQ tests. In the mid-1980s one psychologist reported that the IQ test scores for Japanese children, measured in Japanese schools, averaged eleven points higher than the average IQ score for U.S. students. The study triggered a reaction from U.S. scholars, who argued that the real difference was *only* five to seven points between the children of the two countries. Yet no one in these debates used the higher Japanese scores to argue for the racial superiority in intelligence of the Japanese over, for example, white European Americans.[32]

Some analysts have focused on the cultural bias—specifically, the white middle-class bias—inherent in traditional U.S. achievement and other psychometric tests (including IQ tests). Most psychometric tests measure *learned* skills and *acquired* knowledge (such as linguistic, literary, or geographic subjects)—skills and knowledge not available to the same degree to all racial groups. Researchers have found that test taking itself is a skill white children are more likely to possess. White children with generations of middle-income experience take the tests with a built-in advantage over black children. IQ scores do seem to predict success in school, but this may well be because those children who have been trained to do well on tests are also trained in the same skills necessary for success in schools.[33]

The most fundamental problem with IQ testing is the equation of *intelligence test results* with *intelligence*. From the beginning, intelligence tests have been misnamed. These tests are only measures of certain verbal, mathematical, and/or manipulative *skills*. A number of scholars have argued that intelligence is something much broader than what paper-and-pencil tests can measure. More broadly, intelligence can be viewed as a complex ability to deal creatively with one's environment. (This would include, for example, a farmer's skill in growing foodstuffs.) Only a small portion of that ability can be revealed, even under the best testing conditions, on the typical test.[34]

## Opinion Polls, Prejudice, and Stereotyping

To what extent does the white public still accept the negative stereotypes of black Americans? Surveys have revealed that large numbers of whites believe in the inferiority of blacks. In 1966 half a national white sample felt that blacks had a different odor, were morally inferior, and laughed a lot. Few polls have asked white Americans about biological- and mental-inferiority stereotypes. Belief in inferiority was revealed in a 1965 survey of whites in Los Angeles: 31 percent felt blacks had "less native intelligence than whites," while 27 percent felt that some races are "superior because of the contribution they have made to civilization throughout time." A minority of whites still publicly express racial superiority views.[35]

When whites were asked about segregated schools for blacks in 1972 and 1976 opinion polls, three-quarters said they favored desegregated schools. By the mid-1980s the figure was about 90 percent. The proportion of those interviewed in the 1970s who said whites do not have a right to keep blacks out of their neighborhoods was just over half. About the same proportion thought laws banning racial intermarriages were not a good idea. By the early 1980s the proportion had grown, but in the mid-1980s it decreased a bit to about 75 percent for northern respondents and 45 percent for southern respondents. Support for traditional legal segregation of blacks is no longer publicly expressed by a majority of whites.[36]

Today it may be that for many whites subtle views of cultural and moral superiority have replaced crude theories of biological or intellectual superiority. Some evidence for this shift was found in a study of whites' attitudes in fifteen major cities; the study revealed that the majority thought black job, education, and housing problems resulted from black cultural inferiority, laziness, or lack of ambition rather than from discrimination by whites. Moreover, more recent surveys of whites have found a new type of racial prejudice and hostility, what John McConahay has called "modern racism": the view that blacks have illegitimately challenged cherished white values and are making illegitimate demands for changes in race relations. This is reflected in a large set of negative views of black actions and achievements. McConahay and his associates have demonstrated in a number of studies of whites that old-fashioned race prejudice, which opposes all desegregation and includes extreme negative stereotypes of blacks, has declined. But the research has also found strong support among whites for the following series of "modern racist" views:

1. Government and the news media have shown more respect to blacks than they deserve.
2. Blacks, over the last few years, have gotten more economically than they deserve.
3. Blacks have been too demanding in their push for equal rights.[37]

Other opinion polls have found resentment among whites of gains blacks have made, opposition to vigorous affirmative action, and the view that blacks are not playing by the rules that earlier white immigrant groups played by. Many whites believe that blacks *do not deserve* the gains they have made. Most of these whites publicly state their support for freedom of opportunity for blacks, unlike older racists who believed in across-the-board legal segregation. But the modern racists also feel that "blacks are too pushy, too demanding, too angry; things are moving too fast and blacks are getting more than they deserve."[38] Much of this modern racism targets certain symbols of racial change (such as affirmative action, busing, and fair housing laws). This resentment can be found in both the North and the South.

The ideological position of many white Americans is one of vigorous opposition to any significant government program, whether affirmative action in jobs or prosecution of homeowners and realtors who discriminate. If desegregation means a few black employees at work, a few students in the school room, or a few black families in the larger residential neighborhood, it is acceptable to a majority. But more substantial desegregation brought about by vigorous government action is not acceptable to more than a minority of whites. Between 1964 and 1980 several opinion surveys asked national samples of whites about government intervention to guarantee that blacks get fair treatment in jobs. In no survey did more than 39 percent of whites explicitly support government action, and the most recent of those surveys had the *lowest* percentage. On a question about government intervention to get rid of segregation in schools, the proportion of whites supporting federal action *dropped* from 42 percent in 1964 to only 25 percent in 1978. In surveys from 1973 to 1983 the proportion of whites supporting a law prohibiting race discrimination by a homeowner never reached a majority, but here the percentage did increase, from 34 percent to 46 percent.[39]

# VIOLENT CONFLICT BETWEEN WHITES AND BLACKS

## White Violence Targets Blacks

Just behind the slave system's veneer of civility were the bloody instruments of social control—the whip and the guns. Free blacks also suffered at the hands of whites. Before the Civil War, white-dominated race riots directed at free blacks occurred a dozen times in northern cities. The most serious race riot in American history in terms of human casualties was the 1863 antidraft riot in New York City, staged by a group of white immigrants, including many Irish Americans. Among the targets of their attacks were free blacks, including a black orphanage.

The end of the Civil War brought an increased threat of violence against the legally free Afro-American. Before the Civil War most lynchings were of whites; slaves, as valuable "property," could not be lynched without the lynchers being obligated to pay slave owners. Lynching after the war became a means of keeping blacks "in their place." Recorded lynchings show the following pattern:[40]

|  | White Victims | Black Victims |
|---|---|---|
| 1882–1891 | 751 | 732 |
| 1892–1901 | 381 | 1,124 |
| 1902–1911 | 76 | 707 |
| 1912–1921 | 53 | 533 |
| 1922–1931 | 23 | 201 |
| 1932–1941 | 10 | 95 |
| 1942–1951 | 2 | 25 |
| 1952–1956 | 0 | 3 |

Most killings took place in the South. Between 1892 and 1921, the peak period of segregation, nearly 2400 black Americans were lynched. Cash points out that there was a growing "inclination to abandon such relatively mild and decent ways of dispatching the [lynch] mob's victim as hanging and shooting in favor of burning, often roasting over slow fires, after preliminary mutilations and tortures.... a disposition to revel in the infliction of the most devilish and prolonged agonies."[41]

Studies have shown that at least one-third of the black victims of white vigilante action were falsely accused and that the lynchers were seldom punished. Local police officers were on occasion involved and in most other cases they winked at the lynchings. The decrease since World War II is somewhat misleading, since "legal" and secret lynchings had by then replaced public lynchings. Unnecessary killings by police officers have taken many black lives. Secret attacks resulted in hundreds of deaths of blacks and of white civil rights workers in the South between the 1940s and the 1960s. Moreover, numerous white-supremacy groups, such as the ever present Ku Klux Klan, have periodically played an important role in violence directed against blacks in the 1970s and 1980s.[42]

Many blacks left the South for northern cities to escape oppressive conditions, but the movement north resulted in violent conflict. Clashes with whites became frequent as blacks moved into the central-city areas of border and northern cities. A white riot in 1900 in New York City saw a predominantly Irish police force encouraging working-class whites to attack blacks wherever they could be found. A similar case was the 1917 East St. Louis riot, one of the most serious white-dominated race riots of this century. East St. Louis's white workers, who saw blacks as an economic threat, pressed local government for action. Union organizers placed a newspaper advertisement announcing that Negro labor was being brought into the community by local industries in order to reduce white wages. In the attack on the black ghetto that resulted, thirty-nine blacks and nine whites were killed; ghetto residents had fought back, killing some of their white attackers. This riot was followed in 1919 by a string of riots from Chicago to Charleston, South Carolina.[43]

In the following decades blacks in the North and the South faced the threat of violence from the Ku Klux Klan, which gained strength in the 1920s and again in the 1970s and 1980s. In the mid-1980s the number of white Americans in the various Klan factions was estimated at 10,000. Newspaper reports have documented Klan activities, including violence against minorities and paramilitary training camps where Klansmen are preparing for a "race war." In the 1970s and 1980s Klan members were involved in hundreds of antiblack and anti-Jewish incidents; several have been convicted of the murder or assault of blacks and white liberals. In 1979 Klan and Nazi party members in North Carolina were accused of the murders of five demonstrators who were protesting the Klan. TV cameras captured the killings on film, but a local jury acquitted the accused. In 1981 in Mobile, Alabama, Michael Donald was lynched by Klan members who later testified they selected him at random. Donald's family sued the United Klans of America, the oldest of the KKK groups, and in 1987 won a $7 million award. This was the first time in history that a KKK group had been found guilty of violence. This award signaled the decline of this particular branch of the KKK in the late 1980s.[44]

But it did not signal the end of violence against black Americans. In one year, from mid-1985 to mid-1986, there were 45 known arson and cross-burning attempts across the United States at the homes of minorities who had moved into mostly white residential areas. In addition, during the 1980s there were hundreds of acts of vandalism and intimidation directed at black and other nonwhite Americans. One of the most notorious acts of intimidation occurred in 1986 in the Howard Beach area of New York City, where three blacks were beaten and chased by white youths. One black man died when he was chased into the path of a car. A few days later 5,000 people marched through Howard Beach to protest the attack.[45]

## Black Rioting: Structural Causes?

In the 1930s and 1940s, particularly in New York City, there were a few riots involving pitched battles between black residents and the police. Such rioting revealed the feelings of blacks toward a nonresponsive economic and political system. By the mid-1960s northern cities were seeing ghetto residents rioting against the symbols of white oppression: the police, ghetto businesses, and absentee landlords. Large-scale uprisings occurred in Los Angeles (Watts) in 1965, in Detroit and Newark in 1967, and in Washington, D.C., in 1968. As late as 1970–1971 there were 250 race-related riots across the United States. The impact was felt across the nation, which was confronted by a militant new generation of proud black Americans willing to engage in violent protest. Some government action came on the heels of the riots in the 1960s and early 1970s, sometimes in the significant form of direct economic aid, sometimes in the form of governmental investigative commissions.[46]

In the spring of 1980 there was a major riot in Miami in which black ghetto residents again lashed out against the police and the larger white society with extensive burning and looting. The three days of rioting there took sixteen lives, caused 400 injuries, and resulted in $100 million in property damage. In a *Newsweek* magazine poll conducted after the riot, a nationwide sample of black Americans were asked if they thought the rioting was justified. Twenty-seven percent said "yes" and another 25 percent replied "don't know" or "not sure." Half also said that whites don't care about what happens to blacks or want to "keep blacks down."[47] Black anger at the discrimination and lack of concern of white America broke out in other cities as well in the early 1980s, from Chattanooga, Tennessee, to Washington, D.C. In the fall of 1982 there was a small riot in the nation's capital involving angry blacks and others protesting a Ku Klux Klan demonstration. And there was another riot in Miami late in 1982.

Rioting has been interpreted by media analysts, police officials, and politicians as a rampage by ghetto "riffraff." Criminals, teenage delinquents, and recent migrants have been blamed. Yet research has shown this view to be a myth. Although rioters are typically under thirty, they are not for the most part teenagers. The majority are native-born or long-term residents of the areas they rioted in; most are not convicted criminals. The role of white officials and the police in generating and accelerating rioting, while overlooked by most white Americans, has been significant; police brutality in particular has often precipitated or accelerated rioting by black Americans.

Police malpractice and brutality remain a problem. In a 1986 nationwide poll, nearly 80 percent of the black Americans interviewed said that in most cities the police did not treat blacks as fairly as whites. Significant numbers still view police brutality as a problem. *Time* magazine ran a major news report about two blacks killed while in police custody in Los Angeles and Milwaukee. Under pressure from blacks and other citizens, officials in both cities decided to prosecute the police officers involved in the deaths. In recent years many black communities have reported similar "mysterious" deaths of black youths in police custody.[48]

## THE ECONOMY

An assimilation framework can include the idea of secondary structural assimilation, one aspect of which is the movement of members of racial groups into higher levels of the economy. Whether this assimilation framework can be applied to black and other nonwhite Americans has been disputed by power conflict analysts. A test of the optimistic assimilation theories is the economic progress, or lack of progress, of black Americans since their emancipation from slavery.

Prior to the Civil War the relatively few free blacks sometimes found themselves competing with white immigrants, such as the Irish. In some northern areas blacks found themselves displaced from unskilled and skilled jobs by white immigrants. These patterns continued after the Civil War released a large number of blacks for the free labor market. After the war blacks began to compete directly with whites in the South. Increasingly blacks were segregated in unskilled "Negro jobs" and prohibited from taking skilled employment in the newly expanding industrial sectors in the South.

With no major land reform accompanying the shift to free status, most former slaves were forced to sell their labor to those controlling the agricultural system—their old slave masters. Semislave farm labor became the lot of many. Afro-American laborers in particular were often tied to one farm or one area because of the debts they built up in an exploitative, white-controlled system. Having less money and less legal protection than whites and facing discrimination in land and consumer-product dealings, free blacks in the South, not surprisingly, failed to become independent farmers.[49]

The black population in 1900 was still centered in the South: nine blacks in every ten lived there. But the bustling economy developing in the northern and border cities, especially by World War I, the declining significance of "King Cotton" in the South, and southern oppression in the form of segregation stimulated the migration of blacks to northern cities. With anti-immigrant legislation and the cessation of massive foreign immigration, the demand for black laborers in northern industries increased. Thousands of poor black farmers, unable to finance the technological innovations necessary to circumvent the pestilence of the boll weevil, were driven from their farms to the cities. The major push factors, then, were segregation and the declining importance of cotton; the major pull factor was ready employment.[50]

## The Great Urban Trek to the "Promised Land"

The urban trek north began in earnest around World War I; by the mid-twentieth century millions of black Americans had migrated to what they saw as the economic "promised land." What were their destinations? Large cities in the Northeast, Midwest, and West. Representing the younger and better-educated segments of the black population, these migrants have often been misrepresented. They were not the dregs of the South, as some whites have pictured them. Indeed, such an outflow meant a skill loss for the South just as it was undergoing industrialization; blacks educated in the South became capable workers in other regions.[51]

These migrants generally were forced to settle in low-income areas already occupied by blacks, swelling the size of ghettos. A traditional view of this migration, one fostered by optimistic assimilation theorists, is that it has brought great opportunities for economic mobility: blacks can be viewed as another in a long line of immigrant groups (such as the Irish and the Italians) successfully seeking their fortunes in the city. If we accept this view, we would expect that black economic gains between 1900 and 1980 had dramatically closed the black–white gap. The reality has, however, been quite different.[52]

A persisting division of labor was established in the cities, enforced at first by coercion and discriminatory law, then by subtle institutional mechanisms. The urban economy has been viewed as divided into at least two major sectors. The primary labor market has been composed predominantly of privileged white workers and has been characterized by skilled jobs, high wages, and ladders offering significant mobility. The secondary labor market has traditionally been composed of nonwhite (or, earlier, white immigrant) workers and has been characterized by instability, low wages, and few mobility ladders. The dramatic rise of corporate capitalism after 1900 resulted not only in enormous corporate units but in unionism as well. One method of dealing with the organized expression of worker discontent was to make concessions to the large segment of white workers, separating them from less privileged nonwhites. Positions in the secondary labor market would be for nonwhite minorities. Here we see the split labor market emphasized by Edna Bonacich, a view we examined in Chapter 2.[53]

The increasingly numerous black workers moving out of farm occupations found themselves channeled into the secondary labor market of the cities. There was a slow but steady shift away from tenant farming and sharecropping to unskilled jobs in the industrial sector. In cities the principal occupations of black men became porter, truck driver, janitor, and cook; black women served as maids, restaurant workers, and dressmakers. By 1930 the dominance of agricultural and domestic service jobs could still be seen in Census Bureau figures. Of every 1,000 black workers, 648 were in agricultural or domestic service jobs, compared with 280 of every 1,000 whites. Most of the remainder of blacks were in other unskilled blue-collar positions. Most blacks in the relatively small professional category were teachers, ministers, and physicians serving the black community; likewise, blacks in business usually served a black clientele.[54]

Black incomes were sharply lower than those of whites. For example, the median annual income of black families in Atlanta in the mid-1930s was about one-third that of whites ($632 versus $1,876), a typical situation. In the North, black median incomes were only 40 to 50 percent of the incomes of whites. Most blacks, North and South, were poverty-stricken.

One hopeful sign in the Depression era was the slow opening up of labor unions. Most labor unions had traditionally been segregated. By the late 1930s black pressure and federal legislation had forced many American Federation of Labor (AFL) unions to begin to reduce discrimination in recruiting black workers. The new Congress of Industrial Organizations (CIO) began with an official nondiscriminatory policy in order to attract blacks in the automobile, steel, and packing industries. In 1930 at least twenty-six major unions had officially barred blacks from membership; by 1943 the number had dropped to fourteen.[55]

## From 1940 to the 1980: How Much Mobility?

The 1940 census continued to show a heavy concentration of blacks in agriculture and the secondary labor market of cities. Seventy-three percent of black male workers were in blue-collar jobs, with a heavy concentration in the laborer category and virtually all the rest in other unskilled positions, semiskilled positions, or in farming. Sixty percent of black women were employed in domestic service, and most of the rest were in other service, laborer, or farming positions. During World War II industries with severe labor needs were forced to make significant concessions. In war-related industries the proportion of blacks employed increased from 3 to 8 percent over the war years. Race discrimination in those industries had been lessened by executive orders issued by President Franklin Roosevelt. At the end of the war this interlude came to an abrupt end: layoffs hit blacks much harder than whites.[56]

There has been significant economic progress for black Americans since the 1940s and some of this gain has been translated into better jobs and incomes. Occupational gains have been made by black Americans over the last few decades, most rapidly in the 1960s. Bureau of Labor Statistics data on the proportions of nonwhites among employed persons in specific categories indicate the following changes:[57]

|  | 1955 | 1972 | 1980 | 1986 |
|---|---|---|---|---|
| Professional, technical | 4% | 7% | 9% | 8% |
| Managerial, administrative | 2 | 4 | 5 | 5 |
| Sales | 4 | 4 | 5 | 6 |
| Clerical | 2 | 9 | 11 | 10 |
| Craft and kindred workers | 4 | 7 | 8 | 7 |
| Operatives | 11 | 13 | 15 | 15 |
| Nonfarm workers | 28 | 20 | 17 | 16 |
| Service workers | 29 | 19 | 18 | 18 |
| Private household workers | 49 | 41 | 33 | 39 |
| Farm workers | 14 | 15 | 13 | 12 |

The proportion of nonwhites in white-collar categories grew between 1955 and 1980, with the largest increase in the job category the Census Bureau calls "clerical." There has been little increase in nonwhite representation in the sales category. The growth in the proportion of nonwhites in the higher-level categories was most rapid in the 1960s, but slowed or reversed slightly in the 1980–1986 period. In the Reagan era nonwhite (black) progress in the occupational sphere stalled; indeed, the proportion of nonwhites in the professional–technical and clerical areas actually declined a little.

Some of the pre-1980 gains are not quite as impressive as they may seem. First, these data are for nonwhites, not just for blacks; the Census Bureau includes certain more prosperous Asian American groups in this category. If the data were available for blacks by themselves, the proportions in white-collar jobs would probably be somewhat lower than these figures for nonwhites. Second, nonwhites in white-collar categories are disproportionately concentrated in jobs with lower pay and status. For example, within the professional–technical category, nonwhites today are most commonly found in such fields as social and recreation work, kindergarten teaching, vocational counseling, personnel, dietetics, and health care. They are least often found among lawyers and judges, dentists, writers and artists, engineers, and elite university teachers. Within the managerial–administrative category nonwhites are most commonly found among restaurant and bar managers, health administrators, and government officials. They are least commonly found among corporate office managers, bank and financial managers, and sales managers. And among clerical workers nonwhites are most often seen among file clerks, shipping clerks, postal clerks, keypunch operators, and typists.

The greatest gains came for those young blacks penetrating the labor force at the entry level, although in recessions it is the younger workers who are the most likely to be fired. Gains for black women have come faster than gains for black male workers, but the positions they have attained, such as the white-collar jobs typically held by white women workers, are relatively low-status and low-paying.[58]

All the types of discrimination discussed in Chapter 1 have been documented in studies and court cases dealing with employment practices. An example of isolate discrimination is the white personnel officer in an industrial firm who expresses stereotyped views of blacks by personally defying the company's merit regulations and hiring less qualified whites over better-qualified blacks. This type of discrimination is common.

Small-group discrimination has also been common, North and South. Small-group conspiracies, arranged by prejudiced supervisors or union officials wishing to subvert company or union regulations that require the hiring or promotion of qualified black employees, continue to be omnipresent but hard to document.

Direct institutional discrimination consists of organizationally prescribed actions carried out routinely by people in companies and businesses. Examples are still common; they include relegating blacks to inferior jobs or retarding the job mobility of blacks beyond the entry level. Today they also include disciplinary practices. For example, 1982 Postal Service figures show that black postal workers were fired or suspended four times as often as white workers. Although Post Office officials publicly said that these dismissals and other disciplinary practices were based only on performance, it is likely that such a dramatic racial discrepancy reflects much racial discrimination in this federal agency.

Indirect institutional discrimination is illustrated in now-common practices that harm blacks even though they are carried out with no such intent. A major example is the use of credentials (such as a high school or college degrees) in employment decisions. Institutionalized discrimination, intentional and indirect, in education often handicaps blacks when they compete for jobs having unnecessarily high educational requirements. Moreover, many blacks have suffered because of seniority practices, which were usually established with no intent to harm them. In plants that were intentionally segregated in the past, and where as a result blacks have not been able to build up much seniority, the effect of such practices is to restrict black employment mobility.

## A Public Employment Setting

Shelton examined persisting discrimination at a major state university in the Sunbelt. She found that despite fifteen years of "equal opportunity" as the official policy of the land, specific occupational classifications were segregated, with the majority of black employees concentrated in service or maintenance positions. While there was some racial diversity in each major occupational classification at the university, blacks had only token representation in the professional, managerial, and technical sectors. In the service and maintenance sectors, for example, black employees were concentrated in custodial, food, and grounds-keeping jobs while white employees were clustered in different and better-paying positions. Most wage inequality at the university was a product of discriminatory occupational assignment, rather than different pay for the same jobs. Shelton also found that the interview and hiring process favored whites for better-paying jobs.[59]

## The Business World: Continuing Problems

Significant numbers of minority men and women have moved into corporate America in recent years, especially at entry-level jobs such as low-level managers. But the success of some at the entry level has not carried through to everyday life, or to promotions, in corporate workplaces. In his research on black managers Jones has found that the predominantly white corporate environment, with its pressures for conformity, regularly creates problems. Jones describes one black manager (Charlie) who was working his way up the lower executive ranks. One day he met with same other black managers who wanted his advice on coping with racial discrimination. Here is what happened:

> Charlie concluded that this should be shared with senior management and agreed to arrange a meeting with the appropriate officers. Two days before the scheduled meeting, while chatting with the President at a cocktail affair, Charlie was sombered by the President's disturbed look as he said, "Charlie I am disappointed that you met with those black managers. I thought we could trust you."[60]

It is clear from numerous examples of this type that many black managers in the business world are under heavy pressure *not* to cooperate with or support one another even in the face of blatant discrimination. Yet without this mutual support many may not make it. Examples such as this point up another continuing problem in organizations. The leaders in white-oriented organizations often bring blacks and other nonwhites into important positions only in token numbers and under the existing rules.

Jones has reported striking data on the racial climate of businesses from his nationwide survey of black managers with graduate business degrees from major business schools. Few of those managers had achieved equal opportunity with white managers. More than 90 percent felt there was much subtle or blatant antiblack hostility in corporations; more than 90 percent felt black managers had less opportunity than whites, or none at all, to succeed in their firms solely on the basis of merit and ability. Two-thirds felt that many whites in corporations still believe blacks are intellectually inferior. And most reported that this adverse racial climate had a negative impact on the evaluations, assignments, and promotions of black managers. This extensive research on upper-middle-income blacks who have moved into nontraditional managerial positions clearly documents the firm entrenchment of racial discrimination in the private sector in the 1980s. Entry-level changes have not brought about the necessary changes in corporate climate, in evaluation procedures, in assignments, and in promotions. Blacks are rarely found in middle management and virtually never among top corporate executives.[61]

## Continuing Inequality in the Mass Media

A study of black owners and employers in the mass media found significant underrepresentation. Blacks own less than 1 percent of the 1,138 commercial TV stations and only one of the 50 programming companies. Moreover, blacks own only 1.5 percent of the nation's nearly 9,000 radio stations. Only one of the 1,710 general-circulation daily newspapers is black-owned. Among newspaper executives 97 percent are white. Black representation increases among lower-level employees in the newspaper and broadcast industries. In the mid-1980s in the radio and television industry, for example, blacks constituted 16 percent of the clerical workers and 43 percent of the service workers, but only 8 percent of professional workers.[62]

## Unemployment, Income, and Poverty

In recent decades the nonwhite unemployment rate has consistently been about twice the white unemployment rate:[63]

|      | Nonwhite (or Black) | White | Ratio |
|------|---------------------|-------|-------|
| 1949 | 8.9%                | 5.6%  | 1.6   |
| 1959 | 10.7                | 4.8   | 2.2   |
| 1964 | 9.6                 | 4.6   | 2.1   |
| 1969 | 6.4                 | 3.1   | 2.1   |
| 1975 | 13.8                | 7.8   | 1.8   |
| 1980 | 13.0                | 5.9   | 2.2   |
| 1982 | 20.4                | 9.5   | 2.1   |
| 1986 | 15.0                | 6.6   | 2.3   |

In recent recessions blacks have continued to lose jobs at twice the rate of whites, and they have been recalled at a slower rate than whites. Indeed, in the 1981–1983 recession black unemployment went above 20 percent, the highest rate recorded to that point. By 1986 the black/white unemployment ratio was at a record high of 2.3, yet another sign of continuing economic inequality along racial lines in the United States.

Much higher than the unemployment rate for black Americans is the *subemployment* or *underemployment rate*, which includes those with no jobs, those working part time, and those making poverty wages. One nationwide study in 1980 found that many blacks had part-time work but wanted full-time work, received very low wages, or were *discouraged workers* (they had given up looking for work). In 1980, 3.5 percent of black workers were discouraged workers, 5.4 percent were "involuntary part-time" workers, and 9.5 percent worked for poverty wages. Altogether nearly one-third of black workers fell into these troubled-worker categories; the figure for whites was much less. This situation has persisted. Unemployment and underemployment for blacks worsened between the late 1960s and the early 1980s, then improved somewhat in absolute terms in the late 1980s, but not relative to unemployment and underemployment for white Americans.[64]

Since the 1950s black family income has remained at about 55 to 60 percent of white family income. As indicated in the table on p. 230 blacks have not made consistent gains over this period in income relative to whites. Black family income as a percentage of white family income fluctuated slightly during the 1950s, rose significantly in the late 1960s, then dropped over the 1970s; since 1974 the figure has hovered just below 60 percent.[65]

|      | Nonwhite Income as a Percent of White Income |
|------|------|
| 1950 | 54% |
| 1954 | 56 |
| 1959 | 52 |
| 1964 | 54 |
| 1969 | 61 |
| 1974 | 58 |
| 1980 | 58 |
| 1985 | 58 |

As of 1985 this translated into median-family-income figures of $29,152 for whites and $16,786 for blacks. Between 1970 and 1985 the real income (actual income adjusted for inflation) of white families went up while that of black families declined.[66]

The economic situation of black families varies on several dimensions. Families in which both husband and wife are between twenty and sixty and with both husband and wife working earned 82 percent of comparable white families in 1980. The most severe income differential is between black and white families containing only one parent. In those families black income is only half that of whites. The proportion of black families headed by women increased from 17.6 percent in 1950 to 40.3 percent in 1980. Unemployment for black women has been particularly painful. As Robert B. Hill has concluded, "families headed by black women are primarily poor, not because they do not have husbands, but because they do not have jobs."[67]

Whatever the type of family, blacks pull in fewer dollars than whites and are much more likely than white families to live in poverty. In the mid-1980s about 36 percent of all black Americans, and nearly half of all black children, fell below the official government poverty line. And the extent of black poverty grew between 1980 and 1985. Moreover, a 1984 study of wealth in the United States found that the average white family, with $39,135, had *ten* times the wealth of the average black family, with $3,397. Thirty percent of black families had no wealth or negative net worth because of debts. The comparable figure for whites was only 8.4 percent. The long history of low incomes for black Americans has meant little money for savings and thus for wealth, including home ownership.[68]

## The Debate over the Black Underclass

In *The Declining Significance of Race* William J. Wilson argues that the rise of the black middle class since the 1960s has resulted from shifting economic conditions and new government policies, such as equal employment and affirmative action. In the view of Wilson and like-minded scholars equal employment legislation virtually eliminated the split labor market in which black labor suffered direct racial discrimination. In 1982 Ken Auletta produced a book called *The Underclass.* For Auletta, race and racism play little direct part in the formation of the poor black underclass; rather it is a matter of class culture. Scholars like Auletta argue that there is a growing polarization in the black community between a growing, affluent middle class and a poverty underclass. Since discrimination is being eradicated for middle-class blacks, they argue, there is less need for governmental programs primarily benefitting better-off blacks such as affirmative action. Yet, as we saw earlier in the work of Jones, many middle-income black workers, even corporate managers, face discrimination, a situation revealing the continuing need for governmental civil rights programs and laws. Moreover, in his most recent book, *The Truly Disadvantaged*, William J. Wilson has argued vigorously that the black underclass's major problem is *unemployment*, a structural condition which must be eradicated by massive governmental job training and job creation programs. Whatever its cause, unemployment must be remedied.[69]

The Bureau of Labor Statistics publishes data on three family budget levels—low, intermediate, and high. The proportion of white families with incomes at or above the intermediate budget level increased from 47 percent in 1970 to about half in 1980. The proportion of black families falling into this middle-income range or above increased from 24 to 26 percent. "In short," as Hill puts it, "the proportion of economically 'middle class' families is not significantly different among blacks (one-fourth) or whites (one-half) today than it was a decade ago—due to the unrelenting effects of recession and inflation."[70]

Moreover, a recent analysis of the attitudes and opinions of black Americans found no significant differences between low-income and middle-income blacks. Both groups agreed in their views on government intervention in the economy and on school busing, their identification with the Democratic party, their attitude toward police brutality, and their lack of confidence in the White House and Congress.[71]

In recent years the plight of poor blacks, often called the black underclass, has frequently been discussed as though racial discrimination had little to do with its high unemployment and underemployment, low incomes, and poor housing conditions. The suggestion is that poor black Americans have gotten locked into a lower-class subculture of poverty, with its allegedly deviant value system of immorality, broken families, juvenile delinquency, and lack of emphasis on the work ethic. These arguments are not new, but rather are a resurrection of culture-of-poverty arguments made in the 1960s. If this misconception were true, poor blacks should face the same conditions as poor whites. But this is not the case. Poor blacks do not live in integrated "slums" with poor whites. Poor and near-poor blacks are less likely than comparably *poor* whites to get unemployment compensation when they are unemployed. They tend to hold lower-paying and less secure jobs even than *poor* whites.

The role of past discrimination in current "tangles of underclass poverty" needs to be reassessed. Much past discrimination is not something in the distant past, but is rather recent. *Blatant* discrimination against blacks occurred in massive doses until twenty-five years ago, particularly in the South. All blacks (and whites) over thirty or so were born when the United States still had widespread legal color bars. At least for a few years many blacks over thirty-five were educated in legally segregated schools of lower quality than those of whites, and many have felt the weight of massive blatant racial discrimination in at least the early part of their employment careers. Moreover, most white Americans over thirty-five have benefited, if only indirectly, from all types of racial discrimination in several institutional areas of U.S. society. Put earlier discrimination together with today's blatant and covert racial discrimination and you have a better conception of the causes of much black poverty, unemployment, and underemployment than resurrected poverty-subculture theories provide.[72]

## Is Racial Discrimination Being Remedied?

Government action on discrimination has been a hotly debated issue in recent years. Some argue it has gone too far, even to the point of large-scale "reverse" discrimination favoring nonwhites. Other analysts argue that federal policies have had little impact on discrimination.

Significant government action on employment discrimination began with President Franklin Roosevelt's establishment of a Fair Employment Practices Commission (FEPC) in 1941 in response to heavy pressure from black leaders. Modest gains in war-related employment resulted from FEPC actions, but postwar attempts to make the agency permanent were unsuccessful and blacks lost some of what they had gained. It was not until executive orders were issued by President Johnson in the 1960s requiring government contractors to desegregate that the pressure to remedy discrimination became significant. However, federal contract-compliance agencies, which are supposed to implement the executive orders, have reviewed only a minority of contractors under their supervision. Progress there has in fact been modest.[73]

The 1964 Civil Rights Act and its later amendments prohibit discrimination in employment. The Equal Employment Opportunity Commission (EEOC) was created to enforce the 1964 act, primarily by dealing with employment discrimination by labor unions, private employers, state and local governments, and educational institutions. The EEOC is responsible for investigating complaints, seeking conciliation, and— since 1972—filing suit to end discrimination. However, operating under the conservative philosophy of the Reagan administration in the 1980s, the EEOC drew back from an aggressive position on discrimination. It reduced the number of investigations of class-action complaints and other broad, institutionally focused investigations. The major cutbacks there and elsewhere signaled a federal government retreat from protecting the employment rights of black Americans.[74]

## PARTICIPATION IN POLITICS

Walton has distinguished four levels of political participation by black Americans:

1. *Nonparticipation,* where blacks are excluded
2. *Limited participation,* where a few privileged blacks participate
3. *Moderate participation,* where the majority of blacks participate and where demands are being made
4. *Full participation,* where black priorities become embedded in public policy.[75]

In the slavery period the situation was close to Walton's first category. There was very limited participation by a few free blacks in the North. Between the 1660s and 1860s some black Americans petitioned legislatures and executive officials for redress of grievances; numerous petitions were submitted and, as a rule, ignored. The Civil War brought an end to slavery and a beginning for increased black participation in electoral politics. The 1866 Civil Rights Act made all blacks citizens and proclaimed their civil rights. The Thirteenth Amendment abolished slavery, and the Fourteenth Amendment stated that the rights of blacks cannot be denied by the states. The Fifteenth Amendment guaranteed black males the right to vote.

## From Reconstruction to the 1920s

The Reconstruction era came to the South as a breath of fresh air. Reconstruction was precipitated by a South unwilling to make major changes in its treatment of blacks and insisting that the leaders of the Confederacy be allowed to rule. A brief period of limited federal military occupation resulted. During Reconstruction, blacks made political gains, although the gains were nowhere near as great as southern apologists have suggested. Moderate political participation, to use Walton's term, became the order of the day. After the Civil War, black men gained the right to vote in all states. Southern state constitutional conventions included black delegates, although in most states native white southerners were the majority of delegates.[76]

Between 1870 and 1901 twenty blacks served in the House of Representatives and two in the U.S. Senate. Hiram R. Revel and Blanche K. Bruce were state senators in Mississippi between 1870 and 1881, the first two to serve there and two of the three blacks that have *ever* served there to date. Blacks served in state legislatures, but they attained a legislative majority only for a brief period in the lower house in South Carolina.[77]

The overthrow of white-dominated Reconstruction governments by conservative southern forces came swiftly; the so-called "Redemption" period began with the Hayes Compromise of 1877, which removed federal troops from southern states and withdrew federal protection of blacks. During Reconstruction there was considerable segregation, although it was not the all-encompassing system it would become by the early 1900s. In many areas blacks still voted and continued to hold public office. Sometimes public accommodations, such as hotels, were open to blacks. Freedom here, segregation there, mixing here, exclusion there—such was the fluidity of the period, a fluidity long neglected by social scientists and popular writers.

The threat of black–white coalitions among farmers became too great for the conservative gentry to endure. Agrarian populist movements binding poor blacks and poor whites together reflected an awareness of common problems, but the conservative opposition roared an ugly response. Conservatives appealed to poor whites' sense of racial superiority; populist voters were intimidated by Ku Klux Klan–type violence; election fraud was common. The white populist was attacked as a Negro-loving traitor to the white race, a "renegade to Southern womanhood, the Confederate dead, and the God of his fathers."[78]

Supreme Court decisions nailed the lid on the coffin of southern racial progress. The decision in *Plessy v. Ferguson* (1896) was the major blow, with its doctrine of "separate but equal" facilities for blacks in a case involving the racial segregation of railroad cars. The Court reasoned that "legislation is powerless to eradicate racial instincts or to abolish distinctions based upon physical differences, and the attempt to do so can only result in accentuating the difficulties of the present situation." Moreover, "if one race be inferior to another socially, the Constitution of the United States cannot put them upon the same plane."[79]

In 1922 Mississippi passed a law requiring segregated taxicabs; in 1932 Atlanta passed a law requiring black and white baseball teams to play at least two blocks apart; and Birmingham, Alabama, even prohibited interracial domino playing! [80] Disenfranchisement of black voters was achieved by the rigorous enforcement of discriminatory literacy test laws, poll tax laws, and "grandfather clause" laws—the last of which limited the vote to those who had voted prior to 1861 and their (white) descendants. Between 1896 and 1900 the number of black voters in Louisiana decreased from 130,000 to 5,300. All other southern states followed this lead.[81]

The Supreme Court began a slow swing back to the protection of civil rights in 1915 by declaring grandfather clauses unconstitutional. Voter registration increased very slowly. By the 1920s the movement to the cities had brought a few blacks to the political forefront, particularly in the North. Independent political organizations were constructed in a few cities, but the only major success was that of Adam Clayton Powell, Jr., in New York City. In 1945 Powell became the first black representative in Congress from outside of Chicago in several decades. In the North the black vote was at first strongly tied to the Republican party, but by the 1930s it had begun to shift to the Democratic party.[82]

### The Limits of Black Progress; Political Discrimination

In 1940 only 90,000 of the 3.7 million adult blacks in the Deep South voted in the general election. In 1942 there were only a dozen black state legislators in the entire country, and a few blacks on school and tax boards; none were serving in the South, except for a few in small all-black towns. Blacks benefited little from southern government programs; schools, hospitals, parks, and other public facilities for blacks were inadequate or nonexistent, a situation that would hold true in the South for several more decades. By the late 1940s blacks were again voting in some numbers in the South, with an estimated 600,000 registered. Voter registration increased sharply in the South between the 1940s and the 1970s, from 250,000 to four million voters.

A big jump came after passage of the Voting Rights Act in 1965, an act with a demonstrable impact on black political participation. Social scientists have sometimes suggested that because of inadequate civic training and less education blacks would not be able to organize effectively. Yet with their new enfranchisement blacks have developed effective political organizations and campaigns in the South. In 1965 there were approximately 70 black elected officials in the South. By February 1968 the figure was 248; by the 1980s the figure had increased to 2,500. Blacks were even being elected in some areas where black populations were minorities, most typically from black wards or districts in those areas. Yet blacks have attained proportional equality in *very few* areas of the South. Their proportion among all elected officials is in the neighborhood of 3 percent.[83]

Today blacks face institutionalized attempts to reduce the efficacy of their vote. Davidson has noted several major types of electoral discrimination, such as vote dilution, gerrymandering districts, and disenfranchisement. A major example of vote dilution is the at-large electoral system. In cities across the nation this system has been demonstrated to reduce sharply the participation of black candidates and voters in local campaigns. As long as blacks, for example, are a minority of local voters in a city, it can be difficult for them to elect people to office from their own residential areas. The Supreme Court, in *City of Mobile v. Bolden* (1980), put a burden on minority plaintiffs to prove that at-large electoral systems were *intentionally* set up to discriminate, not just to show that they have a severe negative impact. The Court ruled in effect that indirect or subtle direct discrimination is constitutionally permissible.[84]

Other strategies that have had a discriminatory impact on minority candidates include a run-off rule in at-large elections, decreasing the number of seats in a government body in a system of single-member districts, and local (white) slating groups that hand-pick a token black candidate in order to prevent other minority candidates from having a chance at being elected. Voters face discrimination in the form of purges of voter-registration rolls, changes in polling places with no notice or on short notice, difficult registration procedures, and threats of retaliation to voters. These practices have been documented in Alabama, Mississippi, and Texas in recent years. Candidate diminution is yet another form of political discrimination that black Americans face. This involves attempts to keep minority candidates from running for office. Davidson has noted these examples: changing an office from elective to appointive when a minority candidate has a chance to win (Georgia, Alabama); setting high filing and bonding fees (Georgia); abolition of party primaries (Mississippi); and intimidating candidates with threats of violence or of cutting off credit (Alabama, North Carolina, South Carolina, Georgia).[85]

In the early 1980s the Reagan administration, in response to conservative white supporters, tried to weaken the Voting Rights Act. However, in 1982, after a long battle, Congress approved a twenty-five-year extension of key provisions of the act.

Have black officials in the South been able to accomplish anything? Some argue, with the late Reverend Martin Luther King, Jr., that black votes and officials can end segregation and alleviate poverty. Others see blacks as unable to gain much through the electoral process. Mack Jones has argued that black elected officials have not been able to significantly reorder white priorities in the fields of employment, housing, and education. So far the accomplishments of black officeholders in the South have been more than the pessimists would expect, although much less than justice would require. Relying heavily on federal and private foundation aid, rather than local or state money, black officials have increased public services and expanded economic opportunities somewhat for their constituents. Even where they are in the minority, some have improved services as well as increased the number of blacks hired.[86]

The number of black elected officials in the nation increased sharply between 1964 and 1980, from about 100 to more than 4,900. Since 1967 blacks have won mayoral elections in a number of major cities with large black populations: Washington, D.C., Newark, Philadelphia, Detroit, Chicago, Cleveland, Los Angeles, Atlanta, and Gary, Indiana. Yet black officials continue to be a tiny percentage of all elected officials nationwide. A study of black officials by Conyers and Wallace found them as effective in the North as in the South: the election of blacks typically brought some concrete payoff, usually at the local or state level, in terms of black employment in government, expanded services, and increased respect for black rights by government officials.[87]

## The Federal Government

Between 1933 and 1940 President Roosevelt appointed more than one hundred black Americans to federal positions below the very top levels. Benefits flowing from New Deal actions nonetheless benefited whites considerably more than blacks. New Deal agencies such as the Agricultural Adjustment Administration (AAA) and the National Recovery Administration (NRA) did little to make sure that blacks received their fair share of government aid. Black Americans did receive aid from agencies offering temporary relief, but the more important recovery agencies favored white constituents.[88]

Between World War II and the 1980s, black voters began having a greater impact on the legislative, executive, and judicial branches of the federal government. In the 1950s a third black was finally elected to Congress, joining the two from New York and Chicago. By the late 1980s there were nearly two dozen black representatives, but no black senators, in Congress. The first black *ever* to serve in a presidential cabinet was Robert Weaver, who in 1967 became Secretary of Housing and Urban Development. In the mid-1960s President Lyndon Johnson appointed Andrew Brimmer as the first black on the Federal Reserve Board, Thurgood Marshall as the first black Supreme Court justice, and Patricia Harris as the first black ambassador. Yet even in the Johnson administration few black Americans served at the top in any major executive department or on federal commissions other than the civil rights agencies. The overall pattern in federal legislative, executive, and judicial positions can still be described as one of sharp and continuing discrimination and underrepresentation.[89]

The growing black vote has sometimes been important in close elections. At the local levels moderate whites sensitive to black needs have, with the aid of the black vote, beaten more openly conservative or racist whites. In federal elections the black vote has from time to time loomed large. In 1944 black voters played a role in Roosevelt's election; in the late 1940s they were important to the Truman election.[90] And the black vote in a few key states reportedly decided the Kennedy election in 1960. Black voters played a key role in electing Lyndon Johnson in 1964 and Jimmy Carter in 1976. The black vote has also kept white liberal members of Congress in office when they otherwise would not have survived conservative trends among their white constituents. And in the 1982 congressional elections, blacks increased the number of black representatives in Congress to twenty-one, the largest number in U.S. history. Black voters turned out in record numbers for that off-year election and for the 1984 election; in both these cases and in the 1986 off-year election black voters helped elect a Congress more sympathetic to civil rights issues than the preceding Congress.

## The Future

The future of black political power in the North is tied to the fate of the cities. Numerous observers see increasing black political control of the large central cities, but a decline in the financial strength of those cities may well result in blacks ruling bankrupt fiefdoms. Nonetheless, black electoral victories in cities such as Chicago, Philadelphia, and Los Angeles have caused white politicians to pay more attention to the black vote in national elections. Democratic party successes at the national level depend increasingly on these black votes.[91]

## Nonviolent Protest

Black protest has ranged from legal strategies, to the ballot, to nonviolent civil disobedience, to violent attacks on the system. Criticizing the accommodationist position of such leaders as Booker T. Washington, W. E. B. Dubois and other black and white liberals formed the Niagara movement in 1905. Legal and voting rights, as well as economic issues, were the focus of their activities. Not long thereafter, some of these leaders played a role in creating the National Association for the Advancement of Colored People (NAACP).

Organizations directed at self-help and philanthropic activity, such as the Urban League, were also created in the early twentieth century. The efforts of the new black organizations began to pay off, in providing more philanthropic aid for the poor in cities and in chipping away at the legal edifice of segregation. One of the first major NAACP legal victories was a 1917 Supreme Court decision, *Buchanan v. Warley*, which knocked down a Louisville, Kentucky, law requiring residential segregation and took a first step in reversing the segregationist position the Court had taken since the late 1800s. Most other High Court decisions until the 1930s, however, hurt the cause of black rights, reinforcing segregation in schools, transportation, and the jury system.[92]

Black consciousness grew with new organizations—civil rights groups, educational organizations, and a new press. Against fierce resistance the NAACP began a large-scale attack on segregation in schools, voting, transportation, and jury selection. Beginning in the 1930s NAACP and other lawyers won a series of cases that over the next several decades expanded the legal rights of black defendants, eliminated the all-white political primary, protected the voting rights of blacks, reduced job discrimination by unions, voided restrictive housing covenants, and desegregated schools and public accommodations. The separate-but-equal doctrine of *Plessy v. Ferguson* increasingly came under attack. Dramatically reversing its position in the 1896 case, the Supreme Court in a famous decision in *Brown v. Board of Education* (1954) ruled that "in the field of public education the doctrine of 'separate but equal' has no place."[93]

By the 1940s and 1950s more militant strategies were being generated in black communities. During World War II a threatened large-scale march on Washington, D.C., to be led by A. Philip Randolph and other black leaders, forced President Roosevelt to issue an order desegregating employment. After World War II, Randolph and other leaders organized against the peacetime draft on the basis that blacks should not serve in a Jim Crow army. After unsuccessful attempts to get black leaders to back down on this issue, President Truman set up an agency to rid federal employment of discrimination and a committee to oversee desegregation in the armed forces.[94]

The 1950s and 1960s saw an increase in nonviolent civil disobedience. First came major boycotts, such as that of segregated buses in Montgomery, Alabama, in the 1950s, a successful movement that brought the Reverend Martin Luther King, Jr., into national prominence. In 1960 black students began the sit-in movement at a white-only lunch counter in Greensboro, North Carolina, touching off a long series of sit-ins throughout the South by thousands of black southerners and their white allies. The Freedom Rides on buses came in 1961; blacks and whites tested federal court orders desegregating public transportation and demonstrated the lack of compliance throughout the South. Near Anniston, Alabama, the first bus of Freedom Riders was burned; in Birmingham the riders were attacked by a white mob.

In the spring of 1963 Martin Luther King, Jr., and his associates launched a series of demonstrations against discrimination in Birmingham, Alabama. Fire hoses and police dogs were used against the demonstrators, many of whom were young children, gaining the demonstration movement much national publicity. An agreement desegregating businesses and employment ended the protests, but a round of more aggressive demonstrations was touched off when a black home and motel were bombed. Then came the massive 1963 March on Washington, in which King dramatized rising black aspirations in his famous "I have a dream" speech.[95]

Direct action against segregation in the North began in earnest in the 1960s. There were boycotts in Harlem, sit-ins in Chicago, school sit-ins in New Jersey, and mass demonstrations in Cairo, Illinois. The Nation of Islam ("Black Muslims") aggressively pressed for black pride and black-controlled businesses. The Congress of Racial Equality (CORE) accelerated protest campaigns against discrimination in housing and employment. School boycotts, picketing at construction sites, and rent strikes became commonplace. In 1964 blacks in New York tried to stop traffic by staging a sit-in on a bridge, and threatened a stall-in to disrupt the opening of the World's Fair. New organizations sprang up. Led by Stokeley Carmichael, the Student Nonviolent Coordinating Committee (SNCC) germinated the Black Power movement. There was a growing group of militant organizations oriented toward a Black Power ideology, including the Black Panthers. Pride and consciousness grew in all segments of the black community in the North, particularly among the young.[96]

## Progress and Retreat

During the Johnson administration the civil rights movement brought about three major pieces of legislation prohibiting discrimination in employment, voting, and housing—the Voting Rights Act of 1965 and the Civil Rights Acts of 1964 and 1968. In the 1970s these important acts were amended and expanded, and more effort was put into enforcing them. Yet many of these advances were threatened in the 1980s with the arrival of the Reagan administration. The conservative president radically increased military spending but cut back the federal social programs, such as job training and food stamps, on which many poor blacks and other nonwhites depend. In addition, there were cuts in funding for federal agencies that enforce civil rights laws. Between 1980 and 1983 with inflation taken into account there was a 25 percent drop in support for enforcement agencies. Most civil rights agencies reduced their enforcement activities, such as class-action suits aimed at discriminatory employers and compliance reviews of government contractors, because of the budget cutbacks and the new conservative policy of the Reagan administration. Black civil rights organizations protested; in Washington, D.C. and other cities some staged demonstrations against the cutbacks. A Gallup poll found that 61 percent of whites approved of President Reagan's performance in his first term, versus only 13 percent of blacks.[97]

Ronald Reagan's second term (1985–1988) brought more reactionary plans for civil rights: the administration tried to cut back the Voting Rights Act and federal programs for increasing minority employment. A majority of blacks felt that the federal government had again turned its back on an oppressed nonwhite group in need. Even in this reactionary period civil rights organization continued. In 1985 and 1986 the NAACP Legal Defense Fund, the Leadership Conference on Civil Rights, and other civil rights organizations were able to mount effective public pressure to stop the Reagan administration from implementing some of its radical-right goals. Among other things they helped block appointments of men insensitive to civil rights to federal judgeships, including Supreme Court positions, and helped defeat an attempt to abolish minority-hiring goals for federal contractors.

### A Political Organization with Civil Rights Roots

In 1983 Jesse Jackson announced his candidacy for president of the United States. Jackson and many of his supporters had learned political skills in various civil rights efforts in the past. Despite little money, no wealthy business backers, and insufficient staff, Jackson put together a remarkable campaign grounded in a diverse organization called the Rainbow Coalition.

By the end of his campaign in 1984 Jackson had registered two million new voters and had won nearly four million votes in the primaries, a fifth of all the votes cast. Jackson was able to go to the Democratic party convention in the summer of 1984 with many delegates. He was the first black in U.S. history to make it to that level in the political arena. Although he lost the nomination to Walter Mondale, he succeeded in creating multiracial organizations in states from Vermont to Washington, and he won political power at the party and local levels in some southern states. The voters he registered helped elect numerous moderate whites to the U.S. Congress in 1984 and 1986, people who subsequently voted against some of the efforts of the Reagan administration to roll back civil rights.[98] In 1987 and 1988 Jesse Jackson again campaigned for the Democratic presidential nomination, with the Rainbow Coalition as his base, and took many delegates to the 1988 Democratic national convention.

## EDUCATION

Reconstruction brought former slaves numerous schools sponsored by the federal government or private organizations. Religious organizations and white philanthropists took up the slack when federal aid subsided; schools and colleges increased. By 1900, however, overt institutionalized discrimination was clear in the grossly inferior public educational facilities and programs for blacks; all southern states had legally segregated schools operating on "separate but equal" doctrine.

Yet schools were anything but equal. For many decades little public money was spent on black children. In 1900 some counties in the South were spending *ten* times as much per capita for the education of white children as for that of black children. One study found that as late as the 1930s the average expenditure per pupil in elementary and secondary schools in ten southern states was $49.30 for white children but only $17.04 for blacks, a ratio of nearly three to one for the entire area.[99] A racial discrepancy in school expenditures persists in some areas of the South even in the late 1980s.

In spite of discrimination, blacks pressed on toward their dream of education. By the early 1900s a million and a half black children were in schools. There were thirty-four black colleges in the South. In the late nineteenth century, the nationally known black leader Booker T. Washington advocated vocational education for black youths in the South. He played a significant role in expanding schooling opportunities. Specialized education became a dominant tradition, focusing on industrial skills suitable for an agricultural economy, which, unfortunately, was declining.[100]

After 1900 the proportion of black children attending school in the South continued to increase. And between the 1940s and the 1970s blacks continued to make significant educational progress. Median educational attainment for those over twenty-five went from 5.7 years in 1940 to 9.9 years in 1970. Most of this gain came prior to 1960. By 1986 the black–white differential had narrowed significantly: 12.7 years for whites and 12.3 years for blacks. The educational gap between blacks and whites narrowed much more quickly than the economic gap.[101]

Are increases in educational attainment translated into commensurate occupational and income gains? Since the late 1800s there has been a chorus of opinion that education is *the* solution to black problems. This view is accurate for the period 1940–1965, which saw a significant reduction in black poverty and an improvement in employment. This was due partly to the migration of black Americans from the South to the North, but also to the great increase in the education of black Americans. In 1940 the typical black male entering the labor force had finished the sixth grade; by 1980 he was a high school graduate.

The better quality of education that blacks got in northern schools and the improvement in black schools between 1940 and 1965 brought significant economic gains. However, by the late 1960s these gains had become less dramatic. Studies in the 1960s and 1970s concluded that educational differences accounted for only part of the difference in black and white incomes. One late-1960s study of poverty areas in the twelve largest metropolitan areas found that education and training had a greater economic payoff for whites than for blacks: "In central city poverty areas, whites earn on the average well over twice as much per extra year of schooling as nonwhites."[102] Increased education significantly reduced the likelihood of unemployment for whites—but not for blacks as a group. A more recent RAND study, however, found that among *young* male workers who are employed, blacks get as much benefit from an additional year of schooling as whites. Although young black workers have higher unemployment rates and earn less than comparable white workers, it usually pays for them to get more education.[103]

## The Desegregation Struggle

Early civil rights activity in the twentieth century was directed at improving that education. One of the NAACP's early objectives was a drive to equalize opportunity. The slow movement toward school desegregation began in earnest in the 1930s with the NAACP legal attack. Graduate school cases were the first to show up the "separate-but-equal" doctrine for the sham it was. In the 1930s and 1940s a series of federal court decisions forced the desegregation of the University of Missouri, University of Oklahoma, University of Maryland, and University of Texas law schools. A suit against the University of Oklahoma forced the dismantling of a segregated graduate program. Then in 1954 black parents won the most famous school case of all, *Brown v. Board of Education of Topeka*. Nonetheless, school desegregation came very slowly, with most systems ignoring or circumventing the *Brown* decision. Some of those wishing to avoid school desegregation set up private white academies. Other whites resorted to collective resistance and even violence. In 1956 President Eisenhower was forced to federalize the Arkansas National Guard to desegregate a Little Rock, Arkansas, high school.[104]

A series of court cases over the next three decades expanded the attack on segregated schooling. In *Swann v. Charlotte-Mecklenburg Board of Education* (1971) the Supreme Court upheld the use of limited pupil transportation ("busing") as a legal means of disestablishing a dual school system. In *Keyes v. Denver School District No. 1* (1973) the Court, for the first time in a northern case, ruled that evidence of government-imposed segregation in part of a school district, by such means as selective attendance zones and school-site selection, is sufficient to prove segregation and to require desegregation, including pupil transportation, as a remedy. Segregated schools included those in which local white authorities had taken any significant action to keep nonwhite and white children separate, as by gerrymandering districts or by locating new schools so as to reinforce segregation lines. In other decisions handed down in the 1970s, however, the Supreme Court rejected the inclusion of suburban districts in city desegregation plans except where such districts could be shown to have played a role in perpetuating segregated school systems.[105]

As a result of a long series of court-ordered desegregation actions, large numbers of black children are attending school with whites in formerly dual systems throughout the South. Indeed, desegregation was more extensive in the South than in the North in the 1970s and 1980s. Northern school systems, such as that in Boston, came under court order to desegregate; resistance to such orders—including white violence—has taken place. Some liberal social scientists and politicians who had been vigorous advocates of desegregation now argued that court-ordered desegregation was accelerating the suburbanization of whites, North and South, and thus creating natural dual systems, with blacks in the central city and whites on the periphery. A common conclusion was that school desegregation policy was either a threat or a failure.[106]

Such arguments are problematical, for the suburbanization of white families had been going on for several decades prior to school desegregation. The concentration of blacks in the central cities—sometimes described as a "black neck in a white noose"—would have occurred even without court-ordered school desegregation. In many of the largest cities it is not possible to massively desegregate schools without involving the suburbs. Moreover, one crucial point missed in much of the debate over busing and white flight to the suburbs is that most American cities have populations well below 1 million. Desegregating schools in a city of 100,000 or 200,000 involves much less in the way of organization and transportation problems than it does in the largest cities. Many school boards could do a great deal more to desegregate their public schools without engaging in large-scale pupil transportation. For example, they could redraw gerrymandered districts or locate all new schools on the boundaries of segregated residential areas so as to maximize natural desegregation. Or they could develop more central learning centers, which would draw children from all over the city. Desegregation of a school's staff, extracurricular activities, or curriculum would not require "massive busing."[107]

The failure of many school systems to make these changes suggests that much of the debate over busing is calculated to obscure the real issue—white opposition to white and black children going to the same school. School busing dates back long before the desegregation of schools—in fact, to the beginning of public schools.[108] Even in the 1970s and 1980s an estimated 40 percent or more of all schoolchildren rode to school on school buses, and perhaps two-thirds rode on either school or public buses; less than 4 percent were being bused for the purpose of school desegregation.

Another important issue in the debate over desegregation has been the question of results. While researchers agree that whites in majority-white schools have not suffered a loss in achievement after desegregation, they have debated the results for blacks. A majority of the studies with the most careful methodologies show some gains in achievement for black children as a result of desegregation, but these gains have not been as dramatic as supporters had hoped. A review of 120 studies found that improvement in black achievement in desegregated settings was most likely to be found in the earlier grades, in 50-percent-or-more-white schools, and in arithmetic. Some studies have found few or no achievement gains.[109]

The limited research on aspirations, interracial attitudes, and social mixing in desegregated schools has yielded mixed findings. One of the most impressive studies released in the 1980s was done in Hartford, Connecticut. For fifteen years 318 students at predominantly white schools in the suburbs and 343 students at predominantly black city schools were studied. The black students who had attended the white schools were more likely to graduate from high school, to attended college, and to complete more years of college. They were also more likely as adults to live in integrated residential areas and to have white friends. The study suggests that black students who go to school with whites are more self-confident about dealing with whites as they grow up.[110]

Another result of school desegregation may be housing desegregation. Diana Pearce has reported that cities with metropolitan-area school desegregation plans experienced much more rapid desegregation of housing patterns than cities without such plans. Cities of similar size and racial mix differed greatly in the extent of housing desegregation as a result of differences in the scope of their school desegregation programs. Cities with school desegregation plans only for central cities had less housing desegregation than cities that desegregated both central cities and suburban areas. Pearce concluded from this that busing for school desegregation need not be a long-term program, since metropolitan desegregation of schools may eventually reduce housing segregation—which in turn would mean that schools can eventually be naturally desegregated without busing. Important too is the way in which desegregation is implemented. Much school desegregation has taken place in the face of a rather hostile community and school administration, a situation that might in the short term reduce positive results. Perhaps most important of all, Pearce found that in virtually all school settings *comprehensive school desegregation is a long way from being achieved.*[111]

Russell Irvine and Jacqueline Jordan Irvine have suggested that school desegregation has had effects not only on black achievement but also on the relationships between black children and their teachers, on schools as black community institutions, and on black communities more generally. In regard to pupil–teacher relationships, one result of school desegregation in many areas has been to reduce significantly the number of black teachers with whom a black child comes in contact. One reason for this is that it is often the white schools rather than the black schools that are desegregated. Another reason is that the number of black teachers and principals has been significantly reduced.[112] Picott has found that between 1964 and 1973 the number of black principals in southern school systems decreased to only 200 from 2,000. Fewer black teachers means fewer role models for black children. Moreover, a number of studies have shown that black teachers expect greater education achievement from black pupils than white teachers do, both in schools with high average levels of academic achievement and in schools with lower levels of achievement. Thus, the absence of black teachers means not only an absence of role models but also decreased expectations for achievement from black children.[113]

Since the late 1970s there has been a new factor in school desegregation. Some black leaders in numerous major cities have shifted away from an emphasis on racial balance in local schools, in part for reasons noted in the previous paragraph. For example, in Atlanta, where the school population is 80 percent black, black groups settled their school desegregation suit without a racial-balance plan in exchange for complete desegregation of the faculty and administration. Similar compromises were made in Detroit and Dallas, cities with large black school systems. Many local black leaders have given up on comprehensive desegregation. Nonetheless, most civil rights organizations and leading civil rights lawyers have continued to press for comprehensive school desegregation plans, in spite of massive white resistance to such plans.[114]

## White Resistance in the 1970s and 1980s

In recent years, and particularly in employment discrimination and school segregation cases, the Supreme Court and some other federal courts have led the white resistance, in part by requiring a new standard for proving racial discrimination. The decision in *Griggs v. Duke Power Co.* (1971) had defined remediable discrimination so as to include practices that were "neutral in terms of intent" as long as those practices had a negative effect on black Americans. Yet the conservative Supreme Court of the late 1970s and the 1980s has generally required proof that a particular policy was *intentionally* established to discriminate against members of minority groups. This standard is often difficult and expensive to meet, and thus less progress in fighting discrimination has been made since the mid-1970s. For example, in a 1977–1978 case the Supreme Court upheld the use of a teacher examination in South Carolina that disqualified 83 percent of blacks but only 18 percent of whites, because intent to discriminate had not been proved.[115]

In the 1974 *Milliken* decision the U.S. Supreme Court overturned by a five-to-four vote a lower-court order requiring a combining of the Detroit school system and surrounding (white) suburban school systems according to one metropolitan-wide desegregation plan. The Court ruled that it had not been proved that the segregation in Detroit was caused by the actions of surrounding school boards. Only a few metropolitan-wide desegregation plans have cleared this Supreme Court hurdle.[116]

In the 1980s more than half of all black students still went to schools that were 60 to 90 percent minority, often in central city districts where substantial desegregation is not possible without bringing in the white suburbs. Since the mid-1970s the U.S. Supreme Court has held to a standard of proof that requires minority plaintiffs in desegregation cases to prove that school officials intentionally acted to segregate a school system; only then can dramatic remedies such as busing be used to desegregate the schools.

Nationwide protest against busing and appointments to the Supreme Court by conservative Republican presidents have created this shift of policy on the Supreme Court. Since 1972 most presidents have been hostile to urban desegregation court orders. Moreover, in the 1980s programs designed to aid black and other minority school children were cut back by the Reagan administration, on the grounds that such programs were expensive. On the other hand, the Reagan administration supported private schools by such actions as providing tax deductions for parents who pay private-school tuition. Such actions serve to reduce public support for public schools, particularly in central cities.

## College Attendance

Since the 1950s black students have gone to college in ever increasing numbers. Black Americans had been limited to all-black colleges, but by the 1970s and 1980s three quarters of black college students were going to predominantly white colleges. Students were encouraged by the outreach and affirmative action programs of many colleges. The impossible dream seemed to have come true. But by late 1980s it was becoming a nightmare. In 1980 about 11 percent of all undergraduates were black, but by the late 1980s that figure had dropped to only 8.8 percent. The progress of the previous decade seemed to be coming to an end. In addition, black students in graduate programs decreased by 12 percent between 1980 and the mid-1980s; the percentage of black faculty and administrators also decreased.[117]

Many black students face racial problems on white campuses. There is a higher drop out rate and a lower rate of enrollment in graduate programs than for whites. Walter Allen has reported that black students establish their own social networks because of their exclusion from white networks. In a 1980 University of Michigan study, half the black students questioned said they did not feel part of general campus life. Many reported they were disenchanted with their college environments. Most blacks come to white campuses as the victims of institutional and personal racism. And, as Allen has noted, after they enter the campuses the discrimination does not disappear; and the discrimination causes them to have difficulties in academic performance.[118]

In the University of Michigan survey just cited, 85 percent of the black students questioned reported that they had run into discrimination on campus, including comments by professors that "black students aren't very bright" and blatant forms of discrimination such as "KKK" and "nigger" being painted on a house owned by a black organization. In the late 1980s white students in KKK-type sheets at The Citadel burned a cross in a black student's room. Another cross was burned on the lawn of a black sorority house at Alabama. Racial epithets have often been sprayed on walls at a number of southern and northern universities in the 1980s.

Black students are often blamed by whites for their failure to adjust. In fact, white administrators, faculty members, and students have often failed to adjust their white-oriented college environments to students from different racial and income backgrounds. Black students feel isolated or targeted. Institutionalized racism may be somewhat more subtle in higher education today, but it is nonetheless present.

## RELIGION

The first major stereotyping of black Africans was in terms of what Europeans saw as un-Christian, uncivilized savagery. The irony of militaristic, slave-trading, warring Europeans seeing Africans as savage has been lost on white Europeans ever since. The slaves imported into the colonies brought an array of religions with them. At first slave owners feared that "Christianizing" the Africans would put notions of freedom into their heads. But missionaries were instructed, and laws were passed making it clear, that conversion to Christianity did not bring freedom along with it. Devout slave owners encouraged missionaries, particularly Baptists and Methodists, to convert slaves.[119]

The Christianity of the slaves sometimes became linked to protest. The view of God that many slaves held—stressing the God who led the Israelites out of slavery—was different from what slaveholders had hoped for. In spirituals there was, hidden by symbolism, a religion of yearning to be free. Regular meetings, some held secretly, were fostered by the new religion. In these gatherings slave conspiracies to revolt were sometimes hatched. Blacks were permitted to preach to gatherings, and many of these preachers became leaders, including leaders of slave revolts.

Formal church organizations grew among slaves and free blacks in the cities—a result of their exclusion from white churches. In Philadelphia Absalom Jones and Richard Allen, after being mistreated at a white Methodist church, established their own Free African Society in 1787. Later, Jones established the first Negro Episcopal church, and Allen played a role in the emergence of the African Methodist Episcopal church.[120]

After the Civil War, churches played an important role in black communities. Churches were mutual-aid societies, ministering to those facing sickness and death, and they played a role in the pooling of economic resources. Education often came as religious education. New schools were established after the war, many under religious auspices, and some trained ministers as black leaders. Black churches continued as community and schooling centers, since few such centers were provided by local or state governments.

With the migration to the cities came a shift for some urbanites to a less otherworldly religious style. Social welfare and civil rights activity were ever increasing parts of black religious life, particularly in the mainline churches. At least one urban sect became a major force.Popularly known as the Black Muslims, the Nation of Islam sharply broke with the Christian background of black Americans, pressing hard for a black-oriented theology suffused with major doses of black pride and self-help. Prominent black leaders have arisen from this non-Christian movement, including Malcolm X.[121]

## Black Religion as Protest

Gary Marx has argued that otherworldly religion and protest orientations are not compatible. Basing his arguments on an opinion survey, Marx showed that support for civil rights militancy among his black respondents declined as religious commitment increased. Other scholars have taken issue with Marx's arguments. First, they have noted the public image of black religionists as more religious and otherworldly than whites has not been supported in recent research. One major study by the Nelsens found no black-white differences in reports of religious experience, in prayer frequency, or in conservative theology. Moreover, the same study found that blacks were more likely than whites to feel that their ministers should speak out on social and political issues, an attitude that seems to contradict the opiate-of-the-masses theory of black religion.[122]

The protest motif has been part of black religion from the beginning; religious gatherings and leaders have played a role in spreading protest since the days of slavery. Ministers have long been political leaders. Black ministers have been torn between being protest leaders and defending a discriminatory status quo; many have supported protest. The nonviolent civil disobedience movement from the mid-1950s to the 1970s had religious underpinnings.[123]

Most prominent among the minister-leaders was the Reverend Martin Luther King, Jr. Raised in an intensely religious family with a record of fighting for black rights, King came naturally to his essentially religious view of the legitimacy of nonviolent protests as a way of winning concessions and at the same time healing the wounds of oppressed and oppressor. He led blacks in effective protests and died a hero.[124]

## ASSIMILATION FOR BLACKS?

Milton Gordon argues that his theory of assimilation is applicable to both ethnic and racial groups. Gordon briefly applies this scheme to black Americans, whom he sees as assimilated at the cultural level in terms of language and the Protestant religion, with some black–white differences remaining because of "lower-class subculture." Beyond acculturation Gordon sees modest integration at the structural (primary-group) level, little intermarriage, little erosion of prejudice or discrimination, and no demise of group identity. Substantial acculturation has taken place, but assimilation at the other levels has come slowly.[125] As we noted in Chapter 2, in his recent work Gordon is optimistic about the further assimilation of black Americans, a trend he sees in the allegedly growing black middle class. For that reason, Gordon and other as-similationist authors call for an end to remedial programs such as affirmative action.

### Assimilation Theories: An Evaluation

Optimistic assimilation-oriented analysts have underscored black progress in terms of cultural, economic, and social integration. The prominent sociologist Talcott Parsons argued that the process of racial and ethnic inclusion is basic to U.S. society. One aspect of this process is the increasing inclusion of black Americans in the institutions of the society. Parsons viewed this ongoing process of inclusion as operating earlier for white immigrants. But inclusion for him does not mean slavish Anglo-conformity assimilation. In his view even white ethnic groups have not been prevented by in-clusion from maintaining a distinct ethnic identity. From Parson's inclusion perspec-tive, given the basic egalitarian values of the United States, "the only tolerable solution to the enormous [racial] tensions lies in constituting a single community with full membership for all."[126]

Analysts such as Nathan Glazer have argued that there has been a major col-lapse in traditional racial discrimination, that assimilation of black Americans into the core economy and society is well under way. What they view as dramatic black economic progress is cited as proof of the ongoing assimilation. The major remaining problem is the troubled black underclass, whose difficulties are not primarily ques-tions of current discrimination. While recognizing discrimination as a serious barrier for black Americans, some assimilationists have in effect blamed blacks for their slower economic and social mobility, particularly in the last few decades. In a famous report in the 1960s, Daniel P. Moynihan viewed black families headed by females as a serious retardant to progress. He and scholars such as Wilson have pointed to a sub-culture of poverty among low-income blacks as a major barrier. A general theme of scholars and popular analysts sometimes boils down to "Why can't they be like us?" The suggestion is that blacks, like the urban white immigrant groups before them, are likely to move up through the various levels of the economy, society, and polity—if they will only work hard.[127]

Power-conflict analysts reject this optimistic assimilationist view. From their perspective, the current condition of black Americans is more rigidly hemmed in, more segregated than that of white ethnics because of the character of African incorporation into the English colonies and later into the United States. Once a system of extreme subordination is established, those in the superior position continue to monopolize economic and social resources. Blauner, for example, convincingly argues that there are major differences between blacks and white immigrant groups.[128]

Africans were enslaved and brought across the Atlantic Ocean in chains. Incorporated into the economy against their will, they provided hard labor at the lowest occupational levels, first as slaves, later as tenant farmers, then as urban laborers. Even with the northward migration this status was not altered. Blacks became a subordinate part of the growing urban economic system; they were incorporated at the bottom levels of the economy. This point underscores a major problem in traditional assimilation frameworks, for although incorporation into the society might occur, it might be at the lowest level with modest chances of mobility. Nonwhite minorities have suffered the destruction of their original cultures. Africans were forced to give up many of their traditional ways as part of their incorporation into American work patterns, the Protestant religion, and the English language. In contrast with the assimilation view, there is an emphasis on forced acculturation among power-conflict analysts.

## Barriers to Assimilation

The power-conflict perspective takes a different view of the failure of blacks to move up to economic and social equality. Little relevance is assigned to the black church, matriarchal families, or a subculture of poverty as barriers, but direct and indirect institutionalized discrimination are given great emphasis. For example, when white ethnic groups such as the Irish began coming in, they did *not* gain socioeconomic equality on an equal-opportunity or fair-competition basis: they often displaced free blacks who had been relegated to the lowest-paying jobs. Prior to the Civil War black workers could be found in a number of skilled trades in northern and southern cities. By the mid-nineteenth century white immigrant workers were crowding blacks out of many of these occupations. Blacks were increasingly forbidden by law from entering such crafts as blacksmithing, bricklaying, and mechanics. From Mobile to New York, Irish and German immigrants had begun to fill jobs once filled by blacks.[129]

After the Civil War most blacks in the South remained where they were and became poor tenant farmers and sharecroppers, for the new industrial machine drew workers from southern and eastern Europe, not from the South. Structural assimilation failed in the face of institutionalized discrimination. With the urban trek northward blacks increasingly filled low-level jobs in industry, but it was not until World War II, with its huge labor demand, that a large proportion of blacks encountered the industrial machine for the first time. Yet by the end of that war a decline in demand for black labor had begun, and with it a growing unemployment problem. Thus a second major barrier to mobility for black Americans has been time of entry. Unlike the European immigrants prior to World War I—a boom period for small businesses and for unskilled labor—black migrants after the World War II boom found a declining demand for their labor. Just as the children of the white immigrants had begun to move up the mobility ladder dramatically, blacks were moving into cities in very large numbers. Black migrants found that the opportunity awaiting them was much paler than the promised-land image that had drawn them cityward. Since World War II the demand for black labor in cities has also been reduced by automation.[130]

A third barrier maintaining blacks' subordinate position has been the political situation. Irish, Italian, and other nineteenth- and twentieth-century European immigrants benefited from urban political organizations, which played an important role in providing them jobs and thus in facilitating their upward mobility. When blacks came in during World War II, the period of great public construction in the cities was over. Indeed, because of reform movements the urban machines were on the decline. In most cities blacks were never able to benefit as much as "white ethnics" from the political patronage system.[131]

## The Situation Today

The Civil Rights Acts of 1964, 1965, and 1968 made many formal acts of discrimination illegal, but they did not end the array of blatant, subtle, and covert discrimination in jobs, housing, and education. The spectacle of "slavery unwilling to die" can be seen today: restrictions on black voting continue in the South; most black children still attend segregated schools; most black families live in segregated residential areas; most blacks face informal discrimination by banks, real estate people, landlords, and homeowners; most black defendants are tried by all-white juries; and most blacks face covert and subtle, if not blatant, discrimination in the job market.

Even those blacks moving into better-paying jobs in this society face race discrimination and a new kind of colonialism. For example, sophisticated discrimination has become widespread in recent years. One example, tokenism, has helped slow the dismantling of institutionalized discrimination. Reluctantly tearing down the traditional exclusion barriers over the last two decades, many officials in organizations have retreated to this second line of defense. Part of the tokenism strategy is to hire nonwhite minorities for nontraditional jobs and put them in conspicuous and/or powerless positions. Officials must then be careful not to place too many blacks in one particular unit of their organization. A management consultant, Kenneth Clark, has noted that blacks moving into nontraditional jobs in corporate America have frequently found themselves tracked into "ghettos" within organizations, such as a department of "community affairs" or of "special markets." Many professional and managerial blacks end up in selected staff jobs such as equal opportunity officer rather than in line managerial jobs. Clark notes that "they are rarely found in line positions concerned with developing or controlling production, supervising the work of large numbers of whites or competing with their white 'peers' for significant positions."[132]

## SUMMARY

The social progress of black Americans was severely restricted by slavery, even though at the time of the first great waves of white European immigrants some blacks were already tenth-generation Americans. The slave period was followed by a long epoch, not yet ended, of legal and informal segregation. Jim Crowism frustrated the lives of freed slaves and generations of their descendants. The urban, northward trek reflected protests against southern oppression, protests "by the feet." Other types of black protest against subordination, nonviolent and violent, have punctuated the long course of black-white relations.

In the late 1980s most black Americans were living in cities, North and South. The net migration of blacks from the South had reached zero: no more were leaving the South than were coming in from the North and the West. Those optimistic about black/white relations might point to growing black political power. Yet wherever they live, black Americans face continuing racial discrimination and economic inequality. Attitude surveys between the 1940s and the 1980s have found white support for the old racial stereotypes to be declining.[133] While the decline may to some extent reflect a subtle concealment of white views, it is so steep that it probably reflects as well a genuine change from the blatantly racist attitudes of earlier decades. At the same time, the data on economic inequality along racial lines, taken as a whole, show no dramatic economic improvements for blacks since the 1970s. Subtle and covert forms of discrimination persist. Recent debates over black progress in the economic sphere really seem to be debates between advocates of "no changes" and advocates of "modest changes." Debates over the underclass accent the crisis of black unemployment. Late in the twentieth century black Americans are far from income, occupational, or wealth parity with whites.

## NOTES

1. John Hope Franklin, *From Slavery to Freedom*, 4th ed. (New York: Knopf, 1974), pp.35–36; Winthrop Jordan, *White over Black* (Baltimore: Penguin, 1969), pp 91–98.
2. James H. Dorman and Robert R. Jones, *The Afro-American Experience* (New York: John Wiley, 1974), pp. 72–74; Thomas R. Frazier, preface to Chapter 1, in *Afro-American History: Primary Sources*, ed. Thomas R. Frazier (New York: Harcourt, Brace, & World, 1970), pp. 3–5.
3. Olaudah Equiano, "The Interesting Narrative of the Life of Olaudah Equiano," in *Afro-American History*, ed. Frazier, pp. 18, 20.
4. Dorman and Jones, *The Afro-American Experience*, pp. 80–82.
5. Philip D. Curtin, *The Atlantic Slave Trade* (Madison: University of Wisconsin Press, 1969), pp. 87–93; U.S. Bureau of the Census, *Historical Statistics of the United States* (Washington, D.C.: U.S. Government Printing Office, 1960), p. 770.
6. Carl N. Degler, *Out of Our Past* (New York: Harper, 1959), pp. 161–63; Franklin, *From Slavery to Freedom*, p. 88.
7. Franklin, *From Slavery to Freedom*, pp. 132–33.
8. U.S. Bureau of the Census, *Historical Statistics of the United States*, p. 11; Degler, *Out of Our Past*, pp. 163–64; Ulrich B. Phillips, *Life and Labor in the Old South* (Boston: Little, Brown 1929), pp.

339ff; Kenneth M. Stampp, *The Peculiar Institution* (New York: Random House, Vintage Books, 1956), pp. 383–418.

9. Phillips, *Life and Labor in the Old South*, pp. iv–v; Eugene G. Genovese, *Roll, Jordan, Roll* (New York: Random House, 1974), pp. 56–57. See also Gilberto Freyre, *The Masters and the Slaves* (New York: Knopf, 1956); and Marvin Harris, *Race Patterns in the Americas* (New York: Walder & Co., 1964), pp. 65–90.

10. John W. Blassingame, *The Slave Community* (New York: Oxford University Press, 1972), pp. 155–60.

11. Ben Simpson, "Ben Simpson: Georgia and Texas," in *Lay My Burden Down*, ed. B. A. Botkin (Chicago: University of Chicago Press, 1945), p. 75.

12. Herbert Aptheker, *American Negro Slave Revolts* (New York: International Publishers, 1943), pp. 56–67.

13. Genovese, *Roll, Jordan, Roll*, pp. 5, 362–64; Stanley M. Elkins, *Slavery* (Chicago: University of Chicago Press, 1959), pp. 72–127.

14. Herbert Gutman, *The Black Family in Slavery and Freedom, 1750–1925* (New York: Pantheon, 1976); Stanley Elkins, "The Slavery Debate," *Commentary* 46 (December 1975): 46–47.

15. Elkins, *Slavery*, pp. 84–85.

16. Blassingame, *The Slave Community*, pp. 203–14; Genovese, *Roll, Jordan, Roll*, p. 588.

17. Genovese, *Roll, Jordan, Roll*, p. 650.

18. Aptheker, *American Negro Slave Revolts*, pp. 12–18, 162.

19. Ibid., pp. 165, 220–25, 249–50, 267–73.

20. Herbert Aptheker, *Essays in the History of the American Negro* (New York: International Publishers, 1945), pp. 39, 49–51.

21. Benjamin B. Ringer, *"We the People" and Others* (New York: Tavistock, 1983), p. 533.

22. A. L. Higginbotham, *In the Matter of Color* (New York: Oxford University Press, 1978), pp. 144–149.

23. Thomas F. Gossett, *Race* (New York: Schocken Books, 1965), pp. 42–43.

24. Samuel Cartwright, "The Prognathous Species of Mankind," in *Slavery Defended*, ed. Eric L. McKitrick (Englewood Cliffs, N.J.: Prentice-Hall, 1963), p. 140.

25. Lewis H. Carlson and George A. Colburn, "Introduction," in *In Their Place*, ed. Lewis H. Carlson and George A. Colburn (New York: John Wiley, 1972), p. 99.

26. Duncan J. MacLeod, *Slavery, Race, and the American Revolution* (London: Cambridge University Press, 1974), p. 158.

27. Excerpt from Edward East, *Heredity and Human Affairs*, in *In Their Place*, ed. Carlson and Colburn, p. 103.

28. I. A. Newby, *Jim Crow's Defense* (Baton Rouge: Louisiana State University Press, 1965), pp. 19–23.

29. Thomas F. Pettigrew, *A Profile of the Negro American* (Princeton, N.J.: D. Van Nostrand, 1964), pp. 100ff.

30. Richard J. Herrstein, *IQ in the Meritocracy* (Boston: Little, Brown, 1973); Arthur R. Jensen, "How Much Can We Boost IQ and Scholastic Achievement?" *Harvard Education Review 39* (1969): 1–123.

31. Klinberg's data are cited in I. A. Newby, *Challenge to the Court* (Baton Rouge: Louisiana State University Press, 1967), p. 74. See also Pettigrew, *A Profile of the Negro American*, pp. 123–26.

32. See Horace M. Bond, "Cat on a Hot Tin Roof," *Journal of Negro Education* 27 (Fall 1958): 519–23.

33. Leon J. Kamin, *The Science and Politics of IQ* (New York: John Wiley, 1974), pp. 175–78.

34. N.J. Block and Gerald Dworkin, "IQ, Heritability, and Inequality," in *The IQ Controversy*, ed. N.J. Block and Gerald Dworkin (New York: Random House, 1976), pp. 410–540.

35. William Brink and Louis Harris, *The Negro Revolution in America* (New York: Simon & Schuster, 1964) pp. 140–41; William Brink and Louis Harris, *Black and White* (New York: Simon & Schuster, 1967), p. 136; Richard T. Morris and Vincent Jeffries, "The White Reaction Study," in *The Los Angeles Riots*, ed. Nathan Cohen (New York: Praeger, 1970), p. 510.

36. Howard Schuman, Charlotte Steeh, and Lawrence Bobo, *Racial Attitudes in America* (Cambridge: Harvard University Press, 1985), pp. 86–125.

37. Angus Campbell, *White Attitudes toward Black People* (Ann Arbor, Mich.: Institute for Social Research, 1971), p. 14; John B. McConahay and Willis D. Hawley, "Is It the Buses or the Blacks?" (working paper, Center for Policy Analysis, Duke University, 1981), pp. 35–38.

38. John B. McConahay and Joseph C. Hough, "Symbolic Racism," *Journal of Social Issues* 32 (1976): 38.

39. Schuman, Steeh, and Bobo, *Racial Attitudes in America*, pp. 86–125.

40. U.S. Bureau of the Census, *Historical Statistics of the United States*, p. 218.

41. W. J. Cash, *The Mind of the South* (New York: Random House, Vintage Books, 1960), p. 125.

42. Note a 1940 pamphlet written by a white southerner for U.S. senators and congressmen, quoted in Gunnar Myrdal, *An America Dilemma* (New York: McGraw-Hill, 1964), 2:1198.

43. Gilbert Osofsky, *Harlem: The Making of a Ghetto* (New York: Harper & Row, Pub., 1963), pp. 45–51; Arthur I. Waskow, *From Race Riot to Sit-In, 1919 and the 1960s* (Garden City, N.Y.: Doubleday, 1966), pp. 209–10 et passim; Elliot M. Rudwick, *Race Riot at East St. Louis* (Carbondale: Southern Illinois University Press, 1964), pp. 3–30).

44. John Turner, *The Ku Klux Klan: A History of Racism and Violence* (Montgomery, Ala.: Southern Poverty Law Center, 1982), pp. 48–56; "Going after the Klan," *Newsweek*, February 23, 1987, p. 29.

45. "Tension Rises in New York in March over Black's Death," *Austin American-Statesman*, December 28, 1987, p. A3.

46. Joe R. Feagin and Harlan Hahn, *Ghetto Revolts* (New York: Macmillan, 1973), p. 134.

47. "The Mood of Ghetto America," *Newsweek*, June 2, 1980, pp. 32–34.

48. Ibid., p. 33; "Accidents or Police Brutality?" *Time*, October 26, 1981, p. 70.

49. Ray Marshall, *The Negro Worker* (New York: Random House, 1967), pp. 7–12; MacLeod, *Slavery, Race, and the American Revolution*, pp. 151–53; Pete Daniel, *The Shadow of Slavery: Peonage in the South* (London: Oxford University Press, 1972); Myrdal, *An American Dilemma*, 1:228.

50. Karl E. Taeuber and Alma F. Taeuber, *Negroes in Cities* (Chicago: Aldine, 1965), pp. 12–13.

51. Charles Tilly, "Race and Migration to the American City," in *The Urban Scene*, ed. Joe R. Feagin (New York: Random House, 1973), p. 35.

52. Taeuber and Taeuber, *Negroes in Cities*, pp. 144ff.

53. See Bennett Harrison, *Education, Training, and the Urban Ghetto* (Baltimore: Johns Hopkins, 1972).

54. U.S. Bureau of the Census, *Negroes in the United States, 1920–1932* (Washington, D.C.: U.S. Government Printing Office, 1935), p. 289; Myrdal, *An American Dilemma*, 1:304ff.

55. Marshall, *The Negro Worker*, pp. 23–24, 56–57.

56. U.S. Bureau of the Census, *Population*, vol. 3, *The Labor Force* (Washington, D.C.: U.S. Government Printing Office, 1943). See also Sidney M. Wilhelm, *Who Needs the Negro?* (Cambridge, Mass.: Schenkman, 1970), p. 57.

57. U.S. Bureau of the Census, *Statistical Abstract of the United States: 1980* (Washington, D.C.: U.S. Government Printing Office, 1980), pp. 416–19; U.S. Bureau of the Census, *The Social and Economic Status of the Black Population in the United States, 1974* (Washington, D.C.: U.S. Government Printing Office, 1975), p. 73; U.S. Bureau of the Census, *Statistical Abstract of the United States: 1987* (Washington, D.C.: U.S. Government Printing Office, 1986), p. 137.

58. Andrew F. Brimmer, *The Economic Position of Black Americans, 1976* (Washington, D.C.: National Commission for Manpower Policy, 1976), p. 17.

59. Beth Anne Shelton, "Formal and Informal Mechanisms of Discrimination: A Case Study" (Ph. D. dissertation, University of Texas at Austin, 1984).

60. Edward W. Jones, "What It's Like to Be a Black Manager," *Harvard Business Review* (May-June, 1986): 84–93.

61. Edward W. Jones, "Beneficiaries or Victims? Progress or Process?" (research report, South Orange, N.J., 1985). Cited with permission.

62. Samuel L. Adams, "Blackening in the Media," in *The State of Black America, 1985*, ed. J. D. Williams (New York: National Urban League, 1985), p. 111.

63. U.S. Bureau of the Census, *The Social and Economic Status of the Black Population in the United States, 1971* (Washington, D.C.: U.S. Government Printing Office, 1972), p. 52; Brimmer, *The*

*Economic Position of Black Americans, 1976*, p. 13; U.S. Commission on Civil Rights, *Unemployment and Underemployment among Blacks, Hispanics, and Women* (Washington, D.C.: U.S. Government Printing Office, 1982), p. 5; U.S. Bureau of the Census, *Statistical Abstract of the United States: 1987*, p. 390.

64. Wilhelm, *Who Needs the Negro?* p. 155; U.S. Commission on Civil Rights, *Unemployment and Underemployment among Blacks, Hispanics, and Women*, pp. 5–8.

65. U.S. Bureau of the Census, *The Social and Economic Status of the Black Population in the United States, 1971*, p. 29; Brimmer, *The Economic Position of Black Americans: 1976*, p. 37; Spencer Rich, "New Data Show Blacks' Income Outgained Whites' in 1970s," *Washington Post*, June 3, 1982; U.S. Bureau of the Census, *Statistical Abstract of the United States: 1987*, p. 436.

66. Rich, "New Data"; U.S. Bureau of the Census, *Statistical Abstract of the United States: 1987*, p. 121.

67. Robert B. Hill, "The Economic Status of Black Americans," in *The State of Black America, 1981*, ed. J. D. Williams (New York: National Urban League, 1981), pp. 5–6, 33.

68. Peter T. Kilborn, "U.S. Whites 10 Times Wealthier than Blacks, Census Study Finds," *New York Times*, July 19, 1986, p. 1.

69. William J. Wilson, *The Declining Significance of Race* (Chicago: University of Chicago Press, 1978); Ken Auletta, *The Underclass* (New York: Random House, 1982).

70. Hill, "The Economic Status of Black Americans," p. 34.

71. Franklin D. Gilliam, "Black America: Divided by Class," *Public Opinion*, February/March 1986, pp. 53–60.

72. See Joe R. Feagin and Clairece B. Feagin, *Discrimination American Style*, 2d ed. (Malabar, Fl.: Robert Krieger Publishing Co., 1986), pp. 207–34.

73. Marshall, *The Negro Worker*, pp. 120–24; U.S. Commission on Civil Rights, *The Federal Civil Rights Enforcement Effort, 1974*, vol. 5, *To Eliminate Employment Discrimination* (Washington, D.C.: U.S. Government Printing Office, 1975), pp. 291–92.

74. U.S. Commission on Civil Rights, *The Federal Civil Rights Enforcement Effort: Fiscal Year 1983* (Washington, D.C.: U.S. Government Printing Office, 1982), pp. 53–59.

75. Hanes Walton, Jr., *Black Politics* (Philadelphia: Lippincott, 1972), pp. 14–15, 26.

76. This discussion draws on a course given by Thomas F. Pettigrew at Harvard University.

77. Ibid.; Franklin, *From Slavery to Freedom*, pp. 252–53; Chuck Stone, *Black Political Power in America*, rev. ed. (New York: Dell Pub. Co., Inc., 1970), pp. 30–31.

78. Cash, *The Mind of the South*, p. 174. See also C. Vann Woodward, *The Strange Career of Jim Crow*, 2d rev. ed. (New York: Oxford University Press, 1966), pp. 31ff.

79. *Plessy v. Ferguson*, 163 U.S. 551–552.

80. Woodward, *The Strange Career of Jim Crow*, pp. 115–18.

81. Stone, *Black Political Power in America*, p. 35.

82. Walton, *Black Politics*, pp. 100, 119.

83. David Campbell and Joe R. Feagin, "Black Politics in the South: A Descriptive Analysis," *Journal of Politics* 37 (February 1975): 129–62.

84. Chandler Davidson, *Minority Vote Dilution: An Overview*, Reprint 85-1 (Houston, Institute for Policy Analysis, Rice University, 1985), pp. 17–18.

85. Ibid.

86. Martin Luther King, Jr., in the *New York Times*, February 2, 1965, p. 1; Mack Jones, "Black Office Holders in Local Governments of the South: An Overview" (paper presented at the 68th annual meeting of the American Political Science Association, Los Angeles, September 6–12, 1972), p. 38.

87. James E. Conyers and Walter L. Wallace, *Black Elected Officials* (New York: Russell Sage Foundation, 1976), p. 159; see also pp. 8, 137–40.

88 Myrdal, *An American Dilemma*, 1:503; Raymond Wolters, *Negroes and the Great Depression* (Westport, Conn.: Greenwood Publishing Corp., 1970), p. xi et passim.

89. Stone, *Black Political Power in America*, pp. 68–72.

90. Ibid., p. 47. Stone is drawing here on Henry L. Moon, *Balance of Power* (Garden City, N.Y.: Doubleday, 1948).

91. Campbell and Feagin, "Black Politics in the South," p. 151.

92. Feagin and Hahn, *Ghetto Revolts*, pp. 81–85; Loren Miller, *The Petitioners* (New York: Random House, 1966), pp. 250–56.

93. Miller, *The Petitioners*, pp. 260–347.

94. Lerone Bennett, Jr., *Confrontation: Black and White* (Baltimore: Penguin, 1966), pp. 164–69.

95. Ibid., pp. 223–34; Bryan T. Downes and Stephen W. Burks, "The Historical Development of the Black Protest Movement," in *Blacks in the United States,* ed. Norval D. Glenn and Charles Bonjean (San Francisco: Chandler, 1969), pp. 322–44.

96. Feagin and Hahn, *Ghetto Revolts*, pp. 92–94; Bennett, *Confrontation: Black and White*, pp. 234–37; Inge P. Bell, *CORE and the Strategy of Nonviolence* (New York: Random House, 1968), pp. 13ff.

97. U.S. Commission on Civil Rights, *The Federal Civil Rights Enforcement Effort: Fiscal Year 1983*, pp. 5–7.

98. Sheila D. Collins, *The Rainbow Challenge* (New York: Monthly Review Press, 1986), pp. 128–143.

99. Franklin, *From Slavery to Freedom*, pp. 280–81; Myrdal, *An American Dilemma* 1:337–44; Henry A. Bullock, *A History of Negro Education in the South* (New York: Praeger, 1967), pp. 1–99.

100. Bullock, *A History of Negro Education in the South*, pp. 170–86; Franklin, *From Slavery to Freedom*, pp. 284–86.

101. U.S. Bureau of the Census, *Statistical Abstract of the United States, 1981* (Washington, D.C.: U.S. Government Printing Office, 1981), p. 142.

102. Harrison, *Education, Training, and the Urban Ghetto*, p. 67.

103. James P. Smith and Finis R. Welch, *Closing the Gap* (Santa Monica, Calif.: RAND Corporation, 1986).

104. Bullock, *A History of Negro Education in the South*, pp. 211–12, 225–30; Miller, *The Petitioners*, pp. 347–58.

105. U.S. Commission on Civil Rights, *Twenty Years after Brown* (Washington, D.C.: U.S. Government Printing Office, 1975), pp. 11–41.

106. Nathan Glazer, *Affirmative Discrimination* (New York: Basic Books, 1975); "Busing Backfired" (interview with James Coleman), *National Observer*, June 7, 1975.

107. See the numerous articles on innovative desegregation strategies in the 1966–1976 issues of the journal *Integrated Education*.

108. Nicolaus Mills, "Busing: Who's Being Taken for a Ride," in *The Great School Bus Controversy*, ed. Nicolaus Mills (New York: Columbia University, Teachers College Press, 1973), p. 7. See also U.S. Commission on Civil Rights, *Your Child and Busing* (Washington, D.C.: U.S. Government Printing Office, 1972).

109. Nancy H. St. John, *School Desegregation: Outcomes for Children* (New York: John Wiley, 1975), pp. 119–21.

110. "Study Shows Social Mix Good for Blacks," *Newsweek*, September 18, 1985, p. 3.

111. Diana Pearce, "Breaking Down Barriers: New Evidence on the Impact of Metropolitan School Desegregation on Housing Patterns" (research report, School of Law, Catholic University, 1980), pp. 48–53.

112. Russell W. Irvine and Jacqueline Jordan Irvine, "The Impact of the Desegregation Process on the Education of Black Students: Key Variables," *Journal of Negro Education* 53 (1983): 410–421.

113. R. Picott, *A Quarter Century of Elementary and Secondary Education* (Washington, D.C.: Association for the Study of Negro Life and History, 1976).

114. Feagin and Feagin, *Discrimination American Style*, pp. 201–4.

115. *U.S. v. South Carolina*, F. Supp. 1094 (D.S.C. 1977), affirmed mem. sub nom. *National Educ. Assn. v. South Carolina*, 434 U.S. 1026 (1978).

116. *Milliken v. Bradley*, 418 U.S. 717 (1974).

117. "Is the Dream Over?" *Newsweek on Campus*, February 1987, pp. 10–14.

118. Walter R. Allen, "Correlates of Black Student Adjustment, Achievement, and Aspirations at a Predominantly White Southern University," in *Black Students in Higher Education,* ed. G. E. Thomas, (Westport, Conn.: Greenwood Press, 1981), pp. 128–37; Walter R. Allen, "Black and Blue: Black Students at the University of Michigan" (research report, University of Michigan, n.d.), pp. 8–12.

119. Stampp, *The Peculiar Institution*, pp. 156–62; Aptheker, *American Negro Slave Revolts*, pp. 56–60.

120. Richard C. Wade, *Slavery in the Cities*(New York: Oxford University Press, 1964), pp. 161–63; Jordan, *White Over Black.*, pp. 422–25.

121. E. Franklin Frazier, *The Negro Church in America* (New York: Schocken Books, 1964), pp. 35–39; Myrdal, *An American Dilemma*, 2:938–39; E. U. Essien-Udom, *Black Nationalism* (New York: Dell Pub. Co., Inc., 1964).

122. Gary T. Marx, *Protest and Prejudice* (New York: Harper & Row, Pub., 1967), p. 105; Hart M. Nelsen and Anne Kusener Nelsen, *Black Church in the Sixties* (Lexington: University of Kentucky Press, 1975), pp. 81–123.

123. Frazier, *The Negro Church in America*, p. 44; Joseph R. Washington, Jr., *Black Religion* (Boston: Beacon Press, 1964), pp. 2–29.

124. David L. Lewis, *King* (Baltimore: Penguin, 1970), p. 390.

125. Milton Gordon, *Assimilation in American Life* (New York: Oxford University Press, 1964), p. 78.

126. Talcott Parsons, "Full Citizenship for the Negro American? A Sociological Problem," in *The Negro American*, ed. Talcott Parsons and Kenneth B. Clark (Boston: Houghton Mifflin, 1965), p. 740; see also pp. 714–15.

127. Glazer, *Affirmative Discrimination*, pp. 40–76; Daniel P. Moynihan, *The Negro Family* (Washington, D.C.: U.S. Government Printing Office, 1965); Frazier, *The Negro Church in America*; Myrdal, *An American Dilemma*.

128. Robert Blauner, *Racial Oppression in America* (New York: Harper & Row, Pub., 1972), pp. 51–110.

129. Wade, *Slavery in the Cities*, pp. 273–75; Herman D. Bloch, *The Circle of Discrimination* (New York: New York University Press, 1969), pp. ix–xiii.

130. Wilhelm, *Who Needs the Negro?*; Robert L. Allen, *Black Awakening in Capitalist America* (Garden City, N.Y.: Doubleday, Anchor Books, 1970), pp. 4–6; *Report of the National Advisory Commission on Civil Disorders* (New York: Bantam, 1968), pp. 278–79.

131. *Report of the National Advisory Commission on Civil Disorders*, pp.279–80.

132. Kenneth B. Clark, "The Role of Race," *New York Times Magazine*, October 5, 1980, p. 30.

133. See Herbert H. Hyman and Paul B. Sheatsley, "Attitudes toward Desegregation," *Scientific American* 211 (July 1964): 16–23.

# CHAPTER 9

# *Mexican Americans*

Among Anglo Americans the stereotypical view of Mexicans is of sleepy farmers under big sombreros, mustachioed banditos, a diet of tortillas and tacos, and folk Catholicism. Such popular images are supplemented by treatments of Mexicans and Mexican Americans in schoolbooks that distort the history of the Southwest, as in the myths that glorify freedom-loving, heroic Texans confronting a backward and cowardly Mexican people. Typical too in popular and scholarly accounts of life in the Southwest* is the omission of references to Mexican American contributions to the culture of the United States.

Yet the Mexican American role has been critical in the development of the United States. How did Mexicans initially become incorporated? What has life in the economy and the polity been like for them?

## THE CONQUEST PERIOD, 1500–1853

Early European expansion touched not only the Atlantic coast of North America but also the West. When the Spaniards arrived, they sought to Catholicize the native population in what is now Mexico and the southwestern United States and to concentrate it in agricultural and mining communities for exploitation. A five-level system of European-born Spanish, Criollos (native-born Spanish), Mestizos (mixed Spanish and "Indian"), Mulattoes (mixed Spanish and black) and Negroes, and Indios was established.[1] Because of the small number of Spaniards, the Native American contribution to the population mix was dominant then as it is today. Mexico won its independence from Spain in 1821.[2]

Prior to the 1830s Mexicans had established numerous communities in the Southwest. These were centered in a Mexican way of life. Along the Rio Grande in

*The Southwest* refers here to California, Arizona, New Mexico, Colorado, and Texas.

what would become southern Texas there were several thousand inhabitants living on land grants with a self-sufficient economy. There were an estimated four thousand Mexican settlers in the Texas area in 1821. Soon thousands of European American* settlers from the United States flooded the area. In a few years the new settlers outnumbered the Mexican population.[3]

## The Texas Revolt: Myth and Reality

The Texas province, both its Mexican population and its new United States immigrants, strongly supported a decentralized system of Mexican government. By 1830 some Mexican residents there had joined the new settlers to protest actions by the central government. Some Mexican government actions, including the freeing of slaves and the placing of restrictions on immigration, angered the European American settlers. The causes of the Texas revolt are complex, including not only government policies in Mexico City but also the racist attitudes of the Euro-American immigrants toward Mexicans, the resentment of white slaveholders toward Mexican antislavery laws, and the growing number of Euro-American immigrants coming in *illegally* from the north. Until recently, few analysts have been inclined to see the Texas revolt as territorial aggression by United States citizens against another sovereign nation, which in the end it was, but rather have excused the behavior of the Texans and blamed an oppressive Mexican government.[4]

The Texas revolt has been portrayed in persisting myths about heroic Texans. The legend of the Alamo portrays about 180 principled native-born Texans courageously fighting thousands of Mexican troops. But most of the men at the Alamo mission, in what is now San Antonio, were not native Texans but newcomers. Many were not men of principle defending their homes but adventurers such as James Bowie, William Travis, and Davy Crockett. The Alamo was one of the best-fortified sites in the West; the defenders had twice as many cannons, much better rifles, and much better training in riflery than the poorly equipped Mexican recruits. Another part of the myth suggests that all the defenders died fighting heroically. In fact, several surrendered. After a series of further skirmishes General Sam Houston managed a surprise attack that wiped out much of the Mexican army in the north.[5]

The Texas rebellion was a case of U.S. settlers going beyond an existing boundary and intentionally trying to incorporate new territory into the United States. Texas was annexed in 1845, an action that precipitated the Mexican War. Provocative American troop actions in a disputed boundary area generated a Mexican attack and then a declaration of war by the United States. The poorly equipped Mexican army lost. Some historians have questioned the view of this war as honorable, citing evidence that Mexico fell victim to a U.S. conspiracy to seize territory by force. U.S. soldiers and Texas Rangers murdered civilians and committed other atrocities in Mexico. In 1848 the Mexican government was forced to cede the Southwest area for $15 million. Mexican residents had the choice of remaining there or moving south;

---

The terms *European American, Euro-American,* and *Anglo* are used to designate persons whose ancestry is European. The common term *Anglo* is not fully satisfactory, because many of those involved in subordinating Mexican Americans had non-English European ancestry.

most stayed, assured on paper of protection by Article IX of the Treaty of Guadalupe Hidalgo.[6]

By the 1850s the population of Texas had grown to two hundred thousand, most of whom were in-migrants. Gradually, much land owned by the original occupants was taken away by the immigrants, particularly ranchers and farmers, who used means legal and illegal to do so. Most major Mexican landowners lost their lands.

## California and New Mexico

Prior to conquest California had Mexican-run ranches and missions, with 7,500 residents. After the 1849 gold rush they were outnumbered by incoming Euro-American settlers. The settlers, particularly large Anglo land owners, took over lands and political control from the Mexicans. The means of takeover ranged from lynching to armed theft to legal action.[7]

In New Mexico, villages provided the organization to withstand some of the Anglo onslaught. The villages there are quite old—Sante Fe was established in 1598. The fifty thousand New Mexicans had long maintained their own traditions. The richest 2 percent owned most of the land; the poor held the rest. Many landholders did fairly well under United States rule, continuing to play an important role in commerce and politics in the region. Nonetheless, most Mexicans eventually suffered great losses of private and communal lands.[8]

By the mid-nineteenth century the new United States system of private land ownership was replacing an older Mexican system that emphasized communal lands. The old land grants were ignored in spite of treaty promises and treated as U.S. government land; Mexican landholders ultimately lost most of the land. The invasion of the Southwest was not a heroic period in which United States settlers liberated unused land. It was in fact a period of imperialistic expansion resulting in the colonization of a communal people who already lived in the area.[9]

## THE IMMIGRATION PERIOD

Estimates of the number of Mexicans in the new territorial limits of the expanding United States range up to 118,000 for the 1850s. In the decades to follow, millions of Mexican migrants entered the United States. Two major push factors shaped this immigration: political upheavals and economic conditions. On the pull side were expanding opportunities and the demand for unskilled labor in the fields and factories north of the border. On the pull side too were family ties to what was once old Mexico.

The peak periods have been between 1910 and 1930 and since 1950. There have been five major categories of immigrants: (1) those with official visas ("legals"); (2) undocumented immigrants ("illegals"); (3) braceros (seasonal farm workers on contract); (4) "green-card" commuters (those with official alien visas who live in Mexico but work in the United States); and (5) "border crossers" (those with short-term permits, many of whom become maids).[10] With the exclusion of Asian immigrants by federal action (see Chapter 11) and the industrialization of the World War I era came a sharp decline in the number of laborers available for agricultural work. Mexican labor was drawn into the Southwest by the demand for cheap labor. During World War I more than seventy thousand Mexican workers were legally brought in; immigration restrictions were waived by federal authorities because of U.S. employer pressure.[11]

This Mexican migration increased in the 1920s with 500,000 workers and their families entering on visas. Improved canning and shipping technologies opened new markets for agricultural produce. Cities such as San Antonio had agencies that specialized in recruiting Mexican workers for agriculture as well as for jobs in urban industries—in the North as well as the South. Business opposition to serious restriction of the immigration was intense; temporary work-permit programs were periodically expanded. Mexicans were not excluded by the Immigration Act of 1924, which did restrict most southern and eastern Europeans. Mexico had become a main source of cheap labor for the Southwest and the Midwest.[12]

In the 1920s the Border Patrol of the Immigration and Naturalization Service was created, and in 1929 legislation made it a felony to enter the United States illegally. The Border Patrol came to play a larger and larger role in the lives of Mexicans and Mexican Americans. Although it has had the formal authority to keep out all undocumented workers, it has not always used this authority. Rather it has regulated the flow of Mexican workers so that the number coming in has been sufficient to meet the work demand but not enough to cause political problems. In times of depression and recession between the 1920s and the 1980s, the Border Patrol has conducted exclusion and deportation campaigns; in better times restrictive activity has often been less rigorous.[13]

During the Depression federal enforcement of literacy tests and the prohibition against poor immigrants becoming public charges greatly reduced the flow of immigrants. There was considerable pressure to get Mexicans already here, whether citizens or not, to leave the country. Some left voluntarily; others, undocumented workers (that is, workers without papers), were forcibly deported in massive border campaigns; thousands of others, including U.S. citizens, were expelled in organized caravans by social agencies eager to reduce their costs.[14]

## Braceros and Undocumented Workers

World War II changed the situation. In 1942 an Emergency Farm Labor ("Bracero") agreement between the United States and Mexico was made providing workers for agriculture. Seasonal workers were brought in temporarily to work in the fields. In two decades nearly five million braceros were brought in under contract.

This bracero program stimulated the migration of undocumented workers, and many employers became eager for the cheaper "illegals." Approximately two million documented migrants have come in since the 1860s; between the 1920s and the 1980s somewhere between four and seven million undocumented migrants entered. Many were temporary immigrants who returned to Mexico.[15]

Considerable opposition to this migration has been generated, particularly since World War II. Union officials have called for restrictions that will protect jobs of citizens. But the issue is a very difficult one. The Mexican government has made little effort to stop the undocumented migration, for it relieves severe poverty and population pressures on that side of the border. One study of 493 workers in three detention centers in Texas and California provides a profile of the "illegals." Most had come in without papers. Most were males under thirty with poverty backgrounds and less-than-sixth-grade educations. Their poverty had driven many to desperate measures. Many had come in under the auspices of labor smugglers, who charge $300 to $1,100 per person for their services. Recent research has also made it clear that a significant number of those who have crossed the border are women and children.[16]

Growing opposition led to restrictions in the 1960s, when legal immigration from Mexico was for the first time curtailed. The 1965 Immigration Act, which removed the discriminatory quotas directed at southern and eastern Europeans, incorporated a new limit of 120,000 persons from the Western Hemisphere in an attempt to restrict migrants from Mexico. And in 1976 a limit of just 20,000 persons per year was placed on Mexican immigration. Attempts to deal with undocumented Mexican immigrants have focused on intensified Border Patrol policing and legislation concerning visas.[17]

Because of economic troubles in Mexico, such as poverty and unemployment, a substantial flow of workers continued in the 1970s and 1980s. The best estimates for the number of undocumented Mexican workers in the United States in the 1980s were *substantially less* than the official estimates of 5 to 10 million. Careful research suggests that the real number is closer to 1.5 to 4 million. Public officials exaggerated the estimates for political purposes. Moreover, research has revealed that the undocumented workers do not burden the U.S. taxpayer by going on welfare and using social services for which they have not paid. Numerous studies have shown that they have low rates of use of programs such as welfare, food stamps, and unemployment compensation. They pay out more in income and other taxes than they receive in benefits.[18]

## A New Immigration Act and Undocumented Immigrants

Mexican and other non-European immigrants have long been seen as a "problem" by nativist Anglo Americans; and nativist attempts to limit this immigration were finally successful in 1986. The 1986 Immigration Reform and Control Act has five provisions: (1) legalization of undocumented immigrants resident continuously since 1982; (2) sanctions for employers who hire more recent undocumented aliens; (3) a program to reimburse governments for the added costs of legalization; (4) a program of screening welfare applicants for migration status; and (5) special programs to bring in agricultural laborers. In short, the law established penalties for employers who hire undocumented workers, as well as an identification system and an amnesty program for illegal workers who have resided in the United States for some time. Initial response by undocumented immigrants to the amnesty provision (just over 1.7 million as of early 1988) was far below that predicted by the Immigration and Naturalization Service, which had estimated that three million undocumented immigrants were eligible for amnesty. By mid-1988 there was a debate over extending the amnesty period.[19]

The congressional and public debate over this legislation revived many anti-immigration arguments of the past. Many native-born residents were worried about the character and values of the new immigrants. Native-born workers were concerned that the United States could not absorb so many immigrants, even though the ratio of immigrants to the native-born population was *much* higher in earlier decades than in the late twentieth century. In 1910 the foreign-born constituted 14.6 percent of the United States population; in the late 1980s the figure was only *6.2 percent*. In the 1980s the United States has a smaller percentage of foreign-born than many other nations, including England, Germany, and Switzerland. Australia, Canada, and New Zealand have two to three times as large a proportion of foreign-born as the United States. Given its long history of successful absorption of immigrants, it is unlikely that the United States will be overwhelmed by these new immigrants. Implicit in many discussions of the new immigrants seemed to be a concern that most of them were from Asia and Latin America—that is, not white or European.

## Population and Location

Official census estimates of the Mexican-origin population show an increase from 1.3 million in 1930 to 4.5 million in 1970 and 8.8 million in the early 1980s. By 1980 most Mexican Americans were living in urban areas, especially in the southwestern states. Most were native-born. Many now reside in other regions, particularly the Midwest.[20]

# STEREOTYPING

## Early Images

While competing with and subordinating the Mexican residents of the Southwest, European Americans early came to believe that laziness, backwardness, and poverty were fundamental to the character of the Mexican "race." The slaveholders who came to the Southwest had a well-developed race prejudice rationalizing the subordination of black Americans, so for many it was natural to stigmatize dark-skinned Mexican Americans as inferior .

"Greaser" has been a contemptuous term applied to Mexican Americans since the Mexican War, perhaps deriving from the activities of Mexicans who greased wagon axles. Cowardice was a stereotype that grew after the defeat of the Mexican army in the 1840s. In the 1850s John Monroe reported to Washington that the people of New Mexico "are thoroughly debased and totally incapable of self-government, and there is no latent quality about them that can ever make them respectable."[21] Ironically, it was these Mexicans whose knowledge of ranching, agriculture, and mining had laid the foundation for development of the Southwest.

The heavy Mexican immigration after 1900 triggered attacks on Mexicans by racists. Mexican labor camps were raided by the Ku Klux Klan and other white groups and the workers beaten. The 1911 federal Dillingham Commission on immigration alleged that Mexicans were unskilled and undesirable. In the 1920s a prominent member of Congress stereotyped Mexicans as a mixture of Spanish and "low-grade Indians who did not fight to extinction," plus some slave "blood," a mongrelized people. In 1928 a prominent expert witness appearing before the House Immigration Committee testified to the racial inferiority of Mexicans, branding the "Mexican race" a threat to the "white race."[22] Nativist scholars and popular writers alike expressed fear of "race mongrelization" as a result of contact with Mexicans. In 1925 a Princeton economics professor spoke fearfully of the future elimination of Anglo-Saxons through interbreeding in "favor of the progeny of Mexican peons who will continue to afflict us with an embarrassing race problem."[23]

Much literature since the 1920s has stereotyped the Mexican American as a crime-oriented villain with shifty eyes and a knife in the pocket. For example, a report by a lieutenant in the Los Angeles Sheriff's Department after the 1943 Zoot Suit Riots (see p. 264) alleged that the Mexicans' desire to spill blood was an "inborn characteristic," a view endorsed by the Anglo police chief. Much stereotyping has linked alleged social traits to genetic inferiority: "The Mexican was 'lawless' and 'violent' because he had Indian blood; he was 'shiftless' and 'improvident' because that was his nature."[24]

Since the 1920s the results of IQ testing have been used to argue for the intellectual and racial inferiority of Mexican Americans. As in the case of Jews, Italians, and black Americans, scientists have argued on the basis of paper-and-pencil tests that Mexican American children are of lower intelligence.[25]

## Modern Stereotypes

By the 1960s and 1970s some of the harshest stereotypes were beginning to fade from public view, but prejudicial attitudes were still expressed. One study found that drunkenness and criminality were attributed to Mexican Americans. In a study in a central California city, one-quarter of Anglo respondents reported they would find it distasteful to eat with a Mexican. The statement that "generally speaking, Mexicans are shiftless and dirty" was accepted by 37 percent of the respondents.[26]

Movies have cast Mexicans as banditos. Movies of Pancho Villa's raids in Texas, to take one example, play up the criminal image and ignore the relationship of the raids to prior exploitation by U.S. settlers. With the advent of television came a new medium for circulating stereotypes of Mexicans. Television serials presented the men as "lazy, fat, happy, thieving, immoral creatures who make excellent sidekicks for white heroes."[27] Women have been portrayed as flirting senoritas.

Comedians on television and in night clubs get laughs for stereotyping Hispanic Americans as buffoons who talk with a "funny accent." Television comedy series such as "Chico and the Man" have tried to portray Hispanic figures in terms other than the traditional stereotypes, but these attempts have not offset the prevailing negative stereotypes aired on other shows, not to mention those in movie reruns. Media advertising has also played a role in perpetuating stereotypes. One study found certain major advertisers still showing Mexican Americans in a negative light. Frito Bandito ads suggested that Mexicans were criminals. A deodorant company used a grubby-looking Mexican bandit in an ad that said, "If it works for him, it will work for you." Tequila advertisements in college newspapers had a "game" whose characters represented negative stereotypes of Mexicans—the lazy peon in a large sombrero sleeping on a burro, the border-town prostitute, and the thieving bandito.[28]

George Murphy, former senator from California, alleged that "Mexicans are ideal for 'stoop' labor—after all, they are built close to the ground."[29] Here a biological characteristic is linked to menial jobs. A California judge, ruling against a Mexican American youngster in an incest case, asserted in court:

> Mexican people, after 13 years of age, think it is perfectly all right to go out and act like an animal. We ought to send you out of the country—send you back to Mexico.... You are lower than animals and haven't the right to live in organized society—just miserable, lousy, rotten people. Maybe Hitler was right. The animals in our society probably ought to be destroyed because they have no right to live among human beings.[30]

Here is the criminality image with genocidal overtones.

Numerous government officials have assumed that Mexican Americans are passive and fatalistic. Such a view is based on a stereotype originating in social science studies that viewed Mexican American culture as one of passivity, lack of protest, fatalism, "machismo," and extreme family orientation. Anthropologists such as Robert Redfield and Oscar Lewis portrayed what they thought was a folk culture of fatalism and familism in the villages of Mexico, a view extended to Mexican American life.[31] Other social scientists have criticized these distortions in the traditional views of Mexicans and Mexican Americans and the errors in assuming that life in villages decades ago was the same as life in Mexican American communities today. The point is that the diversity of Mexican American culture from southern Texas to New Mexico to California has been overlooked.[32]

Anglo outsiders have seen Mexican Americans both as an ethnic group and a racial group. Some have accented their cultural characteristics as the major indicators of their distinctiveness. Others have seen them as an inferior race, accenting dark skins and "Indian" features thought to be typical of the group. Recent research in Texas has demonstrated that one likely result of this racial stereotyping is that darker-skinned Mexican Americans do not do as well in occupational and income attainments as lighter-skinned Mexican Americans, whose physical characteristics are closer to those of Anglo Americans.[33]

## VIOLENT CONFLICT

### The Early Period

Coercion was a fundamental factor in the establishment of Anglo domination in the Southwest. Mexican agricultural development was taken over by chicanery and force. The competition for land led to a new system of inequality. Both elite and rank-and-file Mexicans became subordinate to the invaders.

The Mexicans resisted. Such resistance began with the taking of Mexican lands in the 1830s and 1840s. Throughout history there have been bandits whose praises have been sung in folk ballads. Many have been social rebels unwilling to bear quietly the burdens imposed on their peoples. Typically their acts are regarded as crimes by the authorities in the dominant Anglo group, but *not* by people in the subordinate group; they are protected by the common people, in some cases becoming legends.[34]

Among the heroes in Mexican legends are Juan Cortina and Pancho Villa. Cortina has been typed as an "outlaw" and "cattle thief," but he became a Robin Hood figure to many Mexicans. He was certainly more than a thief, for he fought against the oppression of poor Mexicans in the Texas borderlands. In a series of guerrilla raids along the border, his followers clashed with the local militia and the Texas Rangers. In the 1850s and 1860s Cortina fought the injustices of the European American intruders, issuing formal statements of grievances detailing the stealing of land and biased legal systems. Colonel Robert E. Lee was sent to put down Cortina's rebellions, but succeeded only in limiting his activities. There were numerous other raids and clashes along the Texas border from El Paso to Brownsville. Between 1910 and 1925 there were many killings of both Mexicans and Euro-Americans in the Texas border area; estimates of the dead range from five hundred to five thousand.[35]

Lynching and public whipping became ways of keeping Mexicans in line; numerous lynchings were recorded in the nineteenth century. Much of the lawlessness against Mexicans in the Southwest had an official or semiofficial status. Law-enforcement officers such as the Texas Rangers terrorized Mexican Americans. The image of the Texas Rangers has been sugar-coated in exaggerated stories of heroism. Paredes has demonstrated that the myth covers up the oppressiveness of a police force used by Anglos to exploit the Mexican population. The European American rancher and farmer became rich with the aid of the Texas Rangers. In New Mexico the expansion of Anglo ranches at the expense of Mexicans did not come peacefully. Vigilante groups such as *La Mano Negro* (The Black Hand) used whatever means necessary to protect Mexican livestock and land.[36]

## More Anglo Attacks

Later decades in the twentieth century also saw open conflict. The so-called Zoot Suit Riots in the summer of 1943 in Los Angeles began with attacks by Anglo sailors on Mexican American youths, particularly those dressed in baggy "zoot suits." Groups of whites roamed Los Angeles beating up young zoot-suiters. Mexican groups organized retaliatory attacks on the sailors. Why did these riots occur? The local media focussed on Mexican American crime and youth. Police harassment increased, sometimes to the point of brutality. A few biased but well-publicized court trials involving Mexican youths stirred up local prejudices. The unusual dress of these youths became a focus of attention. One study found that in the three years leading up to the riots there was a sharp decline in the *Los Angeles Times*'s use of the term *Mexican* and a corresponding increase in an unfavorable use of *zoot suit* in connection with Mexican Americans. So intense was the paranoia during the rioting that the Los Angeles City Council seriously discussed making the wearing of zoot suits a *criminal* offense.[37]

## Recent Protest

In the 1960s and 1970s groups of young Chicanos, such as the Brown Berets, took to the streets and fought back against police actions they saw as oppressive.* There were three dozen Mexican American protest-oriented riots in southwestern cities. Among the most important were the East Los Angeles riots. In 1970 one hundred people attacked stores in Los Angeles owned mainly by Anglo absentee owners. In August of the same year twenty thousand Mexican Americans went to Los Angeles for a National Chicano Moratorium on the Vietnam War March. During the march, according to the police, some deputies were attacked by demonstrators. Marchers were later attacked by police at a park at the end of the route. Four hundred persons were arrested; dozens were injured; twenty-five police cars were damaged. Another riot occurred along the route of a Mexican Independence Day parade, with one hundred injuries and sixty-eight arrests.[38]

Police forces, with no or few Chicanos in them, have long been used, sometimes illegally, to end legal strikes and protests by Mexican American workers. Some cases have resulted in deaths to innocent civilians. Between 1965 and 1969 the U.S. Justice Department received 256 complaints of police malpractice from persons with Spanish surnames; in the late 1960s the American Civil Liberties Union received 174 such complaints in California alone. The common practice of preventive police patrolling in ghetto areas, with its "stop and frisk" and "arrest on suspicion " tactics, often leads to unfavorable police contacts for Mexican American males. Harassment of this type intensifies negative attitudes toward the police. In a study of three California cities most Mexican Americans interviewed felt the police did not care about protecting their property and lives and were hostile to their needs. Such relations laid the groundwork for rioting.[39]

## THE ECONOMY

We have already traced the outlines of the incorporation of Mexicans into the U.S. economy, first by violent conquest and later by the takeover of lands. An estimated 2 million acres of private lands and 1.7 million acres of communal lands were lost between 1854 and 1930 in the New Mexico area alone. A study of Taos County in New Mexico pointed up what had happened to Chicano lands by 1940: two-thirds of the county's private acreage had originally been land grants to Mexican communities and families, but this land was lost to Anglo settlers or the federal government. In *Stolen Heritage* (1986) Abel G. Rubio tells how his family, who settled in northern Mexico (now Texas) long before U.S. immigrants flooded the area, lost their original land grant. Rubio recounts how his great-grandfather was defrauded of his land, which is now in the middle of one of the largest Anglo ranches in south Texas.[40]

*The term *Chicano* was preferred to *Mexican American* by some activists in the 1960s and early 1970s. By the late 1970s activists were debating its use.

Across the Southwest those who lost their lands, as well as the descendants of such people and new immigrants, became landless laborers. One south Texas study found that in the 1850–1860 period, one-third of Mexican Americans in the rural labor force were ranch and farm owners, one-third were skilled laborers or professionals, and one-third were manual laborers. However, by 1900 the proportion of ranch and farm owners had dropped to 16 percent, while the proportion of manual laborers—many working for large Anglo ranches and farms—had climbed to two-thirds. A similar shift took place in the cities: a predominantly skilled labor force became predominantly unskilled.[41]

Overt, sometimes violent, discrimination played its part in limiting job opportunities. For example, because Mexican miners in California were resented by non-Mexican miners, a Foreign Miners Act placing a license tax on "foreigners" was passed to force them out. In the 1850s a group of two thousand Euro-American miners attacked Mexicans in Sonora, killing dozens and destroying a community. By the 1880s manual laborers were being used extensively in the expansion of railroads. In addition, although displaced by whites, Mexicans were the original vaqueros (cowboys) on the ranches across the Southwest.[42]

Working conditions in agricultural "stoop" labor were so severe that few competed with Mexicans for these jobs before the Depression. Mexican laborers in farming averaged $1.75 a day in Texas and $2.75 to $6.00 a day in California in the late 1920s. In mining, they averaged $2.75 to $4.00 a day. One study of Mexican agricultural workers found that they averaged $600 to $800 per year in income.[43]

## Job Discrimination Persists

Institutionalized discrimination was a major problem. From the 1920s on, agricultural operations, oil companies, mining companies, and other industries paid different rates for "whites" and "nonwhites"; Mexicans were listed under the latter category. Wages for citizens and noncitizens alike could be kept low because of the constant availability of undocumented workers.

Many unions have a record of discrimination against Mexican Americans. In the 1920s and 1930s the California Federation of Labor worked for their exclusion. Numerous industrial unions excluded Mexican Americans from membership. Attempts to create farm labor unions date back several decades, but they were not successful until the 1960s.[44]

By 1930 Mexican Americans were still heavily employed in low-wage manual labor. The 1930 census shows that out of nearly three million Mexican American residents only fifty-four hundred were in clerical positions. During the Depression, the fact that many poor Mexican Americans were on relief led to increasing Anglo hostility toward them. Forced repatriation to Mexico was tried by a number of local welfare agencies. In 1932 more than eleven thousand, citizens and noncitizens, were sent back from Los Angeles communities.[45]

The 1940s saw some improvement in the employment situation, but discriminatory barriers were still severe. One study of San Bernardino, California, found rampant discrimination keeping Mexican Americans in low-wage positions: average annual incomes were $700 to $800. In 1943 President Roosevelt's antidiscrimination order and the tight labor supply finally opened up some jobs at decent wages to Mexican Americans; this development was short-lived. Virtually no qualified workers moved up into skilled or supervisory positions.[46]

Poorly paid jobs meant inferior housing, a situation sharpened by housing discrimination. With the increase in Mexican immigrants came segregated urban ghettos, called *barrios*, which were usually concentrations of deteriorating housing. Restrictive covenants in deeds kept Mexican Americans out of numerous housing areas in the Southwest.[47]

In the 1950s and 1960s many Mexican Americans were in secondary-labor-market positions as farm workers, urban laborers, or service workers. Internal migrant labor streams were important for Mexican Americans (and Mexicans). But the average annual wage for migrant workers in 1956 was only $1,500 in Texas and $2,600 outside of Texas. Even by the late 1960s the average hourly wage for seasonal farm workers was only $1.07 in Texas and $1.50 to $1.70 in the midwestern states. Not only was poverty their lot; several studies found high rates of disabling work injuries among them.[48] Many were living in camps with totally inadequate housing, beds, and sanitation facilities. One author has described the life of a farm worker's family:

> I was never a happy child; in fact I never felt that I was a child since I had to work from an early age.... In 1950 my father, Gustavo, bought a little one shack behind his mother-in-law's house, and here my parents and eight children lived. Dad's economic situation at the time was very bad and since he worked as a farm laborer he was only paid 60 to 70 cents an hour, hardly enough to feed eight kids much less clothe them and provide for medical attention.[49]

Other Mexican Americans worked in industries in southwestern cities. A major problem in the border region has been "runaway" industries, those that have moved from higher-wage areas to this low-wage region to increase profits. Food-processing plants have been a major industry in the Imperial Valley of California, in southern Arizona and New Mexico, and in the Rio Grande Valley. A major garment industry grew up, taking advantage of unemployment in the female labor force. By 1970 there were two thousand manufacturing plants in the border region employing over one hundred thousand people in garment, food-processing, metal-refining, and defense-related industries as well as such local industries as concrete and fertilizers. One study of border cities found that wages were consistently lower on the border than in the interior.[50] Farm wages in Texas and California were lowest in border areas; manufacturing wages were also quite low in Texas border areas.

Many employers in the Sunbelt and the Midwest have sought undocumented workers because they can be exploited more easily than U.S. workers. If they protest oppressive working conditions, an employer can turn them in to the authorities. That threat keeps such Mexican workers more docile than U.S. workers. In the 1970s the *Los Angeles Times* found that 99 percent of employers refused government help in trying to find U.S. workers to replace undocumented Mexican workers who had been caught. The *Times* reporter noted that these employers wanted "workers who can be exploited"—that is, who can be paid less than the minimum wage and who will not *organize.*[51]

## Unemployment, Poverty, and Income

Unemployment rates have been high for decades. In the early 1980s the unemployment rate was still relatively high for Mexican American men—8.5 percent, compared with 5.5 percent for non-Hispanic white men. Rates were similarly high for Mexican American women. Occupational distribution changed slowly between 1960 and 1980. We can obtain a rough idea of this change from data on the Spanish-surname population* in the 1960 census for the five southwestern states and from data on the Mexican-origin population in special surveys in 1970 and 1979.[52]

|  | Mexican American Men | | | Mexican American Women | | |
|---|---|---|---|---|---|---|
|  | 1960 | 1970 | 1979 | 1960 | 1970 | 1979 |
| Professional, technical | 4.1% | 5.3% | 5.5% | 5.9% | 6.4% | 6.4% |
| Managerial, administrative | 4.6 | 4.0 | 6.0 | 2.7 | 1.9 | 3.5 |
| Sales workers | 3.6 | 3.2 | 1.9 | 8.1 | 5.7 | 5.1 |
| Clerical workers | 4.8 | 5.8 | 6.0 | 21.8 | 26.0 | 31.1 |
| Craftworkers | 16.7 | 21.0 | 21.5 | 1.3 | 2.3 | 1.8 |
| Operatives | 24.1 | 27.1 | 26.3 | 26.6 | 26.0 | 25.0 |
| Nonfarm laborers | 15.2 | 13.0 | 13.6 | 1.2 | 1.7 | 1.3 |
| Farm owners, workers | 19.1 | 9.8 | 6.2 | 4.3 | 4.0 | 2.4 |
| Service workers | 7.7 | 11.0 | 12.9 | 28.0 | 26.0 | 23.4 |

Mexican American males were concentrated at the lower job levels, with a majority in the operative, laborer, farmworker, and service worker categories. Women were located primarily in the service, operative, and clerical categories.

In the subsequent 1980 census the occupational statistics for Mexican American men and women taken together showed 6.6 percent in professional and technical positions, compared with 15.4 percent of the population as a whole. The proportion in managerial and administrative positions was 4.7, again much smaller than the 10.4 percent of the U.S. population in such employment. The percentage of Mexican Americans in clerical and sales jobs was 19.9 percent, smaller than the 27.3 percent of the working population in that category. About 31 percent of Mexican American workers were in white-collar jobs, compared with about half of all United States workers, and the percentage in blue-collar categories was larger than that in the total population. Among Mexican Americans 45.6 percent were employed in craft, operative, and laborer jobs, compared with just under one third of the general population. About 16 percent were in service jobs, including domestic work—a little more than the proportion among all workers. And only 7 percent were in farm-related jobs. This last statistic indicates that most Mexican Americans are now living and working in urban areas.[53]

By 1970, Mexican American incomes were still relatively low compared with those of Anglos. At least one-quarter of all Mexican American families fell below the

*In U.S. Census tabulations the category *Spanish surname persons* is predominantly Mexican American.

poverty line in that year. The median family income for Mexican-origin families was $6,972 in 1970, compared with the higher figure for all families of $9,600. In the late 1970s and early 1980s the picture had changed little. In 1980 the median income for Mexican American families was $14,765, about three-quarters of the national figure for all families—$19,917. Additionally, Mexican American families have a large number of workers, which translates into per capita incomes that are much lower than those of Anglo families.[54]

## POLITICS

Mexican American involvement in politics has traditionally been limited by discrimination. Before 1910 some Mexican Americans did hold office in territorial and state legislatures; usually hand-picked by Anglos, they served in the governments of California, Colorado, and New Mexico. There were no political organizations for Mexicans immigrating after 1900, as there were in northern cities to facilitate the mobility of immigrants.[55]

Railroads, mining interests, ranchers, land companies—a few European American groups have dominated local and state politics in the Southwest. Until recently, these interests made sure that Mexican American voting strength was kept low. While there has been considerable variation in discrimination from state to state, a number of devices have been used to reduce voting, including the poll tax, the white primary, and threats of violence. Between the 1910s and the 1940s few Mexican Americans voted, because of discrimination or fear.[56]

### Representation

World War II brought hundreds of thousands out of the barrios of the Southwest into wartime industries or into the armed forces. With this movement came an uphill fight to expand political participation. Numerous examples of slowly expanding, sometimes regressing, participation could be seen in the counties and cities of the Southwest from the late 1940s onward. For example, the Los Angeles City Council finally saw its first Mexican American representative in 1949, but between the early 1960s and the early 1970s there were no Mexican Americans on the council.

By the 1960s Chicanos had moved up significantly from their former position of no representation on school boards: among the 4,600 board members in the Southwest there were 470 Mexican Americans. The number of state legislators with Spanish surnames increased from 20 in 1950 to 67 in 1973. By the late 1980s there were 90 Mexican Americans (123 Hispanics) in state legislatures. And there were significant increases in the number of Mexican Americans and other Hispanics serving at all political levels. For example, in Texas the number of all Hispanic officials increased from 862 in the early 1970s to 1,572 in 1987. However, there were no Mexican American governors as of 1988.

In spite of recent gains the percentage of *all* officials who are Mexican American remains low. In 1968 there were three Mexican Americans in the U.S. House of Representatives, one from California and two from Texas, and one U.S. senator from New Mexico; by 1972 there were only four representatives and one senator. By 1982 there were again only four Mexican Americans in Congress. Between 1982 and 1988 there were some gains in the House: the number of Mexican American representatives increased from four to ten. But there were no senators, as of the late 1980s.[57]

Expanded voting strength was brought about by legal victories in the form of the Twenty-fourth Amendment, which banned the poll tax, and a California court case knocking down an English-only literacy requirement for voting. Expanded voting strength was also the result of the substantial growth in the Hispanic population. In Texas, for example, the Mexican American population grew five times faster than the rest of the population during the 1980s, and the number registered to vote doubled between 1976 and 1986.[58]

## Presidential Voting

At the presidential level, Mexican American voting has traditionally been Democratic. In 1960 Kennedy won an estimated 85 percent of Mexican American votes, which was more than enough to make the difference in New Mexico and Texas. In 1964 Johnson got 90 percent, and in 1968 Humphrey got 87 percent. Hispanics stayed with the Democratic party in 1972, and the 1976 and 1980 elections again saw a substantial Democratic majority among these voters.

In the early 1980s there were 3.2 million Hispanic citizens of voting age in Texas and California, most Mexican American. Most of these voters remained in the Democratic party. In 1980 they voted overwhelmingly for Jimmy Carter and in the 1982 gubernatorial elections in California and Texas 70 to 80 percent of Hispanic voters supported the Democratic candidates. In the 1984 election 75 percent of the Hispanic voters in Texas supported Walter Mondale over Ronald Reagan, and in 1986 79 percent voted for the Democratic candidate for governor of Texas. In 1986 Hispanic voters in California gave two-thirds of their votes to the Democratic candidate for governor—the black mayor of Los Angeles, Tom Bradley—and three-quarters of their votes to the Democratic candidate for senator. In the 1987–1988 national political campaigns Hispanic voters were aggressively courted by Democratic candidates (among whom there were no Hispanics).[59]

## The Courts

Progress in the judicial branch has come slowly; underrepresentation has been common. The first Mexican American federal judge was appointed in the 1960. A 1969 study found that only two of the fifty-nine federal district judges in the five southwestern states, and only 3 percent of the nearly one thousand state judges, had Spanish surnames. An examination of district attorneys and public prosecutors (and assistants) in twenty-two southwest cities found that only 3 percent were Spanish-surnamed. These numbers improved in the 1970s and 1980s, albeit very slowly. Many Hispanic applicants have historically been found unqualified for police positions by the indirect discrimination of height and weight requirements and English-language requirements, as well as by poor scores on conventional qualifying examinations. Moreover, few Mexican Americans have served at the higher levels of the U.S. Department of Justice or other federal law-enforcement agencies.[60]

Given this underrepresentation, it is not surprising that discrimination in the criminal justice system has been documented. Arizona, California, and Colorado have required jurors to be able to speak English, screening out many Spanish-speaking citizens; the pool of jurors in numerous states has until recently been selected by whatever method has suited (usually Anglo) jury commissioner. Mexican Americans charged with crimes have historically been judged by juries containing few of their peers. There is a language problem for some Mexican American defendants in courtrooms where no one, including judges, understands Spanish. Other harmful practices have included excessive bail, the poor quality of legal counsel, the absence of Spanish interpreters in courtrooms, and the negative views of judges toward Mexican American defendants.[61]

## Local Chicano Politics

Lack of influence in mainstream politics led some Mexican Americans to join the more radical La Raza Unida party for a time in the 1960s and 1970s. This party was successful in some Texas towns. Mexican Americans won major political victories in Crystal City, Texas. A city of 10,000 people with a predominantly poor, Mexican American population, Crystal City lies in Zavala County in the profitable Winter Garden area in south Texas. A cannery came to the area in the 1940s, followed in the mid-1950s by the Teamsters' Union. The union gave Mexican American workers job security and some political resources for electoral campaigns. Five Mexican Americans won city council positions in 1963, displacing the establishment. Economic reprisals were taken against the Chicanos, and Anglos regained control of the council in the late 1960s. A massive school boycott in 1969 expressed the discontent of the predominantly Mexican student body in a school system not controlled by Mexican Americans. The new La Raza Unida party became a leading political force in the area. In 1970 Mexican Americans won three of seven school board positions and two of five city council positions. With one already in each body, the Mexican Americans gained political control. Victories were also recorded in nearby towns.[62]

Changes came in the Crystal City schools with the hiring of more Mexican American teachers, teacher aides, and administrators. Bilingual programs were started, and curriculum changes included attention to Mexican American history. Mexican Americans were hired or promoted at all levels of the city bureaucracy, including the police department. Millions of dollars in new federal aid poured in, and important programs were started in health, housing, and urban renewal.[63]

The impact on the Anglo population of Crystal City was far-reaching. Out of power for the first time, they counterattacked. Some Mexican Americans lost their jobs. Anglo parents reacted by withdrawing their children from school; teachers resigned, complaining of discrimination and a redirection of school activities toward Mexican American goals. Financial resources were limited because of a boycott on school taxes. State agencies pressured the school district.

With political experience and activity came divisions within the Mexican American community; tensions in leadership developed. Some of the Mexican American officials were replaced by Anglos in the late 1970s and early 1980s. And some of the militants left the community or moved into the Democratic party. By the 1980s Mexican Americans were identified no longer with the militant La Raza Unida party, but rather with the state Democratic party.[64]

One other local political victory came in San Antonio, whose politics had long been controlled by the Anglo business elite. In 1981 Henry Cisneros was elected mayor there, the first Mexican American mayor of a large American metropolitan area. His victory was the culmination of ten years of organization. In 1977 neighborhood organizers working through Communities Organized for Public Service (COPS), an activist neighborhood organization, and other Mexican American organizations got out the Mexican American vote for a referendum on single-member districts. With this support the referendum passed. A few months later the citizenry elected a city council with a majority of Mexican American and black representatives.[65]

## Organizations and Protest

Protests have a long history among Mexican Americans. Union organization came early. Several organizations of workers came and went between 1900 and 1927, but the first permanent organization was the Confederacion de Uniones Obreras Mexicanas (CUOM), organized in California in 1927 with three thousand members. A 1928 strike by the CUOM was killed by deportation and arrests. Coal miners, farm workers, and factory workers struck in New Mexico, Arizona, and Texas in the 1930s, when Mexican Americans were beginning to make their way into mainstream unions. In the International Ladies Garment Workers Union they participated in strikes. During this period police force was used to break up union meetings and strikes.[66]

Mutual-benefit associations developed early among Mexican Americans. These included worker alliances aimed at pooling resources and providing contexts for social interaction, as well as religious brotherhoods. By the 1920s a number of Mexican American newspapers were being published. The League of United Latin American Citizens (LULAC) was organized in southern Texas in the 1920s and pressed for a better deal for Mexican Americans. Originally oriented toward civic activities, LULAC refused to call itself a protest association. However, since the 1960s LULAC has worked to break down segregation and discrimination on many fronts.[67]

A number of post–World War II organizations reflected growing militancy. After a Mexican American soldier was barred from a Texas cemetery, the American G.I. Forum was established to organize Chicano veterans and to work for expanded civil rights. In Los Angeles the Community Service Organization worked to organize voting strength. Two groups formed about 1960—the Mexican American Political Association, a California organization, and the Political Association of Spanish-Speaking Organizations, a Texas organization—focused more explicitly on political goals. Mexican American protest intensified in the 1960s, reflecting growing political consciousness. "Corky" Gonzales and his associates worked in Denver in support of school strikes and against police brutality. New youth organizations were formed throughout the Southwest, including the Mexican American Youth Organization and the Brown Berets, a militant organization that set forth a program of better education, employment, and housing. A new ideology of *Chicanismo* was developed, espousing a philosophy of decolonization.[68]

Among the most militant protests were those led by Reies Lopez Tijerina. The organization Alianza Federal de Mercedes was created in 1963 by Tijerina after he had spent a number of years researching the old Mexican land grants in the Southwest. In July 1966 a group of Alianza members marched to Santa Fe and presented a statement of land-grant grievances. Another group camped out without a permit on Kit Carson National Forest land, once part of a communal land grant. Forest rangers who tried to stop them were seized and tried for violating the old land-grant boundaries. Tijerina and some others were arrested for this civil disobedience.

In 1967 a local district attorney broke up an Alianza meeting in a small town in New Mexico. News broadcasts were made asking Mexican Americans not to attend, and motorists were stopped by the police and given a notice that alleged the meeting was illegal. Some leaders of the Alianza were arrested and taken to the Tierra Amarilla courthouse. Armed Mexican Americans went to the courthouse to make a citizen's arrest of the district attorney for his actions. A shootout ensued, with some officials wounded. Tijerina was arrested as a result of the Tierra Amarilla raid, but was acquitted.[69]

In the 1980s voter registration became a focus of organization. An important political organization that worked to this end was the Southwest Voter Registration Education Project, located in San Antonio and Los Angeles, and until 1988 was headed by Willie Velasquez, a former activist in the La Raza Unida movement. This organization has participated in eight hundred voter registration campaigns and has joined the Texas Rural Legal Aid organization to file lawsuits seeking to dismantle discriminatory election systems and thereby expand the impact of Hispanic voters.

## Unions for Poor Workers

Developments in unionization took place in the 1960s—the creation of the Agricultural Workers Organizing Committee (AWOC) and Cesar Chavez's National Farm Workers Association (NFWA). By 1964 the NFWA had a thousand members and its own credit union. In 1965 the first big strike came. Workers in AWOC struck the Delano, California, growers; the NFWA met in Delano and voted to go on strike too, demanding hourly wages of $1.40. Growers refused to talk; picket lines went up; guns were fired at pickers; police harassment was a problem. Chavez kept his movement nonviolent in the face of provocation. A grape boycott was also started in 1965 and gradually spread across the country. Picket lines went up wherever the grapes went. There was a massive march on Sacramento. In 1966 AWOC and the NFWA merged into the United Farm Workers Organizing Committee.[70]

Unionization was more difficult in south Texas. The attempt by the United Farm Workers to organize in the Rio Grande Valley in the 1960s and 1970s moved slowly because of imprisonment of strikers and leaders and the intervention of the hated Texas Rangers. Attempts by the Meat Cutters Union to organize Mexican Americans in south Texas did result in some union victories, but much suffering was the price.[71]

In 1973 the largest winery in the United States, Gallo Brothers, chose not to renew its contract with the United Farm Workers and signed with the more conservative Teamsters. Other wineries followed suit. A number of newspaper and magazine articles argued that Chavez and his union were dying. Yet the struggle continued. Governor Jerry Brown of California worked for legislation to protect farm workers, and a labor board was established to run secret-ballot elections, with protection for union activities.[72]

As Jenkins points out in his recent analysis of the United Farm Workers, this was the first successful farm workers' union in U.S. history, one that permanently altered the structure of power in rural California; "it did so by building a permanent membership organization that used the power of organized numbers as a basis for economic and political change." In the late 1980s the charismatic Cesar Chavez was still the leader of the UFW, which was expanding its efforts to the issue of the pesticide spraying of farm products. A nationwide campaign was begun to force large farmers to "stop poisoning workers and consumers," to quote campaign literature. The campaign emphasized studies indicating that many farm workers have chronic skin rashes and liver abnormalities and that much produce in supermarkets has pesticide residues. The union organized a new boycott of table grapes to persuade growers to stop using the most dangerous cancer-causing pesticides and to accept expanded collective bargaining for farm workers.[73]

## EDUCATION

In the first three decades of the twentieth century little attention was given to the education of Mexican Americans. The agricultural economy of the Southwest pressed for cheap labor without the expense of education. Schooling for laborers was minimal—only what was needed for them to learn a little arithmetic and English.[74]

School segregation has been different for Mexican Americans than for black Americans. As a rule, Mexican Americans were segregated not by state law but either by local laws or by informal gerrymandering of school district lines. Discrimination in housing reinforced school segregation. Prior to World War II children were segregated in schools from Texas to California.[75]

### The Problems Persist

A major conference in Texas in 1946 called for an end to segregation, the adoption of a Mexican-oriented curriculum, better teacher training, and better school facilities. Conferences three decades later were reiterating these needs. A few court decisions in the late 1940s began to outlaw segregation. Yet these court decisions did not change the patterns of segregation. In 1970 approximately 17 percent of the children in southwestern schools were Mexican Americans; most lived in California and Texas. Nearly half of these students attended 1,500 predominantly Mexican American elementary and secondary schools. Pupil segregation is only one type of discrimination; underrepresentation among personnel is another. One study found that only 4 percent of the

325,000 teachers in the public schools in the Southwest were Mexican American, only 3 percent of the 12,000 school principals, and 6 percent of the 9,500 nonteaching professionals (such as counselors). Mexican Americans constituted only a small percentage of the 58 members of state boards of education in the five southwestern states.[76]

By the 1980s the proportion of Mexican American children in many of the schools of the Southwest had increased significantly; defacto school segregation was still the rule, largely because of segregated housing patterns. In 1988 most students were still in predominantly minority schools. There were modest increases in the proportions of Mexican Americans among teachers and administrators, but in the late 1980s most school systems still did not have representative numbers of them. In addition, many of the more than one thousand predominantly Mexican American schools had inferior educational resources.

Traditionally, schools with high percentages of Mexican American students were rigid in prohibiting manifestations of Mexican subculture. Schools enforced dress and hair codes on Mexican American students. Teachers anglicized the names of children (for instance, Roberto becomes "Bobby"), downgrading the heritage of the children. School curricula neglected Mexican and Mexican American history.[77]

In Texas and California Mexican American children were overrepresented in classes for the mentally retarded. Most Mexican Americans in these classes were "six-hour" retarded children—capable of functioning in the outside world yet pigeonholed as mentally retarded in schools because of testing procedures, usually conducted in English. A 1970s study in Riverside, California, found that all of the Anglo children in mentally retarded classes showed behavior abnormality, versus less than half of the Mexican American children. Indirect discrimination in the testing procedures was the major reason for this mislabeling.[78]

Although certain discriminatory practices, such as placement in classes for the "mentally retarded," had been eliminated from most schools by the 1980s, vestiges of bias and discrimination remained. Into the late 1980s schools were still placing too many Mexican children in learning-disabled classes, and textbooks were still neglecting Mexican American history. One other persisting problem is the treatment of Mexican American children by Anglo teachers in the classroom. Interaction between students and teachers affects the performance of Mexican Americans. One study of teacher behavior in classrooms found that the average teacher praised Anglo children 35 percent more often than Mexican Americans, questioned them 20 percent more often, and used their ideas 40 percent more often. Teacher practices have been shown to have a strong relationship to student achievement.[79]

## Current Issues: Bilinguilism and Achievement

As recently as 1973, no southwestern state had taken more than token steps in bilingual education. Bilingual programs use children's knowledge of cultural background to link them positively to the learning environment. The 1968 Elementary and Secondary Education Act passed by Congress set up a mechanism for the federal government to fund bilingual programs. Even so, only 5 percent of the Mexican American children in the Southwest were being affected by federally funded bilingual programs in the 1972–1973 school year.

More teeth were put into federal requirements by a 1974 Supreme Court decision (*Lau v. Nichols*), which ruled that school systems could not ignore the English-language problems of national-origin minority groups. The Department of Health, Education and Welfare set up a task force to lay out specific bilingual programs in line with that decision. The Lau Remedies, as they came to be called, were debated into the 1980s. One federal study found that most school systems had few qualified bilingual teachers and had difficulty in accurately assessing the English-language needs of language minority students. The first tentative steps toward adequate bilingual education for Hispanics have been taken. But apart from a few stellar programs in schools with sensitive principals in scattered public school systems, the overall picture of bilingual education is one of snail-like progress. In addition, the passing of English-as-the-official-language laws in a number of states may ultimately pose a serious threat to bilingual education laws and programs.[80]

Median education levels for Mexican Americans increased between 1950 and 1980, but they fell behind Anglo figures. In 1950 the median schooling for adults was 5.4 years. By 1976 the figure had increased to 9 years, decreasing but not closing the gap with the national median. The 1980 census reported the figure to be 9.6 years, much lower than the national median of 12.5 years. Only 37.6 percent of Mexican Americans were high school graduates.[81]

In the 1970s and 1980s a debate has raged over the obligation of school systems to educate the children of undocumented Mexican aliens. State officials in southwestern states have complained that educating these children is a burden on U.S. citizens. State officials publicly exaggerate the number of such children in their schools for political reasons. In Texas a court case arose out of officials' attempts to charge the children of undocumented aliens a special fee to attend school. After an extended struggle in the lower courts, the Supreme Court ruled in 1982 that *all* children had to be provided with schooling and that children could not be discriminated against on the basis of parental condition, such as immigrant status.[82]

## RELIGION

Mexican immigrants to Texas were not accompanied by Catholic priests; nor were the Catholic church and its dogma major factors in the lives of migrants. What has been termed *folk Catholicism*, a blend of Catholicism and certain non-Catholic (native) beliefs, values, and rituals, did play an important role.[83]

Many immigrants were hostile to the established church in Mexico, and most were not ready for a U.S. Catholic church dominated by the Irish. In the first decades little was done for the religious schooling of Mexican Catholics; as late as the 1930s there were only seventy parochial schools in the major dioceses of southern California, where there were several hundred thousand Catholics. Little was done by the church before the 1940s to aid a population troubled by poverty and discrimination.[84]

In the 1950s and 1960s some priests took an active role in union activities. In the 1960s, War on Poverty programs were sometimes operated in connection with church projects, and a number of "lay protest" and "priest protest" groups were formed to deal with urban problems. Yet in some areas priests have been forbidden to aid protesting Mexican Americans. The Los Angeles cardinal refused to provide priests for the Delano farm workers on strike in the 1960s. Moreover, there has traditionally been a pattern of discrimination against Mexican Americans in the hierarchy of the Catholic church. Very few Mexicans had penetrated positions of responsibility prior to the 1960s; the first Mexican American bishop was designated, in San Antonio, in the 1970s.[85]

The Catholicism of most Mexican Americans has been described as being similar to that of Italians, with a general allegiance to the church and little active participation except by women and children. Tuck found that most Mexican Americans in San Bernardino, California, in the 1940s were baptized, married, and buried with a priest in attendance, but participated infrequently in church activities. The power of priests was found to be influential in affecting attitudes on such issues as venereal disease campaigns and unionization. In recent years, however, this influence of the church on secular issues has appeared to be on the wane; rejection of the church position on abortion and birth control has been extensive.[86]

## ASSIMILATION OR COLONIALISM?

An assimilation perspective has been explicit or implicit in the prominent studies of researchers such as Tuck, Sanchez, Madsen, and Grebler. A pivotal idea is that Mexican Americans will move up the mobility ladder just as the European ethnics did, and thus will proceed surely, if a bit more slowly, into the mainstream at all assimilation levels.[87]

An assimilationist looking at Mexican American history might emphasize that only a hundred thousand Mexicans were brought into the United States as a result of military conquest. Most immigrants came later. Most were able to improve their economic circumstances relative to their condition in Mexico. Aspects of Mexican traditional culture began disappearing as acculturation proceeded.

For the first generation of Mexican Americans, the impact of cultural assimilation came mainly in adjustment in language and agricultural values. Religion and basic values were less affected; respect for Mexico remained strong. For later generations there was increased structural assimilation in the economy and considerable cultural adaptation. The traditional view of the Mexican American family depicts a large extended, patriarchal family; this is perhaps most accurate as a description of family patterns in agricultural towns in earlier decades. Urbanization and increased incomes opened up the possibility of separate residences for nuclear families and a decline in the number of extended families. Fertility trends and values became similar to those of other Americans.[89]

From the traditional life of rural villages to the faster-paced life of the urban barrios there has been substantial cultural persistence. Most notable has been language,
which has persisted as a primary language or as part of a bilingual pattern. Closeness
to Mexico has been given as an important reason for the persistence of the language.
Surveys in Los Angeles and San Antonio found that most Mexican Americans wished
their children to retain ties to their Mexican culture, particularly to language, customs,
and religion. A survey of Mexican Americans found that most are bilingual to some
extent, but one-third have little fluency in English. Three-quarters said that Spanish
was a very important aspect of culture to maintain. Most favored bilingual teaching
in public schools. Mexican American parents want their children to know their cultural heritage.[90]

But one should not exaggerate structural assimilation. Even for second and third
generations structural assimilation at the economic level has come slowly; discrimination and the resultant concentration of workers at the lower wage levels persists.
Problematical too has been participation in political institutions, although recent
progress can be seen.

Gordon's dimensions of behavior-receptional assimilation and attitude-receptional assimilation have varied considerably within the Mexican-American group and
over time. Widespread prejudice and severe discrimination faced the Mexicans who
were conquered in the expansion of the United States, as well as the immigrants since
1900. As time passed, some lighter-skinned Mexican Americans in larger cities were
treated with less prejudice and discrimination. Darker-skinned persons have often
been treated just as black Americans have. Today considerable prejudice and discrimination are still directed against Mexican Americans.

## The Limits of Assimilation

Structural absorption at the primary-group level and marital assimilation have not yet
reached the point where one can speak of moderate-to high assimilation for Mexican
Americans as a group. Some increases in interethnic friendship contacts have been
found in recent studies, particularly for children in desegregated environments, although most still have predominantly Mexican American friends. One study found
that less than 5 percent of Mexican respondents in San Antonio had predominantly
Anglo friends; the proportion in Los Angeles was about 15 percent. The majority of
the adult population still seems enmeshed in predominantly Mexican American
primary relations, but the data on children suggest some primary-level assimilation is
under way, at least in desegregated urban areas.[91]

Data on intermarriage indicate that a majority of marriages are still within the
Mexican American group. In San Antonio the proportion of Spanish-surname individuals marrying outside the group went from 10 percent in the 1940–1955 period
to 14 percent in 1964 and to 16 percent in 1973—a slow increase. Studies have found
that in Los Angeles the proportion of individuals marrying outside the group increased
from 9 percent in the period 1924–1933 to 25 percent in 1960–1961. Studies in Texas
and New Mexico have found that in recent years the proportion of Mexican Americans
marrying outside the group has stabilized from 5 to 24 percent. The one exception to

these relatively low outmarriage rates appears in a study for all California counties, which found outmarriage rates to be between 34 and 36 percent for the 1970s. But in that study the outmarriage rates seemed to be stabilizing.[92]

Some conservative assimilation analysts, such as Nathan Glazer, have questioned the extent of Mexican Americans' identification with things Mexican. For example, Glazer has characterized the militant Chicano movement of the 1960s and 1970s as "one of extreme views espoused by a minority for a short period." This view overlooks the fact that the majority of younger Mexican Americans supported the Chicano movement, even if they did not actively participate in its activities, and that many in the older generation—that is, the *families* of the young activists—were quietly supportive. In addition, the perspectives and actions of the Chicano activists, and of activists in the 1980s, reflect themes of militancy rooted deeply in their Mexican cultural heritage. One such theme is the negative appraisal of Anglo police, including the Texas Rangers, in the old Mexican ballads sung on both sides of the border.[93]

Connor has argued that the diversity of ethnic labels used by persons with ties to Mexico—designations such as *Hispano, Chicano, Mexican, Mexican American, Latino, Spanish,*and *Hispanic*—indicate a significant ethnic diversity within this community.[94] Many whose ancestry dates back before the U.S. conquest of northern Mexico seem to prefer terms such as *Spanish*. But other scholars emphasize that pressures brought by outside oppression forced many, particularly in earlier decades, to hide their Mexican origin under the euphemisms of "Spanish" or "Latin" Americans; this is not necessarily a sign of identificational assimilation. Middle-income Mexican Americans in the 1920s began to use such terms to hide from prejudice. In recent years there has been a shift back to Mexican and *Mexican American*. In one survey in Los Angeles the preference of respondents was for *Mexican or Mexican American*, while in San Antonio the majority preferred *Latin American*. Few in either city wanted to be called just *American*. In a survey of households in the Southwest and Midwest, most respondents preferred to be called *Mexican American, Mexican*, or *Chicano*. Pride in Mexican identity remains strong.[95]

Edward Múrguía has argued that the Anglo-Saxon Protestant core society is presently allowing substantial portions of Mexican Americans to assimilate on a more or less equal-status basis. Yet in his view assimilation cannot go as far as it has for other Catholics, such as the Irish. The differences are narrowing, but the processes will stop short of complete absorption. Mexican Americans might conceivably gain near parity at the secondary–structural level—in the economy and politics—although considerable separation would remain at the primary-group level and major cultural differences would persist. Something less than this pluralism is the probable future.[96]

## Applying a Power-Conflict Perspective

Power-conflict analysts would not agree with much in the assimilationist analysis. They would accent the extent to which Mexican Americans have *not* moved toward incorporation in the core society. The best that assimilation analysts can argue is that the trend is toward assimilation, for substantial economic and political assimilation is not a reality for the majority of Mexican Americans.

Internal colonialism analysts accent Mexican American history, particularly its origin in the ruthless conquest of northern Mexico in the 1836–1853 period. The situation for the early Mexican, whose land and person were brought into the United States by force, is one of classical colonialism. Acuña has underscored the parallels between the Mexican American experience and that of the external colonization of other Third World populations: land is taken by military force, the native population is subjugated economically and politically, the native culture is suppressed, and a small native elite is favored in order to maintain the subjugation.[97]

One problem in applying the colonialism perspective to Mexican Americans is that most entered as immigrants after the conquest. Such immigration seems similar to that of European immigrants. Colonialism analysts reply by indicating the differences between this migration and European migration. Unlike Europeans, Mexican migrants did not come into a new environment. People of their background were already here. Socially and culturally, they moved *within* one geographical area, all of which was originally controlled by Mexicans. Moreover, little time was required to move back and forth across the border—in sharp contrast with the time of travel required of European immigrants.[98]

But perhaps the most significant difference was that the heritage of the (external) colonial situation, with its practices of subordination, was inherent in the situation of the immigrants. "The colonial pattern of Anglo domination over the Mexican people was set by 1848 and carried over to those Mexicans who came later to the Southwest, a land contiguous to Mexico and once a part of it."[99] Later subordination by force took the form of deportation and Border Patrol searches.

Later Mexican immigrants were channeled into an environment in which low wages, absentee landlords, inferior schools, and discrimination severely limited their progress and mobility. For many decades residential segregation has reflected discrimination. Mexican Americans are not like European immigrant groups, whose level of segregation has declined significantly with length of residence in the United States. Discrimination in employment and housing persists, even if it is more subtle today.

In Chapter 2 we discussed the book *Race and Class in the Southwest* by Mario Barrera, who analyzes Mexican Americans using a modified internal colonialism model that emphasizes racism and capitalism as factors in inequality. Barrera argues that each of the major classes of capitalism, such as the capitalist class and the working class, contains important segments that are distinguished by characteristics such as race and ethnicity. Each of the major classes contains a racial–ethnic line that separates those suffering institutionalized discrimination, such as Mexican Americans, from those Anglo Americans who do not. Take the example of the working class. While Mexican American workers share a similar *class* position with white workers in that both are struggling against capitalist employers for better wages and working conditions, they are in a subordinate economic position because of structural discrimination along racial and ethnic lines. The dimensions of this discrimination include lower wages for the same or similar work, concentration in certain lower-status occupations, and use as a reserve labor force.[100]

Capitalist employers have created a split labor market from which they as employers have profited greatly; they have focused the attention of Anglo workers on

Hispanics (and blacks) as the threat to Anglo workers. Given the segmentation of the labor force by employers, it is not surprising that Anglo workers try to solidify their positions and keep minority workers out of the privileged job categories reserved for themselves. This is a type of internal colonialism.

Flores has underscored the cultural and psychodynamic aspects of the Mexican American situation. The Mexican American group has been subordinated much more than white immigrant groups. Psychological as well as economic benefits have accrued to the Anglo oppressors. The acculturation of Mexican American children and adults has involved pressure and coercion, as in the public schools. Racial stereotyping of Mexicans has played a major role in establishing and preserving the racial hierarchy of the Southwest. Theories of biological inferiority were introduced to justify taking land and exploiting Mexican American labor. This subordination benefits most Anglos.

> [It] is a complex cultural system of racial and cultural domination which *produces* privileges above and beyond the surplus value generated solely by capitalism—privileges from which all members of the dominant social groups (despite their class) derive benefit directly or indirectly.[101]

Consequently, power–conflict analysts see the real hope for decreased oppression and an improved economic, political, and cultural situation in decolonization movements—the Mexican American protest movements of the past and present.

Moreover, a distinctive aspect of Mexican American communities today is the infusion of undocumented workers. Particularly in the Southwest, this now variable undocumented immigration provides renewal of ties to Mexico and reinforcement of Mexican culture, including the Spanish language and Catholicism. These immigrants provide much cheap labor for the Southwest's Anglo-dominated corporations, farms, and ranches. And their presence has become the center of controversy over U.S. immigration laws and policies. This influx of immigrants creates serious problems for the assimilation perspective on Mexican Americans, because the close ties to the traditional culture—the closest for any immigrant group in U.S. history—significantly slow cultural assimilation.

## SUMMARY

Mexican Americans have an ancient ancestry, predominantly Native American but with a Spanish infusion. Their cultural background is part Native American but heavily Spanish in language, religion, and customs. With the British American conquest, Mexicans became part of the complex mosaic of race and ethnic peoples in the United States. They have suffered racial stereotyping similar to that of other groups of non-European ancestry. Racially motivated discrimination in economics, education, and politics has been part of their lot from the beginning.

In the literature on race and ethnic relations it has been common to compare the situations of black Americans and Mexican Americans, groups considered the largest subordinated minorities in the United States. Both groups face declining prejudice but continuing discrimination and inequality. The apparent decline in white traditional prejudice against blacks has probably paralleled a decline in negative attitudes toward Mexican Americans. But substantial and similar discrimination continues to confront both groups in the last third of the twentieth century, although lighter-skinned, middle-income Mexican Americans probably face less discrimination than middle-income blacks.

At the attitudinal level, blacks and Mexican Americans are often sympathetic to each other's problems. One study of Mexican American attitudes in Texas found more positive feelings toward blacks than were found among Anglos, more sensitivity to discriminatory barriers, and more support for civil rights protest. Differences between blacks and browns appeared in the area of protest strategies. The researchers found that blacks were significantly more militant than Mexican Americans on selected issues, more dissatisfied with civil rights progress, and more approving of civil rights demonstrations.[102] This difference has made it difficult for the two groups to work together against the dominant groups. In some situations the two groups even find themselves competing for limited benefits granted by established groups. Nonetheless, in recent years there have been several attempts to build black–brown coalitions, including the Rainbow Coalition lead by Jesse Jackson.

## NOTES

1. Edward H. Spicer, *Cycle of Conquest* (Tucson: University of Arizona Press, 1962), pp. 4–7; Carey McWilliams, *North from Mexico* (New York: Greenwood Press, 1968), pp. 32–34; Tomas Almaguer, "Historical Notes on Chicano Oppression: The Dialectics of Racial and Class Domination in North America," *Atzlán* 5 (Spring–Fall 1974): 30–33.

2. Spicer, *Cycle of Conquest*, pp. 4–5; McWilliams, *North from Mexico*, pp. 21–31.

3. Américo Paredes, *With His Pistol in His Hand* (Austin: University of Texas Press, 1958), pp. 3–14; Roldolfo Acuña, *Occupied America* (San Francisco: Canfield Press, 1972), pp. 10–12.

4. Acuña, *Occupied America*, p. 15; S. Dale McLemore, "The Origin of Mexican American Subordination in Texas," *Social Science Quarterly* 53 (March 1973): 665–67; Rodolfo Alvarez, "The Psycho-historical and Socioeconomic Development of the Chicano Community in the United States," *Social Science Quarterly* 53 (March 1973): 925.

5. William Lord, "Myths and Realities of the Alamo," *American West* 5 (May 1968): 20–25.

6. Carl N. Degler, *Out of Our Past* (New York: Harper, 1959), pp. 109–10; Acuña, *Occupied America*, pp. 23–29.

7. Leo Grebler, Joan W. Moore, and Ralph G. Guzman, *The Mexican-American People* (New York: Free Press, 1970), pp. 43–44; Acuña, *Occupied America*, p. 105; Joan W. Moore, "Colonialism: The Case of the Mexican Americans," *Social Problems* 17 (Spring 1970): 468–69.

8. Ellwyn R. Stoddard, *Mexican Americans* (New York: Random House, 1973), pp. 9–13; McWilliams, *North from Mexico*, pp. 70–76; Acuña, *Occupied America*, pp. 60–62; Grebler, Moore, and Guzmán, *The Mexican American People*, pp. 43–44; Nancie L. Gonzales, *The Spanish-Americans of New Mexico* (Albuquerque: University of New Mexico Press, 1967), pp. 204ff.

9. Alvarez, "The Psycho-historical and Socioeconomic Development of the Chicano Community in the United States," p. 925.

10. Oscar J. Martinez, "On the Size of the Chicano Population: New Estimates: 1850–1900," *Aztlán* 6 (Spring 1975): 55–56; U.S. Immigration and Naturalization Service, *1975 Annual Report* (Washington, D.C.: U.S. Government Printing Office, 1975), pp. 62–64; Julian Samora, *Los Mojados: The Wetback Story* (South Bend, Ind.: University of Notre Dame Press, 1971), pp. 7–8.

11.  Leo Grebler, *Mexican Immigration to the United States: The Record and Its Implications* (Los Angeles: UCLA Mexican-American Study Project, 1965), pp. 20–21.

12.  Ibid., pp. 23–24; Manuel Gamio, *Mexican Immigration to the United States* (New York: Dover, 1971), pp. 171–74. Gilberto Cardenas, "United States Immigration Policy toward Mexico: An Historical Perspective," *Chicano Law Review* 2 (Summer 1975): 69–71.

13.  Samora, *Los Mojados*, pp. 48–52.

14.  Cardenas, "United States Immigration Policy toward Mexico," pp. 73–75; Grebler, *Mexican Immigration to the United States*, p. 26.

15.  Samora, *Los Mojados*, pp. 18–19, 24–25, 44–46, 57; Joan Moore, *Mexican Americans*, 2d ed. (Englewood Cliffs, N.J.: Prentice-Hall, 1976), pp. 49–51.

16.  Samora, *Los Mojados*, pp. 80–92; Moore, *Mexican Americans*, pp. 49–51.

17.  Cardenas, "United States Immigration Policy toward Mexico," pp. 84–85; Cheryl Anderson, "Immigration Bill under Attack on Several Fronts," *Austin American-Statesman*, December 12, 1982, p. C1.

18.  Wayne A. Cornelius, "Mexican Migration to the United States," in *Crisis in American Institutions*, ed. J. Skolnick and E. Currie (Boston: Little, Brown, 1982), pp. 154–68; Frank Bean, Allen King, and Jeffrey Passel, "The Number of Illegal Migrants of Mexican Origin in the United States," *Demography* 20 (1983): 99–109.

19.  Charles B. Keeley, "Population and Immigration Policy: State and Federal Roles," in *Mexican American and Central American Population Issues and U.S. Policy*, ed. Frank D. Bean, Jurgen Schmandt, and Sidney Weintraub (Austin, Tex.: Center for Mexican American Studies, 1988).

20.  Notes from Gilberto Cardenas.

21.  Quoted in Philip D. Ortego, "The Chicano Renaissance," in *Introduction to Chicano Studies*, ed. Livie I. Duran and H. Russell Bernard (New York: Macmillan, 1973), p. 337.

22.  Cardenas, "United States Immigration Policy toward Mexico," pp. 70–71.

23.  Quoted in Ralph Guzmán, "The Function of Anglo-American Racism in the Political Development of Chicanos," in *La Causa Politica*, ed. F. Chris Garcia (South Bend, Ind.: University of Notre Dame Press, 1974), p. 22.

24.  McWilliams, *North from Mexico*, p. 213.

25.  William Sheldon, "Educational Research and Statistics: The Intelligence of Mexican-American Children," in *In Their Place*, ed. Lewis H. Carlson and George A. Colburn (New York: John Wiley, 1972), pp. 149–51.

26.  Ozzie G. Simmons, "The Mutual Images and Expectations of Anglo-Americans and Mexican-Americans," in *Introduction to Chicano Studies*, ed. Duran and Bernard, pp. 387–97; Robin M. Williams, *Strangers Next Door* (Englewood Cliffs, N.J.: Prentice-Hall, 1974), pp. 29–80.

27.  Livie I. Duran and H. Russell Bernard, introduction to Part 2 of *Introduction to Chicano Studies*, ed. Duran and Bernard, p. 237. See also Stoddard, *Mexican Americans*, p. 6.

28.  Tomás Martinez, "Advertising and Racism: The Case of the Mexican American," *El Grito* 2 (Summer 1969): 31–13; *Daily Texan*, November 5, 1976. See also Stoddard, *Mexican Americans*, p. 6.

29.  Quoted in Guillermo V. Flores, "Race and Culture in the Internal Colony: Keeping the Chicano in His Place," in "Structures of Dependency," ed. Frank Bonilla and Robert Girling (manuscript, research seminar, Stanford, Calif., 1973).

30.  Quoted in Armondo Morales, *Ando Sangrando* (Fair Lawn, N.J.: R. E. Burdick, 1972), p. 43.

31.  Octavio Ignacio Romano, "The Anthropology and Sociology of the Mexican-Americans," *El Grito* 2 (Fall 1968); 13–19; Oscar Lewis, *Five Families* (New York: John Wiley, 1962); William Madsen, *Mexican Americans of South Texas* (New York: Holt, Rinehart & Winston, 1964).

32.  Romano, "The Anthropology and Sociology of the Mexican Americans"; Stoddard, *Mexican Americans*, pp. 42–44.

33.  Edward E. Telles and Edward Múrguía, "Phenotypic Discrimination and Income Differences among Mexican Americans" (typescript, University of Texas, 1987).

34.  E. J. Hobsbawm, *Primitive Rebels* (New York: W. W. Norton & Co., Inc., 1959), pp. 15–16.

35.  Acuña, *Occupied America*, pp. 48–50; McWilliams, *North from Mexico*, pp. 110–12.

36.  Paredes, *With His Pistol in His Hand*, pp. 27–32; McWilliams, *North from Mexico*, p. 127; Moore, "Colonialism," p. 466; Stoddard, *Mexican Americans*, p. 181.

37. Ralph H. Turner and Lewis M. Killian, *Collective Behavior* (Englewood Cliffs, N.J.: Prentice-Hall, 1957), pp. 125–28; McWilliams, *North from Mexico*, pp. 229–38.

38. Morales, *Ando Sangrando*, pp. 100–108.

39. U.S. Commission on Civil Rights, *Mexican Americans and the Administration of Justice in the Southwest* (Washington, D.C.: U.S. Government Printing Office, 1970), pp. 6–10.

40. Abel G. Rubio, *Stolen Heritage* (Austin, Tex.: Eakin Press, 1986).

41. Clark Knowlton, "Recommendations for the Solution of Land Tenure Problems among the Spanish Americans," in *Chicano: The Evolution of a People*, ed. Renato Rosaldo, Robert A. Calvert, and Gustav L. Seligmann (San Francisco: Rinehart Press, 1973), pp. 334–35; George I. Sanchez, *Forgotten People* (Albuquerque: University of New Mexico Press, 1940), p. 61; Arnoldo Deleón, *The Tejano Community, 1836–1900* (Albuquerque: University of New Mexico Press, 1982), pp. 63–91.

42. Almaguer, "Historical Notes on Chicano Oppression," pp. 38–39; Richard del Castillo, "Myth and Reality: Chicano Economic Mobility in Los Angeles, 1850–1880," *Atzlán* 6 (Summer 1975): 153–54; McWilliams, *North from Mexico*, pp. 127–28.

43. Gamio, *Mexican Immigration to the United States*, pp. 39–40; Charles Wollenberg, "Huelga, 1928 Style: The Imperial Valley Canteloupe Workers' Strike," in *Chicano*, ed. Rosaldo, Calvert, and Seligmann, pp. 185–88.

44. Samora, *Los Mojados*, p. 130; Grebler, Moore, and Guzmán, *The Mexican-American People*, p. 91.

45. McWilliams, *North from Mexico*, pp. 193, 220: Grebler, Moore, and Guzmán, *Mexican-American People*, p. 526.

46. Ruth H. Tuck, *Not with the Fist* (New York: Harcourt, Brace, & World, 1946), pp. 173–83.

47. McWilliams, *North from Mexico*, pp. 217–18; U.S. Commission on Civil Rights, *Mexican American Education Study*, vol. 1, *Ethnic Isolation of Mexican Americans in the Public Schools of the Southwest* (Washington, D.C.: U.S. Government Printing Office, 1970), p. 11.

48. Anne Brunton, "The Chicano Migrants," in *Introduction to Chicano Studies*, ed. Duran and Bernard, pp. 489–92.

49. Jesus Luna, "Luna's Abe Lincoln Story," in *Chicano*, ed. Rosaldo, Calvert, and Selgmann, p. 348.

50. Robert R. Nathan Associates, *Industrial and Employment Potential of the United States–Mexico Border* (Washington, D.C.: U.S. Department of Commerce, Economic Development Administration, 1968), pp. 50–51, 125–29; *Report of the Select Commission on Western Hemisphere Immigration* (Washington, D.C.: U.S. Government Printing Office, 1968), p. 116.

51. The *Los Angeles Times* story is quoted in Mario Barrera, *Race and Class in the Southwest* (Notre Dame, Ind.: University of Notre Dame Press, 1979), p. 124. See also *Report of the Select Commission on Western Hemisphere Immigration*, p. 120.

52. U.S. Department of Health, Education and Welfare, *A Study of Selected Socio-economic Characteristics of Ethnic Minorities Based on the 1970 Census* (Washington, D.C.: U.S. Government Printing Office, 1984), p. 63; U.S. Bureau of the Census, *U.S. Census of Population, 1960: Subject Reports— Persons of Spanish Surname*, PC (2)-1B, p. 38; U.S. Bureau of the Census, "Persons of Spanish Origin in the U.S.: March 1979," in *Current Population Reports*, series P-20, no. 354, pp. 1–10.

53. U.S. Bureau of the Census, *U.S. Census of Population, 1980: General Social and Economic Characteristics*, PC80-1-C1, 1983, p. 166.

54. U.S. Bureau of the Census, *U.S. Census of Population, 1980: General Social and Economic Characteristics*, p. 167. See also Dale McLemore and Harley L. Browning, *A Statistical Profile of the Spanish-Surname Population of Texas* (Austin: University of Texas, Bureau of Business Research, 1964); F. Peñalosa and E. C. McDonagh, "Social Mobility in a Mexican-American Community," *Social Forces* 44 (June 1966): 498–505.

55. Moore, *Mexican Americans*, p. 33.

56. Ibid., p. 142.

57. The data on Hispanic officials in this and the proceeding paragraph come from personal communications with Rodolfo de la Garza and Robert Brischetto.

58. Robert R. Brischetto, "Electoral Empowerment: The Case for Tejanos" (typescript, Southwest Voter Research institute, San Antonio, 1987).

59. Southwest Voter Registration Project, *The Hispanic Electorates* (San Antonio: Hispanic Policy Development Project, 1984), pp. 145–49; Robert R. Brischetto, "Chicano Voting and Views in the 1986 Elections" (typescript, Southwest Voter Research Institute, San Antonio, 1987); see also U.S.

Commission on Civil Rights, *Mexican American Education Study, Ethnic Isolation of Mexican Americans in the Public Schools of the Southwest* (Washington, D.C.: U.S. Government Printing Office, 1971) p. 55.

60. U.S. Commission on Civil Rights, *Mexican Americans and the Administration of Justice in the Southwest*, pp. 79–86.

61. Ibid., pp. 66–69.

62. Michael V. Miller and James D. Preston, "Vertical Ties and the Redistribution of Power in Crystal City," *Social Science Quarterly* 53 (March 1973): 772–82; John S. Shockley, *Chicano Revolt in a Texas Town* (South Bend, Ind.: University of Notre Dame Press, 1974), pp. 28–148.

63. Shockley, *Chicano Revolt in a Texas Town*, pp. 162–77.

64. Armando Gutiérrez and Herbert Hirsch, "The Militant Challenge to the American Ethos: 'Chicanos' and the 'Mexican Americans,'" *Social Science Quarterly* 53 (March 1973): 844–45.

65. Robert R. Brischetto, *The Mexican American Electorate: Political Opinions and Behavior across Cultures in San Antonio*, Occasional Paper No. 5, Southwest Voter Registration Education Project and the Center for Mexican American Studies at the University of Texas (San Antonio and Austin, 1985).

66. McWilliams, *North from Mexico*, pp. 191–93; Grebler, Moore, and Guzmán, *The Mexican-American People*, pp. 91–92.

67. Stoddard, *Mexican Americans*, p. 180; Gamio, *Mexican Immigration to the United States*, pp. 135–38.

68. Grebler, Moore, and Guzmán, *The Mexican-American People*, pp. 543–45; Stoddard, *Mexican Americans*, p. 188; Moore, *Mexican Americans*, p. 152.

69. U.S. Commission on Civil Rights, *Mexican Americans and the Administration of Justice in the Southwest*, pp. 15–17; Rees Lloyd and Peter Montague, "Ford and La Raza: 'They Stole Our Land and Gave Us Powdered Milk,'" in *Introduction to Chicano Studies*, ed. Duran and Bernard, pp. 376–78; Frances L. Swadesh, "The Alianza Movement: Catalyst for Social Change in New Mexico," in *Chicano*, ed. Rosaldo, Calvert, and Seligmann, pp. 270–74.

70. Jacques E. Levy, *Cesar Chavez* (New York: W. W. Norton & Co., 1975), pp. 182–201; Peter Matthiessen, *Sal Si Puedes* (New York: Delta Books, 1969), pp. 59–216; John G. Dunne, *Delano* (New York: Farrar, Straus & Giroux, 1967), pp. 110–67.

71. Shockley, *Chicano Revolt in a Texas Town*, pp. 216–17.

72. Levy, *Cesar Chavez*, pp. 495, 522–35.

73. J. Craig Jenkins, *The Politics of Insurgency* (New York: Columbia University Press, 1985), pp. x–xi.

74. Thomas P. Carter, *Mexican Americans in School* (New York: College Entrance Examination Board, 1970), pp. 204–5.

75. George I. Sánchez, "History, Culture, and Education," in *La Raza*, ed. Julian Samora (South Bend, Ind.: University of Notre Dame Press, 1966), pp. 1–26; Paul Taylor, *An American-Mexican Frontier* (Chapel Hill: University of North Carolina Press, 1934), pp. 196–204.

76. Wilson Little, *Spanish–Speaking Children in Texas* (Austin: University of Texas Press, 1944); Tuck, *Not with the Fist*, pp. 185–87; Carter, *Mexican Americans in School*, p. 71; U.S. Commission on Civil Rights, *Ethnic Isolation of Mexican Americans in the Public Schools of the Southwest*, pp. 21–25, 41–51.

77. Carter, *Mexican Americans in School*, pp. 97–102.

78. Jane Mercer, *Labelling the Mentally Retarded* (Berkeley: University of California Press, 1973), pp. 96–189; U.S. Commission on Civil Rights, *Mexican American Education Study*, vol. 6, *Toward Quality Education for Mexican Americans* (Washington, D.C: U.S. Government Printing Office, 1974), pp. 21–22.

79. Thomas P. Carter, "The Negative Self-concept of Mexican-American Students," *School and Society* 96 (March 30, 1968): 217–20.

80. Manuel Ramirez and Alfredo Castaneda, *Cultural Democracy, Bicognitive Development, and Education* (New York: Academic Press, 1974); U.S. Commission on Civil Rights, *Toward Quality Education for Mexican Americans*, pp. 6–8.

81. *Hispanics and Jobs: Barriers to Progress* (Washington, D.C.: National Commission for Employment Policy, 1982), pp. 60–62, 81–82; U.S. Bureau of the Census, *U.S. Census of Population, 1980: General Social and Economic Characteristics*, p. 163.

82. Moore, *Mexican Americans*, pp. 67–69; Carter, *Mexican Americans in Schools*, pp. 30–31; *Hispanics and Jobs*, p. 11.

83. Spicer, *Cycles of Conquest*, pp. 285–365; Patrick H. McNamara, "Bishops, Priests, and Prophecy: A Study in the Sociology of Religious Protest" (Ph.D. dissertation, UCLA, 1968).

84. Moore, *Mexican Americans*, pp. 88–89.

85. Ibid., p. 91; Stoddard, *Mexican Americans*, p. 93; Grebler, Moore, and Guzmán, *The Mexican-American People*, pp. 459–60.

86. Grebler, Moore, and Guzmán, *The Mexican-American People*, pp. 436–39, 473–77; Tuck, *Not with the Fist*, pp. 152–54. See also Jane M. Christian and Chester C. Christian, "Spanish Language and Loyalty in the Southwest," in *Language Loyalty in the United States*, ed. Joshua A. Fishman (London: Mouton & Co., 1966), pp. 296–97.

87. Tuck, *Not with the Fist*; Sánchez, *Forgotten People*; Madsen, *Mexican-Americans of South Texas*; Grebler, Moore, and Guzmán, *The Mexican-American People*.

88. Edward Múrguía, *Assimilation, Colonialism, and the Mexican American People* (Austin: University of Texas Press, 1975), pp. 4–5.

89. Rodolfo Alvarez, "The Unique Psycho-historical Experience of the Mexican-American People," *Social Science Quarterly* 52 (June 1971): 15–29; Stoddard, *Mexican Americans*, p. 103; Benjamin S. Bradshaw and Frank Bean, "Trends in the Fertility of Mexican Americans, 1950–1970," *Social Science Quarterly* 53 (March 1973): 696–97.

90. Grebler, Moore, and Guzmán, *The Mexican-American People*, pp. 384, 430.

91. Ibid., pp. 396–97.

92. Edward Múrguía, *Chicano Intermarriage: A Theoretical and Empirical Study* (San Antonio: Trinity University Press, 1982), pp. 45–51; U.S. Department of Health, Education, and Welfare, *Americans of Spanish Origin*, p. 46.

93. Nathan Glazer, "The Political Distinctiveness of the Mexican Americans," in *Mexican-Americans in Comparative Perspective*, ed. Walter Connor (Washington, D.C.: Urban Institute, 1985), pp. 212–16.

94. Walter Connor, "Who Are the Mexican Americans? A Note on Comparability," in *Mexican-Americans in Comparative Perspective*, ed. Connor, pp. 4–28.

95. Grebler, Moore, and Guzmán, *The Mexican-American People*, pp. 385, 558; "Maintaining a Group Culture," *Institute for Survey Research Newsletter*, p. 8.

96. Múrguía, *Assimilation, Colonialism, and the Mexican American People*, p. 112.

97. Acuña, *Occupied America*, p. 3.

98. Alvarez, "The Psycho-historical and Socioeconomic Development of the Chicano Community in the United States," pp. 928–30.

99. Múrguía, *Assimilation, Colonialism, and the Mexican American People*, pp. 8–9.

100. Barrera, *Race and Class in the Southwest*, p. 213.

101. Flores, "Race and Culture in the Internal Colony," p. 194.

102. Chandler Davidson and Charles M. Gaitz, "Ethnic Attitudes as a Basis for Minority Cooperation in a Southwestern Metropolis," *Social Science Quarterly* 53 (March 1973): 747–48.

# CHAPTER 10

# *Puerto Rican and Cuban Americans*

Piri Thomas, an acclaimed Puerto Rican author, tells this story about his early life:

> I remember my own mother's answer one day when I asked her, "Why can't we have a nice house like this?"—showing her a picture in a magazine. I can remember her now, laughing as she replied, "Of course; we can have it in heaven someday." And I could feel the anger inside me saying, "I want it now."[1]

One of the nation's poorest groups, Puerto Ricans have long suffered at the bottom of the U.S. economic and political pyramids.

## PUERTO RICO AS A COLONY

### From Spanish to U.S. Rule

Borinquén, the original native name for Puerto Rico, had a population of 50,000 in 1493 when Spanish imperialism reached the island. Spain used the native peoples there as forced labor in mines and fields. Forced labor, disease, and violent suppression of rebellions led to a decline in the population, so slaves were imported to fill the gap. By 1530 imported black slaves were the majority of the population. Plantation agriculture replaced the earlier craze for gold, and slaves worked the fields.[2]

In 1897 Puerto Ricans pressured the Spanish government into granting them some autonomy, including the right to elect their house of representatives. In 1898 U.S. troops landed during the war with Spain. In the peace treaty (1899) Spain gave the island to the United States, which saw it as a useful station for warships and a profitable agricultural enclave. Puerto Rico moved from one empire, the Spanish, to another, that of the United States, without input from the inhabitants.[3]

A U.S. governor was appointed by the U.S. president. Acts of the local legislature were subject to veto by the U.S. Congress, and English became the mandatory language in schools. In 1917 the Jones Act awarded U.S. citizenship to all Puerto

Ricans. Islanders were split over ties to the United States, with the majority party (the Unionist party) favoring greater autonomy.[4]

In 1948 Puerto Ricans were permitted to elect their own governor, and in 1952 the Commonwealth of Puerto Rico, with its own constitution (approved by the U.S. Congress), was created. Considerable home rule was granted, and Puerto Ricans elected their own officials, made their own civil and criminal codes, and ran their own schools. In 1948 Spanish became the official language in schools, and the Puerto Rican flag was allowed to fly. However, this was only permitted by the U.S., the colonial power overseeing Puerto Rico.

## Operation Bootstrap

When the U.S. took over Puerto Rico, much land was owned by small farmers who raised coffee, sugar, and foodstuffs. In 1899 Puerto Ricans owned 93 percent of the farms, but by 1930 land-ownership was changing dramatically. Large absentee-owned companies soon controlled 60 percent of sugar production, and they monopolized tobacco production and the shipping lines. The independent farmers growing coffee were driven out by the U.S.-forced devaluation of the Puerto Rican peso and the closing of European markets that came with U.S. occupation. Many peasants were forced to seek jobs with the absentee-owned sugar companies. Puerto Ricans became cheap labor for international corporations, and in the slack seasons thousands endured terrible poverty.[5]

Until the 1930s Puerto Rico was an agricultural colony based on the sugar plantations; it was ruled under various U.S. decrees that determined life in the island, from currency exchange to the amount of land a person could own. When New Deal reforms came to Puerto Rico, U.S. governor Rexford Tugwell envisioned a program for the island that would include agricultural and industrial development. But after World War II, agricultural development was forgotten, and a program called Operation Bootstrap, designed to attract U.S. industrial corporations to the island, was implemented.

Nathan Glazer and Daniel P. Moynihan have seen Operation Bootstrap as a great help to Puerto Rico because it opened up "access to American investment capital."[6] Actually, U.S.-dominated agribusiness took much land that could have been used for growing food locally, forcing this island to import food. Operation Bootstrap lured multinational corporations to Puerto Rico through a system of tax breaks and other concessions. Government programs provided electricity, land, and roads for the multinationals. Urban industry was emphasized and agriculture neglected, so that the island tilted farther away from its heritage of locally owned farms and the rural population was pressured to migrate to industrial areas. The absence of taxes and the presence of cheap labor led to the development of many industries in Puerto Rico. "Modernization" brought with it massive unemployment. Capital investments grew from $1.4 billion in 1960 to $24 billion in 1979. Yet at the same time, the official unemployment rate grew from 13 percent to 19 percent. Industrialization helped create large numbers of unemployed workers, despite migration to the mainland.[7]

More recently, numerous industries have left the island, some looking for cheaper labor and tax exemptions elsewhere. This has created even greater unemployment. One Puerto Rican immigrant said at a U.S. Commission on Civil Rights hearing that he came to the United States because the company he worked for had used up its fifteen-year exemption from taxes, and its executives had decided to move rather than pay taxes.[8] Recessions have brought cutbacks in the petrochemical plants, increasing unemployment rates and federal payments for unemployment compensation, welfare, and food stamps.

# MIGRATION TO THE UNITED STATES

## Migration Streams

Puerto Ricans migrated to the mainland before 1940, but the number of migrants was small until World War II. In 1940 there were 70,000 Puerto Ricans on the mainland. For later periods the net number of migrants to the mainland has been as follows: 1946–1955, 406,000; 1956–1965, 179,000; 1966–1971, 121,000. At first most went to New York; later they went to the other cities on the eastern seaboard; and in the 1960s they migrated to the Midwest and West.[9]

Many a tourist who has seen Puerto Rico has probably asked, "Why would anyone want to leave such a beautiful island?" Piri Thomas answers succinctly: "Bread, money, gold, a peso to make a living … Diggit, wasn't that the greatest reason all the other different ethnic groups came to America for, freedom from want?"[10] Indeed, it was the Operation Bootstrap industrialization of the 1950s that created pressures for migration. One in five Puerto Ricans left. Thousands of farm workers, forced out of work by changes in agriculture, migrated. The Puerto Rican government encouraged migration as a safety valve reducing the pressures of unemployment. Pull factors were important. With the U.S. economy booming in the 1950s, corporations sent recruiters to Puerto Rico seeking cheap labor, such as workers for textile sweatshops.[11]

In the 1970s and 1980s opportunities in the United States deteriorated; a series of recessions prompted many Puerto Ricans to leave the mainland each year. Ironically, since the 1970s many Puerto Rican workers who could not find work on the island because of declining industrialization there have migrated to U.S. cities that are also plagued with unemployment.[12]

## Population Distribution

In 1900 there were 2,000 Puerto Ricans on the mainland, and the number grew slowly until World War II. At the beginning of the war about 70,000 Puerto Ricans resided here, but in the next two decades the number increased more than tenfold, to 887,000. By 1980 the number of people of Puerto Rican descent had doubled again, to more than 2 million. Between the 1940s and the 1980s the Puerto Rican population gradually fanned out to cities across the nation. In 1940 most Puerto Ricans lived in New York City, but by 1980 there were large communities in New Jersey cities as well as in Chicago, Cleveland, and Los Angeles. Today Puerto Ricans make up one eighth of all Hispanic Americans.[13]

## STEREOTYPING

Puerto Ricans have been stereotyped like Mexican Americans and black Americans have. The first Anglo American stereotypes were developed by U.S. military officials and colonial administrators. In the 1890s, a U.S. captain noted that "the people seem willing to work, even at starvation wages, and they seem to be docile and grateful for anything done for them. They are emotional...."[14]

Images of lazy, submissive Puerto Ricans persist, particularly among officials who deal with Puerto Rican clients. Anglo teachers have held images of Puerto Ricans as lazy and immoral. Lopez reports on being at a college meeting in New York where an experienced teacher from a ghetto school spoke on instilling the "middle-class values" of thrift, morality, and motivation in the children. Lopez asked the teacher about her image of Puerto Rican children:

> It was when I asked what morality was and where it was practiced among middle-class people or what motivation was lacking in our people and how she discovered this, or finally, how the hell a person could be thrifty on eighty-four dollars a week, that she began to do some thinking.[15]

Often referred to by the derogatory term *spics*, Puerto Ricans have been viewed, as were the Italians and Chicanos before them, as a criminal lot. A 1980 Aspen Institute conference report noted that the English-language news media emphasize selected aspects of Puerto Rican and Chicano life—poverty, gang violence, and illegal immigrants. Crimes by Puerto Ricans have been sensationalized in the New York City newspapers and other mass media; this has helped foster the image of Puerto Ricans as criminals. J. Edgar Hoover, former director of the FBI, promulgated this stereotype:

> We cooperate with the Secret Service on presidential trips abroad. You *never* have to bother about a President being shot by Puerto Ricans or Mexicans. They don't shoot very straight. But if they come at you with a knife, beware.[16]

Hoover's stereotype of Hispanic peoples as dumb-but-sinister knife carriers is still circulating in the United States.

In the 1950s, when large numbers of migrants began coming to the United States, the Puerto Rican government circulated pamphlets trying to prepare migrants for prejudice on the mainland. One read as follows:

> If one Puerto Rican steals, Americans who are prejudiced say that all Puerto Ricans are thieves. If one Puerto Rican doesn't work, prejudiced Americans say all of us are lazy....we pay, because a bad opinion of us is formed, and the result may be that they discredit us, they won't give us work, or they deny us our rights.[17]

This pamphlet recognizes the ways in which Anglo Americans unfairly generalize from one Puerto Rican's actions to those of the entire group, and it implies that negative stereotypes are translated into discrimination against Puerto Ricans looking for jobs.

Stereotypes of Puerto Rico and Puerto Ricans have been circulated by social scientists as well. For example, Nathan Glazer and Daniel Moynihan argued in 1963 that Puerto Rican society was "sadly defective" in its culture and family system. Families were weak and disorganized. Glazer and Moynihan suggested that this alleged weak family structure was the reason Puerto Ricans on the mainland did not move into better-paying jobs.[18]

## Racism

As with other non-European groups, stereotyping continues to be harmful. It is reflected in Anglo discrimination, and in Puerto Ricans' negative self-images. Americans of white European descent tend to lump Puerto Ricans with black Americans or Chicanos. They are seen as a nonwhite group. Physical distinctiveness is emphasized even more than cultural distinctiveness. The discrimination and segregation on the mainland come as a shock to many immigrants. Color discrimination is less blatant on the island than in the U.S. Until they come to the mainland, most Puerto Ricans have seldom had to deal with overt color-based discrimination.[19]

## ECONOMIC CONDITIONS: THE MAINLAND

Jesús Colon, an early immigrant, wrote a book on his experiences. Puerto Ricans did the dirty work of the society, and poverty was their lot. Jesús and his brother worked different hours, and to save money they even shared their working clothes. Jesús notes that "we only had one pair of working pants between the two of us."[20]

Discrimination faced the immigrants, with the darker-skinned immigrants usually suffering the most. Piri Thomas grew up in Spanish Harlem (El Barrio) and eventually became well known as the author of *Down These Mean Streets*. He recounts an interview in 1945 for a job as a door-to-door salesperson. He did not get the job, but a lighter-skinned friend did. Dark-skinned Puerto Ricans, he discovered by asking other applicants, were discriminated against by the white employer; they were treated like blacks.[21]

## Occupation and Unemployment

The increase in migration after 1950 did not change conditions. Mainland Puerto Ricans still did the "dirty work" for other Americans. They cleaned up New York City as busboys and janitors; they worked in sweatshops that paid low wages. Many have faced unemployment. The occupational distribution for employed Puerto Ricans in the continental United States has been as follows:[22]

| | MEN | | | WOMEN | | |
|---|---|---|---|---|---|---|
| | 1950 | 1970 | 1979 | 1950 | 1970 | 1979 |
| Professional, technical | 5.3% | 4.7% | 8.2% | 3.4% | 7.2% | 10.4% |
| Managers, administrators | 5.4 | 4.2 | 4.6 | 1.2 | 1.6 | 4.2 |
| Clerical and sales | 9.6 | 14.9 | 12.2 | 11.0 | 34.1 | 42.0 |
| Skilled blue-collar (crafts) | 11.2 | 15.7 | 14.4 | 1.7 | 2.4 | 2.2 |
| Operatives | 33.0 | 33.5 | 28.1 | 72.5 | 39.7 | 23.4 |
| Service workers | 25.1 | 17.5 | 19.5 | 6.5 | 12.5 | 16.1 |
| Domestic work | 0.2 | 0.1 | | 2.3 | 1.0 | |
| Nonfarm laborers | 7.3 | 8.0 | 10.1 | 1.0 | 1.1 | 0.8 |
| Farmers, farm workers | 2.9 | 1.5 | 3.0 | 0.4 | 0.4 | 0.9 |

In 1950, 1970, and 1979 we find male workers concentrated in blue-collar jobs, especially in lower-paying jobs as laborers, service workers (e.g., busboys), and assembly-line workers ("operatives"). A major shift of Puerto Rican women into the clerical and sales fields, particularly as lower-level typists, retail sales clerks, and keypunch operators can be seen by the late 1970s.

The 1980 census data show a pattern similar to that in the 1979 census survey. Among the 600,266 Puerto Rican men and women employed, 14 percent were in managerial, administrative, professional, or technical jobs, compared with 25.7 percent of the general population. About 26 percent were in the other white-collar categories of clerical and sales, compared with 27.3 percent of the U.S. population. In 1980 the proportion of Puerto Rican workers in service, including domestic, work was 17 percent, the proportion in craft jobs was 11 percent, in operative work 24 percent, and in laborer positions 7 percent—all of these percentages but the one for craft jobs being much higher than corresponding figures for the general population. Just 1 percent were in farm work. As in earlier censuses, the majority (60 percent) were in blue-collar work, particularly the males, who make up two-thirds of all Puerto Rican workers. Among the 235,000 women workers the majority were in white-collar jobs, particularly clerical and retail sales positions.[23]

In many East Coast areas Puerto Rican laborers have done much of the low-paid field work that has put vegetables on American tables. In the late 1970s in Vineland, New Jersey, 15,000 Puerto Rican farm workers were working for low wages, often seven days a week and in inhumane, barracks-like housing. Nearby farm workers were fired for attempting to organize to improve their working conditions.

Many Puerto Ricans are "operatives," a category that includes factory workers and seamstresses. The proportion of Puerto Rican men and women in these jobs has declined since 1950. Puerto Ricans were hard hit in the late 1960s and the 1970s by a decline in New York City's clothing industry that increased unemployment for apparel workers. Many men have moved into work as dishwashers, orderlies, janitors, health-care aides, and recreational facility attendants. Women have moved into service jobs and jobs as file clerks, typists, cashiers, and teacher aides. Puerto Ricans in professional and other white-collar jobs tend to be at the lower-paid levels, which include such workers as teachers, librarians, and health, personnel, and recreational professionals.[24]

For Puerto Ricans on the mainland unemployment has been high. In 1976 over 16 percent of Puerto Rican men and 22 percent of women were unemployed, figures up sharply from 1970. In 1980 the unemployment rate was 12 percent for all Puerto Rican workers and 12.7 percent for the women. In the 1981–1983 recession the unemployment rate increased. At all points the rate has been much higher than that for white workers. Over the 1980s Puerto Rican men and women continued to have unemployment and subemployment rates that were among the highest of any racial and ethnic group in the northeastern cities. Unemployment rates are only the tip of the iceberg, for they reflect no more than half the numbers of Puerto Ricans who are either unemployed or subemployed—that is, working part time, discouraged from looking for work because of long-term unemployment, or making very low wages.[25]

## Employment Discrimination and Other Barriers

Institutionalized discrimination can be seen in the restriction of Puerto Rican access to certain job categories. In New York City, for example, Puerto Ricans have been very underrepresented (relative to their percentage of the population) in local and state government jobs. This is at least in part because of their being less well integrated into traditional job information networks, dominated by white New Yorkers. In many cases, Puerto Ricans are screened out of jobs by tests that are, unnecessarily, given only in English. This occurs where Puerto Rican applicants are capable of doing the jobs, but the screening tests are not job-related. Even trash collection jobs, for example, have sometimes required screening tests, on which those who speak English and have a high school diploma score better. As with Mexican Americans, many Puerto Ricans find themselves unfairly stigmatized as of "low intelligence" because their command of English is not very good.[26]

Puerto Ricans have suffered discrimination because they are U.S. citizens. As a Puerto Rican woman in California said in a 1978 Civil Rights Commission interview,

> I've had about six or seven jobs since I came here. What happens is that they hire you temporarily and get rid of you as soon as possible because you don't belong to the right race. I'd even say that bosses here prefer Mexicans (particularly illegals) because they know that unions don't represent them, so they can be exploited easier. At least Puerto Ricans have citizenship and can get into unions.[27]

Some have been asked by local government officials to prove that they are U.S. citizens—that is, to prove that Puerto Rico is part of the United States.

Institutionalized discrimination can also be seen in height and weight requirements, which have disqualified some Puerto Rican applicants for police and fire department jobs; these requirements use as their standards Anglo males. Racial discrimination is important. Although only 9 percent of Puerto Ricans classify themselves as of Afro-American or African ancestry, most white Americans classify the majority of Puerto Ricans as nonwhite and discriminate against them for the same reasons they discriminate against blacks. Several studies have found that with few exceptions the skilled blue-collar trades remain virtually all-white. Less-skilled jobs, such as those of concrete laborers and mason tenders, have been controlled so that token numbers of blacks and Puerto Ricans are hired; union, private, and governmental authorities have collaborated in these practices.[28]

## Restructuring

Another problem for Puerto Ricans workers on the mainland has been corporate flight. Rodriguez notes that both automation and the movement of manufacturing jobs to the New York City suburbs and to the South have caused a major decline in the number of blue-collar positions available to Puerto Ricans in New York City. This "sectoral decline combined with insufficient educational opportunities and retraining of blue-collar workers to produce blue-collar structural unemployment." The lack of retraining and education for white-collar jobs means that Puerto Rican and other minority workers in New York are increasingly part of a large surplus labor force.[29]

In 1987 there was a discussion in the *New York Times* about the economic situation of Puerto Ricans. Marta Tienda, a sociologist, and William Diaz, a program officer at the Ford Foundation, argued that the reasons for the sharp deterioration in the economic position of Puerto Ricans were primarily the decline of inner-city manufacturing in the northeastern cities and the continuing circular migration to Puerto Rico. The most important reason for the rising poverty and unemployment faced by Puerto Ricans between the late 1970s and the late 1980s was the "drastically reduced job opportunities in industrial Northeastern cities like New York, Newark, and Pittsburgh, as well as on Puerto Rico. "In their view circular migration, the constant movement of Puerto Rican workers back and forth between Puerto Rico and the mainland in search of jobs, causes significant disruption to families and educational attainment. It also makes worse the more fundamental economic problems created by economic dislocation, capital flight, and racial discrimination in the northeastern cities. Robert Garcia, a member of Congress from New York, wrote a letter to the *Times* praising the accuracy of Tienda and Diaz in assessing the social and economic problems of Puerto Ricans and pointing out that both blacks and Puerto Ricans in New York City face common problems of poverty and discrimination.[30]

## Income and Poverty

Puerto Ricans are the poorest of American minorities except for Native Americans. Between 1959 and 1974 Puerto Rican family incomes declined from 71 percent of the national average to only 59 percent. In the 1980 census median family income for Puerto Ricans was only $10,734, less than half the Anglo median family income. Poverty and near poverty are the lot of most families. In 1980 about 35 percent of Puerto Ricans fell below the federal poverty line; accounts of oppressive conditions are not unusual. Filipe Luciano describes life as a Puerto Rican:

> You resign yourself to poverty—my mother did this. Your face is rubbed in shit so much that you begin to accept that shit as reality… my stomach rumbling. My mother beating

me when I knew it was because of my father...the welfare investigator cursing out my mother because what she wants is spring clothing for her children....[31]

The economic situation became critical during the 1980s. We have just noted the high level of poverty among Puerto Ricans in 1980. This figure did not improve significantly over the 1980s. Unemployment increased and real incomes declined. Median family income fell in real terms (adjusting for inflation) 18 percent between 1979 and 1984, more than the huge 14 percent drop for black Americans and the 9 percent decrease for Mexican Americans. In 1984 the median family income for Puerto Ricans was only $12,282, and the per capita income for Puerto Rican families was half that of whites. Given this desperate situation, the use of public assistance increased substantially over the 1970s and 1980s for both couple-headed and single-parent families.[32]

## Housing

Discrimination against Puerto Ricans is conspicuous in the area of housing. A Rutgers professor of law testified at a Civil Rights Commission hearing that Puerto Ricans have suffered even more than blacks from housing discrimination. Blacks are "steered" by real estate agents to certain housing areas. But Puerto Ricans generally have been excluded from all decent housing markets. Puerto Ricans get the "housing scraps" no one else wants. Overcrowding and deteriorating housing—these are primary characteristics of many ghetto areas. Housing displacement and blatant housing discrimination have been serious problems for Puerto Ricans. The Puerto Rican Legal Defense and Educational Fund won a major court victory over housing discrimination in four new housing developments in Brooklyn, where racial quotas limited the number of nonwhite residents. In *Williamsburg Fair Housing Committee v. New York City Housing Authority*, the court found that discrimination against Puerto Ricans did exist, and legal remedies were provided that eliminated racial quotas. Moreover, a large number of poor families, the majority of them being Puerto Ricans, were forced to move out of a residential area in the city of Lyons, New York, as part of a downtown renewal project.[33]

## EDUCATION

In mid-1970s, average educational attainment for Puerto Ricans was only 8.7 years, well below the national average. The 1980 census listed 10.5 as the median years of schooling completed by Puerto Ricans over 25. Only 40 percent were high school graduates. In 1980 just 79 percent of 16-and 17-year-olds were enrolled in school, compared with the national figure for non-Hispanic whites of 89 percent. A Chicago study found that large numbers of Puerto Rican children leave before they finish high school. In 1980 only 6 percent of males and 5 percent of females completed college, compared with a fifth of Anglo males. Still, the number in college has increased. For example, the percentage of Puerto Ricans in the City University of New York increased during the 1970s.[34]

## Barriers to Mobility

The high dropout rate, or rather the *pushout* rate, for Puerto Rican children has a number of causes, including the need to work to support families and discriminatory barriers in school systems. Few teachers are Puerto Rican or Hispanic. One study found a sharp disparity in many urban school systems between the percentage of Hispanic teachers and the percentage of Hispanic students. While 27 percent of the students in New York City were Hispanic, only 2 percent of the teachers were. In addition, most Puerto Rican children and teachers are in very segregated schools having large minority enrollments.[35]

The representation of Puerto Ricans among administrators is similarly small. Only a few Puerto Ricans have moved into influential positions in higher education. A few have served on local and state boards of education in New York; in 1978 the school system in New York City had two Puerto Rican district superintendents and forty-five Puerto Rican principals.[36]

Puerto Rican students are often assigned to low-ability groups, to "language-disabled" classes, or to lower grades. A number of New York and New Jersey studies have found racially identifiable tracking systems and placement of children in classes for the mentally retarded without sufficient justification. In New York City these classes were disproportionately made up of Hispanic children. As a recent Civil Rights Commission report put it, "the rationale for such practices is that students will benefit from special instruction in low-level classes, but the correlation between such placement and improved academic performance is dubious. In fact, the lower level of curriculum and the absence of stimulation from higher-achieving students may be negative factors that further retard the student."[37]

## Curriculum and Language

The school curriculum often seems irrelevant to Hispanic children. Anglo authorities frequently are insensitive to Hispanic history and cultures. Neglect of Puerto Rican history by the schools contributes to a lack of self-esteem.[38]

U.S. schools are generally not structured to deal with students who do not speak English. The fault is in the schools, not in the children; in Europe many schools are more hospitable to language diversity among students. Puerto Rican students, on the average, do not do as well on achievement tests as Anglo students. One reason for this is that most tests are given in English. A psychologist in Philadelphia commented on the inaccuracy of English-language tests scores:

> In my clinic, the average underestimation of IQ for a Puerto Rican kid is 20 points. We go through this again and again. When we test in Spanish, there is a 20 point leap immediately—20 higher than when he's tested in English.[39]

Moreover, many of the new Spanish-language achievement and "IQ" tests are translations of English-language tests, a practice that passes along whatever cultural bias exists in the tests.

Some Puerto Rican educators argue that children should be taught to read and write well in Spanish first, taught subjects in that language, and then be taught English as a second language. Civil rights groups have actively pressed for bilingual education programs for Hispanic children. Herman La Fontaine, a Puerto Rican educator, phrased it this way: "Our definition of cultural pluralism must include the concept that our language and our culture will be given equal status to that of the majority population."[40] In the 1980s bilingual programs were heavily cut by the Reagan Administration. Conservative officials viewed them as luxuries. A leader of Philadelphia's Puerto Rican Alliance argued that this showed a "blatant disregard of a right the courts have already recognized."[41] In such states as New Jersey and Massachusetts attempts have been made to cut back or eliminate bilingual education laws. And in New York major cutbacks have been implemented.

## POLITICS

In Puerto Rico voting participation by those registered runs to 60 percent or more. In the United States, voting rates are as low as 20 percent in some urban areas. Since the early 1940s Puerto Ricans have participated in Democratic party politics in such states as New York and New Jersey, but that participation has usually been token. So far in New York, Puerto Ricans have been able to dominate only one congressional seat, that originally held by Herman Badillo. In 1965 Badillo became the first Puerto Rican to be elected president of a New York City borough; six years later he became the first of Puerto Rican background in the U.S. House. In the 1970s, however, Badillo lost the race for mayor of New York. In the 1980s there was still one Puerto Rican holding a regular voting position in Congress, Robert Garcia, who held the House seat previously occupied by Badillo.

Garcia has played a role in building political bridges between blacks and Puerto Ricans in New York. In 1965 he and several other state legislators, including the prominent black leader Shirley Chisholm, formed a black-Puerto Rican caucus in the New York state legislature. In the late 1980s that caucus was still bringing black and Puerto Rican legislators together on issues of importance to both communities. Similar coalitions have periodically appeared at Democratic party conventions. In 1987 Garcia, then a member of Congress, noted that "blacks and Puerto Ricans are natural allies as defined by our common position on the bottom rung of the socioeconomic ladder."[42] In the future we may see more of this type of "rainbow coalition" in the northeastern cities.

In 1937 the first Puerto Rican was elected to the New York state assembly; it would be fifteen more years before another was elected. In the late 1970s New York had two state senators, four members of the state assembly, and two members of the New York City Council who were Puerto Ricans. Today Puerto Ricans are significantly underrepresented in appointed political positions as well. Puerto Ricans have as yet had little political impact outside New York City. In 1980 Mayor Kevin White of Boston made a gesture toward Hispanic voters by appointing a Cuban American as deputy mayor for Hispanic affairs. But there was little direct representation in Massachusetts politics for the Puerto Rican population. And a study in Chicago concluded that as of the mid-1980s Puerto Ricans and other Hispanics "have not been included in the politics of the city, nor have they been able to show the political strength that would force the political powers to bring them into political leadership."[43] In 1982 there was only one Puerto Rican in the local population of 130,000 on the Chicago city council and not one Puerto Rican served on the county board, in the state legislature, or in the U.S. Congress. With the election of Mayor Harold Washington, a black American, in 1983 (with the help of Hispanic voters), Chicago's black and other minority populations gained new power. But Washington's death in 1987 brought a new struggle for political power between the remnants of the old white machine and the newly enfranchised minority voters.

The effects of discrimination can also be seen in New York state and New York city government employment, in which Puerto Ricans are significantly underrepresented. As a result, Puerto Ricans frequently feel they are not part of the political system. The U.S. Commission on Civil Rights interviewed 120 members of the Puerto Rican community in California. These Puerto Ricans felt that they were treated as nonpersons by government and private agencies. Government officials serving or surveying minorities are usually not Puerto Rican and seldom speak much Spanish. Government services have historically been less accessible to Puerto Ricans. Job training and employment services have been slow in coming to Puerto Rican communities.[44]

Toward the end of 1987 the governor of Puerto Rico announced that he was starting a half-million-dollar campaign to register mainland Puerto Ricans to vote. At that time an estimated 400,000 eligible Hispanics, mostly Puerto Ricans, in the New York City alone were unregistered. The campaign was expected to use direct mail and telephone canvassing, as well as advertising. Local leaders welcomed this unique intervention by a nonmainland Puerto Rican leader, which demonstrated the close political alliances between the mainland and island communities. One local leader pointed up the need to couple this voter registration effort with a get-out-the-vote effort because turnout has been a problem for Puerto Rican voters, especially when there are no candidates articulating policies relevant to Puerto Rican needs.[45]

## PROTEST

### In Puerto Rico

In Puerto Rico the period of U.S. rule has been punctuated with protest. In the 1930s there was a mass attack by Puerto Ricans on the colonial government buildings, and in 1934 there were strikes in the sugarcane fields. The Nationalist party, led by a Puerto Rican hero, Harvard-educated Pedro Albizu Campos, began pushing for expanded freedom and for independence. In March 1937 there was a massacre of Nationalist party marchers who had joined a legal march in Ponce. By bringing in 200 heavily armed police, the governor had set the stage for violence. A shot was fired, probably by the police, and a pitched battle ensued, with twenty dead and one hundred injured, mostly marchers and bystanders.[46]

In the fall of 1950 police raided Nationalist party meetings and houses. This precipitated an armed revolt that spread to five cities. Hundreds of people were killed. Two thousand people were arrested for actively advocating or pressing for independence. On the mainland Puerto Rican nationalists attacked the residence of President Harry Truman and the U.S. House in session. The future of Puerto Rico is a major political issue on the island and the mainland. The platforms of both the Republican and the Democratic parties have supported statehood for Puerto Rico. Pro-statehood sentiment is very strong on the island; "statehood for the poor" is the slogan of this movement. But there are substantial pressures against statehood as well. There is still a significant pro-independence movement, representing perhaps 10 percent of the voters. Some continue to use violence against U.S. officials and military personnel in an attempt to drive the colonialists, as they see them, from the island.[47]

## Organizational Protest on the Mainland

The mainland Puerto Rican community has always had service organizations that deal with community problems. There are the Puerto Rican Legal Project, the Puerto Rican Legal Defense Fund, the League of Puerto Rican Women, the Puerto Rican Teachers Association, the Puerto Rican Forum, and the Puerto Rican Family Institute. The Puerto Rican Teachers Association has worked to increase representation of Puerto Ricans among teachers and principals and to expand bilingual programs.[48]

Puerto Ricans have been active in labor and union organizations in the United States since the late 1800s. In the 1960s and early 1970s Puerto Rican protest and political activity increased; there were riots in some Puerto Rican ghettos.

Chicago was the birthplace of the Young Lords, which began as a street gang and evolved into a militant protest group. In the spring of 1969 the Young Lords, patterned after the Black Panthers, occupied the administration building of McCormick Theological Seminary to publicize poverty in Chicago. They took over a Methodist church, opening a day-care center and school for the community. They broke up a meeting in order to protest the use of the urban-renewal land for a tennis club, and they set up a "people's park" on other urban-renewal land.[49] A New York group formed the Young Lords Party. In December 1969 these Young Lords occupied the First Spanish Methodist Church in New York City for eleven days and organized a day-care center, a breakfast program, and a clothing distribution program. They created a newspaper, *Palante* (Forward), and led a demonstration of two hundred Puerto Ricans protesting squalid conditions at a local hospital.[50] The Young Lords developed their own protest style. Children of poor immigrants, they articulated a thirteen-point program for a democratic socialist society. They called for "liberation and power in the hands of the people, not Puerto Rican exploiters." This group envisaged a multi-ethnic, democratic-socialistic society. At the peak of their influence, the Young Lords had chapters in twenty cities.[51]

The police repressed black and Puerto Rican groups. The groups were infiltrated, their leaders prosecuted, sometimes in frame-up trials. Other leaders were co-opted into government anti-poverty programs. Internal divisions helped splinter the groups as well. Nonetheless, there are still some militant protest groups in Puerto Rican communities. There is, for example, the Puerto Rican Solidarity Committee, with chapters in numerous cities on the mainland and in Puerto Rico.[52]

## Community Protest

There have been community protests against discrimination. In Cleveland, Orlando Morales, a young prisoner serving two life sentences was viewed by community groups as innocent. Three hundred angry Puerto Ricans met in a protest meeting at Cleveland's Spanish American Committee Hall. Much evidence indicated that Morales did not commit the murder for which he was convicted. Many in the Puerto Rican community felt the twenty-two-year old Puerto Rican had been railroaded and actively protested what they saw as discrimination in the criminal justice system.[53]

Some protests have brought changes. Pressures from Puerto Rican activists led to the founding of a community college in the South Bronx and helped create an open admissions program at the City University of New York. City and state governments provided more funds for community projects. More Puerto Ricans were hired into city governments. More Puerto Rican studies and bilingual programs were added to the schools, and more Puerto Rican teachers were hired.[54]

Coalitions of grass-roots organizations and older established groups were created in the 1980s, among them the National Congress for Puerto Rican Rights in 1981. Through such mechanisms traditional and militant leaders have been trying to bridge the long-standing gap between them and improve the conditions of Puerto Ricans. A source of tension between the federal government and Puerto Ricans is Puerto Rican support for independence organizations. A number of grand jury investigations of the independence-for-Puerto-Rico movement have been conducted in the United States and Puerto Rico. There have been community protests over these investigations.

# RELIGION

Most Puerto Ricans are Catholic, but in the United States they have generally been led by clergy from backgrounds other than Puerto Rican. The supportive framework that parishes gave to previous Catholic groups has largely been missing. One exception to this dependence on non-Puerto Rican clergy has been the Bishop of Puerto Rico, who regularly visits Puerto Rican parishes on the mainland.

Scholar Joseph Fitzpatrick argues that Puerto Rican religion is more a religion of the community than of the parish. Community celebrations and processions are important, as is reverence for the Virgin Mary and the saints. As is the case for Italian Americans, formal worship is less important than communal celebrations and home ceremonies. On the mainland Puerto Ricans have shared parishes with blacks and other

Latin American groups. Hispanic caucuses have developed within the Catholic church to press for Hispanic services and more priests of Hispanic background. In Fitzpatrick's words, "the principal demand of the Puerto Ricans and other Hispanics is for a policy of cultural pluralism in the church that will provide for the continuation of their language and culture in their spiritual life and the appointment of Puerto Ricans and other Hispanics to positions of responsibility."[55]

# ASSIMILATION OR COLONIALISM?

## Assimilation Reconsidered

In his influential book on Puerto Ricans, Fitzpatrick relies on an assimilation model to interpret Puerto Rican experiences. In his 1964 work Gordon, the prominent assimilation theorist, had found little assimilation of Puerto Ricans into the core culture and society; in his later work Fitzpatrick reports a significant degree of assimilation. Fitzpatrick notes substantial cultural assimilation, particularly for many mainland-born Puerto Ricans who identify with U.S. society and who have adopted English as a second language. This cultural adaptation creates family problems when Spanish-speaking parents must depend on English-speaking children in order to get along in mainland society. In *Up from Puerto Rico*, Elena Padilla argues that second-generation Puerto Ricans often have a different reference group, the mainland society rather than island society, and many hide their Spanish-language facility in an attempt to assimilate.[56]

The pressure to assimilate culturally has been intense, as Maldonado-Denis notes: "Regardless of what Glazer and Moynihan argue in *Beyond the Melting Pot*, the American ethic is a messianic one, and all ethnic groups are required to assimilate culturally as a condition for achieving a share in the material and spiritual goods of American society."[57] For Puerto Ricans these cultural assimilation pressures begin in Puerto Rico, where for decades the colonial government pressured Puerto Ricans on the island to assimilate culturally, as in requiring the use of English in the schools.

Fitzpatrick notes significant Puerto Rican resistance to Anglo-conformity cultural assimilation. The Puerto Rican quest for identity, he finds, "is taking the form of a strong assertion of the significance of Puerto Rican culture, including language, and also the definition of Puerto Rican interests around militant types of political and community action."[58] Among Puerto Rican groups themselves, some argue that Puerto Ricans in the U.S. must assimilate and become Americans in order to find better jobs and achieve a higher position in this society; some argue that this can be done with a minimum of soul selling—that is, with a strong persistence of Puerto Rican culture. Other groups worry about the heavy cost of assimilation in terms of the identities of Puerto Ricans; they worry that assimilation pressures, as with other race and ethnic groups, will lead to rootlessness.

While there seems to be some decline in blatant prejudice and discrimination against Puerto Ricans, subtle forms continue in housing and employment. For the most part, the level of assimilation in this regard is relatively low. Moreover, secondary-structural assimilation at the level of higher-paying white-collar jobs has been slow; there remains a disproportionate concentration of Puerto Ricans in blue-collar and lower-wage white-collar jobs, as well as among the unemployed. Problematical too has been the low level of participation of Puerto Ricans in mainland political institutions.

Structural assimilation of Puerto Ricans at the primary-group level and marital assimilation have not reached levels comparable to those of European immigrants. A New York study of four hundred Puerto Ricans found "almost incessant interaction between the parents and their married children." In spite of, or perhaps because of, their wrenching experiences of migration to the mainland and three decades in the United States, the first generation of immigrants maintained a high level of social integration with their children and grandchildren. The better jobs and educations of many in the second generation did not break up this family integration. However, outmarriage seems to be significant for the second generation. Over half of the U.S.-born Puerto Ricans who are married have a Puerto Rican spouse, compared to over 80 percent of the island-born migrants. Numerous outmarriages, however, are to other Hispanics and to black Americans rather than to Anglos.[59]

Generational conflict has been a problem for Puerto Rican families. Children grow up in the U.S. culture and pick up values that often conflict with traditional values. The traditional chaperoning of girls has given way to the less restricted mainland dating patterns. And the street life of boys in large ghettos is more difficult to supervise. Moreover, identificational assimilation has come slowly for Puerto Ricans. Most, whether island-born or mainland-born, still see themselves as Puerto Rican. A study of two generations of Puerto Rican families in New York City found that both had acculturated to some extent to the mainland culture, "but internally, in the symbolisms linking them to the island, they experienced less change." Even those born on the mainland retained strong symbolic ties to the island of Puerto Rico. More than half of the first generation of migrants to the mainland and 45 percent of their children saw themselves as solely Puerto Rican in terms of values. The rest saw themselves as partly Puerto Rican and partly North American. Not one of the four hundred persons in the sample identified himself or herself as purely North American in terms of values. The second generation apparently had as strong an allegiance and sense of identity with Puerto Rico as the first generation.[60]

## Power–Conflict Views

Power–conflict analysts would agree that there has been heavy Anglicization pressure on Puerto Ricans, but they would stress how colonized Puerto Rican Americans remain. Assimilation into the economic and political mainstream has been rather slow, which suggests that non-European migrants such as Puerto Ricans are not, contrary to the views of some assimilation analysts, like the European immigrants in earlier periods.

There is also the distinctive Puerto Rican experience of external colonialism. Unemployment in Puerto Rico has often been cited as a major reason for out-migration; the prosperity of the mainland economy has been cited as an important pull factor. But unemployment and mainland prosperity would not have created the long streams of migration from this Caribbean island without the long colonial relationship. The economic history of Puerto Ricans is grounded in the history of the colonial relationship between the United States and the island of Puerto Rico. After the war with Spain the United States took the island by force as an external colony. Since that time the inhabitants have been subject to economic and political intervention. Thus it was the creation of a one-crop agricultural society dominated by U.S. absentee sugar companies that originally created a large group of agricultural workers seeking other work.

With the later industrialization of Puerto Rico, under the auspices of large U.S. firms, many Puerto Rican workers became part of a growing surplus labor population, one that made its way to the industrialized northeastern cities on the mainland. These immigrants from an external colony became part of the internal colonialism of the inner cities. Puerto Ricans live, for the most part, in segregated ghettos. And there seems to be a co-opted Puerto Rican elite that, like colonial elites in the Third World, has, at least in part, a social control function.[61]

Internal colonialism can be seen in the "urban enterprise zone" proposals of the Reagan Administration. These proposals would significantly reduce taxes and regulations on corporations that decide to open plants in poverty and ghetto areas in U.S. cities. This plan recognized nonwhite ghettos as areas for economic exploitation. Bonilla and Campos have compared this "puertoricanization" of central-city ghettos to the economic colonialism of Operation Bootstrap in Puerto Rico. Under Operation Bootstrap, Puerto Rico's poverty and low wages became its main assets as far as multinational corporations were concerned. In the 1980s President Reagan's advisers explicitly used Puerto Rico as an example of the reindustrialization they had in mind for mainland "urban enterprise zones."

In Puerto Rico corporations were encouraged by various incentives to come in and profit from exploiting cheap labor. The "puertoricanization" of central-city ghettos makes them corporate havens of profitability similar to the island of Puerto Rico. Bonilla and Campos note that various urban-renewal schemes, new and old, to exploit Puerto Rican and black workers show the logic of capitalistic expansion, which leads "not only to the introduction of the peoples and problems of colonialism into the metropolis, but also to the transfer there of colonial 'solutions' [such as urban enterprise zones] and practices."[62]

## THE CASE OF CUBAN AMERICANS

The fastest-growing segment of the U.S. population in the late 1980s is the Hispanic population. Mexican Americans make up 60 percent of that population, Puerto Ricans 14 percent, and Cuban Americans 5.5 percent. Other Hispanic groups, such as Central Americans, many of whom are refugees from political turmoil and persecution, make up the rest. In the last two chapters we have focused on the two largest of these groups; we can now briefly survey the situation of the next largest, the Cuban Americans.

## Immigration and Conflicts

The nineteenth-century wars of Cuban independence brought the first Cuban immigrants to the United States, to be followed in the 1950s by refugees from the Batista dictatorship. However, the largest immigration (600,000 people) took place in the 1960s as middle- and upper-income Cubans fled the revolution; many settled in Florida. With substantial federal aid in the form of relocation and job assistance, they built their own communal and economic infrastructure. Between 1965 and the 1970s another quarter million Cubans came to the United States; only a sixth of these could be described as middle-income.[63]

In 1980 there was an influx of 124,000 Cubans. These recent immigrants are generally poorer and less educated than the earlier waves of Cuban refugees. Substantial federal aid was required for resettlement of these recent immigrants; many remained in detention camps years after arrival because the U.S. government feared that many were criminals. These immigrants have created serious tensions, even riots, in prison communities.

One result of the various Cuban migrations over the last few decades is a major change in the population mix of south Florida. By the late 1980s a majority of the population in Miami was Hispanic.

The 1980 Cuban migration swelled Miami welfare rolls, increased overcrowding in the schools, and created $30 million in expenses for local governments already hurting from cutbacks in federal programs. The millions of dollars paid out to care for the new influx of Cubans angered many whites; the latter unfairly blamed all Cubans for local social problems. Tensions also accelerated with blacks because of the growing Cuban American presence in south Florida. Miami's 1980 Liberty City riot and 1982 Overtown riot by poor blacks were precipitated in part by Hispanic (and white Anglo) police involvement in the killing of black men. After the Liberty City riot white landlords and white businesses that had been damaged were replaced by Hispanic landlords and businesses. One former black school official complained that "after a generation of being Southern slaves, blacks now face a future as Latin slaves." Blacks argued that Cuban Americans were taking jobs away from them. The larger and more affluent Cuban American community controls many of its own businesses, small and large; Cubans are usually preferred in hiring there. Not surprisingly, then, in a 1980s mayoral election 95 percent of black voters voted *against* the Cuban American candidate. Intergroup rivalry and competition can be seen clearly in south Florida today, with a very old immigrant group (Afro-Americans) losing a power struggle with a new immigrant group (Cuban Americans).[64]

## The Economic Situation: An Enclave Economy?

Compared with other Hispanic groups, Cuban Americans have relatively high levels of education and income, much entrepreneurial activity, and a large percentage of older persons. In the 1980 census the occupational statistics for male and female Cuban

American workers taken together showed 41.7 percent in white-collar positions—more than the 31 percent of Mexican American workers but less than the half of all U.S. workers in those jobs. The percentage in blue-collar categories was larger than in the total population. Among Cuban Americans 46.9 percent were employed in craft, operative, and laborer jobs, about the same as for Mexican Americans, but more than in the general population. About 11 percent were in service jobs, including domestic work—about the same as for all workers. Very few were in farm-related jobs. The Cuban Americans are an urban population. While less affluent than Anglo Americans, they are more affluent than other Hispanic groups.[65]

Portes and Bach have discussed the development of the Cuban American enclave in Miami. They suggest that a critical reason the Cubans have done relatively well economically is that they migrated not as poor individuals in isolated circumstances but rather as a group with substantial resources, with access to important social networks, and with support from governmental programs. Many of them came with educations and credentials that enabled them to become doctors and other professionals, as well as entrepreneurs. Once created, the ethnic enclave economy of the Cuban Americans gave entrepreneurs access to a stream of cheap labor from Cuba. Appeals to ethnic solidarity, to the Cuban identity of the laborers, helped the business people to exploit their own laborers.[66]

## Politics

Politically, Cuban Americans tend to be more active than other Hispanic groups and more conservative. For example, in the 1980 and 1984 presidential elections most voted for the Republican candidate. As the Cuban American marketing director of the *Miami News* put it, "Cuban-Americans are definitely super-conservative. Communism for us is the enemy. On domestic issues, we will be more toward the center…but the Cuban business community is still more in favor of Reaganomics than Mexicans or Puerto Ricans."[67] Today in Miami there are more than half a million Cubans, many of whom are still psychologically involved in the politics of Cuba. Some have been involved in paramilitary training and plans for terrorist acts against the Cuban government.

## Assimilation Pressures

Cultural assimilation pressures on the Cuban immigrants have created cross-generational problems similar to those of earlier European immigrants. Among Miami's Cubans the young reportedly prefer to listen to English-language programs on radio and TV, whereas their parents switch back and forth between English and Spanish programs. The grandparents prefer to hear and speak Spanish. Parents and grandparents worry about the excessive freedom and lack of parental respect of teenagers in U.S. cities. They worry that dates between Cuban American young people are not chaperoned the way they were in Cuba. Parents and grandparents tend to emphasize Cuban traditions and food; children often prefer things American. Moreover, the older generations seem to be more strongly committed to overthrowing Cuba's Communist government and returning home. Home for the less politically active youth is the United States. Nevertheless, family and community ties remain strong, and the young are proud of their Cuban identities.[68]

## SUMMARY

Puerto Ricans are a distinctive American group with an ancient heritage. Like Mexican Americans, they represent a fusion of Native American, Spanish, and African heritages. Puerto Ricans are a divided nation, with one foot on the mainland and one foot in Puerto Rico. The existence of an island population in a more or less external-colony situation just off the mainland complicates the picture. There has been a debate among Puerto Ricans as to whether they are one nation with one set of problems with a few variations or rather two nations with different sets of problems.

The issue of class also comes into this debate. The Caribbean island is a self-contained society with a variety of classes, including both a local capitalist class and a local working class, as well as a small elite of U.S.-based multinational capitalists. Some argue that island problems are different in terms of class from those on the mainland. On the mainland, Puerto Ricans tend to be primarily poor working-class people; there are few capitalists. Others play down the class divisions and stress that there is only *one* Puerto Rican nation. As one Puerto Rican social scientist put it, "No matter how we see ourselves internally, the Yanqui always sees us and deals with us as one class and one people with the same problems. Therefore we should band together and not divide ourselves to fight for our nation against the colonizer."[69]

In addition to the Puerto Ricans, a number of other important Hispanic groups have experienced varying degrees of discrimination in the United States. In the late 1980s the fastest growing segment of the population was Hispanic. Hispanic groups today include the Cuban Americans, many of whom are political refugees from governments with U.S. military backing. The third largest Hispanic group, the Cuban Americans, are concentrated in the southeastern United States. Compared to other Hispanic groups, Cuban Americans have relatively high levels of education and income and are basically an urban population. A distinctive aspect of this important Hispanic community has been the development of the politically powerful urban community centered in Miami. A major reason why Cuban Americans have done relatively well is that most of the early immigrants did not migrate as poor individuals but rather as a group with resources and access to important networks. The achievements of the Cuban Americans underscore the advantages of migrating under the auspices of strong family and friendship networks and governmental support.

## NOTES

1. Piri Thomas, "Puerto Ricans in the Promised Land," *Civil Rights Digest* 6 (no. 2, n.d.):7.
2. Manuel Maldonado-Denis, *Puerto Rico, A Socio-historic Interpretation,* trans. Elena Vialo (New York: Random House, Vintage Books, 1972), pp. 13–19.
3. U.S. Commission on Civil Rights, *Puerto Ricans in the Continental United States: An Uncertain Future* (Washington, D.C.: U.S. Government Printing Office, 1976), pp. 11–12.
4. Ibid., p. 12.

5. Maldonado-Denis, *Puerto Rico·*, pp. 305–6.

6. Nathan Glazer and Daniel P. Moynihan, *Beyond the Melting Pot* (Cambridge: MIT Press and Harvard University Press, 1963), p. 95.

7. Maldonado-Denis, *Puerto Rico*, pp. 311–12; Frank Bonilla and Ricardo Campos, "A Wealth of Poor: Puerto Ricans in the New Economic Order," *Daedalus* 110 (Spring 1981): 135.

8. Thomas, "Puerto Ricans in the Promised Land," p. 19.

9. Adalberto Lopez, "The Puerto Rican Diaspora: A Survey," in *Puerto Rico and Puerto Ricans: Studies in History and Society*, ed. Adalberto Lopez and James Petras (New York: John Wiley, 1974), p. 318.

10. Thomas, "Puerto Ricans in the Promised Land," p. 20.

11. U.S. Commission on Civil Rights, *Puerto Ricans in the Continental United States*, p. 25.

12. Ibid.

13. Ibid., pp. 19–21; Juan Gonzalez, "Puerto Ricans on the Mainland," *Perspectives* 13 (Winter 1982): 10.

14. Quoted in Frank Bonilla, "Beyond Survival: Porque Sequiremos Siendo Puertoriquenos," in *Puerto Rico and Puerto Ricans*, ed. Lopez, p. 439.

15. Alfredo Lopez, *The Puerto Rican Papers* (Indianapolis: Bobbs-Merrill, 1973), p. 120.

16. Quoted in Ibid., p. 211.

17. From a "What Is Prejudice?" pamphlet prepared by the Puerto Rican government; reprinted in *The Puerto Ricans: A Documentary History*, ed. Kal Wagenheim (Garden City, N.Y.: Doubleday, Anchor Books, 1973), p. 291.

18. Glazer and Moynihan, *Beyond the Melting Pot*, pp. 88–90.

19. Lopez, "The Puerto Rican Diaspora," pp. 328–29.

20. Jesús Colon, "The Early Days," in *The Puerto Ricans*, ed. Wagenheim, p. 286.

21. Piri Thomas, *Down These Mean Streets* (New York: Knopf, 1967), as quoted in *The Puerto Ricans*, ed. Wagenheim, pp. 314–20.

22. U.S. Commission on Civil Rights, *Puerto Ricans in the Continental United States*, p. 54; Bonilla and Campos, "A Wealth of Poor," p. 158; U.S. Bureau of the Census, *Persons of Spanish Origin in the United States: March 1979* (Washington, D.C.: U.S. Government Printing Office, 1980), p. 29.

23. U.S. Bureau of the Census, *U.S. Census of Population, 1980: General Social and Economic Characteristics*, PC80-1-C1, 1983, p. 166.

24. Gonzalez, "Puerto Ricans on the Mainland," p. 16; U.S. Commission on Civil Rights, *Puerto Ricans in the Continental United States*, p. 52; Bonilla and Campos, "A Wealth of Poor," p. 160.

25. U.S. Commission on Civil Rights, *Social Indicators of Equality for Minorities and Women* (Washington, D.C.: U.S. Government Printing Office, 1978), p. 30; U.S. Bureau of the Census, *Persons of Spanish Origin in the United States*, p. 25; U.S. Bureau of the Census, *U.S. Census of Population, 1980: General Social and Economic Characteristics*, p. 165.

26. U.S. Commission on Civil Rights, *Puerto Ricans in the Continental United States*, pp. 59–62.

27. Western Regional Office, U.S. Commission on Civil Rights, *Puerto Ricans in California* (Washington, D.C.: U.S. Government Printing Office, 1980), p. 17.

28. Herbert Hill, "Guardians of the Sweatshops: The Trade Unions, Racism, and the Garment Industry," in *Puerto Rico and Puerto Ricans*, ed. Lopez, pp. 386–88.

29. U.S. Commission on Civil Rights, *Puerto Ricans in the Continental United States*, p. 60; Clara E. Rodriguez, "Economic Factors Affecting Puerto Ricans in New York," in *Labor Migration under Capitalism: The Puerto Rican Experience*, ed. History Task Force (New York: Center for Puerto Rican Studies, 1979), pp. 208–10.

30. Marta Tienda and William A. Diaz, "Puerto Ricans' Special Problems," *New York Times*, August 28, 1987, p. A30; Marta Tienda and William Diaz, letter to the *New York Times*, October 10, 1987, p. A30; Robert Garcia, letter to the *New York Times*, September 17, 1987, p. 34.

31. Felipe Luciano, "America Should Never Have Taught Us To Read, She Should Have Never Given Us Eyes To See," in *Puerto Rico and Puerto Ricans*, ed. Lopez, pp. 430–31.

32. Tienda and Diaz, "Puerto Ricans' Special Problems."

33. Testimony by Jose A. Rivera, printed in "Fair Housing and the Spanish Speaking," *Civil Rights Digest* 8 (Fall 1975): 35–36; Gonzalez, "Puerto Ricans on the Mainland, " pp. 15–17.

34. Bonilla and Campos, "A Wealth of Poor," p. 163; Joseph P. Fitzpatrick, "Puerto Ricans," in *Harvard Encyclopedia of American Ethnic Groups*, ed. S. Thernstrom (Cambridge: Harvard University Press,

1980), p. 863; U.S. Bureau of the Census, *U.S. Census of Population, 1980: General Social and Economic Characteristics*, p. 163.

35. U.S. Commission on Civil Rights, *Puerto Ricans in the Continental United States*, p. 104.
36. Fitzpatrick, "Puerto Ricans," p. 863.
37. U.S. Commission on Civil Rights, *Puerto Ricans in the Continental United States*, p. 100.
38. Lopez, *The Puerto Rican Papers*, p. 119.
39. Quoted in U.S. Commission on Civil Rights, *Puerto Ricans in the Continental United States*, p. 99.
40. Quoted in Ibid., p. 103.
41. Gonzalez, "Puerto Ricans on the Mainland," p.11.
42. Garcia, letter to the *New York Times*, p. 34. In the sections on politics and protest I draw on some insights provided by Maria Merrill-Ramirez in comments on this chapter.
43. James Jennings, "Puerto Rican Politics in Two Cities: New York and Boston," in *Puerto Rican Politics in Urban America*, ed. James Jennings and Monte Rivera (Westport, Conn.: Greenwood Press, 1984), pp. 75–90. See also Isidro Lucas, "Puerto Rican Politics in Chicago," in *Puerto Rican Politics in Urban America*, ed. Jennings and Rivera, pp. 102–7.
44. Lopez, "The Puerto Rican Diaspora," p. 329; Fitzpatrick, "Puerto Ricans," p. 866; Western Regional Office, U.S. Commission on Civil Rights, *Puerto Ricans in California*, p. 16.
45. David E. Pitt, "Puerto Rico Expands New York Voter Drive," *New York Times*, October 14, 1987, p. A18.
46. Lopez, *The Puerto Rican Papers*, pp., 55–58.
47. Bonilla and Campos, "A Wealth of Poor," pp. 166–67.
48. Fitzpatrick, "Puerto Ricans," p. 866.
49. John Adam Moreau, "My Parents, They Cry for Joy," in *The Puerto Ricans*, ed. Wagenheim, pp. 327–30.
50. Lopez, "The Puerto Rican Diaspora," p. 331.
51. Ibid., pp. 331–32.
52. Michael Abramson, *Palante: Young Lords Party* (New York: McGraw-Hill, 1971), pp. 34–36.
53. Gonzalez, "Puerto Ricans on the Mainland." p. 17.
54. Lopez, "The Puerto Rican Diaspora," p. 332.
55. Fitzpatrick, "Puerto Ricans," p. 865.
56. Joseph P. Fitzpatrick, *Puerto Rican Americans: The Meaning of Migration to the Mainland* (Englewood Cliffs, N.J.: Prentice Hall, 1971), pp. 22–43; Milton Gordon, *Assimilation in American Life* (New York: Oxford University Press, 1964), pp. 75–77; Elena Padilla, *Up From Puerto Rico* (New York: Columbia University Press, 1958).
57. Maldonado-Denis, *Puerto Rico*, p. 319.
58. Fitzpatrick, *Puerto Rican Americans*, p. 43.
59. U.S. Commission on Civil Rights, *Puerto Ricans in the Continental United States*, p. 29; Lloyd H. Rogler and Rosemary Santana Cooney, *Puerto Rican Families in New York City: Intergenerational Processes* (Maplewood, N.J.: Waterfront Press, 1984), p. 204.
60. Rogler and Cooney, *Puerto Rican Families*, pp. 76–79.
61. Compare Lopez, "The Puerto Rican Diaspora," p. 343.
62. Bonilla and Campos, "A Wealth of Poor," p. 172.
63. "U.S. Hispanics: Who They Are, Whence They Came, and Why," in *The Hispanic Almanac* (Washington, D.C.: Hispanic Policy Development Project, 1984), pp. 17–18.
64. "Trouble in Paradise," *Time*, November 23, 1981, pp. 24–32.
65. "Characteristics of the Cuban American Population," in *The Hispanic Almanac*, pp. 46–48.
66. Alejandro Portes and Robert L. Bach, *Latin American Journey* (Berkeley: University of California Press, 1985), pp. 200–220.
67. Quoted in "Widespread Political Efforts Open New Era for Hispanics," *Congressional Quarterly*, October 23, 1982, p. 2709.
68. "Trouble in Paradise," pp. 30–31.
69. Maria Merril-Ramirez, private communication to author, July 1982.

# CHAPTER 11

# *Japanese Americans*

For many non-Asian Americans, thinking about the Japanese conjures up stereotypes of crafty "Orientals," of militaristic expansionism, or of "yellow" skins. Political speeches and the graffiti of vandals have in recent years included such phrases as "fat Japs" and "little Japs." Negative views are prevalent among the World War II generation of European Americans, whose memories of the Japanese sometimes remain couched in war propaganda. In the 1970s and 1980s we have seen a renewed stereotyping of Japanese Americans as the "model minority." We have also experienced a hostility toward things Japanese because of growing Japanese competition with the United States in world trade.

## MIGRATION: AN OVERVIEW

In 1853 U.S. commodore Matthew Perry sailed warships into Tokyo Bay, and with a show of force won a treaty granting the United States trading rights with Japan. In a few decades trade and labor migration would characterize shipping between the two nations.

Hawaii was the first destination for Japanese migrants coming within the sphere of the United States. European planters sought low-wage laborers for the sugarcane fields. At first, Chinese laborers were brought in under five-year contracts; typically they were one step away from slavery, since quitting a job meant a stay in jail. Between 1885 and 1894 thirty thousand Japanese laborers were brought to the Hawaiian plantations under contract labor agreements. When the agreements expired in 1894, immigration decreased. Most immigrants stayed on, laying the basis for the large present-day Japanese American community. Propertied European Americans strove to ensure their control of the islands, many hoping for annexation by the United States. In 1898, their hopes came true: Hawaii came under the territorial control of the United States government.[1]

## Mainland Migration

Between the 1880s and the so-called Gentleman's Agreement in 1908 more than 150,000 migrants entered; between then and the 1920s another 100,000 came. The immigrants to the mainland United States came under more diverse auspices than did the immigrants to Hawaii. Some came under contract to capitalists, others under the auspices of relatives and friends, and yet others on their own. The pre-1908 Issei* had a harder time than those who came afterward, because later immigrants were brought into a Japanese American community.[2] The decline in Chinese immigrants and a sharp demand for low-wage labor, particularly in agriculture, accelerated the Japanese migration. (For a further discussion of the Chinese, see Chapter 12.)

Soon agitation was sprouting on the West Coast. Employers favored the immigration; many white workers and unions opposed it. The mayor of San Francisco campaigned against the Japanese, arguing they were "unassimilable" and a competitive threat. In 1905 California newspapers began a campaign against the "yellow peril," which they saw as a threat to everything from public schools to non-Asian women. In the same year, both houses of the California legislature passed a resolution calling for exclusion on the grounds that the Japanese Americans would not assimilate, given their racial differences. Because of this agitation, President Theodore Roosevelt arranged for a government prohibition of Japanese migrants. In negotiations in 1907–1908 Roosevelt persuaded the Japanese government to assent to the infamous Gentleman's Agreement, whereby no passports would be given by the Japanese government to any workers except those already in the United States and their close relatives.[3]

Between 1910 and 1919 the majority of immigrants were former residents or parents, wives, and children of residents. The number leaving the United States was significant, about one-third the total number of immigrants. In contrast with the earlier Chinese immigrants, who were virtually all male, more of the Japanese immigrants were family members.

Hate groups argued that the Japanese Americans were taking over, that their birth rate was so high they would overpopulate California, that they were disloyal, and that they were an alien race. A fierce pamphlet and speech battle was waged over these issues, with European Americans railing against the "yellow peril" and a few Japanese scholars counterattacking with carefully documented pamphlets and books.[4]

## Racist Agitation

The writers who proclaimed the threat posed by southern and eastern Europeans to "Anglo-Saxon" superiority often expressed fear of Asian migration. Organized groups, including the American Legion, the American Federation of Labor, and the California Farm Bureau Association, pressed for exclusion of the Japanese. By the 1920s Congress had succumbed to the agitation. The 1924 Immigration Act, which established racist quotas based on a formula giving preference to "Nordic" nations,

---

*Issei, Nisei, Sansei,* and *Yonsei* are Japanese terms for the first four generations of Japanese Americans. The Issei were born in Japan.

*excluded* Japanese immigration with an amendment prohibiting all "aliens ineligible for citizenship." A Supreme Court decision, *Ozawa v. United States* (1922), had paved the way by ruling that only those immigrants of white or African origin could become citizens of the United States—that is, Asians could not become citizens.[5]

Government action against Asians, spurred by labor unions and hate groups, persisted. Until after World War II much of the U.S. labor movement, fighting for survival, supported direct discrimination and exclusion, including discriminatory legislation. Not until the 1950s was action taken to provide a token quota for the Japanese, and not until 1965 were anti-Asian restrictions taken out of U.S. immigration law.[6]

In 1880 there were 148 Japanese in the United States. By 1920 the number had grown to 111,000. By 1970 Japanese Americans were the largest Asian group; the 1965 Immigration Act had resulted in a new flow of immigrants. However, by the 1970s other Asian and Pacific peoples predominated in the migration streams from the East. According to the U.S. census there were 3.7 million Asian Americans in 1980, an increase of more than 100 percent from 1970. Among these were 716,331 Japanese Americans.[7]

## STEREOTYPING

The sentiments of non-Asian Americans toward Japanese Americans have contained positive and negative stereotypes. Stereotypes, as we have seen, are half-truths or gross exaggerations with little or no empirical support. In the earliest years, comparisons with the negatively stereotyped Chinese immigrants led many to evaluate the new Japanese migrants more positively, as less threatening and more family-oriented. The Japanese were more likely to bring along their families. Yet early images contained negative notions that the Japanese were docile and servile.[8]

Around 1900, European Americans worried about exaggerated claims of Japanese American land ownership, which was growing but never involved more than a small percentage of all West Coast farmland. Another widespread view was that the Japanese Americans were incapable of being shaped by the Anglo-Saxon core culture because of their different culture. V.S. McClatchy, a Sacramento editor, argued that the Japanese were "for various reasons unassimilable, and a dangerous element either as residents or citizens."[9]

Above all, their "race" was seen as problematical: "He is brown; we are white; and this difference, they [whites] insist, carries with it such psychological, social, and civilizational differences that any attempt to live together is sure to be disastrous."[10] The ultimate outcome of mixing was seen as "race degeneracy." From presidents and U.S. senators to ordinary westerners, many whites belabored the point of racial differences. James Phelan, U.S. senator from California, argued that the Japanese Americans were a great threat to the "future of the white race, American institutions, and Western civilization."[11]

As early as 1905 some even saw a military threat; the victory of the Japanese in the Russo-Japanese War evoked fears of an invasion from Japan. Paranoia reached a fever pitch in white fears that spies were coming in disguised as immigrants. A related stereotype targeted the alleged Japanese American disloyalty to the United States, said to be due to a prior loyalty to the Japanese emperor.[12]

Movie images were part of a broader smearing of the Japanese Americans as treacherous, villainous, and immoral. In the formative period of the movie industry, Chinese and Japanese characters were consistently pictured as villains, often by white actors. The Asian was stereotyped as "inscrutable," as speaking little English, as cunning and treacherous.[13] Between 1900 and 1920s the image of the forward, buck-toothed "Jap" exploded in the mass media. In his widely circulated "Letters of a Japanese Schoolboy," Wallace Irwin stimulated stereotypes about Japanese Americans, including a mode of speech parodied with phrases such as "honorable sir" and "so sorry please." Magazines and newspapers complained about the dirty conditions Japanese Americans allegedly lived in. Legislators spoke of their early alleged immorality, bringing up the apelike image applied earlier to the Irish and the blacks.[14]

Attitude surveys in the 1920s and 1930s suggested that anti-Japanese prejudices were accepted by most white Americans, especially those on the West Coast. In a survey of white students' attitudes in California in 1927 the frequently mentioned stereotypes were negative: Japanese were thought to be dishonest, treacherous, and unfairly competitive, and to have low standards of living. Another West Coast sample of whites expressed negative attitudes towards the Japanese and Chinese in regard to such matters as friendships and desirability as neighbors.[15]

## War Propaganda

From the 1890s to the 1930s there was much anti-Japanese racism in the United States; the Japanese people were considered an inferior race of people with the brashness to challenge European and American actions in Asia. Even *before* the attack on Pearl Harbor, West Coast leaders were portraying Japanese Americans as disloyal, as potential spies. This image escalated after Pearl Harbor, with rumors of spying and sabotage circulating by the thousands, including such stories as Japanese American farmers planting flowers in a pattern that would guide attacking airplanes.[16]

Major political figures repeated stereotypes to a public inclined to accept them. California's attorney general (later U.S. chief justice), Earl Warren, depicted Japanese Americans as dangerous and threatening. In 1943 General John L. DeWitt, the West Coast military commander, argued, "A Jap's a Jap...The Japanese race is an enemy race and while many second- and third-generation Japanese born on United States soil, possessed of United States citizenship, have become 'Americanized,' the racial strains are undiluted."[17] The national press presented the image of numerous enemy agents in the "large alien population." The irony is that the reason for the large alien population was the racist prohibition on Japanese Issei becoming citizens under U.S. law.

Surveys by the War Relocation Authority after the war revealed that stereotypes continued to be commonplace. Yet with the changes in Japan's position from enemy to ally, the stereotypes slowly began to change. By the 1960s new stereotypes developed, many with apparently positive aspects. Magazines and newspapers praised the Japanese Americans for being highly acculturated.

Some came to see Japanese Americans as the foremost example of nonwhite success. However, Ogawa has noted that the "highly Americanized" and "successful citizens" stereotypes are not entirely positive. The stereotypes suggest that one must become "white" in order to be a good citizen. In the "success" view, since the Japanese Americans have become English-speaking models of the Protestant ethic, they can be accepted by whites as sterilized members of the "Oriental race." The "superior, successful citizen" image has been used to defend the U.S. record with other minorities: other nonwhites can make it too if they become like the Japanese Americans.[18]

## Textbook Distortions, Stereotypes, and Omissions

A study of the images of Japanese Americans in history textbooks found not only this success stereotype but also numerous distortions of Japanese American history. One prominent U.S. history textbook used in public schools tiptoes around the oppressive circumstances of early Japanese American history, speaking of Japanese being "added" to the population. There is a serious omission in such textbooks—the fact that U.S. employers in Hawaii and California actively recruited and exploited Japanese laborers. These textbooks also do not deal with the impact of the racist 1924 Immigration Act on Japanese Americans. That act violated the earlier Gentleman's Agreement with Japan and stopped the immigration of Japanese entirely, over the objections of the Japanese government.

The internment of Japanese Americans in concentration camps during World War II (to be discussed shortly) is not adequately portrayed. The textbooks see the camp experience as part of the "hysteria of war" and do not discuss the long history of anti-Japanese agitation as a prelude to the illegal imprisonment of American citizens of Japanese descent. Moreover, one textbook suggests that Japanese Americans "have forgiven the government for violating their rights during World War II." The fact is that the imprisonment is well remembered by Japanese Americans, who are still pressing the government for fair compensation for the great damage done. They have neither forgotten nor forgiven.[19]

## REPRESSION AND VIOLENT ATTACKS

Japanese Americans have suffered not only from stereotyping but from discrimination and physical attacks as well. The first major acts of violence against the Japanese came within a decade of their arrival in large numbers. White groups, particularly on the West Coast, used a variety of means to stop Japanese migration and competition. Violence was aimed at keeping Japanese Americans subordinate.

After the 1906 San Francisco earthquake the violence directed at Japanese Americans increased. Scientists sent by Japan to help with earthquake relief were attacked by groups of men and boys; local newspapers condoned the actions as pranks. In the wake of growing anti-Asian hostility, Japanese businesses were boycotted; windows were broken; shopkeepers were attacked. Two dozen were attacked on the streets and in places of business in San Francisco. Japanese American resistance was active but inadequate; the police seldom intervened on their behalf.[20]

The anti-Japanese exclusion movement sometimes turned to violence, as in California in 1921, when large numbers of Japanese farm workers were driven out of certain farm areas. Japanese workers and farmers were harassed by exclusionists, and the farmers formed protective organizations. In the 1930s white farmers in Arizona petitioned the governor to throw out Japanese farmers. When this failed, attempts were made to drive them out by force. The threat of such violence spreading to California led the legislature to consider a bill restricting Japanese American agricultural enterprises. At the beginning of World War II violent attacks escalated. In 1942 newspapers and radio broadcasts were reporting dozens of attacks on Japanese Americans and their property from Seattle to San Diego.[21]

## The Horror of Concentration Camps in the United States

In this century only one U.S. racial or ethnic group has been imprisoned as a group—Japanese Americans. The military victories of the Japanese government in the 1930s and 1940s, including the attack at Pearl Harbor, increased fears of a Japanese invasion of the American mainland. We have noted the increase in stereotyping among whites at the time. Members of Congress and the news media parroted the stereotypes and escalated fear across the United States. By January 1942 evacuation and imprisonment were being suggested as the solution. In addition, white-dominated organizations such as the Farm Bureau and the Western Growers Protective Association seemed committed to destroying Japanese American business competition.[22]

The California legislature passed a bill aimed at reducing the presence of Japanese Americans, including the native-born, in state government. State and federal police raids on Japanese aliens, which had begun directly after Peal Harbor, were intensified in a frantic search for spies; more than two thousand aliens were arrested, most without tangible evidence. Japanese American businesses were forced to close. Citizens were illegally detained by local police, evicted by landlords, and fired by employers.[23]

In the first phase of federal action a small number of Japanese, German, and Italian aliens were moved from certain sensitive military areas and their travel was restricted. Then came the second stage. On February 19, 1942, Executive Order 9066 was issued by President Franklin Roosevelt and validated by Congress. It ordered the secretary of war to establish military areas from which any person could be excluded. The West Coast military commander established the western parts of California, Washington, and Oregon, as well as the southern part of Arizona, as areas where no Japanese, Italian, or German aliens could reside. But *only* the Japanese were pressured to resettle outside coastal areas. The two hundred thousand Italian and German aliens there did not have to endure forced movement from their homes. Japanese Americans were detained in assembly centers and later transported under guard to barbed-wire concentration camps.[24]

Businesses and farms were sold at losses. By the fall of 1942 inland areas in the West housed more than 100,000 Japanese, *two-thirds of them native-born U.S. citizens*, in ten camps watched by armed guards. The camps were in barren areas. Barracks were bare-board buildings with few furnishings. [25] At the Tule Lake Camp in

California the white administration arranged for camp inmates to be hired out to white personnel as cooks and domestics at the extraordinarily low wage of $30 a month for a forty-hour week. Part of this wage was taken by the camp administration and spent on recreational facilities for white personnel. Low-price barber shops and cafeterias for whites working in the concentration camps were staffed by Japanese Americans paid semi-slave wages, such as $16 a week to waitresses.[26]

Soon political screening was implemented; the disloyal were to be ferreted out by means of background checks. As a result, protest movements, demonstrations, and riots were generated in the camps. Six thousand prisoners renounced their U.S. citizenship. A few thousand college students and workers for special agricultural assignments were released. Others were released to the U.S. Army, where, ironically, many served with extraordinary valor in segregated units under white officers. By 1944 one-third had been allowed to leave the camps.[27]

Late in 1944 an order was issued rescinding the original order to evacuate; the War Relocation Authority, which had supervised the removal of Japanese Americans, planned to close all the camps within a year. Most evacuees returned to the West Coast, though during late 1945 and 1946 eight thousand returned in despair to Japan. Those who returned to the West Coast found farms and businesses in ruin, household goods destroyed, and local residents hostile; some even experienced attacks by their white neighbors.

The cost of this entire episode was enormous. The government (including the army) spent about $250 million on the evacuation; Japanese American economic losses have been set at more than $400 million.[28]

## Why the Camps Were Created

Why were the Japanese Americans imprisoned? Some emphasize the military angle. Others focus on anti-Japanese prejudice or on the role of white business elites in their struggle with Japanese American competitors. Yet others have accented the role of West Coast politicians who sought public favor by selecting an issue supported by popular prejudices. The U.S. Supreme Court upheld the military decision without investigation—even though *two-thirds* of those evacuated were U.S. citizens. Justice Robert M. Jackson dissented in these Supreme Court decisions, pointing out that the Court had validated "the principle of racial discrimination in criminal procedure." Here was a violation of the rights guaranteed by the Constitution.[29]

Research by Thorne and Drinnon has demonstrated that Franklin Roosevelt and other high officials held racist attitudes. On occasion, Roosevelt made derogatory references to the inferior Asians, including the Vietnamese and Burmese. He believed that the Japanese had less developed skulls and thus believed in their racial inferiority. As a result of this pre-existing racism, Roosevelt and other top leaders saw the emerging struggle and later war in the Pacific as racial. And these racist attitudes made it easy for top U.S. government officials to order the internment of American citizens of Asian descent in concentration camps.[30]

A number of Japanese Americans fought valiantly but unsuccessfully in the courts to prevent their forced evacuation. Vigorous demonstrations were also held. There was a confrontation between Japanese American evacuees and authorities at the

Santa Anita Assembly Center in California over the rumored appropriation of personal property. Property was destroyed and a police officer was attacked by a group of angry Japanese; two hundred armed military police suppressed the rioting. At the Poston camp in the fall of 1942 there was a strike over the imprisonment of two Japanese Americans; more than two thousand persons met in a protest rally.[31]

A similar situation occurred at Manzanar in east-central California, where there were ten thousand relocatees. In December 1942 an assault on a Japanese American who had collaborated with whites and the imprisonment of the attacker led to a mass meeting of four thousand people and to demands for an investigation of conditions at the camp. The camp director, escorted by military police armed with machine guns, met the crowd. A crowd again formed at night at the jail and was fired upon when it did not disperse. Two inmates were killed.

There was also protest at the Tule Lake camp in California after it became a segregation camp for those Japanese Americans considered especially disloyal. A series of conflicts between inmates and the authorities erupted over police attempts to break up crowds, over arbitrary work decisions, over poor working conditions, over a public funeral, and over camp living conditions. In 1943, as a result of a fight between a white officer and evacuees, the latter were arrested, the Army brought in tanks to restore order, and martial law was declared.[32]

## THE POLITICAL ARENA

Because of the racist character of U.S. naturalization laws in the late 1800s, the Issei could not become citizens. In 1922 the Supreme Court reaffirmed that Japanese Americans could not become citizens because citizenship was limited by law to "free white persons" and those of African ancestry. Great pressure was directed against Japanese American participation in U.S. politics. Most second-generation Japanese Americans did not become old enough to vote until the 1940s. Just as these Nisei were coming of age, World War II brought a severe setback in the struggle for political participation. Because they had no leading politicians and few votes, there was no political peril involved in uprooting them.[33]

After World War II, political gains began accruing to Japanese Americans. Some organization had begun in the 1930s. The Japanese American Citizens League (JACL), controlled by Nisei leaders, was pressing moderately for civil rights and for citizenship for the Issei. Voter registration campaigns were inaugurated, but attempts to get candidates to run generally stopped at the planning stage. The JACL has been the largest voluntary association among Japanese Americans. In recent decades it has come under attack as too establishment-oriented and conformist.[34]

### Compensation Pressures and Political Progress

In the decades after World War II the JACL, together with other Japanese American groups, played a role in winning political victories. The first victories came in the area of legal and political rights. By 1946, together with newer organizations, the JACL was pressing for compensation for evacuation losses, for citizenship for the first generation, and for changes in discriminatory laws. Meager compensation finally came in the form of the 1948 Japanese American Evacuation Act. By the 1950 deadline nearly 24,000 claims had been filed for $132 million. Ultimately the Japanese American victims of this constitutional deprivation of rights were paid $38 million, less than 10 percent of losses.[35]

These token payments did not end Japanese American pressures. Since the mid-1970s a number of Japanese American organizations and officials have pressed the United States government for more adequate repayment for the substantial economic losses suffered. In 1980 Congress established the Commission on Wartime Relocation and Internment of Civilians. The commission recommended that the 66,000 survivors of imprisonment receive compensation of $1 billion to $2 billion.

On September 17, 1987, the 200th anniversary of the signing of the U.S. Constitution, the U.S. House passed a law including a formal apology to Japanese Americans for internment and providing $1.2 billion in compensation for the 66,000 internees still alive. The bill admits that the "basic civil liberties" of Japanese Americans were violated as a result of "racial prejudice." The Senate finally passed the bill on April 20, 1988. The House bill was passed after years of foot dragging by congressional leaders, opposition from the conservative Reagan White House, and intense opposition from many non-Asian Americans, many of whom still hold racist attitudes about Japanese Americans.[36]

In 1952 the Japanese *exclusion* provision of the 1924 Immigration Act was repealed, only to be replaced with a racist small-quota restriction; the Japanese now had a token quota. Asian background was removed as a barrier to naturalized citizenship. The racist quota on Japanese immigration was not eliminated until the 1965 Immigration Act.[37]

In the early 1970s, in response to pressure from organized Japanese Americans, Title II of the 1950 Internal Security Act was finally repealed. That provision had permitted government imprisonment of citizens deemed potential collaborators with an enemy in time of crisis. Old anti-Japanese laws and ordinances were repealed. In the mid-1970s a symbolic political gain was achieved when President Gerald Ford rescinded the infamous Executive Order 9066 which had resulted in the wartime imprisonment.[38]

While these belated gains were being won, political activity aimed at electoral victories was increasing. Major gains came first in Hawaii. Some Nisei were registered to vote in Hawaii as early as 1917, and a few made early unsuccessful bids for office in the territorial legislature. In 1930 the first were elected to office, one as a county supervisor and two as members of the territorial legislature; by the late 1930s nine Japanese American officials were among the nearly one hundred elected officials in Hawaii.

Returning Japanese American World War II veterans, intent on expanding their political participation, became active in Democratic attempts to overthrow the traditional Republican domination of the islands. Several were elected to the Hawaii legislature; in the late 1950s their activities facilitated Congress's conferral of statehood, finally overcoming the anti-Asian sentiment that had kept Hawaii from achieving this status. Daniel Inouye, a war hero, was elected the first U.S. representative from the new state and the first Japanese American in Congress. Spark Matsunaga became the second to serve in the House, in 1962, when Inouye became senator. In 1964 a second House seat was won by Patsy Takemoto Mink, the first Japanese American woman to serve in Congress. Since the 1960s local and state offices in Hawaii have seen a growing number of Japanese American occupants.[39.]

Mainland Nisei cut their political "teeth" serving in the prison camps of World War II, but victories have been made difficult by the dilution of votes in the heavily European American populations of the western states. Clarence Arai made unsuccessful attempts at election to the Washington legislature in the 1930s. Only one Nisei was elected to a state legislature between that time and the late 1960s. In 1953 the first Japanese American became a judge on the mainland. In the 1960s a few were elected to city council offices in Los Angeles County, Oakland, and San Jose and to mayoral posts in two or three towns.[40] In the 1980s there were only a handful of Japanese Americans in elected positions at the higher levels of local, state, and federal governments on the mainland. In 1976 Samuel I. Hayakawa, a Canadian-born semanticist, was elected senator from California, the first Japanese American senator from the mainland. The same year, Norman Mineta of California became the first mainland representative. In 1982 Hayakawa retired from the Senate and was replaced by a non-Asian senator. In 1988 both senators from Hawaii, Inouye and Matsunaga, were Japanese Americans, as were the two representatives to the U.S. House. In addition, two survivors of the camps, Mineta and Robert Matsui, California Democrats, led the House effort in 1987 to pass the aforementioned compensation bill.

## Politics, Stereotyping, and Competition with Japan

During the 1970s and 1980s there have been incidents of vandalism and violence against Asian Americans, including Japanese Americans. For example, the word *Jap* was spray-painted on the garage of a Japanese American state legislator in California. A Chinese American woman was pushed in front of a subway train in New York City by a man who said he had a "phobia about Asians." In Flint, Michigan, an exhibit at an auto show showed a car with a Japanese face falling like a bomb on Detroit, a portrayal suggestive of the classic racist view of the "Oriental hordes" threatening white America.[41]

A new form of anti-Japanese agitation was spreading across the United States. Japan's development was surpassing that of the United States in a number of industries, such as steel and automobile manufacturing. As a result, the United States was importing large quantities of manufactured goods from Japan. Buy-American cartoons caricatured "wily Japs" and "crafty Orientals." Old stereotypes appeared again in conversations and in newspaper articles. Unemployment fueled the tendency to make the Japanese scapegoats for U.S. troubles. Anti-Japanese protectionist bills were introduced in Congress. And Japanese Americans were blamed for the actions of the Japanese. Yet Japan was not the major cause of recessions in U.S. capitalism; the real causes lay elsewhere—in poor U.S. corporate management, for example.

## Protest Organizations and Nonviolent Protest

Research has dramatized the forgotten protests of Japanese Americans against oppression. At the turn of the century white delegates arriving at a Chinese Exclusion Convention were met at the door, much to their surprise, by Japanese Americans with leaflets arguing against attempts to exclude the Japanese. This was the beginning of a long series of books, speeches, and pamphlets over the next two decades by Japanese and Japanese Americans protesting exclusion attempts. A few voluntary associations, such as the Japanese Association, were formed in the early 1900s to combat white exclusion activities and other manifestations of anti-Japanese discrimination.[42]

Organized worker activity was part of the early Japanese experience. Japanese workers in Hawaii participated in at least sixty work stoppages in the five decades after 1870. On the mainland there was substantial worker organizing. A few strikes occurred in the 1890s; after 1900 their number increased. A few socialist groups were formed by Japanese immigrants in the early 1900s; most pressed for better wages and working conditions. In 1903 more than one thousand agricultural workers, Japanese and Mexican, struck farmers in Ventura, California. Japanese American workers were involved in agricultural and mining strikes in California, Utah, Colorado, and Washington. Up to the 1940s, Japanese American and Mexican American workers cooperated in strikes against exploitative white farmers in south-western states.[43]

Japanese Americans protested during the prison camp period. Thousands renounced their citizenship and returned to Japan. There were numerous demonstrations and even a few riots against oppressive conditions.

In the 1960s, an Asian American movement developed, this time led by the Sansei. The students active in the movement questioned older views and leaders. Programs in Asian American studies were established; new journals were created, such as the *Amerasia Journal*, with papers urging collective Asian American action and attention to problems of that group. Sugar-coated images of Japanese success were challenged as a renewed sense of group pride and collective consciousness developed. The young have been sensitive to the price paid for acculturation—acquiescence to European-American values, which they see as frustrating creativity. By the 1980s some of the militancy had died down. But the concern for Asian American problems has persisted.[44]

# THE ECONOMY

Most immigrants started out at the bottom levels of the pyramid, filling the hard jobs on farms and in the cities along the West Coast. Contract labor from Japan went first to the agricultural plantations in Hawaii. On the mainland many Japanese went into agricultural work and other work in rural areas, such as logging and working for lumber mills and railroads. Most had farming backgrounds and so were receptive to this type of labor. One California study in 1909 found 65 percent of Japanese American workers in agriculture, 15 percent in domestic service work, 15 percent in small businesses, and 5 percent in other lines of work.[45]

In the first decades the new residents worked for as little as 50 cents to a dollar a day in agriculture. Japanese workers received less than European Americans. While white sawmill laborers got $2.60 to $3.50 a day in the state of Washington, Japanese laborers got only $1.75 to $2.75. This pattern of differential wage rates was true for many, if not most, job categories along the West Coast. Here intentional discrimination can been seen.

In cities Japanese Americans became service workers and laborers. Some gained a toehold in the economy as servants of whites, at wages of $1.50 a week plus board. By 1910 there were several thousand domestics in San Francisco alone. As in the case of the Italians and Irish, the immigrants were aided in their entry by those who had preceded them.[46]

## Finding an Economic Niche

Gradually the Issei began to buy or lease land to farm on their own. In urban areas, where direct discrimination kept the Japanese out of manufacturing and white-collar employment, some went into small businesses. In the view of Bonacich and Modell, the Issei came to play a middleman-minority role in the California economy. By 1909 there were at least 3,000 Japanese American businesses in the western states, and by 1929 there were nearly 2,000 in Los Angeles alone. An estimated 30 percent of Japanese Americans were involved with Japanese American businesses as employers or employees. Operated on a small scale, some enterprises catered primarily to a Japanese American clientele, but many eventually serviced a non-Asian clientele. The Issei's ethnic solidarity helped them create the ethnic economy, and this small-business economy in turn reinforced their solidarity. Bonacich and Modell conclude that "the Japanese minority filled a particular and specialized niche in the general economy and was important to it, providing key products and services."[47]

Most Japanese immigrants came from eleven southern prefectures in Japan, each with its associations in the United States. These prefectural clubs could act as mutual-aid associations for immigrants in a hostile environment. Prefectural associations aided the movement of immigrants into the economy by providing training for workers and directing clients to businesses. Restaurants and cleaning operations succeeded because the networks could be drawn on for workers and for economic aid. Pooling resources in informal money-raising organizations called *tanomoshi* provided capital for entrepreneurs who could not secure funds from banks. Mutual-aid associations helped half of all foreign-born Japanese secure the capital necessary for establishing businesses.[48]

White opposition built swiftly and had a clear economic thrust. In urban areas the labor movement led the opposition, even though Japanese Americans seldom sought jobs in unionized industries. Boycotts and anti-Japanese advertising were used by white groups, as in the 1908 Anti-Jap Laundry League attempt to drive Japanese Americans out of the laundry business. Laborers and farmers were accused of every conceivable "vice." But the basic problem was that the Japanese immigrants were hard-working and, frequently, successful competitors.[49]

The 1913 California Alien Land Law, passed under pressure from white farmers, stipulated that aliens could not buy land or lease it for more than three years; nor could they pass on land to their children. As we have seen, all Issei were forced to remain "aliens" because of discriminatory naturalization laws. While this California land law did interfere with agricultural activity, ways were found to circumvent it, such as registering ownership of lands under the names of children. In response, in the 1920s new discriminatory laws prohibited Issei from leasing land and from holding it in the names of children.

The impact of these land laws was to reduce the number of Japanese American farms from over five thousand in 1920 to four thousand in 1930. Those who remained in farming relied on tenant or truck farming, raising vegetables for urban markets. New organizations such as the Japanese Cooperative Farm Industry organized the flow of farm products to Japanese retailers in cities. Using ingenuity, Japanese American farmers were again demonstrating their knack for success; then the wartime evacuation destroyed their farming again.[50]

Forced out of farming by land laws, and attracted to the demand for landscaping in the booming cities of California, many displaced farmers and farm workers became gardeners or nursery operators. The 1930 census of California showed that 54 percent of male Japanese workers were still in agriculture or gardening, 25 percent were in trade or business, 2 percent were in the professions, and a large percentage of the rest were in other urban occupations.[51]

By the beginning of World War II some Japanese Americans in cities were moving into white-collar positions. One study estimated that 51 percent of the males in highly urbanized Los Angeles County in 1940 were in white-collar positions and about 40 percent were in semiskilled and unskilled blue-collar positions.[52] Then the bottom fell out. Median economic losses per family in Los Angeles from the forced wartime evacuation were estimated at about $10,000 in goods, property, income, and expenses (in 1940 dollars). The figures were similar elsewhere. There were heavy losses to small businesses. One official estimate put total economic losses at $400 million. Many of those who could not regain their businesses and farms after 1945 went into contract gardening and private household work. Some groceries and restaurants were reestablished, and the "Little Tokyos" of West Coast cities again became vibrant areas.

## The Postwar Economy

The booming postwar economy was more willing to accept Japanese American workers with experience, particularly experience outside the West Coast and in professional and civil service areas. Social and economic discrimination continued to affect the second generation; after the war certain occupations and industries were still off limits. For more than a decade University of California education departments discouraged Japanese American students from considering the teaching profession because of the difficulty of placement.[53]

Self-employment continued to be important. By 1960 there were seven thousand Japanese-owned businesses in the Los Angeles area, most of them gardening businesses. Hotels, groceries, and laundries made up the next largest categories. According to Bonacich and Modell, the middleman-minority model, which we discussed in Chapter 2, seems to fit best the Issei generation. The second and later generations have gradually moved away from the ethnic economy of small businesses and "trading" to professional and other white-collar jobs in the larger economy. The Nisei were split into two groups. In 1960 about half were still involved in ethnic businesses, but many others used the education provided by parents to move into jobs in the larger society. It was the older and less educated Nisei who had stayed in the ethnic economy.[54]

## Occupational Mobility and Problems

Since 1960 a number of books and articles have related the Japanese American experience as a remarkable success story of achievement in the face of enormous odds. The usual socioeconomic indicators in census data do indicate that Japanese American progress since the 1950s has been dramatic. For example, compared with the total U.S. male population, in 1970 Japanese American men occupied white-collar levels in somewhat larger proportions. In 1960 about 40 percent of Japanese American men were in white-collar positions, a proportion that increased to nearly half by 1970. Similarly, the majority of women were in white-collar positions in both 1960 and 1970, with the percentage also increasing over that decade. Japanese American women were concentrated in clerical and service occupations.[55]

In the 1980 census Japanese Americans were found to be concentrated in white-collar jobs. About 20 percent were in professional and technical jobs, compared with 15.4 percent of the population as a whole. The proportion in managerial and administrative positions was 12.8 percent, larger than the 10.4 percent of the general population. The proportion in clerical and sales jobs was 29.9 percent, again larger than 27.3 percent of the general population in that category. Altogether, over 60 percent of Japanese American workers were in white-collar jobs, compared with about half of the general population. The percentages in most blue-collar categories were smaller than comparable percentages in the total population. Among Japanese Americans, 19.9 percent were employed in craft, operative and laborer jobs, compared with about one-third of the general population; about 12 percent were in service jobs, about the same as for the U.S. population.[56]

A study by the U.S. Commission on Civil Rights found a significant degree of occupational segregation for Japanese American workers, when compared with white workers. Examining 441 major jobs categories, the commission found that 42 percent of Japanese American males and a third of Japanese American females would have to change occupations to have the same occupational distribution as white workers. Even though Japanese Americans have made major occupational gains since World War II, they are disproportionately concentrated in certain job categories. They do not hold as wide an array of jobs as do European-American workers. The niches occupied by many Japanese Americans reflect past and present exclusion from other job categories.[57]

The income picture seems to generally support the success argument as well. In 1970 the median income for Japanese American families was $12,500, compared with $9,600 for all families. By 1980 it was $27,354, substantially greater than the national figure for all families of $19,917. In addition, only a small percentage of Japanese American families (6.6 percent) fell below the federal poverty line, a figure lower than those for whites and for all other Asian groups. While these income attainments are impressive, some troubling problems remain. The income figures relate to current income and do not include property and other types of wealth. Japanese American families average *more* workers *per* household than the typical white family, and Japanese American workers are concentrated in states (Hawaii, California) with both high wages and a high cost of living. Moreover, Japanese families with *foreign-born* heads, many of whom are recent immigrants, have had incomes below the national median for families.[58]

The income levels of Japanese Americans are lower than they should be, given this group's high level of education. Some statistics suggest this discrepancy between occupation and education. In 1970 in the United States as a whole, for every male aged 25 to 34 with at least four years of college there were 1.5 males making $10,000 or more; among Japanese Americans the comparable ratio was much lower, only 0.9 males making $10,000 or more for everyone aged 25 to 34. Among older males, those 35 to 44 the national ratio of 2.4 was still higher than the Japanese ratio of 1.8. For a given level of education, Japanese American men got less on the average than non-Japanese men.

Moreover, a study by the U.S. Commission on Civil Rights found the same pattern. This study calculated what Japanese American workers would have been earning if they had been white workers with the same level of education, state of residence, age, and level of work effort. They found that Japanese workers earned only 88 percent of the amount earned by white males with comparable characteristics. Discrimination is suggested in these imbalances between education and income.[59]

In a recent survey of Japanese Americans in three California cities, the majority of the respondents *disagreed* with the statement "Currently, Japanese [Americans] do not experience job discrimination." Majorities of both the Nisei and the Sansei in the sample felt that Japanese Americans still face job discrimination.[60]

In the 1980s Japanese Americans have continued to face subtle exclusion from prominent positions in businesses, movies and television, politics, and certain civil service areas, such as police and fire departments. Indirect discrimination in the form of height and weight requirements has played a role in some occupational areas. Positions at higher administrative, managerial, and professional levels are often closed to Asians, particularly on the West Coast. In recent years some Japanese have complained that whites with poorer credentials or lesser ability have been promoted at a faster rate. One study of employment in private industries in the San Francisco metropolitan area found Asian Americans to be underrepresented in manufacturing, construction, and wholesale trade. Asian Americans were found to be underrepresented in better-paying jobs (such as managerial jobs) and overrepresented in lower-paying jobs (such as clerical jobs).[61]

A *Newsweek* review of Asian Americans noted that "Asians tend to be underemployed for their levels of education and are underrepresented in corporate executive suites." Overall trends in the economy have affected the employment patterns of Japanese Americans. For example, although elementary and secondary education has been a popular college major in the postwar period, the demand for teaching jobs slackened in the 1960s and 1970s. Past discrimination channeled Asian Americans into a few occupations, such as teaching, thus setting some of them up for serious problems in times of category-specific recessions.

That Japanese Americans have achieved remarkable economic success against enormous odds is clearly indicated in socioeconomic data obtained since the 1940s. What they could have achieved without the persisting direct and indirect discrimination can only be imagined.[62]

# EDUCATION

## Racism and Segregation

Japanese Americans have had a commitment to education. Issei parents sent their children to school more often than parents in most other groups. Many Issei pursued formal education. Forty-five percent of a large sample of Issei who had come after 1907 reported they had secured some formal education in the United States; many developed a facility with English early.[63]

In 1906 the mayor of San Francisco, in a move supported by local newspapers, got a resolution from the board of education setting up a separate school for Asian children. There were at the time fewer than 100 Japanese American children in two dozen schools. One member of the California legislature spoke of the danger to the "pure maids of California" posed by older Japanese students in primary grades. The Japanese government protested, and the federal government took court action to force the San Francisco Board of Education to give Japanese American children the equal rights promised to them by an 1895 treaty.

Some anti-Japanese Californians were so angered about this rare federal support of Japanese Americans that they began to talk about secession. A compromise was worked out between President Theodore Roosevelt and San Francisco officials. After three months out of school, most Japanese American children were allowed to return; the compromise meant the exclusion of over-age Japanese pupils. In return, the infamous Gentleman's Agreement, aimed at stopping migration, was executed by President Roosevelt.[64]

In this period of racist agitation a common stereotype was that Japanese immigrants' children were displacing other children in California schools. The fact was that in 1920 Japanese Americans outnumbered whites only in one village school in the town of Florin. Even by the late 1930s Japanese children were present only in small proportions in all but two or three schools in California. One result of this agitation over schools was an increase in segregation pressures. Several attempts were made by California legislators to segregate Japanese children, and by 1930 there were segregated schools for Asian Americans in four school districts.[65]

## Language Schools and Japanese Educational Progress

Japanese Americans developed private "language schools," which focused on training in the Japanese language and in traditional values. The schools played an important role in teaching such values as industry, courtesy, and an intensified respect for elders.

The Issei established the language schools as a way of strengthening community bonds. By 1920 there were at least 54 language schools in California, with 2,000 pupils; by 1928 there were more than 4,000 pupils in 118 language schools. Anti-Japanese exclusionists vigorously attacked the schools as centers of emperor worship and Buddhism aimed at making children disloyal to the United States. The California legislature passed a bill, fortunately vetoed by the governor, abolishing the schools. The exclusionists' stereotyped view of these schools was racist and sharply out of touch with reality.[66]

By the 1930s Japanese Americans were making great strides in public education, from the primary grades to the college level, in spite of entrenched discrimination. At several branches of the University of California the ratio of Japanese American students to the Japanese American population was a little greater than the figure for the total California population. A 1930 survey of a large number of Japanese Americans in California showed the average educational level for males over 20 born in the United States to be 12.5 years. The figures for females were also relatively high. The educational attainments of Japanese Americans were at least equal to those of California whites.[67]

The war evacuation sharply interrupted these educational attainments. Students were forced to leave public schools. Americanization schools were provided in prison camps. Second- and third-generation Japanese Americans got part of their schooling in the camps. After the war, educational discrimination against Japanese Americans was relaxed, so that major gains continued again. Enrollment in Japanese language schools gradually declined, and public schools became central to Japanese American education.

By 1970 the median educational levels for adult Japanese American males and females were 12.6 and 12.4 years, respectively, compared with a combined national figure of 12.1 years. The proportion of Japanese Americans who had completed high school and college was larger than the proportion of the population as a whole; school enrollments were also higher. Between 1970 and 1980 Japanese educational attainment increased further. By 1980 the median educational level for all Japanese Americans was 12.9 years, substantially greater than the 12.5 years for all adult Americans. Most (82 percent) were high school graduates.[68]

Yet the educational picture still contains more than a few traces of discrimination. Japanese Americans continue to be underrepresented in some graduate programs and departments at the University of California. Further, while Japanese Americans made up a representative proportion of administrators and teachers in the Department of Education in Hawaii in the 1970s, they were underrepresented on the faculty of the University of Hawaii. And although the education levels of Japanese Americans are higher than those of the white population, their income levels are lower than one would predict on this basis. The financial payoffs of college can still vary according to race and ethnicity.[69]

## RELIGION

Japanese immigrants brought Buddhism and Shintoism with them as they crossed the Pacific. These religious traditions remained strong in the United States. Once the Japanese had arrived, Protestant missionaries converted many to Christian beliefs. The Protestant missions provided support for immigrants establishing themselves in a difficult environment. They were crucibles of acculturation in which young Japanese Americans began to absorb the language and values of the core culture. When the missions grew, they became full-scale Japanese Protestant churches segregated from other churches. By the 1920s there were thousands of practicing Japanese American Protestants.[70]

Buddhist temples were founded in all major coastal cities in the decade after 1900. By 1920 there were two dozen temples in the West. Buddhist groups made significant adaptations to the new environment, with Christian-style Sunday schools and church organizations. As with the Japanese language schools, white exclusionists made the grossly exaggerated claim that the temples were hotbeds of emperor worship and antipatriotic teaching. Ironically, Buddhism does *not* involve emperor worship.[71]

A survey of Japanese Californians in the 1930s found that while three-quarters of first-generation immigrants were Buddhist, only 39 percent of the second generation were. A majority among the Nisei were Christian. The Japanese Americans were becoming a Christian group. A study in Seattle found the community there roughly split between Christian churches and traditional Japanese religious groups. Yet the division was not as great as it might have appeared. Adoption of Christian practices did not entail a break with the past, for many considered themselves Christian and Buddhist.[72]

Before and during World War II there was jingoistic agitation branding Buddhism and Shintoism un-American. The evacuation closed churches on the mainland; Buddhist temples were closed in Hawaii and priests imprisoned. World War II brought destruction to Buddhist temples; many were vandalized during the war. After the war Buddhist temples grew in number across the United States; Buddhism regained its important position in Japanese American communities.[73] By 1980 there were several dozen Protestant churches in the Japanese Southern California Ministerial Fellowship, with numerous others scattered up and down the West Coast and across the country. The Jodo Shinshu Buddhist Churches of America had many churches; there were dozens of smaller Buddhist sects. One study of Japanese Americans in San Francisco found that churches were second in importance only to the family in cementing the community; two-thirds of those interviewed were at least occasional participants in church activities. Buddhist groups tended to attract older, more conservative members, while younger Japanese Americans preferred Presbyterian and Methodist churches.[74]

## ASSIMILATION?

An assimilation perspective has predominated in much analysis of Japanese Americans. This group has been seen as the most adaptive of non-European immigrant groups. Cultural assimilation came at an early point for most Issei, although some acculturated more rapidly than others. One group sought to survive by isolating themselves from the outside world and immersing themselves in things Japanese; the other group sought to acculturate rapidly, at the same time maintaining social, and some cultural, ties.[75]

Cultural assimilation, in regard to language and religion, came rapidly for later generations. In one survey, although most Issei reported they could get along in English, many reported some language difficulty. The influence of the Issei in the Japanese community has been wide-ranging, while their ability to cope in the core culture has been restricted. The Nisei have equally wide-ranging adaptive patterns in the two spheres. Several studies of the Sansei have underscored the apparent closing of the gap with the outside white culture. For example, Feagin and Fujitaki found that Nisei and Sansei respondents showed substantial acculturation in regard to speaking English at home and not reading Japanese literature.[76]

### Structural Assimilation

Structural assimilation at secondary levels has been dramatic for the Japanese, particularly in the *economic* sphere. Many analysts have dramatized this aspect of assimilation. Petersen, among others, has argued that Japanese Americans represent a remarkable success story in the economic progress they have made against intense discrimination. Relatively high levels of occupation, income, and education are characteristic of the Nisei and even more characteristic of the Sansei. Explanations for this success have tended to focus on Japanese Americans' values, ethical background, and community organization. Light has opted for a traditional-culture explanation in examining successful small businesses and has argued that the development of the small-business economy among Japanese Americans sets them apart from other non-European Americans such as blacks and Mexican Americans. He accents the role of a "culturally preferred style of economic organization," by which he means the rotating-credit associations brought over with the immigrants from Japan.[77]

What Milton Gordon refers to as behavior-receptional assimilation and attitude-receptional assimilation showed little change until after World War II. Intense discrimination and prejudice marred the lives of the Issei and Nisei for the first fifty years. Since World War II discrimination and prejudice directed at Japanese Americans have decreased. The fact that ideal adaptation has not been reached in these areas was pointed up in a recent study. In this survey, a significant number of Japanese Americans reported discrimination. One-fifth of their sample (31 percent of the Nisei and 13 percent of the Sansei) reported that they had experienced considerable discrimination as adults, and another 65 percent reported a little discrimination. Only 13 percent reported *never* having experienced discrimination. In addition, three-quarters of the sample felt that Japanese Americans today experience social discrimination, and, as we noted earlier, the majority disagreed with the statement that Japanese Americans do not face job discrimination today. Given the reluctance of Japanese Americans to speak ill of their country, these responses are likely to be an underestimate of the subtle and blatant discrimination actually faced today by Japanese Americans.[78]

Assimilation at the level of primary social ties and voluntary associations is an important dimension; for the Japanese this assimilation has not proceeded as far as integration in the economic sphere. The Issei immigrated under the auspices of family members already in the United States. Employment and small-business relationships were their main contacts with non-Japanese; most remained isolated socially, in part because of discrimination. In recent decades, surviving Issei have tended, much more than later generations, to reside in extended families and to localize their ties within Japanese networks.

A number of researchers have found that primary-group integration with outsiders has been limited for the Nisei and modest for the Sansei. One study of 148 Japanese American males looked at the primary-group level. Two-thirds had mostly Japanese Americans as close friends; the Sansei were only slightly more integrated with whites than were the Nisei. However, majorities in both groups reported they lived in neighborhoods where 50 percent or more of their neighbors were white. According to a major study of Japanese Americans by Montero and associates, the proportion of Japanese Americans living in heavily Japanese neighborhoods declined from 1915 to 1967. By the late 1960s over half lived in predominantly non-Japanese neighborhoods, while 40 percent lived in mixed neighborhoods. Residential segregation has declined very significantly for these Asian Americans.[79]

In their study Feagin and Fujitaki found that only a minority of the Nisei and Sansei samples preferred that their children associate only with other Japanese; most preferred mixed associations. Data since the 1960s suggest a trend toward primary-group assimilation. There does seem to be an increased movement among the Sansei into wider social circles.[80]

Until the late 1940s antimiscegenation laws in western states made Asian European marriages *illegal*. Aside from the Japanese war brides of returning soldiers, there was almost no intermarriage with outsiders until the 1950s. Los Angeles data showed an outmarriage rate of 2 percent in the 1924–1933 period and a rate of 11 to 20 percent for the 1950s. Several surveys in the 1950s and 1960s showed strong but declining preferences among the Nisei and the Sansei for Japanese American marriage partners. In 1967 a national survey of the Sansei discovered that one-third had outmarried or were planning to outmarry; studies of recent marriage licenses in Los Angeles and Fresno counties found the proportions outmarrying to be closer to half. And a study of three generations of Japanese Americans by Levine and Rhodes concluded that the predilection of half the Sansei for white mates will mean that it will be difficult to preserve a vibrant Japanese American community in the future, especially outside Los Angeles.[81]

However, a recent analysis of 1980 census data found that just 34 percent of Japanese Americans in the United States had married outside their group. Indeed, only 23 percent of native-born men and 24 percent of native-born women had married out. Among the native-born Japanese Americans the intermarried women were older on the average than inmarried women, whereas intermarried men were a bit younger on the average than inmarried men. These data suggest that the younger generation of men are somewhat more likely to intermarry than older men, but that among women the opposite is the case. The importance of this study is that its sample is national and therefore larger than the samples used by studies showing higher rates of outmarriage. The data on intermarriage for Japanese Americans, at this point, are too inconsistent to argue strongly for the full marital assimilation of Japanese Americans in the near future.[82]

## Japanese Identity

When it comes to identificational assimilation, few Japanese have rejected their Japanese heritage for a purely "American" identity. The sense of "Japaneseness" has been strong in all generations. Most have seen themselves as having a foot in both worlds. A 1969 study found more than 60 percent of the Sansei and more than 80 percent of the Nisei saying they were very proud of their Japanese background. Indeed, in recent years some of the Sansei and Yonsei have developed a renewed interest in that heritage, to the extent of some activists emphasizing the need for militancy.[83]

An assimilationist might see Japanese Americans as well on the road to comprehensive assimilation to the outside white culture and society. On major levels there has been some movement toward greater inclusion, though candor would require an assimilationist to contrast the substantial integration in such areas as the economy with the more modest integration at the primary-group level.

Japanese Americans might also be viewed as a clear-cut example of ethnogenesis—partly in but partly outside the dominant white culture and society. No analyst has yet developed this perspective on Japanese Americans, although Petersen has argued that this group has become a "subnation" in the United States, achieving integration in the economic sphere and making some cultural adaptation, but maintaining a distinctive and cohesive family-centered community.[84]

Connor's study of three generations of Japanese Americans in Sacramento suggests the persistence of Japanese American ways. Connor found that the third generation (the Sansei) still had many psychological and family traits that were characteristic of the first generation (the Issei). The Sansei had a greater sense of duty and family obligation, closer family ties, and a greater tendency to be deferential than the whites who were surveyed. A more recent study asked Japanese American respondents whether or not they saw differences in "Japanese and Caucasian ways" in social affairs, church life, and family relations. Large percentages saw significant differences between the majority group and their group, from 42 percent for social life to 65 percent for family life and 75 percent for church life. Interestingly, the Sansei were more likely to see differences than the Nisei. The authors of this study suggest that Japanese Americans do *not* see themselves as assimilating rapidly to the core culture in such spheres as social, family, and church life.[85]

## The Power–Conflict View

Few analysts have interpreted the Japanese American experience systematically from a power–conflict point of view. One leading power–conflict thinker, Robert Blauner, has suggested that Japanese Americans might be viewed as partially colonized. Many early Japanese immigrants worked in a position of debt servitude or migrated to the United States under substantial pressure. This was particularly the case for thousands of contract laborers who went to Hawaii and later moved on to the mainland.

Bonacich has underscored the intimate economic relationship between the labor needs of capitalism and the streams of immigrant workers employed over the centuries in the United States. Asian labor filled the needs of a booming frontier capitalism on the West Coast. Chinese and Japanese laborers became the "colored" labor, with fewer rights than their white counterparts. The United States was an imperial power in the Pacific region; as a result, U.S. agents had easy entry into Asian countries and could more or less dictate treaties and labor agreements benefiting employers. U.S. capitalists actively recruited Asian laborers because they could be made to work for very low wages. Employers thus had the backing of their government in securing cheap labor from countries such as Japan and China where the United States had the greatest influence. Neither China nor Japan had the clout that European nations had to protect immigrant workers. Moreover, the Japanese immigrants could not become citizens under U.S. law, so they could easily be excluded if they later became "unsuitable" to West Coast employers.[86]

In the beginning Japanese Americans, much like Mexican Americans, were often forced by means of discrimination to become cheap laborers in the fields. The alien-labor laws barring land ownership for Issei, the complete exclusion of Japanese immigrants in 1924 on the grounds of race, and the massive imprisonment in World War II underscore the semi-colonial treatment that Japanese Americans—unlike virtually all European immigrant groups—have endured. Their structural experiences were not the same as those of most European immigrants, on whose experiences the assimilation models are grounded.

Acculturation might be viewed a bit differently in a systematic power–conflict analysis. The pressures to acculturate were coercive. Commitment to some cultural assimilation in Japanese communities can be seen as a reaction to severe white discrimination. By the 1910s and 1920s numerous Japanese American leaders were exhorting their constituents to be exemplary in their hard work and deference in order to command some acceptance of dominant groups. In the public schools, acculturation pressures took the form of attacks on the Japanese cultural heritage. Japanese Americans, while in some ways the most integrated of non-Europeans, have many experiences essentially similar to the forcible exploitation of black, Mexican, and Native Americans.

Some social scientists have been critical of assimilationist perspectives. They have not as yet, however, developed a systematic alternative to it. Some have questioned the origins of the assimilation model itself. For example, Takagi argues that the assimilation theory of Robert Park and other early social scientists emerged in a period of intense agitation over Japanese immigration and reflected those scholars' *racist* views of the Japanese. Defending against charges of a group's unassimilability even led some assimilationists to Eurocentric views of Japanese culture, views that have persisted into present-day theorizing.

Paramount among the weaknesses in the assimilation perspective has been the "model minority" stereotype. The success of Japanese Americans, seen as rooted in their values and family styles, has been cited by numerous writers as a paramount example of what other nonwhites, particularly blacks and Mexicans, could achieve if they would only conform to these patterns. Stereotyping that sees the Japanese as paragons of hard work and docility carries a negative undercurrent.[87]

Suzuki has suggested that the "model minority" image of Asian groups such as Japanese Americans was not created from within these groups but rather was developed by white American outsiders, including non-Asian scholars and media analysts (for example, in a 1966 story in *U.S. News & World Report*), for ideological reasons.[88] As black Americans protested in the streets during the 1960s, some non-Asian, white intellectuals created the model-minority image in order to suggest that nonwhite groups could achieve the "American dream" simply by working hard. Coupled with this was the idea that the values of Asian Americans were more like those of whites in regard to the work ethic. In the 1980s this model minority theme continues in the mass media and in the writings of neoconservative scholars.

Yet, as we have noted, recent scholarship has questioned much of this imagery. For example, Suzuki argues that American educational opportunities, greater than those of segregated blacks, helped prepare them for the white-collar jobs opening up after World War II. It was not Asian "values" that brought success so much as good access to education and the great increase in white-collar jobs opening up in the U.S. economy after the war. Critics of this cultural-background interpretation have also noted a number of other factors in economic success: the early role of the Japanese government in supporting immigrants and the availability of a small-business niche on the West Coast.

Japanese Americans, at an early point, created small businesses to serve one another and the basic economic needs of a frontier economy. In this hostile situation both Japanese American employers and employees saw themselves as a single group confronting the outside world. Out of dire economic necessity employers and employees, many having kinship or regional ties, worked together against white competitors. Success came at the price of being ghettoized in the small-business economy and, later, in certain professions. As with Jewish Americans, Japanese Americans have "made it" as a group in American society in a distinctive "niche" way, a process of adaptation not completely in line with idealistic assimilation models. Thus the long-term effects of discrimination are still reflected in the concentration of Japanese Americans in the small-business economy and in certain professional occupations.

Japanese Americans lead all Asian American groups in their integration into the U.S. economy. But their movement into white-collar jobs does not signal complete emancipation from discrimination. Thus a recent study of Japanese American workers in the San Francisco metropolitan area found that those in lower-tier white-collar jobs were clustered in such positions as computer programming, office clerks, architects, engineers, chemists, dentists, and pharmacists. Upper-tier white-collar jobs, such as managers, financial officers, and management analysts, still tended to be held by white males.[89]

Moreover, a study of minority-owned businesses found that most of those owned by Asian Americans were in retail trade (such as grocery stores and restaurants) and selected services (such as laundries). Gross annual receipts were modest for the majority of Japanese American firms. And as we have seen, research has also revealed that Japanese Americans do not get as much payoff from their high levels of education as do comparably educated whites. One study found that Japanese American males with four years or more of college earned only 83 percent of the incomes of white males with similar educations. For Asian American females the disparity was worse.[90]

Takagi has pointed to another bias in the traditional cultural-background explanation of Japanese American success—the idea that those racial and ethnic groups whose values are closest to the dominant groups' culture are the ones who will be, and should be, successful. In this sense, success is evaluated only in terms of values prized by the dominant white culture. While Japanese Americans have acculturated in numerous ways, the price paid in terms of their own conformity and lost creativity and in lost contributions to this society has been great.[91.]

## SUMMARY

Japanese Americans are a distinctive non-European group. In the beginning, they were a severely exploited minority. Many entered as laborers, facing violence and intense discrimination. They endured complete exclusion as a result of immigration legislation. They endured laws against land ownership. They suffered the only large-scale imprisonment of U.S. citizens in concentration camps in the mid-twentieth century. Against terrible odds they moved up. Here is a non-European group whose economic mobility has been remarkable. Yet, for all their acculturation and economic assimilation, Japanese Americans have a way to go before they are fully included in North American society. Whether they will be the first non-European group to be fully included, politically and socially as well as economically, in the dominant white culture and society remains to be seen.

It is important for students of racial and ethnic relations to realize that the success story of Japanese and other Asian Americans is partially myth. Japanese Americans have suffered from neglect by government and from discrimination in the private sector. Fewer Japanese Americans than whites can fully realize the earnings levels that parallel their education levels. Few rise high in Fortune 500 corporations or in government agencies. In general, they have been neglected by insensitive state and federal government officials. For example, Lionell Van Deerlin, California representative and head of the House Subcommittee on Communications, commented that Asian Americans did not need to be considered a disadvantaged minority group because they were "more prosperous than [majority] Americans." Yet in the communications industry, as of that date there was not one television or radio station owned by a Japanese or other Asian American, and a survey of four San Francisco television stations showed that Asian American males were underrepresented, relative to their proportions in the local labor force, at three of them. These data suggest that Japanese and other Asian Americans have not yet achieved equal opportunity in the communications industry or in many other American industries. In spite of hard work and impressive achievements this "model minority" continues to suffer subtle discrimination.[92]

As we will see in the next chapter, in recent decades Japanese Americans have been joined by a large number of other groups coming from Asia.

# NOTES

1. Roger Daniels, *The Politics of Prejudice* (New York: Atheneum, 1969), pp. 3–6; Hilary Conroy, *The Japanese Frontier in Hawaii, 1868–1898* (Berkeley: University of California Press, 1953), passim.

2. U.S. Immigration and Naturalization Service, *1975 Annual Report* (Washington, D.C.: U.S. Government Printing Office, 1975), pp. 62–66.

3. Arinori Mori, *The Japanese in America* (Japan Advertiser Press, 1926), pp. 19–21; Kaizo Naka, *Social and Economic Conditions among Japanese Farmers in California* (San Francisco: R & E Research Associates, 1974), p. 6; John Modell, "On Being an Issei: Orientations toward America" (paper presented to the American Anthropological Association, San Diego, November 1970), p. 4.

4. T. Iyenago, *Japan and the California Problem* (New York: Putnam's, 1921), pp. 100–106; Roger Daniels, "Japanese Immigrants on the Western Frontier: The Issei in California, 1890–1940," in *East across the Pacific*, ed. Hilary Conroy and T. Scott Miyakawa (Santa Barbara, Calif.: ABC-CLIO, 1972), pp. 82–86; V.S. McClatchy, *Japanese Immigration and Colonization*, reprint ed. (San Francisco: R & E Research Associates, 1970), pp. 42–44; Kiyo Sue Inui, *The Unsolved Problem of the Pacific* (Tokyo: Japan Times, 1925).

5. Jacobus tenBroek, Edward N. Barnhart, and Floyd W. Matson, *Prejudice, War, and the Constitution* (Berkeley: University of California Press, 1968), pp. 42–43; *Takao Ozawa v. United States*, 260 U.S. 178 (1922).

6. Hilary Conroy and T. Scott Miyakawa, "Foreword," in *East across the Pacific*, ed. Conroy and Miyakawa, pp. xiv–xv.

7. The statistics are from U.S. Census publications.

8. E. Manchester-Boddy, *Japanese in America* (San Francisco: R & E Research Associates, 1970), pp. 25–30.

9. McClatchy, *Japanese Immigration and Colonization*, p. 42.

10. Sidney L. Gulick, *The American Japanese Problem* (New York: Scribner's, 1914), p. 16.

11. Quoted in Edward K. Strong, Jr., *The Second-Generation Japanese Problem* (Stanford, Calif.: Stanford University Press, 1934), p. 133.

12. tenBroek, Barnhart, and Matson, *Prejudice, War, and the Constitution*, pp. 26–28; Carey McWilliams, *Prejudice* (Boston; Little, Brown, 1944), pp. 30–45; Dennis M. Ogawa, *From Japs to Japanese* (Berkeley: McCutchan Publishing Co., 1971), pp. 16–19.

13. tenBroek, Barnhart, and Matson, *Prejudice, War, and the Constitution*, p. 31.

14. Ogawa, *From Japs to Japanese*, p. 12; Carey McWilliams, *Brothers under the Skin*, rev. ed. (Boston: Little, Brown, 1964), pp. 148–49; Stanley Sue and Harry H. L. Kitano, "Stereotypes as a Measure of Success," *Journal of Social Issues* 29 (1973): 83–98.

15. C. N. Reynolds, "Oriental–White Race Relations in Santa Clara County, California" (Ph.D. dissertation, Stanford University, 1927); E.S. Bogardus, "Social Distance: A Measuring Stick," Survey 56 (1927); 169ff. Both are cited in Strong, *The Second-Generation Japanese Problem*, pp. 109, 128.

16. tenBroek, Barnhart, and Matson, *Prejudice, War, and the Constitution*, pp. 66–70.

17. Quoted in Ogawa, *From Japs to Japanese*, p. 11.

18. U.S. War Relocation Authority, Department of the Interior, *Myths and Facts about the Japanese American* (Washington, D.C.: U.S. Government Printing Office, 1945), pp. 7–8; Ogawa, *From Japs to Japanese*, pp. 35–54. Survey data document attitude changes in the period 1942–1961. See also Roger Daniels, "Why It Happened Here," in *The Social Reality of Ethnic America*, ed. R. Gomez et al. (Lexington, Mass.: Heath, 1971), p. 236.

19. Council on Interracial Books for Children, *Stereotypes, Distortions and Omissions in U.S. History Textbooks* (New York: Racism and Sexism Resource Center for Educators, 1977), pp. 42–46.

20. Herbert B. Johnson, *Discrimination against the Japanese in California* (Berkeley, Calif.: Courier Publishing Co., 1907), pp. 73–74; Daniels, *The Politics of Prejudice*, pp. 33–34; Howard H. Sugimoto, "The Vancouver Riots of 1907: A Canadian Episode," in *East across the Pacific*, ed. Conroy and Miyakawa, pp. 92–110.

21. Jean Pajus, *The Real Japanese California* (San Francisco: R & E Research Associates, 1971), pp. 164–66; Daniels, *The Politics of Prejudice*, p. 87; tenBroek, Barnhart, and Matson, *Prejudice, War, and the Constitution*, p. 73.

22. Lemuel F. Ignacio, *Asian Americans and Pacific Islanders* (San Jose, Calif.: Pilipino Development Associates, 1976), pp. 95–96; tenBroek, Barnhart, and Matson, *Prejudice, War, and the Constitution*, passim.

23. Dorothy Swaine Thomas and Richard S. Nishimoto, *The Spoilage* (Berkeley: University of California Press, 1946), pp. 5–10; tenBroek, Barnhart, and Matson, *Prejudice, War, and the Constitution*, pp. 82–84.

24. Thomas and Nishimoto, *The Spoilage*, pp. 8–16; tenBroek, Barnhart, and Matson, *Prejudice, War, and the Constitution*, pp. 118–20.

25. tenBroek, Barnhart, and Matson, *Prejudice, War, and the Constitution*, pp. 120, 126–29, 130; Thomas and Nishimoto, *The Spoilage*, pp. 10–20; Edward H. Spicer et al., *Impounded People* (Tucson: University of Arizona Press, 1969), pp. 141–241.

26. Richard Drinnon, *Keeper of Concentration Camps* (Berkeley: University of California Press, 1987), pp. 47, 153.

27. Thomas and Nishimoto, *The Spoilage*, pp. 54–71; tenBroek, Barnhart, and Matson, *Prejudice, War, and the Constitution*, pp. 126–32; 149–55; Spicer et al., *Impounded People*, pp. 252–80.

28. Leonard Bloom and Ruth Riemer, *Removal and Return* (Berkeley; University of California Press, 1949), pp. 124–57, 198–204; tenBroek, Barnhart, and Matson, *Prejudice, War, and the Constitution*, pp. 155–77, 180–81.

29. Bradford Smith, *Americans from Japan* (New York; Lippincott, 1948), pp. 10–12, 202–76; McWilliams, *Prejudice*, p. 4; tenBroek, Barnhart, and Matson, *Prejudice, War, and the Constitution*, pp. 211–23; Harry H. L. Kitano, *Japanese Americans*, 2nd ed. (Englewood Cliffs, N.J.: Prentice-Hall, 1976), pp. 82–88; S. Frank Miyamoto, "The Forced Evacuation of the Japanese Minority during World War II," *Journal of Social Issues* 29 (1973): 11–29.

30. Drinnon, *Keeper of Concentration Camps*, pp. 255–56; see also Christopher Thorne, *Allies of a Kind* (New York: Oxford University Press, 1978).

31. Kitano, *Japanese Americans*, p. 73.

32. Gary Y. Okihiro, "Japanese Resistance in America's Concentration Camps: A Re-evaluation," *Amerasia Journal* 2 (Fall 1973): 20–34; Arthur A. Hansen and David A. Hacker, "The Manzanar Riot: An Ethnic Perspective," *Amerasia Journal* 3 (Fall 1974): 112–42. See also Roger Daniels, *Concentration Camps, U.S.A.* (New York: Holt, Rinehart & Winston, 1971).

33. Daniels, *The Politics of Prejudice*, pp. 104–5.

34. Ivan H. Light, *Ethnic Enterprise in America* (Berkeley: University of California Press, 1972), pp. 174–79; Bill Hosokawa, *The Nisei* (New York: Morrow, 1969), pp. 199–200; Kitano, *Japanese Americans*, pp. 55–58.

35. Hosokawa, *The Nisei*, pp. 439–46; Kitano, *Japanese Americans*, pp. 89–90.

36. Nathaniel C. Nash, "House Votes Payments to Japanese Americans," *New York Times*, September 18, 1987, p. 15A.

37. Hosokawa, *The Nisei*, pp. 452–55.

38. Rodolfo Acuña, *Occupied America* (San Francisco; Canfield Press, 1972), pp. 212–13.

39. Kitano, *Japanese Americans*, pp. 174–86; Daniel Inouye and Lawrence Elliot, *Journey to Washington* (Englewood Cliffs, N.J.: Prentice-Hall, 1967), pp. 248–50; Hosokawa, *The Nisei*, pp. 460–69.

40. Hosokawa, *The Nisei*, pp. 486–87.

41. U.S. Commission on Civil Rights, *Recent Activities against Citizens and Residents of Asian Descent* (Washington, D.C.: U.S. Government Printing Office, 1986), pp. 3–6.

42. Daniels, *The Politics of Prejudice*, pp. 23–24

43. Yuji Ichioka, "A Buried Past," *Amerasia Journal* 1 (July 1971): 1–25; Karl Yoneda, "100 Years of Japanese Labor History in the U.S.A.," in *Roots*, ed. Amy Tachiki et al. (Los Angeles: UCLA Asian American Studies Center, 1971), pp. 150–57.

44. See articles in *Roots*, ed. Tachiki.

45. Cited in Gulick, *The American Japanese Problem*, p. 11.

46. Japanese Association of the Pacific Northwest, *Japanese Immigration* (San Francisco: R & E Research Associates, 1972), pp. 22–25; Daniels, *The Politics of Prejudice*, pp. 7, 10–12.

47. Edna Bonacich and John Modell, *The Economic Basis of Ethnic Solidarity* (Berkeley: University of California Press, 1980), pp. 38–47.

48. Kitano, *Japanese Americans*, pp. 19–21; Light, *Ethnic Enterprise in America*, pp. 27–29; S. Frank Miyamoto, "An Immigrant Community in America," in *East across the Pacific*, ed. Conroy and Miyakawa, pp. 223–25.

49. Gulick, *The American Japanese Problem*, pp. 11, 32–33; Light, *Ethnic Enterprise in America*, p. 71; Daniels, "Japanese Immigrants on the Western Frontier," p. 85.

50. Pajus, *The Real Japanese California*, pp. 147–51; Light, *Ethnic Enterprise in America*, p. 76.

51. Bloom and Riemer, *Removal and Return*, pp. 115–17; Strong, *The Second-Generation Japanese Problem*, pp. 209–11.

52. Bloom and Riemer, *Removal and Return*, pp. 17–20.

53. Ibid., pp. 44, 144; Forrest E. LaViolette, *Americans of Japanese Ancestry* (Toronto: Canadian Institute of International Affairs, 1945), pp. 162–67.

54. Bonacich and Modell, *The Economic Basis of Ethnic Solidarity*, pp. 256–59.

55. U.S. Bureau of the Census, *Population, 1960: Nonwhite Population by Race* (Washington, D.C.: U.S. Government Printing Office, 1963), p. 108. The "occupation not reported" data have been excluded for the purpose of calculating percentages. The 1970 data are from U.S. Department of Health, Education and Welfare, *A Study of Selected Socio-economic Characteristics of Ethnic Minorities Based on the 1970 Census* (Washington, D.C.: U.S. Government Printing Office, 1974), p. 83.

56. U.S. Bureau of the Census, *U.S. Census of Population, 1980: General Social and Economic Characteristics*, PC80-1-C1, 1983, p. 160.

57. U.S. Commission on Civil Rights, *Social Indicators of Equality for Minorities and Women* (Washington, D.C.: U.S. Government Printing Office, 1978), pp. 42–45.

58. U.S. Bureau of the Census, *U.S. Census of Population, 1980: General Social and Economic Characteristics*, p. 161.

59. U.S. Department of Health, Education and Welfare, *A Study of Selected Socio-economic Characteristics*, pp. 105–8; Gene N. Levine and Darrel M. Montero, "Socioeconomic Mobility among Three Generations of Japanese Americans," *Journal of Social Issues* 29 (1973): 33ff. U.S. Commission on Civil Rights, *Social Indicators of Equality for Minorities and Women*, pp. 42–45.

60. David J. O'Brien and Stephen S. Fugita, "Generational Differences in Japanese Americans' Perceptions and Feelings about Social Relationships between Themselves and Caucasian Americans," in *Culture, Ethnicity, and Identity*, ed. William McCready (New York: Academic Press, 1983), pp. 235–36.

61. U.S. Commission on Civil Rights, *Success of Asian Americans: Fact or Fiction?* (Washington, D.C.: U.S. Government Printing Office, 1980), pp. 14–15.

62. Kitano, *Japanese Americans*, pp. 92–93, 95; Levine and Montero, "Socioeconomic Mobility," pp. 45ff; Dale Minami, "Testimony to U.S. Commission on Civil Rights in *Civil Rights Issues of Asian and Pacific Americans* (Washington, D.C.: U.S. Commission on Civil Rights, 1979), pp. 420–22; "Asian Americans: A 'Model Minority,' " *Newsweek*, December 6, 1982, p. 41.

63. K. K. Kawakami, *The Japanese Question* (New York: Macmillan, 1921), pp. 143–45; John Modell, "Tradition and Opportunity: The Japanese Immigrant in America," *Pacific Historical Review* 40 (May 1971): 163–82.

64. Johnson, *Discrimination against the Japanese in California*, pp. 3–20, 40–47; Franklin Hichborn, *The Story of the Session of the California Legislature of 1909* (San Francisco: James H. Barry Press, 1909), p. 207; Pajus, *The Real Japanese California*, pp. 170–78; Kawakami, *The Japanese Question*, pp. 168–69.

65. Pajus, *The Real Japanese California*, pp. 180–81; Kawakami, *The Japanese Question*, pp. 162–63.

66. William Petersen, *Japanese Americans* (New York: Random House, 1971), p. 183; Strong, *The Second-Generation Japanese Problem*, pp. 201–4; Kawakami, *The Japanese Question*, pp. 146–51; Pajus, *The Real Japanese California*, p. 181.

67. Pajus, *The Real Japanese California*, p. 183; Strong, *The Second-Generation Japanese Problem*, pp. 185–88.

68. U.S. Department of Health, Education and Welfare, *A Study of Selected Socio-economic Characteristics*, pp. 70ff; U.S. Commission on Civil Rights, *Social Indicators of Equality for Minorities and Women*, pp. 12–14; U.S. Bureau of the Census, *U.S. Census of Population, 1980: General Social and Economic Characteristics*, p. 157.

69. Kitano, *Japanese Americans*, pp. 93, 174–75; U.S. Commission on Civil Rights, *Social Indicators of Equality for Minorities and Women*, pp. 24–26.

70. E. Manchester-Boddy, *Japanese in America*, p. 118.

71. Petersen, *Japanese Americans*, p. 177; Manchester-Boddy, *Japanese in America*, pp. 114–18.

72. Strong, *The Second-Generation Japanese Problem*, p. 229; Shotaro Frank Miyamoto, "Social Solidarity among the Japanese in Seattle," *University of Washington Publications in Social Sciences* 11 (December 1939): 99–102; Petersen, *Japanese Americans*, pp. 174–75.

73. Andrew W. Lind, *Hawaii's Japanese* (Princeton, N.J.: Princeton University Press, 1946), pp. 212–57; Petersen, *Japanese Americans*, pp. 177–78, 185.

74. Hosokawa, *The Nisei*, p. 131; Kitano, *Japanese Americans*, p. 115; Christie Kiefer, *Changing Cultures, Changing Lives* (San Francisco: Jossey-Bass, 1974), pp. 34–38; Petersen, *Japanese Americans*, p. 187.

75. Modell, "On Being an Issei," pp. 1–2, 19–20.

76. John Modell, "The Japanese American Family: A Perspective for Future Investigations," *Pacific Historical Review* 37 (February 1968): 79; Joe R. Feagin and Nancy Fujitaki, "On the Assimilation of Japanese Americans," *Amerasia Journal* 1 (February 1972): 15–17; Abe Arkoff, "Need Patterns in Two Generations of Japanese–Americans in Hawaii," *Journal of Social Psychology* 50 (1959): 75–79.

77. Petersen, *Japanese Americans*, pp. 6–7; Light, *Ethnic Enterprise in America*, passim; William Caudill, "Japanese American Personality and Acculturation," *Genetic Psychology Monographs* 45 (1952): 3–102.

78. O'Brien and Fugita, "Generational Differences," pp. 235–360.

79. Darrel Montero, *Japanese Americans: Changing Patterns of Ethnic Affiliation over Three Generations* (Boulder, Colo.: Westview Press, 1980), p. 80; Petersen, *Japanese Americans*, pp. 220–24; Modell, "The Japanese American Family," pp. 76–79; Kitano, *Japanese Americans*, pp. 189, 196; George Kagiwada, "Assimilation of Nisei in Los Angeles," in *East Across the Pacific*, ed. Conroy and Miyakawa, p. 273.

80. Feagin and Fujitaki, "On the Assimilation of Japanese Americans," p. 23.

81. Akemi Kikumura and Harry H. L. Kitano, "Interracial Marriage: A Picture of Japanese Americans," *Journal of Social Issues* 29 (1973): 67–81; John N. Tinker, "Intermarriage and Ethnic Boundaries: The Japanese American Case," *Journal of Social Issues* 29 (1973): 55; John W. Connor, *Tradition and Change in Three Generations of Japanese Americans* (Chicago: Nelson-Hall, 1977), p. 308; Gene N. Levine and Colbert Rhodes, *The Japanese American Community* (New York: Praeger, 1981), p. 145.

82. Sharon M. Lee and Keiko Yamanaka, "Intermarriage in the Asian American Population" (typescript, Cornell University, 1987).

83. Feagin and Fujitaki, "On the Assimilation of Japanese Americans," pp. 25–26.

84. Petersen, *Japanese Americans*, pp. 214–21.

85. Connor, *Tradition and Change in Three Generations of Japanese Americans*, pp. 304–8; O'Brien and Fugita, "Generational Differences," pp. 231–35.

86. Edna Bonacich, "United States Capitalist Development: A Background to Asian Immigration," in *Labor Immigration under Capitalism*, ed. Lucie Cheng and Edna Bonacich (Berkeley: University of California Press, 1984), p.82.

87. This section draws on Robert Blauner, *Racial Oppression in America* (New York: Harper & Row, Pub., 1972), pp. 54–55; Paul Takagi, "The Myth of 'Assimilation in American Life,'" *Amerasia Journal* 2 (Fall 1973): 149–58; Peter Uhlenberg, "Demographic Correlates of Group Achievement: Contrasting Patterns of Mexican-Americans and Japanese-Americans," *Demography* 9 (February 1972): 119–28.

88. B. Suzuki, "Education and the Socialization of Asian Americans," in *Asian Americans: Social and Psychological Perspectives*, ed. R. Endo, S. Sue, and N. Wagner (Palo Alto: Science & Behavior Books, 1980), 2:155–78; William Petersen, "Success Story, Japanese-American Style," *New York Times*, January 9, 1966, p. 21; "Success Story of One Minority Group in the U.S.," *U.S. News & World Report*, December, 1966, pp. 73–76; Thomas Sowell, *Ethnic America* (New York: Basic Books, 1981).

89. Amado Cabezas and Gary Kawaguchi, "Empirical Evidence for Continuing Asian American Inequality: The Human Capital Model and Labor Market Segmentation," in *Reflections on Shattered Windows* (Pullman: Washington State University Press, 1988, forthcoming).

90. Amado Cabezas, "Testimony to U.S. Commission on Civil Rights," in *Civil Rights Issues of Asian and Pacific Americans* (Washington, D.C.: U.S. Commission on Civil Rights, 1979), pp. 389–93.

91. Takagi, "The Myth of 'Assimilation in American Life,' " pp. 149–58; Ogawa, *From Jap to Japanese*, pp. 43ff.

92. U.S. Commission on Civil Rights, *Success of Asian Americans: Fact or Fiction?* p. 21.

# CHAPTER 12

# Recent Immigrant Groups: Chinese, Pilipino, Korean, and Vietnamese Americans*

In the 1980s the fastest-growing immigrant groups were Asian, including Chinese, Pilipino,** Korean, and Vietnamese Americans. Table 12-1 illustrates the changing scale of this immigration since the early nineteenth century.

## MIGRATION: AN OVERVIEW

For the Pilipino, Korean, and Vietnamese groups there was little immigration before the 1960s. Thereafter the numbers of immigrants increased dramatically. In just over twenty years, the number of Pilipino, Korean, and Vietnamese immigrants rose from so few immigrants that records were not kept of their arrival to a total of well over a million. Chinese immigration has followed a different pattern, with two major periods. The first began about 1850 and lasted until the passage of the 1882 Chinese Exclusion Act, which prohibited direct immigration. Although there was some immigration in the years following the act, large-scale immigration did not resume until the immigration reforms in 1965. Most Chinese immigrants to the United States have come recently.

The combination of the Exclusion Act and the 1924 Immigration Act, which essentially prohibited Asian immigrants, served to exclude persons of Asian origin from immigrating to the United States. The 1952 Immigration and Nationality Act superseded previous laws and eliminated *some* of the anti-Asian racism inherent in the 1924 national-origins act. The Immigration and Nationality Act established three principles for immigration policy: (1) the reunification of families; (2) the protection of the domestic labor force; and (3) the immigration of persons with needed skills. This act made immigrants from Asia eligible for citizenship for the first time. Moreover, in

*This chapter was written with Suzanne Harper.
**Among those Asian Americans traditionally called *Filipino*, *Pilipino* is the preferred name because there is no *F* sound in the native language of the Philippines.

**TABLE 12-1** Immigration by Country

| | 1820–1900 | 1901–1920 | 1921–1940 | 1941–1960 | 1961–1980 | 1981–1985 | Total |
|---|---|---|---|---|---|---|---|
| Chinese** | 305,455 | 41,833 | 34,835 | 41,910 | 347,564 | 205,525 | 977,122 |
| Pilipino | * | * | * | 19,307 | 453,363 | 230,542 | 703,212 |
| Korean | * | * | * | 6,231 | 302,164 | 165,054 | 473,449 |
| Vietnamese | * | * | * | 335 | 177,160 | 211,914 | 389,409 |

SOURCE: Immigration and Naturalization Service, *1985 Statistical Yearbook* (Washington, D.C.: U.S. Government Printing Office, 1986), pp. 2–5.

*Data not reported before 1951.
**Figures include Hong Kong after 1951.

1965 Congress took a major step toward providing Asians the opportunity to become American citizens. The 1965 Immigration Act abolished the national-origins system and established higher quotas for individual countries. The percentage of Chinese, Pilipino, Korean, and Vietnamese immigrants among the total number of immigrants to this country rose from .2 percent for the years 1901–1920 to 28.3 percent for the years 1981–1985.[1]

## The Chinese

The Chinese have been the largest single group of Asian immigrants to this country. Chinese migration to the United States began in substantial numbers in the decade just before the Civil War, with the largest number, a quarter of a million, coming in during the three decades after 1860. Most entered as low-wage workers, brought in to do the "dirty work" along the West Coast, including mining, railroad, and service work. Many were recruited to remedy labor shortages in railroad work and service employment, to fill menial positions in such areas as laundry and restaurant work that the European American miners and settlers did not want.

As the 1870s began, the U.S. economy entered a depression; at the same time, the Chinese Americans were becoming numerous and more successful. Resentment of these immigrants spread throughout the country; labor leaders, newspapers, politicians, and the general public accused the Chinese Americans of driving wages to a substandard level and taking jobs away from whites. Whites also blamed them for the country's economic plight.[2] The attacks on Chinese Americans led to official government exclusion under the 1882 Chinese Exclusion Act. Direct immigration was prohibited. Over the next few decades the Exclusion Act effectively restricted the flow of Chinese immigrants, which had reached a high of 123,201 in the years 1871–1880, to a record low of 4,928 for the years 1931–1940.[3] The Chinese Exclusion Act was extended for ten years in 1892 and indefinitely in 1904. In 1905 President Theodore Roosevelt affirmed his support of the act, stating that the Chinese laborer must be kept out of this country "absolutely."[4]

The second major period of Chinese immigration—by far the largest immigration—took place after the 1960s immigration legislation. Between 1961 and 1980 nearly 348,000 Chinese, mainly from Hong Kong and Taiwan, came to the United States; they were followed in the 1980s by an even larger number of immigrants, totaling more than 205,525 between 1981 and 1985. This large-scale immigration (especially from Taiwan) is related to U.S. involvement overseas, including military support of the political dictatorship in Taiwan. In addition, the U.S. individual and corporate presence in Taiwan has given the Chinese people there an impression of the United States as a place of economic opportunity and political freedom.

## The Pilipinos

When the Philippines were handed over to the United States by Spain at the end of the Spanish-American War, a direct colonial relationship began that lasted half a century. Almost immediately after the U.S. gained possession of the islands, a U.S. commission arrived to determine how best to Americanize the Philippines. Between 1901 and 1913 a more democratic and Americanized form of government was established, and a new system of public education was introduced in which American teachers taught Pilipino children American values and attitudes.

William Howard Taft, the first civil governor of the Philippines and later a U.S. president, inspired a plan to further Americanize the colony by sending young men to college in the United States. These students were taken into American homes; after they finished their studies in such fields as education, agriculture, and medicine, they were to return to the Philippines to teach American ways. Approximately 14,000 Pilipinos had enrolled in U.S. schools by 1938.

However, by the 1920s and 1930s the overwhelming majority of immigrants to the United States were peasants who sought employment as unskilled laborers. Since the Philippine Islands was a territory of the United States, Pilipinos were exempt from the racist exclusionary provisions of the 1917 and 1924 Immigration Acts. This exemption allowed them to immigrate freely to the United States; they were recruited by whites to work in the sugar plantations of Hawaii and along the West Coast. Few came to the mainland in the early years; by 1924 only 6,000 lived in the continental United States.[5]

After the passage of the 1924 Immigration Act, there was additional pressure to recruit Pilipinos as laborers on the West Coast to replace the Asian and other workers excluded by the act. Between 1924 and 1929, 24,000 Pilipinos came to California. As their numbers increased, so did anti-Pilipino sentiment. In 1934 Congress responded to this sentiment by passing an act granting deferred independence to the Philippines and simultaneously imposed an annual immigration quota of 50 persons per year.[6]

Although Pilipinos could enter the United States without restriction until 1934, almost all advantages ended there. Pilipino Americans held an ambiguous legal position that was not resolved until 1946, when they were finally declared eligible for citizenship. Most states did not allow them to practice law, medicine, or other professions. As noncitizens Pilipinos did not qualify for federal relief funds. At the outbreak of World War II, Pilipinos were unable either to volunteer for, or be drafted into, the armed forces; their status as noncitizens exempted them. Congress began moving toward citizenship for Pilipinos during the war, since it made little sense for the United States to fight for freedom for the Philippines from Japanese rule; while denying Pilipino Americans the rights of citizenship.

Between 1950 and 1970 the number of Pilipinos residing in the U.S. almost doubled. Immediately after World War II, most Pilipinos still found themselves restricted largely to jobs as unskilled or semiskilled laborers, mostly in agriculture. Whereas the earlier Pilipino immigrants had been predominantly male workers and had not established families or communities in the United States, these newer immigrants were men and women between twenty and forty, who brought their children with them, hoping to find better job opportunities.[7] Many came to be united with family members who had already migrated. Most Pilipinos have come to the U.S. for economic reasons. An expert on Pilipino migration has noted that "most people leave the Philippines to get a job."[8] The immigration of Pilipinos continued into the 1980s. Altogether the 1980 census counted approximately 782,000 Pilipino Americans.

## The Koreans

Immigration of Koreans to the United States began in small numbers in the early 1900s. Approximately 7,000 had emigrated to Hawaii between 1903 and 1905; by 1905 approximately 1,000 Korean Americans lived in California. Most came seeking better living and working conditions, but they were confronted with deplorable working conditions and low wages. After learning of these conditions, Japan, which occupied Korea beginning in 1910, pressured the Korean government to ban all emigration. This ban effectively restricted the entry of Koreans into the United States for many years.[9]

Even after these restrictions were imposed a small number of Koreans—mainly "picture brides" and students—were able to emigrate to the United States. Since most who arrived in the U.S. before the 1905 restrictions were single men, and since interracial marriage was not an option because of white prejudice, the picture-bride system was developed. The men would send pictures of themselves to prospective brides in their homeland. From 1910 to 1924, a total of over 1,000 brides came to the U.S., with the largest number settling in Hawaii. In addition, despite the restrictions on migration from Korea to the United States, several hundred students entered between 1899 and 1940, some as political refugees.[10]

After U.S. involvement in the Korean War in the 1950s, the people of South Korea saw prosperous Americans up close and came to regard the United States as a place to be admired. The strong U.S. support for the South Korean government, which allowed little political freedom in the country, built strong ties between the two countries. The political dictatorship in the country drove out some Koreans who dissented from the regime; some migrated to the United States. Many others came for economic or educational reasons. With the growing economic and political power of South Korea in Asia in the last decade has come a growing migration of business people and students to the United States.

Most Koreans who immigrated from 1950 to 1965 were wives of American servicemen; as such they escaped the immigration quota system. These wives continued to migrate after 1965 as the United States maintained troops in Korea, but the changes in the immigration laws in 1965 opened new possibilities for immigration. Lack of economic or educational opportunities in Korea compared with those in the U.S. has regularly stimulated emigration. Moreover, many of the recent immigrants have been from urban middle-income groups opposed to the political regime in South Korea or students who completed their education and stayed. Once the first immigrants were established, they used the family reunification clause of the immigration laws to bring in others. Korean migration to the United States grew annually. Between 1960 and 1965 only a few thousand Koreans entered each year, but by 1969 the number had reached over 6,000. By 1977 Korean immigration was exceeding 30,000, with about one-third being nonquota family members. In the decade after the 1965 act, the number of Korean immigrants increased tenfold to 160,000; between 1975 and 1985 well over 300,000 Koreans immigrated to this country.[11]

In addition to the Americanizing effects of the U.S. military presence in South Korea, religion sometimes draws Koreans to the United States. Korea has one of the largest Protestant Christian populations of any Asian nation, and many Korean immigrants are Christians. These immigrants have established new churches here; in Chicago in 1981 Korean Americans supported eighty to one hundred Christian churches, which combine Western practices with Korean ceremonies and Korean-language services.[12]

## The Vietnamese

The Vietnamese do not have a long history of immigration to the United States. Most immigrants arrived after 1975, when American involvement in the Vietnam War ended abruptly. The United States first became involved in Vietnam in an attempt to aid the French military forces trying to maintain their colonial control in the area. When the French forces pulled out in 1954 and the country was divided in two, the United States became a military ally of the South Vietnamese government, a non-Communist dictatorship. American troops and dollars flowed to a war that became increasingly unpopular in the United States. In Saigon, the capital of South Vietnam, American military and civilian authorities made plans to evacuate a great number of South Vietnamese because of the advancing Communist forces. Included in the planned evacuation were family members of U.S. citizens and those Vietnamese and their families who were employed by the American government or American businesses, or those who might be at risk of losing their lives when the Communists took over. As Communist troops rapidly approached Saigon in April 1975, the controlled evacuation that had been planned became instead a confused and tragic event. In one week, thousands of Vietnamese left their country. People jammed the airport and the United States embassy, climbing fences and clinging to helicopters. Those who could not get on the airplanes sometimes pushed their children on, believing they were sending them to a better life in the U.S. Others, then and later, fled by sea in fishing boats.[13]

In the spring of 1975 over 130,000 refugees from Southeast Asia entered the United States. The Vietnamese were admitted to the U.S. under "parole status" outside the usual immigration process because they were considered political refugees.[14] As Table 12-1 shows, there was very little immigration from Vietnam prior to 1961, in part because of the restrictive immigration laws. Changes in immigration laws, U.S. military involvement in Vietnam, and the precipitous fall of Saigon in 1975 contributed to the increase in immigrants. There has been a large increase in the number of Vietnamese immigrants, from 335 for the years 1941–1960 to 211,914 between 1981 and 1985.

## STEREOTYPES AND DISTORTIONS

There is a long history of anti-Asian sentiment in the United States. There are widely held stereotypes about Asian Americans that are not supported by empirical evidence.

One common misconception about Asian Americans is that they are essentially the same physically and culturally. Japanese Americans are taken for Chinese Americans, who in turn may be mistaken for Vietnamese Americans. Asian Americans are often viewed as foreigners rather than Americans because of their distinctive non-European appearance. The media frequently portray Asians as faceless, fanatic, maniacal, or willing to die because they do not value life. Images such as the "evil Jap" of World War II and the "Communist gook" in China, Korea, and Vietnam have been recycled as U.S. foreign policy changed from decade to decade. This uninformed and stereotypical way of thinking, sometimes called *Orientalism*, is common among white European Americans and affects discrimination directed at Asian Americans.[15]

Another common stereotype of Asian Americans or of particular Asian groups, one especially emphasized by the mass media, is that they are a "model minority." We noted this image in our discussion of Japanese Americans. The stereotype is that Asian Americans are moving ahead within American society, essentially unhindered by prejudice or discrimination, by applying the traditional values of hard work, thrift, and morality. They are also perceived as especially ambitious. *Fortune* magazine, in an article entitled "America's Super Minority," went so far as to assert that Asian Americans are "smarter and better educated and make more money than *everyone else*." While there are certainly exemplary members of the Asian American community, this is an overstatement of the situation, and this stereotype, like all stereotypes, does not hold true for the entire population of Asian Americans. One unfortunate result of what is seemingly a positive stereotype is that in addition to misrepresenting Asian Americans, it may create resentment and jealousy among other Americans.[16]

## Some Specific Images

The first Chinese laborers on the West Coast soon became the subjects of much derision and suspicion. They were known as "coolies" and were perceived to be dirty and immoral. The stereotypes of Pilipino immigrants have tended to fluctuate with their usefulness to the capitalists recruiting them as cheap labor, especially in the sugar plantations of Hawaii. When European American employers were recruiting the young, single men they characterized them as "not too intelligent" and "docile." But when the workers were no longer needed by the employers, they were viewed as "lazy, shiftless, and unmanageable."[17]

The Vietnamese arrived in the United States at a time when unemployment was high, and many Americans feared that the refugees would take jobs from them or be a drain on the public assistance rolls. This anti-Vietnamese sentiment was reflected in a Gallup poll that reported 54 percent of Americans felt the Vietnamese should not be permitted to stay in the United States.[18] Many Americans seemed to wish they could forget Vietnam and its people. Some have even perceived all Vietnamese to be "the enemy" because of the United States' experience in Vietnam and have persisted in referring to them as "Viet-Cong" or calling them by the derogatory term *gooks*. Vietnamese Americans represent a very different culture to a large segment of American society, and many people regard them as strange, clannish, and hard to approach.[19]

## REPRESSION AND VIOLENT CONFLICT

Violence, harassment, intimidation, and vandalism against persons of Asian descent have periodically been reported in various rural and urban areas across the United States. New York lawyer Nicholas Chen, a board member of the Asian American Legal Defense and Education Fund, was recently quoted as saying, "We are seeing a trend of racially motivated violence directed against Asians which we believe is a national phenomenon."[20]

### Chinese Americans

In the first waves of immigration in the nineteenth century, Chinese immigrants were violently attacked by white Californians. The recent wave of immigrants has not been immune from such attacks. Careful monitoring and reporting of racially motivated actions against Asian Americans began in 1982 with the death of Vincent Chin, a Chinese American, in Detroit. Two white men started an argument with Chin in a bar, and then used a baseball bat to beat him to death. The two men were laid-off auto workers and apparently believed Chin was Japanese—and therefore to blame for the layoffs in the auto industry. Each man received the extraordinarily lenient sentence of three years' probation and a fine of $3,780. Asian Americans expressed outrage. The U.S. Department of Justice investigated the case and recommended charging the two assailants with civil rights violations. On June 28, 1984, a U.S. district court jury found one of the defendants guilty of violating Chin's civil rights, underscoring the racial motivation of the attack. The guilty defendant was sentenced to twenty-five years in prison. The other defendant, apparently not directly involved in beating Chin, was acquitted.[21]

### Korean Americans

Koreans are relatively recent immigrants. A number of Korean American businesses have recently been the targets of violence. In several major cities Korean entrepreneurs operate small stores in predominantly black neighborhoods. As with the white merchants in ghetto areas, these Korean merchants have faced black hostility. Korean and black community leaders in Los Angeles have debated whether the killings of four Korean business people in three separate incidents were racially motivated. And in New York City, interethnic tensions led to a black boycott of Korean shops along a major street in Harlem, where Korean Americans own approximately one-fourth of the small businesses. Blacks complain that Korean Americans treat them rudely and refuse to hire black employees or extend credit. One source of bitterness is the unfounded belief that the federal government helps Korean Americans start businesses; in fact they usually pool their resources to purchase businesses in poor neighborhoods.[22]

### Pilipino Americans

Pilipino Americans, among the oldest of Asian immigrants, have endured violent attacks. In the early period of immigration there were many clashes in California between Pilipino and white farm laborers. In 1929 the Imperial Valley, the Sacramento Valley, and the San Joaquin Valley depended heavily on migratory Pilipino labor; by 1930 Pilipinos represented 42 percent of all non-European labor working on California farms. Pilipino wages were considerably lower than those of their American counterparts. As a consequence of the heavy use of Pilipino labor from 1924 to 1929, the atmosphere was conducive to fights between Anglo and foreign laborers over menial farm labor work once the Great Depression hit California.[23]

On October 24, 1929, the first anti-Pilipino riot took place in Exeter, a small farming community in the San Joaquin Valley. The riot resulted from long-standing bitterness over the use of Pilipino labor for harvesting crops. It began at a local carnival where young Pilipinos were being shot at with rubber bands as they walked with local girls. After a few days of harassment, a young Pilipino farm laborer knifed a white man and slashed a group attempting to corner him. He escaped, but a mob formed. The mob went to a nearby labor camp and ordered all Pilipinos out. The labor camp, which usually housed the Pilipinos, was burned to the ground. The chief of police refused to take action despite the destruction of the barn, a tractor, and fifteen tons of hay that were burned.

Perhaps the most highly publicized and prolonged anti-Pilipino riot in California occurred in the Pajaro Valley near Watsonville in January 1930. This riot reflected a decade of increasing tension between white and Pilipino workers. The tension in Watsonville was exacerbated by an interview in the local newspaper with a white official who condemned the Pilipinos and blamed them for the increasing tensions. A series of anti-Pilipino demonstrations then erupted. At one point, a vigilante mob of five hundred white youths marched on a Pilipino dance hall. The police stepped in to curtail the violence. Not surprisingly, the press reported the incident as Pilipinos marching and rioting in the streets.

On January 22, 1930, the riots reached a peak when four hundred vigilantes attacked the Northern Monterey Pilipino Club. One person was killed in the scuffle, and a large number of Pilipinos were severely beaten. Law enforcement officials who tried to protect the Pilipinos were taunted with cries of "Goo Goo Lovers." The local paper added to the tension by printing stories that condemned the dance halls frequented by Pilipinos and the practice of socializing with white women. After this massive white attack, the confrontations subsided.

Perhaps because of less direct competition with whites for jobs, few anti-Asian attacks that single out Pilipino Americans have been reported in recent decades.

## Vietnamese Americans

Many recent Vietnamese immigrants engaged in fishing as a livelihood in their homeland, and thus it has seemed a natural choice for an occupation in their new country. To pursue this dream, some Vietnamese Americans moved to fishing communities on the Texas Gulf Coast. Originally, in the late 1970s, they were encouraged to move to that area because of its labor shortage. They generally took low-paying jobs such as cleaning fish or working in restaurant kitchens, and in that capacity they were tolerated within the community. But as they began to buy shrimp boats and offer considerable competition to the other fishermen, attitudes toward them changed. Many European American natives of the area resented the success of the Vietnamese Americans and blamed them for the increasing economic downturn along the Gulf Coast.

These Vietnamese Americans have experienced open hostility from their white and Hispanic counterparts since they began fishing. For example, a 1979 conflict between Vietnamese Americans and local fish catchers in Seadrift, Texas, culminated in the shooting death of a white fish catcher. Two Vietnamese refugees were arrested for the shooting, which followed an argument over the placement of crab traps. Within hours of the death, three Vietnamese boats were burned, one house was fire-bombed, and an attempt was made to bomb a packing plant where many Vietnamese Americans worked, causing most of the refugees to flee to another town. The Vietnamese American crabbers were eventually acquitted of the shooting. In response to this verdict, some white fish catchers turned to the local Ku Klux Klan for "protection of their industrial interest."[24]

## THE POLITICAL ARENA

As mentioned in the chapter on Japanese Americans, some Asian Americans have distinguished themselves politically, such as Senators Daniel Inouye and Samuel I. Hayakawa. But these senators were elected from states with a larger proportion of Asian American voters than the nation as a whole. Until recently, there has been no national political organization specifically addressing the concerns of Asian Americans. In 1986 the first national pro-Asian political effort began with the founding of the Asian-American Voters Coalition. The coalition includes twelve national and seven local organizations representing Japanese, Chinese, Indian, Pilipino, Korean, Vietnamese, and Thai Americans. The organization seeks to consolidate Asian American citizens into a more effective bloc of votes—a bloc that could have a significant impact on elections in California, Texas, New York, and Illinois. According to the president of the organization, Jane Hu, the group's most important issue in the late 1980s is protecting the civil rights of Asian Americans from anti-Asian legislation, distorted media images, racial violence, and employment discrimination.[25]

### Chinese Americans

Perhaps because Chinese Americans have had the longest history of immigration of the four groups studied in this chapter, they also have been the most politically active of these groups. Chinese American political activity in the United States seems to have increased in the period 1917–1920, shortly after the revolution in China. Chinese Americans became involved in a wide variety of political organizations and spent much time discussing developments in China rather than in their U.S. communities. There were a number of labor-oriented organizations, several of which tried to organize laborers in New York's Chinese communities, where the largest concentration of Chinese Americans lived. These attempts proved unsuccessful, however, because most of the labor was organized around family ties.[26]

The second period of Chinese immigration, after the immigration reforms of 1965, revived political activity among Chinese Americans. Some Chinese Americans began to explain their problems to the U.S. Congress. Irving Chin, then chair of the Chinatown Advisory Committee to the Borough President of Manhattan, told a U.S. Senate committee in the 1960s that the Chinese had not protested much because of their problems with English, their fear of and lack of familiarity with government, and a cultural reluctance to engage in political activity. In addition, Professor Ling-chi Wang, a San Francisco community activist and later the chair of the Asian American Studies Department of the University of California, Berkeley, spoke to the same committee. Wang spoke in support of governmental training programs, which he said were sorely needed and long overdue. Wang testified that the unemployment rate in San Francisco's Chinatown was almost double the citywide average, that available housing was substandard, and that the incidence of tuberculosis was six times the national average. This testimony signalled a growing willingness to speak openly of Chinese American problems.[27] The growth of the Chinese American population coincided with a recognition of the importance of ethnicity throughout the country, a social movement in behalf of civil rights for all minorities, and a demand for self-government by oppressed groups. Chinese American youth were examining their values and their place in U.S. society. Their careers and opportunities were doubly limited, first by the traditional elites who held sway in the older Chinese American communities, and by the prejudice and discrimination in the larger society. This dissatisfaction sparked in some cases the rise of militant youth gangs, in other cases a move to establish programs in Asian American studies at colleges and universities.[28]

## Korean and Pilipino Americans

Like those of the Chinese Americans, Korean American political actions were sometimes inspired by events in the homeland. During the years 1905–1919 many Korean Americans were active in the fight for Korean independence from Japan. Japan, however, maintained its dominance of Korea, and after 1919 the Korean independence movement began to decline. Korean Americans who had devoted time and energy to the cause of independence could not sustain the political movement; many organizations reemerged as nonpolitical organizations.[29]

In the chapter on Mexican Americans we discussed Cesar Chavez and the United Farm Workers Union. This union was the result of a merger between a Mexican American organizing drive and a Pilipino labor organization, the Agricultural Workers' Organizing Committee (AWOC). The head of AWOC was Larry Itliong, a Pilipino American activist.[30] There have been a few other Pilipino political organizations in the U.S. In the 1970s the Pilipino Organizing Committee was created in the San Francisco area to address issues of concern to Pilipino Americans participating in the U.S. political system.[31] Perhaps one reason Pilipino Americans have not been more active in politics in this country is because they represent such cultural diversity— several religious groups, for example. Even in their own country, effective political coalitions are difficult to build. The Pilipino Americans are divided by religious differences, language differences, ideological rifts, and subgroup cultures. Because of the strength of local groups and their competing loyalties, overall organizations are difficult to form. In many instances—at least at present—Pilipino American political organizations seem to multiply, rather than unify.

## Suburban Development and Politics

As the number of Asian American immigrants in the United States continues to increase and as many of these immigrants and their children concentrate in particular geographic areas, they are becoming more significant in U.S. politics. Recent Asian immigrants, concerned about events in the United States, are involving themselves politically in order to try to influence events in their communities.

One example is Monterey Park, California, a Los Angeles suburb of 60,000 people, three-fourths of them Asian and Hispanic. After New York's Chinese American communities it is the largest place of settlement for Asian immigrants, particularly those from Taiwan and Hong Kong, in the U.S. Although Chinese Americans are the most numerous, a number of other Asian groups are well represented in the community. When white city council members passed a resolution that Monterey Park does not consider itself a sanctuary for illegal aliens and that English should be the official language of the United States, many members of the community were outraged. No fewer than 4,000 people signed petitions demanding that the city council rescind the resolution, which it did. The controversy over the resolution was indicative of a much bigger rift within the community between fearful and prejudiced whites, who contend that the Asian Americans are not making efforts "to assimilate" and are "taking over," and the Asian Americans, many of whom are now affluent suburbanites with successful businesses.[32]

## THE ECONOMY

### Chinese Americans

In the nineteenth century Chinese immigrants were recruited to fill the lower rungs of the occupational ladder in the United States. While some were merchants and craftworkers, most were unskilled. Chinese workers had been employed to build railroads in California as early as the 1850s, but the first large-scale use of Chinese labor, more than 12,000 workers, was in the construction of the transcontinental railroad, completed in 1869. By 1880 there were at least 105,000 Chinese Americans; most lived in California, and there they became an important factor in the economy. They converted swampland in California to rich farmland; their skills in planting, cultivating, and harvesting were used extensively at vineyards, orchards, and ranches. Some farmed as sharecroppers; others raised their own vegetables for the market.

Chinese factory workers were an important part of the California economy after the Civil War. By the early 1870s, Chinese workers made up 70 to 80 percent of the labor force in woolen mills and 90 percent of the cigar makers in San Francisco; by the mid-1870s they were a majority of the shoemakers and garment makers. Chinese American entrepreneurs developed shrimp fisheries, which by the 1880s were exporting a million pounds annually; they were leaders in developing abalone fisheries. Chinese workers were a mainstay of canneries, especially the salmon canneries in the Pacific Northwest. Thousands more operated or worked in laundries and served as cooks or domestic servants. Many worked long hours in poor conditions for low wages.[33]

The prospects for many of the recent Chinese immigrants have not been much better than those for the early immigrants because many lack money, skills, and the ability to speak English. Most have settled in Chinese American communities in larger cities such as New York and San Francisco. There many of the men work long hours in restaurants, while thousands of women labor in the hundreds of garment shops located either in, or near, the Chinese residential areas. A 1979 study noted that the garment industry in New York provided Chinese American women with their main source of employment. Conditions in nonunion factories are substandard or dangerous. These contemporary sweatshops pay poorly, often below the minimum wage, and lack decent working conditions. Some immigrants do own or manage some of the garment shops and restaurants.[34]

Some of the postwar Chinese immigrants have been better educated; among these immigrants there have been engineers, doctors, mathematicians, and scientists. Some were trained in China and fled after the Communist victory in 1949; others received their education in Taiwan, where schools prepared them for emigration to the United States. Still others completed their advanced studies in the United States and found employment in American industries and universities. This group of elite immigrants found better jobs and generally had an easier time adjusting to their new country than their poorer brethren.[35]

Data from the 1980 census reveal that Chinese Americans were heavily concentrated in white-collar jobs, with 39 percent in professional, technical, and managerial jobs compared with 26 percent for the population as a whole. This is also the highest concentration in white-collar jobs among the four Asian groups considered in this chapter. The proportion in clerical and sales jobs was 24 percent, compared with 27 percent for the population as whole. The proportion in blue-collar jobs was only 19 percent, versus about one-third of the general population. Chinese Americans are underrepresented in blue-collar jobs other than service jobs.[36]

Even though the median family income for Chinese Americans is $22,559, higher than the $19,917 average for the general population, it would still appear to be lower than expected. Considering that 39 percent of Chinese Americans hold white-collar occupations, compared with only 26 percent of the general population, one would expect to find a greater difference in median income. The Chinese American community seems to be represented at both extremes of the economic spectrum. Of the first one hundred people on *Forbes*'s 1983 list of the wealthiest Americans, two were Chinese. Fifth on the list was An Wang, head of Wang Laboratories, reported to be worth $1.6 billion; and Kyupin Philip Hwang, head of TeleVideo Systems, was reported to be worth $575 million. At the other extreme, the 1980 census estimated that 14.8 percent of Chinese Americans live below the poverty line. A partial reason for this split may be because of the length of the immigrants' stay in this country. Chinese Americans themselves sometimes distinguish between "ABCs" and "FOBs," that is, between American-born Chinese and Fresh-off-the-boat immigrants. The former tend to be better educated, hold managerial or professional jobs, and live outside the Chinatowns. The more recent immigrants tend to have less education, be unemployed or hold low-wage jobs, and live in inner-city Chinatowns.[37]

## Pilipino Americans

Pilipinos were first recruited as farm workers for the sugar plantations in Hawaii and farms along the West Coast beginning in the 1920s. The vast majority of these workers were single men who endured a grueling schedule and meager wages. Their typical day began at 4 a.m.; with one fifteen-minute break for breakfast and a half hour for lunch, the men worked until three or four in the afternoon. Dinner was eaten by 6 p.m., and most were asleep by 8:00 p.m. The wage for this labor remained the same from 1915 to 1933—eighteen to twenty dollars a month.[38]

A 1987 analysis of 1980 census data for Pilipino Americans in California found that there was still considerable occupational and economic inequality between Pilipino Americans and white U.S.-born Americans. Pilipino men, whether U.S.-born or foreign-born, had only about two-thirds the income of white men. Pilipino women had only about half the income of white men. When income distributions were compared, the inequality was more pronounced. In the lowest income bracket, about 30 percent of white men had an annual income below $10,000, compared with about 50 percent of Pilipino men and women.

The same study revealed inequality in the occupational distribution of Pilipino Americans compared with the white population. In the managerial and professional ranks, Pilipino men were mostly accountants, civil engineers, and electrical engineers, while women were mostly registered nurses, elementary school teachers, and accountants. Few Pilipino Americans were found among public administrators, financial managers, marketing managers, physicians, attorneys, architects, aerospace, industrial, and mechanical engineers, and social scientists—occupations that showed high concentrations of native white men.[39]

According to the 1980 census, the proportion of Pilipino Americans in upper-tier white-collar jobs is 31 percent, higher than the national average of 26 percent. The proportion of Pilipino Americans in clerical and sales work is roughly the same as the national average of 27 percent. Twenty-five percent of Pilipino Americans are blue-collar workers, lower than the national average of 33 percent. The proportion of service workers among Pilipino Americans is 17 percent, higher than the 12 percent for the population as a whole. The median family income for Pilipino Americans is the highest among the four Asian groups, at $23,687. This is also higher than the average for the general population, which is $19,917.[40]

## Korean Americans

The language barrier and racial discrimination kept most early Korean immigrants from obtaining employment in accordance with their abilities and skills. In the early twentieth century immigrants engaged in hard physical labor for extremely low wages. Many, including professionals, worked in agriculture as laborers or as dishwashers, kitchen helpers, houseboys, or janitors in urban areas. During the First World War, a few Korean Americans began to open small, family-operated shops—laundries, shoe-repair shops, and used-furniture stores, mainly in Hawaii. By the Second World War, more than fifty small and medium-sized businesses had been set up on the mainland. However, in the total Korean population of ten thousand, just 5 percent were engaged in business.[41]

The immigrants arriving after the 1965 immigration reforms have included mathematicians, scientists, and medical professionals. A number of recent immigrants were entrepreneurs who established small businesses. A study in Los Angeles found that 40 percent of Korean American heads of household were self-employed in 1978, compared with 8 percent of the general population of Los Angeles County. An additional 40 percent were employed by these entrepreneurs, so that fully 80 percent of employed Korean Americans in Los Angeles County worked in Korean-owned firms, mostly service and retail proprietorships.[42]

The 1980 census statistics for Korean Americans are closer to the statistics for the general population than any other group discussed in this chapter. For example, the proportion of Korean Americans in professional, technical, and managerial jobs is 29 percent, versus 26 percent for the general population. Twenty-four percent of the general population is in clerical and sales work, while 27 percent of Korean Americans pursue such occupations. Thirty-one percent of Korean Americans are in blue-collar occupations, compared with approximately 33 percent of the population as a whole. The proportion of the general population in service occupations is 12 percent, compared with 16 percent of Korean Americans. The median family income for Korean Americans, $20,459, is also close to the national average of $19,917.[43]

## Vietnamese Americans

Because the Vietnamese are such recent immigrants to this country, they do not have a long economic history. Most arrived after 1975, so there is still not much information available on their economic adaptation to this country. The information that is available shows a pattern of downward occupational mobility. A 1977 study showed that there was considerable downward occupational mobility for Vietnamese American heads of households. Of the 319 Vietnamese in the survey who held white-collar jobs in Vietnam, more than six in ten held blue-collar jobs at the time of the study. The remainder held white-collar jobs, with the largest category being clerical and sales positions. This downward mobility is true among professionals as well. Of the 142 Vietnamese Americans surveyed who were employed as professionals in Vietnam, fewer than one in five had been able to find similar work in the United States.[44]

The 1980 census data for Vietnamese Americans reveal that they lagged far behind the other Asian immigrants in occupational attainment. These figures can be misleading, though, when compared with the figures for the nation as a whole or with figures for other Asian immigrants, because most Vietnamese are very recent immigrants. The proportion in upper-tier white-collar occupations is 21 percent, compared with the national average of 26 percent. The proportion in clerical and sales work is 19 percent, compared with 27 percent for the general population. The proportion of Vietnamese Americans in blue-collar work, 44 percent, is substantially higher than the national figure of 33 percent. And the proportion in service work is 15 percent, also higher than the national figure of 12 percent. Vietnamese Americans are concentrated at the lower end of the occupational ladder, with almost 60 percent in blue-collar and service work. This is reflected in the median family income for Vietnamese Americans, which is $12,840. This is substantially below both the national average of just under $20,000 and the median incomes of the other Asian groups.[45]

# EDUCATION

## Achievement: A Mixed Blessing?

In 1987, for the first time, the top five of ten scholarships awarded in the prestigious Westinghouse Science Talent Search were won by teenagers of Asian parentage.[46] However welcome the scholarships were to the student winners, they were a mixed blessing for Asian Americans as a group. Winning the national science competition serves to reinforce popular stereotypes of Asian Americans as "naturally" gifted in science and as a "model minority." Asian Americans are critical of these stereotypes, for many Asian Americans excel in areas other than science. Others are in great need because they are poor and uneducated.[47]

In 1980 the median years of school completed by Chinese Americans was 13.4, higher than the median of 12.5 years for the general population. Seventy-one percent of Chinese Americans have graduated from high school. Pilipino Americans' median years of school competed was 14.1, the highest of the Asian groups in this chapter and well above the national average. Three quarters of Pilipino Americans have completed high school. Close to the Chinese American median were Korean Americans, with a median of thirteen years of school completed; 78 percent had graduated from high school. Vietnamese Americans ranked the lowest among the Asian groups in educational attainment, yet they were still very close to the national average. Vietnamese Americans completed a median of 12.4 years of school in 1980, barely under the national average of 12.5; 62 percent had graduated from high school.[48]

## Controversy in Higher Education

At the nation's top universities, Asian Americans, who make up only 2 percent of the college-age population, accounted for 11 percent of the 1986–87 freshman class. Asian American leaders, however, have suggested that there is discrimination against Asian American students; colleges have apparently imposed ceilings to keep them out. The Ivy League institutions began admitting large numbers of Asian Americans in the mid-1970s, but as their applications increased, by as much as 1,000 percent, the acceptance rate dropped. At Yale, the acceptance rate for Asian Americans fell from 39 percent to 17 percent from 1977 to 1986.[49] Critics have accused the colleges of using such pretexts as lack of alumni parents to keep Asian American students out, somewhat like the "grandfather clause" prevented blacks in the southern states from voting unless their grandfathers had voted.

The reasons for the Asian American success are often speculated upon. Some say it is rooted in a traditional reverence for learning in Asian culture, the fierce support of family, and in some cases a head start gained in schools in their homeland. Others point to those Asians who learn English at a young age and say they gain additional benefits from bilingualism, which may help them understand new concepts.[50] One writer points out that policy makers who attribute the educational success of Asian immigrants to family structure and cultural values should consider that Asian Americans have access to educational institutions, such as those in California, that facilitate economic and educational mobility better than the schools attended by blacks and Hispanics in southern areas. Moreover, even though Asian American students reside in large metropolitan areas, they are not segregated from the mainstream of the educational system. On the contrary, Asian American students, unlike blacks and Hispanics, are typically well integrated into public schools with white majorities.[51]

## ASSIMILATION FOR ASIAN AMERICANS?

### An Optimistic Assimilation View

As we have noted throughout this book, Milton Gordon has argued that his theory of assimilation is applicable to a wide range of ethnic and racial groups. However, Gordon himself does not explicitly apply the stages of his assimilation scheme to recent Asian American groups, groups whom other assimilationists have generally viewed as already on their way to assimilation at the core–cultural level in terms of language and at the secondary–structural level in terms of job placement. Beyond acculturation there appears to be only modest integration with the European American core society at the primary-group level and little intermarriage. Substantial acculturation in language and American values has taken place, but assimilation at the other levels for most groups has come slowly. Assimilationists tend to be very optimistic about the assimilation of Asian Americans, including the trend toward a growing middle class in suburban areas such as Monterey Park.

Optimistic assimilation-oriented analysts have underscored Asian American progress in terms of cultural and economic integration. The sociologist Talcott Parsons argued that racial and ethnic inclusion is a basic process in U.S. society; one aspect of this process is the increasing inclusion of various racial and ethnic groups in the institutions of the society. Analysts such as Thomas Sowell and Nathan Glazer have asserted that there has been a collapse in traditional discrimination, that assimilation of nonwhite Americans, especially Asians, into the core society is well under way.

Indeed, traditional assimilationist scholars and other analysts of European origin see Asian Americans as "model minorities." Success occurs when a minority attains some economic privileges broadly comparable to those of the dominant group, attainments measured by quantitative socioeconomic indices such as education, occupation, and income. Setting up Asian Americans as a model minority sends the message that if they can make it through their own efforts and without government intervention, then so can blacks and other minorities. This message is used to affirm that the United States is a just and fair society, where any group can succeed if its members are willing to work hard enough. In turn, it is argued, government programs such as affirmative action are harmful and counterproductive.[52]

Recently, Kitano and Daniels applied this assimilation model to Asian Americans in a more complex and differentiated fashion. They have developed a model of assimilation and ethnic identity that distinguishes between four types of adaptation: (1) high assimilation, low ethnic identity; (2) high assimilation, high ethnic identity; (3) low assimilation, low ethnic identity; and (4) low assimilation, high ethnic identity.

Asian American individuals who fall into the category of high assimilation and low ethnic identity are more core American than ethnic Asian. Their language, lifestyle, and expectations are core American, and their traditional culture and language are all but forgotten. High rates of marriage to non-Asians occur in this group, and females are more likely to belong to this group than are males. This group is often the focus of "model minority" advocates.

Those in the second category of high assimilation, high ethnic identity differ from the previous category by retaining a strong ethnic identity. The individuals move easily in and out of both cultures, and their friendship patterns, group memberships, and interests reflect a bicultural perspective. They tend to be comfortable with their ethnic identity and also their questioning of ethnic prejudice and discrimination.

The category of low assimilation, low ethnic identity includes those Asian Americans who are alienated, disillusioned, and disenchanted. These people have acquired little of the core American culture but are also uncomfortable with their original ethnic identity. Very few Asian Americans fall into this category.

Those in the fourth category, persons with low assimilation, high ethnic identity, are often newly arrived immigrants or Asian Americans who have spent most of their lives in the ethnic enclaves in U.S. cities. Some of them may have attained a nominal level of adaptation to the dominant culture, but they prefer their ethnic communities. These individuals tend to form friendship and marriage bonds with people in their own ethnic group. Many feel that the dominant society will never treat them as equals, so they are better off opting for their enclave adaptation.[53]

Kitano and Daniels's approach indicates the complexity in patterns of adaptation depending on length of stay in the United States, particular ethnic group, and strength of in-group ethnic commitment. But it does not pay sufficient attention to such external factors as continuing prejudice and discrimination, which also handicap Asian Americans and affect assimilation probabilities.

## Some Questions from the Power–Conflict Perspective

Power–conflict analysts reject the overly optimistic assimilationist view of Asian Americans, especially the view of them as model minorities. The model-minority view exaggerates Asian Americans' progress and downplays the problems of prejudice and discrimination. The model-minority label began to be generally applied to Asian

Americans in the 1960s, a time of much unrest among blacks protesting and rioting to demand the protection of their constitutional rights. As we noted in the chapter on Japanese Americans, the model-minority image for Asian groups was not created from within the groups but rather was intentionally created by outsiders, including scholars and the media, substantially for ideological reasons. With black Americans protesting, certain white leaders and scholars broadcast this image to suggest that nonwhite groups could achieve the American dream simply by working hard. In the 1960s the term *model minority* was used in a speech by Democratic politician Hubert Humphrey at a Chinese American high school, during which remarks Humphrey praised the Chinese Americans for not rioting and demonstrating. And in 1966 an article appeared in *U.S. News and World Report* entitled "Success Story of One Minority Group in U.S.," which compared the Chinese Americans with blacks. The tone of the article is negative toward blacks: while it sings the praises of the hard work, thrift, and morality of Chinese Americans, it clearly implies that if blacks simply possessed these virtues it would not be necessary to spend "hundreds of billions [of dollars] to uplift" them. ("Billions" is, of course, an extreme exaggeration.)[54]

## Hidden Economic and Education Problems

The secondary–structural integration of Asian Americans into the U.S. economy is not as untroubled as the assimilation analysts may suggest. For example, a recent study of the income differentials among Asian Americans, whites, and blacks demonstrates that the Asian American success story is overstated. In examining 1980 census data for California, researchers have found that Asian Americans earned $20,790, compared with $19,552 for whites and $12,534 for blacks. However, this differential should be analyzed in relation to the number of workers per household. The Asian American families had 1.70 workers per household, compared with only 1.28 for whites and 1.20 for blacks. Therefore, Asian Americans earned only $12,229 per worker, while whites received $15,275. That means Asian American income per worker was only 80 percent of white income. This gap was even wider in urban areas, where most Asian Americans reside. Another important point in this research was that many of the Asian immigrants have resources such as education, skills, and finances that many comparison groups, such as black Americans, lack. There is also a regional bias inherent in these figures. Most Asian Americans live in New York and California, two areas that have much higher pay rates than the rest of the United States.[55]

Asian Americans still suffer discrimination in education. We have cited the informal quotas used to reduce Asian penetration of some U.S. universities. In addition, many Asian Americans who have excelled in the U.S. educational system are finding a barrier once they finish school. This barrier is employment discrimination. While many get white-collar jobs, the jobs are often not as good as their possessors' credentials. Although Asian Americans tend to excel in their studies, they still receive a lower rate of return on their investment in education, especially higher education, than whites do.[56] Moreover, although many Asian Americans are hired by major companies, most find that promotions into upper management are rare. Once hired, Asian American workers complain, they soon reach a point of no promotion. In 1985, according to the

Equal Employment Opportunity Commission, Asian Americans made up 4.3 percent of all professionals and technicians in the United States, but just 1.4 percent of all supervisory officials and managers. Many point to racial discrimination as the explanation.[57]

The model-minority stereotype also obscures the presence of many poor, uneducated, and unsuccessful Asian Americans. Several recent studies have shown that many Southeast Asian immigrants, especially those from rural backgrounds with little education, are facing severe economic strain in the economically troubled 1980s.

## Other Problems

Asian Americans may be experiencing some backlash born of their success. As the section in this chapter on violence has demonstrated, Asian Americans have been the victims of vicious attacks—the death in 1982 of Vincent Chin, the attack on Vietnamese Americans by the Ku Klux Klan and other whites in Texas, and the Asian–black tensions in some cities, including those arising from the killings of four Korean American entrepreneurs in Los Angeles. Some point to the model-minority stereotype as one possible factor in these attacks.[58]

## SUMMARY

Chinese, Korean, Pilipino, and Vietnamese Americans are among the most recent of the immigrant additions to the American melting pot. Yet, as with other immigrants before them, they have been the targets of much prejudice and hostility, and not a little violence in the past and in the present. In general, their success has been so dramatic that they have often been stereotyped, like the Japanese Americans, as model-minorities. To some extent, this portrayal has had an ulterior motive, even for social science analysts. Asian Americans have often been compared with other non-European Americans as an example of what hard work can accomplish in the United States. Assimilation-oriented social scientists have been inclined to accent Asian American progress in the U.S. economy, but to neglect or downplay persisting problems.

We have documented the problems that still confront Asian Americans today. From the power–conflict perspective, a non-European minority group has not achieved success until it can fully participate in the mainstream of U.S. life without paying higher social or psychological costs for that participation than the dominant group. No Asian American group has attained that comfortable equality with the oldest white immigrant groups, such as Scottish and German Americans. The model-minority stereotype has distorted the reality of the Asian American experience: as distinct racial and ethnic groups, Asian Americans have actually remained a disadvantaged and discriminated minority with persisting economic problems, periodic violent discrimination, and little actual political power—so far at least—in the United States.[59]

## NOTES

1. Immigration and Naturalization Service, *1985 Statistical Yearbook* (Washington, D.C.: U.S. Government Printing Office, 1986), pp. 2–5.
2. U.S. Commission on Civil Rights, *Recent Activities against Citizens and Residents of Asian Descent* (Washington, D.C.: U.S. Government Printing Office, 1986), p. 7.
3. Immigration and Naturalization Service, *1985 Statistical Yearbook*, pp. 2–5.
4. U.S. Commission on Civil Rights, *Recent Activities against Citizens and Residents of Asian Descent*, p. 8.
5. Stephan Thernstrom, ed., *Harvard Encyclopedia of American Ethnic Groups* (Cambridge: Harvard University Press, 1981), pp. 357–59.
6. U.S. Commission on Civil Rights, *Recent Activities against Citizens and Residents of Asian Descent*, p. 9.
7. *Harvard Encyclopedia of American Ethnic Groups*, ed. Thernstrom, p. 359.
8. Tim Schreiner, "Philippine Brain Drain," *American Demographics* 8 (December 1986): 14.
9. U.S. Commission on Civil Rights, *Recent Activities against Citizens and Residents of Asian Descent*, p. 9.
10. Warren Y. Kim, *Koreans in America* (Seoul: Po Chin Chai Printing Co. 1971), pp. 22–25.
11. David M. Reimers, *Still the Golden Door: The Third World Comes to America* (New York: Columbia University Press, 1985), pp. 110–111; Immigration and Naturalization Service, *1985 Statistical Yearbook*, pp. 4–5.
12. Reimers, *Still the Golden Door*, p. 111.
13. Darrel Montero, *Vietnamese Americans: Patterns of Resettlement and Socioeconomic Adaptation in the United States* (Boulder, Colo.: Westview Press, 1979), pp. 1–3.
14. Morrison G. Wong and Charles Hirschman, "The New Asian Immigrants," in *Culture, Ethnicity, and Identity*, ed. William C. McCready (New York: Academic Press, 1983), p. 381.
15. Harry H.L. Kitano and Roger Daniels, *Asian Americans: Emerging Minorities* (Englewood Cliffs, New Jersey: Prentice Hall, 1988), p. 176.
16. U.S. Commission on Civil Rights, *Recent Activities against Citizens and Residents of Asian Descent*, pp. 32–33; Anthony Ramirez, "America's Super Minority," *Fortune*, November 24, 1986, p. 148 (italics added). David J. Hellwig, "Black Reactions to Chinese Immigration and the Anti-Chinese Movement: 1850–1910," *Amerasia Journal* 6 (Fall 1979): 26.
17. Miriam Sharma, "Labor Migration and Class Formation among the Filipinos in Hawaii, 1940–1946," in *Labor Immigration under Capitalism*, ed. Lucie Cheng and Edna Bonacich (Berkeley: University of California Press, 1984), pp. 583, 593.
18. Montero, *Vietnamese Americans*, pp. 3–4.
19. Paul Sweeney, "Tolerance in a Texas Town," *Texas Observer*, September 17, 1982, pp. 7–9.
20. Quoted in Terry E. Johnson et al., "Immigrants: New Victims," *Newsweek* 107 (May 12, 1986): 57.
21. U.S. Commission on Civil Rights, *Recent Activities against Citizens and Residents of Asian Descent*, pp. 43–44.
22. Johnson et al., "Immigrants," p. 57.
23. Howard A. DeWitt, *Anti-Filipino Movements in California: A History, Bibliography and Study Guide* (San Francisco: R and E Research Associates, 1976), pp. 27–66.
24. U.S. Commission on Civil Rights, *Recent Activities against Citizens and Residents of Asian Descent*, pp. 50–52; Sweeney, "Tolerance in a Texas Town," pp. 7–10.
25. Paul Sweeney, "Asian Americans Gain Clout," *American Demographics* 8 (February 1986): 18–19.
26. Peter Kwong, *Chinatown, N.Y.: Labor and Politics, 1930–1950* (New York: Monthly Review Press, 1979), pp. 45–67.
27. Kitano and Daniels, *Asian Americans*, p. 49.
28. Stanford M. Lyman, *Chinese Americans* (New York: Random House, 1974), pp. 161–2.
29. Bong-youn Choy, *Koreans in America* (Chicago: Nelson-Hall, 1979), pp. 141–89.

30. John Gregory Dunne, *Delano: The Story of the California Grape Strike* (New York: Farrar, Straus & Giroux, 1967), p. 77.

31. Lemuel F. Ignacio, *Asian Americans and Pacific Islanders* (San Jose, Calif.: Pilipino Development Associates, 1976), pp. 11–56; Kitano and Daniels, *Asian Americans*, p. 86.

32. Nicholas Lemann, "Growing Pains," *Atlantic Monthly* 261 (January 1988): 57–62.

33. *Harvard Encyclopedia of American Ethnic Groups*, ed. Thernstrom, pp. 218–20.

34. Reimers, *Still the Golden Door*, p. 107.

35. Ibid.

36. U.S. Bureau of the Census, *U.S. Census of Population, 1980: General Social and Economic Characteristics*, PC80-1-C1, 1983, p. 160.

37. Ibid., pp. 157, 162; Kitano and Daniels, *Asian Americans*, pp. 48–50.

38. Sharma, "Labor Migration and Class Formation among the Filipinos in Hawaii, 1906–1946," p. 589.

39. Amado Cabezas, Larry Hajime Shinagawa, and Gary Kawaguchi, "New Inquiries into the Socioeconomic Status of Pilipino Americans in California," *Amerasia Journal* 13 (1986–87): 3–7.

40. Ibid.

41. Choy, *Koreans in America*, pp. 123–33.

42. Reimers, *Still the Golden Door*, pp. 111–12; Ivan Light, "Immigrant Entrepreneurs in America: Koreans in Los Angles," in *Clamor at the Gates*, ed. Nathan Glazer (San Francisco: ICS Press, 1985), p. 162.

43. U.S. Bureau of the Census, *U.S. Census of Population, 1980: General Social and Economic Characteristics*, p. 160.

44. Montero, *Vietnamese Americans*, p. 39.

45. Ibid.

46. Sam Howe Verhovek, "Two Girls Win Westinghouse Competition," *New York Times*, March 3, 1987, p. C1.

47. Dennis A. Williams et al., "A Formula for Success," *Newsweek* April 23, 1984, pp. 77–78.

48. U.S. Bureau of the Census, *U.S. Census of Population, 1980: General Social and Economic Characteristics*, p. 160.

49. Eloise Salholz et al., "Do Colleges Set Asian Quotas?" *Newsweek*, February 9, 1987, p. 60.

50. "A Formula for Success," *Newsweek*, April 23, 1984, p. 78.

51. Gary Orfield, Franklin Monfort, and Rosemary George, "School Segregation in the 1980s," *International Development Research Association Newsletter*, November 1987, p. 5.

52. Ronald Takaki, "Is Race Surmountable? Thomas Sowell's Celebration of Japanese-American 'Success,' " in *Ethnicity and the Work Force*, ed. Winston A. Van Horne (Madison: University of Wisconsin Press, 1985), pp. 218–20.

53. Kitano and Daniels, *Asian Americans*, pp. 190–192.

54. Ishmael Reed, "America's Color Bind: The Modeling of Minorities," *San Francisco Examiner*, November 19, 1987, p. A-20; "Success Story of One Minority Group in U.S.," *U.S. News & World Report*, December 26, 1966, pp. 73–76.

55. For a summary of research, see Patricia A. Roos and Joyce Hennessy, "Assimilation or Exclusion? Attainment Processes of Japanese, Mexican Americans, and Anglos in California" (paper presented at the American Sociological Association meetings, San Antonio, 1984); and Ronald Takaki, *From Different Shores* (New York: Oxford University Press, 1987).

56. Gloria Luz R. Martinez and Wayne J. Villemez, "Assimilation in the United States: Occupational Attainment of Asian Americans, 1980" (paper presented at the American Sociological Association meetings, Chicago, August 1987), pp. 31–32.

57. John Schwartz, "A 'Superminority' Tops Out," *Newsweek*, May 11, 1987, pp. 48–49.

58. Beverly McLeod, "The Oriental Express," *Psychology Today* 20 (July 1986): 48–52.

59. Kwang Chung Kim and Won Moo Hurh, "Korean Americans and the 'Success' Image: A Critique," *Amerasia* 10 (Fall/Winter 1983): 15.

# CHAPTER 13

# *The Future of the American Dream: An Inclusive Melting Pot?*

## AN INCLUSIVE MELTING POT?

A major image of U.S. society has been the "melting pot." In the early 1900s Israel Zangwill made an influential statement of this idea in his popular play, *The Melting Pot*. In that play a struggling Russian immigrant vigorously argues that

> America is God's Crucible, the great Melting-Pot where all races of Europe are melting and re-forming! Here you stand, good folks, think I, when I see them at Ellis Island, here you stand in your fifty groups, with your fifty languages and histories, and your fifty blood hatreds and rivalries. But you won't be long like that, brothers, for these are the fires of God. ... A fig for your feuds and vendettas! Germans and Frenchmen, Irishmen and Englishmen, Jews and Russians—into the Crucible with you all! God is making the American.[1]

Here is the idealistic image of the great crucible which melts fifty divergent groups together to form the new "American blend." This is a rosy view of a mutual adaptation process in which old and new groups freely blend together on an *equal* basis. Yet this is a pipe dream that glosses over the reality of unequal intergroup relations in the United States. The omission of nonwhite groups from the boiling cauldron, just to cite one flaw, suggests how optimistic the image is.

## A NATION OF IMMIGRANTS

The United States is, nonetheless, a nation of immigrants. Tens of millions of immigrants have come to these shores from all over the globe, in numbers and diversity unparalleled in the rest of the world. Dozens of languages, scores of cultures, a great diversity in resources, and a remarkable array of physical characteristics have characterized these millions of immigrants. This diversity can be seen in something as simple as the array of Asian, African, European, Middle Eastern, and South American restaurants, or something as complex as voting patterns and debates over bilingual education in U.S. schools.

The 1987 national survey by the University of Chicago's National Opinion Research Center (NORC) reveals the countries of origin of immigrants to the United States. The NORC researchers interviewed a random sample of 1,466 adults; of these 1142 emphasized one country in reply to the question "From what countries or part of the world did your ancestors come?" Countries listed by at least 1 percent of these respondents were:

| | | |
|---|---|---|
| Africa | Germany | Poland |
| Austria and Hungary | Ireland | Russia |
| Canada | Italy | Spain |
| Czechoslovakia | Mexico | Scotland |
| England and Wales | The Netherlands | Sweden |
| France | Norway | |

Dozens of other countries were mentioned by less than 1 percent. The list clearly shows that the major infusions of immigrants to this country originated in Africa, Mexico, Canada, and certain areas of Europe, particularly northern Europe.[2] Conspicuously absent in this 1987 list are countries in the Middle East and Asia.

The peculiarities in this list of countries, as well as the total number of immigrants from each, have been shaped by the distinctive economic and political conditions that characterized the United States and the sending countries in particular historical periods of immigration. In the homeland economic conditions and political situations were often distressing or inhospitable to personal and family development. While variable, the U.S. economy, often a booming one with many low-wage jobs, attracted poor immigrants, such as the Irish, the Jews, the Koreans, and the Italians—all studied in this book. Most came more or less voluntarily. The Africans came in chains.

The political situation in the United States was also important. White, usually Anglo-Saxon, Protestant control of the national political institutions meant that white Protestants controlled important state mechanisms, such as the power to launch military invasions overseas or draft restrictive immigration laws at home. Imperialism overseas, as in the Philippines or Puerto Rico in the late nineteenth century, also shaped immigration. Tough immigration laws could be used to control the streams of migration to the United States. White Protestant leaders, capitalists and politicians, permitted or restricted immigration according to their preferences and prejudices.

Particularly important have been the discriminatory restrictions on immigrants in U.S. immigration laws, such as the Chinese Exclusion Act and the 1924 Immigration Act with its restrictive national-origin quotas. These laws were constructed by white Protestant Americans and thus guaranteed that by the late twentieth century the United States would have relatively few Asian Americans and fewer Americans from southern and eastern Europe than otherwise would have been the case. The discriminatory 1924 law, for example, sharply reduced the number of Catholic immigrants from Italy and Poland, as well as the number of Jews from eastern Europe.

As a result, the United States is today overwhelmingly Protestant; only a quarter of the population is Catholic or Jewish. The provisions excluding Asians insured that the United States would have fewer than 4 million Asian Americans in a population of 250 million by the late twentieth century. It is ironic that those responsible for *anti-immigrant* discrimination in one period always included descendants of *immigrants* to the United States of a previous period. Only the Native Americans can claim that they are the real natives and that all others are intruders.

More recent U.S. immigration acts, those passed in 1965 and 1986, have no directly and blatantly discriminatory provisions along racial or national-origin lines, but they do intentionally limit the number of immigrants who can come to the United States from any one country. This is in contrast, for example, to the unlimited numbers of Irish and German immigrants allowed in the mid-nineteenth century.

The most recent immigrant act, the 1986 Immigration Reform and Control Act, aims at restricting the flow of immigrants from south of the U.S. border, particularly from Mexico. As we have seen, that act has some provisions regarded as troubling by Hispanic and other Americans, including intrusive governmental documentation of legal work status, employer sanctions to prohibit employment of undocumented aliens, a governmental program of screening welfare applicants for migration status, and governmental programs to bring in low-wage agricultural workers.

It was clear from the congressional and public debate over this 1986 legislation that many native-born, and especially white, business leaders, politicians, and other residents of the United States were worried about the character and values of the new Hispanic and Asian immigrants. These native-born leaders were concerned, as were most earlier nativists, that the United States could not absorb so many new immigrants. Interestingly, however, the ratio of immigrants to the native-born population was *much* higher for the United States in earlier decades of the twentieth century. As we noted previously, today this country not only has a smaller percentage of foreign-born than in the 1920s, but also has a smaller percentage of foreign born immigrants in its makeup than such nations as France, England, Germany, and Switzerland.

Given its long history of successful absorption of immigrants and its size in geographical terms, it is unlikely that the United States will be overwhelmed by these or future new immigrants. Implicit in many discussions of restricting immigrants is a concern that the new immigrants from Asia and Latin America are not compatible with, or assimilable to, a core American culture and society that has been substantially white and European-American. This too is an old worry of nativist advocates. The real agenda of the anti-immigrant forces appears to be the preservation of white European-American cultural and structural dominance. For many anti-immigrant groups the American experiment as a "nation of immigrants" is over. However, the future of such anti-immigration efforts is unclear, because it faces fierce opposition from those Americans who hold other sentiments—"great crucible" views that are also fundamental to this society. Pro-immigrationists believe that Zangwill was right, that the American crucible can still be enriched, can still blend in, preferably with increasing equality, the racial and ethnic groups made up of new immigrants who have recently come to these shores.

As we have underscored throughout this book, the United States still is a "golden land" of promise for the poor and oppressed peoples of the world, those from such areas as Asia, Mexico, and Central America seeking a haven here from economic or political troubles. They, like their predecessors, bring intelligence, creativity, hard work, and cultural invigoration to the boiling racial and ethnic melting pot of the United States. A true understanding of this immigrant contribution and a recognition that most of us are ourselves immigrants or the descendants of immigrants should make us welcome these and the next waves of immigration that will undoubtedly wash the American shores. Only such hospitality will make the inscription on the Statue of Liberty, the words of Jewish American poet Emma Lazarus, ring true:

> Give me your tired, your poor,
> Your huddled masses, yearning to breathe free,
> The wretched refuse of your teeming shore,
> Send these, the homeless, tempest-tost to me:
> I lift my lamp beside the golden door.

## RACE, ETHNICITY, AND EQUALITY

The equality sought by immigrants and their children has been viewed in different ways in the United States in the years since 1776. The philosophy that "all men are created equal" held by some of the founding fathers meant equality of political participation for white, northern European, male immigrants and their descendants, especially those with property. Even this equality of access to the political institutions was a dramatic step for its day, but such a limited view of equality obviously excluded such groups as women, black slaves, Native Americans, and to some extent Jewish and Catholic immigrants.

Over the next two centuries U.S. conceptions of equality would change, so much so that numerous commentators have seen equality as an ideal whose driving force has been extraordinarily great in American history. In this view the historical process has seen the progressive "egalitarianization" of the economic and political system. Gradually, the idea of equality came to include equality of worth among individuals, equality of opportunity for all individuals, and equality before the law (civil rights). Numerous authors have praised the egalitarian trend in the United States. Poor ethnic and racial groups experienced ever greater equality in some or all of these categories—according to this optimistic perspective. Between the early 1800s and the early 1900s capitalistic development came dramatically and swiftly to the United States. Rapid expansion gave substantial economic opportunity to millions of white immigrants; they became the prospering labor for this economic miracle. Although they suffered, success came to the majority of white ethnic Americans who entered as low-income individuals. From the most optimistic perspective, white ethnics finally "made it." Today nonwhites are seen as moving toward full inclusion in the society.

Yet such a view of the egalitarianizing society is a series of half-truths. Substantial economic and political mobility did indeed come for many white groups. But this optimistic view ignores the great poverty and misery that white ethnics and nonwhites endured as poorly paid laborers in an exploitative capitalistic system. We have documented this exploitation for white groups such as the Italians, Irish, and Jews; and this was also the picture for many white ethnic groups we have not examined. Racist immigration laws aimed at restricting the entry of whites from southern and eastern Europe were not abolished until the mid-1960s.

This portrait does not take into account the significant discrimination, often subtle and institutionalized, still experienced by groups such as the Italians and the Jews. This rosy picture also glosses over the continuing subordination of many nonwhite and non-European Americans in the lower social, political, and economic tiers of the society. To some extent, the egalitarianizing trend has affected the majority of nonwhite Americans, especially as concerns legal rights and formal opportunity. But in terms of political and economic advancement, most run as hard as they can to keep from becoming more unequal than they currently are.

It was only a century ago that a decade or two of great progress in expanding opportunities for black Americans (1865–1885), the Reconstruction period, was followed all too soon by a dramatic resurgence of reaction, the Redemption period. Although there are major differences between then and now, it is also true that only two decades or so after public policy shifted significantly in favor of expanded opportunities for nonwhite Americans, we moved in the Reagan years, the 1980s, in a reactionary direction. Powerful leaders cut back or eliminated affirmative action, equal opportunity, and other supportive programs. The bottom line on evaluating racial progress is that decades into affirmative action and equal opportunity programs no fundamental changes can be seen at the top levels in most major institutional sectors in the United States. White males, mostly of Anglo-Saxon or Protestant heritage, overwhelmingly dominate upper-level and middle-level positions in most major bureaucratic organizations in the United States, from the Department of Defense, to Fortune 500 corporations, to state legislatures, to local banks and supermarket chains. In the late 1980s the dominant white concern has shifted away from patterns of institutionalized discrimination facing blacks, Native Americans, Hispanics, and many Asian Americans. Those hurt most by the shift have been the nonwhite Americans who have long suffered from traditional institutionalized discrimination. In the best scenario one can envision for the 1990s, nonwhite equality or parity with whites still seems generations in the future.

Equality has long been an authentic American dream. Whether it can ever be a reality in the sphere of racial and ethnic relations remains to be seen. The likelihood of true racial and ethnic equality becoming reality is in part conditional on the protest and political activities of those American immigrants and their descendants who are committed to the ideal of equality.

## NOTES

1. Israel Zangwill, *The Melting Pot* (New York: Macmillan, 1925), p. 33.
2. National Opinion Research Center, University of Chicago, *1987 General Social Survey*. Tabulation by author.

# Index